THE MEDIA WERE AMERICAN

D0144965

Also by Jeremy Tunstall

The Fishermen

The Advertising Man

Old and Alone

The Westminster Lobby Correspondents

Journalists at Work

The Media Are American

The Media in Britain

Communications Deregulation

Television Producers

Newspaper Power

Studies on the Press
with O. Boyd-Barrett and C. Seymour-Ure

Media Made in California
with David Walker

Liberating Communications
with Michael Palmer

Media Moguls
with Michael Palmer

The Anglo-American Media Connection
with David Machin

Media Sociology
editor

Sociological Perspectives
editor with Kenneth Thompson

The Open University Opens
editor

Media Occupations and Professions
editor

THE MEDIA WERE AMERICAN

U.S. MASS MEDIA IN DECLINE

Jeremy Tunstall

New York   Oxford
OXFORD UNIVERSITY PRESS
2008

Oxford University Press, Inc., publishes works that further Oxford University's
objective of excellence in research, scholarship, and education.

Oxford   New York
Auckland   Cape Town   Dar es Salaam   Hong Kong   Karachi
Kuala Lumpur   Madrid   Melbourne   Mexico City   Nairobi
New Delhi   Shanghai   Taipei   Toronto

With offices in
Argentina   Austria   Brazil   Chile   Czech Republic   France   Greece
Guatemala   Hungary   Italy   Japan   Poland   Portugal   Singapore
South Korea   Switzerland   Thailand   Turkey   Ukraine   Vietnam

Copyright © 2008 by Oxford University Press, Inc.

Published by Oxford University Press, Inc.
198 Madison Avenue, New York, New York 10016
http://www.oup.com

Oxford is a registered trademark of Oxford University Press

All rights reserved. No part of this publication may be reproduced,
stored in a retrieval system, or transmitted, in any form or by any means,
electronic, mechanical, photocopying, recording, or otherwise,
without the prior permission of Oxford University Press.

ISBN: 978-0-19-518147-0 (pbk.)
        978-0-19-518146-3 (cloth)

9 8 7 6 5 4 3 2 1

Printed in the United States of America
on acid-free paper

CONTENTS

PART 4   NATIONAL MEDIA AND WORLD REGION MEDIA   327

ACKNOWLEDGMENTS

Early versions of some of these chapters were tried out on students (many from the United States, Asia, and mainland Europe) at City University, London, from 1990 to 2005. Thanks to them and to City University colleagues and library staff.

Thanks to the 50 media people in China, India, and Kenya who agreed to recent interviews. Especially helpful over the years have been Reuters and Associated Press bureau chiefs and correspondents in Algiers, Beijing, Bogotá, California, Delhi, London, Mexico City, Mumbai, Nairobi, New York, Shanghai, Tunis, and Washington, DC.

The following read some or all of this book in first draft and provided sage advice together with encouragement: Oliver Boyd-Barrett, Jean Chalaby, John Cowley, Winston Fletcher, Petros Iosifidis, John Landell-Mills, Graham Mytton, Colin Seymour-Ure, Christopher Sterling, Rodney Tiffen, Howard Tumber, Frank Webster, and Rex Winsbury.

Khushwant Singh, way back in 1972, provided extraordinary hospitality (in both Bombay and Delhi) and a unique introduction to Indian media.

Carol Lasbrey was a marvelous host and guide when my wife and I visited Guatemala.

Diana Livesey, Rob, Jessica, and Cecilia have repeatedly welcomed us in Columbus and Connecticut and provided me the opportunity to read the *New York Times* in beautiful surroundings.

Thanks also to my colleagues, since 1982, in the Euromedia Research Group who taught me about Europe's media: Werner Meier, Josef Trappel, Denis McQuail, Gianpietro Mazzoleni, Kees Brants, Els de Bens, Olof Hultén, Mary Kelly, Hans Kleinsteuber, Rosario de Mateo, Helge Østbye, Bernt Østergaard, Vibeke Petersen, Karen Siune, and Wolfgang Truetschzler.

My family—Sylvia, Paul, Helena, and Rebecca—have been endlessly tolerant and supportive. Especially helpful and happy was our 3,000-mile drive in 1988 across what was still the Soviet Union (but is now Russia, Ukraine, Georgia, and Moldova).

Thanks to Frances Bruce for her expert secretarial support over a number of years.

Finally, my editor at Oxford University Press, Peter Labella, has dealt diplomatically and effectively with an awkward author five time zones away.

Jeremy Tunstall

INTRODUCTION

In my previous book *The Media Are American*,[1] published in 1977, the central argument was that the media *are* American because most new mass media were industrialized for the first time within the United States. That book considered the period from 1890 to 1970. In each case—newspaper, movies, radio, and TV—much of the pioneer work was done in Europe; but it was in the United States (and especially in and around New York City) that most new media were first successfully industrialized and sold to the bulk of the population.

This book makes a quite separate (and different) argument—namely, that the U.S. media on the world scene peaked in the mid-twentieth century. The *Media Are American*, while not predicting the big continuing relative decline, did specify that U.S. media in the world had probably peaked around 1947–1948.

The Media Are American did discuss India and China and the threat of separatism in the Soviet Union, but I anticipated neither the scale of economic and media growth in India and China nor the collapse of the Soviet Union.

This book discusses the importance of population size in general, and of China's and India's populations in particular. Much talk and writing on American media emphasizes the large foreign revenues earned by Hollywood movies and TV series. Impressive numbers of billions of dollars are still earned from other countries. Hollywood's export business system ensures that a large fraction of all movie theater box office revenue, from around the world, flows back to California. But the great majority of people in the world spend less than six hours per year in a movie theater; hundreds of millions of people in Asia and Africa have never seen even one Hollywood film.

More than 60 percent of the world's people live in countries with populations of over 100 million people. Most of these big-population countries are only modest media importers. In terms of billions of audience hours, the U.S. media have continued to grow on the world scene. However, China's and India's population and media have grown very much faster than those of the United States and Hollywood. For example, the U.S. audience spends over

---

[1] Jeremy Tunstall, *The Media Are American: Anglo-American Media in the World*, London: Constable, and New York: Columbia University Press, 1977.

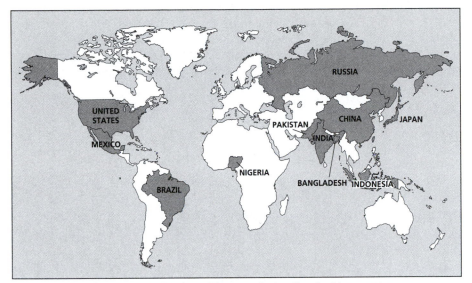

Figure 1 Over 60 percent of the world's population live in 11 countries.

one billion hours each day watching television; but the Chinese audience spends over three billion hours each day watching television.

Even though U.S. media have been in relative decline on the world scene since the 1950s, it is difficult for U.S. citizens not to believe in the continuing dominance of American media across the entire world. When an American citizen visits Canada, Mexico, or Europe, he or she sees much evidence of a big American media presence. In the downtown areas of most capital cities Hollywood movies are visibly present; in the tourist hotels *USA Today*, the *Wall Street Journal*, and *Time* are on sale; each hotel guest room TV set offers CNN, MTV, Discovery, and much other American media output. Within a short distance are American fast-food outlets. Many of the natives on the streets speak more-or-less understandable English. Even the pop music playing in retail stores, and on car radios, sounds familiar. Surely, then, American media are exerting global dominance? Surely Hollywood *vincit omnia*? No, not so. Visiting Americans who consult the natives—or resident Americans—in that same country will hear a different story.

CNN is indeed available around the world. But who, apart from American tourists, is viewing CNN? In the Netherlands, for example, English-language ability is extraordinarily widespread; but in each recent year CNN's Dutch audience share has been either 0.0 percent or 0.1 percent (one-thousandth of all Dutch TV viewing).

In Britain—another country where a version of English is widely spoken—a lot of American material is available. One junior-year-abroad U.S. student told me recently that most British students watch mainly American TV shows; if this referred to students viewing TV after midnight and before midday, it probably made a fair point. American TV shows are heavily available (in Britain as elsewhere) at times (and on channels) characterized by very, very small audiences. In recent years in Britain a few U.S. shows—such as *The Simpsons* and *Desperate Housewives*—have had a strong niche audience; but in a typical week only one or two of the 75 largest British audiences is achieved by an American import.

Most people around the world prefer to be entertained by people who look the same, talk the same, joke the same, behave the same, play the same games, and have the same beliefs (and worldview) as themselves. They also overwhelmingly prefer their own national news, politics, weather, and football and other sports.

Many people have argued that the media have become globalized and Americanized. This book points to the resilience and (probably) increasing strength of national culture, national sentiment, and national media—especially in the Asian and other countries where most of the world's people happen to live.

In the last two decades the United States has become a large-scale media importer (primarily from Mexico) and now more closely resembles other big-population nations, in which typically about 10 percent of audience time is devoted to media imports. However, the United States remains unique in that the great majority of its (non-Spanish-speaking) people devote almost all of their media consumption to domestic (U.S.) media output.

Most people in almost all other countries spend a tenth or more of their media time with media imported, typically, from the United States and/or from one or two other countries. Consequently, most of the world's people have some sustained exposure to the history, culture, and mythology of one or two other countries. The United States remains unique in that most Americans are exposed almost entirely to their own nation's history, culture, and mythology. What do they know (of a supposedly global reality) who only American media know?

A global or world level of media certainly does exist. But world media, or American media, play a much smaller role than national media. I also argue that in most, or many, cases, "Euro-American" is a more accurate description than "global" media. World regions—such as India and southern Asia, or China and eastern Asia—play salient media roles. "Euro-American" refers to the entire European continent and the entire American continent (north and south); I argue that Euro-America possesses a single media industry that, at least for some years, will be the leading single force in world media.

PART 1

AMERICAN MEDIA IN DECLINE

1

Anglo-American, Global, and Euro-American Media Versus Media Nationalism

"Globalization" does not adequately describe today's worldwide pattern of media exporting and importing. Media trade varies from very direct sales to more ambiguous transactions, such as TV format sales, or piracy.

Although Anglo-American media have been world leaders since before 1900, today's leading media force is Euro-American. The European and American continents are the main importers, as well as exporters, of media. But the world's people spend very much more time with their own media than with imported media.

English language, Anglo-American media already led the world's media in 1900. Until 1913 Britain was probably still the world's leading media power. From 1914 to 1918 the U.S. media became the leading partner in the Anglo-American media. Through the twentieth century this Anglo-American combination depended upon several key, but gradually changing, factors.

By 1913 the United States already had a larger population (97.6 million) than did any western European country. This was crucial in the media industries, where scale economies tend to take an extreme form. In 1918 the United States had just become the leading producer of films; in film additional audience millions can often be reached at the low additional cost of printing more copies. This fact meant that film was always likely to be a winner-takes-all industry.

Around 1900 in much of western Europe, and in Japan, the press was still only just emerging from state control; but in both the United States and Britain newspapers experienced very few governmental constraints.

In the United States the commercial element (including advertising) continued to predominate. Nevertheless the Anglo-American media also included important not-for-profit elements. Reuters (British) and the

Associated Press (U.S.) were leading wholesalers of news around the world through the twentieth century, and neither was a conventional commercial enterprise. The London-based BBC was the most successful international radio broadcaster of the years 1940–2000, and it also was not-for-profit.

In 1913 the U.S. population was over twice that of Britain's; by 2005 the U.S. population was nearly five times that of the United Kingdom. But the trend toward ever-increasing U.S. dominance within English-language media occurred gradually and relatively smoothly. In practice the U.S. media were able to infiltrate the British empire and later the (British) Commonwealth in pursuit of export markets. Already in the 1920s Hollywood was the dominant film power in India.

In recent decades, as the United Kingdom has become an increasingly weaker player within the Anglo-American media, other countries in which all, or most, of the population speak English as their first language have become more significant. By 2005 the United States, the United Kingdom, Canada, Australia, New Zealand, and Ireland had a combined population of 417 million (about 90 percent of whom spoke English as their main language). In recent decades the United States media industries have been able to use not only the United Kingdom, but also these other four English-speaking countries, as junior partners in the Anglo media enterprise.

Today the United Kingdom, Canada, Australia, New Zealand, and Ireland all have film industries that operate in partnership with Hollywood. This includes Hollywood offshore productions in all five countries and the production of Hollywood TV series and New York TV commercials in Canada. These five countries also have some of the most Americanized of the world's media systems. These are the main locations where Hollywood products are sold without the need for translation. The United Kingdom, Canada, Australia, New Zealand, and Ireland can be seen as leading examples of media globalization; these nations' newspaper presses also exhibit high levels of market concentration and foreign ownership.

Anglo-American media exert world influence through their status as mother-tongue speakers of the world's leading international language. Although many other countries (especially in Asia and Africa) have their own versions of the English language, it is the United States, with some British help, that develops the concepts and usages that enter the conceptual frameworks of international trade and of many other international activities and organizations. English is in practice the main working language not only of the European Union but also of the United Nations.

Small- and Large-Population Countries: Globalized and Nonglobalized Media

"Globalization," another term of U.S. origin, became more and more heavily used during the 1990s; politicians, journalists, and public relations people were prominent as proponents and definers of globalization. Academics also in the 1990s used the term in thousands of academic papers and in the titles of hundreds of books.[1]

Most definitions of globalization gave a prominent place to finance (including banking) and to communications (including both telecommunications and mass media). Clearly finance, banking, and credit do operate on a much more global basis than in the past. This does have some impact on mass media; for example, foreign acquisition and ownership of media companies is now more widely tolerated. Nevertheless, a solely financial focus can be misleading. Just as much "global trade" is in fact between neighboring countries inside the European Union, so "global media exports" from Hollywood also rely financially mainly on the affluent markets of western Europe, Japan, Canada, and Australia.

Telecommunications (not mass media) has the most global potential— since the Internet, consumer credit, and plain old phone calls use telecommunications networks. Many of these global transactions focus on trade names and numbers and on cash amounts. The network aspect of globalization has been stressed by Manuel Castells and by Armand Mattelart.[2] The potential global reach of telecommunications was obvious to the thousands of Americans who worked for NASA in the 1960s; as NASA's funding was reduced in the 1970s, many NASA personnel went into telecommunications. One of the main public relations arguments for the break-up of AT&T was that smaller and more commercial telecom companies would be better able to exploit the global potential for the United States.[3]

The global potential for mass media is again strong,[4] especially if we focus only on technologies—such as space satellite systems. However, the global *export* potential for mass media content—movies, TV series, news stories—is inevitably lower. Words and cultural assumptions are central to most major forms of mass media, including movies and pop songs. And most people around the world prefer most of the time to be entertained and informed by people from their own culture and nation.

One of the oddities of the globalization literature is that there are relatively few references to population size or to the differences between large and small population nation-states. There are, however, marked differences between, for example, China and Jamaica. China has a population of over 1,300 million and supplies most of its own TV, print, and other media output in, of course, Mandarin and a few other Chinese languages. Jamaica has less than three million people and, like its big neighbor the United States, speaks

---

[1] David Held and Anthony McGrew (eds.), *The Global Transformations Reader*, Oxford: Polity Press, 2003 ed.

[2] Manuel Castells, *The Rise of the Network Society*, Oxford: Blackwell, 2000; Armand Mattelart, *Networking the World, 1794–2000*, Minneapolis: University of Minnesota Press, 2000.

[3] An interesting book from this period is Joseph Pelton, *Global Talk*, Boston: A.W. Sijthoff, 1981.

[4] Terhi Rantanen, *The Media and Globalization*, London: Sage, 2005; Symposium: "What Is Global About Global Media?" *Global Media and Communication*, Vol. 1/1, April 2005: 9–62.

English; not surprisingly, Jamaica is a massive importer of media, although even here "globalized" is not really the correct term. Jamaica's media intake includes huge amounts of material from its close neighbor the United States, some 500 miles away.

Population size has a central place in the arguments found in this book. Some 42 percent of the world's population live in China and three Indian subcontinent countries (India, Pakistan, and Bangladesh). In none of these countries do media imports from the United States or western Europe have a big market share. This is also true of six other countries—Indonesia, Japan, Brazil, Mexico, Nigeria, and Russia—each of which has a population of over 100 million people. Taking these 10 countries together, probably not more than 10 percent of their entire audience time is spent with foreign media.

The most globalized media systems—the systems that do the most importing—fall into three categories. One group is small-population countries in sub-Saharan Africa (where most imports are from the United States, United Kingdom, and France). Second, in the Caribbean and Central America, small countries do a lot of importing, mainly from their big neighbors, the United States and Mexico. Third, the best export market for the United States in financial terms continues to be Europe; the smaller-population European countries do the most importing—not only from the United States but also from their bigger neighbors such as France, Germany, and the United Kingdom.

Direct and Indirect Media Exports

Some media exports are very direct, but other exports are so indirect as perhaps not to qualify as exports.

The media product that is *exported without any alteration* is the most direct and least ambiguous. Examples include a Hollywood movie or TV series going to another English-speaking country or a German production going to another German-speaking country. Here there is usually no need for translation and also no (or minimal) editing. In this most direct case, the importing country's audience sees the same product that the audience in the exporting country sees. But this does not ensure an identical impact; Australians may not experience a Hollywood TV series in the same way that an American audience does. A Swiss-German audience will be well aware that a German TV series carries German, and not Swiss, accents, values, and characters.

A *translated or edited* version of a Hollywood product is needed in all non-English-speaking markets. In general the wealthier TV markets dub the sound by employing local actors;[5] this in itself subtly alters the film or TV

---

[5] Bob Jenkins, "Mind Your Language," *Television Business International*, September 2001: 49–51.

series, especially if, for example, a Texas accent in the Hollywood product is dubbed into a German regional accent such as Bavarian.

In less affluent and smaller countries, foreign language imports are usually subtitled. These words under the picture are typically a much-shortened version of the spoken dialogue; this process of abbreviation can lose certain subtleties and also split the audience's attention between subtitles and pictures. Both forms of translation make quite radical changes, and there may also be editing—for example, to remove or shorten scenes that are regarded as too obscene, too sexy, too boring, or too obscure.

Versioning is another variety of both editing and translation. Not uncommonly an importing TV network buys eight hours of a TV mini-series but then edits it down to perhaps five hours. Often one purpose is to conceal from the audience that the series is a 100 percent import; this can be done by using a local national performer who appears on screen and/or does the (translated) commentary. Such versioning can make a Japanese series about the Pacific seem like a British or French series about the Pacific. Or a production that was originally 90 percent American can be made to seem a 50/50 co-production.

Foreign financing can include a very wide range of situations. Ownership (in whole or in part) sounds fairly unambiguous; but some foreign owners of newspapers, magazines, or satellite TV channels claim not to interfere with the local editorial team. This may seem to be wise business practice, but a foreign owner will normally "interfere" to the extent of selecting the top local personnel, while also establishing the broad financial guidelines. In many cases foreign ownership will go much further; for example, a foreign edition of an American (or French) magazine will probably operate on some specific ratio of local content to American (or French) material from the main edition.

Foreign commissioning of television programming is a common practice of export versions of American satellite channels that are seeking to become more local. An American channel operator such as Discovery does seek to commission good quality local material, but it also enforces some of its own key editorial guidelines—for example, historical characters may appear in period costume, but will not be allowed to speak.

A *script-sale or format sale* in practice usually involves a smaller editorial input from the exporter. One cheap device for a new channel is to purchase the scripts of an American or British comedy or soap opera; the purchased script will then be rewritten into the local language and culture. These arrangements often last only for one or two seasons.

Format sales are especially common in game and reality shows.[6] The sum of money that changes hands is relatively modest; an "importing" TV

---

[6] Marie-Agnès Bruneau, "When Is a Format Not a Format?" *Television Business International*, January/February 2000: 44–51.

network, by buying the format for its national market, acquires access to useful production details and advice. However, the key ingredient of many such shows is the "host"—often an already popular local comedian or entertainment star.

Copying of a genre or editorial formula probably does not involve a contractual sale, and the end-product may be only very loosely related to any single existing model. For example, if an African or Asian TV network is about to make its first hospital drama, it may well look at episodes of American, British, Mexican, or Indian hospital dramas; but the key influences could come from nearer to home in the form of a well-known hospital novel or from a hospital radio series.

Finally, *media policies or media systems* may be imported. Such imports may be very important, but particular examples are likely also to be ambiguous. Many countries in the 1980s and 1990s moved their radio and TV systems toward a greater commercial emphasis and away from various kinds of "public" broadcasting. However, these trends, toward privatization and commercializing and Americanizing the national media, typically led to revised systems that were still significantly different from supposed American models. Often such adoption of foreign media policies and media systems is most strongly influenced not by America or Europe, but by the example of close neighbors, whose popular media output may be leaking across the border. Both India and Israel initially decided not to introduce television; but India changed its mind because of nearby Pakistani trans-missions, and Israel changed its policy because of nearby Arab TV.

Euro-American, Eastern Asian, Southern Asian, and Arab Media

This book argues that the world splits into four major media regions, which are largely self-sufficient. Each of these four is based on geography, on religious and cultural tradition, and on one main language or one main group of languages.

Euro-America (the whole of America, north and south, and most of Europe) is the largest and most affluent of these groupings. Euro-America (minus Russia) has some 27 percent of the world's population. It includes most of the world's leading media exporters—not only the United States, but also Brazil, Mexico, France, Germany, and the United Kindom. Europe and Latin America include most of the United States' best media export markets. Although the predominant flow is eastward across the Atlantic, there is a substantial (but smaller) reverse flow into the United States—especially from Mexico, France, Germany, and the United Kingdom (and from Japan). There is substantial European ownership of U.S. media, as well as substantial U.S. ownership of European media. Euro-America relies on common European-based history, culture, and religion. Euro-America is the home not only of large numbers of English and Spanish speakers but also of other major world languages, including French, German, and Portuguese. There is even a degree of common regulation, as the Justice Department in Washington cooperates with the competition Directorate in Brussels.

Many European and American television executives meet their transatlantic colleagues three times each year at MIP-TV (International TV Program Market) in France, at MIPCOM (International Film and Program Market for TV, Video, Cable and Satellite) also in France, and at NATPE (National Association of TV Programming Executives) in Las Vegas.[7] All three annual sales conventions are dominated by Europeans, Americans, and Latin Americans.

China has some 20 percent of the world's population and has become a major media power. China does do some importing of media, but it balances modest American imports with imports from culturally (and geographically) closer places such as Taiwan, Hong Kong, and South Korea. In China a simultaneous TV audience of 200 million people is commonplace. China is, of course, protected by its unique history, culture, and cuisine and by the Mandarin language.

India alone has 17 percent of the world's population; India possesses the leading mass media industries of southern Asia, and much of its output leaks across the borders into Pakistan and Bangladesh. When these latter two countries are added, southern Asia has nearly 22 percent of the world's population. India possesses the world's most complex national media system, which really involves a collection of 10 separate-language media systems. Since its independence in 1947, India has done little media importing.

A fourth distinctive media grouping is the *Arabic-language media*, which stretch from Morocco on the Atlantic to the Persian Gulf. This grouping consists of 20 countries, whose media intake is mainly in Arabic; again, of course, there is a distinctive cultural history, a distinctive religion, and a language that foreigners find very difficult. The Arabic-speaking countries (including Sudan) had a combined population of only about 346 million in 2005.

These four regional groupings (Euro-America, China, southern Asia, and the Arab countries) currently have about 74 percent of the world's population.

Among these four big groupings the Europeans are the most avid media importers. Globalization does not seem the most apt description. Europe is perhaps the leading example of American media exporting. But rather than refer to either Americanization or globalization, this book will regard the combined Euro-American media as world leaders.

---

[7] Timothy J. Havens, "Exhibiting Global Television: On the Business and Cultural Functions of Global Television Fairs," *Journal of Broadcasting and Electronic Media*, Vol. 47/1, March 2003: 18–35.

National and Regional Media Are Stronger Than International Media

Foreigners visiting big cities such as Beijing, Delhi, Paris, or Berlin have little difficulty in observing the relevant national media, as well as American and other international channels available in hotel bedrooms. But in the larger-population countries where most of the world's people live, the main tension tends to be between national media (based in the capital or largest city) and big regional media (based in the leading cities of the larger regions).

Domestic, or nonglobal and non-American, media in fact exist in many countries at four different levels. First are the *national media* coming from the biggest city and using the main national language. Second are the *regional media* based in that region and often using the regional language, as well as reflecting regional policies and politicians. Third are often the *local media*, such as newspapers and radio stations, which may appeal to a smaller minority, distinct from the regional media and language. Fourth are often the foreign media coming from a *neighboring nation-state*; often a language group straddles an international frontier—for example, people in both eastern India and in Bangladesh speak the same Bengali language. Added together, these four different categories of domestic media typically attract much bigger audiences than do the current crop of Euro-American imports.

New technology has helped to make media available from far-off places. But technology has also made possible a huge increase in local FM radio stations, and new printing systems make it easier to produce local newspapers. Even in the United States, where the national media are strong, many people rely heavily on nonnational media (local radio, a local newspaper, and local TV news-weather-sport-crime) and follow their local teams on regional sports networks.

Even in small population countries the majority of audience time goes to national media. In larger population countries the national, regional, local, and across-the-border media typically achieve audiences between 6 and 12 times those of global or American media.

2

Television Soap Operas, *Telenovelas*, Brazil

Two major aspects of relative U.S. media decline are considered in this chapter. First, the United States in the mid-twentieth century had a near monopoly of formats for cheap-to-produce popular television programming —such as game shows and soap operas. But the evolution of the soap opera has included its reinvention in other lands, most notably in the form of the Latin American *telenovela*.

Brazil—along with Mexico a leading exponent and exporter of the *telenovela*[1] —is also considered in this chapter. Brazil, a leading example of another wider phenomenon, is one of 11 countries that now has a population of over 100 million people as well as its own significant mass media industry.

Television's Cheap Genres: Rise and Fall of U.S. Dominance

By around 1960 the United States was far ahead of the rest of the world in producing cheap TV genres. The United States had had three decades of commercial radio and then commercial TV experience, especially in the case of quiz/game shows. In the 1950s and 1960s, new television services around the world mostly did three things, in sequence. First, they simply imported game/quiz and other cheap American productions; second, they acquired the right to make a local national version of, for example, an American game show; third, networks in other nations began to build on these American models by creating their own new shows.

---

[1] Kate Large and Jo Anne Kenny, "Latino Soaps Go Global," *Television Business International*, January/February 2004: 38–41.

These cheap formats seemed in their origins to be 100 percent American TV shows. However, a local national version—peopled with local participants and a national celebrity host—quickly came to seem native to its new national location. These cheap formats made heavy use of ordinary people, modest citizens of the particular nation-state speaking their own language.

Most "new" game/quiz shows adopted by TV networks around the world in the 1950s and 1960s were in fact local versions of American formats. Because the United Kingdom was the second world TV power of the period around 1950, it (along with the Latin America) was an early big importer of U.S. game/quiz formats. For example, *Twenty Questions*, which began on BBC radio in 1947, was modeled on the American ABC radio show of the same name, which began in 1946. *What's My Line?* began on CBS TV in February 1950 and on BBC TV in July 1951. *This Is Your Life* (BBC TV, 1955 onward) was based on the U.S. show of the same name, which began on NBC radio in 1948 and NBC TV in 1952.[2]

"Talk shows" became a television staple in Britain and in numerous other countries. These shows usually followed the format of a comedian-host interviewing two or three show-biz celebrities; this was the American NBC *Tonight* show format, which began in 1954 with Steve Allen as the host (Johnny Carson took over from Jack Paar in 1961).

Candid Camera began in the United States in 1948 and was the pioneer of "reality," hidden cameras, and "surprise." Many of these cheap-to-produce shows, when they achieved strong ratings, became enormously profitable. A number of independent producers and on-camera hosts controlled the rights to the shows, and some became seriously wealthy. One such entrepreneur was Mark Goodson, who created *The Price Is Right* and *What's My Line?* He produced 42,000 half-hour TV episodes and, at his 1992 death, had an estimated wealth of $450 million.

After the 1960s, there were fewer fresh U.S. exports of cheap formats. Many foreign networks were breathing long life into what they had already imported. Within the United States, successful old shows (like the soaps) just ran and ran five days a week. The American cheap shows were locked into the rigid framework of "dayparts" operated by the three big U.S. networks in the 1970s—soaps in early afternoon, game shows before prime time, and talk shows after prime time.

The next big burst of American cheap TV format exporting was around 1990. In the late 1980s and early 1990s many American soaps were exported around the world to new, or newly commercial, networks. A new type of talk show began in the 1980s—with hosts such as Oprah Winfrey in 1986, Sally Jessy Raphael in 1983, and Jerry Springer in 1992. These afternoon talk shows became steadily more confessional, more outlandish, more freak show–like,

---

[2] Maxene Fabe, *TV Game Shows*, Garden City, NY: Doubleday, 1979; Asa Briggs, *The History of Broadcasting in the UK. Volume IV. Sound and Vision*, Oxford: Oxford University Press, 1979.

and more confrontational;[3] audiences around the world were offered these shows, and many marveled and gasped at the "only in America" antics.

American game show exports also had a revival around 1990,[4] not least because new networks had great difficulty scheduling 18 or 24 hours of programming per day. As an example, just one American game show company (Fremantle) was licensing 10 different game shows to various German networks in 1992. One of the new German networks (RTL+) at 4:40 pm, five days a week, was showing *Riskant!*, a German version of *Jeopardy!* At 5:15 pm the same network was showing *Der Preiss ist Heist* (*The Price Is Right*). At 5:05 pm, also five days a week, the SAT-1 network was showing *Geh Aufs Ganze* (*Let's Make a Deal*). One remarkable fact was the age of these U.S.-German games; these three games were all launched in the United States between 1956 and 1963, which gave them an average age (in 1992) of 31 years.

In 1990, however, a first batch of American "reality" exports were in a more active phase. In 1990–1991 there were some 25 "reality" shows on American television. The year 1990 saw the launch of *America's Most Wanted* and *America's Funniest Home Videos*. Such shows were both cheap to make in the United States and easy to export. Networks in importing countries could use some of the American video, while adding some of their own (and their audiences') video efforts.

From about 1995 on came a decline in American exports of some of these cheap programming formats. Some newer networks in Europe now seemed more agile at developing new formats. The Australian Grundy company developed expertise in making sophisticated national versions of soaps and games for a range of European countries. In the Netherlands two TV format innovators eventually joined together in Endemol; this company had a big presence in Germany and then in Britain and subsequently in many other countries.

Endemol was a leader in developing new mixes of the game-reality formats. Often this involved a dozen or so youngish people being isolated from the world, but surrounded by cameras. Formats such as *Big Brother* claimed to break old taboos and to push the envelope. Their various audience participation "interactive" innovations (which allowed "voting," text messaging, and the like) contributed to the sense of excitement and to the audience level. Successful shows of this kind opened up fresh revenue streams (premium priced phone calls and merchandizing). They also generated a crescendo of press and other media interest.

---

[3] Joshua Gamson, *Freaks Talk Back: Tabloid Talk Shows and Sexual Non-conformity*, Chicago: University of Chicago Press, 1998; Jane M. Shatuc, *The Talking Cure: TV Talk Show and Women*, New York: Routledge, 1997.

[4] The arrival of *Wheel of Fortune* in Europe is analyzed in Michael Skovmand, "Barbarous TV International: Syndicated Wheels of Fortune," in Michael Skovmand and Kim Christian Schrøder (eds.), *Media Cultures*, London: Routledge, 1992: 84–103.

New reality game shows achieved big audiences on European and American TV—especially during 1999–2001—thus paralleling the dot-com bubble of the same years. Many of these shows were created in the Amsterdam or London suburbs.[5] Especially in 2000 and 2001 the big American TV networks (traditionally reluctant to import anything from anywhere) placed several of these European shows into prime time. *Who Wants to Be a Millionaire?* was created by a British company (Celador) and appeared on (U.K.) ITV in 1998; it was on the ABC network in the United States in 1999 and by 2000 was achieving huge audiences in India. Several such shows were really reworkings of ancient American formats; the British *The Weakest Link* was a traditional quiz show with some add-ons; the British *Pop Idol* (U.S. version, *American Idol*) was the old talent show idea in new clothing.[6] The BBC's *Strictly Come Dancing* was a much exported and copied version of the ancient ballroom dancing format.

But it was the Dutch company Endemol that created *Big Brother*[7] and many other successful reality formats. Why was Endemol so successful in the years both before and after 2000 in creating shows that could be sold to many other countries? Based in a small population country, the founders of Endemol became adept at creating Dutch shows that would also work in Germany. Endemol was highly successful at licensing its formats in the United Kingdom and in most other European countries. In the United States (by contrast) much of the creative focus was upon creating new formats for new niche cable channels.

Most of these reality shows had a quick rise and quick fall in terms of audience appeal. The founders of Endemol were aware of this pattern and sold their company to the Spanish phone company Telefonica for $4.8 billion in 2000.

From U.S. Soap to Hispanic and Brazilian *Telenovela*

Telenovelas, the Latin American version of the TV soap opera, illustrate several aspects of the growth, and subsequent decline, of U.S. media

---

[5] Of 32,625 format hours exported during 2002–2004, 32.1 percent came from the United Kingdom, 20.9 percent from the Netherlands, 18.2 percent from the United States, and 8.3 percent from Australia. In "balance of trade" terms the United Kingdom was the biggest net exporter, followed by the Netherlands and the United States. "World Trade in Television Formats: UK and the Netherlands Are Ahead of the USA in Exports," *Screen Digest*, April 2005: 100–101.

[6] Rana Forodhar, "Hello, 'Good Bye': Why British Shows Are the Hottest Thing on US TV," *Newsweek International*, May 7, 2001: 48–9.

[7] Donald Koeleman, Elena Ruiz Argüello, and Michael Sedge, "Big Designs on Big Brother," *Multichannel News International*, October 2000: 40–42; Richard Kilborn, *Staging the Real: Factual Programming in the Age of Big Brother*, Manchester, UK: Manchester University Press, 2003: 75–88.

dominance. Brazil, like many other countries, was initially a big importer of U.S. television programming. Subsequently, however, Brazil increasingly made its own programming; its *telenovelas* (TV stories) became Brazil's most popular programming and also a major export.

Producing a national soap opera was more expensive than making a game/quiz show. But Brazil and Mexico gradually emerged as leading producers and exporters of *telenovela*-soap TV drama. Brazil has the world's fifth largest population, and it also illustrates a wider point. In the 1950s and 1960s the world's highest output (TV) soap factory was in the United States; but by the 1980s and 1990s the biggest soap factories were in Brazil, Mexico, India, and China.

The U.S. TV soaps around 1960 were "daytime" shows (usually shown between 12 noon and 4 pm); they were commercially driven—with soap companies, especially Procter & Gamble, still in charge of the production of some of them. They had a target audience of "at-home" women, preferably youngish women with middle-class house-proud spending habits. The American soaps ran on weekdays around the year (five a week, 260 a year). Initially on radio the soaps had been only 15 minutes;[8] on television they were 30 minutes or 60 minutes.

These U.S. TV soaps were super-popular with their target audiences. If a new soap was not popular, it was quickly killed off. Surviving soaps seemed to run forever. Of the soaps on U.S. television in 1982, six had each been running for two decades.[9] Viewers could feel that their own lives ran alongside those of the soap characters; the soaps lived in the same time frame and referred to current events in the news. The soap writers were reading the same daily newspapers as were their viewers. When the soaps were exported, the foreign audience lost much of this original sense of intimacy.

The first British TV soap, *Coronation Street*, was launched by Granada in 1960; it copied some, but not all, of the U.S. characteristics. *Coronation Street* was commercially driven, but it was scheduled in an early evening time slot and was targeted at a mass audience; within the British "public" system it was also more working-class oriented. *Coronation Street* did only two episodes a week (100 a year). It had a higher rating than any U.S. soap; it was in a bigger audience time slot and it had less competition. *Coronation Street* seemed blessed with huge rating (and share) numbers and near-everlasting life.

Latin American *telenovelas* were different from both U.S. and U.K. soaps. The *telenovela* was scheduled into evening prime time; it also had a radio

---

[8] Rudolph Arnheim, "The World of the Daytime Serial," in Paul F. Lazarsfeld and Frank N. Stanton (eds.), *Radio Research, 1942–1943*, New York: Duell, Sloan and Pearce, 1944: 34–85.

[9] Muriel G. Cantor and Suzanne Pingree, *The Soap Opera*, Beverly Hills, CA: Sage, 1983: 50; Mary Cassata and Thomas Skill, *Life on Daytime Television: Tuning-in American Serial Drama*, Norwood, NJ: Ablex, 1983; Marilyn J. Matelski, *The Soap Opera Evolution*, Jefferson, NC: McFarland, 1988; Robert C. Allen, *Speaking of Soap Operas*, Chapel Hill: University of North Carolina Press, 1985.

Table 2.1   Starting Domestic TV Soap Production

START DATE	COUNTRIES
Early 1950s	United States
Late 1950s	Cuba, Argentina, Mexico
Early 1960s	United Kingdom, Brazil, Japan
Late 1960s	Venezuela, Colombia, Peru, Chile, Australia
Early 1980s	India
Mid-1980s	China
Early 1990s	Western Europe

prehistory and was targeted at a mass audience and women in particular. The Brazilian *novelas* claimed (and probably delivered) unusually high quality for a daily drama product. But their key difference from both U.S. and U.K. soaps was that Brazilian *telenovelas* only lasted for about 150 or 200 daily episodes (Mexican *telenovelas* were shorter). Partly because of its briefer life span, the successful *telenovela* seemed to pack a knock-out emotional punch, and many *novelas* became major media "events" in their home country.

American-made soap operas were exported to many countries from the 1960s onward. But (as Table 2.1 shows) most western European countries did not make these high episode numbers series until some four decades after the United States did. Western European systems, until around 1990, were mainly public service systems that wanted little daytime popular programming; U.S. soap-style output was still regarded as low quality, or trash, TV.

The worldwide spread of soap factory TV production is a complex topic, not least because of the widely varied definitions of "soap."[10] Some TV networks experimented with daily, or near daily, series. There were numerous false starts. Most countries already had their own radio soap operas. Some national networks began experiments at the same time with short series (such as six episodes), weekly series (perhaps 26 episodes), and soap series (100 episodes or more); depending on its perceived success, one of these series could be switched to a different category. But most countries still preferred to fill the early afternoon hours with educational or children's output.

Nevertheless, the international soap production sequence certainly saw the United States in the lead (with numerous TV soaps running by 1955). Next came Latin America in three phases. The leading "mixed" (public-commercial) systems in the United Kingdom and Japan both began in the 1960s, but on a small scale and in their own idiosyncratic manners; Japan's public service NHK scheduled 15-minute daily soaps at breakfast-time. Next

---

[10] Robert C. Allen (ed.), *to be continued . . . soap operas around the world*, London: Routledge, 1995.

came India and China, the population giants, and in the 1990s the main western European soap effort.[11]

Like other mass media genres, television soaps changed over time. Those American soaps that were launched in the 1950s and survived into the 1970s changed significantly along the way; during the 1970s, for example, U.S. soaps became much sexier.[12]

The Latin American *novelas* also changed over the decades. In the 1960s and 1970s the *telenovelas* were closely linked to the metropolis (Mexico City; Rio and Sao Paolo in Brazil). By the 1980s television was reaching out into the hinterland. Brazil, which in 1970 had imported most of its programming, was by 1983 importing only 23 percent of its prime-time schedule.[13]

The U.S. soaps reached their high point in terms of domestic audience size (and profitability) around 1980, before the big subsequent fragmentation into new networks and cable. In 1981 each of the three big networks (ABC, CBS, NBC) was transmitting four daytime soap operas, five days a week. ABC had the three top soaps, *General Hospital*, *One Life to Live*, and *All My Children*; clearly some people were watching two or three soaps each afternoon.[14] Even NBC's less popular soaps were profitable; ABC's popular soaps were super-profitable.

As the domestic U.S. audience steadily fragmented during the 1980s and 1990s, some of these U.S. daily soaps found new customers in the form of newly launched channels around the world. In the early 1990s *Santa Barbara* was showing in, for example, France and Russia; *The Bold and the Beautiful* was showing in Italy, Denmark, Greece, Australia, and many African and Asian countries.[15] Also popular on the world scene was *The Young and the Restless*, which completed its 8,000th episode on November 1, 2004.

But by the 1990s U.S. soap exporters found themselves competing with popular *telenovelas* from Brazil and Mexico. By 1990 Brazilian *telenovelas* had been shown in over 100 countries. The U.S. soaps continued to appear on schedules around the world; but the glitzy fantasy representations of affluent Americans were inevitably remote from reality as experienced in much of the world. Despite their rags-to-riches plots, the Brazilian (and Mexican) *telenovelas* seemed more relevant to the lives of many people in many countries.

---

[11] Kate Bowles and Sue Turnbull, *Tomorrow Never Knows: Soap on Australian Television*, Melbourne: Australian Film Institute, 1994; Paul A. S. Harvey, "Nonchan's Dream: NHK Morning Serialised Television Novels," in D. P. Martinez (ed.), *The Worlds of Japanese Popular Culture*, Cambridge, UK: Cambridge University Press, 1988: 133–151; Hugh O'Donnell, *Good Times, Bad Times: Soap Opera and Society in Western Europe*, London: Leicester University Press, 1999.

[12] Dennis T. Lowry and David E. Towles, "Soap Opera Portrayals of Sex, Contraception, and Sexually Transmitted Diseases," *Journal of Communication*, Vol. 39/2, Spring 1989: 76–83.

[13] Tapio Varis, *International Flow of Television Programmes*, Paris: UNESCO, 1985: 19.

[14] "ABC Keeps on Packin' Daytime Dynamite," *Variety*, December 30, 1981.

[15] Angela Ndalianis "Style, Spectacle, Excess and the Bold and the Beautiful," in Kate Bowles and Sue Turnbull (eds.), *Tomorrow Never Comes to Australian Television*, Melbourne: Australian Film Institute, 1994: 25–41.

Figure 2.1
Marketing three
Globo *telenovelas*.
(Image provided by
the author.)

Brazil as Globo-lized *Telenovela* Nation

The year 1964 marked the beginning of two decades (1964–1984) of military
rule in Brazil. Also in 1964, domestic Brazilian TV production of daily *novelas*
was beginning. The *telenovelas*, and the Globo company (the main producer
of *novelas*), had an especially intimate relationship with the military. In 1984,
after 20 years of military rule, Globo decided to switch its political allegiance.
The Brazilian military smoothed the way to Globo's commercial success;
Globo eventually showed the military the way to the political exit.

Brazil's population more than trebled from 1950 to 2000. But in 1964
Brazil had only 81 million people; these people were split between a narrow
urban-coastal fringe and a vast rural, and rain forest, interior. The military in
the mid-1960s planned to develop this vast interior. Like other groups of

generals-in-power, the Brazilian military worked to develop national technology, and they wanted to control a bigger and more nationally spread mass media system. Brazil focused on several highish technology fields, such as smaller passenger jet aircraft; the generals also annoyed the United States by developing and protecting a Brazilian computer industry. There was a heavy focus on telecommunications—both microwave and satellite systems were extended, initially into all of the provincial capitals. Television was seen by the military both as fitting into this technology vision and as the best way to build Brazilian national identity.

Globo was a well-established newspaper and radio company that did not start in television until 1965. Globo's television activities initially involved the American company Time Inc. Globo soon developed a structure reminiscent of U.S. TV networks of that era; Globo owned and operated TV stations in five major cities and established a national network of "affiliated" local stations in all of the provinces.

The number of Brazilian TV households steadily rose—from 1.8 million (1960) to 6 million (1970) to 16 million (1980). Television was soon attracting about half of all Brazilian advertising expenditure; gradually the amount of U.S. programming in prime time reduced, and by 1980 Globo's own productions were getting most of the top 10 TV ratings each week. By the mid-1980s audience research and ratings numbers indicated that *telenovelas* were the most popular, and most viewed, genre; second were the (weekend) variety shows; third was the national news; and fourth were films (the main remaining Hollywood foothold). Brazilian comedies were also popular, as, of course, were big football games.

The national news got high ratings not least because it was sandwiched in mid-evening between two currently super-popular *telenovelas*. The military had little difficulty in censoring the news into a broadly upbeat and positive account of Brazil's economic growth and dynamic development. Press censorship was more difficult and tense, with several Brazilian newspapers engaged in the classic games of testing the censorship laws and placing messages between the lines.[16]

Telenovelas were especially easy to censor. In most cases the writing of perhaps 170 one-hour episodes was dominated by a single well-known writer (aided by a very small team of assistants). Episode scripts were normally written only a few weeks ahead of final transmission; this situation obviously put the script censor in a very strong position. Leading *novela* writers often came from *radionovelas* (or the theater) and were widely known as skilled professionals. But *telenovelas* had to be long on melodrama and

---

16 Dov Shinar and Marco Antonio Rodrigues Dias, "Communications Policy in Brazil," in Majid Teheranian, Farhad Hakimzadeh, and Marcello L. Vidale (eds.), *Communications Policy for National Development*, London: Routledge, 1977: 225–41.

short on social message.[17] (In recent years social messages have become more common.)

Brazilian newspapers followed the Latin American tradition of being upmarket, elitist, urban, and as political as censorship allowed.[18] Radio never became a nationally spread (as opposed to local) mass medium. So television in general, and *telenovelas* in particular, became the main national mass media. Successful *novelas* received huge amounts of press coverage. Many anecdotes claim that, as Brazilian *novelas* approach their final days, "everything stops" and urban traffic jams melt away.

Telenovelas seem to have mopped up much of Brazil's acting and writing talent; these people, especially from 1964 to 1984, found themselves unable to comment on the extremes of inequality in Brazilian culture. In fact, in 1980 more Brazilians had a TV set in their household than had either clean water or a primary school education; the same was still true in 1990.[19]

Brazil, like other Latin American countries, has experience of the real-life political scandal/*telenovela*. Presidential elections in Brazil in both 1985 and 1989 had many melodramatic twists and turns; in both elections Globo TV itself played a central role in the reality *telenovela* on which it was reporting.

The 1984–1985 election in Brazil marked the handover from (two decades of) military power to civilian rule. The military wanted an indirect form of presidential election via an electoral college. As the 1984 presidential elections approached, Globo TV began to distance itself from the military; Globo gave much news coverage to protestors demanding a direct election by the electorate of the president. Globo TV also split from the military by opposing the generals' preferred candidate. Globo in effect supported an "opposition" candidate who was elected president (under the indirect rules). But the president elect, Tancredo Neves, then died before taking office.

According to the Constitution this meant that the next in succession, the speaker of the Lower House, would become president. Globo TV, however, argued that the next-but-one successor—the newly elected vice president (Jose Sarney) should become president; and this is what did, indeed, happen.

The 1989 presidential election produced its own ration of melodrama. The election was eventually won by Fernando Collor de Mello, who was at the time age 39; the youthful, good-looking Collor (of German descent) could

---

[17] Thomas Tufte, *Living with the Rubbish Queen: Culture and Modernity in Brazil*, Luton, UK: University of Luton Press, 2000; Michèle and Armand Mattelart, *The Carnival of Images: Brazilian Television Fiction*, New York: Bergin and Gavey (Greenwood), 1990; Nico Vink, *The Telenovela and Emancipation: TV and Social Change in Brazil*, The Netherlands: Royal Tropical Institute, 1988; Conrad Phillip Kottak, *Prime-Time Society: An Anthropological Analysis of Television and Culture*, Belmont, CA: Wadsworth, 1990; Robert Mader, "Globo Village: Television in Brazil," in Tony Dowmunt (ed.), *Channels of Resistance*, London: British Film Institute, 1993: 67–89.

[18] Anne-Marie Smith, *A Forced Agreement: Press Acquiescence to Censorship in Brazil*, Pittsburgh: University of Pittsburgh Press, 1997.

[19] *The Economist*, April 29, 1995.

easily have been a *telenovela* hero. His main opponent, "Lula" (Luis Inácio da Silva), was the candidate of the Workers Party; Lula had risen from dire poverty to become a trade union leader—but on television he looked fat, bearded, ethnically nondescript, and sloppily dressed, in contrast to Collor. The conservative Collor promised to attack corruption and to privatize state-owned industries.

But even before his successful election there were some press stories to the effect that Collor (first as a city mayor and then as a provincial governor) had his own track record of corruption. His family controlled Globo TV's affiliated TV company in the northeastern region of Alagoas. After Collor was installed as president, these corruption stories multiplied; Globo TV in due course changed sides once more and repeated its previous tactic of giving massive news coverage to street demonstrations (which demanded Collor's impeachment). Collor was duly impeached and was removed from office in late 1992.

Globo continued to be an extremely active player in Brazilian politics.[20] It supported Fernando Cardoso (president, 1995–2002) and subsequently made another adjustment to support the nondescript and leftist "Lula," who was elected president of Brazil in 2002. Soon President Lula and his Workers Party were being accused, by Globo TV and the press, of political bribery and corruption.

U.S. Loss of Dominance over Cheap TV Genres and of Big-Population Nations' Media

The Brazilian *telenovela* exemplifies two ways in which U.S. media leadership, or dominance, steadily declined from the 1960s onward. Cheap genres—such as the soap opera, the quiz/game show, and the talk show—were developed for mid-twentieth-century American commercial radio and TV. All of these genres and formats were then adopted, and adapted, by other countries.

Adopted genres, such as the Procter & Gamble soap opera, were adapted and altered into distinctive local national versions. Although based on an original North American model, the *telenovela* became ever more Brazilian; the *telenovela* came to reflect Brazilian, not U.S., values. This pattern paralleled the Brazilian adoption of the British-invented game of association soccer football. Brazil became a world leader in the world's leading sport.

[20] Elisabeth Fox, *Media and Politics in Latin America: The Struggle for Democracy*, London: Sage, 1988; Elisabeth Fox, *Latin American Broadcasting: From Tango to Telenovela*, Luton, UK: University of Luton Press/John Libbey, 1997; John R. Dassin, "Press Censorship and the Military State in Brazil," in Jane Leftwich Curry and Joan R. Dassin (eds.), *Press Control Around the World*, Westport, CT: Praeger, 1982: 149–86; Alexander Cockburn, "Hot About Collor," *New Statesman*, September 1, 1989; "Collor Television," *The Economist*, August 19, 1989.

Brazilian teams played football in a bravura Brazilian style, which seemed to retain fairly few residues of Victorian Britain.

In 1945 Brazil was still a giant coffee republic (a banana republic writ large). By 2005 Brazil was a major player on the world scene. The people and politicians of big population countries do not want to be culturally beholden to the United States or to any other nation-state. Brazil now generates at home the great bulk of the media it consumes. Brazil's media have long focused on the samba and much other made-in-Brazil popular music. The national language, Portuguese, is important. Also significant have been Brazil's entertainment and football stars. The funeral of Ayrton Senna (the Formula One racing driver killed at Imola on May 1, 1994) attracted one million people onto the streets of Sao Paulo. A decade after his death (on live television), Senna was still revered; his name was attached to freeways, streets, schools, and over 200 commercial products, whose profits were plowed back into social projects.

Brazil's main population centers are remote from the rest of the world. It is over 4,000 miles from Rio or Sao Paulo to New York; relatively few Brazilians have travelled north or west of Florida.

The centrality of television meant that Roberto Marinho (1904–2003) and his sons—through their Globo TV-radio-press empire—exerted extraordinary power over Brazil's politics, culture, and life. For four decades (1965–2005) Globo was probably more powerful than any group of Brazilian generals or any political party.

Globo has played a major political role in selecting (and electing) Brazilian presidents. Globo has also been active (with other electronic and print media) in destroying political incumbents with lurid stories of scandal, corruption and cash-in-suitcases.[21] While adept at encouraging massive street demonstrations, the Brazilian media could also be accused of sensationalizing crime and making some of the world's most freaky reality shows, while downplaying massive urban poverty and exploitation. But all of this was predominantly Brazilian and South American, not North American.

[21] "Brazil's Bribery Scandal: Jeffersonian Democracy, Tropical Style," *The Economist*, June 25, 2005: 65–66; Richard Lapper, "Media Battle to Win Readers Fuels Brazil's Corruption Scandal," *Financial Times*, July 19, 2005.

3

From B2B to Bedroom and from the United States to the World

As a new mass medium gradually moves toward maturity, it typically follows two parallel paths. First, most new media begin on a business-to-business (B2B) basis and are used by wealthy individuals; next they become available in semi-public places such as reading rooms or Internet cafes; then comes a mass move into households; and finally the (now mature) medium reaches individuals in their private spaces and bedrooms.

Parallel to this sequence is another, international, path to maturity. Typically the new medium first reaches industrial scale in the United States; it is then exported, in various ways, to northern Europe and to the rest of the world.

Of course these two paths to maturity do not exhaust the history of the mass media in the world. Several other dimensions are clearly important. One is politics. Another is technology; the mass media can be seen as beginning with the application of steam power to the printing of newspapers in the years after 1800. Subsequent master technologies included electricity, radio and electronics, space satellites, and digital computerization. "New media" and new technologies derive from commercial competition and take several decades to mature. Early promotional hoopla often exaggerates the prospects for rapid growth; typically the resulting burst bubble in turn leads to underestimation of the longer term significance of the "new medium."

"Death of the Newspaper" and of Other Old Media

"New media" are always arriving and posing a serious challenge to existing or "old" media. The "death of the newspaper" has been frequently predicted over the last hundred years.

Despite their predicted deaths, several other media—such as magazines, movies, recorded music, and radio—are all still alive. But how is it possible for so many new mass media to appear without killing off established media? First, old mass media survive by adjusting to new media. Second, human beings devote more and more of their time to "following" the media; people often follow the medium as a secondary activity—they view, listen, or read while they work, travel, cook, and so on. Third, people squeeze in more media consumption by following two media at the same time; when Americans watched TV in 2004, 54 percent also talked on the phone, 38 percent also read a newspaper, 17 percent also used the Internet, and 9 percent also listened to the radio.[1]

Whenever television in a particular country became a major mass medium the imminent "death of radio" was asserted; but this death did not happen. From the 1920s until at least the 1980s, each decade saw more and more millions of human hours devoted to radio. Even in the media-saturated United States, household members spend nearly one-third of total media time with their radios.

As cable grew dramatically in the United States after 1980, it was widely predicted that cable would blow television away. Some people today argue that cable has indeed mortally wounded television; but most household consumers probably see cable and television as two elements of the same thing.

The movies' golden years came to an end in the 1950s and since then the film has been in decline. Right? Wrong, at least in terms of audience numbers. More people watched more films in the 40 years after 1960 than in the 60 years before 1960. People now see more films on their TV screens than the golden age audience saw in the movie theater. Also, the film audience—both theatrical and TV—hugely expanded, especially in Asia, in the second half of the twentieth century.

As the oldest of the mass media, the newspaper has had its death proclaimed the most frequently. In fact, world daily newspaper sales continued to grow up to, and past, the year 2000. Substantial sales increases in China, India, South America, and Africa more than compensated for modest declines in Europe, the United States and Japan. From 1999 to 2004 world sales of daily newspapers grew by over 5 percent to 395 million daily sales in 2004. Many newspapers today find that the Internet cuts their revenue (especially classified advertising) and also increases their costs (supplying web services for free). Nevertheless, many newspapers around the world still deliver generous profits.

---

[1] "Crowned at Last: A Survey of Consumer Power," *The Economist*, April 2, 2005: 9; Ron Lembo, *Thinking Through Television*, Cambridge, UK: Cambridge University Press, 2000.

From B2B via Café to Bedroom

Twenty-four Chinese students died in Beijing in June 2002 when fire destroyed an Internet café. The café was locked (presumably for security purposes). The time was 2:40 am, when the computers were available at cheaper rates.[2]

The Internet café phenomenon occurred in many different countries around the world before and after the year 2000. This semi-public access to the new medium was most popular at an intermediate phase in the Internet's local history—a point when many students and others wanted to access the net but did not have, and could not yet afford, their own personal computer. The Internet café provides echoes of the eighteenth-century European coffeehouse where men went to read the newspapers and to gossip with other men.[3]

The *daily newspaper* in eighteenth-century Europe was primarily a business-to-business or government-to-government product; merchants and officials read the newspaper in order to keep up with news of shipping, war, and court politics. From 1800 onward daily newspapers sold increasingly to affluent (and literate) individuals. Both in Europe and America much newspaper reading in the mid-1800s was done in bars, taverns, reading rooms, and coffee shops; these were predominantly male places. Between 1850 and 1900 a particularly spectacular growth in newspaper sales occurred in the United States; by 1900, Pulitzer, Hearst, and other popular newspaper owners were appealing strongly to women readers—and the daily paper had become a family medium. More than one daily newspaper per American household was sold in all the decades between 1900 and 1960. But around 1960 the American daily entered a phase of (relative) decline. Research still showed that daily newspapers were read heavily both before 9 am and between 5 and 9 pm.[4] The newspaper already made separate appeals to different family members. Newspapers increasingly were sectionalized to allow individuals to read separate sections in their own personal spaces. But already by the early 1980s, significantly fewer young adults (ages 18–29) were reading the daily newspaper as opposed to those age 45 and over.[5] The American daily newspaper has largely lost the evening hours, and the young

---

[2] Erik Eckholm, "Fire in Illegal Internet Café Kills 24," *International Herald Tribune*, June 16, 2002 (from *New York Times*); Erik Eckholm, "Chinese Seizing an Opportunity to Chat," *International Herald Tribune*, August 6, 2000; (from *NYT*); "China Cracks Down on Internet Cafes," *Screen Digest*, November 2001.

[3] "The Internet in a Cup: Coffee Fuelled the Information Exchanges of the 17th and 18th Centuries," *The Economist*, December 20, 2003: 48–50.

[4] Chilton R. Bush, *News Research for Better Newspapers*, New York: American Newspaper Publishers' Association Foundation, 1966.

[5] Newspaper Advertising Bureau, *Newspapers in American News Habits: A Comparative Assessment*, New York: Newspaper Advertising Bureau, 1985.

adult audience, to the electronic media. Today only one American daily is sold for every two households.

The *movies* have a radically different history from other mass media. After the movies began in the late 1890s there was no B2B phase and the early audience was not an affluent one. The movie audience before 1914 did, however, use very small local venues (converted shops, and then small halls and nickelodeons) that conformed loosely to a semi-public phase.[6] As with other new media, the early movies often had predominantly male audiences—because the movie venues were often insufficiently respectable to attract women. The movies initially faced no formal censorship and (as Kevin Brownlow reveals) the early silent movies covered strong subjects such as drugs, prisons, poverty, and political corruption; there was more overt sex than censorship subsequently allowed and the early silent cinema also offered soft pornography and covered topics such as prostitution and abortion.[7] During the 1920s the Hollywood movie industry began to pursue a family audience and adopted strict puritanical censorship. Only after a pause of several decades did the movies eventually become, with the videocassette, a household and then bedroom medium.

Recorded music's history conforms broadly to the B2B-to-bedroom trajectory. The 1890s saw a brief business-to-business phase because office dictaphone recording was regarded to be the potentially most profitable application. Much of the early history of recorded music followed the semi-public pattern. In penny arcades the great urban American public was offered a choice between brief sound recordings or a one-minute movie show;[8] this was a nonrespectable and, in the late 1890s, a predominantly male activity. However, the new industry after 1900 made a big effort to reach women and affluent families. The gramophone became an expensive, large, and heavy (hardwood) piece of domestic furniture; big publicity was focused on Enrico Caruso and other opera singers, although most recorded fare consisted of popular songs. In the 1920s this continued to be an expensive medium, and the 1930s saw huge falls in annual record sales. Even in the United States recorded music continued to have a significant semi-public element. People danced to recorded music; during the 1930s the new juke boxes were a major outlet for the record companies. Not until the 1940s did recorded music, even in the United States, become a genuinely mass medium.[9]

---

[6] John L. Fell (ed.), *Film Before Griffith*, Berkeley: University of California Press, 1983.

[7] Kevin Brownlow, *Behind the Mask of Innocence*, London: Jonathan Cape, 1990. See also Ben Singer, *Melodrama and Modernity: Early Sensational Cinema and Its Contexts*, New York: Columbia University Press, 2001.

[8] David Nasaw, *Going Out: The Rise and Fall of Public Amusements*, Cambridge, MA: Harvard University Press, 1993: 120–34.

[9] William Howland Kenney, *Recorded Music in American Life: The Phonograph and Popular Memory, 1890–1945*, New York: Oxford University Press, 1999.

Radio had before 1940 overtaken recorded music as a mass medium, although it had done this largely by playing recorded music over the air. Radio conformed to the initial B2B pattern because until 1920 it was seen as having mainly commercial (including ship-to-ship) and also military applications. Radio was initially seen as a medium for men.[10] Early "crystal" sets were difficult to operate, and batteries needed recharging, often at the car garage. But as radio sales (and household electricity) rose, radio became a female as well as male medium. The set was often in the kitchen. (But where radios still remained scarce, as they did in Africa into the 1990s, the new transistor radio/cassette player tended to be carried around by a proud male owner.) In the United States by 1940 there were radio sets in 81 percent of homes and in 27 percent of cars.[11] The march toward the family as the owner of several, or numerous, radio sets had begun.[12]

Television did not have a genuinely B2B phase, but it had a lengthy prehistory in the 1920s and 1930s; in the 1940s much of the relevant industrial capacity went into wartime electronics. After 1945 the American television industry initially reached fairly affluent customers; there was a brief phase during which many Americans viewed television in their friends' and neighbors' homes and in bars and other semi-public places. By 1954 some 58 percent of U.S. homes were equipped with a TV set. By 1962 there were television sets in 90 percent of U.S. homes, while 14 percent already had two or more TV receivers. This move beyond the single household set continued, and by 1979 half of all U.S. homes had at least two sets. By 2000 most American children age eight or older had not only a TV set but also a radio and a tape/CD player in their bedroom.[13]

Home video had a brief B2B phase; initially, when the technology was both noisy and expensive, video was seen as having a major application in industrial training and education. The United States was hesitant about this new technology; in the 1970s Hollywood saw the videocassette as a fiendish Japanese sneak attack. In the 1970s home video was still a predominantly male amusement; the technology was far from user-friendly, and much early viewing (as with other new media) was of pornography. However, the home

---

[10] Richard Butsch, "Crystal Sets and Scarf-Pin Radios: Gender, Technology and the Construction of American Radio Listening in the 1920s," *Media, Culture and Society*, Vol. 20/4, 1998: 557–72; William Boddy, *New Media and Popular Imagination*, New York: Oxford University Press, 2004: 16–43.

[11] Richard Butsch, *The Making of American Audiences: From Stage to Television, 1750–1990*, Cambridge, UK: Cambridge University Press 2000: 173–92.

[12] Alan B. Albarran and Gregory G. Pitts, *The Radio Broadcasting Industry*. Boston: Allyn and Bacon 2001.

[13] Christopher H. Sterling, *Electronic Media*, New York: Praeger, 1984: 236–37; Donald F. Roberts and Ulla G. Foehr, *Kids and Media in America*, Cambridge, UK: Cambridge University Press, 2004: 42–48.

video soon became a primarily family and household medium. By 2003 there was more world spending on DVD than on VHS.[14]

From the United States to the World

Alongside the B2B-to-bedroom sequence, most new media have first reached mass scale, and been industrially developed, within the United States.

But although this latter generalization remains broadly true, in most cases the initial—not yet mass scale—developments did not occur in the United States; the new medium and its technology, typically, was pioneered in Europe.

The American colonial newspaper closely followed London models. It was more than a century after 1776 before American newspapers came to be seen as models for Europe and the world. Around 1900 the popular newspapers of Britain, France, Germany, Russia, and Japan were certainly copying some American press practices; but the influence was still in both directions. However, by 1919 the United States had easily the world's most influential and largest newspaper press (33 million daily sales).

The movies also were invented in Europe, especially in France.[15] Much traditional film vocabulary is French, as are several industry standards (such as 35mm film). But the United States was the leader in building a coherent movie industry, in fine-tuning technology, and in controlling domestic competition. The U.S. movie industry then led, by systematically attacking the entire world market. By 1925 Hollywood movies amounted to 60 percent or more of all movies shown in the United Kingdom, Germany, France, Italy, Hungary, Czechoslovakia, Scandinavia, Austria, Spain, Portugal, Australia, Canada, New Zealand, Argentina, Brazil, and Mexico.[16]

There was a bigger American participation in developing commercial sound recording; but the invention process again prominently involved Europeans. The American industry's rapid growth also relied heavily on Caruso, and numerous other European opera stars, to persuade affluent American customers to pay premium prices for very short recordings. Like the U.S. movie industry, the U.S. recorded music industry made big advances from 1914 to 1918. Competition was effectively controlled (with Victor and Columbia losing a cartel case in 1919), and in 1920 the United States industry sold 100 million records. There was always close Euro-American combination, both in terms of ownership and in the licensing of musical talent. But the United States maintained its lead, selling 150 million records in 1929 versus

---

[14] "World Video Markets Shuffle: World Spending on DVD Overtakes VHS for the First Time," *Screen Digest*, November 2003: 329–36.

[15] Alan Williams, *Republic of Images: A History of French Filmmaking*, Cambridge, MA: Harvard University Press, 1992; Kerry Segrave, *American Films Abroad*, Jefferson, NC: McFarland, 1997: 1–19.

[16] Jeremy Tunstall, *The Media Are American*, London: Constable, 1977: 284.

60 million for the United Kingdom and Germany combined. In the 1920s recorded American dance music and jazz had a big impact in Europe. The 1930s Depression hit both the U.S. and European recording industries. While Europe was going to war, the three years from 1938 to 1941 saw a massive growth in U.S. record sales; and this leadership—indeed dominance— continued into the 1950s. Gradually U.S. production dominance declined, and by 1974 the United Kingdom, Germany, France, and Japan together manufactured more records than did the United States.[17]

Radio is another example of a mass medium whose technology was largely developed in Europe but whose commercial potential was exploited in the United States. A public, government-controlled radio system developed in most other countries, but in the United States the federal government encouraged an initially totally unregulated commercial radio system. Consequently in 1930 the United States had 43 percent of the world's radio receivers. Combined American leadership in both commercial radio and in recorded music was extremely influential around the world in the mid- and late 1930s.

Television was another mass medium that relied upon Europe for much of its basic technology. Several European countries (the United Kingdom, Soviet Union, Germany, and France) operated quite substantial TV transmissions from 1936 to 1939. But it was the United States that, after 1945, took a huge world lead in all aspects of television.

Home video followed a different pattern. Here Japan was the chief technology innovator and was also the leading early user in terms of home video household penetration. The home video has its own complex history, with, for example, some Arab countries being early leaders in levels of household penetration. U.S. interests (Hollywood in particular) were anxious about the implications of home video for Hollywood's products. In the early 1980s the United States had fewer VCRs per hundred households than did Japan, the United Kingdom, and West Germany.[18] Subsequently the source of U.S. anxiety—its Hollywood movie and TV industry—was to prove, once again, to be a big advantage. American movies were to play a big part in the history of the JVS/VCR and also in its successor technology, the DVD.

Internet: From B2B to Bedroom and from the United States to the World

The Internet has an important mass media element; much Internet material is seen by large numbers of scattered individuals within a brief time frame

---

[17] Pekka Gronow and Ilpo Saunio, *The International History of the Recording Industry*, London: Cassell, 1998 (first published in Finnish in 1990).

[18] Gladys D. Ganley and Oswald H. Ganley, *Global Political Fallout: The First Decade of the VCR, 1976–1985*, Norwood, NJ: Ablex, 1987: 149–55.

—roughly comparable with the audience of a magazine, newspaper, or radio show. We will be looking at this mass media element and not at other large, or larger, aspects, such as the business-to-business and business-to-consumer Internet and e-mail.

The Internet has a unique history involving American big science, Department of Defense funding, and libertarian culture.[19] When the Internet moved beyond this bureaucracy-to-bureaucracy beginning, it grew quickly, but was, of course, dependent on the preexisting spread of personal computers in both businesses and homes. There followed the familiar semi-public phase with much Internet access involving semi-public locations such as universities, libraries, schools, and Internet cafés. In 1995 some 77 percent of U.S. and Canadian Internet users were male.[20] These numbers included many young men accessing pornographic sites. In the later 1990s both personal computers and the Internet made big advances into American homes—advances that then continued into individual bedrooms.

The Internet also broadly followed the international diffusion pattern found in previous mass media. Once again, Europe and Europeans played key roles in giving birth to the Internet. The "World Wide Web inventor" was a British citizen, Tim Berners-Lee, who was working in Geneva at CERN, the European high-energy physics research center. However, the main industrial development of the Internet (in its many mass media and non–mass media forms) took place in the United States.

Broadly in line with the history of earlier mass media, the 1990s saw the United States dominate the large-scale emergence of the consumer Internet. The rapid U.S. growth was assisted by many factors—including the widespread existence of personal computers and the recent deregulation of telecommunications, which created a huge surplus fiberoptic cable capacity; this fiberoptic surplus made possible the huge capacity involved in the rapid growth of the Internet "backbone."

During the 1990s the Internet developed as a predominantly American phenomenon. This was evident in the governance of the Internet[21] and in the predominance of American locations, users, finance, and terminology. Through the 1990s most of the material available on the net was in American English; this was loosely comparable to Hollywood silent films in the 1920s or to American television series in the late 1950s and early 1960s.

In its early years, several basic characteristics of the Internet played into traditional U.S. international advantages. Although in 1993 the net was only two years old, the United States was already "the first nation in cyberspace,"[22] with some 50 other countries participating. The early Internet

---

[19] Manuel Castells, *The Internet Galaxy: Reflections on the Internet, Business and Society*, Oxford, UK: Oxford University Press, 2001.

[20] Nielsen and other data, *Variety*, November 13–19, 1995: 6.

[21] Brian D. Loader (ed.), *The Governance of Cyberspace*, London: Routledge, 1997.

[22] Philip Elmer-Dewitt, "First Nation in Cyberspace," *Time*, December 6, 1993.

Figure 3.1 Eating and surfing in a Taipei (Taiwan) Internet café. (Chris Stowers/ Panos Pictures.)

Figure 3.2 Internet Café/Travel Agency and cows, Udaipur (Rajasthan), India. (Chris Stowers/Panos Pictures.)

Figure 3.3 Internet café, Beijing. (AP.)

seemed even to surpass the early movie business in terms of extreme scale economies. Soon American search engines not only were searching across English-speaking countries but were also offering searches in many other languages. The Internet required early entrepreneurial faith, engineering expertise, and generous finance; all of this fitted neatly with U.S. West Coast capitalism. The mass consumer Internet quickly came to depend on advertising finance—presumably another American advantage—at a time when American advertisers were looking for alternatives to both print and regular television. These financial characteristics also pointed toward probable dominance by only one or two big search engines[23] and only one or two leading specialists in each of books, travel, event tickets, and so on.

In line with what happened in other mass media, the 1990s level of American dominance was highly unlikely to be maintained. While net users in the United Kingdom and other English-speaking locations were still offered huge amounts of U.S. material, Japan by 2000 had already established its very own, very Japanese, Internet. In 2000 Japan already had 47 million Internet users, while both China and South Korea were not far behind.[24] By the end of 2002 there were more Internet users in Europe than

[23] Gary Rivlin, "Seeing Google with the Eyes of Forrest Gump," *New York Times*, August 10, 2004: C1, C6.
[24] K. C. Ho, Randolph Kluver, and C. C. Yang (eds.), *Asia.com: Asia Encounters the Internet*, London: RoutledgeCurzon, 2003.

in the United States; since then Asia has gone far ahead of both Europe and the United States.

As in many other media areas, there is a major difference between small population and large population countries. The large population countries (where most of the world's people live) are already well advanced in developing their own Internets in their own (major) languages. Many studies show that the most heavily visited websites deal with things like news, music, education, personal finance, weather, sport, jobs, cars, houses, and health. These popular websites are predominantly national and local, not international.

4

Freakish Media Finances
Benefit Number One

The media are financed from a bizarre variety of sources—including advertising, subscription, legally enforced license fees, subsidies, and bribes of various kinds. The prevailing financial picture varies drastically between media and between countries.

Freakish finances in the mass media are caused especially by the extreme economies of scale. It is the production of the "first copy" of a movie, newspaper, audio or video disk, or TV episode that accounts for the bulk of costs. Additional copies can be manufactured relatively cheaply. Once the cost of making the "first copy" is covered, a high proportion of subsequent revenue "drops to the bottom line" as profit. These industries aim at big audiences, best-sellers, and million-sale music because a big seller can generate a hundred times more profit than does a merely good average seller. It is because of these huge potential profits (from scale economies) that star performers earn star salaries.

Extremes of scale economies in the media typically benefit the number one in each national market or market niche. Similarly, scale economies operate internationally and benefit the United States as the number one media producer and exporter.[1] It only requires one copy of a movie or TV series to be shown on a foreign TV network to another national audience; much of this additional foreign revenue is clear profit.

These broad advantages, for the market number one, translate into several more specific financial benefits. The market number one can usually charge advertisers more (than its competitors) for each thousand audience members reached; if a market leading publication or cable channel has 60 percent of the specific audience, this typically translates into a 70 percent or more share of

---

[1] Colin Hoskins, Stuart McFadyen, and Adam Finn, *Global Television and Film: An Introduction to the Economics of the Business*, Oxford, UK: Oxford University Press, 1997.

the available advertising money—because advertisers seek to reach the majority of the target audience.

Bulk discounts are also salient in the media. The bigger a cable system operator, or the bigger the advertiser, the better the price. Meanwhile, in order to acquire attractive programming, small local broadcasters or cable operators may be compelled to accept other less attractive movies or series from the same strong supplier. This is a present-day version of the "blind buying" of the old movie industry (in which theater operators were compelled to rent some films they hadn't seen, and didn't want, in order to be allowed to rent popular movies).

In many media markets there is a trend toward market domination by the number one player. Despite the large number of new and hopeful cable offerings, the cable landscape includes several well-known examples of specific niches that are dominated by one supplier.

The mass media are not only the industry that is most dependent on advertising; the mass media are also exceptionally dependent on audience, and market research, numbers. There is a huge apparatus of research numbers, the best known of which are the Nielsen ratings for television and cable audiences. Nielsen operates in over 70 separate countries. Some of its numbers —for example, those for African-American and Spanish-language audiences in the United States—have been bitterly contested in recent years. Ratings points potentially represent large amounts of money.

Despite much billion-dollar talk about mass media imports, world import spending on programming, news, and entertainment is only about 1 percent of total world trade. The hardware—TV sets, audio and video players, personal computers—takes up a bigger slice of world trade.

There is also a huge difference in media expenditure between the world's most affluent and poorest people. Very little advertising is directed at the world's poorest two billion people; advertising promotes brands, and the poorest people in Asia and Africa mostly don't buy branded goods or branded food. In 2001 American exports of movies, TV, and video earned an average of about $2.50 from each of the world's six billion people. Wealthier people spend far more than this on multiplex visits, home video, and premium movie channels. In 2004 the French and Germans spent about $7 per movie theater visit, while Americans spent $6. But Indians spent only 20 U.S. cents per movie theater visit,[2] and very few Indian cinema visits involved a Hollywood film.

The mass media overall depend upon a bewildering array of financial sources. *Subscriptions* operate for most cable TV and satellite services, as well as for old media such as magazines. *One-off* (single) *sales* are typical of buying tabloid newspapers, recorded music, books, and cinema visits. *Advertising* prevails in commercial radio and TV, while *classified advertising* finances most

---

[2] "China's Cinema Prices Rise Fastest," *Screen Digest*, June 2005.

newspapers. A compulsory *license fee* commonly finances public service television and radio. Computer games rely upon a (cheapish) console. A mix of *commission and fee* finances advertising agencies. Much selling of syndicated television and cable programming relies on *barter*; no money changes hands, but the payment is made in advertising minutes.

In addition to this big range of financial arrangements, media political power and prestige also attract noncommercial finance in the forms of subsidy and bribery. Across the world, political subsidies have been common, especially for the political party's (loyal) newspaper; governments have often provided direct cash subsidies or the indirect subsidies of government official advertising. Media have also often been subsidized by foreign governments; the CIA gave American government financial assistance to media in many foreign countries in the decades after 1950. There are, of course, also commercial subsidies—the loss-making newspaper, or cable channel, maintained as the prestige flagship of a commercial media group. Moreover, across several continents, commercial and political bribes (in envelopes) to journalists allow media owners to save money by paying lower salaries.

Global and Freakish Advertising Finance

The media industry's heavy dependence on advertising revenue is a major source of financial freakishness. Advertising factors lie behind many media oddities. Two magazines may look fairly similar but one has a hefty cover price, while the other magazine is financed solely by advertising and is provided free to a "controlled circulation" list; or two competing media may reach a similar audience size, but one gets much more advertising because it has what the advertising world sees as "good demographics" (a young and affluent audience).

The United States has long been the world's biggest advertising spender,[3] and in 2005 about $500 was spent on advertising for each American man, woman, and child. Both U.S. society itself and the U.S. media industry are the world's most advertising saturated. To take just two examples, American children and American sports fans are subjected to more advertising messages and channel promotion than are children and sports fans elsewhere in the world.[4] Old media in America, such as newspapers and radio, are typically more advertising dependent than are old media elsewhere in the world.

American media companies—such as Time Warner and Disney—not only depend on advertising but are themselves among the biggest advertisers in

---

[3] Ingomar Kloss (ed.), *Advertising Worldwide*, Berlin: Springer, 2000.
[4] Susan Tyler Eastman (ed.), *Research in Media Promotion*, Mahwah, NJ: Lawrence Erlbaum, 2000.

the world. Big budget Hollywood movies are launched in the United States with an advertising blitzkrieg, and the same movies also receive heavy advertising launches in foreign markets.[5]

Since the 1930s leading American advertising agencies have expanded in two ways—they have bulked up at home and have also moved out onto the world scene. Advertising agency globalization has occurred in several waves. By 1930, for example, the McCann-Erickson agency was handling Esso (Exxon), Del Monte, and General Motors advertising in Europe. From 1955 to 1965 came another global wave as New York agencies followed the growth of television advertising in Europe, Latin America, and Japan; by 1965 McCann-Erickson had agency offices in 13 western European countries.

It was in the 1980s that leading American and British advertising agencies developed a major new bulking-up strategy. Previously "professional" rules had prevented an advertising agency from handling more than one car-maker or more than one detergent manufacturer. However, this "no competing accounts" rule was circumvented by new super-agencies that now included two or three, previously independent, big agencies. This super-agency development began cautiously around 1960 (as McCann-Erickson became part of the Interpublic super-agency). In 1985 and 1986 a frenetic round of Interpublic agency mergers led to a group of six super-agencies—all of them based in the United States, United Kingdom, France, and Japan.

Since the 1980s these same six agencies have remained in place, although —as with the six leading Hollywood companies—there have been many new acquisitions, management crises, and company recoveries. The three largest super-agencies have been Omnicom (U.S.), Interpublic (U.S.) and WPP (U.K.).

These super-advertising groups (and their constituent agencies) have for several decades been leading examples of the extent (and limitations) of media and cultural globalization; their networks of agencies across the world have for decades been involved in the complexities of thinking globally, but acting (sometimes very) locally. In many cases one advertising agency acts for one advertiser in from 10 to 30 countries (not usually in just 2 and not in 100 countries). Even when one agency acts for one advertiser in 20 or 30 countries, there will often be different campaign themes both within continents and between continents.

In terms of media finance, a key development in the 1990s was the emergence of huge media buying agencies, typically owned by one of the super advertising agencies. In 2000 the three largest such buying groups (each owned by one of the three super-agencies) together placed $53 billion

---

[5] Matthew P. McAllister, "From Flick to Flack: The Increased Emphasis on Marketing by Media Entertainment Corporations," in Robin Anderson and Lance Strate (eds.), *Critical Studies in Media Commercialism*, Oxford, UK: Oxford University Press, 2000: 101–22; Julian Stringer (ed.), *Movie Blockbusters*, London: Routledge, 2003; Justin Wyatt, *High Concept: Movies and Marketing in Hollywood*. Austin: University of Texas Press, 1994.

of advertising. The big buying groups offer to place advertising for their own mother super-agency's clients and also for other advertisers. The big buying groups use their huge advertising expenditure to obtain significant bulk discounts from media companies; the big buyers also offer research analysis expertise and original research data. When a media buying agency confronts one of the largest media companies, this becomes a gorilla versus gorilla negotiation. The size of media buying agencies also constitutes a continuing pressure on the media gorillas to bulk up still further.

Much of the media industry's finance is now channelled through these advertising super-agencies. But the super-agencies have hugely expanded their portfolios of subsidiary companies into a much wider range of activities. The super-agencies together own most of the world's biggest market research companies and most of the biggest public relations companies. In addition, they have expanded into a bewildering number of specialist marketing fields—company branding and identity and consultant activities in health, finance, sport, and other lucrative fields.

The super-agencies remain, of course, experts, especially in advertising; they also have expertise on key media issues like the loss of the advertising audience (as new gadgets increasingly facilitate skipping commercials). The big agencies are in the lead in generating types of advertising that are more difficult to escape. This means things like "infomercials," "advertising funded programming," and the four minute "webisode"; in one pioneering example of the webisode, Jerry Seinfeld did a four-minute Internet comedy appearance during which he joked about his American Express card.[6] There's an element here of déjà vu all over again; back around 1950 New York advertising agencies played an active production role in American TV programming. The advertising agencies seem likely to generate directly more entertainment programming in the future.

Media Gorillas Bulk Up

In 1980 just three networks (ABC, NBC, CBS) still had about 90 percent of the American prime-time evening television audience. By 2005 six TV networks had less than half the national audience; about 35 of the most popular cable and broadcast networks achieved a 90 percent share of the national TV audience. In 2005 there were also many other small cable offerings with national audience shares of 0.1 percent and less.

But competition in 2005 was less than this might suggest because three previously separate industries—TV networks, Hollywood studios, and cable—had been allowed (under new deregulatory rules) to merge into a single industry. Five giant companies (Disney, Time Warner, Viacom, News

---

[6] Gary Silverman, "A Moment of Your Time, Please," *Financial Times*, April 15, 2004.

Corporation, and NBC-Universal) were each heavily engaged in broadcast TV, cable TV, filmed entertainment, publishing, and other media.[7]

The total number of cable offerings continued to increase, especially as the spread of both digital cable, and digital satellite, opened up much new household capacity. But several kinds of bunching and bundling gave huge financial advantages to the few gorilla companies. First, most of the strongest cable channels belonged to the biggest companies; for example, both Nickleodeon and MTV belonged to Viacom, while ESPN was in the same Disney ownership as the sports-strong ABC network. Cable channels such as ESPN, with a committed audience, could charge local system operators high carriage fees and were also attractive to advertisers; ESPN's combined 2004 revenue was over $3 billion. Second, successful networks could offer a bundle of several ESPN or MTV channels, thus tapping into audience subgroups. Third, big gorilla owners of local cable systems (such as Time Warner) had (through swaps and acquisitions) focused their ownership into a limited number of cities and states, which thus offered management and marketing economies.

Big new media offerings involve big financial risks. But a media gorilla can spread the risk of high budget movies across more than one would-be blockbuster. For the media gorilla there is not much risk in adding one new cable subnetwork to an existing dozen; local multiple system operators who want the gorillas' big popular channels may have to accept also the new, untried, channel. But all of this is different for a small company perhaps launching its very first cable offering. The small company will not only receive no carriage fees, but may have to pay local operators to be allowed carriage on the system. Despite this financial hazard, lone new cable networks have been successfully developed. The Weather Channel, for example, faced major financial difficulties after its 1982 launch, but it had the support of Landmark Communications, an established newspaper, magazine, and TV company.[8] Home and Garden Television (HGTV) launched successfully in 1994—and indeed expanded into the Food, DIY, Fine Living, and Shop At Home networks; but HGTV had the backing of the long-established Scripps Howard print and TV group.[9]

In addition to the five broadcast/cable/film combinations, there are a few other gorillas. These include the newspaper-and-TV Gannett company (owner of *USA Today*) and the rapidly bulked up Clear Channel, owner of some 1,200 American local radio stations.

---

[7] In 2003 Disney, Time Warner, Viacom, and News Corporation averaged 24 percent of revenue from broadcasting, 18.25 percent from cable, 33.5 percent from film and publishing, and 24.25 percent from other businesses (mainly entertainment media). Meredith Amdur and Jill Goldsmith, "Biz Girds for Chain Reaction," *Variety*, February 16–22, 2004.

[8] Frank Batten, *The Weather Channel*, Cambridge, MA: Harvard Business School Press, 2002.

[9] Home and Garden Television, 10th anniversary supplement to *Broadcasting and Cable* and *Multichannel News*, June 14, 2004.

These big media companies were involved in the dot-com bubble period of 1999–2001, during which their debt levels rose, while their share prices rose and then fell. To many executives within these media gorillas, the outlook may have been threatening, turbulent, and too competitive for comfort. But competitors in the United States and in the world beyond could argue that Hollywood + network + cable constituted a new cartel. Already in the late 1990s there were many elements: cross-ownership of many cable channels by two gorilla companies; co-production by two big companies of a big budget movie; revenue sharing as developed by Blockbuster (Viacom), which assisted the other gorillas and discriminated against smaller companies; swaps of local outlets (mainly cable and radio) to allow the lower costs of "clusters"; and co-purchasing of movies, by which, for example, Time Warner would supply one of its movies to its own cable networks (TNT and TBS) and also to a selected major TV network.[10]

Small Finance, Big Reach: News Agencies and Public Broadcasters

Pay-per-view (video-on-demand) pornography in the United States had a 2005 revenue of nearly $1 billion. This was approximately the same as the combined revenues obtained by both the Associated Press (AP) and Reuters for delivering fast news to nearly all of the world's leading print and TV news media.

Pornography is revenue rich because its customers are willing to pay premium prices. American local cable operators charge more for pornography than for regular pay-per-view (PPV) movies, and the local cable operator typically keeps over 75 percent of this cash.[11] Another key point about video pornography is that, although its production is centered on northwest Los Angeles, the productions are super-cheap.

While PPV pornography sells cheap productions at high prices, the news agencies sell large quantities of complex material at low prices. Both Associated Press and Reuters do something in addition to world news. AP is also the main U.S. domestic news agency. Reuters is a London-based agency, 90 percent of whose revenues in recent decades have come from financial data and financial transactions (which boomed in the 1990s and crashed in the early 2000s). Less than 10 percent of Reuters' revenue comes from its international news operations. At a conservative estimate some AP and some Reuters news (text, still picture, video news) is seen by at least one billion people around the world each week. AP and Reuters together receive

---

[10] Jeremy Tunstall and David Machin, *The Anglo-American Media Connection*, Oxford, UK: Oxford University Press, 1999: 53–67.
[11] "Special Report: Adult TV," *Multichannel News*, June 14, 2004: 41–46.

about one U.S. dollar per year for each of these one billion audience members per week.

Other examples of super-cheap services include National Public Radio, listened to by about 22 million Americans each week. With an annual budget of somewhat over $100 million per year, NPR revenue is about $5 annually per each at-least-once-a-week listener.

Another public radio example is the BBC World Service (radio), which receives about $2.50 per year for each of 163 million at-least-once-a-week listeners, plus its weekly on-line audience, around the world (mostly in Asia and Africa). These BBC customers in fact pay nothing because the British government pays the full cost.[12]

It is difficult to make exact comparisons of revenue-per-hour, not least because many PPV pornography viewers prefer to view in several short sequences per day. However, one hour's PPV pornography seems to generate about 160 times as much revenue as does one hour of BBC world service radio.

Similarly huge financial differentials can also be found outside the media, especially when comparing luxury with basic versions of many products. However, the media may be unusual in that such huge revenue differentials are so substantial across the whole media industry landscape.

New Media and Freakish Finance

Freakish financing in general—and extreme media scale economies in particular—have assisted both media market leading companies and also the United States as the world media market's leading nation. But does this show signs of continuing? After the dot-com boom and bust of 1999–2001, the consumer (and mass media) Internet settled down into yet another example of combined dependence on subscription and advertising. Following a fall in advertising revenue in 2001–2002, Internet advertising became quite buoyant —for example, on the Google search engine. In addition, the consumer Internet showed its potential for attracting revenue from pornography and gambling.

What has been widely proclaimed as the arrival (at last) of digital convergence raises questions as to which digital gadgets will prevail in the office, in the home, and in the car and what combination of computer, music, and phone gadgetry will be carried around by individuals. Another key issue is how much of the prevailing technology will derive from the U.S. Pacific Coast and how much will derive from Europe, Japan, Korea, China, and India.

---

[12] *BBC World Service, Annual Review* 2005/2006, London: BBC, 2006.

Media exporting may well continue to be financially freakish. While barter export deals may continue, Hollywood is finding it increasingly difficult to finance movies with pre-sales, which once meant that affluent European customers often carried much of the Hollywood risk.

Another idiosyncratic type of pre-buying continues to prevail when foreign buyers arrive in Los Angeles each year to bid for national rights to new Hollywood movies and TV-cable series. Back in the 1960s and 1970s much of this buying was done by a very few people. Britain, for example, had two main buyers; one individual, Leslie Halliwell, was employed, from 1967 to 1987, by Britain's only two advertising-funded networks to buy Hollywood movies and miniseries.[13] Today the much bigger number of foreign networks has generated a total of some 1,300 buyers who descend on Hollywood each year. Their decisions can be extremely hit-and-miss because they are often looking at "pilots" for TV series, not the actual episodes. Also, since there will be only one main buyer per importing nation, the competition (or collusion) between competing buyers from the same nation inevitably has a big impact on the ultimate price paid. One study looked at how foreign networks buy Hollywood-made African-American comedies; European buyers preferred such comedies as *The Cosby Show*, which portrayed middle-class black people who spoke and behaved much like middle-class white people. Some network buyers show potential imports to selected focus groups, while others test the audience appeal of potential imports by showing them to friends and family members.[14]

Finally, it's worth remembering three long-term financial idiosyncrasies that have assisted U.S. media on the world scene since the early twentieth century. These were the star system, military finance, and copyright.

The star system has been crucial in projecting American media across the United States and the world. Because they are crucial, stars (with effective agents) claim large slices of total revenue.

Military finance, for U.S. media, dates back to the U.S. Navy's early twentieth-century support for radio and RCA. Military funding was also key to U.S. leadership in space satellites (and satellite TV) from the 1960s onward. Then the Defense Department funded ARPANET, the forerunner of the Internet.

Property rights in entertainment products ("intellectual property"), and hence copyright legislation, are central to media finance.[15] The U.S. media

---

[13] Basil Comely, "Leslie Halliwell. V: Sign of Times in TV Acquisition," *Broadcast*, August 24, 1984: 66–71; Richard Brooks, "Halliwell's Farewell Guide to Buying Films for TV," *The Observer*, March 22, 1987.

[14] Timothy Havens, "'It's Still a White World Out There': The Interplay of Culture and Economics in International Television Trade," *Critical Studies in Mass Communication*, Vol. 19/4, December 2002: 377–97.

[15] Richard Haynes, *Media Rights and Intellectual Property*, Edinburgh, Scotland: Edinburgh University Press, 2005; Cees J. Hamelink, *The Politics of World Communication*, London: Sage, 1994: 108–35.

industries have been adept at persuading the U.S. Congress to extend and strengthen copyright protection, both for companies and also far beyond the death of individual performers. In recent decades the defenders of such rights—in music,[16] movies, TV series, and print media—have found themselves in a loose lobbying alliance with the pharmaceutical and computer industries in their proclaimed war on "piracy."[17] Big media, big pharma, big data, and big government share financial interests (at home and abroad) in big knowledge and big information.

---

[16] Geoffrey P. Hull, *The Recording Industry*, New York: Routledge, 2004: 69–96.

[17] Majid Yar, "The Global 'Epidemic' of Movie 'Piracy': Crime-wave or Social Construction?" *Media, Culture and Society*, Vol. 27/5, September 2005: 677–96; Lee Marshall, "The Effects of Piracy upon the Music Industry: A Case Study of Bootlegging," *Media, Culture and Society*, Vol. 26/2, March 2004: 163–81.

5

Media Moguls Are National

The financial freakishness of the media industries encourages the emergence of billionaire mogul ownerships. The oddities of media finance—especially the salience of advertising revenue—tend to deliver special benefits to number one market leaders. This media market leadership often reaches a level of dominance that in other industries and other markets would be seen as monopolistic.

But most media moguls only achieve such market dominance, or leadership, in their own national home market. The leading American media moguls typically get 80 percent or more of their total revenue from the U.S. domestic market. Moguls who achieve dominance in one media market earn enough monopoly (or semi-monopoly) profit to finance a move into other media markets.

Media organizations can be retargeted by new orders introduced at the top. A new owner—of a newspaper or TV network—can quickly set new goals (such as a much younger target audience and new types of news or entertainment). A media organization can be made to change direction almost immediately—in contrast to the possibilities in many other industries. This enables a successful media mogul quickly to project a media organization away from loss and (perhaps) toward profit.

A media mogul is defined here as a person who owns and operates major media properties, who takes entrepreneurial risks, and who conducts these media businesses in a personal and idiosyncratic style.[1] A media mogul is often supported by barons, who are senior managers; media barons may operate, but they do not own, media companies.

Media moguls are among the United States' richest individuals; names such as Cox, Kluge, Malone, Murdoch, Newhouse, Redstone, and Roberts (of Comcast) have appeared high on the United States rich lists in recent years.

---

[1] Jeremy Tunstall and Michael Palmer, *Media Moguls,* London: Routledge, 1991: 105–222.

In other countries media moguls are also among the super-rich. The number of media billionaires is greater than the relatively modest financial size of the media industries might otherwise suggest.

The media's financial peculiarities mean that the media are especially suitable territory for the demonstration of entrepreneurial skills. Also important are the political skills necessary to obtain friendly regulatory decisions. But even more relevant are acquisition skills; successful media moguls tend to be acquisition and "turnaround" artists, who buy existing media properties and then transform them by such familiar artistic devices as cutting costs and boosting revenue.

A Distinctive Risk-taking and Acquisition Style

The classic media mogul is a first generation owner-operator. But even moguls who are "self-made" billionaires may well have inherited something —one newspaper, one radio company, a small group of movie theaters— from their fathers or families. A common feature of the media mogul career is experience of ownership and general management from a young age, such as the early or mid-twenties.

The media mogul almost invariably is male; because he is an owner-operator, he does not need to conform to discipline from controlling shareholders. Media moguls are relatively free to build their companies around their own personality, their own business skills, and their preferred working habits. This in turn leads to very idiosyncratic management styles.

A number of media moguls—including William Randolph Hearst and Rupert Murdoch—seem to have been trying to prove themselves to their fathers, while being emotionally close to their mothers. (Hearst was also financially close to, and financially dependent on, his mother until she died, when he was age fifty-six).

The media mogul's urge to maintain control has typically shaped his approach to acquiring fresh companies. Rupert Murdoch often relied upon large bank debt, leaving his News company with massive repayment (or rescheduling) obligations. Murdoch stepped ever westward—building his expansion on the Australian–U.K.–U.S. axis of cultural similarity. Murdoch also liked to exert tight control over his increasingly far-flung media properties; he consequently targeted a small number of big properties because it's easier to control six big properties rather than 60 or 100 small media entities.

John Malone's entrepreneurial style (as king of cable) was quite different, reflecting his own talents and preferences. Malone had an engineering background and a deep understanding of telecommunications and cable technology; Malone also preferred to be an investor/controller rather than a manager of cable programming. Malone focused on growing company and share value and deliberately avoided making taxable profits. Malone specialized in buying and selling numerous companies of all shapes and sizes. Malone also preferred to spend most of his time in Denver, within sight of a mountain skyline.

Despite their very different and very personal management styles, all media moguls have been risk-takers. There may well have been one key successful bet-the-farm risk in a mogul career; Sumner Redstone, for example, spoke in this way about his acquisition of Viacom in 1987. But as experienced risk-takers, these media acquisitors do not expect to win every bet. Some bets will be lost, and in each mogul's career there have been some massive mistakes—often failures to buy (or failures to sell) a media property at a particular moment. The successful media mogul's entrepreneurial failures are outweighed financially by his successful bets, his quick perception of media promise and future profitability.

Media moguls can contrast themselves with the more staid management styles of baronial managers who run more conventional and older public companies. Media moguls also can compare themselves with failed moguls whose risk-taking was less successful and involved too many bad bets. The successful media mogul can see his own success as an example of the survival-of-the-fittest entrepreneur. With a previous career of risks successfully taken and of entrepreneurial intuition justified, the media mogul may continue to take big—or bigger—risks. Canadian media mogul Roy Thomson[2] recalled in his book *After I Was Sixty* how he had acquired a string of British television and newspaper properties after his sixtieth birthday. Both Sumner Redstone at Viacom and Rupert Murdoch at News made some of their biggest gambles after their sixtieth birthdays. Some previously successful media moguls—such as Leo Kirch in Germany—have made some unwise bets after they were 60. But in a youth-oriented industry, in which many careers are quite short, the successful media mogul may remain entrepreneurially active and successful for 50 years or more. Many youngish journalists, as well as editors and apprentice moguls, are in awe of the fittest and richest surviving media moguls; one consequence is a continuing flow of exaggerated news coverage. Elderly media moguls attract more news attention than the financial scale of their business success really deserves.

After they passed age 60, several media moguls deliberately reduced their ownership below 40 percent of the media companies they supposedly "own." In some cases the mogul owns perhaps 35 percent of the main company, which itself owns only 35 percent of a supposedly "owned" subsidiary. Often the mogul owns a higher proportion of voting shares. The mature mogul may need the loyal support of two or three key minority shareholders. Financial journalists, in particular, are aware that the own-and-operate mogul's grip is less firm than his confident entrepreneurial style might suggest. This is perhaps another reason why financial journalists focus on the reigning mogul's

---

[2] Lord Thomson of Fleet, *After I Was Sixty*, London: Hamish Hamilton, 1975.

current moves, as well as upon his children and other possible successors (or acquisitors).

The Cross-Media Jump to Market Dominance

A common pattern finds the media mogul jumping from one media market into a second media market, in which he then establishes a dominant position. Two of the earliest media moguls were William Randolph Hearst (born in 1863) and Lord Northcliffe (born in 1865 as Alfred Harmsworth). By their early thirties both men owned nationally significant publications. Northcliffe's first publication was the weekly magazine *Answers to Correspondents*; with profits from *Answers* he acquired the *London Evening News* (1894), and by 1908, when he acquired *The Times*, Northcliffe was Britain's leading owner of London and provincial dailies.[3]

William Randolph Hearst's big jump was from a small San Francisco daily (*The Examiner*) to acquire in 1895 the *New York Journal* (later *N.Y. American*). By 1912 Hearst had become the leading newspaper owner across the six largest U.S. cities. Hearst became a big owner of magazines (*Cosmopolitan*, *Harper's Bazaar*); he owned a Hollywood movie production studio (Cosmopolitan); he established International News Service (INS) as a national and international news agency; and he controlled King Features.[4] However, Hearst's peak of newspaper dominance was reached in the 1920s. He failed to meet the challenge of the 1930s Depression and by 1941 Hearst bore little resemblance to his fictional portrayal in the movie *Citizen Kane*. Despite his political eccentricities, his bitter opposition to President Franklin Roosevelt, and his interviews with prominent Nazis, Hearst's key achievements lay in editorial recycling. Hearst demonstrated how material from his New York daily could be recycled across his 24 other U.S. dailies and then re-used by either his news or feature agency. He was also a pioneer in the simultaneous use of fiction in newspapers and movie serials, such as *The Perils of Pauline* (1914).

Another news recycler was Henry Luce,[5] who in 1923 launched *Time* magazine (with his partner Briton Hadden) as a weekly digest of the daily

---

[3] Reginald Pound and Geoffrey Harmsworth, *Northcliffe*, London: Cassell, 1959; *The History of The Times, Volume 3, The Twentieth Century Test, 1885–1912*, London: The Times, 1947: 509–86; *Volume 4, The 150th Anniversary and Beyond, 1912–48*, London: The Times, 1952: 446–86, 623–46, 678–710.

[4] David Nasaw, *The Chief. The Life of William Randolph Hearst*. Boston: Houghton Mifflin, 2000; Ben Procter, *William Randolph Hearst. The Early Years, 1863–1910*, New York: Oxford University Press, 1998; Louis Pizzitola, *Hearst over Hollywood*, New York: Columbia University Press, 2002; Marion Davies, *The Times We Had: Life with William Randolph Hearst*, New York: Ballantine Books, 1977.

[5] "Henry R. Luce: End of a Pilgrimage," *Time*, March 10, 1967: 22–29; "Henry R. Luce: His Time and His Life," *Newsweek*, March 13, 1967: 42–47; W. A. Swanberg, *Luce and His Empire*, New York: Dell, 1973.

press. Subsequently *Time* made the jump into original reporting in a fresh (brief, personalized, narrative) style. After *Time* came *Fortune* (1930) and *Life* (1936); Luce also jumped with his *March of Time* into radio (1931) and movies (1935). In the 1930s, 1940s, and 1950s Luce's Time Inc. was the dominant national weekly purveyor of news and accompanying national advertising. Eventually in the 1960s, Time Inc.'s market dominance was dented by competition from TV news and magazine competitors (such as *Newsweek*).

One of the most spectacular media mogul jumps was made by William Paley from owning CBS radio to owning the CBS television network.[6] The other major radio-TV company, NBC, was presided over by David Sarnoff, who was a salaried (and very successful) baron, not an owning mogul.[7] Paley, like other media moguls, was given his start by a generous father. William Paley first learned his father's (cigar) business—not least the sales and advertising aspects; his father next bought him (for $250,000) CBS—a then smallish radio company. Paley, who both owned and operated CBS, was adroit in network relations with affiliated radio stations, in music and comedy entertainment, in handling stars, and in setting up CBS radio news. Paley was also an accomplished radio industry politician who achieved the big jump into television (at a time when most other countries either had just one state-controlled TV network or no TV at all). CBS television was, of course, not a monopoly, but in the early years of American television the old NBC-CBS duopoly remained in place. William Paley presided over CBS as an owner-operator from 1929 until he came out of retirement to "rescue" CBS (in 1986) 57 years later.

A very different media mogul was Walt Disney, whose big jump was from animated movies first into television (with the ABC network) and then into the theme park business with Disneyland (which opened in Anaheim, California, in 1955). In addition to this jump into a three-ringed circus of movies-TV-theme parks Walt Disney achieved further dominance of the animation business by controlling rights in Donald Duck, Mickey Mouse, and the other Disney creations.[8]

Sumner Redstone (of Viacom) was another media mogul who made big, and successful, jumps into new media fields after he passed age 60; only when he reached age 80 (in 2004) did he announce that he would retire. Redstone had a classic, all-American, mother-loving, media mogul career background. His family was in the movie exhibition business, and Redstone spent much of his adult life expanding this business, and the valuable underlying real estate. In 1987 Redstone acquired Viacom—"I bet my life on that deal." A second massive deal (1994) was the acquisition of Blockbuster

[6] David Halberstam, *The Powers That Be*, New York: Knopf 1979: 124–28, 148–55, 420–28; Erik Barnouw, *The Golden Web: A History of Broadcasting in the United States, Volume II—1933 to 1953*, New York: Oxford University Press, 1968: 55–69.

[7] Eugene Lyons, *David Sarnoff: A Biography*, New York: Harper and Row, 1966.

[8] Richard Shickel, *The Disney Version*, London: Pavilion Books, 1986 (first pub. 1968).

Video. Third he acquired Paramount (1995). Fourth (1999–2000) he "merged" with CBS, while already controlling the mini-network UPN. Redstone's mantra was, "Content is king." But Viacom's (and Redstone's) success could also be explained in terms of broad market strength in all the main aspects of movies, television, cable, and video. This involved vertical strength from Hollywood production through to local TV, cable, and video outlets. Redstone's Viacom developed dominant positions with some of the most profitable satellite channels such as MTV and Nickelodeon. Redstone and Viacom were also deeply involved in the unromantic, but lucrative, business of outdoor advertising.[9]

Rupert Murdoch was another mother's boy who jumped between media with great agility. Alongside Murdoch's westward progression (Australia, United Kingdom, United States, Hong Kong) went another progression from newspapers to television and movies and then to satellite television. Murdoch's core skill lay in acquiring and "turning around" newspapers. His route into each of his key locations was via newspapers. In each location he then made the risky jump from newspapers into television. Murdoch's preference for a small number of big media properties with short names (News, Sun, Post, Fox, Sky, Star) was also a preference for market dominance. He eventually achieved market dominance or market leadership in four areas—Australian newspapers, British national (London based) newspapers, British direct-to-home (BSkyB), and finally (after a long and bitter struggle) DirecTV, the US direct-to-home satellite TV leader. Murdoch also pursued the goal of market dominance by paying very heavily for premium content—especially sports and movies in the United Kingdom (for BSkyB) and sports in the United States. In India he even paid big bucks for the quiz show services of a Bollywood superstar. Murdoch's seemingly reckless investment in selected premium content was based on the insight that such content could boost the channel's entire audience and perhaps lead to the premium advertising rates that reward market dominance.

John Malone's unique mogul career included a unique pattern of jumping between media. The first jump was from local cable systems to the acquisition of small slices of channels. Market scale enabled Malone to purchase equipment at big discounts and to acquire slices of faltering channels in return for carrying the channels on his TCI local systems. A second leap occurred when Malone sold TCI to AT&T management, who hoped Malone's local cable systems could be used for telephony and digital on-line services. John Malone's third big jump—with the AT&T billions—was back into cable both in the United States and Europe. Market dominance was an especially strong theme in John Malone's career because the local cable customer faces

[9] Jay Greene, "Sumner's Star Rises," *Variety*, February 21–27, 1994: 1, 184–85; Hank Kim, "Sumner Redstone's Global Sprawl," *Advertising Age Global*, July 2002: 12–13; "Multichannel Mogul: Sumner Redstone's Viacom," *Multichannel News International*, June 2001: 12–14; Linda Moss, "Viacom Split-Up Becomes a Reality," *Multichannel News*, June 20, 2005.

a monopoly local cable supplier. As Discovery distributed 15 factual cable channels, some commentators saw him as seeking to dominate nonfiction cable. But John Malone continued to change his channel portfolio, which included slices of Time Warner, Viacom, and News Corp.[10]

Failed media moguls tend to fail because they do not succeed in jumping from market dominance in one media segment, such as newspapers, to establish some market dominance in another media area, such as television or cable. Some successful television moguls failed to complete the jump into another area of television. Ted Turner emerged onto the U.S. national scene through his local Atlanta TV station, WTBS (initially WTCG). Ted Turner the apprentice mogul made three successful decisions; first he turned WTBS into a superstation (showing his local Atlanta output) across the United States; then he launched a lean and mean CNN (against the bloated big New York networks) by relying heavily on a cheap Atlanta staff and news film from agencies and European networks (such as ITN in London); and finally Turner acquired MGM's film library. This enabled Turner to offer an attractive bundle of cable entertainment channels, with CNN as the prestige money-loser. But by 1987 Turner ran out of finance and luck and had to be rescued by fellow cable owners; Turner became a big shareholder within Time Warner (and then AOL Time Warner) but no longer an owner-operator.

One final example of failed media moguldom is Canadian Conrad Black, who in 1991 was described (in a Murdoch newspaper) as "one of world's biggest newspaper barons."[11] At this time Black controlled a large number of very small dailies in Canada and the United States, the *Daily Telegraph* group in London, the *Jerusalem Post* in Israel, and other press interests in Australia. But Conrad Black's acquisition of the Telegraph group in London was his one big, lucky, successful deal; when Black acquired it in 1986, the *Daily Telegraph* was starting to lose its commanding dominance of U.K. up-market broadsheet newspaper advertising, but its circulation was still more than double that of its nearest competitor, *The Times*. Black installed much younger editors and managers and the Telegraph papers were for about five years highly profitable.[12] But in 1993 *The Times* (Murdoch controlled) began a fierce cover price war. Conrad Black failed to anticipate this and did not reinvest his (market domination) profits of 1988–1992. Black had not been born into a media-owning family, although he nevertheless acquired his first newspaper (a small rural weekly in Quebec) at age 22. But Black was not fully dedicated to media moguldom; he, in effect, pursued two careers—one was buying and "turning round" small city Canadian and U.S. newspapers, and the other was as a scholarly biographer of a Quebec politician, Maurice Duplessis. Black

---

[10] "John Malone's Biggest Gamble," *Multichannel News International*, January 2002: 13–14, 48–53; Martin Peers, "Liberty Ends Up Home Malone," *Variety*, June 29–July 12, 1998: 1, 52; Tim Burt, "The Cable Guy," *Financial Times Magazine*, May 21, 2005: 14–15.

[11] Andrew Davidson, "Conrad Goes Global," (London) *Sunday Times*, December 22, 1991.

[12] *The Daily Telegraph plc: Report and Accounts, 1988*.

made a series of business decisions that rendered major media mogul success ever less likely. Black was determined to be an important newspaper owner in both Canada and the United States; but his most prestigious property, the *Chicago Sun Times*, was a money loser. He acquired the English-language *Jerusalem Post* and switched it from left to right in Israeli domestic politics.[13] Black admitted enjoying the "perquisites" and status of being the owner of the *Daily Telegraph*; but, unlike many other newspaper owners, he failed to use the accompanying cash and political influence to diversify into television. Black recruited a trophy board of nonexecutive directors including Henry Kissinger and several British former cabinet ministers. Black continued to see himself as a leading intellectual figure; he specialized in writing critical, and invariably pompous, letters to his own publications. He also continued his other career as heavyweight political biographer. In 2003 while his key company, Hollinger, was experiencing financial meltdown,[14] Conrad Black (now Lord Black) published a massive biography of Franklin D. Roosevelt.

Acquiring, Owning, and Operating the Assets: Murdoch at Work

Rupert Murdoch's print beginnings and jumps into electronic media have attracted a big batch of biographies from Australian, British, and American journalists.[15] Murdoch's liking for hands-on journalism and for off-the-record gossip has endeared him to selected senior journalists.[16] Murdoch also found journalists to be useful sources of information, and several journalists who interviewed him have subsequently edited one of his publications. Consequently more is known about Murdoch's working methods than about those of any other media mogul.

For Murdoch as acquisitor and "turnaround" artist, the first phase was achieving the purchase, which could often best be accomplished by stalking older media owners; Murdoch systematically pursued owners such as Walter Annenberg (easy to meet when U.S. ambassador in London), from whom he

[13] Richard Siklos, *Shades of Black: Conrad Black and the World's Fastest Growing Press Empire*, London: Heinemann, 1995: 193–210.

[14] Jamie Doward, "Fall of a Tycoon: Canadian Clubbed," *The Observer* (London), November 23, 2003: Business Focus, 3–5; Stephanie Kirchgaessner, "Hollinger Trial Makes It a Black Thursday for Newspaper Baron," *Financial Times*, February 28/29, 2004.

[15] Bruce Page, *The Murdoch Archipelago*, London: Simon and Schuster 2003; William Shawcross, *Rupert Murdoch: Ringmaster of the Information Circus*, London: Chatto and Windus 1992; Neil Chenoweth, *Rupert Murdoch: The Untold Story of the World's Greatest Media Wizard*, New York: Crown Business 2001; Simon Regan, *Rupert Murdoch: A Business Biography*, London: Angus and Robertson, 1976: 26–119; Michael Leapman, *Barefaced Cheek: Rupert Murdoch*. London: Coronet, 1983; Peter Elman, John Winsley, and Rex Winsbury, "Campaign Interview: Rupert Murdoch," *Campaign* (London), September 19, 1969: 34–39; Peter Chippindale and Chris Horris, *Stick It Up Your Punter! The Rise and Fall of the Sun*, London: Mandarin, 1992.

[16] Peter Bart, "All Hail Rupert the Reticent," *Variety*, August 12–18, 2002.

acquired *TV Guide* in 1988. During the stalking phase, Murdoch's charm was at high volume; even so, he was often judged to have "paid too much." The second phase was of actually taking control; typically this involved selling off and "letting go" buildings, equipment, editors, and other unwanted personnel. Fresh commercial and editorial managers were installed; often the acquired media property was relaunched at a younger audience and with more downmarket content. Third came another phase with another relaunch. At this stage the initial new manager and new editor[17] choices might be discarded.

Murdoch learned to focus on journalists and politicians. In his early meetings with journalists (at an about-to-be-acquired property) he exuded charm and typically agreed to most of their anxious demands; initially he was highly accessible to journalists and others. But Murdoch was also adept at playing on the fears and insecurities of his editors. A small number of key editors received regular phone calls, in which Murdoch discussed recent issues of the publication. Murdoch personally recruited key editors. Typically it was also Murdoch who, some years later, sacked the editor, with a lesser job offered elsewhere in the empire.

Managers were treated similarly. Here Murdoch kept in touch, not by reading the publication but by looking at financial reports, which he received every weekend for the Australian, U.K., and U.S. businesses. Murdoch typically appointed already successful managers to top managerial positions; these manager barons were then given large salaries, large bonus targets, and share options and were told to grow the business. In some cases the plan could involve several years of heavy investment, but, whether this investment did or did not lead to big profits, the baron manager knew that his reign would probably not last a decade. This uncertainty seems to have turned both editors and managers into insecure workaholics. Typically the top managers were supported by a team of managerial rottweilers—with tabloid (Australian, British, American) experience to the fore.

Murdoch started his American career in 1973; he had spent 20 years (from age 22 to 42) learning to be a media mogul in Australia and in London. After a decade of somewhat faltering American newspaper and magazine progress,[18] Murdoch in 1985 entered upon a phase of dramatic U.S. growth, profit, turbulence, and then loss. In 1991 (age 60) he came close to commercial collapse and bankruptcy, although, in 1985–1991, Murdoch had built a major new American media company. In 1985 Murdoch made two huge

---

[17] A lengthy (and entertaining) account of one example of the process comes from the editor: Harold Evans, *Good Times, Bad Times*, London: Coronet, 1984. Another readable account from a Murdoch ex-editor is Andrew Neil, *Full Disclosure*, London: Macmillan, 1996.

[18] Thomas Griffith, "Rupert Murdoch Fights to Hold His US Beachhead," *Fortune*, January 15, 1979: 66–72; Chris Welles, "The Americanization of Rupert Murdoch," *Esquire*, May 22, 1979: 51–59; Richard I. Kirkland and Gwen Kinkead, "Rupert Murdoch's Motley Empire," *Fortune*, February 20, 1984: 60–71; "Rupert Murdoch: Is America a Leap Too Far?" *The Economist*, February 25, 1984: 69–73.

acquisitions—first the Twentieth Century Fox movie and TV production business and then the Metromedia group of TV stations, which included local stations in New York, Los Angeles, and Chicago. In 1986 Murdoch did something that seemed impossible—in terms both of commercial viability and regulatory legality; he launched Fox as the fourth national TV network. In 1998 Murdoch also acquired *TV Guide* and the whole of Triangle Publications for $3 billion.[19] This rapid expansion, and Murdoch's insistence on financing by bank debt (which left him still in control of the voting shares), led to the financial crisis in 1991.[20] Because the big banks laid off slices of debt to smaller banks, Murdoch had to negotiate with over 100 banks for debt rescheduling.

The 1991 near-bankruptcy was also partly caused by another Murdoch jump into unknown territory; this was the British BSkyB satellite effort, which in 1990 was experiencing gushing financial losses. Satellite TV was an area in which Murdoch had already notched up two failures. Skyband was an American exercise that in 1982–1983 went nowhere; the notion—to transmit TV programming via one-meter dishes to a domestic U.S. public—was hopelessly underprepared, underfinanced, and underpublicized.[21] But Murdoch could perhaps consider the modest loss as a pilot, or self-training, entrepreneurial exercise. A second and quite separate Sky television exercise was based in London and directed at Europe via an Astra (Luxembourg) satellite. Several other European operators were attempting the same thing in 1985–1986; in November 1986 the Murdoch "Sky Channel" was in 7.3 million homes across western Europe. But it was in the English language only and was generating almost no revenue (either advertising or subscription). Murdoch also closed down this Sky operation with a significant loss and with some addition of knowledge and wisdom. Murdoch now launched his third Sky offering; this one was aimed only at the United Kingdom. By 1990 Murdoch's unofficial (Luxembourg-regulated) Sky service had outplayed the official, U.K.-regulated British Satellite Broadcasting. In late 1990 the two systems merged into one, BSkyB. It was this BSkyB that contributed to Murdoch's high level of debt and loss in 1990–1991. A key extravagant cost for BSkyB was the overgenerous amounts being paid to Murdoch's Hollywood competitors for premium TV channel (Sky Movies) rights to their movies. This particular "British" innovation—which subsequently became highly profitable—depended heavily on two Anglo-American elements—live U.K. football and new U.S. movies.[22]

After he was 60 (in 1991), the major focus of Murdoch's continuing growth was upon the U.S. domestic market. This involved building the Fox network,

[19] Jerome Tuccille, *Rupert Murdoch*, New York: Donald I. Fine, 1989.
[20] Richard Belfield, Christopher Hird, and Sharon Kelly, *Murdoch: The Decline of an Empire*, London: Macdonald, 1991.
[21] "Murdoch into DBS to Tune of $75 million," *Broadcasting*, May 9, 1983: 34; Michael Schrage, "Murdoch Reaches for the Sky," *Washington Post* (Business and Finance), October 9, 1983, G1, 4.
[22] Mathew Horsman, *Sky High: The Inside Story of BSkyB*, London: Orion, 1997.

developing fresh Fox cable offerings, and providing high-priced major sport. Also, in line with career-long Murdoch interests, there had to be an all-news channel; this emerged in the highly successful tabloid Fox News Channel— devoted to rottweiler interviewing (of liberals) and shock jock super-patriot conservative ideology.[23] A further big Fox addition was another large batch of local TV stations, the 10 Chris-Craft local stations, acquired, against strong opposition, in year 2000. And then there was DirecTV—the satellite TV service after which Murdoch had lusted for some years and in which in 2003 he finally acquired a controlling position. In 2005 Murdoch's acquisition of MySpace.com and other sites made News Corporation into a major Internet company.[24]

The Anglo thrust in general, and the U.S. thrust in particular, absorbed most of Murdoch's new investment in the years before and after 2000. But it is also true that these years saw serious efforts in Asia and Latin America. Murdoch's first significant media property in Asia was, once again, a newspaper; he acquired the Hong Kong, English-language *South China Morning Post* in 1987; it was a full six years later (1993) that he bought into Star Television. But the initial Star programming was mainly in English (repeating the mistake made in 1980s Europe). It was only after a lengthy English phase that Star began serious efforts in Asian languages, and then decided to focus on China and India. In both cases, there was some genuine success but very much less than the many wild claims suggested. Australia, not Asia, continued to be Murdoch's and News Corporation's third main revenue source; the United Kingdom continued to be second, and the U.S. market continued to generate about 80 percent of total News revenue.

Mogul Political Connections and Regulatory Benefits

Just as Murdoch became skilled at charming and then chilling "journos" and managers, so too did he develop parallel skills in relation to politicians. Murdoch had observed as a child that politicians live in fear of newspaper attacks. Murdoch learned to charm (first) and frighten (later) Australian politicians. The friendly phase might last four or five years—or even longer —but a succession of Australian prime ministers and opposition leaders experienced both the warmth and the frightening hostility of Murdoch's newspapers. In Britain also many politicians received Murdoch press praise,

---

[23] Alexander Kitty, *OutFoxed: Rupert Murdoch's War on Journalism*, New York: Disinformation, 2005.
[24] James Harding and Tim Burt, "Sound and Fury as Murdoch Withdraws Offer," *Financial Times*, October 29, 2001; Jill Goldsmith and Adam Dawtrey, "Murdoch: Sky's the Limit," *Variety*, August 2–September 3, 2000; John Dempsey, "Sky Is No Longer the Limit," *Variety*, February 12–18, 2001; Wendy Goldman Rohm, *The Murdoch Mission: The Digital Transformation of a Media Empire*, New York: John Wiley, 2002: 3–82; "News Corporation: Old Mogul, New Media," *The Economist*, January 21, 2006: 67–69.

and subsequently maintained a frozen silence as they experienced the dreaded and humiliating tabloid denunciation.

Margaret Thatcher was an exception; she received 15 years of uninterrupted Murdoch newspaper adulation during her tenure as opposition leader and then prime minister (1975–1990). But Thatcher used U.K. prime ministerial "presidential" power to give Murdoch several astonishing (and apparently illegal) commercial boosts. First Thatcher waived the monopoly rules to allow Murdoch to acquire *The Times* and *Sunday Times* (in 1981) and *Today* (in 1987). Second, Thatcher provided advance help (trade union legislation and the provision of massive London police numbers) for Murdoch's strike-breaking move to new technology and the new Wapping printing plant in 1986. Third, Mrs Thatcher also "looked the other way" as Murdoch in 1990 merged with the regulated and official service to establish BSkyB as the U.K. satellite TV monopolist.[25]

Murdoch's experience in both Australia and the United Kingdom was that ownership of newspapers could lead to key politician support in navigating the always foggy grey areas of media regulation and legality. Murdoch anticipated that his ownership of U.S. newspapers would also smooth his way to further U.S. acquisitions. He was friendly toward an assortment of Republican and Democrat politicians (including President Ronald Reagan and New York Mayor Ed Koch). As Murdoch attempted to navigate around the TV network regulations, his relationship with the Federal Communications Commission (and the relevant subcommittees in Congress) became significant and was mostly positive. Senator Edward Kennedy was Murdoch's most high-profile political enemy; Kennedy received much abuse from the *Boston Herald* when it was under Murdoch ownership.

On several occasions Murdoch's American plans seemed to run counter to current law and FCC regulation. But Murdoch usually received friendly regulatory treatment because he and his lobbying team convinced the FCC, and most of the relevant Congressional committee members, that they were all swimming in the same direction—toward more competition and less regulation. Murdoch was allowed, seemingly against the rules, to own a Hollywood studio (Fox) and a new TV network because initially the Fox network only supplied 14 hours a week of programming and thus did not meet the definitional threshold. Murdoch was permitted to keep News Corporation based in Australia, which was against the current rules. Murdoch also received remarkably generous waivers on his cross-ownership of both a daily newspaper and a major TV station in both Boston and New York.

The prevailing FCC view was that Murdoch and News were welcome because they reduced the market domination of the old NBC-CBS-ABC TV network trinity. Murdoch also managed to convince the Washington authorities that he should be allowed to control DirecTV because in the 2000s

---

[25] Jeremy Tunstall, *Newspaper Power*, Oxford, UK: Oxford University Press, 1996: 251–53, 385–88, 411–12.

it would be competition for the now too powerful cable Multiple System Operator (MSO) business.[26]

Media Moguls Are National

Despite their bold talk about global media enterprises, Sumner Redstone and Rupert Murdoch built media engines in which the national (United States)—not the global—was dominant. Both Viacom and News Corporation in the early 2000s took about 80 percent of their revenue from inside the United States.

Rupert Murdoch was a partial exception, but an exception who also helped to prove the general rule. His success in Australia and the United Kingdom depended on cultural similarity within the Anglo countries; it also depended, in part, on the media policy shambles that existed in both Australia and the United Kingdom.

These U.S.-based, mogul owned-and-operated companies depended on the U.S. market. Like other successful media moguls, both Redstone and Murdoch—in addition to a helpful family start and an elite education (Harvard, Oxford)—served a lengthy apprenticeship. As mature media moguls they could rely upon a long career of contacts established, experience gained, and finance accumulated. Deeply embedded into American society, culture, politics, and business, these moguls in their fifties and sixties were well trained (and well financially supported) enough to make big, quick jumps into fresh media areas of high risk and high potential.

Market strength or dominance—first in one media area, then in others—is fundamental to the successful mogul career in which financial accumulation is vital. It is very difficult to achieve strength, let alone dominance, in any foreign market. In many countries foreign media corporations are regarded with suspicion because they seem to threaten the national culture that politicians and their populations want to defend. There is one, and only one, major exception—Hollywood's "high-end" output. Much of Viacom's and News Corporation's export success depends on the familiar old names of Paramount and Fox.

---

[26] Michael Cieply, "Metromedia and Fox Film Weigh Possible Combination," *Wall Street Journal*, May 2, 1985; "US Agency Clears Sale of TV Stations to Murdoch," *Wall Street Journal*, November 15, 1985; Jeanne Saddler, "Murdoch Seems Bent on Seeking Clearance to Retain US Newspapers, TV Stations," *Wall Street Journal*, January 13, 1986; "Rupert Murdoch Faces Hurdles in Bid to Start a TV Network in US," *Wall Street Journal*, February 26, 1986: 1, 8; Robert Homan and Richard Tedesco, "Murdoch Sparks Debate over Cross-Ownership," *Electronic Media*, January 11, 1988; Dennis Wharton, "Murdoch Romancing D.C.," *Variety*, June 13–19, 1994; Dennis Wharton, "Murdoch and Co Do D.C. Shuffle," *Variety*, February 13–19, 1995; Pamela McClintock, "Chris-Craft OK Signals Rift in FCC," *Variety*, July 30–August 5, 2001; "Satellite Television: Hit or Bust," *The Economist*, November 2, 2002; Demetri Sevastopulo and Peter Thal Larsen, "FCC Staff Back News Corp/DirecTV," *Financial Times*, December 4, 2003; "Satellite Television: Hit or Bust," *The Economist*, November 2, 2002; Ronald Grover and Tom Lowry, "Rupert's World: With DirecTV, Murdoch Finally Has a Global Satellite Empire," *Business Week*, January 26, 2004: 58–63.

6

Anglo-American World News, Public Relations, and Unreported Mass Killings

Throughout the twentieth century, the British and the Americans were the leading suppliers of international news around the world. In the years up to 1918, the British and the Americans were approximately equals in world news. From 1918 onward the Americans were in the lead, with the British following at some distance.

Public relations is yet another field in which the United States—borrowing from European precedents—became the world leader. Public relations (like advertising) is larger, and more pervasive, in the United States than in any other country. Public relations is central to American life from high school graduation onward.

Anglo-American news and public relations both made significant advances during the twentieth century's two world wars. The Anglo-American media—both factual and fictional—tend to portray Great Britain and the United States as having "won the war." Nevertheless, the low casualty figures of both the Americans and the British in World War II are remarkable. Over 50 million service people and civilians were killed in World War II. A large majority of these were citizens of the Soviet Union, China, Germany, and Poland. Less than 1 percent of the dead were British, and an even smaller proportion were American.[1]

While national media in general, and Anglo-American national media in particular, seem to have exaggerated their own countries' sufferings, the international media have greatly understated—or entirely failed to report at the time—numerous mass killings, genocides, and massacres. For example,

---

[1] Jan Palmowski (ed.), *A Dictionary of Twentieth Century History*, Oxford, UK: Oxford University Press, 1998 ed.: 663–66.

there was little reporting at the time when several million people died in the Congo around 1900, and again when several million people were killed or died in the Congo around 2000.

English-Language News: The Free Flow of American Imagery and Concepts

During the twentieth century the English language became ever more obviously the world language or, more precisely, the dominant second language of the world. Like any other language, the English language carries the values, assumptions, and prejudices of the language's native speakers. The English language inevitably carries the values, assumptions, and pre-judices of the United States. This is especially true of new formulations, new phrases, and new slang. These English innovations flow in particular from the northeastern United States, the main location not only of the New York media business, but also the World Bank and IMF. The United Nations is based in New York and uses English as its lead language; as the UN seeks to grapple with the world's current problems, its personnel adopt relevant new English language (American) terminology. Diplomats and other people who speak English as a second language tend to defer—in matters of correct usage—to native speakers of the language. In the case of the UN this means that in addition to Americans and Britons, English-language educated citizens of (British) Commonwealth countries have been extremely prominent.

The communications and media industries are one leading example of this more general tendency. The term "free flow" of media and communications was adopted in the early days of the UN (and its communications agency, UNESCO) in the late 1940s. The term "free flow" was a classic example of American terminology; "free flow" has an attractive simplicity and brevity and seems to be merely a new and broader version of "press freedom." But free flow also included a basic assumption that some post-1945 diplomats failed fully to grasp. The assumption was that free trade in media was self-evidently desirable; the unstated assumption was that any attempt to tax or to control the importing of movies, news, or music would be a deviant and perverse transgression of the free flow of media, ideas, truth, and democracy.

Free trade values lay behind a number of key American communications terms that became, in the decades after 1945, part of the conceptual frame-work of international discussions of communications. "Free TV," for example, sounded like a good thing for the purchaser of a TV set, but it also carried the assumption of television funded entirely by advertising. The "deregulation" of communications promised cheaper telephone calls and more video channels; but deregulation is a 100 percent American term because it refers to the Washington, DC, tradition of regulatory agencies—and, in the case of communications, the Federal Communications Commission (FCC). Previous to 1980 the concept of deregulation was an alien one in most of the world's nations, where quite different governmental arrangements operated (i.e., state-owned industries and "public" broadcasting systems).

Also 100 percent American was the "information highway," a key 1980s concept that in practice prepared the way for the largely "unregulated" Internet growth of the 1990s. "Information highway" sounded neutral enough (especially to American ears), but it was another public relations term; "highway" is an all-American term (it is not used in British English), and "information highway" suggested an ordered two-way system useful to all (car owners) and not interrupted by red traffic lights. Behind the information highway lay the information industry.

Much new Anglo terminology comes from the American computer industry, from the American space industry and NASA, from the Internet, from the pharmaceutical industry, from military high technology, and from video gaming.

Many other terms have crept into world English from sport and American sporting terminology. Baseball terms such as "stepping up" (to the plate) and "three strikes" are used by people who have never seen or played baseball. Some cricket terms such as "on the back foot" are still used by non-Anglos and noncricketers.

Survival of the fittest new Anglo slang—or Darwinnowing via public relations and headline-writing—features many terms that are short and zippy in English. But terms such as choice, pro-life, hard drugs, soft porn, road map, cold war, or twin track may not translate quite so briefly into German, Hindi, Spanish, or Mandarin. This can be one reason for adopting the original snappy Anglo term without translation.

In the early development of these new concepts, several professional groups are involved—public relations people, journalists, politicians, and White House speech writers. "War on terror" was a late 2001 term that originated in Washington, DC, and New York and carried with it much ideological and other baggage.

Embroidered News: Anglo-American Public Relations

Public relations is about making you look good by stressing your positives and concealing your negatives. You can be a government, company, charity, or individual. Public relations has a massive literature, and most American authors see PR as overwhelmingly American.[2] The European contribution to public relations was significant especially before 1918. British and European public relations tended to catch up before and during both world wars; the American contribution was especially strong after 1950 and also before 1900.

The 1,900 American daily newspapers of 1900 provided a big, almost unmissable, target for the eager press agent. The American circus originated

---

[2] For example, Stuart Ewen, *PR! A Social History of Spin*, New York: Basic Books, 1996.

much larger-than-life publicity hoopla. Also contributing was "Buffalo Bill" and his Wild West Show, which began in Saint Louis in 1884. Buffalo Bill went on his first transatlantic tour only three years later in 1887; he arrived in London with 200 people (including "Sitting Bull" and the sharp shooting "Annie Oakley"), 180 horses, and 18 buffalos. Queen Victoria was amused and even delighted. Buffalo Bill went to numerous cities outside London and also across France and Germany on a series of European tours.[3] Many European publicists discovered the almost unlimited possibilities for embroidering, mythologizing, and inventing the recent past.

 Also important were several self-styled inventors of the "public relations counsel," such as Edward Bernays and Ivy Lee (aka, Poison Ivy).[4] They drew upon current American election publicity (from marching bands to special newspapers); other sources of PR practice were Broadway and the new movie industry. The PR "counsels" covered the top end of the market, which included such wealthy monopolists as John D. Rockefeller and Pierpoint Morgan. Before 1914 many American industrial strikes were violent and the new PR counselors found themselves having to explain away the killing of strikers. But one company in particular, AT&T, followed the new enlightened PR gospel. From 1907 Theodore Vail set out to establish the giant phone company as genuinely more concerned with long-term customer happiness than with short-term profits; long distance calls were priced so as to let business subsidize households. AT&T showed that (at least in a growing business) positive public relations could be successful.[5]

 In Europe before 1914 two other factors caused public relations to develop primarily as a governmental, and not so much as a commercial, activity. The British during the South African Boer War (1899–1902) were heavily criticized in the press across Europe;[6] so, after 1900, were the Belgian king and the German government. These European imperial powers relied on such public relations devices as carefully designed visits for carefully selected visitors. A second factor was the anticipation during 1900–1914 of major war. The British, French, German, Russian, and Italian governments all tried to control military publicity at home and to repel suspicious journalists as potential spies. These same governments also carried on public relations activity in each others' countries; and several countries—not least the Germans and British—also tried to influence pre-1914 opinion in the United States.[7] One common method was to finance, or subsidize, a friendly

---

[3] Alan Gallop, *Buffalo Bill's British Wild West*, Stroud, UK: Sutton Publishing, 2001.
[4] Edward L. Bernays, *Biography of an Idea*, New York: Simon and Schuster, 1965; Ray E. Hiebert, *Courtier to the Crowd: The Life Story of Ivy Lee*, Ames: Iowa State University Press, 1966.
[5] John Brooks, *Telephone: The First Hundred Years*, New York: Harper and Row, 1975: 127–55.
[6] Keith Wilson (ed.), *The International Impact of the Boer War*, Chesham, UK: Acumen, 2001.
[7] Ken Ward, *Mass Communication in the Modern World*, London: Macmillan, 1989; Robert Park, *The Immigrant Press and Its Control*, New York: Harper, 1922; Joel Wiener (ed.), *Papers for the Millions: The New Journalism in Britain*, Westport, CT: Greenwood, 1988.

newspaper inside the United States. A number of German-language dailies inside the United States were accused (especially by the British) of accepting German government funding.

The 1914–1918 war accelerated this government involvement in the media and public relations. British and French troops fought the Germans for 50 months, whereas the first U.S. troops landed in France in June 1917, only 17 months from the November 1918 end of the war. In 1914–1917 the French and British went deeply into the new business of total publicity as a subbranch of total war. In practice the newspaper owners and the governments jointly worked out censorship arrangements that in turn led to one-sided news; enemy casualties were emphasized, while most news about friendly casualties was censored.[8] New forms of positive publicity were developed in newsreels[9] and shown in cinemas. The British not only cut the German submarine cables but also listened in to German radio traffic.

The United States, having had a much slower start in 1914–1916 public relations, made great leaps forward in 1917–1918. In April 1917 President Woodrow Wilson set up the Committee on Public Information (CPI) under the prominent journalist George Creel. The CPI put out publicity on a massive scale; it recruited some 75,000 "Four Minute Men" to each give two local speeches per week; guidance on the speeches' content was provided. The CPI also aimed at the big immigrant, foreign language newspaper press; positive inducements were generous government advertising and much free editorial material. Newspapers not loyal to the U.S. war effort found their revenue drying up, especially in the patriotic excitement of 1917. But, by 1918, the American and British PR efforts were learning much from each other. The British were more sophisticated about Europe, not least because *The Times*, and other London newspapers, had for many years followed both French and German politics very closely. The leading British newspaper owner (*The Times*, *Daily Mail*) Lord Northcliffe had been a hyperactive traveler around Europe, and in 1917 he visited the United States for the eighteenth time (his first visit was in 1888). In 1917 Northcliffe had good access to U.S. Secretary of State Robert Lansing and some access to U.S. President Woodrow Wilson.[10] American media emissaries had good access in London. An "Inter-Allied Propaganda Conference," held in London on August 14, 1918, was chaired by Northcliffe. Americans attending the meeting included the young (Captain) Walter Lippmann (protégé of President Wilson) and Lieutenant Charles Merz (later editor of the *New York Times*).[11] Harold Lasswell, having studied the 1914–1918 war, concluded that

8 Philip Knightley, *The First Casualty*, London: Andre Deutsch (and Quartet), 1975.
9 Luke McKernan, *Topical Budget: The Great British News Film*, London: British Film Institute, 1992.
10 Reginald Pound and Geoffrey Harmsworth, *Northcliffe*, London: Cassell, 1959: 526–91.
11 *The History of the Times: The 150th Anniversary and Beyond. 1912–1948. Volume 4/Part I, 1912–1920*, London: The Times, 1952: 366.

propaganda "is the new dynamic of society, for power is subdivided and diffused and more can be won by illusion than by coercion."[12]

From 1918 to 1939 American public relations expanded hugely; most big American companies took public relations increasingly seriously, not least after 1933 when Franklin Roosevelt became president. The following year a 1934 California election produced the first multimedia attack advertising campaign; it was directed against Upton Sinclair, a famous left-wing muckraking journalist who was running for governor. The attack campaign was organized by a new publicity company, Campaigns Inc. (later Whitaker and Baxter). Upton Sinclair was ferociously attacked in press editorials, in press advertising, and on the radio. The campaign saw the wholesale invention of news and its presentation on film (by the Hollywood owners). Disreputable-looking marchers were also hired to carry placards on the streets "supporting" Sinclair.[13] By 1934 rent-a-crowd public relations had begun.

Alongside these, and other, startling American developments, the Europeans were making their own advances, especially in political public relations. As described in Chapter 10, the British government in India had already by 1920 drawn on London's 1914–1918 experience to establish a complex press relations operation. In the 1930s big advances were made in Germany, Japan, and the Soviet Union in various kinds of publicity misinformation and dirty tricks. A key German dirty tricks campaign was mounted for the January 1935 plebiscite in which the people of the Saarland voted to return to Germany. A blitzkrieg of Nazi disinformation was broadcast from German radio transmitters close to the Saar border; Saarland newspapers were also on the receiving end of an extraordinarily belligerent pro-German campaign. A similar German media blitzkrieg was quickly established against the Dollfuss government in Austria.

The Europeans were ahead of the United States in the 1930s also in terms of foreign language radio broadcasting. By 1935 Germany was broadcasting in relevant languages to Africa, eastern and southern Asia, Australia, Spanish-speaking South America, and Central America. Mussolini's Italy conducted a vigorous radio war against French interests in Morocco, Algeria, and Tunisia. The British aimed at their empire and then at the Middle East; by the outbreak of war in 1939 the BBC was broadcasting radio services in 16 foreign languages.[14]

While the Soviet Union, Japan, and Germany all had big wartime efforts, the 1939–1945 external radio leaders were initially the British and then

---

[12] Harold D. Lasswell, *Propaganda Technique in the World War*, London: Kegan Paul, Trench and Trubner, 1927: 222.

[13] Curt Gentry, ". . . Right Back Where We Started From," *Columbia Journalism Review*, September/October 1992: 60–62; Garth Jowett, *Film: The Democratic Art*, Boston: Little, Brown 1976: 294–96; Carey McWilliams, *California: The Great Exception*, Santa Barbara, CA: Peregrine Smith, 1949: 171, 182, 205–7.

[14] Harwood L. Childs and John B. Whitton (eds.), *Propaganda by Short Wave*, Princeton, NJ: Princeton University Press, 1942:3–48.

the combined British and Americans. Having closely studied especially the German/Nazi style of belligerence and big lies, the British decided on two contrasting forms of propaganda radio. First were the BBC's European and other external radio services; the European service transmitted in most of Europe's larger and smaller languages. A reputation for truth-telling was cultivated as the BBC broadcast bad news, especially bad news that would already be broadly known to the Germans (such as the precise number of British planes "which failed to return" from last night's raid on Germany). The largest services were in German and French, and the BBC French Service was run by French citizens.

In addition to these truthful (or "white") services, the British also ran "black" stations—which happily transmitted lies and disinformation. By the end of 1941 there were already four separate British-controlled black stations operating in French, each purporting to be coming from inside France.[15]

The U.S. wartime radio effort was designed broadly to complement, rather than to compete with, the BBC's. The U.S. radio effort was extremely active in Latin America and in the Pacific. But while the BBC continued with its multilanguage operation around the world—and especially in Europe—the United States developed several complementary efforts. First, the United States was allowed (by the British government) to set up the American Forces Network for U.S. military personnel; this steadily expanded into an increasingly Europewide (and then worldwide) effort. Second, the United States became the leader in taking over radio stations (for example, in Luxembourg) when these were abandoned by the retreating Germans. Third, the black radio phenomenon attracted much active American interest and subsequently was adopted by the CIA for Cold War anti-communist purposes.

After 1945 the United States quickly reclaimed its leadership of the public relations business. This was obviously supported by the big move into the world of American companies and advertising agencies and the continuing strength of Hollywood and Hollywood exports. Emphasis on the brand image was seen as now requiring long-term public relations sustenance of the brand.

One of many American innovations was the use on a large scale of public relations by the American military. Senator William Fulbright wrote *The Pentagon Propaganda Machine* in 1970, when he was chairman of the Senate foreign relations committee and when U.S. involvement in Vietnam was drawing toward its end. Fulbright had little difficulty in showing that each of the U.S. armed services had its own substantial public relations effort aimed at boosting its own budget and projects. The U.S. Navy and U.S. Air Force claimed together to employ 1,990 PR people but then admitted to having 3,105 PR people. There were other big PR efforts at the Department of

---

[15] Asa Briggs, *The War of Words: The History of Broadcasting in the United Kingdom*, Volume 3, Oxford UK: Oxford University Press, 1970: 379–441.

Defense and in the Army and Marine Corps. One of the U.S. Navy's secret weapons was special visits by important people to aircraft carriers at sea; another was the offer of a free Hawaii trip to visit U.S. Navy ships at Pearl Harbor. The U.S. Navy had many publicity efforts based in that great naval city, Chicago; one such activity involved the U.S. Navy distributing across Latin America six tons of chewing gum generously donated by the Wrigley company.[16]

In recent decades Washington, DC, has become the world leader in publicity campaigns mounted by some of the world's most notorious and least democratic regimes. An African or Arab dictator may well choose to invest a few million dollars in employing a Washington, DC, political public relations firm. A Washington-based publicity effort can target not only the State Department and relevant congressional committees but also the World Bank and the International Monetary Fund.

Buried News: Unreported Mass Killings

Journalists tend to regard violent deaths as neatly matching the requirements of news values ("three people were killed today when . . ."). But paradoxically some of the twentieth century's largest mass killings received little, if any, immediate news coverage. Hundreds of thousands died, but few news stories appeared.

One common circumstance is that the mass killings occur in remote and far-away places where no Anglo-American correspondents or even local journalists are stationed. Often there is a deliberate cover-up by a government that wishes to keep secret the horrible deeds committed by its soldiers, prison guards, or death squads. Strict censorship may prevent journalists from visiting the relevant location and may also make sending the story impossible; when large numbers of people are being killed, inquisitive strangers may be in deadly danger. Even if we exclude wartime military deaths and casualties, many of these events happen in the shadow of war—civilians are deliberately bombed or executed, or civilians may fail to survive the chaos of military defeat.

Another news reporting difficulty is that often the worst of the mass killing event happens in the first days or weeks. In its all-out attack, an army may kill every enemy soldier and every civilian in sight; in an "anti-guerrilla" campaign numerous villages may be attacked at dawn on the same day. Even if journalists are able to get to the scene of the massacre, genocide, or ethnic cleansing, it may be difficult to decide how many killings occurred. After mass killings, bodies may be burned, buried, or eaten by animals; dead

---

[16] Senator J. William Fulbright, *The Pentagon Propaganda Machine*, New York: Vintage Books ed., 1971 (first publ. 1970).

bodies are often thrown into rivers and washed downstream to resting points far from the original place of death.

Here we will consider very briefly some eight cases of mass killings. Only three or four of these eight cases fall within the United Nations Genocide Convention's definition: The Convention refers to acts committed with intent "to destroy in whole or in part, a national, ethnical, racial or religious group."[17] The following list contains examples that might be classified as genocides, massacres, mass killings, or perhaps ethnic cleansing. One particular mass killing may include elements of several of these categories. Some mass killing episodes may begin with deliberate genocide or mass killing of certain subgroups (such as men), while other subgroups (such as women) may be punished by rape, beatings, starvation, and expulsion from their homes.

Another relevant problem—which may be significant both for contemporary and for retrospective reporting—is the difficulty of establishing the who, when, and where of a mass killing. The precise date and location are often problematic. Nor is the identity of the mass killers always self-evident; the army may claim that two factions, or ethnic groups, attacked each other in tribal warfare. Here are eight very varied examples of mass killings, each of which was either unreported or very inadequately reported at the time.

1. *The Congo, around 1900.* Several million people died in the Belgian Congo from sleeping sickness but also from executions and a particularly brutal form of forced labor amounting to semi-slavery. The Belgian colony had no civil administration but was administered by commercial interests; the colony was effectively the personal possession of King Leopold, who was a public relations pioneer. Leopold perfected the practice of (very carefully) guided tours for selected journalists.[18]

2. *In the Soviet Union,* Stalin's purges and the German invasion killed millions of civilians.

   a. Around 1932 some 5 or 6 million people were starved to death, or executed, mostly in Ukraine, the North Caucasus, and Kazakhstan.

   b. In Stalin's great terror (1937–1938) some 650,000 (including many senior communists and thousands of military officers) were killed.

[17] Israel W. Charny (ed.), *Encyclopedia of Genocide*, 2 vols., Santa Barbara, CA: ABC-Clio, 1999; Robert Gellately and Ben Kiernan (eds.), *The Specter of Genocide: Mass Murder in Historical Perspective*, Cambridge, UK: Cambridge University Press, 2003; Samantha Power, *"A Problem from Hell": America and the Age of Genocide*, New York: Basic Books, 2002.

[18] Neal Ascherson, *The King Incorporated: Leopold the Second and the Congo*, London: Allen and Unwin 1963 and London: Granta Books, 1999; Adam Hochschild, *King Leopold's Ghost*, London: Papermac, 2000.

    c. From 1941 to 1945 some 16 million civilian Soviet citizens were killed or starved to death in the fighting between the Soviet Union and Germany.

    d. Especially during Stalin's remaining years (1945–1953), more millions died in the Gulag of labor camps.[19]

A few of these cases were deliberately publicized in "show trials"—especially of Stalin's political enemies and rivals in 1937–1938. But the vast majority received no coverage in the fiercely censored Soviet media; from 1930 to 1953 there were only a very few foreign reporters based in the Soviet Union and they were largely confined to Moscow. The Soviet public relations people were adept at selecting sympathetic foreign journalists and intellectuals, who—after a brief visit—typically wrote positive stories about Stalin and the Soviet Union.[20]

3. *About six million Jews—and five million Poles, Roma, communists, and other "undesirables"*—were killed in the Holocaust. Although the concentration camps began in 1933, the majority of killings occurred in 1942 and 1943. All of the extermination camps (as opposed to labor camps) were in Poland; three million died in Auschwitz-Birkenau. Numerous well-researched books on this large subject discuss the issues of who knew what and when.[21] Roosevelt, Churchill, and Stalin knew long before 1945 that what the Germans (and allies) were doing to the Jews (and others) went far beyond a somewhat larger version of the old Pogrom.

    In December 1942, the U.S. and U.K. governments and nine others (the then 11-country United Nations) issued a statement confirming the existence of a German campaign to exterminate all Jews.

    What was happening to Europe's Jews in 1939–1945 was not ignored by the U.S. and U.K. media, but it was played down. Laurel Leff in *Buried by The Times* explores in detail how and why the *New York Times* deliberately played down the Jewish extermination story. The family publisher, Arthur Hays Sulzberger, preferred to see the Nazis' mass killings as targeted at several groups, including the Jews. Sulzberger, nevertheless, made special personal efforts to help his own Jewish relatives in Europe. Cyrus Sulzberger, the publisher's nephew, was a talented and flamboyant *Times* correspondent in Europe, but he was not especially interested in Jewish issues. During the European war

---

[19] Jan Palmowski, *Dictionary of Twentieth Century History*, Oxford, UK: Oxford University Press, 1997.

[20] Malcolm Muggeridge, *The Thirties: 1930–1940 in Great Britain*, London: Hamish Hamilton 1940; and London: Weidenfeld and Nicolson, 1989: 202–11; Douglas McCollam, "Should This Pulitzer be Pulled? Seventy Years After a Government-Engineered Famine Killed Millions in Ukraine, a New York Times Correspondent Who Failed to Sound the Alarm Is Under Attack," *Columbia Journalism Review*, November/December 2003: 43–48.

[21] Robert Gellately, *Backing Hitler: Consent and Coercion in Nazi Germany*, Oxford, UK: Oxford University Press, 2001.

the *New York Times* carried 1,186 stories that dealt in whole or in part with Jews in Europe; but most of these were short pieces "buried" deep inside the paper. Only 26 such stories reached the front page in 1939–1945. Although *The Times* had a well-resourced Berlin bureau in 1939–1941, no single journalist back in New York (or in London) was subsequently designated as a specialist on Hitler and the Jews. The Jewish extermination story was often covered by *The Times* with AP and UP stories—an indication of lower importance in an elite newspaper. The *New York Times* was also relatively reluctant to use stories from the Polish government in exile (in London); *The Times* did not subscribe to the specialist Jewish Telegraphic Agency (to which the New York *Post* and *Herald Tribune* did subscribe). On April 22, 1943, listeners in Stockholm and London heard a radio transmission from inside the Warsaw ghetto, which said that 35,000 Jews were about to be killed by the German army. Although the Warsaw ghetto uprising had all the classic ingredients of a huge, and tragic, news story,[22] the *New York Times* gave it the usual low-key, brief, and undramatic coverage.[23]

4. *The British and American targeted bombing of civilians in Germany and Japan* took place especially during 1942–1945 and probably killed between three and four million civilians. The two atomic bomb raids on Japan in August 1945 killed about 200,000 people (with more dying later). The news media certainly reported hundreds of air raids, each involving several hundred aircraft dropping thousands of tons of bombs. The air crew members themselves were well aware that increasingly the prime objective was to burn down entire cities,[24] while the precise and accurate destruction of a major war factory was relatively rare. Any British or American journalist who looked around London could see that bombing was a somewhat inexact science. There was some criticism of "Bomber Harris," who was Britain's bombing supremo; most of this criticism, however, occurred after the war was over. The city-bombing policy had been coordinated and agreed to by Britain, the United States, and Canada in late 1941. In retrospect American and British journalists could claim that several wartime conditions—censorship and self-censorship, patriotic support for our brave bomber crews, shortage of paper for lengthy background stories—would have made it difficult to get anti-bombing stories published.

---

22 Martin Gilbert, *The Holocaust: The Jewish Tragedy*, London: Collins, 1986: 557–67.
23 Laurel Leff, *Buried by The Times: The Holocaust and America's Most Important Newspaper*, Cambridge, UK: Cambridge University Press, 1995: 1–48, 173–4, 330–58.
24 Max Hastings, *Armageddon: The Battle for Germany, 1944–45*, London, Macmillan, 2004: 343–88; Hermann Knell, *To Destroy a City: Strategic Bombing and Its Consequences in World War II*, Cambridge, MA: De Capo/Perseus, 2003; Ian Buruma, "The Destruction of Germany," *New York Review of Books*, October 21, 2004: 8–12.

5. *In China during Mao's "Great Leap Forward" campaign (1958–1960)* probably between 15 and 30 million people died of starvation and related illness. Although this was not a deliberately planned disaster, it does seem to qualify as a mass killing because Mao persisted with the policy well after its consequences were fully apparent. There was no coverage at all in the Chinese media, and almost none in any foreign media. (This episode is discussed at greater length in Chapter 12).

6. *In Guatemala some 200,000 civilians were killed* by the army in several phases between the late 1970s and late 1980s. The great majority were Maya (the traditional inhabitants), so this qualifies as genocide targeted at a specific ethnic group. Many of the killings occurred in remote villages in mountainous areas, some of which were near the Mexican border; many Mayans crossed the international border to evade the army. There was very little accurate coverage of these events in Guatemalan media; coverage did occur in foreign publications, but it tended to focus on specific individual cases, such as a murdered nun who happened to be a U.S. citizen (more on this in Chapter 18).

7. A significant fraction of the entire population of the *small African country of Rwanda* was murdered, mainly with clubs and machetes in a few weeks in 1994. Estimates of the total deaths vary between about 400,000 and nearly one million. (More on this Rwanda case appears in chapter 15.)

8. *Around 2000 the Congo experienced violence* that probably produced over three million deaths. This conflict had elements of an invasion (supported by other African governments) leading to civil war; much of the conflict seems to have involved local armed bands fighting each other to control local territories. This was a classic example of a conflict too obscure, too complex, and too dangerous to allow reliable reporting. Much of the reporting was done from, and related to, the extreme west and extreme east of the Congo, with little about the 900,000 square miles in between (more on this in chapter 15).

Although these—and other—mass killings were underreported at the time, several cases of mass killings have received more attention some years, or even decades, later. The Holocaust—after being heavily reported in 1945 in all the media (including cinema newsreels)—for some years attracted relatively little media attention. It was not until 1961 (and the televised trial of Adolf Eichmann in Jerusalem) that "the Holocaust" became the accepted phrase and media (and scholarly) coverage greatly increased.[25]

---

[25] Peter Novick, *The Holocaust in American Life*, New York: Houghton Mifflin, 1999; Jeffrey Shandler, *While America Watches: Televising the Holocaust*, New York: Oxford University Press, 1999.

In other cases a major change of political regime led to a process of literally digging up the bodies contained in secret burial grounds. This kind of development is marvelously described by Victoria Sanford in *Buried Secrets*. Sanford and her colleagues have used the new science of forensic archaeology to dig up "clandestine cemeteries" resulting from some 600 massacres conducted by the army in rural Guatemala.[26] This process of digging up the dead reveals a complex pattern; the army killed some villagers (suspected of being guerrilla fighters) and also ethnically cleansed (or destroyed) the village—thus forcing villagers to depart higher up into the mountains or across the border into Mexico. Some of these villagers were then killed as they fled.

Some further revelations may surface several decades after the violent events. In some cases old soldiers publish their memoirs and confess the torture and killings of their youth. Some trials are held of prominent people. Other prominent people establish some kind of truth and reconciliation procedure. In Spain the bodies of political opponents killed by General Franco in the late 1930s were being dug up by villagers in the early 2000s. For example, clandestine cemeteries were being dug up in 2002–2003 near Segovia, about 50 miles north of Madrid. In three villages some 240 Republican sympathizers were killed (and buried) in December 1936 by Franco soldiers, assisted by Franco-supporting villagers. The location of the unmarked graves were well known to the victims' relatives.[27]

DNA and forensic archaeology techniques will continue to look back at past horrors; we will have further opportunities to marvel at mass killings, which make the news today, but were not reported when they happened some decades ago.

---

[26] Victoria Sanford, *Buried Secrets: Truth and Human Rights in Guatemala*, New York: Palgrave Macmillan, 2003.

[27] Giles Tremlett, "Spanish Civil War Comes Back to Life. Old Divisions Resurface Across the Country as Descendants Dig Up Mass Graves," *The Guardian*, March 8, 2003; Antonio Feros, "Civil War Still Haunts Spanish Politics," *New York Times*, March 20, 2004: A15, 17.

7

U.S. World Media Peak Around 1950

Around 1950 the United States was in an exceptionally dominant position on the world media scene. This dominance was so great that a big subsequent decline was inevitable.

The greatest peak was in two years, 1947 and 1948, and was largely caused by temporary postwar conditions. From 1939 to 1945 Berlin, Hamburg, Warsaw, Moscow, and Tokyo had all been devastated by bombing; their media output would not return to 1938–1939 levels until well into the 1950s.

In 1948 the United Kingdom had the world's second biggest media industry. But even the United Kingdom suffered severe shortages of paper,[1] raw film stock, and advertising. In the United Kingdom in 1948 the number of TV sets, the consumption of newsprint, and the number of movies produced reached 7 percent, 8 percent, and 16 percent of U.S. levels. The Soviet Union was at 1 percent, 7 percent, and 4 percent of U.S. levels.[2]

By 1947–1948 Hollywood and other U.S. media had had time to regain export markets. As of 1947–1948 the "Iron Curtain" (referred to by Winston Churchill in a 1946 speech in Fulton, Missouri) had not yet chopped off all media trade between eastern and western Europe. In 1948 Czechoslovakia still imported more movies from the United States, United Kingdom and France (48 percent) than from the Soviet Union (23 percent). Hungary in 1948 imported 30 percent of its movies from the Soviet Union but 55 percent from the United States, United Kingdom, and France combined.[3]

While the U.S. media in 1947–1948 were in their peak phase of global influence, the United States itself had emerged from World War II with the world's only large and healthy economy.

---

[1] J. Edward Gerald, *The British Press Under Government Economic Controls*, Minneapolis: University of Minnesota Press, 1956.

[2] UNESCO, *World Communications. Press, Radio, Film*, Paris: UNESCO, 1950.

[3] UNESCO, *World Communications*, Paris: UNESCO, 1950.

The United States in midcentury grappled with three major international opponents: (1) It had fought against fascism (Japan, Italy, and Germany); (2) around 1947–1948 it switched toward a new anti-communist, anti–Soviet Union, and anti-China orientation; and (3) it was against empires, not least the still existing empires of the United Kingdom and France.

An important event in confirming the reality of the East-West Cold War was the Berlin Airlift from June 1948 to May 1949; when Soviet forces blocked access to the western sectors of Berlin, the American and British air forces flew 200,000 flights into Berlin, carrying goods and food. The key event that marked the heating up of the East-West confrontation was the north Korean invasion of south Korea on June 25, 1950. From 1950 to 1953 33,000 American service people were killed in Korea; deaths of north and south Koreans (military and civilian) totalled 1.3 million. As in 1941, in 1950 the United States found itself involved in simultaneous confrontations in both Asia and Europe.

John Fousek has argued in *To Lead the Free World* that the U.S. government and people became committed, not to promoting international capitalism or international freedom, but to promoting American nationalism. This was an ideology of "American nationalist globalism." America, according to Fousek, now saw itself as the leader, not just in Asia and Europe, but on a global scale.[4] Fousek awards a prominent role in American nationalism to media mogul Henry Luce and his concept of the "American century." Fousek also stresses the importance of the mass media in general.

The year 1950 marked the beginning of the McCarthy period; Senator Joseph McCarthy accused the State Department of having employed communists who assisted the communist victory in China. The media also were given a leading role in the McCarthy period, with the House Un-American Activities Committee (HUAC) targeting Hollywood, and in particular Hollywood screen writers.

But the great fear of the McCarthy period settled over all of the American media—old, newish, and new—at a time when the media (especially with the arrival of television) were becoming more central to American life, leisure, and politics. The old media of press and film supported the belligerent anti-communist stance; so also did the newish media of radio and of factual magazines, such as *Time*.[5]

The new medium of television, in 1950–1955, was also careful to be correctly anti-communist.[6] One of the first politically significant televised events was the return of General Douglas MacArthur in 1951 to the United

---

[4] John Fousek, *To Lead the Free World: American Nationalism and the Cultural Roots of the Cold War*, Chapel Hill: University of North Carolina Press, 2000.

[5] Michael Emery and Edwin Emery, *The Press and America*, Boston: Allyn and Bacon, 1996 ed.: 363, 367, 372–75.

[6] Fred J MacDonald, *Television and the Red Menace*, New York: Praeger, 1985; Ella Taylor, *Prime Time Families: Television Culture in Post-war America*, Berkeley: University of California Press, 1989.

States after he had been sacked by President Truman (for advocating the use of nuclear weapons against China). Kurt and Gladys Lang studied "MacArthur Day" in Chicago on April 26, 1951; they concluded that the television coverage stressed the positive and the patriotic and presented the viewer with an exaggerated impression of MacArthur's actual support among voters on the streets of Chicago. The following year, in 1952, the Republican and Democratic national conventions were televised on a substantial scale for the first time.[7]

New media moguls also came to prominence in the mid-twentieth century. Henry Luce can be said to have played his part in establishing the popular American perception that "America lost China." Henry Luce's parents had been Christian missionaries in China, and Luce was a passionate opponent of the Chinese communists; he was able to pursue his anti-communism, not only in *Time* and *Life* but also in his *March of Time* news features that began on radio, moved into cinemas, and then switched to television in 1951.[8] Another anti-communist media mogul was William Paley, who eventually allowed his CBS TV network to show the famous *See It Now* (Ed Murrow) attack on Senator Joe McCarthy. This TV show aired on March 9, 1954, marking the beginning of the end of a four-year period in which McCarthy's hysterical—and largely fabricated—accusations received only sporadic criticism from the American media.[9]

The period around 1950, during which American media reached their peak of world influence, also saw the establishment of several popular mythologies; as the foreign policy elite were, of course, aware, these media-derived mythologies ignored important complexities.

One media and Hollywood myth was that America "won the war" in Europe. This formulation ignored the fact that the German military was defeated primarily by the Soviet Union. In 1944–1945 the Soviet Army faced three German divisions for each German division deployed in France against the American and British Commonwealth armies.

A second myth was that in 1945–1948 America "lost China" because of inadequate American commitment. This myth ignored the fact (well known to General Stilwell and to American journalists on the ground, such as Theodore White and Jack Belden) that America lost its influence in China

[7] "The Unique Perspective of Television" and "The First Televised Conventions: 1952," in Kurt Lang and Gladys Engel Lang, *Television and Politics*, New Brunswick, NJ: Transaction, 2002: 29–96 (first publ. 1984).
[8] W. A. Swanberg, *Luce and His Empire*, New York: Dell, 1973; David Halberstam, *The Powers That Be*, New York: Knopf, 1979: 45–93.
[9] William S. Paley, *As It Happened*, New York: Doubleday, 1979; Sally Bedell Smith, *In All His Glory: The Life of William S. Paley*, New York: Simon and Schuster, 1990; Fred W. Friendly, *Due to Circumstances Beyond Our Control . . .* , New York: Random House, 1967; Thomas Doherty, *Cold War, Cool Medium: Television, McCarthyism and American Culture*, New York: Columbia University Press, 2003.

because it allied itself with the deeply reactionary Chiang Kai-shek, who was reluctant to fight corruption—or the Japanese or the communists.[10]

A third myth propagated by the media in general, and by Hollywood in particular, was that wars were won by heroic individuals. Movies such as *Sands of Iwo Jima* (1949), which starred John Wayne, were loosely based on genuine, and genuinely heroic, battles.[11] But this focus on heroes, which presented the United States as the preeminent military power, distracted attention from the fact that the United States was only the preeminent bombing power. Heavy use of bombing frequently lay behind the relatively low American casualties. Success in bombing in 1942–1945 led to even more bombing in Korea in 1950–1953. "The firebombing continued until nearly every North Korean city had been substantially destroyed and thousands of civilians killed";[12] the napalm bomb was used, on a large scale, to burn people (Koreans and Chinese) to death.

1947–1948: U.S. Media Bestride the World

Across all major mass media categories, the United States in 1947–1948 had a huge lead against almost all possible rivals. This leadership was especially obvious in movies and popular music; American leadership in magazine journalism and advertising probably had its main impact on journalists and advertising professionals across the world. The American lead in television was well known, even though in 1950 most of the world's people had never seen a television set. Perhaps the most potent American media influence of all lay in the news agencies, which were selling their news on a daily basis in many corners of the world.

The Hollywood movie industry around 1950 was in a state of internal turmoil, involving censorship of communism and sex, the court-ordered break-up of the old Hollywood monopoly, and a background of criminal racketeering in the Hollywood trade unions.[13] But none of this inhibited Hollywood's aggressive selling of its movies in most of the world's cinemas. In most countries there was a hunger for entertainment. Tens of millions of cinemagoers looked forward to their weekly movie visit as a—or the— highlight of their week; and in most cases this was a Hollywood movie.

[10] Barbara W. Tuchman, *Stilwell and the American Experience in China, 1911–45*, New York: Grove Press, 1985 (first publ. New York: Macmillan, 1970); Jack Belden, *China Shakes the World*, London: Penguin, 1973 (first publ. 1949); Theodore H. White and Annalee Jacoby, *Thunder out of China*, New York: William Sloane, 1946.

[11] Lawrence H. Suid, *Guts and Glory: Great American War Movies*, Reading, MA: Addison-Wesley, 1978: 91–109.

[12] Michael S. Sherry, *In the Shadow of War: The United States Since the 1930s*, New Haven, CT: Yale University Press, 1995: 181.

[13] Mike Nielsen and Gene Mailes, *Hollywood's Other Blacklist: Union Struggles in the Studio System*, London: British Film Institute, 1995.

In Germany and Japan—and in the many countries they had invaded—Hollywood's wartime movie output had been excluded; in these countries Hollywood in 1947 could offer not just its current output but its entire unseen output of the six or seven previous years.

In radio and music the United States also had an unassailable lead. As American military bases set up American Forces Network (AFN)[14] stations in Germany and other countries in Europe and Asia, the local population could, and did, listen in. The American record companies pursued their normal business practice by supplying free records to radio stations across the world. In 1954 Elvis Presley made his first recording in Memphis, and in 1955 rock-and-roll was playing on radio in many countries.

American magazines also had a huge lead at this time. At its 1936 launch, *Life* magazine incorporated European and British innovations; by 1945–1955 *Life* (and its competitor *Look*) was admired and venerated by journalists around the world. *Life* was printed lavishly on expensive glossy paper, and its team of celebrated photojournalists were given the space to tell a story with a sequence of several photographs. Magazines were the leading medium in the United States for national advertising (in the years before TV was established). American women's magazines—both their editorial content and their lush advertising—were a revelation in impoverished Europe. Most politically influential was *Time* magazine, which had a major national news significance (at a time when no American daily yet reached beyond its local base). *Time* was a pioneer of modern nontabloid gossip—not least in its early and accurate reporting of the Mrs. Simpson–Edward VIII royal romance story of 1936. Henry Luce, as the editor and publisher of *Time* (and *Life*), had a huge impact on the public, especially on American perceptions of China and the "loss of China to communism." *Time*'s editorial format also was immensely influential; after 1945 national newsmagazines quickly became important in Germany, Italy, and France and subsequently elsewhere. Luce's device of presenting complex issues via a personality (whose face filled the front cover) was influential. *Time* also—unlike much American journalism—was brief and well written (and rewritten); this brevity and readability spoke to many journalists across the world who, around 1947–1948, were still restricted to four or six daily pages.

In television the United States had an enormous world lead in the years around 1950. In 1948 the United States and the United Kingdom had 98 percent of the world's television receivers; U.S. TV sets outnumbered U.K. TV sets by 14 to 1. In 1948 the Soviet Union and France each had 1 percent of the world's TV sets.[15] As Table 7.1 indicates, even by 1954 U.S. TV dominance had only been modestly eroded. In 1954 the United States still had about 82 percent of all the world's TV sets, and U.S. TV sets outnumbered Soviet Union TV sets by 72 to 1.

---

[14] Patrick Morley, *"This Is the American Forces Network,"* Westport, CT: Praeger, 2001.
[15] UNESCO, *World Communications: Press, Radio, Film*, Paris: UNESCO, 1950.

Table 7.1   American Leadership in World Television, 1954 (Top 10 Countries in Number of Television Sets)

	TOTAL NUMBER OF TV SETS, THOUSANDS	NUMBER OF TV SETS PER THOUSAND POPULATION
United States	32,500	199
United Kingdom	4,156	81
Canada	1,125	74
Soviet Union	450	2
Cuba	135	22
France	125	3
Brazil	125	2
Mexico	93	3
Italy	88	2
West Germany	81	2

Source: UNESCO, *Statistics on Radio and Television, 1950–1960*, Paris: UNESCO, 1963: 77–82.

Through the years 1948–1954 the U.S. TV industry grew increasingly strong, as the rapid increase in audience numbers allowed higher and higher advertising rates to be charged. The U.S. production industry began in New York, doing live television; but from 1952 onward the production industry moved to Los Angeles and to series such as *I Love Lucy*, which were recorded.[16] These increasingly expensive recorded productions could now be conveniently exported. American series were made available to foreign TV networks at realistically cheap prices; imported American series quickly became essential in countries where the total revenue (and number of TV sets) remained too low to finance much domestic production.[17]

The Peak of Anglo-American International News Agencies

American international news agencies around 1950 were much more dominant than they had been in the 1920s and 1930s and than they would be in the late twentieth century.

A UNESCO report gives us a convenient picture of the world news wholesalers in 1952. All three of the strongest world agencies were Anglo-American. In terms of fast news, aimed at daily newspapers, two big American agencies—Associated Press (AP) and United Press (UPA at that time)—were approximately equal to the British Reuters. Then roughly equal in fourth place were another American agency, the Hearst-owned

---

[16] Christopher Anderson, *Hollywood TV: The Studio System in the Fifties*, Austin: University of Texas Press, 1994.

[17] UNESCO, *Television: A World Survey*, Paris: UNESCO, 1953; Wilson P. Dizard, *Television: A World View*, Syracuse, NY: Syracuse University Press, 1966.

International News Service (INS), and Agence France Presse (AFP). Trailing in sixth place was the Soviet Tass.[18]

By 1952 news globalization meant that the big Anglo-American agencies pumped news around the world. Major specific services offered 30,000 words a day. With different versions of the service going to different world regions, up to one million news agency words could go out on a single day. The majority of American foreign correspondents at this time worked for the agencies.[19]

In 1952 the UP service went out each day to 1,183 foreign customers—941 newspapers and 242 radio stations in 76 foreign countries and territories. In addition to news for newspapers and radio stations, both AP and UP offered a fast wirephoto picture service; these still pictures were heavily used (then as now) by newspapers and were also used by infant TV news operations. Big news agencies have long been the technology innovators of the news business. Feature stories in 1952 still went by airmail, but teleprinters were the main technology (60 words a minute) used by these big agencies. (The hot new technology of teletypesetting was just arriving for domestic U.S. services). The teleprinter services printed out the news in each customer's office and depended in 1952 on either cable or radio. The Soviet Tass did not compete with the western agencies in terms of speed, technology, or news. Tass news was also slowed by censorship. Tass news was supplied free to communist countries and also provided a special Arabic service, which in some newspaper offices in the Middle East arrived by bicycle.

The 1939–1945 war played a big part in the postwar Anglo-American news agency dominance. By 1944 the American media had by far the largest number of foreign and war correspondents in action; the United States also had the most media organizations doing extensive war reporting—three news agencies, three radio networks, and about 10 newspapers.[20]

Meanwhile in Europe the previously important French Havas agency, which had collaborated with the Germans, was closed down. Agence France Presse was born in 1944 and was heavily funded in its early years by the French government.[21]

Reuters, the British agency, also had severe postwar problems—including the total loss of its strong China market and a big reduction in its revenue from India.[22] But Reuters maintained its strength in the Arab world and

[18] UNESCO, *News Agencies: Their Structure and Operation*, Paris: UNESCO, 1953.
[19] The news agencies employed 169 American correspondents in Europe, versus 69 employed by newspapers, 34 by magazines, and 14 by radio networks. Theodore E. Kruglak, *The Foreign Correspondents*, Geneva: Libraire E Droz, 1955, reprinted by Greenwood Press, 1974: 72.
[20] Robert W. Desmond, *Tides of War: World News Reporting, 1931–1945*, Ames: University of Iowa Press, 1982: 448–65.
[21] Oliver Boyd-Barrett, *The International News Agencies*, London: Constable and Beverly Hills, CA: Sage, 1980: 122–30.
[22] Donald Read, *The Power of the News: The History of Reuters*, Oxford, UK: Oxford University Press, 1992: 234–82.

worked hard in Europe. The old German Wolff agency was no more, but Reuters agreed to a big news exchange with the German national agency, DPA—which itself was a merger of post-1945 news agencies in each of the occupation zones. Reuters' news was used heavily in the Netherlands and other European countries—partly on the basis of the BBC's wartime performance. Reuters lacked a picture service, but made up for this in part with a strong financial news service (Comtelburo).

AP strength in 1952 can be seen from a list of AP's bureaus; all news agency terms and statistics are somewhat flexible, but, generally speaking, a "bureau" is an office that not only collects news but also sells the agency's services to news media in that particular city and country. In 1952 AP had 12 bureaus in Canada, 29 bureaus in Europe (of these one was in Moscow, one in Yugoslavia, six in Italy, and seven in Germany),[23] 13 bureaus in Asia (including three in India), and 18 bureaus in Latin America (including five in Colombia, two in Brazil, and two in Venezuela). In total, AP had 72 foreign news bureaus in 1952, none of which was in Africa.

Commercial Media and U.S. Government International Alliance

Even before the December 7, 1941, Japanese attack on Pearl Harbor, an informal wartime alliance was being prepared between the commercial mass media, the news agencies,[24] and the U.S. government. This alliance continued through the 1940s. The big news agencies, the new radio networks, and the Hollywood studios all waged propaganda and information war first against the fascist powers and then, from about 1947, against the communist powers. Hollywood made many patriotic movies about winning the war and later switched to belligerent anti-communism. The top men at both CBS (William Paley) and NBC radio (David Sarnoff)[25] were prominently engaged in Europe following the June 1944 Normandy landings.

Latin America in 1940 saw the first large example of this U.S. alliance of government and commercial media. Nelson Rockefeller (as coordinator of Inter-American Affairs) was in charge of a broadly successful Washington effort to persuade Latin American media into the U.S. and Allied camp (see Chapter 18).

Italy in 1943 was the first of the Axis powers to be invaded by American and British forces. As they moved up the Italian peninsula the Allied powers established approved, licensed, nonfascist newspapers. Italy was to some

---

[23] This AP targeting of Germany was successful; AP still has an important German language news service.

[24] Jean-Luc Renaud, "US Government Assistance to AP's World-Wide Expansion," *Journalism Quarterly*, Spring 1985, Vol. 62/1: 10–16, 36.

[25] Eugene Lyons, *David Sarnoff, a Biography*, New York: Harper and Row, 1966: 232–67.

degree used as a test market for the bigger German and Japanese operations yet to come. But in Italy, as in subsequent cases, one or two polite fictions (or public relations formulations) were adopted; a key polite fiction was to the effect that Italy had never really been fascist and thus only required quite gentle guidance back to democratic ways.

Germany was seen as a much tougher case, and media policy issues, especially in 1945–1950, were contested with some belligerence. The Americans and the British cooperated against German Nazis and Soviet communists but disputed among themselves. American State Department and Department of Defense views did not always coincide. Moreover, while the alliance between U.S. commercial media and the U.S. government was extensive, it was not always tranquil. The State Department wanted to revive the German film industry, but Hollywood's hard men—determined to dominate the German movie scene—got what they wanted.[26]

The Americans played a leading role in their large south and southwest German occupation zone, as did the British in their large northwest zone. While the Americans in effect designed six German regional systems modeled loosely on U.S. states, the British went for just one big system modeled loosely on London's national media. The British approach broadly prevailed in newspaper[27] publishing (with the northern city of Hamburg becoming the press capital); the German radio broadcasting (and subsequently TV) system loosely followed the British public service (and noncommercial) model of that time. However, Hollywood won a big victory in post-1945 Germany; so also did the New York advertising agencies.

But not all Germans agreed that the German media had been Anglo-Americanized. Certainly the early licensed newspapers were run by (approved) Germans from 1946. The Anglo-Americans deliberately avoided both politicians and media people who had prospered during the 1933–1945 Hitler period. The Allies' early choices for political office were mostly elderly men, like Konrad Adenauer (later elected chancellor); he was aged 69 in 1945 and had been imprisoned by the Nazis. Most Germans who held prominent media positions in 1946–1949 belonged either to this elderly (and pre-Nazi) club or were too young to carry the Nazi taint. Rudolph Augstein was 26 years old when as editor of *Der Spiegel* in 1950 he revealed a major bribery scandal that involved legislators in the new federal capital of Bonn. The period of approved and licensed media ran only until 1949. By 1949 American and British concerns were more with communism than with de-Nazification; some of the new media owners from 1949 onward were less free of the Nazi taint. But although the ultimate extent of Americanization remains contested

---

[26] Jeremy Tunstall, *The Media Were American*, London: Constable and New York: Columbia University Press, 1977: 149–53, 156–60.

[27] Kurt Koszyk, "The Press in the British Zone of Germany," in Nicholas Pronay and Keith Wilson (eds.), *The Political Re-Education of Germany and Her Allies*, London: Croom Helm, 1985: 107–38.

or ambiguous, the (West) German media around 1950 could be broadly seen as a win for America (and Britain), and most especially as a win for Hollywood.[28]

The Hollywood moguls knew that France was going to be difficult. Their two key European markets were Germany and the United Kingdom, and in both Hollywood used its familiar mix of skill and bargaining belligerence. Both the British film industry and Hollywood-in-Britain had had a good war, with the highest ever weekly cinema attendances. The movie business in Britain looked to be prosperous and successful; this appearance attracted a large increase in taxation on cinema visits in August 1947. Hollywood had met this situation previously in other rebellious movie markets around the world. The Hollywood response to the tax increase was swift and terrifying —an absolute and immediate embargo; there would be no new U.S. movies for U.K. movie audiences until the U.K. government dropped the tax. The British government—out of its depth in the movie business—surrendered after seven months of the embargo (in March 1948). Now millions of British film fans could again see fresh Hollywood movies.[29]

The European countries that Hollywood regarded as its leading foreign markets—United Kingdom, Germany, France, and Italy—were also the countries that received the bulk of Marshall Aid from Washington ($8.8 billion out of a total $13.2 billion). The year 1947 marked the switch from de-Nazification to anti-communism. President Truman propounded the "Truman Doctrine" (March 12, 1947) in his speech to a joint session of the U.S. Congress; this effectively marked Truman's recognition of the Cold War.[30] Although Winston Churchill's Iron Curtain warnings of 1946 were quite heavily criticized in the U.S. media, from 1947 onward the U.S. media and the Truman administration were broadly in agreement as to the severe communist threat. Media and government also broadly agreed on the conduct of the Korean War.

In the two decades from 1940 to 1960 this loose alliance of the U.S. commercial media and the U.S. government continued jointly to promote the United States as not only a great, but a good, power. The United States had been against the Nazis, then against both the Soviet and Chinese communists. Finally, the United States was applauded widely in Asia and Africa for its opposition to the British and French, and other European, empires.

---

[28] Henry P. Pilgert with Helga Dobbert, *Press, Radio and Film in West Germany, 1945–1953*, Bad Godesberg-Mehlem: Historical Division, Office of the Executive Secretary, Office of the US High Commissioner for Germany, 1953; Anna J. Merritt and Richard L. Merritt (eds.), *Public Opinion in Occupied Germany: The OMGUS Surveys, 1945–1949*, Urbana: University of Illinois Press, 1970; Ralph Willett, *The Americanization of Germany, 1945–1949*, London: Routledge, 1989; Jessica C. E. Gienow-Hecht, *Transmission Impossible: American Journalism as Cultural Diplomacy in Postwar Germany, 1945–1955*, Baton Rouge: Louisiana State University Press, 1999.

[29] Ian Jarvie, *Hollywood's Overseas Campaign: The North Atlantic Movie Trade, 1920–1950*, Cambridge, UK: Cambridge University Press, 1992: 213–72.

[30] Harry S. Truman, *1946–1952, Years of Trial and Hope. Memoirs of Harry S. Truman (Vol. 2)*, New York: Signet/New American Library, 1965: 126–44 (first publ. 1956).

Aligning Japanese History and Media

In Japan the postwar occupation (1945–1952) was dominated by the United States and General Douglas MacArthur. In less than one year after the August 1945 Japanese surrender, MacArthur had brokered a gentlemen's agreement (largely unspoken) with Japanese Emperor Hirohito and a few others. The war, in effect, was blamed on Japanese General Tojo Hideki, who was Japanese war minister (1940–1944) and prime minister (1941–1944); Tojo was tried as a war criminal and hanged in 1948.[31]

Under this MacArthur-Hirohito agreement, Japan would not complain about the merciless American bombing, including atomic bombs on Hiroshima and Nagasaki. MacArthur would pretend that Emperor Hirohito had always been a "constitutional" monarch with no real powers, although Hirohito had been—behind the scenes—an autocrat and militarist who actively supported, and gave his semi-divine approval to, Japanese aggression. Hirohito would from 1945 to 1946 onward need to behave as a constitutional monarch and was also required to lose his semi-divine status. MacArthur would ignore the massacres and mass killings conducted by the Japanese, especially in China. The Japanese mass media would be allowed to resume, largely unpurged, as long as they followed the new democratic rules. All of this happened.

MacArthur also badly needed the support of President Truman and of the U.S. media. Despite some turbulence, the autocratic MacArthur broadly received this support. Not only Washington, but also the U.S. media, looked the other way and accepted the political theater and the deliberate and calculated falsification of history. MacArthur and Washington did this because occupying a Japan of (then) 80 million people was no simple task. The *New York Times*, AP, and UP[32] broadly went along for patriotic reasons; lack of Japanese language ability, admiration for MacArthur, and anxieties about China and the Soviet Union may also have been relevant.

The MacArthur-Hirohito version of the Japanese war effort lived on for decades. In *Language, Ideology and Japanese History Textbooks*, Christopher Barnard shows that Japanese schoolchildren were still, 50 years later, being taught a version of history that followed the MacArthur-Hirohito agreement by glossing over major elements of Japanese history. For example, the schoolbooks do refer to the December 1937 events in Nanking (not far from Shanghai), but the schoolbooks do not mention that Japanese soldiers killed some 400,000 Chinese people and raped tens of thousands of women. None

[31] Ray A. Moore and Donald L. Robinson, *Partners for Democracy: Crafting the New Japanese State Under MacArthur*, New York: Oxford University Press, 2002.

[32] Herbert P. Bix, *Hirohito and the Making of Modern Japan*, New York: William Morrow, 2000, and London: Duckworth, 2001: 546–53, 561–62, 572.

of the books mention Japan as having attacked any foreign country in 1941. Most of the books do not record that Japan surrendered in 1945.[33]

During the American occupation, a determined effort was made to democratize Japanese media content. For example, films were not to glorify militarism, medieval-style authority, or the subordination of women. Positive encouragement was extended to new Japanese films that showed baseball, kissing between males and females, and crime á là Hollywood.[34]

As in the German case, disagreement exists as to how American the Japanese media are (or how Japanese the American media are) today. But certainly in the years immediately after 1945 General MacArthur and the U.S. media walked tall in Tokyo.

[33] Christopher Barnard, *Language, Ideology and Japanese History Textbooks*, London: Routledge Curzon, 2003; Erna Paris, *Long Shadows: Truth, Lies and History*, London: Bloomsbury, 2002: 122–63 (first publ. by Knopf, Canada, 2000); David McNeill, "Textbook War Escalates as China and Korea Vent Their fury at Japanese Rewriting of History," *The Independent* (London), April 11, 2005.

[34] Kyoko Hirano, *Mr. Smith Goes to Tokyo: Japanese Cinema and the American Occupation, 1945–1952*, Washington, DC: Smithsonian Institution Press, 1992.

8

Since 1950

The United States Looking Superlative While Losing World Media Market Share

Most adults alive today do not remember the years around 1950, and thus do not remember that peak period of American media dominance. This may make it difficult for them to accept that American dominance in world media not only is declining now, but has been declining since the 1950s. There is also some reluctance to acknowledge that, from 1953–1954 onward, CIA covert action and bribery were used in many countries to undermine popular media and to overthrow popular regimes.

Much foreign news was, and still is, available within American households. Associated Press, the biggest supplier of foreign news to American households, shifts huge quantities of daily news around the world as well as into the domestic United States. But this world news is heavily edited and re-edited before it reaches the household, and most of it is not read or viewed by most people. Much of the foreign news that does reach American households is really "home news abroad." All countries' news media tend to focus upon those foreign countries that are closest, or most significant, to their own citizen public. But, because the United States is such an important world power, it presents other nations and world regions almost entirely through the spectacles of U.S. interests and foreign policy.

Foreign countries are seen in terms of friendship/hostility, trade with the United States, and military involvement with the United States. Since the collapse of the Soviet Union in 1991, all of these relationships are usually presented in terms of a superior United States and an inferior other country. There is a standard assumption that the United States is the number one power in the world.

Three different types of power are spread mainly across three cities—Washington, New York, and Los Angeles. Each of these cities has very important, and very extensive, international involvement; but within each of these cities the key powerful community is also inward-looking and oddly remote from its constituencies. The Manhattan financial elite is one rather closed world; the Washington "inside the beltway" political class is another separate world; and Beverly Hills also is a separate ghetto, walled off by money from greater Los Angeles. Foreign visitors to these locations often meet a lot of charm, expert knowledge, and generosity; they may also notice a lot of arrogance, ignorance, and belligerence.

Even State Department personnel in Washington, DC, seem to regard much of the world as a difficult and dangerous place. A 2002 report from the (politically neutral) General Accounting Office found that 60 percent of all U.S. embassies and consulates were officially regarded as hardship posts; this included much of Africa as well as China, Russia, and all of the ex-U.S.S.R. new states. In major countries such as China, Russia, and Ukraine, many U.S. diplomats did not speak the local language and were working in posts too senior for their qualifications and experience. Despite additional hardship payments (up to 25 percent on top of basic salary) even postings such as the Philippines (a former U.S. colony) were unpopular. The most highly sought posts included London, Toronto, Madrid, The Hague, and Canberra.[1] Four years later (2006), some of these weaknesses were being addressed by Secretary of State Condoleezza Rice.

American citizens are repeatedly told that the United States is number one. The U.S. media are leading players in the national activity of constructing superlatives. Many superlatives focus on the United States itself—the world's biggest, best, richest, strongest, deadliest, most feared, most admired, and most copied nation in history. Many other nations claim their own national superlatives. But the United States does more; its production of superlatives is itself superlative.

Within the forest of media statistics is often one very big number as well as one very small number. The average (nonspecialist) journalist has a strong preference for that newsworthy big number[2]—the total audience that views the channel for at least 10 minutes per month. The very, very much smaller number is the number of people actually viewing the channel now, this evening, or at any other specific time.

The Hollywood Academy Awards, it is sometimes reported, are seen by a billion people around the world each year. If this includes a generous four minutes on many national news shows in many countries, then perhaps a billion could be correct. But it is quite a small number, outside the United States, who actually view live (or recorded) most or all of the lengthy

---

[1] Christopher Marquis, "State Dept Finds That Few New Diplomats Will Take Hardship Posts" (from *New York Times*), *International Herald Tribune*, July 23, 2002.

[2] For example, this statement about CNN: "It reaches more than a billion people worldwide . . . ," Neil Hickey, " 'Chicken Noodle News,' " *Columbia Journalism Review*, March/April 2001: 67.

Academy Awards show. The West-Coast-for-East-Coast timing alone makes it unsuitable for live transmission in much of the world.

The extent to which the United States is numero uno in the world tends to be exaggerated by the U.S. mass media. Quite often a more sober assessment (on a per population, or other, basis) is that the United States tends to be in the top three or four places on many world league tables. But to point out that Europe has a bigger economy and wins many more Olympic medals, or that China has a bigger army, or that Nestlé (the "world's largest food company") is not in fact American, but Swiss—all of this can be a shade dull. At best it's too long-winded and at worst it somehow seems a trifle unpatriotic.

When Ronald Reagan was president one of his most used anecdotes concerned how, as a young radio station employee, he commented on baseball games; he did not actually attend the baseball games but read incoming news agency reports. He then used his imagination and creative skills to invent a ball-by-ball running commentary. Reagan justified his reporting style as merely presenting the truth "attractively packaged."[3]

Exporting American TV Series

Between 1950 and 1966 television arrived in most of the larger and mid-sized nations in Latin America, Asia, and Africa. Nearly all of these nations also found themselves importing about half of their entire programming output; with half or more of these imports coming from the United States, about 30 percent of their entire programming by 1970 was coming from Hollywood.

Previous to 1951 there was no reliable way of recording (or exporting) television programming; the years from 1947 to 1952 were thus the golden era of live TV drama in both New York and London. Then in the 1951–1952 TV season two pioneering shows, *I Love Lucy* and *Dragnet*, demonstrated how to record television series on film (not yet videotape). These and other recorded shows quickly found an export market in the United Kingdom, the other main TV nation of 1952. But the big impact of these shows came a few years later—as more countries adopted TV and as the Hollywood shows built up a fat backlog of episodes. In 1951–1955 the initial run of *I Love Lucy* made 179 episodes (25 minutes); *Dragnet* (1951–1958) made about 300 episodes. To importers around the world, from about 1955 onward, these shows were enormously attractive. A network in Latin America could schedule *I Love Lucy* for 179 weekdays or 36 weeks. The production standard remained high, and the price low, while the schedule slot was securely filled.

Elihu Katz and George Wedell in *Broadcasting in the Third World* reported that most of the new television systems were modeled on the United States,

---

[3] On one such occasion, President Reagan was speaking at the Voice of America's fortieth anniversary celebrations in Washington, DC, February 24, 1982.

the United Kingdom, or France. The first wave of new TV systems were modeled on the United States, with Cuba (1950) and Brazil (1950) in the lead. These systems broadly followed the U.S. commercial model (and their own existing commercial radio). Other early TV nations were Mexico (1951), Argentina (1951), and Venezuela (1952). Also starting in 1951 was the Philippines, which followed the Latin American pattern.[4]

The second big wave of new television nations were mostly colonies of Britain or France, which were acquiring their independence and setting up television at about the same time. Particularly influential was Nigeria, which began television in 1959, one year before its independence. During the decade from 1956 to 1966, other former British colonies to launch television were India (1959) and Pakistan (1962); French territories included Algeria (1956) and Morocco (1962); the former Dutch colony Indonesia (1962) and the former Belgian colony Zaire (1966) followed this broad pattern. These ex-European colonies diverged from the commercial Latin American pattern; in following various European models, these newly independent nations all developed "public" television systems that were in fact state owned and state controlled.

Most of these new television systems had a fairly chaotic first decade of operation. In particular there was not enough finance to build the television system, and there was not enough household income to purchase many of the (expensive) receiving sets. In Latin America the advertising revenue was inadequate; a mushroom growth of hopeful new stations quickly came to an end. Major engineering and technical standards problems existed, often not helped by large gifts of equipment from competing American, European, Japanese, and Soviet equipment suppliers. Governments wanted to have a big say in programming, and quite often a military coup led to a new government with its own fresh programming requirements. Always a key dilemma was the need to entice audiences (and more TV set purchasing) with attractive programming, while lacking the finance to make such programming. Long runs of expensively made American series, available at semi-token prices, constituted salvation for many anxious scheduling executives.

Arguably the figures in Table 8.1 tend to exaggerate the levels of TV imports from the United States. In most of these countries in 1971–1972 most people still did not have television. Even Brazil and Mexico both had less than 100 TV sets per 1,000 population; there were still very few TV sets in India or China or in any African country.

In summarizing his comparison of television exporting in 1973 and 1983, Tapio Varis suggested that the broad picture had stayed much the same over that decade. But his study included many very small population countries, some of which even increased their importing levels. In a group of big population countries (China, Pakistan, Philippines, Nigeria, and Egypt) the

[4] Elihu Katz and George Wedell, *Broadcasting in the Third World: Promise and Performance*, Cambridge, MA: Harvard University Press, 1977.

Table 8.1   Television Imports as an Approximate Percentage of All Television Time, 1971–1972

	PERCENTAGE OF TV PROGRAMMING FROM THE UNITED STATES	OTHER MAIN SOURCES OF TV PROGRAMMING	IMPORTS AS A PERCENTAGE OF ALL TV PROGRAMMING
Central America and Spanish Caribbean	35%	Mexico, Argentina, West Europe	60%
South America	35	Mexico, Argentina	50
South and East Asia (excluding China and India)	30	United Kingdom	50
Egypt	30	Eastern Europe, France	40
Western Europe	10	United Kingdom	20
Eastern Europe	3	Soviet Union, Eastern Europe	35

Source: UNESCO, *World Communications: A 200 Country Survey*, Paris: UNESCO, 1975.

overall level of imports dropped from about 35 percent (1973) to about 24 percent (1983).[5]

Since 1970–1975 American television programming has continued to be exported in huge total quantities; but it has had a declining share of the world market and of world audience time. After 1975 China and India became major television players. Moreover, the original modeling on the American and European patterns became less immediate.

Good/Bad/Inward-looking United States; and *MASH*

The United States presents various different versions of itself to the world. But most of these versions have been designed primarily for the home market; most offer a good/bad vision of American society. This good/bad element is found in four different views that are briefly indicated here—the showbusiness or entertainment view, the hard news view, the consumerist view, and a more sophisticated view.

Studies of the reception of the *Dallas* TV series (which began in 1978) indicated considerable enthusiasm for what became a popular series in many countries in the 1980s. Foreign audiences seem to have missed some of the ways in which *Dallas* (as a weekly soap opera) poked fun at "real" every-afternoon soaps.[6] Views obviously varied across countries, and, even within

---

[5] Tapio Varis, "The International Flow of Television Programs," *Journal of Communication*, Vol. 34/1, Winter 1984: 143–52.

[6] Alessandro Silj, *East of Dallas: The European Challenge to American Television*, London: British Film Institute, 1988; Ien Ang, *Watching Dallas*, London: Methuen, 1985.

the small nation-state of Israel, there were quite different interpretations. One popular Israeli response to *Dallas* was to the effect that "businessmen and rich people are often unhappy." But recent Russian immigrants into Israel tended to suspect more devious American manipulation: "They are telling us that the rich are unhappy, because that's what they want us to believe."[7] The producers of *Dallas*, needless to say, denied all of this.[8]

Much Hollywood output both flatters and critiques American society. Hollywood has always accompanied its product with an endless flow of showbiz gossip. In succeeding decades this gossip has tended increasingly to focus on scandal of one kind or another. Even under the puritanical rules of 1930s Hollywood, much of this publicity focused on the love life of the stars. Leo Rosten pointed out that many "romances" were highlighted, or completely invented, in order to publicize male and female stars appearing together in a new film.[9] While at least some American adults must surely have recognized such "romance" as public relations, movie fans in other parts of the world were perhaps more likely to think that Hollywood's publicity represented standard American reality.

A hard news view of America is carried across the United States by the Associated Press and by other news media. Versions of this domestic hard news view are also available to subscribing AP customers elsewhere in the world. The "two-sides" factual approach includes, along with the United States as number-one theme, a lot of bad-boy United States. During the 1960s, news organizations around the world, which subscribed to the Associated Press (and other U.S. media services), were supplied with massive quantities of negative news and images about the U.S. military effort in Vietnam. Since the 1960s AP has carried much "good United States" material; but AP has also carried much news about U.S.-funded death squads and military regimes and U.S.-funded collateral damage to various peoples around the world. American hard news has tended to portray American presidents in a good/bad framework, as being either nice-but-simple or brilliant-but-flawed.

A good/bad mix is found also in the consumerist or marketing view. Here America is bright and beautiful because it offers all kinds of consumer goodies from computers to Coca-Cola, which the rest of the world finds hard to resist. America is the home of benign high technology; however, "junk food" is an American (not a foreign) term for fast food that contains too much salt, fat, sugar, cream, and dubious meat. One oddity of many of the most famous all-American consumer brands is that they are cheap and

[7] Tamar Liebes and Elihu Katz, "Once Upon a Time in Dallas," *Intermedia*, Vol. 12/3, 1984: 28–32.
[8] I interviewed the executive producer of *Dallas*, Leonard Katzman, in Los Angeles in May 1979; this was soon after the completion of the first season of the *Dallas* series. Asked whether Dallas was intended as a parable of Hollywood's own history, Katzman asserted that most American industries had histories of corruption and skulduggery.
[9] Leo Rosten, *Hollywood: The Movie Colony, the Movie Makers*, New York: Harcourt, Brace, 1941: 109–32.

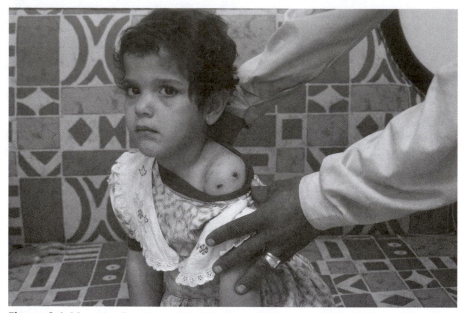

Figure 8.1 Negative Iraq image in AP photo. When wounding this four-year-old Iraqi girl, American Marines killed her parents and three of her siblings; her family were trying to flee Fallujah in their family car on April 27, 2004. (AP.)

"down-market." But expensive products like Nike[10] shoes and clothing also reach the world accompanied by (American-written) critiques about underpaid Asian child workers and excessive levels of profit and paid promotion.

More sophisticated views of America also circulate in the world. But these again present a good/bad mix of images. One of the core ingredients of a more sophisticated view must be, and is, plenty of criticism. Those in foreign lands—including journalists, academics, and politicians—who follow the more sophisticated U.S. media are supplied with generous helpings of negative facts about U.S. pollution, poverty, prisoners on death row, politicians buying elections, and the like.

Many Americans are surprised if and when they encounter sharp criticism of, and deep antagonism toward, the United States. But they should recognize that much (even most) of this criticism is made in the United States and carried abroad by AP, the *New York Times* service, CNN, blockbuster movies, MTV, Madison Avenue, and the Internet.

To outsiders the major American media—especially Hollywood—can seem extraordinarily cautious and inward looking. One example was the TV series *MASH* (1972–1983). It was unusual to have a long-running American

---

[10] Robert Goldman and Stephen Papson, *Nike Culture: The Sign of the Swoosh*, London: Sage, 1998.

television series supposedly located in a foreign country; very little Korean reality, however, and few Koreans, were seen in *MASH*.[11] The series (following the successful 1970 movie directed by Robert Altman) used the more distant Korean War to comment on the then more recent (and controversial) Vietnam War. Much of the comedy involved revealing that young medical doctors swore, drank, flirted with drugs, and pursued women; but, despite all this, the young doctors were portrayed as brave and dedicated professionals, working under difficult wartime conditions near the front line.[12] The hospital focus in *MASH* was on the American wounded, with little reference to the deaths of 1.3 million Koreans. This was also true of almost all of the 90 English-language Korean War movies; one of the most successful of the Korean War movies was *The Bridges at Toko-ri* (1955), which (like several other Korean bombing movies) showed the skilled and dangerous bombing of bridges,[13] not the carpet bombing of cities, towns, and people.

U.S. Covert Action Against Foreign Media and Governments

While Hollywood was offering the world the first episodes of *I Love Lucy*, Washington was offering the world a different media experience. In Iran (1953) and Guatemala (1954), the CIA was perfecting its covert techniques of regime change, which involved destabilizing and undermining the struggling mass media of fragile democracies. These techniques—developed during the early Cold War and at the height of domestic U.S. McCarthyite anti-communism—were to be used in numerous other regime change exercises in subsequent decades.

The existing regimes in Iran and Guatemala in 1953–1954 were fragile elected democracies, which by then current European standards were broadly centrist, but with some socialist and communist involvement. However, to leading members of the Eisenhower administration, installed in January 1953, these hesitant democracies looked to be in danger of "going communist."[14]

To Secretary of State John Foster Dulles and his CIA brother Allen Dulles, regime change seemed urgently needed. The CIA goal was to precipitate

---

[11] James H. Wittebols, *Watching M*A*S*H*, Watching America: A Social History of the 1972–1983 Television Series*, Jefferson, NC: MacFarland, 1998.

[12] The key writer on *MASH* was Larry Gelbart. Gene Reynolds was executive producer until 1977, when he was succeeded by Burt Metcalfe. I interviewed both Gene Reynolds and Burt Metcalfe in Los Angeles in early 1979.

[13] Robert J. Lentz, *Korean War Filmography: 91 English Language Features Through 2000*, Jefferson, NC: MacFarland, 2003.

[14] For the place of Iran and Guatemala in early Eisenhower Cold War strategy; see Odd Arne Westad, *The Global Cold War: Third World Interventions and the Making of Our Times*, Cambridge, UK: Cambridge University Press, 2005: 110–57.

a military coup. The military (in Iran and Guatemala) were to be drawn into the coup by three linked devices—by bribing prominent people, by destabilizing the mass media with various media dirty tricks and covert operations, and finally by rent-a-crowd street demonstrations and marches.

Money, bribery, and small cash payments were traditional in countries like Iran and Guatemala, but financial inducements also had been successfully used by Nelson Rockefeller to persuade the Latin American media in 1940–1945. In 1953 and 1954 the dollar was still in its almighty era; all other currencies were either weak, or very weak, by comparison. An envelope of cash could rent a surprisingly large number of street demonstrators; a suitcase of cash could persuade significant numbers of national politicians, army officers, and most of the small number of newspaper editors and senior journalists. The CIA found that, in 1953–1954, bribery was easy to distribute, effective, and cheap.

Iran had about 18 million people, Guatemala only 3 million. But John Foster Dulles (as secretary of state from January 1953) saw both countries as vulnerable to communism; Iran bordered the Soviet Union and Guatemala might infect the rest of Latin America. Both capital cities had very small populations compared with today, and most—even of these people—were illiterate. Guatemala was the main base (and virtually the property) of the United Fruit company; Iran had big oil and had nationalized the Anglo-Iranian oil company in 1951. In both cases land and property were controlled by a small elite; in Guatemala the owners of huge plantations held their indigenous (Maya) workers in various forms of semi-slavery.[15] In both countries the incumbent head of government was a democratically elected politician. In Iran Mohammed Mossadegh was a scholarly and eccentric nationalist politician, very popular on the oil issue,[16] and in Guatemala Prime Minister Jacobo Arbenz was a centrist former soldier whose main political goal was land reform.[17] Both of these politicians had flirted with, and also clashed with, their country's smallish Communist Party. President Eisenhower and his administration were determined to intervene, initially by attacking both the Iran and Guatemala economies via sanctions and trade boycotts (organized with Wall Street help). In both cases the CIA had specific approval from President Eisenhower to bring down the government. Winston Churchill (as British prime minister in 1953) also personally approved—and expressed his admiration for—the operation in Iran.

The still young CIA had already intervened in several countries (not least in Italy in 1947–1948). Most senior CIA people had been in the wartime Office of Strategic Services (OSS) and had been at Ivy League universities. Several had worked previously as journalists; both Richard Helms (CIA director,

---

[15] David McCreery, *Rural Guatemala, 1760–1940*, Stanford, CA: Stanford University Press, 1994.
[16] Brian Lapping, *End of Empire*, London: Granada, 1985: 191–226.
[17] Deborah J. Yashar, *Demanding Democracy: Reform and Reaction in Costa Rica and Guatemala, 1870s–1950s*, Stanford, CA: Stanford University Press, 1997: 96–100, 130–37, 203–7.

1966–1973) and Joe Goodwin (CIA station chief in Teheran in 1953) had worked as journalists for American news agencies. A Special Forces (or James Bond) style was cultivated by many CIA people, such as Kermit Roosevelt, the CIA man who led the successful Iran coup of 1953.[18] The CIA also liked to finance (or bribe) its future coup leaders. The CIA chose in advance the coup leader in Iran (General Zahedi on behalf of the shah) and in Guatemala (Castillo Armas). American policy, and CIA activity in particular, carried a large element of self-fulfilling prophesy. Trade boycotts and financial measures, and aggressive American criticism, destabilized the governments of both Iran and Guatemala. Instability was then seen as justifying direct intervention aiming at regime change.

In this destabilization process, the CIA saw the mass media as playing a leading role. The mass media in both countries were very small, but the whole effort was aimed at the capital city, and especially at the army officers—in the case of Guatemala the army had 5,000 men and perhaps 300 officers.

The main established media were newspapers and radio. In Teheran about 50,000 newspapers were sold each day; probably more than half of all the working journalists were receiving CIA money by summer 1953. Six new newspapers suddenly appeared that summer, and the buildings of three pro-government newspapers were burned by a crowd on August 19, 1953.

Radio was an important medium in both capital cities, although there were only about 70,000 radios in Guatemala in 1954. In both capitals the radio was government dominated. Radio stations were attacked from the ground and bombed by the CIA from the air. The CIA pursued the black radio route; black radio stations supplied information and disinformation supposedly from inside the country; in fact, it came from nearby countries (such as Honduras and El Salvador in the case of Guatemala). One new black station, calling itself La Voz de la Liberación, recorded its programming at CIA premises in Miami, Florida (the recorded material was then flown by Pan American to central America).[19]

The CIA used various public relations (and U.S. election-style) dirty tricks. Fake newspaper clippings were circulated; leaflets were handed out on the streets (or dropped from the air) and then reprinted as news. The CIA by 1953 had at least one publication in each of numerous countries, and these CIA papers were then quoted in Iran and Guatemala publications as evidence of "international opinion." Much material was written at the CIA in Washington, or in Miami, and appeared in translation in Teheran and in Guatemala City one or two days later.

In addition to cash bribery and media manipulation, the third key regime change mechanism was rent-a-crowd. Large crowds (aka, mobs) could be hired

---

[18] Stephen Kinzer, *All the Shah's Men: An American Coup and the Roots of Middle-East Terror*, Hoboken, NJ: John Wiley, 2003.
[19] Nick Cullather, *Secret History: The CIA's Classified Account of Its Operations in Guatemala, 1952–1954*, Stanford, CA: Stanford University Press, 1999.

for quite modest amounts of cash. In Teheran the CIA adopted the device of two opposing rented crowds; one crowd was anti-government, while a "competing" crowd was seemingly pro-government. Crowd violence of this kind killed several hundred people in Teheran—more than did the military.

Although bribes, media, and crowds proved to be an effective regime change combination in both Iran and Guatemala, the CIA operations were nevertheless badly planned and tended to descend into chaos and farce. Aircraft pilots didn't know how to drop bombs, and the old World War II bombs often failed to explode. When the bombs did explode they tended to hit the wrong targets such as British and French ships and capital city gardens. Top secret information leaked out quickly; many people employed by the CIA were adventurers and gross incompetents. In both Iran and Guatemala the army officers reluctantly agreed—in view of the chaos and American threats—to stage the requested coup; but very few soldiers or officers fired their weapons or put themselves in danger. When the coups were completed, searches of government buildings revealed no evidence at all of Soviet involvement; in fact, there was not even a Soviet embassy in Guatemala City. Stalin died in February 1953, which may partly explain why there was almost no Soviet activity of any kind in Teheran before or during the coup of August 1953.

It was not only the Washington government that was involved in these dubious schemes. The British played a big part in Iran, not least in making available to the Americans a small group of "reliable" businessmen/agents through whom cash and orders could be efficiently passed. Both the British and French governments in 1953 and 1954 were reluctant to criticize the Americans because both governments needed U.S. support in their numerous colonial problems in Africa and Asia.

In both Iran and Guatemala the coups (of 1953 and 1954) were followed by decades of authoritarian rule. The Iranian coup led to the shah's regime (1953–1978), which was notorious for its human rights abuses. In Guatemala the succeeding decades were marked by repression, military dictatorship, civil war, and genocide. But at the time the two coups were regarded, especially in Washington, as a win-win situation. Most of these techniques were used more widely after 1954—in Vietnam, Chile, and numerous other places. The biggest growth in CIA expenditure on political action and propaganda occurred in 1964–1967, when a third of such CIA projects were aimed at influencing elections; about 30 percent were media and propaganda projects.[20]

Although the U.S. media did speak up in protest over Vietnam and Chile, before and after 1970, the entire half-century after 1953 found the elite U.S. media often reluctant to reveal all that they knew. One remarkable 1950s case was that of U.S. overflights of the Soviet Union. On May 1, 1960, an American U-2 pilot (Gary Powers) was shot down and captured while flying across the

---

[20] John Prados, *Lost Crusader: The Secret Wars of CIA Director William Colby*, New York: Oxford University Press, 2003: 157–58.

Soviet Union (from Pakistan to an intended landing in Norway). A detailed study of these overflights indicates that at least 252 air crewmen were shot down on spy flights from 1950 to 1970, mostly over the Soviet Union. This broad picture was known to *New York Times* and other journalists but was not revealed for the usual Cold War "patriotic" reasons.[21]

These failures to report of the *New York Times*, Associated Press, and others extended across the coverage of the Iran and Guatemala coups. Stephen Dorril even publishes the names of two prominent American reporters who, he says, found time actually to hand out CIA propaganda leaflets in Teheran in 1953.[22]

Newspaper journalists were not alone in being close to the CIA. In another (unintentionally) comic initiative, the CIA decided to participate in the cultural side of the Cold War. It financed (through the "Congress for Cultural Freedom") an international chain of elite intellectual publications including *Encounter* (London), *Preuves* (Paris), *Cuadernos* (Latin America), *Forum* (Vienna), *Tempo Presente* (Italy), *Quadrant* (Australia), *Quest* (India), and *Jiyu* (Japan).[23] Literally hundreds of the world's most celebrated writers of the 1940s and 1950s wrote in, and accepted generous payment from, these politically centrist CIA publications. Many must have guessed that these publications were funded by Washington, DC, but very few complained.

While these intellectual publications had few consequences, the CIA interventions in Iran (1953) and Guatemala (1954) did have serious, and long-term, consequences. While the U.S. State Department demanded that foreign countries develop free and democratic media, the CIA was undermining free and democratic media in two ways. First, the CIA was actively undermining, through bribery and attacking the offices of, the freest and most democratic media currently available under elected regimes, in places like Iran and Guatemala. Second, the CIA and State Department were undermining leading domestic U.S. media by persuading them to suppress ugly truths and to print deliberate untruths.

The United States Loses UNESCO and the Moral High Ground

By the 1980s the United States had lost much of the moral high ground in terms of world media. This loss was exemplified by the 1984 U.S. withdrawal from the main world body concerned with mass media, the United Nations Educational, Scientific and Cultural Organization (UNESCO). One year later,

---

[21] Philip Taubman, *Secret Empire: Eisenhower, the CIA, and the Hidden Story of America's Space Espionage*, New York: Simon and Schuster, 2003: 46–47.

[22] Stephen Dorril, *MI6: Fifty Years of Special Operations*, London: Fourth Estate, 2000: 558–99.

[23] Frances Stonor Saunders, *Who Paid the Piper? The CIA and the Cultural Cold War*, London: Granta Books, 1999 (also publ. in the United States as *The Cultural Cold War: The CIA and the World of Arts and letters*, New York: The New Press, 2000).

in 1985, Margaret Thatcher's U.K. government also departed; Singapore, the only other nation to withdraw from UNESCO, was already notorious for its exceptionally restrictive media laws. The failure of the United States and United Kingdom to attract any other countries to follow them constituted a spectacular diplomatic failure. This failure also indicated a worldwide reluctance to accept at face value the protestations of the Reagan and Thatcher governments that they were dedicated to media freedom, while UNESCO was not.

The main arguments of both the U.S. and U.K. governments were directed against a UNESCO commission report, *Many Voices, One World*;[24] this commission was chaired by Sean MacBride, a former Irish foreign minister. The Reagan and Thatcher governments claimed to find the MacBride report guilty of seeking to restrict media freedom and media democracy. The Report, it was claimed, reflected the views of repressive and authoritarian "Third World" governments, now in a voting majority in UNESCO and the United Nations.

But, the real reasons

> for leaving UNESCO were, firstly, there was a desire in Washington to hit back at the supposed humiliation of the US in various forums, and UNESCO was chosen as the agency which the US could leave least painfully. Second, there was US hostility to several UNESCO policies and practices, but in particular to UNESCO criticism of the Western news media. The third US reason for leaving UNESCO was the belief that it had come under the control of a clique of francophone Africans hostile to the US. This criticism focused especially on the UNESCO director general, Mr M'Bow of Senegal. His predecessor had been a Frenchman and these two French-speaking chief executives, based in Paris, seem to have established a fairly dictatorial management style.[25]

Amadou-Mahtar M'Bow, the UNESCO director-general (1974–1986), was from the former French west African colony of Senegal. Both the American and British governments were suspicious of him on several grounds. Mr. M'Bow was the first black African to head a UN agency; he was a Muslim (at a time when the U.S. government saw anti-Israel and anti-Semitic prejudice featuring large in the UN agencies). M'Bow was also French educated and intellectually self-confident in both English and French.[26] Finally, M'Bow, as a former education minister in Senegal, came from the educational world (as did several MacBride commission members) and was thus suspected of naivety in relation to the hard-ball world of the media. However, it was the British (Thatcher) government that was the more hostile (not least to most things French). Washington gave the issue much more detailed analysis, with several congressional subcommittees conducting investigations.

---

[24] Sean MacBride (chairman), *Many Voices, One World*, Paris: UNESCO, 1980.
[25] Jeremy Tunstall, *Communications Deregulation*, Oxford: Basil Blackwell, 1986: 213.
[26] For example, Amadou-Mahtar M'Bow, *Building the Future: UNESCO and the Solidarity of Nations*, Paris: UNESCO, 1981.

The Anglo-American decisions to leave UNESCO were made by the governments but were encouraged by the mass media. The publishers and chain owners of U.S. and British newspapers were then (and are now) politically conservative in general and belligerently opposed to "government control" of any kind.[27] Most members of Congress also shared these beliefs.

However, it was the international news agencies that believed themselves to be in the firing line. The news agencies saw several MacBride suggestions as likely to restrict their ability to collect news, and to operate, in Africa and Asia. MacBride commission members and UNESCO personnel admitted that the report was somewhat vague and self-contradictory, but they said that it did not intend to undermine the news agencies. It was also claimed that any objectionable points in the interim report (1978) had been removed in the final report (1979–1980).

The Anglo-American news agencies were not convinced. They maintained a campaign[28]—through their worldwide news services—against UNESCO and the MacBride proposals. This is a shameful episode, especially in the history of Reuters.[29] The Associated Press pursued its traditional low profile approach, but AP and Reuters undoubtedly conducted a combined campaign. News organizations (like other organizations) pursue their own interests, and one cannot expect them happily to publicize policies that they believe to be threatening. Nevertheless, these two big agencies did campaign on their own behalf; they did support the conservative views of Reagan and Thatcher; and in this anti-UNESCO campaign they lived up to the capitalist and monopolistic conspiracy stereotype that they claimed to be an Afro-Asian caricature and fantasy.

Both Associated Press and Reuters vacated the moral high ground. But Reuters was especially guilty. Gerald Long, chief executive at Reuters, was famous for his blunt speaking, but in this case he excelled himself. He described the UNESCO-MacBride Report as

> filled with ill-founded judgements on matters about which most of the Commission members knew little or nothing. . . . It is a gallimaufry of undigested ideas about information and ideas in general, mostly written by the UNESCO Secretariat from the viewpoint of those who do not believe in freedom of the press.[30]

---

[27] M. L. Stein, "UNESCO Controversy Continues," *Editor and Publisher*, November 10, 1984: 12–13; James H. Scheuer, "Western Allies Should Pressure UNESCO," *Wall Street Journal*, November 19, 1984; Paul Lewis, "US and UNESCO in a New Clash on Special Fund," *New York Times*, August 15, 1984; "Tell It to M'Bow," *The Economist*, October 13, 1984; "Time to Quit," *The Economist*, November 16, 1985; "Farce and Failure at UNESCO," *The Times* (London), October 8, 1985.

[28] Crucial in this campaign was a meeting of news agencies and other media organizations at Talloires, France, in May 1981. This was attended by media representatives from 20 countries, including five Third World "moderates"—Nigeria, India, Malaysia, Mexico, and Egypt.

[29] Donald Read, *The Power of the News. The History of Reuters*, Oxford, UK: Oxford University Press, 1992: 326.

[30] William G. Harley, *Creative Compromise: The MacBride Commission*, Lanham, MD: University Press of America, 1993: 180.

9

Decline

U.S. Media, Moral Authority, "Sole Superpower"

The previous chapter argued that the U.S. media underwent a relative decline on the world scene in the 1970s and 1980s; this chapter argues that the decline continued after 1990. Despite the wide acceptance of the United States as the "sole superpower," the years after the Soviet Union's collapse in 1990–1991 saw U.S. declines in international economic, military, and media terms. In particular the moral authority and credibility of the United States—and its news media—declined in the eyes of the world.

Many polls indicated, from 2001 onward (after an upward sympathetic blip after the September 11, 2001, terrorist attacks in the United States), the international unpopularity of George W. Bush and the U.S. 2003 invasion of Iraq. For instance, a 2005 poll by the (U.S.-based) Pew Global Attitudes Project found that, of 16 nations polled, only 5 had a majority positive to the United States. In 10 countries a majority held broadly negative attitudes toward the United States. Moreover, when asked, "Where would you go to lead a good life?" the citizens of only one country (India) chose the United States. Four countries' citizens chose Australia, three (United States, France, China) chose Canada, two chose Britain (Poland and Spain), and two (Turkey and Russia) chose Germany.[1]

Despite these declines, hundreds of millions of people (including this author) still have a positive opinion of the United States and its people. Despite a slow overall decline in world market share, American video entertainment (including music) remains very popular. Despite the heat, millions of European children are taken to Florida each summer to visit the theme parks; this summer sale is itself an astounding triumph of American marketing skill.

---

[1] "How Others See Americans. Still Not Loved. Now Not Envied," *The Economist*, June 25, 2005; Brian Knowlton, "The US Image Abroad: Even China Is Better," *International Herald Tribune* (from *NY Times*), June 24, 2005.

The (world-perceived) decline in America's credibility and moral authority included the American news media. The 1972–1974 Watergate scandal (leading to the resignation of President Richard Nixon) marked a high point in the international reputation of American journalism. But by the early 2000s many foreign journalists offered sweeping criticisms. For example, Richard Lambert, the *Financial Times* (*FT*) editor who played a big part in boosting the *FT*'s U.S. sales, denounced U.S. media "hero worship" of entrepreneurs such as Bernie Ebbers of WorldCom. Harold Evans, formerly editor of *The Times* (London) and the *Sunday Times*, criticized the American press for its "slavish" hypocrisy in allowing George W. Bush in 2000 to hide his "shady side" (including business impropriety and lies about his drunk-driving record).[2] There was also much European and Asian comment on the uncritical coverage of the U.S. 2003 invasion of Iraq (both before and after it occurred).

The term "sole superpower" was yet another new U.S. term, which (in 1991) was quickly accepted by much of the world. Numerous authors and politicians asserted that the United States was not merely a "sole super-power" but now presided over a sole empire.[3] Many American journalists, in eagerly adopting the "sole superpower" rhetoric, failed to notice several potentially self-disproving complexities:

- Could not the Soviet demise indicate the end of all empires and superpowers?

- "Sole superpower" was another example of American delight in superlative, tabloid, and self-congratulatory exaggeration.

- How could a sole superpower put its power in evidence? Most easily, perhaps, by handing out overwhelming military defeat to a small bad nation led by a big bad guy?

- A sole superpower also needed a "War on Something General"—to follow the previous "War on Poverty" and "War on Drugs." Terrorism (both before and after 2001) presented itself as the obvious choice.[4] But a "War on Terrorism" had to confront the ancient truism that one nation's terrorist is another nation's freedom fighter; the United States itself would inevitably be seen in some parts of the world as a terrorist state.

- The sole superpower imagery included rhetoric about the United States as the only military superpower. But could the United States not more accurately be described as the bombing, missiles, and covert

---

[2] Jon Slattery, "Lambert Slams US Media over WorldCom Scandal," *Press Gazette*, July 5, 2002; Harold Evans, "A Slavish Press Connives to Hide GW's Shady Side," *The Guardian*, November 6, 2000.

[3] For example, David Harvey, *The New Imperialism*, Oxford, UK: Oxford University Press, 2003.

[4] Ross Glover, "The War on _____," in John Collins and Ross Glover (eds.), *Collateral Language: A User's Guide to America's New War*, New York: New York University Press, 2002: 207–22.

action superpower? These have the attraction of low U.S. casualties, but the United States also suffers the collateral damage of being seen as equating one American death with hundreds or thousands of Korean, Vietnamese, Cambodian, or Arab deaths.

- Central to sole military superpower rhetoric were high technology weapons. One critique of American air power refers to this as a "Technological Fanaticism;"[5] another critique is of U.S. "Military Theatricality."[6] U.S. military public relations seems to present war as a video game in which the enemy are zapped off the screen; enemy dead bodies and—even more so—dead U.S. bodies are not seen.

It has often been argued that, to combat these critiques, the U.S. government needs to pursue "public diplomacy" and to market "brand USA" on a suitably global scale. A somewhat more sophisticated version of this argument has been presented by Joseph S. Nye (of Harvard University and the Clinton Department of Defense). Nye has argued repeatedly for an emphasis on American "soft power" (including the mass media, education, and culture). But during the years in which Joseph Nye made these arguments, U.S. soft power continued to melt. Or, to change the metaphor, Nye wants to shut the stable door after the horse has bolted.[7]

What are the origins of these critiques of the United States and its media? Many of them derive from books written by American academics and journalists; of every 100 American books attacking George W. Bush, perhaps 20 or 30 were widely available and read in other countries.

Much media criticism of the United States in the 2000s relied heavily on the video (and text) output of Associated Press and Reuters. It is hard to overstate the impact of locally edited and voiced video material (often from the Western agencies) when played and replayed to Arab or Asian audiences.[8] A single unwise choice of words—such as Bush's advocacy of an American "crusade"—can, with frequent repetition, be quickly and negatively imprinted on the worldview of many millions of people.

The output of cartoonists and late night comedians from the U.S. mainstream media also travels abroad. But cartoonists and comedians around the

---

[5] Michael S. Sherry, *The Rise of American Air Power: The Creation of Armageddon*, New Haven, CT: Yale University Press, 1987: 219–300.

[6] Emmanuel Todd, *After the Empire: The Breakdown of the American Order*, New York: Columbia University Press, 2003: 14–21, 134–43 (first publ. as *Après l'empire*, Paris: Editions Gallimard, 2002).

[7] Joseph S. Nye, "Soft Power: Bombs Can't Do It All," *International Herald Tribune*, February 14, 2003; Joseph S. Nye, *The Paradox of American Power*, New York: Oxford University Press, 2002; Joseph S. Nye, *Soft Power: The Means to Success in World Politics*, New York: Public Affairs, 2004.

[8] "As the Iraq war moves into its third week . . . rage against the United States is fed by this steady diet of close-up color photographs and television footage of dead and wounded Iraqis, invariably described as victims of US bombs." Susan Sachs, "In Arab Media, War Shown as a 'Clash of Civilizations,'" *International Herald Tribune* (from *NY Times*), April 5–6, 2003.

world found plenty of easy raw material in President Clinton's womanizing and President Bush's struggles with the English language.

Most Americans, and many Europeans, would probably answer yes, if asked whether the United States is the leader in distributing news around the world. There are, however, strong arguments to be made for two other propositions—that the world news flow is dominated by a Euro-American news combination and that within this combination it is Europe (and not the United States) that is the main leader. The latter assertion does rest on the perhaps controversial assumption that the United Kingdom is part of Europe; the United Kingdom is important in this connection because it is the home base of the BBC, Reuters, the *Financial Times*, and *The Economist*. These British news purveyors are widely regarded in several parts of the world as being a little more objective, or a little less nationally biased, than the *Wall Street Journal* or *USA Today*.

In the international sale and syndication of newspapers the United States may seem to be well in the lead. Among U.S. printed news exporters are the *New York Times* (through its now fully owned subsidiary, the *International Herald Tribune*), the *Chicago Tribune* and *Los Angeles Times* grouping, the *Washington Post*, the *Wall Street Journal*, *USA Today*, *Time*, and *Newsweek*. Collectively these publications have a substantial syndication business. But the direct sales figures are quite modest; these international sales figures include significant sales to Americans traveling and living abroad, and substantial numbers of copies are given away by hotels and airlines.

Europe's main print competition is led by the *Financial Times* (which in 2005 printed in 21 locations outside the United Kingdom) and its linked publication *The Economist*. At first glance this looks like a very uneven contest. However, while about 12 U.S. daily newspapers do have their own team of foreign correspondents, Europe collectively has about 25 daily papers that employ their own team of staff correspondents. Not only capital city, but big provincial city, newspapers in Germany, France, Spain, and Italy employ a few foreign correspondents. Media in other parts of the world republish material from European newspapers—not least from such nonconservative papers as *Le Monde* (France), *El Pais* (Spain), and *The Guardian* (United Kingdom). German dailies sell copies in eastern Europe; and French papers are flown each day to northwest and west Africa. Nevertheless, the United States probably still beats Europe in daily newspaper exporting.

It is news agencies that do the really large-scale news distribution around the world, and here the U.S. dominance of 1950 has been lost. In 1950 three U.S. agencies opposed just one strong European agency, Reuters. The third U.S. agency (Hearst's INS) was folded into UP in 1958, which then became UPI. But UPI was sold by Scripps-Howard in 1982, and it lasted as a major world agency only until 1985, when it filed for Chapter 11 bankruptcy protection. UPI was now acquired by a Mexican businessman who owned the *El Sol* newspaper group. UPI continued to operate (minus its vital picture service) but it was no longer a major player.[9] By now Agence France Presse was a major agency. By 1985 Europe had other important agencies; the Spanish agency, EFE, began to take the lead in Latin America. The German agency, DPA, was (and is) especially strong in central and eastern Europe.

That the European agencies were taking the lead from the American agencies could already be seen in a 1979 study of world news. Only within the United States was Associated Press in a dominant position. In Latin America the French agency was a leader; in Africa Reuters and Agence France Presse were first equal; in both Asia and western Europe Reuters and AP shared the lead. But the two leading European agencies (Reuters and AFP) were well ahead of the two U.S. agencies (AP and UPI) outside the United States.[10]

By 1990 UPI had slipped further, even in its one remaining strong region of Latin America. A study of the use of news agency copy by 33 big Latin American newspapers showed the European agencies outgunning the U.S. agencies. The same was true of a smaller group of 15 elite Latin American newspapers. Combining the two newspaper groups, the European agencies outgunned the U.S. agencies by 48.5 percent to 30.4 percent. The U.S. Associated Press was just ahead of the Spanish EFE, with Reuters third, UPI fourth, AFP fifth, the Italian ANSA sixth, and DPA seventh.[11]

A third area is international television news services. This is an area in which CNN was very prominent and was brilliantly promoted by its founder, Ted Turner. CNN's prominence was widely exaggerated—even around 1990–1991 and the first Gulf War. It subsequently suffered a relative decline, both in the United States and in the world (except Africa). CNN— and other U.S. all-news TV services—now have to compete with domestic 24-hour TV news services in all of the larger population countries; European all-news leaders have included France with La Chaine Info (LCI) launched in June 1994. In the United Kingdom CNN faces strong domestic all-news channels (BBC, Sky); the British public regards CNN as much less "fair to all" than the British news services.[12] Europe also has two other important TV news services. One is the 24-hour news channel Euronews, available in several languages and in many countries beyond Europe. There is also the daily Eurovision news exchange (launched 1950), which swaps TV news each day between European public broadcasters. The Eurovision news exchange

---

[9] "UPI Sale Confirmed," *Wall Street Journal*, November 14, 1985; Richard M. Harnett and Billy G. Ferguson, *Unipress: United Press International Covering the 20th Century*, Golden, CO: Fulcrum Publishing, 2003: 305–30.

[10] Annabelle Sreberny-Mohammadi, "The 'World of the News' Study," *Journal of Communication*, Vol. 34/1, Winter 1984: 121–33.

[11] Fernando Reyes-Matta, "Journalism in Latin America in the '90s: The Challenges of Modernization," *Journal of Communication*, Vol. 42/3, Summer 1992: 74–83.

[12] Independent Television Commission research in 2003 reported only 46 percent of U.K. respondents finding CNN "fair to all," compared with 75 percent for Sky News.

is the world leader in swapping TV news each day with similar exchanges in other world regions. Finally, BBC World—and similar services from France, Spain, and Germany—are available as 24-hour television news services across the world. Despite predictable dissent from CNN, Europe is the comfortable winner here.

A fourth news field (and a third field in which Europe leads) is radio news. BBC Radio in 2005 claimed 163 million listeners per week (most of them in Africa and Asia)—substantially more than the American equivalents. Deutsche Welle and Radio France International are also extremely strong world radio services, and other countries (not least Spain) are strong here as well. These European radio services together reach very much bigger audiences than does the Voice of America; this is especially so in the Arab world, Africa, and South Asia.

Europe thus probably beats the United States in three out of the four fields of world news provision. What about the countries covered in the news? Does the United States get the most news coverage? One would predict that the United States is the single country that gets the most world news coverage. But European countries get more news coverage than the United States. This, of course, is an awkward comparison, and it would require a specially designed study to produce a more reliable answer. One study by Denis Wu covered news media in 44 countries in 1995.[13] The United States received 15.57 percent of the coverage; however, 6 of the top 10 countries were in Europe, and these 6 alone accounted for 30.34 percent of all news stories. Just France and Britain together (14.76 percent) almost equaled the United States, despite together having less than half the U.S. population.

Perhaps more striking than any European or U.S. "wins" in international news is the extent to which Europe and America combine in many ways. The news media of the United States and Europe depend upon each other, operate in each others' countries, swap material, and sometimes share the same foreign correspondents. Even correspondents who work for quite unrelated news organizations on different sides of the Atlantic may work together; a European and an American correspondent will often share a car, share interviews, swap quotes, and exchange insights.

Similar things happen with senior personnel. British Reuters has employed many Americans (as well as many Europeans) and has appointed an American chief executive. Similarly, Associated Press employs many British (and European) personnel. AP's late move into the fast video news business depended heavily on senior British personnel (hired from Reuters), and the AP world video news operation also chose London as its headquarters.

---

[13] H. Denis Wu, "Homogeneity Around the World?" *Gazette*, Vol. 65/1, February 2003: 9–24; H. Denis Wu, "Systematic Determinants of International News Coverage," *Journal of Communication*, Vol. 50/2, Spring 2000: 110–30.

The United States was the sole world news superpower back in 1950, but that is true no longer. The world news flow has been Euro-American dominated since the 1970s.

Slowing the TV Export Decline: Cable/Satellite Channels

Since around 1990 many U.S. cable/satellite channels have established local versions in Europe, Asia, and around the world. But the U.S. cable channels' achievement in establishing successful niche markets in many countries has been outweighed by the bigger decline of Hollywood export sales to major conventional networks. The success of many countries in making much more of their own—soap, reality, sports, and other—entertainment programming has substantially reduced Hollywood shares of foreign TV markets. MTV and all the other U.S. cable channels have succeeded only in slowing this overall decline in American market shares around the world.

Inside the United States, the combined cable networks by 2005 had a bigger market share than the combined seven traditional broadcast networks. But while in 2005 some 20 U.S. cable channels each had at least a 1 percent share of the total U.S. TV market, these same 20 channels' export versions typically had a 0.1 percent share (or less) of the world TV audience time. To put this in very round numbers: When (in the mid-2000s) U.S. cable had a 50 percent plus share of domestic U.S. audience TV time, U.S. cable had a 4 percent minus share of world audience time.[14]

MTV has been the most successful U.S. cable exporter. In 2005 MTV launched its one hundredth export offering. MTV Europe alone had 45 regionalized channels with nine targeted solely at the United Kingdom; MTVE had dedicated offerings that included MTV Romania, MTV Nordic, and MTV Russia. MTV's Asian offerings included MTV Cricket. MTV had gradually expanded from music TV to a mix of music and youth lifestyle programming. MTV typically launched new offerings with a 70/30 mix of American and local music; but this usually switched to something more like 30 percent U.S. and 70 percent local.

MTV had successfully exploited some unique opportunities—much (high quality) free material, the acceptability of endless musical repetition, the wide availability of weekly audience chart data, and the strong appeal to advertisers of a youthful and affluent audience. MTV was a major exception to the rule of modest niche appeal for U.S. cable channels abroad. But despite its stunning 2005 numbers—it was "available in 189 languages and 164 territories"—MTV's (doubtless exaggerated) claim to be in 412 million homes

---

[14] In the United Kingdom in 2003 the four most popular U.S. programming bundles (Cartoon Network total, Hallmark, Nickelodeon total, and Discovery total) had a combined 1.57 percent share of U.K. TV audience time. Phillip Reevell, "Digital TV Passes the Tipping Point," *Broadcast*, January 9, 2004: 16–17.

would mean that MTV was available in fewer than 25 percent of the world's (non-U.S.) homes.[15]

Perhaps more typical of the world overall was a 2004 study from 11 Southeast Asian nations that showed Discovery reaching 21.9 percent of households, at least once a month, followed by National Geographic (15.3 percent), CNN (14.6 percent), and MTV (12.4 percent). But this sample was city-based and included affluent cities such as Tokyo, Singapore, Kuala Lumpur, Jakarta, and Seoul; like many such surveys, this sample was merely a thin slice of wealthy Asians; these households' average income was $62,500 in 2004.[16]

Another big American cable/satellite export success was ESPN. But ESPN has to face the difficulty that several top U.S. sports (such as American football, ice hockey, and baseball) are not the world's top sports. However, ESPN across the world has adroitly presented a mix of U.S. and local sport. ESPN has also been adept at reaching agreements with major competitors. ESPN was for some years involved in Eurosport (which has access to the sports programming of the European public broadcasters). ESPN also joined its competitor, Fox, in an Asian merger that kept down the cost of acquiring sports like cricket (the top sport in southern Asia).[17]

One other big American success has been Discovery, the documentary and factual group of channels. On the world scene Discovery mixes its voluminous American output with British and other "local" material. Top-of-the-line documentary is expensive to produce, but it can then be cheaply "localized" with a translated commentary and/or a local personality to front the show. Documentary can also be repeated endlessly over 24 hours and through the years.

Nevertheless, even the most successful American cable channels have had to struggle hard (and not always profitably) for their international success. Channels that have been fine-tuned (and retuned) for a domestic U.S. niche

---

[15] Johnny Davis, "The Beat Goes On," *The Independent*, review section, February 22, 2005; Andy Fry, "Face the Music," *Cable and Satellite Europe*, November 2003: 26–29; Special Issue on MTV, *Journal of Communication Inquiry*, Winter 1986, Vol. 10/1; Jack Banks, *Monopoly Television: MTV's Quest to Control the Music*, Boulder, CO: Westview Press, 1996; Marta Wohrle, "Music Video. Promos: A Green Light in a Grey Area," *Broadcast*, February 10, 1984: 16–17; Raymond Snoddy, "In at the Start of a TV Revolution," *Financial Times*, July 6, 1987; Jane Harbord, "Europe Pops the Question," *Invision*, August/September 1987: 14–16; Glyndwr Matthias, "Face the Music," *Cable and Satellite Europe*, September 1987: 24–28; Don Groves, "MTV Europe Enters USSR," *Variety*, November 12, 1990; Steve Clarke, "MTV Europe: Rock Conquers Continent," *Variety*, November 16, 1992: 35–36; Sarah Walker, "Music TV: Make War, Not Music," *Television Business International*, April 1994: 30–34; Mike Galetto Speaks with Bill Roedy, "Making the Music Video World Go Round," *Multichannel News International*, May 2001: 38; Bill Carter, "An 'Inner Teen' Takes the Helm at MTV," *International Herald Tribune* (from *NY Times*), July 27, 2004.

[16] Jo Bowman, "Discovery Leads Asia's Pax Pack," *Media* (Hong Kong), December 17, 2004.

[17] Michael Freeman, *ESPN: The Uncensored History*, Dallas: Taylor Publishing Company, 2000; Michael Williams, "Jock Lock Rocks the Box," *Variety*, April 27, 1992: 1, 102; Tim Burt, "Raising Their Game," *Financial Times*, "Creative Business," January 24, 2004.

audience cannot possibly fit so neatly on the world scene. A successful U.S. channel may claim to be in, for example, "90 million homes in 100 countries." This will mean, in many of these specific countries, in fact being in very few homes.

When an American channel commissions "local content," it typically pays the local producer only a small fraction of the rate paid in the United States. In more affluent markets, especially in Europe, this local programming then has to compete against higher budgeted output from major national broadcasters.[18]

The overall picture becomes even more complex.[19] Many channels have audience shares too small to research with the current technology. The ever-increasing flood of American cable programming means that many cable hours are acquired by national channels (both broadcast and cable/satellite) and shown at very low audience times. In many cases the "one million households" reached by a particular channel in a particular country refers only to a two-hour or four-hour block well away from any high audience time; also, the million figure refers to availability in households, while actual viewer numbers may never rise above a few thousand.

Exceptionalism, Bombing, Loss of Moral Authority

The United States has long prided itself on being an (or the) exceptional nation, uniquely founded on universal principles, which the rest of mankind may follow. Exceptionalism has continued to be a theme in America's view of its place in the world,[20] but since 1990 the world's citizens and the world's media have increasingly seen American exceptionalism as a negative.[21]

Especially during the Roosevelt and Truman years (1933–1953) the United States had moral authority on the world scene. Presidents Eisenhower, Kennedy, and Johnson (mainly in 1964) wielded some (reduced) moral authority.[22] The United States in the Cold War years did some horrible things, but they were perhaps a little less horrible than the Soviet Union's horrible deeds.

In the mid-1990s there was some admiration for the success of President Clinton's deft management of U.S. diplomatic relations with Russia and with

[18] "The Discovery Channel: 10th Anniversary," *Variety*, April 3–9, 1995: 1–36; Justine White, "What's Really Happening to the Discovery Brand," *Cable and Satellite Europe*, December 1997: 41; Andy Fry, "Documentary Channels: The Hard Facts," *Cable and Satellite Europe*, March 2002: 23–27; Michael Rosser, "Making the Factual Fun," *Broadcast*, April 16, 2004: 17.
[19] An excellent worldwide account is Jean Chalaby (ed.), *Transnational Television Worldwide*, London: I.B. Tauris, 2004.
[20] "A Nation Apart: A Survey of America," *The Economist*, November 8, 2003: 1–18.
[21] Claes G. Ryn, *America the Virtuous: The Crisis of Democracy and the Quest for Empire*, New Brunswick, NJ: Transaction, 2003.
[22] Anthony Woodiwiss, *Postmodernity USA: The Crisis of Social Modernism in Postwar America*, London: Sage, 1993.

a heavy-drinking Boris Yeltsin. However, by around 1997–1998 this phase of admiration was largely over. The consequent decline in U.S. moral authority was—according to opinion poll data—exacerbated by President George W. Bush's decision to invade Iraq in early 2003. Gunter Grass (the German Nobel prize–winning novelist) was one of many who from April 2003 onward mourned "the moral decline of a superpower."[23]

The U.S. Iraq invasion of 2003 was seen widely as reflecting a previous U.S. liking for preventive action—most frequently "covert" preventive action. Now the Bush administration was proclaiming its badly thought out doctrine of full-scale "preemptive" war.[24] The choice of Iraq, for a clinical demonstration of sophisticated preemptive war, was seen widely as an extremely unwise choice. Several American institutions suffered a loss of international reputation. The major American media—as observed from abroad—seemed largely to fail to see the gaping holes in this preemptive war exercise. Many journalists (and politicians) in the world expressed that criticism of nearly all of the mainstream U.S. media. Several of the major U.S. media subsequently apologized and broadly admitted their failure to see what millions of people demonstrating on the streets of London, Paris, Berlin, and Madrid had been able to see (before the invasion occurred).

All "democratic" political systems—not least European ones—have obvious weaknesses and inadequacies. In recent years, however, newspaper readers and TV viewers in Europe (and elsewhere) have become familiar with several critiques of U.S. "political corruption." These criticisms increasingly include the U.S. mass media for being too conservative, too self-satisfied, too monopolistic, and too cautious. For example:

- Four recent two-term presidencies ended in massive corruption, scandal, or disaster: Nixon (Watergate), Reagan (Iran-Contra), Clinton (Lewinsky), and George W. Bush (Iraq).

- *Capital Corruption*, a book by internationally respected social scientist Amitai Etzioni, was published in 1984; its main argument remains true today. Washington was, and still is, corrupted by campaign contributions channeled by lobbyists to senators and congressmen who oversee those lobbyists' specific industries. Adlai Stevenson welcomed Etzioni's book and commented that it was with the "advent of television" that "money took over politics."[25] The Jack Abramoff scandal of 2006 pointed to corrupt behavior within the lobbying industry itself.

---

[23] Gunter Grass, "Pre-emptive War: The Moral Decline of a Superpower," *International Herald Tribune*, April 10, 2003; Thomas Fuller and Brian Knowlton, "Losing High Ground on Moral Leadership," *International Herald Tribune*, July 5, 2004.

[24] Ivo H. Daalder and James M. Lindsay, *America Unbound: The Bush Revolution in Foreign Policy*, Washington, DC: Brookings Institution Press, 2003.

[25] Amitai Etzioni, *Capital Corruption: The New Attack on American Democracy*, New York: Harcourt Brace Jovanovich, 1984; "Selling America to the Highest Bidder," *The Economist*, November 11, 2000; Thomas B. Edsall, "Fundraising Doubles the Pace of 2000," *Washington Post*, August 21, 2004.

- Electoral corruption (and electoral redistricting in favor of incumbents)[26] was well illustrated by the 2000 presidential election in Florida; in particular, the part played by partisan local officials seemed less than democratic and transparent.
- The role of the "political consultant," long established across all levels of U.S. politics, is largely unknown in the rest of the world. The central role of Karl Rove (aka Turdblossom) at the 2000 and 2004 elections, and in White House policy, made excellent "only in America" shock-and-horror material for foreign journalists.[27]
- Companies such as Enron, WorldCom, and Halliburton have became internationally notorious as examples of business corruption, with political overtones.

These five types of corruption have been reported widely by the national media in many nations. With the major exception of Nixon and Watergate, the performance of the U.S. media has been widely regarded as inadequate. Why does the U.S. press not challenge capital corruption and in particular the relentless grip on electoral finance exerted by the National Association of Broadcasters (the TV equivalent of the National Rifle Association)? Many European and other journalists who descended on Florida in November 2000 were astonished, not least at the complex arrangements for discouraging African Americans from voting. In the Enron and WorldCom scandals the U.S. media in general, and cable news and financial news stations in particular, were seen as having boosted dishonest and overpaid company executives.[28]

Despite their excellent past record, the American media are widely seen as having in recent years paid insufficient attention to human rights and inequality issues. The U.S. media frequently carry stories that originate with such organizations as Human Rights Watch and Amnesty International; stories about the rich getting richer, while the poor still lack health insurance, are commonplace. But many foreign journalists were themselves surprised in 2005 that the U.S. media seemed surprised by the extreme poverty and inequality in New Orleans revealed by Hurricane Katrina. Why had the U.S.

---

[26] "Behind Closed Doors': The Recurring Plague of Redistricting," in Steven Hill, *Fixing Elections: The Failure of America's Winner Take All Politics*, New York: Routledge, 2002: 78–93; "Tom DeLay's Chef d'Oeuvre: A New Low in the Abuse of Electoral Rules for Partisan Advantage," *The Economist*, October 18, 2003: 54; Sasha Abramsky, "The Redistricting Wars," *The Nation*, December 29, 2003: 16–19.

[27] Jerry Hagstrom, *Political Consulting: A Guide for Reporters and Citizens*, New York: The Freedom Forum Media Studies Center, 1992; Dennis W. Johnson, *No Place for Amateurs: How Political Consultants Are Reshaping American Democracy*, New York: Routledge, 2001; Turdblossom was George W. Bush's pet nickname for Karl Rove. Lou Dubose, Jan Reid, and Carl M. Cannon, *Boy Genius: Karl Rove, the Brains Behind the Remarkable Political Triumph of George W. Bush*, New York: Public Affairs, 2003; James Hardine, "The Smell of Success2," *Financial Times* magazine, October 2, 2004: 16–21; Howard Fineman and Michael Isikoff, "King Karl," *Newsweek International*, February 21, 2005: 22–3.

[28] "Editorial: Let Us Count the Culprits," *Business Week*, December 17, 2001.

media not previously campaigned about this, as well as the poor showing of the United States in world data concerning infant mortality and life expectation? Were the media too afraid of the medical industrial complex?

U.S. retention of the death penalty attracts a particularly large amount of media criticism, not least from Europe. Here the United States finds itself alongside China and Saudi Arabia. Franklin Zimring argues that legal execution is most common in those same southern American states in which, in the past, mob lynchings were most common. Capital punishment is a familiar Hollywood theme. America's overpopulated prisons and the death penalty are popular subjects with foreign TV documentary makers, and "Texas Executes Mentally Ill Killer" fits international tabloid news values to perfection.[29] In a few cases the condemned person is a citizen of another country. Such a case may attract little media attention in Texas or Mississippi, but it may get big media coverage around the world. In particular cases the pope, prime ministers, and presidents have appealed for mercy; this typically generates no mercy, but it does generate massive new waves of "Barbaric America" headlines and TV news coverage.

Many American politicians began as lawyers and sharpened their belligerence as court lawyers and prosecutors. As politicians, they experience "attack" electioneering and internalize the aggressive style of Washington committee politics. When they step out onto the international stage, American politicians tend to continue with their belligerent style. One resulting tendency may be a preference for bending the letter of the law, so as to tolerate "torture lite" and "extraordinary rendition"[30] (kidnapping suspects and transporting them to third countries to be interrogated with heavy torture).

Another strand of influence that feeds into the U.S. use of torture (lite and heavy) comes from the last days of the British and French empires. The aggressive measures used by the British in Malaya and Kenya[31] attracted Washington interest and admiration. One of the several attractions of torture lite was that supposedly it could be kept secret from a not very inquisitive American media.

Bombing also involved strong British and World War II influences. It was the British who initially showed the greater enthusiasm for burning down entire German cities; the British dropped their heaviest weight of bombs

[29] Franklin E. Zimring, *The Contradictions of American Capital Punishment*, New York: Oxford University Press, 2003; Lee Hockstader, "Texas Executions Are So Routine That Few Notice," *International Herald Tribune* (from *Washington Post*), September 24, 2004; Alan Berlow, "The Texas Clemency Memos," *The Atlantic Monthly*, July/August 2003: 91–96; Kat Allen, "Hi, Death Row . . . ," *Amnesty*, March/April 2004: 8–9; Patti Waldmeir, "US Court to Be Asked: How Grisly Can Execution Be?" *Financial Times*, October 30/31, 1999; Andrew Buncombe, "Executed, by Lethal Injection: The 74-Year-Old So Stricken by Dementia He Forgot Who He Was," *The Independent*, August 7, 2004; Helen Prejean, "Death in Texas," *New York Review of Books*, January 27, 2005: 4–6.
[30] Bob Herbert, "Outsourcing Torture," *International Herald Tribune*, February 12–13, 2005.
[31] David Anderson, *Histories of the Hanged: Britain's Dirty War in Kenya and the End of Empire*, London: Weidenfeld and Nicolson, 2005.

on Germany in the twelve months of 1944–1945, after which the British did nothing subsequently on such a large scale. But the Americans, of course, continued on occasions over the next six decades to bomb on a massive scale. The British pioneering of aerial bombing had involved the Royal Air Force bombing of Iraqi villages in the 1920s.[32] Eight decades later, American bombs were falling on Iraqi centers of population. Contrary to the widely accepted rules, the United States dropped napalm[33] and cluster bombs and also used uranium depleted weaponry in Iraq. Bombing continued to have its traditional (short-term) attractions; it was cheaper and less dangerous (to U.S. personnel) than ground action. Bombs and missiles also had (short-term) publicity advantages.

The "shock and awe" of 2003 neatly reflected contempt for the local people and indifference to their fate. Bombing could still, to a considerable degree, be hidden from the American and foreign media; the full effects of bombing can only be seen close-up on the ground. American journalists were, understandably, cautious about visiting places where civilians had just been slaughtered by American bombs; and few journalists wanted to step on an unexploded cluster bomb. But British and other European journalists (perhaps because of their nations' strong historic memories of bombing) were more inclined to believe the worst, when confronted with ambiguous evidence. If the American military said they had destroyed a village full of rebels, American journalists seemed inclined to report this. But, if the locals said that the Americans had attacked a village wedding party, European (and even more so, Arab) journalists were more likely to believe the villagers.

In the nineteenth century American exceptionalism involved the United States in seeing itself as different from Europe and Europe's empires. American exceptionalism was evident before 1914 in the field of telecommunications; but America's insistence on pursuing its own way with the telephone and telegraph business was rooted in real differences. The United States had indeed diverged from the European pattern of state and post office control of telecommunications.

After 1990 the U.S. positions on international criminal courts and global climate change seemed—to most of the rest of the world—to be based on short-term and blinkered self-interest. These two cases generated much domestic media criticism of Washington's policies. Some American critics argued that "rogue America"[34] was now a more accurate description than "exceptionalist America."

---

[32] Sven Lindqvist, *A History of Bombing*, London: Granta, 2001 (first publ. in Swedish, 1999): 102–33.

[33] Andrew Buncombe, "US Admits It Used Napalm Bombs in Iraq," *The Independent on Sunday*, August 10, 2003.

[34] Clyde Prestowitz, *Rogue Nation: American Unilaterism and the Failure of Good Intentions*, New York: Basic Books/Perseus, 2003.

Monopoly Dilemmas: *New York Times*, Associated Press

The year 2003 was a bad one for the *New York Times*. A *Times* reporter, Jayson Blair, was revealed to have systematically invented and plagiarized at least half of all his pieces in the paper; also in 2003 the *New York Times*—after pre-invasion hesitation—gave an overenthusiastic and overpatriotic account of the invasion of Iraq. The *Times* subsequently apologized at length for both errors.

But 2003 did not mark the start of a decline in the international and national reputation of the *New York Times*; the 1960s saw the peak of its reputation and performance. The *Times* could be satisfied with how it had covered the Vietnam War. Famously in 1963 the *Times* refused President John Kennedy's suggestion that a critical reporter should be moved from Saigon; this reporter was David Halberstam, who later wrote the trenchant *The Making of a Quagmire*.[35] In the 1960s there were still many foreign correspondents based in New York,[36] and they—like American journalists—tended to rely heavily on, and to write flattering things about, the *New York Times*. But in 1967 the *Times* acquired a monopoly of the serious newspaper market in New York City, when the *World Journal Tribune* collapsed and died. Since 1967 many of the *New York Times*' weaknesses (and strengths) have been those of monopolistic dominance.

Since the 1960s the whole concept of the elite newspaper of record has been challenged in Europe, Japan, India, and Latin America—as well as in the United States. All of the other supposedly elite U.S. newspapers have become more commercial and more part of a large diversified media group.[37]

The elite prestige newspaper can now be seen to have been a myth, although—like all good myths—this one did contain elements of empirical truth. The elite paper is supposed to be independent of political party; it must have an enlightened and hands-off owner; its chief editor has sovereign control of editorial content; the elite paper is a "paper of record" to which historians and others can refer. Finally, the elite newspaper competes through its superior quality, which earns it strong support from both advertisers and readers.

Editorial "independence" needs to be put in evidence. The *New York Times* was not a party paper and has endorsed Republicans, as well as Democrats, in recent presidential elections. But the "sovereign editorship" element has

---

[35] David Halberstam, *The Making of a Quagmire*, London: Bodley Head, 1965.

[36] In 1968 the British print and broadcast media had 61 staff correspondents on the U.S. East Coast; 27 were in Washington and 34 in New York. Jeremy Tunstall, *Journalists at Work*, London: Constable, 1971, and Beverly Hills, CA: Sage, 1974.

[37] For example, Dennis McDougall, *Privileged Son: Otis Chandler and the Rise and Fall of the LA Times Dynasty*, Cambridge, MA: Perseus, 2001; Christopher Parkes, "LA Times Confesses to Breach of Ethics," *Financial Times*, December 21, 1999; Jennifer Saba, "Will Tribune Tower Again?" *Editor and Publisher*, February 2005: 29–32.

Figure 9.1 *Time* magazine celebrates the *New York Times*, June 1971. (Image provided by the author.)

always had strict limits, since the real sovereign is the chief owner or publisher; and, whether the humble journalists realized this or not, *New York Times* publishers were far from being hands-off. The *New York Times* did make an especially big attempt to be a paper of record, but electronic archiving has now transformed this area (with both benefits and losses to the *Times*). Also the detail of politics has increased; in recent decades *New York Times* Washington coverage has focused on presidents, the presidents' cabinets, and the White House, with less and less prominence devoted to the House of Representatives.[38]

---

[38] In 2001 the *New York Times* devoted 8.6 percent of its political front page stories to the House of Representatives, compared with 36.3 percent to president, White House, and cabinet; Stephen J. Farnsworth and S. Robert Lichter, "The Mediated Congress: Coverage of Capitol Hill in the New York Times and Washington Post," *Press/Politics*, Vol. 10/2, Spring 2005: 94–107.

New York Times attempts to compete, through quality, face two severe difficulties. First, there is no comparable competitor in the key market within 50 miles of New York City. Second, the *Times* finds itself competing for diminishing classified advertising against strong suburban and exurban dailies outside New York City, and also against strong city dailies in all of the larger U.S. cities (where its non–New York City editions are on sale). Increasingly the elite-and-prestige daily is only two or three sections within a multisection bundle of showbiz, shopping, and other consumer offerings. The *Times*, now more dependent on a national audience and upon movie advertising, has boosted its Hollywood celebrity coverage.

Anyone who has talked with, or interviewed, chief editors will be aware that the phone call from the publisher is crucial. The publisher hires and fires the editor. Like other family ownerships, the *New York Times* ownership has a history of just a few generations. In 110 years (1896–2005) the *Times* had just five publishers (one of whom died after two years on the job). These five publishers took office at an average age of 42. The last two publishers—Arthur Ochs Sulzberger senior and junior—had both been well prepared for the job. The standard pattern has been that the youngish new publisher introduces major business changes, especially during his first decade. The *New York Times* has thus had a few dynamic decades of change. The founder of the present dynasty, Adolph S. Ochs, was the publisher for 39 years, but his dynamic decade was his first 10 years—1896–1905—during which he cut the cover price from three cents to one cent and established the (previously sinking) paper's reputation.[39] Subsequent dynamic decades (led by new publishers) were from 1935 to 1945 and during the 1960s. Especially if he appoints a new executive editor (the top editor post), the publisher has an initial advantage. The publisher has had some training in advertising, circulation, and printing as well as editorial, while the new editor only knows editorial. In his first dynamic decade the publisher tends to dominate; it is only after this decade that the publisher may become less active, while the executive editor—who normally continues up to age 65—uses his superior energy, skill, and intellect to become at least somewhat more sovereign. But for much of its history the *New York Times*—with a tradition of long-staying executive editors and publishers—has been run with caution by men in their fifties and sixties.

The *New York Times* had its last dynamic decade in 1992–2002; one year later came the crisis year of 2003. In his first decade as publisher of the *New York Times*, Arthur Ochs Sulzberger, Jr., who became chairman of the entire *NYT* company in 1997, introduced many business changes that contrasted sharply with the last two decades (1970s and 1980s) of his father's three-decade reign (1963–1992) as publisher. The 1990s saw major changes and

[39] Meyer Berger, *The Story of the New York Times, 1851–1951*, New York: Simon and Schuster, 1951, 70–201.

major investments in the *New York Times*. The "good grey lady" of tradition became a significant Internet news provider and adopted color and more showbiz, sports, entertainment, and consumer sections. There were also major developments in the New York Times company, which had previously stuck to its long-time ownership of local TV stations and its other (mainly small southern) daily newspapers. Two big investments were the acquisition of the *Boston Globe* and taking full control of the (Paris-based) *International Herald Tribune*. Most important for the *New York Times* newspaper was a massive and expensive roll-out of local printing operations across the entire United States. All of this made the 1990s a decade of growth and accomplishment. The young publisher was fortunate also in his executive editor of this era, Joseph Lelyveld—a man of great intellectual ability and originality and with a deep feeling for both South Africa and India (where he had worked as a foreign correspondent). However, Lelyveld was succeeded, as executive editor, in 2001 by Howell Raines. In 2002 the *New York Times* received seven Pulitzer prizes. But Raines—who was widely praised for the *Times'* coverage of September 11, 2001, and after—lost his executive editor job in 2003, as a result of the Jayson Blair affair.[40]

The aggressive business moves of the 1990s may have resulted in senior managers and editors failing to scrutinize the work of young reporters like Jayson Blair. But senior editors and managers may also have failed to notice that, despite the end of the Cold War and the Soviet Union, *New York Times* foreign news still tended to follow Washington foreign policy quite closely. The *Times*—like other U.S. media—had failed to kick the Cold War habit of seeing the entire world through the spectacles of U.S. politics. Having adopted that framework (How is this story relevant to American policy and interests?), *New York Times* foreign coverage was forced to rely heavily on State Department guidance in Washington and on U.S. Embassy guidance in foreign countries. The chief editor of one major Delhi newspaper noted that all American coverage of India adopted the same narrow, Washington, perspective.[41] An academic content analysis of 2001 coverage of China shows a similar pattern. Both the *New York Times* and *Los Angeles Times* covered China through a narrow and negative framework of U.S. national interest.[42]

[40] "After Sept 11, Howell Raines Helped Lift His Paper—and His Profession—to New Heights," *Editor and Publisher*, April 2, 2002: 14–20; Dave Astor, "Prized Above All Else," *Editor and Publisher*, April 15, 2002: 9–20; "Special Report: Perspectives on The Times," and Brent Cunningham, "Re-Thinking Objectivity," *Columbia Journalism Review*, July/August 2003: 14–32; Gerard Baker, "The News About the Man Who Made It Up," *Financial Times*, May 15, 2003.

[41] Author interview with V. N. Narayanan, chief editor of *Hindustan Times*, Delhi, April 7, 1999.

[42] Zengjun Peng, "Representation of China: An Across Time Analysis of Coverage in the New York Times and Los Angeles Times," *Asian Journal of Communication*, Vol. 14/1, March 2004: 53–67.

The foreign news coverage of the *Times* has been studied in depth by academic content analysts. Inspection of six books and seven articles that deal partly or wholly with *New York Times* foreign coverage[43] suggests that during the Cold War 1980s and after the end of the Soviet Union, the *Times* usually stayed fairly close to the current Washington administration's foreign policy.

William Dorman and Mansour Farhang studied some 1,600 items about Iran that appeared in the *New York Times* between 1951 and 1978; this period included the CIA-engineered coup of 1953 and all of the shah's repressive regime (1953–1978). Throughout this 25-year period the *New York Times* broadly followed Washington policy, broadly supported the shah, and portrayed in a negative light the political opposition that eventually led to the massive popular uprising against the shah in 1978.[44]

Some of the biggest "scandal" revelations about newspapers, as about politics, appear in books, and this proved to be the case for the *Times* in the years around 2003. Prior to 2000, numerous books had been written about the *New York Times*. Many of them dealt with conflicts and intrigue between *Times* journalists and their editors. At least four books have presented sharply different views of Abe Rosenthal, whose career followed a classic post-1945 *New York Times* pattern. After a successful foreign correspondent career (in India, Poland, and Japan) he returned in 1963 to run the metropolitan (New York City) desk. For 10 years (1976–1986) he held the top journalist post, executive editor. The four books about Abe Rosenthal include portraits of him both as a charismatic journalist genius and also as a mean-spirited, vicious executive who ruled the newsroom by fear and

---

[43] Daniel C. Hallin, *The "Uncensored War": The Media and Vietnam*, Berkeley: University of California Press, 1989 (first publ. New York: Oxford University Press, 1986); Andrew K. Semmel, "Foreign News in Four US Elite Dailies: Some Comparisons," *Journalism Quarterly*, Vol. 53/4, Winter 1976: 732–36; Lee Becker, "Foreign Policy and the Press," *Journalism Quarterly*, Vol. 54/2, Summer 1977: 364–68; David Daugherty and Michael Warden, "Prestige Press Editorial Treatment of the Mideast During 11 Years of Crisis," *Journalism Quarterly*, Vol. 56/4, Winter 1979: 776–82; Trevor Brown, "Did Anybody Know His Name? US Press Coverage of Biko," *Journalism Quarterly*, Vol. 57/1, Spring 1980: 31–38, 44; J. V. Vilanilam, *Reporting a Revolution: The Iranian Revolution and the NIICO Debate*, New Delhi: Sage Publications, 1989; W. Lance Bennett, "Towards a Theory of Press–State Relations in the United States," *Journal of Communication*, Vol. 40/2, Spring 1990: 103–25; Nicholas O. Berry, *Foreign Policy and the Press: An Analysis of the New York Times' Coverage of US Foreign Policy*, New York: Greenwood Press, 1990; Daniel Riffe, Charles F. Aust, Rhonda J. Gibson, Elizabeth K. Viall, and Huiuk Yi, "International News and Borrowed News in the *New York Times*: An Update," *Journalism Quarterly*, Vol. 70/3, Autumn 1993: 638–46; Kristen Alley Swain, "Proximity and Power Factors in Western Coverage of the Sub-Saharan AIDS Crisis," *Journalism and Mass Communications Quarterly*, Vol. 80/1, Spring 2003: 145–65; Jack Lule, *Daily News, Eternal Stories: The Mythological Role of Journalism*, New York: The Guilford Press, 2001; Joshua Muravchik, *Covering the Intifada: How the Media Reported the Palestinian Uprising*, Washington, DC: The Washington Institute for Near East Policy, 2003.

[44] William A. Dorman and Mansour Farhang, *The US Press and Iran: Foreign Policy and the Journalism of Deference*, Berkeley: University of California Press, 1987.

ridicule. The most balanced portrait of Rosenthal is in Edwin Diamond's *Behind the Times*; Diamond also realizes that the Sulzbergers, as the controlling family, call the shots.[45]

The year 2003 saw the publication of two damaging books about the *New York Times* and the foreign world. John F. Stacks in *Scotty: James B. Reston and the Rise and Fall of American Journalism* described how Reston—the top *Times* political journalist of the 1960s and 1970s—allowed himself to become a media mouthpiece for John Kennedy and Henry Kissinger.[46] Another 2003 book was a self-inflicted wound; *"A Time of Our Own Choosing": America's War in Iraq* was a book digest of *New York Times* stories written before and after the U.S. invasion of Iraq in March 2003. The *Times* subsequently apologized for the patriotic zeal and generous self-congratulation reflected in this book. Previous to the 2003 invasion, the *Times* sat on the fence, arguing for diplomatic caution and the UN route. But when the invasion was about to commence, the paper slipped into its familiar pro-Washington mode and also into patriotic support for our boys in the military. The *New York Times* deployed a large number of journalists to cover the invasion both inside and outside Iraq. The paper's reporters come across as hard-working and mildly skeptical; but overall the tone is patriotic, proud to be American, and equally proud to be reporting the big invasion for the great newspaper. The leading players in this book's drama are George Bush, the United Nations, Saddam Hussein, weapons of mass destruction and nuclear weapons, Colin Powell, Donald Rumsfeld, the 3rd Infantry Division, General Tommy Franks, and the CIA. Receiving many fewer mentions are civilian casualties, suicide bombings, oil, and electricity problems.[47]

Frank Bruni's 2002 book *Ambling into History* was another self-inflicted wound. Bruni was the *New York Times* reporter assigned to follow George W. Bush on the 2000 election campaign trail.[48] Bruni also covered Bush during the early months of his presidency. Alexandra Starr, writing in *Business Week* (April 12, 2002), accurately described the Bruni book as "The Seduction of a Campaign reporter." Bush is reported in the book as being long on charm, running, sleep, and leaving it to the team. Not only Bush but also Bruni seem to be ambling along—each has little to say about politics, but engages in plenty of amusing anecdotes. The *New York Times* reporter presents himself (and thus his newspaper) as self-satisfied and lazy. As a reporter Bruni compares badly with, for example, Bill Minutaglio in his 1999 book *First Son*.[49]

---

[45] Edwin Diamond, *Behind the Times: Inside the New York Times*, New York: Villard Books, 1994.

[46] John F. Stacks, *Scotty: James B. Reston and the Rise and Fall of American Journalism*, Boston: Little, Brown, 2003: 314–34.

[47] Todd S. Purdum and the staff of the New York Times, *"A Time of Our Choosing": America's War in Iraq*, New York: Times Books, Henry Holt, 2003; See also Michael Massing, "Unfit to Print?" *New York Review of Books*, June 24, 2004: 6–10.

[48] Frank Bruni, *Ambling into History: The Unlikely Odyssey of George W. Bush*, New York: HarperCollins, 2002: 193–96.

[49] Bill Minutaglio, *First Son: George W. Bush*, New York: Three Rivers Press, 1999: 99–100.

The reporter from the *Dallas Morning News* outplayed the reporter from the *New York Times*.

Kathleen Hall Jamieson and Paul Waldman, in their 2003 book *The Press Effect*, show how the *New York Times* accepted White House definitions of a "War on Terror" against bad people in Afghanistan and Iraq.[50] Perhaps the *Times* was led into this by its own super-patriotic and massive post–September 11 coverage. Starting September 15, the paper published "Portraits of Grief" (short obituaries of those who died on September 11); these obituaries continued everyday for 15 weeks.[51] This massive *New York Times* coverage may have contributed to the excessive national response—not least because the national TV networks (also based in New York and with allied New York City local stations) followed the same pattern. This super-patriotic response was presumably just what the planners of the attacks had hoped for.

But the most myth-shattering of these numerous books was *The Trust: The Private and Powerful Family Behind the New York Times* by Susan A. Tifft and Alex S. Jones.[52] This husband-and-wife team were given "official" access; their 870-page book is yet another *Times* self-inflicted wound. Unlike the numerous previous *Times* books, this one is 90 percent about the family and 10 percent about journalists and managers. This is the United States' royal family, frequently behaving in soap opera mode. There are hundreds of pages of family gossip and bitter feuds, many failed marriages, and parents and children who cannot communicate with each other. There are plenty of strong female parts and even more numerous rogue males and male chauvinists. The soap opera's key "central place" is to the east of Central Park (near the Metropolitan Museum of Art), where most of the Sulzberger family members have lived. With a mix of luck and skill the family succeeded in picking passable family publishers and talented executive editors.

The Trust leaves its readers in no doubt at all that "The Family" dominated the general direction of the *New York Times* from 1896 onward. Although the word "monopoly" is not used, the book makes clear that, because the paper was so prestigious, monopolistic, and (usually) highly profitable, *The Family* could—especially in 1970–2000—afford to make plenty of business mistakes.

The Trust's portrait of a dominant family and dominant publisher is reinforced by Laurel Leff's 2005 book, *Buried by the Times*. This makes clear in massive and painful detail how the *Times* covered what became known as the Holocaust. Arthur Hays Sulzberger, the then youngish publisher (48 years old in 1939), dictated the frame through which the *New York Times* covered

[50] Kathleen Hall Jamieson and Paul Waldman, *The Press Effect: Politicians, Journalists and the Stories That Shape the Political World*, New York: Oxford University Press, 2003.

[51] Janice Hume, " 'Portraits of Grief', Reflections of Values: The New York Times Remembers Victims of September 11," *Journalism and Mass Communication Quarterly*, Vol. 80/1, Spring 2003: 166–82.

[52] Susan E. Tifft and Alex S. Jones, *The Trust: The Private and Powerful Family Behind the New York Times*, Boston: Little, Brown, 1999.

the story; the story was to be seen as one of persecution of several subgroups —and the Jews were only one of these groups. It was not seen as one of the really big stories of World War II and was thus to be covered in frequent, but brief, news stories on inside pages. The *New York Times* must be seen as an American paper, not a Jewish or Zionist paper.[53]

The reputation of the *New York Times* has been degraded not only by the damning revelations of a succession of high profile books. There is also an extensive pamphleteering literature—of magazine articles, short books, and Internet material. Many of these pamphleteering critiques are by recent ex-employees of the *New York Times* who have rushed rapidly and bitterly into print. In 2003 both Jayson Blair (the plagiarist reporter) and Howell Raines (the sacked executive editor) exploded in bitter pamphleteering statements. Some ex-employees feel able to deliver love-plus-hate memoirs. One such is John L. Hess, whose *My Times: A Memoir of Dissent* covers his *Times* career as finance reporter, Paris foreign correspondent, rewrite man, investigative reporter, and food correspondent. This amusing and delightfully written book is a reminder of the strength of journalist talent lurking inside the *Times* bureaucracy.[54]

The fact of monopoly may have contributed to the ferocity of feuds and love-hate within the *Times*. Journalism operates at speed, which makes hierarchy and quick decisions essential. In such a large news bureaucracy, the hierarchy is steeper, more ruthless, and more resented than in a smaller newspaper. The *Times'* monopoly situation meant that there was no direct New York competition to provide alternate news frameworks or to provide alternate career opportunities. The resulting bitterness and aggression can be expected to continue and probably to increase in the uncertain era ahead.

The international reputation of the *New York Times* will probably never return to the heights of 1961–1971. But paradoxically the Associated Press— an even larger monopoly news bureaucracy—may have been gaining a somewhat enhanced reputation, at least in the world outside the United States. Within the general news agency field AP exercises monopolistic dominance across the United States; AP delivers national, regional, and state news to smaller American newspapers. It's a monopoly that can boast that it gives U.S. newspapers most of their news from the world, and the nation, and also from their own state.

But outside the United States, the Associated Press is—and is seen as—a *competitor* agency. AP competes aggressively, especially with Reuters, in fast TV video news, as well as photographs and text news. It competes also with AFP, EFE, and others. Like these latter international news agencies—but unlike the *New York Times*—the Associated Press is widely used on an

---

[53] Laurel Leff, *Buried by the Times: The Holocaust and America's Most Important Newspaper*, Cambridge, UK: Cambridge University Press, 2005.
[54] John L. Hess, *My Times: A Memoir of Dissent*, New York: Seven Stories Press, 2003.

everyday basis around the world. AP also employs many non-U.S. citizens. Many news customers around the world may prefer Reuters and AFP— partly because they are British and French, and not American. But many news customers probably regard AP as "less American" or "less American ideological" than the *New York Times'* syndication service.

Despite recent turbulence, both the *Times* and Associated Press have major continuing strengths. They are among the fairly few old and conventional news media that may ultimately benefit from the electronic news revolution.[55] Each has what any news service needs—big amounts of good quality news output.

After 2001: American Journalism's Declining Reputation

The *Washington Post* and the *New York Times* both apologized for the inadequacy of their coverage of the Iraq invasion. Along with other elite elements of the U.S. media, these two newspapers published news stories that should have been treated with skepticism. Ten top U.S. news media (including the *Times* and the *Post*) unanimously accepted the lead of the Bush administration during the four weeks after September 11, 2001; not a single editorial argued against military intervention in Afghanistan.[56] The patriotic stance was accepted by all 10 media. For some months after September 11 the U.S. media looked back in anger[57] and accepted the Bush administration's binary framework of good/evil and security/peril.[58]

Reuters was seen by some as un-American and hostile because, unlike the U.S. media, it did not accept the Bush administration's loose use of the term "terrorist."[59] The U.S. media allowed the Bush administration to get away with using the term "war" when this was convenient (for example, when bombing villages) and also to use the term "terror" (for example, when claiming that the Geneva Convention rules of war did not apply).

The U.S. media accepted too easily much dubious pro-war "information" about weapons of mass destruction. A dubious news source such as Ahmad Chalabi (convicted as a fraudster in U.S.-friendly Jordan) managed—with the help of generous U.S. government funding—to place stories in the *New*

[55] Anthony Bianco, "The Future of the New York Times," *Business Week*, January 24, 2005: 52–55.
[56] Michael Ryan, "Framing the War Against Terrorism," *Gazette*, Vol. 66/5, October 2004: 363–82.
[57] Barbie Zelitzer and Stuart Allan (eds.), *Journalism After September 11*, London: Routledge, 2002.
[58] Kevin Coe, David Domke, and others, "No Shades of Gray: The Binary Discourse of George W. Bush and the Echoing Press," *Journal of Communication*, Vol. 54/2, June 2004: 234–52.
[59] Kathleen Hall Jamieson and Paul Waldman, *The Press Effect*, New York: Oxford University Press, 2003: 140.

York Times and in other major media.[60] The U.S. media also accepted the US military approach of "embedding" journalists with specific military units; this term itself should have aroused skepticism, not least because *The Concise Oxford Dictionary's* first meaning for "embedded" is "fix firmly in a surrounding mass (*embedded in concrete*)."

American reporters in Iraq seem to have been more careful of their own safety than were journalists of other nations. British journalist Robert Fisk coined the term "hotel journalism" to describe the performance of *New York Times*, NBC, and other U.S. journalists; some U.S. journalists, he claimed, not only seldom left their hotel, but were forbidden by their security guards even to visit the hotel restaurant or swimming pool.[61] Some of this caution was doubtless required by news executives back home (and also by insurance contracts); the effectiveness of such U.S. caution is illustrated by the fact that, from March 2003 to January 2005, of 62 journalists killed in Iraq only 1 was an American; 8 were Europeans and 45 were Iraqis.[62] Both American and European correspondents used Iraqi journalists (as reporters, photographers, and camerapersons) to cover the more dangerous stories. Consequently it was the Iraqis—and certainly not the Americans—who covered the worst of the violence (which in conventional news terms was the core of the story). This reluctance of U.S. journalists to get out on the streets must have contributed to the long time it took for the U.S. media to acknowledge that torture lite occurred from the occupation's very earliest days. Since torture lite was used against large numbers of people, tens of thousands of relatives of the prisoners and other Iraqis must have known about the torture.[63] Within four months of the invasion, Amnesty International reported the use of torture. Anya Schiffrin (of Columbia University) suggested several reasons why the U.S. media were far behind the media of other countries in reporting the prevalence of torture at the Abu Ghraib prison, near Baghdad.[64] Subsequent revelations (by Human Rights Watch) show that elite soldiers in the U.S. 82nd Airborne Division were involved in torture at least from September 2003 onward.[65]

The U.S. media were also remarkably accepting of the Department of Defense's playing of the death card. "We don't do body counts" was surely unacceptable from a U.S. military supposedly bringing democracy and

---

[60] Douglas McCollam, "The List: How Chalabi Played the Press," *Columbia Journalism Review*, July/August 2004: 31–37; James Moore, "How Chalabi and the White House Held the Front Page. The New York Times Has Burned Its Reputation on a Pyre of Lies About Iraq," *The Guardian*, May 29, 2004.

[61] Robert Fisk, "Hotel Journalism Gives American Troops a Free Hand as the Press Shelters Indoors," *The Independent* , January 17, 2005.

[62] Doreen Carvajal, "Media Death Toll on Rise in War Zones," *International Herald Tribune*, January 27, 2005.

[63] "Torture: A User's Manual," *Index-on-Censorship*, Vol. 34/1, 2005: 22–81.

[64] Anya Schiffrin, "Heads in the Sand," *Financial Times* magazine, September 11, 2004.

[65] "Torture in Iraq," a report by Human Rights Watch, *New York Review of Books*, November 3, 2005: 67–72.

minimizing collateral damage; it was certain to be perceived by Iraqis and other Arabs as grotesque and racist. Meanwhile, of course, U.S. casualties and coffins were not to be photographed. All of this was traditional. George H. Roeder has documented the U.S. military's careful censorship in World War II. He describes how, in "playing the death card," the U.S. military from 1941 to 1945 largely prevented the U.S. media from using the thousands of available photographs of dead American servicemen.[66]

Some of this excessively cautious and accepting response to official U.S. guidance can probably be traced back to the standard American media preference for seeing all world events through a framework of U.S. policy relevance. This U.S. policy framework has led the U.S. media in Washington to rely on government sources; a study of late Cold War (1988) national security reporters found that 81.4 percent of story sources were governmental.[67] The dependence is sometimes said to be upon an iron triangle of Defense, State, and CIA.

Foreign reporting (both from Washington and from other countries) traditionally plays down its dependence on CIA sources. Until at least 1970 this was done for patriotic, Cold War, reasons. The CIA was subjected to massive criticism and massive revelation in the 1970s; and much was revealed about the CIA both in Congress (by the Church Committee in the U.S. Senate) and in books like Philip Agee's *Inside the Company: CIA Diary*; Agee published the names and activities of some 400 people and organizations friendly to, employed by, or working secretly as agents (full-time or part-time) for the CIA in Latin America.[68] For a few years the CIA was in retreat, but under President Reagan The Intelligence Identities Protection Act (of 1982) made revealing a CIA identity a criminal offense. So for all of the years since 1982, and most of the years since the late 1940s, journalists have not referred to their dependence on CIA sources. But an American foreign correspondent needs to be friendly with people in the local U.S. embassy (a substantial fraction of whom are CIA, under rather thin cover). A correspondent who critiques the local CIA "station" and its local performance will obviously be blacklisted by the entire embassy staff. This would then make it difficult or impossible to report according to the required framework of U.S. official policy and interest.

The CIA never goes away, and the CIA has always cultivated favorable publicity as well as rigid secrecy.[69] In the "War on Terror" era, from September

---

[66] George H. Roeder, Jr., *The Censored War: American Visual Experience During World War Two*, New Haven, CT: Yale University Press, 1993.

[67] 58.2 percent were executive branch, 15.1 percent congressional, 3.6 percent former executive, and 4.5 percent government contractors or Justice Department. Daniel C. Hallin, Robert Karl Manoff, and Judy K. Weddle, "Sourcing Patterns of National Security Reporters," *Journalism Quarterly*, Vol. 70/4, Winter 1993: 753–66.

[68] Philip Agee, *Inside the Company: CIA Diary*, London: Penguin, 1975: 599–624.

[69] Rhodri Jeffreys-Jones, *Cloak and Dollar: A History of American Secret Intelligence*, 2d ed., New Haven, CT: Yale University Press, 2003; John Prados, *Lost Crusader: The Secret Wars of CIA Director, William Colby*, New York: Oxford University Press, 2003.

11, 2001, onward, the CIA at the Washington level was a focus of much publicity and criticism. At least some of this criticism of the CIA should probably have been directed at Special Forces operations and at intelligence agencies other than the CIA. Nevertheless, U.S. correspondents (in Baghdad and elsewhere) obviously continued the traditional practice of talking quietly with CIA personnel.

Three aspects of this correspondent dependence on CIA sources contributed to the American correspondents' inadequate reporting. First, as numerous subsequent investigations revealed, the CIA was not well informed about Iraq; CIA misperceptions thus showed up in American reporting. Second, the CIA had a long history of undermining and bribing the local media. Many books on the CIA indicate the casual manner in which CIA personnel mixed with selected local journalists, supplying them with cash payments, black propaganda, and "news stories."[70] This could mean that when foreign correspondents relied on local media, they were relying on stories planted by the CIA. A third CIA-related problem was that the CIA always aimed for "plausible deniability." But CIA denials did not convince the Soviet government when it shot down American U-2 spy planes. Similarly, when an American bomber crashed in northern Indonesia on May 18, 1958, American denials were not credible; the Indonesian authorities knew that the pilot was American because he was carrying with him (against orders) his American passport.[71] Quite often "plausible deniability" will have been plausible only to the domestic U.S. audience and media. When the prevailing framework—especially in 2003 and early 2004—was patriotic support for our fighting men and women, correspondents may sometimes have suspended their own disbelief to report statements that would still seem plausible to the U.S. audience.

When considering the U.S. news media's loss of reputation in the context of the Afghanistan and Iraq wars, one can conclude that the U.S. media were unlucky to be largely alone in what was initially seen as a patriotic war. In any popular war the media normally tend toward patriotic applause, while largely dispensing with skepticism and negative news values. Journalists from most other countries lacked this patriotic involvement and remained skeptical. Consequently, skepticism about the U.S. military effort soon spread to include skepticism about the seemingly feeble U.S. media performance. Even in Britain (which was the only other significant player in the so-called Coalition Forces) both the print and electronic media were much more skeptical and much less patriotic than the U.S. media.

All of this is very different from the situation in the 1940s and 1950s when American journalism was highly regarded, and quite widely copied, in the

---

[70] For example, Howard Frazier (ed.), *Uncloaking the CIA*, New York: Free Press/Macmillan, 1978.

[71] Kenneth Conboy and James Morrison, *Feet to the Fire: CIA Covert Operations in Indonesia, 1957–1958*, Annapolis, MD: Naval Institute Press, 1999.

rest of the world. In all of the defeated Axis countries—Italy, Germany, Japan—the impact of Anglo-American journalism models was seen by some as being very strong, while others saw it as only temporary. Latin America has often been quoted as the world area where U.S.-style "professional" journalism education was especially influential in the 1950s and 1960s.

But university-level journalism education had begun in Argentina in 1934, in Mexico in 1936, in Cuba in 1942, and in Brazil in 1943; by 1947 there were also journalism schools in Peru, Venezuela, and Chile. While post-1950 influences from North America were important, Latin American journalism schools reflected a "professionalism" that involved influences from the government, from the Roman Catholic Church, and also from the trade unions. The "colegio" system—a closed profession based on a standard university qualification—was contrary to American conceptions of journalism as an open occupation. Brazilian newspaper publishers seem to have deployed U.S. concepts such as "fourth branch" and "objectivity" as part of attempts to discipline the literary and leftist inclinations of their journalists.[72]

The U.S. journalism school model was, perhaps, most influential in encouraging other nations to set up journalism schools in which the particular nation's own national style of journalism could be taught and learned. Theodore Glasser has pointed out[73] that the values assumed in American journalism education are indeed American and do not travel comfortably into other cultures. What at home inside the United States looks like professional neutrality can in the outside world look like rabid partisanship.

The typical American university journalism school—in Texas, Iowa, Missouri, or California—must take account of the requirements of those local media that hire fresh student talent. The preferences of small local American media differ from those of national media in the United States and in other countries.

The star system has, of course, made big advances at all levels of the U.S. news media.[74] But Dan Rather, Tom Brokaw, and Peter Jennings—long-serving

---

[72] Afonso de Albuquerque, "Another 'Fourth Branch': Press and Political Culture in Brazil," *Journalism*, Vol. 6/4, November 2005: 486–504; Juan S. Valmaggia, "Latin America," in UNESCO, *The Training of Journalists: A Worldwide Survey of Training of Personnel for the Mass Media*, Paris: Unesco, 1958: 122–38; Jerry W. Knudson, "Licensing Journalists in Latin America: An Appraisal," *Journalism and Mass Communication Quarterly*, Vol. 73/4, Winter 1996: 878–89; Mary A. Gardner, "Trend Toward Colegiación of Journalists in Latin America and Its Impact on Freedom of the Press," in Harold E. Hines and Morris Charles M. Tatum (eds.), *Studies in Latin American Culture*, Vol. 6, 1987: 235–43.

[73] Theodore L. Glasser, "Professionalism and the Derision of Diversity: The Case of the Education of Journalists," *Journal of Communications*, Vol. 42/2, Spring 1992: 131–40; Theodore L. Glasser and Lise Marken, "Can We Make Journalists Better?", in Hugo de Burgh (ed.), *Making Journalists*, London: Routledge, 2005: 264–76; Jeremy Tunstall (ed.), *Media Occupations and Professions: A Reader*, Oxford, UK: Oxford University Press, 2001.

[74] Howard Kurtz, "When the Press Outclasses the Public," *Columbia Journalism Review*, May/June 1994: 31–34.

news anchors of the three traditional TV networks—were not well known in the wider world. Reports that Peter Jennings was paid $10 million annually by ABC and left an estate worth $50 million (when he died in 2005) attracted little international interest.

Nevertheless, some stars of Anglo-American journalism do have an international following. Three quite different examples are Bob Woodward of Watergate fame, who specialized in Washington politics; another is Seymour Hersh, who revealed the 1968 My Lai village massacre in Vietnam and subsequently completed a number of other explosive investigations of political and military scandals; a third is British journalist Robert Fisk, who lived in Beirut for three decades and reported on the Middle East's numerous massacres and wars. These three journalists are very different from each other and have different admirers (and enemies). But they all share extraordinary dedication to the subject in hand; all play the long game and are willing to suffer abuse and skepticism; and all also write books that achieve big readerships both at home and abroad. Woodward, Hersh, and Fisk all took risks (and were vindicated) in their coverage of the Bush-Afghanistan-Iraq adventure. Woodward "embedded" himself in the Bush administration and with two fat books—*Bush at War* and *Plan of Attack*—produced remarkable detail for both supporters and opponents of the Bush policies. Seymour Hersh wrote a series of explosive pieces about prisoner abuse, Abu Ghraib, and "extraordinary rendition." Robert Fisk correctly predicted the Iraq insurgency on April 17, 2003—shortly before it began;[75] Fisk was also unique, as an interviewer of Osama bin Laden and close-up chronicler of mayhem who also put the Afghanistan-Iraq events into 1,366 pages of historical context.[76]

While the moral authority of American politics and journalism has declined, the moral authority of certain journalists has increased. A few journalists have become multimedia stars (or should it be brands?). Woodward, Hersh, and Fisk all worked on big newspapers but subsequently achieved wider fame and authority via books, magazines, television, public speaking, and the Internet. The Internet has the potential to take this phenomenon still further.

---

[75] *The Independent*, April 17, 2003.
[76] Robert Fisk, *The Great War for Civilisation: The Conquest of the Middle East*, London: Fourth Estate, 2005.

PART 2

BIG-POPULATION COUNTRIES

INDIA AND CHINA

10

The Rise of Big-Population Nations and Their Media

Most of the world's people live in countries that have populations of over 100 million and are broadly self-sufficient in media exports and imports. This chapter first indicates some common characteristics of the (non-U.S.) big-10-population countries. Then some shared media features of the two population giants—India and China—are suggested (as an introduction to the subsequent individual chapters on these two countries). Next this chapter focuses on Japan, a big-population country that was heavily media dependent on the United States, but only for a relatively brief period after 1945. Finally, post-independence Indonesia is considered. Indonesian media and politics have been through a succession of distinct phases, several of which have also been experienced in other large-population countries.

In 2005 some 61 percent of the world's people lived in the United States and 10 other countries with populations of more than 100 million. The big-two-population nations (China and India) together in 2005 had 37 percent of the world's population. Both China and India have done only very modest media importing since 1950; their media imports (especially from the United States) peaked in the 1920s and 1930s. The same is true of Pakistan and Bangladesh (which in the 1920s and 1930s were part of colonial India).

Of the other big-10-population countries (excluding the United States), Japan's media imports from the United States peaked during 1945–1955, Brazil's and Mexico's media imports peaked during 1930–1970, and Nigeria's imports had peaked by 1980. Russia had two major peaks—one in the 1920s and another in the 1990s.

By 1983 India was importing only 7 percent of its television programming, while China and the Soviet Union were importing 8 percent. Data for 1983 are available for four other big-population countries—Pakistan, Brazil, Mexico, and Nigeria—and these had higher proportions of imports. But taking these seven countries together (and weighting for China and India's bigger populations) the overall level of imports was 10.7 percent of all television broadcasting in 1983.

Only a quarter (26 percent) of year 2005's total world population lived in countries with fewer than 50 million people. It is these countries and especially the very lowest-population countries that do the most importing. Obviously a nation-state with only a few million people is penalized in terms of media scale economies and cannot generate much revenue for expensive television or film production. The Tapio Varis study of 1983 television importing reported that its 10 smallest-population cases (Brunei, Iceland, Singapore, New Zealand, Ireland, Tunisia, Zimbabwe, Ecuador, Uganda, and Algeria) had a then average population of 6.8 million and imported a weighted average of 64.4 percent of their television programming.[1]

Table 10.1 gives a quick sketch of media trading in the world's 11 most populous nations in the early twenty-first century. The "Media Trading" column indicates whether the particular nation is a net media importer or net exporter. According to this (author's) quick sketch, the United States was still the only "very big exporter." Net media importers (−) included Indonesia, Pakistan, Bangladesh, and Nigeria. In approximate balance (=) were China, India, and Russia. But net exporters (+) included Brazil and Mexico, with Japan especially being a big exporter.

Leaving aside the United States, the other big-10-population countries are extremely diverse but still have some common characteristics and tendencies:

- Each of the big 10 occupies a very distinctive, or eccentric, territory. Brazil is big, some 60 times bigger than flood-prone Bangladesh. Indonesia includes three large islands, part of two other large islands and an additional 13,672 smaller islands.

- All of these big-10 countries (except Nigeria) have one leading language and/or one main religion. Their governments, to a greater or lesser extent, attempt to extend this basis of national culture and national identity; the governments look toward the media to support these goals.

- Most of these big-10 countries have had military or other autocratic governments in the years since 1950. Japan and India are the two main exceptions.

- In most, or all, of these countries the media are more democratic (or less undemocratic) than in the 1960s and 1970s.

- Each of these big-population countries now has an educated middle class of at least several million people who oppose and resist extremes of censorship.

- In all big-10 countries the national media were, after 2000, more commercial and less government dominated than in the years after 1950.

---

[1] Tapio Varis, *International Flow of Television Programmes*, Paris: UNESCO, 1985.

Table 10.1   Big-Population Nations: Mass Media Trade Balance, 2000–2005

COUNTRY	2005 POPULATION (IN MILLIONS)	MEDIA TRADING	IMPORTS MAINLY FROM	EXPORTS TO
China	1,306.3	= Balance, largely self-sufficient	Taiwan, United States, South Korea, Japan	Asia and Chinese diaspora
India	1,080.3	= Balance, largely self-sufficient	United Kingdom, United States	Pakistan, Bangladesh, Africa, Indian diaspora
United States	295.7	+ Very big exporter, modest importer	Mexico, Latin America	Whole world, especially small population (including Europe)
Indonesia	242	– Substantial importer	United States, Japan, Hong Kong, India	Southeast Asia
Brazil	186.1	+ Big exporter, modest importer	United States	Most of the world, especially fringe Europe and Latin America
Russia	143.3	= Biggish importer and exporter	United States, Europe, Latin America	Central Asia, Russian diaspora
Pakistan	162.4	– Biggish importer, modest exporter	India, United States	Mid-East and Pakistan diaspora
Bangladesh	144.3	– Net importer	India, United States	Bangladesh diaspora
Japan	127.4	+ Big exporter, modest importer	United States	Most of world, especially Asia
Nigeria	128.8	– Net importer	United States, Europe, Latin America	Africa
Mexico	106.2	+ Big exporter, substantial importer	United States	Most of world, especially United States, Latin America, fringe Europe

Source: CIA, *The World Factbook*, for July 2005 population estimates. (http://www.cia.gov/cia/publications/factbook/rankorder/2119rank.html accessed February 7 2006)

- All big-10 countries by the early 2000s had substantial domestic media industries that typically involved more radio and TV households, more daily newspaper sales, and more movie production than in the smaller western European countries.

- Most big-10 countries have had big enough domestic markets to generate the necessary scale economies for a sizeable movie production industry. India led the world with some 17,000 movies produced between 1980 and 2000. Japan and Hong Kong each made over 6,000 movies in these 21 years; China and Bangladesh each made over 2,000; and Indonesia, Mexico, and Brazil each made at least 1,000 movies.[2]

Media Similarities in India and China

Both India and China are famously complex and are, in many ways, different from each other. During India's early years of independence, the ruling Congress Party and the prime minister, Jawaharlal Nehru, moved the media along slowly and cautiously, in low gear. In China, Mao Zedong and the Communist Party drove the media along in high gear, rapidly, often recklessly; occasionally Mao slammed on the media brakes and changed into reverse gear, again at high speed. But here we can briefly note some similarities and, in particular, the broad media self-sufficiency of the two countries.

Both India and China have quite strong national identities. In both India and China, most people are aware of belonging to a subcontinental entity that has an impressive and lengthy history. In both nations there is the sense that Europe arrived on the world scene only quite recently. China was, in fact, the world's largest economy up to the early 1800s.

Both Delhi and Beijing are anxious about potential breakaway, or separatist, regions. China has several such areas around its inland borders, and India has separatist anxieties across its long northern border (mainly in the northwest and far northeast). But in both cases the total numbers of people are small, compared with the population of regions that seem happy to remain part of India or of China.

Although the colonial histories were very different in detail, both India and China experienced European colonization. In both cases the modern mass media were launched by Europeans; but both Indian and Chinese people were already media active before 1900 (primarily in producing newspapers). In the first half of the twentieth century both China and India followed a similar media pattern in terms of imperial involvement. Very simply: From 1900 to about 1930 outside colonial domination was in place.

The peak of foreign media domination occurred in both India and China around 1930. Why? By 1930 the local national Indian and Chinese media were reaching a substantial size, buoyed up by increasing levels of education and literacy; various "indirect rule" imperial procedures also involved a growing bureaucracy of Indian and Chinese administrators and clerical

---

[2] *Screen Digest*, December 2001: 377–80.

workers. After 1930 the European-language newspapers in India and China were hit by economic depression, by the turbulence of invasion and civil war (in China), and then by world war.

The early 1930s saw the arrival of the talking film, and this ending of the silent film was the high water mark for Hollywood films in both India and China. From 1930 onward Indian films proliferated in numerous genre and language combinations. China also in the 1930s developed multiple film industries.

India became independent in 1947, and two years later the People's Republic of China came into existence. For the next three decades both countries looked inward to domestic economic development; and both China and India deliberately cut themselves off from foreign mass media. Two leading examples of this were film and television. Hollywood films were completely excluded from China, while India allowed in a very small token number of foreign films.

Television is an equally striking case. A number of smaller countries around the world decided not to have television. But China and India were the only two large countries that until the late 1970s kept television back to an "experimental" level, with almost no TV importing.

In both China and India the 1950s, 1960s, and 1970s were three turbulent decades in which the existing media were highly active. The communist regime in China combined modern mass media with traditional media, in a series of spectacular political propaganda campaigns. Indian governments tried hard to use the same modern-plus-traditional media for purposes of general education and nation building. Both China and India relied on print, film, radio, and traditional media, such as posters. But this 30-year media effort was in both cases unremittingly domestic and national.

Both China and India from the 1950s to the 1970s had relatively small media systems, which focused heavily on the current charismatic office-holders. The detail of the Indian and Chinese cases is very different indeed. But the combination of a still small media industry plus one dominant current political personality made it difficult for political rivals to acquire national "name recognition" and to command more than merely local or factional support.

In the late 1970s everything changed. In the Indian general election of 1977 Indira Gandhi and the Congress Party lost power. Also in 1976 Mao Zedong died, and his death finally terminated the bizarre events of the Cultural Revolution. After 1977 both India and China took the capitalist road toward commercialization, consumerism, and dramatic economic growth. The Chinese economy grew by about 10 percent a year in the 1980s and 9 percent a year in the 1990s. India's 1990s economic growth was only a little behind this. In both countries media growth, on most indicators, ran well ahead of general economic growth. In advertising, in television, in cable, and also in the newspaper press, both Chinese growth and Indian growth surpassed most previous media growth spurts around the world. By year

2000, China and India (the former TV laggards) had 354 million households containing at least one television set.[3]

In both China and India today the media incorporate much of the same turbulence as the whole national society is experiencing. Social dislocation takes many forms. In both India and China many millions of people move back and forth between country and city in search of work; there are big and increasing differences in prosperity between regions and between people. Both countries experience thousands of local riots, strikes, and protests each year; most of these concern local taxation, the closure of factories, local planning decisions, and other economic/financial happenings. Many protests are linked to local government corruption.

Media corruption seems especially common within the booming advertising industry of both China and India. Bribes, kickbacks, and bought editorial coverage are endemic. One consequence is that in both China and India there seem to be few reliable data about advertising or media finances.

Japan: From Media Dependence to Independence

Of all the countries with over 100 million population, Japan was once (1945–1955) the most dependent on U.S. media. After its 1945 defeat, Japan both imported much American media material and had its own media (not least Japanese television) launched along an American-style commercial path. Nevertheless, by the 1960s Japan was increasingly making nearly all of its media at home. Movies are the one exception; most movie theater visits today are still to see Hollywood, not Japanese, films—but the average Japanese person makes only one such visit per year. The Japanese population devote less of their TV viewing to TV imports than does the United States. Japan has since 1980 imported only 3 or 4 percent of its networked TV from the United States, and most of this programming has been scheduled out of prime audience times.[4]

Although many aspects of Japanese media have been modeled on (mainly) the United States, the Japanese version typically differs from the American. Many Western-made media practices have been remade in Japan;[5] the result is a long list of Japanese practices that may seem odd or quirky to the Western eye, but are also nationally distinctive, un-American, and un-Western.[6]

---

[3] *Screen Digest*, October 2000; "China and India: The Challenge and the Opportunity," *Business Week*, August 22/29, 2005: 29–104.

[4] Shigeru Hagiwara, "The Rise and Fall of Foreign Programs in Japanese Television," *Keio Communication Review* (Tokyo), 17, 1995: 3–26; P. Gould, J. Johnson, and G. Chapman, *The Structure of Television*, London: Pion, 1984.

[5] Joseph J. Tobin (ed.), *Re-Made in Japan*, New Haven, CT: Yale University Press, 1992.

[6] Anne Cooper-Chen with Miiko Kodama, *Mass Communication in Japan*, Ames: Iowa State University Press, 1997.

Since 1914, Japan has had a big newspaper press; in the late 1930s it had some 1,400 dailies. Japan by the 1990s had the world's biggest daily newspaper sale—bigger than the daily sale in the United States (which had more than double Japan's population). Japan also now has the world's most formidable collection of high sale dailies. The big dailies claim political neutrality, but are accused of being both excessively left/liberal and excessively submissive to Japan's long sequence of conservative governments.[7]

The *manga* is another distinctively Japanese point product. These *manga* "comics" are aimed at a children's and youth market, but some are extremely violent and sexually explicit by Western standards. At their peak (in the 1980s) over two billion *manga* were sold annually (equivalent to 16 *manga* comics per Japanese man, woman, and child).[8]

Japan has for decades also had the most commercial, and best funded, national television outside the United States. But Japan's NHK is also a world leader in public television and is funded by substantial (but, amazingly, voluntary) public subscriptions. With very few exceptions, Japanese TV audiences do not view imported programming. However, the Japanese have imported the soap opera and other American formats; Japanese families, indeed, developed a big appetite for (Japanese-produced) soaps at breakfast time.

Japan's modern media history has involved three major phases, quite unlike those of the United States, although perhaps more comparable to Germany. Up to about 1930 Japanese media grew rapidly both in scale and in terms of creative freedom. But 1931–1945 marked a sharply authoritarian phase in which the Japanese media did the bidding of the military. Then in 1945 everything again altered, in line with the requirements of the U.S. occupation; many directors who had made anti-American war movies, for instance, quickly switched to make pro-American peace movies.[9]

The "Americanized" Japanese media developed in the 1950s into a much more centralized system than the one that then prevailed in the United States. A major element of cross-ownership developed between the leading national newspapers and the leading commercial television networks. The Japanese system was centralized geographically as well as across media. Further elements of the system—such as the "press clubs" whose journalist members monopolized access to their particular government department—also seem

---

[7] Peter J. S. Dunnett, *The World Newspaper Industry*, London: Croom Helm, 1988: 172–87; Gregory J. Kasza, *The State and the Mass Media in Japan, 1918–45*, Berkeley: University of California Press, 1988; Jung Bock Lee, *The Political Character of the Japanese Press*, Seoul: National University Press, 1985; Susan Jo Pharr and Ellis S. Krauss (eds.), *Media and Politics in Japan*, Honolulu: University of Hawaii Press, 1996.

[8] Mariko Sanchanta, "Manga Publishers Look Overseas for Growth," *Financial Times*, September 30 2002.

[9] Donald Richie, *Japanese Cinema: Film Style and National Character*, London: Secker and Warburg, 1972; Peter B. High, *The Imperial Screen: Japanese Film Culture in the Fifteen Years' War, 1931–1945*, Madison: University of Wisconsin Press, 2003 (first publ. in Japanese: 1995).

highly centralized and elitist to many outsiders.[10] Even the advertising arrangements were highly centralized—with one dominant advertising agency,
Dentsu, whose media activities stretched beyond advertising.

Japan has continued—even in the multichannel era of cable and satellites
—to be a very modest importer in terms of market share of national audience
time. But Japan has gradually become a substantial media exporter. Some of
Sony's foreign media activities are very visible—including Sony's Hollywood
company (Columbia) and Sony music.[11] But other Japanese media exports are
largely invisible or clandestine. Japan is a big exporter of cartoons, animation,
and anime; NHK is an active coproducer with foreign broadcasters; and
Japan is a major seller of game show, and other television, formats.[12] These
clandestine, or low profile, exports deliberately reverse the U.S. practice.
Whereas American media exporters like to emphasize Hollywood and other
American origins, Japanese media exporters (still mindful of World War II)
prefer to play down the national origin of their products.

Nevertheless, Japan's media products are widely accepted around the
world. Despite long memories of Japanese aggression and war crimes,
Japanese media exports are gradually becoming more welcome in Taiwan,
South Korea, China, and elsewhere.[13]

From Colony via National Culture to Commercialization: Indonesia

Indonesia has a unique history, but we can list six stages in Indonesian
mass media history since the mid-twentieth century, some or most of which
have been shared with such other big-10 countries as India, China, Pakistan,
Bangladesh, and Nigeria. Between 1950 and 2005 Indonesia's population
trebled (from 79 million to 242 million).

Colonial Past

Indonesia was a colony, the Dutch East Indies. Indonesia achieved independence in December 1949, after four chaotic years that included the departure of

---

[10] William De Lange, *A History of Japanese Journalism: Japan's Press Club as the Last Obstacle to a
Mature Press*, Richmond, Surrey: Curzon Press, 1998, Young C. Kim, *Japanese Journalists and
Their Work*, Charlottesville: University Press of Virginia, 1981; Charles Pomeroy (ed.), *Foreign
Correspondents in Japan*, Rutland, VT: Charles E. Tuttle, 1998.

[11] Yasuhiro Inoue, "Hard and Soft Mega-Media Conglomeration: Has Sony's Strategy Created
synergies?" *Keio Communication Review* (Tokyo), 25, 2003: 39–54.

[12] Koichi Iwabuchi, "Feeling Global: Japan in the Global Television Format Business," in Albert
Moran and Michael Keane (eds.), *Television Across Asia: Television Industries, Programme
Formats and Globalization*, London: RoutledgeCurzon, 2004: 21–35.

[13] Koichi Iwabuchi, "Japanese Popular Culture and East Asian Modernities, *Media Development*,
3/2001: 25–30.

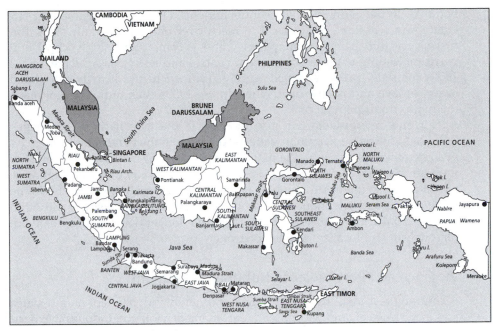

Figure 10.1 Indonesia and Malaysia.

the Japanese, as well as the Dutch, and a substantial independence war. Like other newly independent nations, Indonesia inherited two press traditions— newspapers established by the colonizers and newspapers that had campaigned for independence. As early as 1920 there were 21 Dutch-language (very small) daily papers.

The Netherlands authorities had cultivated a federal approach that involved local government and local semi-autonomy, combined with a strong capital city (Jakarta) central administration. This Dutch approach to both government and media carried over into independence.

National Independence, Media Growth, Regionalism

Other new nations (large and small) were led to independence by their own father of the new nation; in Indonesia's case this was Achmad Sukarno, president of Indonesia (initially self-styled) for 22 years, from 1945 to 1967.

As in other big newly independent nations, there was an early honeymoon phase during which the new president's prestige and charisma were dominant; this allowed an initially tolerant official approach to politicians and journalists and to political debate. Independent Indonesia also had its early mushroom growth of small new newspapers, whose editors (often owner-editors) were eager to enjoy the newfound freedom. By late 1949, many Dutch newspapers had closed, while Indonesian language dailies boomed. In the eight years after independence (1949–1957) newspaper circulation increased by 250 percent to reach over one million daily sales. But these very thin papers (four pages daily) became increasingly shrill and partisan, leading to more government control and less critical debate. In the 1950s the daily press remained largely confined to the heavily populated island of Java and its few main cities. In the 1950s even radio did not reach the main (rural) population.

Not only mass media, but also the newly selected "national language" (Bahasa Indonesian) was not widely used—even in the rural areas of Java. As in some other new nations, the national language was not spoken by most of the nation's people. Indonesia had (literally) hundreds of local languages, which acquired increased numbers of speakers via population growth. In the 1950s interisland telephone service was still largely nonexistent. Although Java and Jakarta were now Indonesian (no longer Dutch) administered, regionalism and localism remained strong.

Violence and Post-Violence National Settlement

A common feature of large population and newly independent nation-states was experience of, and widespread fear of, major violence. Indonesia experienced major violence before and during independence and on numerous occasions after independence. As elsewhere, this included violence against domestic ethnic minorities. As also happened in other nations, the Indonesian government of President Mohamed Suharto (1968–1998) established what was intended to be a new national settlement, the "New Order," which stressed national unity and attempted to outlaw (especially) ethnic violence.

The Dutch colonial authorities had used significant violence against both communists and nationalists; there were also fascist-style elements among the Dutch settlers. The Japanese period (1942–1945) had its violence, while in 1947 and 1948 Dutch "police actions" resulted in many deaths. After independence the Indonesian military put down a number of local uprisings. In 1965 an attempted Communist Party (PKI) coup was put down by then General Suharto and the army, with some assistance from the American CIA. Both before and after 1965 there were numerous major racist attacks on Chinese Indonesians (often resented, and scapegoated, for their financial and business success).

Once president, Suharto launched his attempt at a new national settlement (the New Order) and a set of new national goals called Pancasila.[14] This was overtly designed to encourage the Muslim majority to tolerate the Chinese and Christian minorities. The New Order supported these five components: belief in one god, humanitarianism, a united Indonesia, democracy guided by wisdom, and social justice for all. Behind these wholesome sentiments,

---

[14] Michael R. J. Vatikiotis, *Indonesian Politics Under Suharto*, London: Routledge, 1994 ed.

obviously lay some harsher political realities, one of which was control of the entire mass media.[15]

During Suharto's three decades as president, newspapers and magazines were controlled by licensing, by (telephone) "advice," and by closures of publications. Broadcasting was for many years a government monopoly; when technology (microwave and Indonesia's Palapa satellite, launched in 1976) allowed, national television was projected across the entire Indonesia archipelago.[16] Suharto adopted the familiar practice of requiring all television channels to carry the national news simultaneously; he himself, of course, was the leading performer on the TV news.

For the 50 years up to 1998, the two long-serving presidents (Sukarno and Suharto) wanted to develop a new Indonesian national culture; this involved the use of the Indonesian language in the school system. Local and regional critics saw this as Javanization because the new "national" culture was really based on the (politically) core island of Java. The new national culture slotted the national media into place alongside the new national (and semi-military) regime.

In promoting the two long-serving presidents, the mass media also conferred name recognition and historical legitimacy on just two political dynasties.[17] These family dynasties remained active even after Suharto's departure in 1998. Suharto's children were major players in Indonesian media and politics. President Megawati Sukarnoputri (2001–2004) was the daughter of father of the nation, Sukarno. However, the era of dynastic politics appeared to terminate with the 2004 popular election of a nondynastic president, Susilo Bambang Yudhoyono (aka, SBY).

Media Imports, Up and Down

Indonesia has been a bigger importer of American media output than have most of the other big-population countries. Compared with most former British and French colonies, Indonesia has not imported much from Europe. Indonesia long had a weakish film industry,[18] which has provided an unusually big opportunity for Hollywood; but Indonesia has also been a substantial importer of both movies and TV from Hong Kong, India, and Japan.

Indonesia has had a succession of importing ups and downs. In the 1920s and 1930s Indonesia was a big importer from Hollywood and was dependent

---

[15] Karl D. Jackson and Lucian W. Pye (eds.), *Political Power and Communications in Indonesia*, Berkeley: University of California Press, 1978.

[16] Willy Moenandir, "Indonesian telecommunications development: an overview", *Telematics and Informatics*, Vol 2/1, 1985: 79–89.

[17] Theodore Friend, *Indonesian Destinies*, Belknap Press of Harvard University Press, 2003.

[18] Marseth Sumarno and Nan Triveni Achnas, "Indonesia: In Two Worlds," in Aruna Vasudev, Latika Padganonkar, and Rashmi Doraiswamy (eds.), *Being and Becoming: The Cinemas of Asia*, Delhi: Macmillan, 2002: 152–70.

on Dutch material and models in the press. In the early years of independence (1949–1965) Indonesia did little media importing. Television began in 1962, and in the 1960s much TV programming was imported. But in the 1970s and 1980s, imports from Hollywood reduced; television was still very restricted and the Indonesia film industry around 1980 was still making about 120 films a year. However, in the early 1990s the launch of several new commercial TV channels led to greatly increased importing, which subsequently declined from about 1995, when domestic TV production (including drama) greatly expanded.[19] In the early 2000s, rapidly expanding advertising expenditure further fueled television production.

Western popular music was banned until 1965; subsequently much American music reached Indonesian audiences. But most recorded music sold in the 1990s was produced in Indonesia.[20] Most Indonesian popular music was based either on Western models or Asian models (such as Dangdut, which is heavily influenced by Indian film music and Arab popular music). Indonesia (with its big population) has received targeted attention from MTV; but MTV Indonesia—in order to maintain its Indonesian credentials—plays a lot of Indonesian music.[21]

Democratization and Commercialization

Indonesia, like other large population nations, saw a big growth in commercial media from the 1980s onward. There was some increase in democracy—on almost any definition; the increasingly large media industry was increasingly dominated by commercial factors, with control by politicians now considerably diminished.

In the early 1980s Indonesian TV was still quite small in scale. Very few rural homes had even a black-and-white TV set. There was no television advertising (banned in 1981); the only television came from the public service broadcaster. But the Suharto regime was worried that too many Indonesians in outlying (and potentially separatist areas) were picking up conventional TV signals from nearby Malaysia. In 1988–1995 President Suharto launched no less than five new national television networks; Suharto aimed to keep control by awarding these new networks to his children and to other relatives and close allies. There was a huge growth in television advertising and a huge switch from nation-building to profit-seeking programming. There was also a massive increase, around 1990, in programming imports from the United States and Asia.

---

[19] Marselli Sumaro and Don Groves, "Indonesia TV Production Sees Windfall," *Variety*, July 17–23, 1995.
[20] Krishna Sen and David T. Hill, *Media, Culture and Politics in Indonesia*, Melbourne: Oxford University Press, 2000: 164–93.
[21] R. Anderson Sutton, "Local, Global or National? Popular Music on Indonesian Television," in Lisa Parks and Shanti Kumar (eds.), *Planet TV*, New York: New York University Press, 2003: 321–40.

From the mid-1990s onward, however, the bulk of the most popular TV programming was Indonesian produced—with Indonesian soap operas, Indonesian-style kung fu, and Indonesian comedies in the lead.[22]

This new media commercialism was one factor in President Suharto's removal from power in 1998. Suharto's three decades in power ended partly because he lost military support. However, the media also, somewhat tentatively, "changed sides." Leading journalists, mogul owners, underground press operators, and Internet activists all began, in their different ways, to lean away from Suharto.[23] The new, more skeptical, media mood helped to generate popular street talk opposition, which in turn contributed to the delegitimization of the now 76-year-old president.[24]

The 1998 departure of Suharto led to a relaxation in press controls. *Tempo*, Indonesia's leading weekly newsmagazine, returned after being banned for four years. The freer climate quickly generated a fresh mushroom growth of hundreds of new newspapers and magazines. The new survival-of-the-commercially-fittest publications made journalists less politically dependent but also less secure[25]—as a new generation of multimedia moguls bought and sold media (and other) properties.

Regional Media Growth and Indonesian National Culture

In Indonesia, as in other big-population countries, media commentators tend to focus on the bigger cities and the bigger media. Much "national" audience research in these countries ignores the rural areas where the bulk of (non-brand-buying) citizens reside. An early exception was a BBC survey that involved 8,500 interviews and revealed that in 1991 47 percent of Indonesian rural households and 61 percent of "small town" households had a radio set.[26]

Especially since 1990, Indonesian, and other, governments have paid more attention to rural areas. Since independence, all Indonesian governments have been aware of separatist problems in some outlying areas—such as the far east of the country (West Papua) and Kalimantan (Borneo). Aceh, in the

[22] Krishna Sen and David T. Hill, *Media, Culture and Politics in Indonesia*, Melbourne: Oxford University Press, 2000: 108–36.

[23] Jeffrey A. Winters, "The Political Impact of New Information Technologies in Indonesia," Effendi Gazali, "The Suharto Regime and Its Fall Through the Eyes of the Local Media," and Victor Menayang, Bimo Nugroho, and Dina Listiorini, "Indonesia's Underground Press," *Gazette*, Vol. 64/2, April 2002: 109–19, 121–40, 141–56.

[24] Dedy N. Hidayat, " 'Don't Worry, Clinton Is Megawati's Brother': The Mass Media, Rumours, Economic Structural Transformation and Delegitimization of Suharto's New Order," *Gazette*, Vol. 64/2, April 2002: 157–81.

[25] Ariel Heryanto and Stanley Joseph Adi, "Industrialized Media in Democratizing Indonesia," and Kukuh Sanyoto, "Indonesian Television and the Dynamics of Transition," in Russell H. K. Heng (ed.), *Media Fortunes, Changing Times*, Singapore: Institute of South East Asian Studies, 2002: 47–82, 83–105.

[26] Graham Mytton, *Global Audiences for Worldwide Broadcasting*, London: BBC, 1993, 224–525.

extreme north of Sumatra, has been the focus of a separatist struggle since the 1950s, with many locals killed. But most Indonesians do not live in these separatist-inclined areas.[27]

Since the 1970s, Indonesian governments have been trying to put more resources into regional development. Such development is seen to be needed for numerous reasons, not least as a counterattraction to the overpopulated cities and Java (640 people per square kilometer). Radio (which into the 1990s was the mass medium with the biggest reach) has always been the most localized of the media and the only medium that has made a big effort in regional languages. But a bigger regional output on television and in the press can be expected. This may mean that media and cultural tensions between Jakarta and the national regions will become more salient than cultural tensions between Indonesia and other countries such as Australia, Malaysia, the Philippines, and the United States.

[27] Margaret Scott, "Beyond the Dirty Wars?" *Times Literary Supplement*, July 21, 2000: 26–27; Navid Kermani, "The Flower Children of Banda Aceh," *Times Literary Supplement*, November 1, 2002: 16–17; Timothy Mapes, "No Solution in Sight of Aceh," *Far East Economic Review*, September 25, 2003: 21–22; "What Did Mobil Know? Mass Graves Suggest a Brutal War on Local Indonesian Guerrillas—in the Oil Giant's Backyard," *Business Week*, December 28, 1998: 24–28; "Thousand-Island Dressing: How Far Should Regional Autonomy Go?" *The Economist*, "Time to Deliver, a Survey of Indonesia," December 11, 2004: 8–11.

11

India's Multi-Ring Media Circus

Nation-states with large populations, and large territories, tend to be inward-looking and broadly self-sustaining in terms of mass media. India was dependent on the British press and British radio until its 1947 independence. India was dependent on Hollywood films, especially in the 1920s, and decreasingly in the sound era of the 1930s. But since 1947 India has imported very little print, radio, film, or television from other countries and in non-Indian languages. True, the Indian film industry has often borrowed movie plots from Hollywood, but (as with such plot-borrowing elsewhere) the resulting product is about 95 percent domestic Indian and only 5 percent foreign.

Most of present-day India's people—one-sixth of the world's population—have had little or no exposure to made-in-America or made-in-Europe media.

India's language map is more complex than Europe's. India has more than 20 separate languages, each of which is spoken by over a million people, as their mother tongue. India also has 11 different scripts, each used by separate daily newspaper and magazine presses. These language (and related cultural) differences ensure that India has the world's most complex single national media system.

India's diversity encompasses what the outside world can see as many extremes, many marvels, many horrors, and many paradoxes. Here are a few in which the mass media have played a significant part:

- Jawaharlal Nehru (prime minister of India, 1947–1964) led the invention of a new form of government—mass democracy in a then predominantly illiterate country. Nehru was able to gain—without autocratic compulsion—a semi-monopoly of national media attention; the prominence he gave to his daughter, Indira Gandhi, enabled her subsequently also to become and to remain Indian prime minister for 15 years. Yet neither father nor daughter saw the development of the mass media

139

as a priority. Both presided over regimes that expanded literacy; but, because of rapid population growth, both Nehru and Indira Gandhi presided over an increase in the total number of illiterate Indians.

- There was rapid media growth in the years after 1991. This was in sharp contrast to India's first 44 independent years of deliberately slow growth.

- Despite the dominance of "The Centre" (the Delhi capital) and the Nehru dynasty, the regions and the big states gradually became more powerful. Especially after Indira Gandhi's 1984 assassination, India was increasingly governed by national coalitions, in which a few regional political bosses played commanding roles. Alongside the regional political bosses also emerged regional movie stars, regional media, regional media moguls, and regional television. In some cases a single individual doubled as movie star and regional political star.

- Extremes of wealth and poverty are highly visible in India's cities and countryside. The "green revolution" increased India's wheat crop by at least five times (from the late 1960s onward), and there has been big economic growth since 1991. India's super-rich flaunt their wealth with million-dollar weddings, while the financially comfortable enjoy air-conditioning, servants, and satellite television. But close to the five-star hotel, close to the airport, close to the rail track, and very close to many streets, people are sleeping rough and begging.[1] In villages and city slums, tens of millions of children don't go to school[2] and are still inadequately fed; fewer than 10 percent of Indians had access to a flush toilet in 2002.[3]

- The affluent top 10 percent receive a big supply of media at semi-token prices, while the bottom 30 percent (300 million) have little or no media and often cannot afford the batteries for a radio. Official data showed real earnings falling after 1994,[4] and anthropologists saw the increased casualization of work—both urban and rural—as having further impoverished many low caste Indians.[5] The Indian media gave more and more attention to consumption, shopping malls, movie stars, big prize television quiz shows, and the stock markets.

- Indian society and Indian media are remarkably tolerant and also intolerant. In 2004 the Indian head of state was a Muslim; the national

[1] Gita Dewan Verma, *Slumming India: A Chronicle of Slums and Their Saviours*, New Delhi: Penguin, 2002.
[2] Soma Wadhwa, "Pencil Erasure," *Outlook*, March 1, 2004: 58–62.
[3] Sulabh Shauchalaya, "Toilet Training," *India Today International*, August 19, 2002.
[4] Bibek Debroy, "India Must Reform Farming Next," *Far East Economic Review*, May 27, 2004: 24.
[5] Jan Breman, *The Labouring Poor in India: Patterns of Exploitation, Subordination and Exclusion*, New Delhi: Oxford University Press, 2003.

Figure 11.1 India: population by state, 2001 census. *Sources*: The Economist; census of India; India Ministry of Finance.

election was won by the Congress Party, which was led by an Italian-born woman (Sonia Gandhi); and the prime minister, who emerged from the election, was Manmohan Singh—from the very small Sikh community. But the period since 1991 has also seen deadly racist-religious attacks, mainly against Muslims. While the Indian media traditionally play down ethnic divisions, some major media elements—especially some of the big Hindi newspapers in north India—gave vocal support to the Hindu nationalist "Hindutva" movement. Tolerance also extends to the invasion of both politics and the movie/TV industry by criminals and the Indian mafia.

- India has a talent for fictional melodrama (as seen in the movies and TV) and also for factual melodrama (as seen in the newspapers and the TV news). The two sorts of melodrama overlap when, for example, a drunken movie star's expensive car kills a poor street sleeper. The rags-to-riches biographies of some populist Indian politicians make the Hollywood equivalents seem staid and conventional. Real-life and movie melodrama merged in the story of Phoolan Devi, a low caste woman who suffered multiple rapes, revenged her partner's murder by personally killing 22 upper caste men, became a bandit, served a long prison term, was then an elected national politician, and finally became the subject of a big movie, *Bandit Queen*, before herself being murdered.

- On a slightly more modest level of melodrama and publicity, business and political leaders invite movie stars and photographers to their parties and displays of conspicuous wealth. Meanwhile out on the urban streets huge advertising portrayals of the stars of movies, TV, and music are to be seen floating and hovering above the traffic lights, above the passing crowds, and above the street sleepers.

- What of "media imperialism" in India? The term has never been in widespread use—but the term "media imperialism" might well be used by southerners objecting to the attempted invasion of the south by Bollywood and other north Indian and Hindi media.

Hindi Bollywood Versus Indian Regional Movies

Hollywood film dominance in India declined in the 1930s and disappeared in the 1940s. In the years 1955–1962, for example, India provided less than 1 percent of Hollywood's foreign revenues.[6] There was some "copying" of fashions, plots, and genres from Hollywood and also from Hong Kong, Bertholt Brecht, British documentary, the Soviet Union, France, Germany, and Japan. But within a world film industry so given to importing and copying, the Indian film industry was extraordinarily self-dependent and inward looking. Indian film has been through five historical phases.

1896–1930: The Silent Era

As elsewhere, American silent films gradually became dominant. Hollywood followed its usual combination by offering better quality films at lower rental prices. But in the 1920s an Indian silent film industry developed, peaking with 200 silent feature films produced in 1931.

---

[6] Manjunath Pendakur, "Dynamics of Cultural Policy Making: The US Film Industry in India," *Journal of Communication*, 35/4, 1985: 52–72.

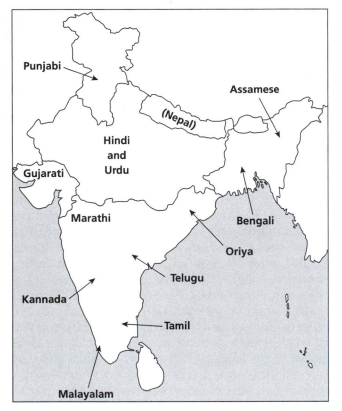

Figure 11.2 India and Bangladesh: main location of 12 major languages.

1930–1947: Talkie Era to Independence

The first Indian talking films appeared in 1931; most used Hindi. By 1935 India's multilocation and multilanguage film industry was already evident and Hollywood was in retreat. Already before Britain's (and thus India's) entry into world war in 1939, India had three main film-making locations. In the years 1935–1939 India averaged 112 films each year in Hindi (made in Bombay, now Mumbai), 37 films in Tamil (made in Madras, now Chennai) and 18 films in Bengali (made in Calcutta, now Kolkata). Bombay made both Hindi and also Marathi films, giving it in 1935–1939 about 64 percent of all productions. But Madras was also emerging as a major film location—for films in Telugu, Malayalam, and Kannada as well as in the Tamil language. Madras was making 47 films a year, or 24.6 percent of the Indian total. Third, Calcutta's Bengali-language industry was making 18 films a year, or 9.4 percent of Indian output.

1947–1970: Building India After Independence

In these first two decades after independence the film industry grew steadily, producing 300 films for the first time in 1963 and 400 in 1971. The standard film of this period often incorporated six or eight songs, dancing, fights, some comedy, and a bit of tragedy, garnished with lots of (nonkissing) romance. Hindi films had the biggest budgets and audiences, while other languages (especially Tamil and Telugu) made more (but lower budget) films. In the early independent years, Nehru's government wanted to develop agriculture and industry; film had a low priority and was lumbered with high taxation levels, severe censorship (political, ethnic, sex), and restrictions on imports of film and equipment.

The "studio system" largely disappeared and was replaced by a new generation of "independent producers" who employed film personnel for one film at a time. These (several hundred) new producers were driven by a wide range of motives; some were nationalists, others wanted sexual adventures with starlets,[7] and some had artistic ambitions. Probably the commonest motivation was entrepreneurial—the film industry looked like a risky, but glamorous, business in which profits could be made. Around 1950 there was a lot of illegal cash available from smuggling, postwar profiteering, and other tax-evading activities; the film industry (located in major business and smuggling locations) was an ideal money-laundering mechanism. Cash could be used for various kinds of bribes and kickbacks—such as extra (tax-free) payments to star actors and inducements to cinema exhibitors to show the film. Many of these ambitious entrepreneurs ran into serious difficulties (as their films flopped); they might, then, borrow cash at shamefully high short-term interest rates. The consequent extreme lack of financial transparency also contributed, many said, to the prevailing short-termism, industrial chaos, and commercial cynicism.

1970–1990: The Film Boom Years

The number of feature films made in India more than doubled between 1970 and 1990. These were the real film boom years before the popular emergence of television. There was a big increase in the numbers of cinemas and cinema seats; the northern Hindi film expanded, but the southern film locations expanded faster. In the years 1985–1989 the four main south India language film industries made 517 films per year, versus only 170 in Hindi-Bollywood (Bombay-Mumbai). Another 132 films were made annually in yet other languages (Table 11.1). At least 10 films per year were being made in 10 separate languages—the big five (Hindi, Telugu, Tamil, Malayalam, and Kannada) plus another smaller five (Bengali, Marathi, Oriya, Gujerati, and Bhojpuri).

---

[7] A major motive, I was told in 1972, by the then editor of *Filmfare*, the leading film publication.

Table 11.1 Film Production in Indian Languages, 1935–1939 and 1985–1989

	AVERAGE NUMBER OF TALKIE FILMS PER YEAR, 1935–1939	AVERAGE NUMBER OF FILMS PER YEAR, 1985–1989
Hindi	111.8	170
South India		
Tamil	37.4	162
Telugu	9.4	173
Malayalam	0.2	110
Kannada	0.2	72
South total	47.2	517
Bengali	18.0	39
Marathi	10.4	23
Oriya	0.2	14
Gujerati	1.0	12
Bhojpuri	—	11
Assamese	0.4	8
Punjabi	2.0	6
Haryanvi	—	6
Rajasthani	—	4
Nepali	—	2
English	—	2
All others	0.6	5
Total	192	819

Source: Ashish Rajadhyaksha and Paul Willemen, *Encyclopaedia of Indian Film*, New Delhi: Oxford University Press, 1994: 31–33.

1990 Onward: India's TV Era

A significant television impact on film audiences was not felt until around 1990; this was closely linked to India's deliberately delayed entry to the television era. In all of the main production locations, the film industry now converted itself into a combined film-and-television industry. By 1990 films were reaching the public by new illegal methods that generated no industry revenue. Illegally copied films were appearing on local cable TV; across India by 1990 there were hundreds of thousands of "video parlours" showing films for about a quarter of the cinema ticket price.

India had plenty of film industry hype and hope. But behind the hoopla about the "world's biggest and most star-studded" lay some awkward, contrary, facts. Poverty was inevitably a major fact in the film business. Attendance at cinemas has never risen above about five or six annual visits per person. Tens of millions of urban Indians have been weekly or frequent attendees; but hundreds of millions of rural Indians have averaged perhaps one attendance per year. Between 1950 and 1980 the average number of attendances per person only doubled; a doubling of India's population, and a trebling of the number of films made, meant that by 1980, the average Indian film was seen by only five million people (or less than 1 percent of the population). Some successful and super-successful films had much bigger numbers, big stars, and big profits. But most Indian films (like most films everywhere) had low production budgets and still made a financial loss; most film employees received (if lucky) very low (trade union) minimum rates of pay.

Even this degree of poverty left India's film industry well ahead of most other nations' industries. The Indian industry had faced the reality of language diversity and recognized that Indians wanted films in their own languages. The Indian industry had also succeeded in delivering entertainment and avoiding many awkward subjects. The centrality of song, dance, fights, and visual spectacle broadened the appeal and reduced language difficulties. The films also focused obsessively on young love, unattached youth, and Cinderella plotting, with evil and conflict often personified into super-villains. Most films understated awkward realities of Indian arranged marriage, intrafamily conflict, and the subordination of women. The film industry also avoided the minefields of interethnic conflict—partly in conformity with official censorship requirements but also in line with commercial instinct and producer political belief. Nevertheless, intercaste conflict was seen as good box office material, especially in south India, where bad guy Brahmin characters became commonplace.

But a massive weakness was the Indian film industry's relative failure in marketing its films either across India or even within each region. The several film industries remained based in their headquarters cities and a very few other larger cities. Box office success was often defined within the industry as a film that was shown in a single city cinema for over 100 continuous days. There was no national or regional release strategy linked to national and regional media publicity and advertising. Even though films were shown in small town cinemas, most rural families could not get to the small town cinema and could not afford the entrance price. Urban cinemas dominated and bigger city cinemas carried greater weight because admission prices and revenue were higher.

The weakness of the other Indian mass media—especially in the three decades after 1947—also made film mass marketing difficult or impossible. Much cinema publicity and advertising appeared mainly in city newspapers, where few Indians saw it. The huge street hoardings obviously had some impact. Literally hundreds of different fan magazines were published; however, they all had low circulations and these magazines—like so much Indian film publicity—still today reach predominantly male readerships. Radio could have been the best publicity channel, but even radio did not become a real mass medium until the 1970s. Then, at last, it was possible to release film

Figure 11.3 Mumbai movie, 2006. (Image provided by the author.)

songs ahead of the film and thus to boost film appeal. The remarkable late surge of Indian film audience numbers after 1970 was greatly helped by heavy radio play of film music. There was another late late surge in the late 1980s assisted by the then newly widespread radio/audiocassette players.

India's exaggerated film star system is closely linked to this marketing weakness. In practice marketing and publicity—and the Indian film industry overall—focus heavily on a few current superstars. The box office performance of the star's previous film generates media publicity and positive word-of-mouth anticipation of the next film. Because successful stars make several or a dozen films a year, it is possible for a movie fan to follow just one or two chosen stars. The top stars can take up to half the total production cost of the film. The star being paid 1,000 times as much as a dancer or set carpenter and 10,000 times as much as a film extra can be seen as a filmic parody of an unjust and unequal society; it is widely quoted as an indication of "chaos" —especially because the star who insists on performing in eight films a year is required in several different studios at the same time. However, this "chaos" originated from a truly chaotic system not just of marketing, but of distribution, cinema exhibition, and finance. The star-focused system does exploit a genuine commercial asset; some stars are themselves producers and/or directors and they typically work with their own team of key professionals, such as a director, and a popular playback singer. Even if the star does make 8 or 10 films in a year, this still allows for four or five full weeks per film. Even if this means 25 hours of finished screen-time per year, it is not much different from traditional Hollywood television norms for weekly one-hour series.

The highly variegated Indian film industry has had an extremely varied output. From extreme high budget to extreme low budget there are three broad categories. First is *the big budget movie* typically made in Bombay (Mumbai) and in Hindi. This major production employs a current superstar who may be making as few as two films a year, like Raj Kapoor in the 1950s. Another superstar, Amitabh Bachchan, made 88 films during 1971–1990, or only 4.4 films per year.

Second is *the medium budget film* as made by the larger regional industries. The superstars of Tamil and Telugu films have tended to make 10 or even 15 films a year at the height of their careers. Some of the highest star output per year has occurred in Kerala's (small) Malayalam film industry, whose biggest star—Prem Nazir—averaged over 20 films a year during 1972–1984.

Third is *the small budget "art" film* exemplified by Satyajit Ray, the celebrated Bengali director; he himself averaged about one film a year during 1955–1991. He could not pay star salaries and relied in part on amateur actors. Ray's films were popular with Bengali speakers but largely unknown elsewhere in India. When he died in 1992 very few of his films had appeared (either subtitled or dubbed) in Hindi or in any other Indian language.[8]

The total number of superstars at any point in time is quite small, and most, even of these, remain at their peak of high pay and high productivity for only one decade or less. The highest productivity and longest success is found among the leading playback singers who combine famous voices with professional speed and studio efficiency. One heroic figure in Telugu (and Tamil) film music was V. R. Ghantasala, who went to prison in 1942 for singing patriotic anti-British songs; in a 30-year subsequent career he sang over 10,000 songs and also composed for 125 films. Some music composers have a huge successful output; the Laxmikant-Pyarelal partnership composed the music for 487 Hindi films during 1963–1998.[9]

Since 1990 the separate Indian film industries have become combined film and TV industries; and especially in the southern states people are offered on cable and satellite TV a wide choice of channels in Tamil, in Telugu, and in other major regional languages.

But in many other respects the separate film industries still follow most of their familiar patterns of the 1980s. Mafia financing is still common, while cinema audience sizes are substantially lower. But television, cable, and video generate additional finance. In 2001 India produced over 1,000 films for the first time; however, some of these films might be regarded as made primarily

[8] Andrew Robinson, *Satyajit Ray: The Inner Eye*, London: André Deutsch, 1989: 323–25; "Satyajit Ray," *Sight and Sound*, August 1992: 28–37.

[9] *Encyclopaedia of Indian Film*, New Delhi: Oxford University Press, 1994.

Figure 11.4 Indian movie stars. (Image provided by the author.)

for TV and anticipating only a modest theatrical showing. The average Indian movie production budget has been very low by international standards.[10]

Indian movie statistics are today even less reliable than previously. Some data suggest that movie theater attendance fell below three billion in 2000–2001, but the real number may have been higher; on top of this, video piracy now operates on a massive scale.[11] Probably more accurate than any movie industry data are figures from the well-established National Readership Survey. This latter source confirms that Telugu and Tamil movie fans attend

---

[10] In 2002 the average Indian movie budget was $160,000, versus $1.5 million in Mexico. The European Union average was $3.88 million, and the U.S. average was $27 million. "Average Film Budgets in the US Soar Ahead," *Screen Digest*, October 2003: 228.

[11] While pirate versions dominated the VHS rental market, piracy was less dominant in the DVD rental market. *Screen Digest*, March 2003: 83.

much more frequently than do people in the northern Hindi-speaking heart-land (and highly populated) states of Uttar Pradesh and Madhya Pradesh.[12]

South India now has four distinctively separate movie industries in four separate locations. Three of these are located in three of India's most dynamic cities—Chennai, Hyderabad, and Bangalore. All four of these southern states now have an established state policy of supporting their film industry. These policies include lower taxation and special support for artistic merit. The southern states—partly because of state government support—tend to have more modern production facilities, and the southern movie industries are better at maintaining commercial discipline, including much shorter production schedules.

In the Mumbai Hindi movie industry many of the old excesses continue. But there is now more involvement by major "corporates" such as Tata, and bank finance is now possible, following government recognition of movies as an industry. However, criminal involvement still leads critics to claim that Bollywood's own reality is more dramatic than its high decibel fictions. Although everyone claims that the era of the Hindi superstar is now past, top Hindi movie stars seem to have bigger images and higher earnings than ever. Stars still work on several films simultaneously; one reason why producers now like to make part of their film in far-off Scotland, Switzerland, Las Vegas, or New Zealand is that they can then get the big star's full attention for several whole days in succession. Stars, the print media are now agreed, have become "brands"; this involves expensively endorsing several product lines, and it can involve film financing.

The main competition in the India-wide movie industry is between the Hindi industry in Mumbai and the main regional industries, especially in south India. This is much more salient than any competition from Hollywood; most Indian film people are more interested in exporting to, rather than importing from, the United States.

Framing Anglo-Indian Slow Change: Media, Dynasty, and Regional Language to Independence

What held India together? Several brief answers might include the army, the civil service, the Nehru-Gandhi dynasty, the Congress Party, caste, the railways, and the federal system.

Another answer is that all of these factors spanned the 1947 independence and that all of them were bolstered by the English language and the media. Large numbers of Indian soldiers fought with Britain in the 1939–1945 war; and after independence India's nonpolitical military were seen by India's

---

[12] Vanita Kohli, *The Indian Media Business*, New Delhi: Response Books/Sage Publications, 2003: 108–54; Manjunath Pendakur, *Indian Popular Cinema: Industry, Ideology, and Consciousness*, Cresskill, NJ: Hampton Press, 2003.

media as national heroes—not least in the three wars with Pakistan (1947–1949, 1965, and 1970–1971). The Nehru-Gandhi dynasty was media supported, as was the Congress Party in the early years. The caste system, and attempts to reform it, were a major political and media issue. The railways—a British project—became the classic Indian mode of transport and carried big city newspapers into the hinterland. India's federal government system derived from the British "indirect rule" (which had involved many "independent" principalities).

For several decades before 1947 independence, a small British governing elite had begun preparing a small educated Indian governing elite. This included elite Indian schools modeled on the fee-paying schools of Britain. Many members of independent India's senior civil service, and media and political elites, received a British-style education at the Doon School[13] and others of its kind. There was continuity across 1947 also in many commercial and industrial enterprises. For example, the Tata group—an Indian industrial giant of today—was founded by J. N. Tata (1839–1904), who set up India's first steel mill and India's first hydroelectric project. Another Indian industrial pioneer was G. D. Birla, who built his first Jute mill in 1919; his company and his leading newspaper (*Hindustan Times*, launched 1924) were major forces both before and after Indian independence.

The most active phase of Indian nationalist protest began in 1919. Mahatma Gandhi had returned (from South Africa) to India in 1915 and was already a major nationalist figure by 1919. In early April there were "riots" in Delhi. Then on April 13, 1919, nearly 400 unarmed Indians were killed by British soldiers at Amritsar in the Punjab. The British authorities used their censorship powers to keep this massacre out of the newspapers. One (British) editor of a nationalist newspaper, the *Bombay Chronicle*, who did carry the news was immediately deported by ship to London.

From 1919 onward the British speeded up their previous policy of Indianization. This policy generated more Indian lawyers and legislators (in the various national and regional legislative bodies) and many more Indian civil servants, policemen, soldiers, clerks, and translators. Gandhi himself was a lawyer-journalist who ran several weekly newspapers aimed at "untouchables." Jawaharlal Nehru followed his own father (Motilal Nehru) into this lawyer–nationalist politician–journalist combination. Like other wealthy nationalists, Motilal Nehru launched his own newspaper, *The Independent*; when Jawaharlal returned from his English education, he briefly edited this newspaper, and two decades later (1938–1939) he himself launched his own paper, the *National Herald* (Lucknow), which became a key Congress Party supporter.[14]

---

[13] Sanjay Srivastava, *Constructing Post-Colonial India: National Character and the Doon School*, London: Routledge, 1998; Edward Luce, "Liberal Streak," *Financial Times* magazine, January 3, 2004: 23–25.

[14] Moti Lal Bhargava, *Role of Press in the Freedom Movement*, New Delhi: Reliance Publishing, 1987: 169–74.

Already in the 1920s there were increasing numbers of Indian-owned newspapers; but daily circulations were at most only a few thousand, and the big majority of Indians were illiterate. The Congress Party consequently needed to develop additional publicity methods. The British did gradually expand Indian involvement in legislative bodies and the (restricted) elections provided one type of platform. Leading Indian nationalist politicians increasingly attracted huge crowds to hear their formal speeches. By the late 1930s Jawaharlal Nehru was indulging in several speeches a day tours using air, as well as rail and road, travel. Nehru, before he became prime minister in 1947, had been seen and heard by tens of millions of people. This tradition continued; Nehru's daughter, Indira Gandhi, was similarly seen in the flesh by tens of millions of Indians; at her often immense meetings the crowds were "warmed up" with loud film music.

Both Gandhi and his younger disciple Nehru managed astutely both their onstage entrances and their offstage exits to prison. This was the era of the still photograph. They recognized the importance of visual appeal; Gandhi was sparsely dressed in peasant clothing and wore simple wire-framed glasses, while his spinning wheel was often in the picture. Nehru himself, when recalling Gandhi 20 years after the event, summoned up a visual image— Gandhi marching, staff in hand, to Dandi on the Salt March in 1930.[15] This 1930 protest march was one of the world media events of the 1918–1939 period.

Gandhi was known by journalists to provide excellent material in interviews, "but it was essential to tell him in advance the subject for the interview."[16] Gandhi was adept at staging newsworthy events. His Salt March of 1930 straddled the Bombay–Ahmadabad–New Delhi rail and road routes; the final section of the march to the sea at Dandi was from Navsari, 150 miles from Bombay on a major rail route. Many Indian and foreign journalists made the easy journey.

By the 1930s India had its own sizeable film industry, but British censorship restricted the possibilities for overt nationalist propaganda. The censors looked out for more unobtrusive propaganda such as a film scene in which a picture of Gandhi was shown pinned to a household wall. However, it was more difficult for the British censors to eliminate nationalist references in film music and songs. In 1930s Indian musicals, song references to the gods, house, home, hearth, land, the Himalayas, heroes, East-West slavery, freedom, wake up and stop sleeping, and the spinning wheel—these and others—were nationalist sentiments that the film censors often missed but the film audience recognized and applauded.

When the British relaxed most censorship during the years 1938–1939, newsreel censorship was also relaxed. Cinemas were now free for the first

---

[15] Sarvepalli Gopal, *Jawaharlal Nehru: A Biography* (abridged ed.), Delhi: Oxford University Press, 1989: 76.

[16] Milton Israel, *Communications and Power: Propaganda and the Press in the Indian Nationalist Struggle, 1920–1947*, Cambridge, UK: Cambridge University Press, 1994: 117.

time to show newsreels of Gandhi's Salt March of 1930, "Mahatma Gandhi's Return from London," and other nationalist events of recent years. Now millions of Indians saw, for the first time, moving images of their nationalist leaders.[17]

Indian radio, which was relaunched under British (BBC) leadership in 1935, might seem to have been a highly suitable medium for the nationalist leaders. Lionel Fielden, the BBC producer who ran All India Radio (AIR) in the late 1930s, was in fact eager to put Gandhi and Nehru on the air as a means of boosting AIR and selling more radio sets. But the Congress leaders were unwilling to appear on a British-controlled medium. Both Gandhi and Nehru wrote friendly letters expressing their sincere regrets; in his January 1937 letter Nehru even invited the boss of British imperial radio to come and stay a few days in Allahabad ("Both my sister and I would be happy to have you").[18]

The Congress leaders saw just one major media avenue for political propaganda and progress; this avenue was the newspaper press and the related news agencies. They focused on all three main categories of newspaper—the British-owned English language papers, the Indian-owned English language papers, and the papers in Hindi and other Indian languages. In the 1920s the British-English papers were the most prominent—especially the *Times of India* (Bombay), *The Statesman* (Calcutta), and *The Mail* (Madras). These papers had an obvious pro-British and (by later standards) racist bias, but they did, for example, carry stories (and pictures) reporting—in slightly amused style—"Mr. Gandhi's Latest March."

In the 1920s the few Indian-owned newspapers consisted of weak papers with small staffs, very small circulations, and little advertising. But the Congress Party's attention (and its sympathizers' finances) focused mainly on such Indian-owned, English-language dailies as *The Bombay Chronicle*, the *Amrita Bazar Patrika* (Calcutta), *The Hindu* (Madras), and the *Hindustan Times* (Delhi).

Both the Anglo-British and Anglo-Indian newspapers tended quite explicitly to follow London models. The British-owned papers supported the government, while the Indian-owned papers were, especially in the 1920s, the opposition press. However, especially after the 1929–1930 economic downturn, the British press itself slumped somewhat. Meanwhile, from 1930 onward, the Indian-owned (opposition) English-language press continued to grow—with increasing numbers of English-educated Indians and more Indian-business advertising and subsidy. Also in the 1930s the nationalist movement became more outspoken; during the 1930s Gandhi increasingly came to be seen as a world-class political personality. Nehru and other younger Congress leaders also grew in news terms and took on a more heroic

---

[17] Gautam Kaul, *Cinema and the Indian Freedom Struggle*, New Delhi: Sterling Publishers, 1998: 34–37.

[18] Lionel Fielden, *The Natural Bent*, London: Andre Deutsch. 1960: 197–98.

gloss, not least through their now frequent court appearances plus prison entrances and exits. The Government of India (GOI), which now employed thousands of Indian Congress supporters and probably hundreds of British (and Irish) Congress sympathizers, was a very leaky body. Increasingly British officials had to read the Indian-owned English papers to find out what was going on inside the British GOI.

Even before the Amritsar massacre of April 1919, the GOI had established one of the world's then largest press relations operations. By 1919 the government of India had set up a Central Bureau of Information (CBI), which each week supplied 10 newspaper articles to the press, sent out frequent news telegrams, wrote private letters to editors, and supplied press photographs and cinema films. Foreign visitors were welcomed (one per week in hot weather, three per week in cool weather); already in 1919 250,000 leaflets in Indian languages were distributed each month. A press cuttings operation indexed 50,000 items per year.[19] The understaffed Indian-owned newspapers of the 1920s (the press cuttings revealed) used a lot of this officially supplied British material. However, the Congress Party itself built up its own press relations, and during the 1930s major Congress gatherings reserved large working areas for the increasing numbers of journalists, both from India and from around the world.

All of the larger British-owned and Indian-owned 1930s newspapers had correspondents in Delhi, covering the activities of the GOI and increasingly the Congress Party. Much of the GOI bureaucracy trekked north to the cooler heights of Simla in the hot months; journalists also moved between Delhi and Simla.

The agency wholesaling of news inevitably played a big role in tracking and reporting the British-Indian ship of state. At first glance there were four separate news agencies, each dominating a different news market. But in fact all four key news agencies were located in one office, owned by one imperial agency (Reuters) and operated by a very small group of British and Indian journalists. The four agencies were the Eastern News Agency (ENA), which distributed foreign news to the entire press of India; the Associated Press of India (API), no relation to the AP of the United States, which distributed domestic Indian news inside India; the Indian News Agency (INA), which distributed Indian news to the GOI; and "Reuters," used for sending Indian news to London and onward to the world.

India's numerous small newspapers, the GOI, and the Congress Party were all drawing their basic supplies of daily news and features from the Reuters' twin offices in Delhi and Simla. The British viceroy and his staff, Gandhi and Nehru, and other leading political players were well aware of the news agency monopoly. During the 1930s, senior British officials were increasingly unhappy about the amount of positive publicity the agency grouping gave to

---

[19] Milton Israel, *Communications and Power*, Cambridge, UK: Cambridge University Press, 1994: 32–35.

the Congress; but these officials realized that a rival Indian-owned agency would generate even more pro-Congress (and anti-British) news.

This Reuters-controlled news operation was, during 1923–1951, presided over by just two general managers. William Moloney (1923–1937) was himself Irish and sympathetic to Indian nationalists; William Turner (1937–1951), who was also quietly sympathetic to Indian nationalism, had an informal agreement with Gandhi that the API agency would have exclusive rights to Gandhi's personal news. Reuters (Delhi-Simla) thus maintained special privileged relationships with both the British GOI and what looked increasingly like the government of the future, the Congress Party. Reuters was simply pursuing the traditional news agency tactics of monopoly combined with market orientation. While in the 1930s the British GOI was still in control (and still the biggest financial subscriber to Reuters in India), it seemed obvious that the growing Indian press, and probably an independent "Dominion" Indian government, would prevail in the not too distant future.

While the Reuters Delhi office was managed by a European general manager, in the 1930s most of the senior journalists were Indians. K. C. Roy had himself founded the Associated Press of India in 1899; after selling out to Reuters, Roy continued as the chief API correspondent in Delhi until 1931. He was trusted and respected both by British officials and the moderate Congress leaders. The Congress leaders preferred Roy's "professionalism" and restraint and gave news items to him rather than to more militant nationalist journalists (whose stories they saw as often sinning in the direction of parochialism, ethnic communalism, and squabbling between rival nationalists). Roy was typical of many leading 1920s Indian journalists in supporting Indian nationalism, while also admiring the British in general and the serious end of British journalism in particular. Roy seems to have exhibited a rather British mixture of diplomacy and mild eccentricity. J. N. Sahni (then of the *Hindustan Times*) saw Roy as a skilled journalist and a master practitioner of "refined sycophancy." During the summer Roy occupied a Simla hotel suite where, often wearing "silk pyjamas in garish stripes," he entertained a steady flow of well-informed informants. Roy was friendly with (and seemingly sympathetic to) Congress nationalists and minority communalists, as well as highly placed British civil servants.[20]

In the late 1920s and early 1930s the mainstream flow of Indian political news was controlled by a team of five senior journalists in the Reuters grouping; four of these journalists were Indian and only one British. These journalists not only sent out stories through the four different Reuters news pipelines; the same few journalists often also wrote separate "special" articles, personally commissioned (and paid for) by particular newspaper editors.

[20] J. N. Sahni, *Truth About the Indian Press*, Bombay: Allied Publishers, 1974: 55–56; also on Reuters in India: Chandrika Kaul, "Imperial Communication, Fleet Street and the Indian Empire c. 1850s–1920s," in Michael Bromley and Tom O'Malley (eds.), *A Journalism Reader*, London: Routledge, 1997: 58–86.

Yet another key newsgathering practice in the late 1920s and onward was a mini-copy in Delhi of the London-Westminster press "lobby," which allowed for privileged daily informal access to the Delhi Legislative Assembly. Of the three journalists allowed this privilege, two were Indian Reuters men (K. C. Roy and his deputy); the third was the (British) editor of the *Times of India*. When J. H. Sahni became editor (at age 26) of the then new publication the *Hindustan Times*, he brashly demanded the lobby privilege for himself. By 1930 there were four privileged political journalists in Delhi, three of them Indians.

This Delhi/Simla newsgathering scene looks in retrospect to have been amazingly small and obsessively inward-looking. The Indian press was undoubtedly very small; precise circulation figures are unavailable (not least because a lot of copies were given away free, and not actually sold). Even as late as 1952 India sold only 2.5 million dailies. The 1938 daily sale was probably about 1.5 million—or one daily for every 250 people in the population.

This mismatch of huge electorate and small newspaper readership favored the emergence of just one or two national leaders. The initial beneficiary of this system was Gandhi, the saintly demi-god and virtuoso self-publicist. The other early beneficiary of this publicity system was Jawaharlal Nehru, who was Gandhi's political heir. The importance of dynasty and national name (or image) recognition continued after 1947, through four family generations. First was Motilal Nehru, the important Congress leader. Second was his son, Jawaharlal Nehru (prime minister, 1947–1964). Third was Nehru's daughter Indira Gandhi, whose husband, Feroze, was another journalist/politician, but no relation to the mahatma; Indira was prime minister in two spells (1966–1977 and 1980–1984). Fourth was Indira's son, Rajiv Gandhi, who also was prime minister (1984–1989). Even after Rajiv's assassination, the potency of the magic name was evident in the rise of Sonia Gandhi (Rajiv's Italian-born widow), who led the Congress Party to election coalition victory in 2004.

Two years after Nehru died in 1964, the Congress Party chose his daughter, Indira Gandhi, to be his successor as prime minister because she was the only Congress politician with a truly national reputation and image. All other Congress politicians had only a regional appeal or some other electoral disadvantage. Morarji Desai was too close to big business; Jagiwan Ram was a Harijan (untouchable). In the national election of 1967 the still relatively inexperienced Indira Gandhi attracted vast crowds across India and led the Congress Party to victory.[21]

The centrality of the Gandhi-Nehru-Gandhi dynasty was not the only characteristic of twentieth-century India, which was linked to the big politics/small political media combination. Parallel to India's great political dynasty were a few newspaper-owning families who also controlled industrial

---

[21] Krishan Bhatia, *Indira: A Biography of Prime Minister Gandhi*, London: Angus and Robertson, 1974: 198–99; Tariq Ali, *The Nehrus and the Gandhis: An Indian Dynasty*, London: Pan Books, 1985: 145–77.

interests. These three families owned the *Times of India, Hindustan Times,* and *Indian Express* and were major players in India's first 50 years of independence.

In the three decades previous to independence in 1947 the Congress Party to a great extent spoke (and also thought) through the elite newspaper press. From the 1919 Amritsar massacre onward, the Congress and the Indian-owned press drew upon "bad news" values to highlight brutality and killings by British soldiers. But, even before the mass ethnic killings of 1947, the "responsible" Indian press, while playing up the dangers of violence, also tried to play down the facts of violence. This (perhaps unavoidable) duality continued through three wars with Pakistan and through separatist and ethnic violence in the Punjab, in Kashmir, and in several large cities. An obsession with the fearsome consequences of ethnic violence was almost impossible to avoid in a sequence of political assassinations—Mahatma Gandhi (1948), Indira Gandhi (1984), and Rajiv Gandhi (1991). The last two assassinations involved members of ethnic minorities (Sikh, Tamil) and were followed by ethnic rioting and killings.

The centrality, power, and independence of a small newspaper press in the years before and after 1947 had another obvious consequence. Governments that could not control the press were determined to control the radio; the BBC-created All India Radio was, during Indira Gandhi's premiership, known as "All Indira Radio" for good reason. An element of this tradition lingered on until the 1990s, not only in radio but also in television.

Before Television: More Slow Change

For 30 years after independence the media grew only a little faster than the Indian economy, and the economy grew only a little faster than the population. Were these three decades, then, years of media "stagnation"? In 1974 (27 years after independence) less than two daily newspapers were sold per 100 population; a large majority of households still did not have a radio receiver. Even the supposedly super-popular cinema business was a mainly urban medium.[22]

The Indian media industry and government are often accused of wasting these post-independence decades, of failing to provide popular entertainment, of snobbish obsessions with "high" literary versions of Hindi and of lecturing an uncomprehending rural audience about "development," literacy, and family planning. However, the Indian media reflected the multiple shocks and deep trauma of the 1947 independence period. At independence, millions of Muslims trekked west into Pakistan and millions of Hindus and Sikhs trekked east into India; at least half a million (perhaps one

---

[22] Chanchal Sarkar, *Challenge and Stagnation: The Indian Mass Media,* New Delhi: Vikas Publications. 1969.

million) people were killed before, during, and after the partition of India and Pakistan. Media people were amongst the refugees. *The Tribune* was an established English-language daily based in Lahore. Staffed mainly by Sikhs, the paper was read by both Muslims and Hindus, as well as Sikhs, across the Punjab. From the late nineteenth century *The Tribune* had been the main Indian-owned competitor to the British-owned *Civil and Military Gazette*, the Lahore paper for which Rudyard Kipling had worked as a young reporter. But in 1947 Indian partition involved the partition of the Punjab, leaving Lahore on the Pakistan side, close to the new frontier with India. In early August 1947 as the day of independence and partition approached, ethnic violence erupted in Lahore and several *Tribune* employees were killed. On August 15 most of the staff departed. The office truck carried 80 people and a small car carried 14. As they traveled east on the Lahore-Amritsar road, they witnessed buses and trucks being stopped and the passengers being killed. [23]

Politicians and media people in Delhi were acutely aware of these ethnic massacres, not least because the Pakistan-Indian border was so near. In Delhi itself three-way violence (Hindu-Muslim-Sikh) was severe; journalists (such as Doon Campbell of Reuters) went out onto the streets for twice daily body counts. For some days in mid- and late August 1947 simply removing (and burning) the dead bodies from the Delhi streets was a major logistical problem. Many youthful witnesses of the killings of 1947 were still, five decades later, remembering with anguish (and with various degrees of accuracy) what had happened.[24]

Whether the numbers killed in summer 1947 were one million or "only" half a million, the big fear was that this was just the beginning. Indeed the next year saw the assassination of Mahatma Gandhi and also the first India-Pakistan war. From 1949 onward there were some calmer times; but those who predicted more trouble with Pakistan were later proved right by two more India-Pakistan wars (1965–1966 and 1971).

From the very first days of independence in 1947, Pakistan and also the Indian Muslims posed acute anxieties. The Congress Party had, only a few years earlier, expected to preside over both India and what in 1947 became (two wings of) Pakistan. Now after 1947, not only did the conception of India have to be radically revised, the Congress Party found itself at war with Muslim Pakistan, while at home seeking (and depending on) the Indian Muslim vote. From the late 1940s onward Nehru (who was both foreign minister and prime minister) and his cabinet looked out on what they saw as a threatening world. Soon India was cultivating a defense relationship with the Soviet Union, while attracting the antagonism not only of Pakistan but of the United States and also China. (In a brief 1962 war on the Indian-Tibet border, the Chinese army triumphed over the Indian army.)

[23] Prakash Ananda, *A History of the Tribune*, Chandigarh: The Tribune Trust, 1986: 124–28.
[24] Gyanendra Pandey, *Remembering Partition: Violence, Nationalism and History in India*, New Delhi: Cambridge University Press, 2001.

Although Prime Minister Nehru cultivated India's "nonaligned" leadership status at the United Nations, very few Indians in the 1950s and 1960s traveled outside India. Indian politicians and media people focused obsessively on maintaining India. To the Indian elite Pakistan was both an enemy and a dreadful warning. At all costs India must hold together as one geographical and political entity. Those who claimed that India was not a nation, and would not remain one nation-state, must be proved wrong.

Big domestic policies were introduced. Five-year plans, industrial investment, and nationalization accompanied a major policy pronouncement in land reform. Education (especially higher education) was hugely expanded. Not all of this was successful; some would say that all of these policies—plus population control—were policy disasters. But, it can be argued, the real drama was of India's survival as a single democratic state with the world's largest democratic electorate; India also achieved a balance between national and regional identities (and loyalties), which was acceptable to most of its billion population of the year 2000 and after.

What did the media do in all this? India could have pursued its own version of China's highly activist and aggressive use of the media. In fact, Nehru's government chose the opposite approach to that of China. Nehru's somewhat vague admiration for the Soviet Union did not extend to the Soviet media system. India after 1947 went for a cautious, low profile media approach. The media were not allocated a high priority in the five-year plans. Both overt policies and lack of policies in effect ordained that the Indian media should remain small and speak quietly; the only big sound would be movie song and dance, and even this would be heavily censored, heavily taxed, and somewhat looked down upon.

India was dependent on imports for such basics as paper and printing equipment. Central and regional governments and state-owned industries also accounted for between one-third and one-half of all advertising expenditure.

Which language or languages should India's independent media use? From at least the eighteenth century onward India's numerous different scripts, languages, and dialects had been one of the wonders of the world. India was known as the country where the language changes every eight miles. The Congress Party in the 1890s was already anxious about the language problem. So was Mahatma Gandhi on his return to India in 1915; he spoke English and his mother tongue of Gujarati, but his Hindi was weak. Three decades later when Jawaharlal Nehru gave his famous independence speech ("While the world sleeps, India awakes") Nehru spoke in English, a language few Indians understood. Indeed, some of Nehru's poetic eloquence ("tryst with destiny") already had archaic overtones suggestive of pre-1914 Edwardian England.

India, both before and after 1947, had an awkward logjam of languages: English (spoken well by about 2 or 3 percent, read and understood by more); Hindi (spoken, written, and understood in one form or another by a large minority of all Indians); then a group of the next 11 largest languages (Bengali,

Telugu, Marathi, Tamil, Urdu, Gujarati, Kannada, Malayalam, Oriya, Punjabi, Assamese), together spoken by about 50 percent of the Indian population.[25] Finally were a much larger number of much smaller languages—found across India but especially in the mountainous northeast—which were the mother tongues of about 10 percent (or 100 million in year 2001) of India's people.

Most of the founding fathers of the new India were Congress Party politicians from north central India, the main location of Hindi. They made the logical point that English was not an Indian language. Hindi was much the biggest single Indian language; already by 1950 Hindi had a strong position in film, newspapers, and All India Radio as well as in Delhi politics and the Indian constitution.

However, the spectacle of northern Congress politicians trying to expand Hindi in south Indian administration, and in south Indian schools, duly met determined opposition. Gradually state boundaries were redrawn around the bigger languages; Telugu, Tamil, Gujarati, and Marathi all became the lead language of newly drawn states (Andhra Pradesh, Tamil Nadu, Gujerat, Maharastra). This rejigging of state languages in practice tended to fix and maintain the strength of all the larger languages, each of which would now have its own educational and media systems.

Why did such a large and politically well supported language as Hindi not manage to become a more dominant political and media force? Most of the answers are to be found in the 1947–1977 period. One key difficulty was the conflicting lobbies pushing different high, middle, and low—and Hindu and Muslim—versions of Hindi. In practice each of the three main mass media used a different "level" of Hindi. The Hindi film industry used the most popular street level version of Hindi, namely Hindustani, which included a lot of Urdu and Persian words. The Hindi-language newspapers used respectable, modern, school Hindi. Third, All India Radio—in the years immediately after 1947—favored a "high" or classical, traditional (and archaic) form of Hindi; Minister for Information and Broadcasting Dr. B. V. Keskaz, who held this post for most of the 1950s, preferred classical Hindi and classical Indian music. He was especially opposed to the words in Hindi film music, the very words (in Hindustani) that were most widely used and best understood across India in the 1950s. By 1960 this policy was changing, but it was too late.

A much more determined attempt to popularize and spread some kind of Hindustani-Hindi from 1947 might (but might not) have been successful. One recurring problem (or opportunity) was that Hindustani was always seen as a combination of Hindi and Urdu; the "Hindi heartland" of the north Indian plain had long also been the location of a significant Muslim, and Urdu-speaking, population. Although Hindi and Urdu had different scripts, much of the vocabulary was common; thus numerous attempts were made to

[25] Robert W. Stern, *Changing India: Bourgeois Revolution on the Subcontinent*, Cambridge, UK: Cambridge University Press, 2003 ed.: 107–27; Paul R. Brass, *The Politics of India Since Independence*, Cambridge, UK: Cambridge University Press, 1994 ed.: 116–227.

combine and codify the two languages into one. First a Scottish physician, John Gilchrist, soon after arriving in India in 1782 decided that Hindustani was (and should be confirmed as) the language of all of India; Gilchrist prepared an English-Hindustani dictionary, adopting the same method as Dr. Samuel Johnson in his (then) recently published English dictionary—a heavy reliance on literary quotations (supplied by both Hindi and Urdu scholars).[26] Other such efforts were made over the next 150 years. When Hindi films needed to talk in the talkie film era after 1930, the scriptwriters of Bombay quickly commenced the creation of film Hindustani; this film Hindustani was intended to appeal to both Hindi and Urdu speakers and also to generate film songs that speakers of other languages (in eastern and southwestern India) could follow.

All India Radio's failure to take a commanding lead with its own version of Hindustani dates at least from 1940. Lionel Fielden's successor as head of AIR was a Muslim, A. S. Bokhari, who held the post from 1940 to 1947, until he moved to Pakistan. Bokhari was a strong believer in Hindustani, but (Indian critics said) his Hindustani was dominated by Urdu. After 1947 there was a policy change in direction toward a more Hindi Hindustani (before the subsequent 1950s retreat from any Hindustani).

The failure during the 1947–1977 period significantly to shift the existing pattern meant that the language pyramid stayed in more or less the same shape. Most educated Indians can speak two or three languages—often English and Hindi and perhaps a third mother tongue language.

The preservation of independent India involved not only the preservation of the language pattern. In seeking to maintain a nonreligious, secular state, Indian politicians found themselves seeking only gradual change. India avoided Pakistan's pattern of frequent military coups and China's pattern of policy great leaps. India's lack of aggressive policy on sensitive social and religious issues was illustrated by the growing Indian population, which almost trebled between independence in 1947 and the census of 2001.

In India inequality was linked to caste and corruption as well as to the media. In the years immediately after 1947 most senior politicians were high caste Brahmins; the Congress Party was really an upper caste socialist party —led by Brahmins who depended on the votes of "untouchables" (Dalits), other lower castes, "tribals," and Muslims. Even the nationalist Hindu Bharatiya Janata Party (BJP), who were in power in Delhi during 1998–2004, were another Brahmin-led party.

Caste in India works at national, regional, and local levels. Caste is connected to work and employment as well as landholding. Caste inequality —including the domination of landless and marginal small farmers by

---

[26] David Lelyveld, "The Fate of Hindustani: Colonial Knowledge and the Project of a National Language," in Carol A. Breckenridge and Peter van der Veer (eds.), *Orientalism and the Post Colonial Predicament: Perspectives on South Asia*, Philadelphia: University of Pennsylvania Press, 1993: 189–214.

landlords and larger farmers—was especially persistent in the traditional Hindi heartland of the north. Although lower castes did eventually break through into political power in the north, this happened earlier in the south. That caste difference was reflected in many ways, including the more dynamic mass media of southern India.

As upper caste dominance was gradually reduced in the 1970s and 1980s, corruption in many forms increased. International monitors of "transparency" found India to be one of the most corrupt countries in Asia. Remarkably few people in India paid income tax. Poor people—in both city and countryside —often found that a bribe was required if one wanted to talk with a local government official. Increasingly commercialized elections, at both state and national level, involved large scale bribery; consequently politicians required access to substantial amounts of cash. Criminals, who had traditionally bribed politicians, in recent years have been directly elected in significant numbers into state and national legislatures.[27]

There are arguments to the effect that both caste and corruption helped to preserve India. Caste was the glue that held the society together; corruption was the lubrication that allowed the wheels to turn. Certainly both corruption and caste affected the growth of the Indian media. Especially at the local level, Indian journalists are offered bribes. One of the costs faced by candidates at elections is the bribing of reporters. But media corruption also happens at higher levels. The "License Raj"—the micro-management of the economy by government in the early decades—meant that key licenses were often provided on a corrupt basis. Even during the "liberalization" of the 1990s, licenses to operate (for example, in cable TV) were for sale in at least some cities.

Even the highly respectable (and largely corruption free) English language press has had a few corrupt episodes. One example was the *Times of India* in the independence era. In 1945 Ramkrishna Dalmia purchased the *Times of India* (and associated publications) from its British owners. Dalmia was a poorly educated but very successful, and very corrupt, businessman who served time in prison.[28]

The Indian media were also, inevitably, deeply involved with caste. Brahmins were long dominant in the large newspapers and important in the other media. Moreover, media readerships and audiences are heavily

---

[27] Christoph Jaffrelot, "Indian Democracy: The Rule of Law on Trial," *India Review*, Vol. 1/1, January 2002: 77–121; Alyssa Ayres and Philip Oldenburg (eds.), *India Briefing: Quickening the Pace of Change*, Armonk, NY: M.E. Sharpe, 2001; Pradip N. Thomas, "Beyond the Pale: Poverty in an Era of Cutting-Edge Communications. A View from India," *Media Development*, 2, 2002: 50–58; P. Sainath, "Poverty, Development and the Press in India," *Media Development*, 1, 2000: 9–13; Edward Luce, "Indians Greet Runaway Graft with Sadness but No Surprise," *Financial Times*, August 8, 2002; M. N. Srinivas (ed.), *Caste: Its Twentieth Century Avatar*, New Delhi: Penguin, 1997; Pavan K. Varma, *The Great Indian Middle Class*, New Delhi: Penguin, 1999.

[28] J. N. Sahni, *Truth About the Indian Press*, Bombay: Allied Publishers, 1974: 194–201, 207–14.

skewed toward the upper castes. Even though this Brahmin domination has weakened since the 1980s there is still a critique that sees Brahmin political leaders (however corrupt) as supported by Brahmin owned-and-operated media; however, the critique continues, when lower caste, more populist, politicians do achieve power, they tend to be labeled as "corrupt" by the major media and some of them end up in prison.

By the year 2000, India had a daily newspaper sale of 40 million. But at independence in 1947 the daily sale was about two million. In the early 1970s Prime Minister Indira Gandhi always looked at six English-language dailies each morning before starting work.[29] On June 25, 1975, Gandhi declared an emergency; special powers were targeted at three enemy groups—the courts, opposition politicians, and the newspapers, in particular English-language newspapers such as the *Indian Express*. While this latter paper and some others resisted, most newspapers did not. However, the emergency ended in 1977 with a general election that Gandhi and the Congress Party lost. Journalists today say that Gandhi's 1975–1977 emergency was a wake-up call.[30] Certainly the general tone of the newspapers has changed radically since the early 1970s. The papers have become much more aggressive and assertive in pursuing news, in terms of critical comment, and also in terms of boosting circulation. The gradual relaxation of government regulations and import restrictions means that the press can no longer be controlled by cutting off its vital supplies.

When Rajiv Gandhi as prime minister a decade later (in 1988) tried to legislate to curb the power of newspapers, he was met with vigorous opposition. The owners, journalists, and editors of all the leading publications engaged in strikes, marches, and protests to support their case, and within two weeks the government backed down.[31]

But, while India's newspapers after 1977 were bigger and more assertive, they continued to look obsessively inward. Such foreign stories as were carried tended mainly to be Indian home news abroad (not least India's relations with Pakistan, Bangladesh, Sri Lanka, and China); advocates of "development" news (about the rural economy, farming, water supplies, birth control) found very little such news in the major newspapers.[32]

---

[29] Krishan Bhatia, *Indira: A Biography of Prime Minister Gandhi*, London: Angus and Robertson, 1974: 277.

[30] Sol. J. Sorabjee, *The Emergency, Censorship and the Press in India, 1975–77*, London: Writers and Scholars Educational Trust, 1977; Michael Henderson, *Experiment with Untruth*, New Delhi: Macmillan, 1977. George Verghese, "Press Censorship Under Indira Gandhi," in Philip C. Horton (ed.), *The Third World and Press Freedom*, New York: Praeger, 1978: 220–30; S. K. Aggarwal, *Media Credibility*, New Delhi: Mittal Publications, 1989.

[31] K. K. Sharma, "Press Law Outrages Indian Opposition," *Financial Times*, September 1, 1988; David Housego, "Indian Press Wins a Moral Crusade," *Financial Times*, September 13, 1988.

[32] A study of two big English-language dailies and two big Telugu dailies in 1995 found that only 5.8 percent of content dealt with "development". D. V. R. Murthy, "Developmental News Coverage in the Indian Press," *Media Asia*, Vol. 27/1, 2000: 24–29, 53.

Broadly the big newspapers reflect their urban, affluent, educated, and high caste readerships. In all countries, of course, the press has its hierarchical aspects that are linked to general inequality, education, and hierarchy. In India the hierarchical and pyramidal aspect is especially salient for additional reasons: The leading newspapers are mostly entrenched publications, older, for example, than many of the daily newspapers of continental Europe. The most recently launched of the leading general English-language dailies was the *Indian Express*, which began in 1932. In contrast, the two current main political parties are relatively new creations. There was a traditionally sharp hierarchy within the press in terms of English, Hindi, and other languages. Also deeply affecting the Indian press is the very uneven spread of education (with large numbers of university graduates and huge numbers of illiterates).

The Indian national newspaper industry's general elite emphasis has been reflected in the higher prestige of English-language publications, in its urban character, and in its reliance on advertising finance. The elite emphasis has been marked by international standards. Film and women's interest magazines are plentiful but modest in circulation. The political capital, Delhi, is a bigger publisher of magazines than is the entertainment and commercial media capital of Mumbai. The most dynamic magazine sector of recent years has been the newsmagazine, exemplified by *India Today*.

Figure 11.5 *India Today* newsmagazine in Hindi (March 2006) and in English (November 2005). (Images provided by the author.)

By 2005 English-language daily newspapers had only 17 percent of total daily sales (and a lower percentage of daily readers). Hindi dailies had 32 percent of sales, and daily papers in other Indian languages accounted for 51 percent of daily sales. But the traditional salience of the English-language newspaper readership can scarcely be exaggerated. Many urban people (both at work and at home) speak "Hinglish"—a mix of Hindi, or Hindustani, and English. Similar mixes also occur in southern India (where more people read English than Hindi daily papers).

Speaking English was traditionally the key to a job in the British administration of India; an English education still is a key to high level jobs in central government and to many "corporate" jobs. English speaking correlates strongly with high caste background as well as the family's ability to pay the fees for English education.

Newspapers in India are overwhelmingly urban. Research indicates that nearly half of all urban adults in India do some reading of newspapers; in Delhi and Mumbai the proportion is about one-half, and in Kerala and Punjab more than half of urban adults read a daily. Other studies confirm that some slumdwellers manage to read a daily paper, but only a few percent of India's huge "rural" population read a daily paper. Studies of villages for several decades have indicated only a few lone newspaper purchasers per thousand villagers; often each village newspaper copy has reached more than a dozen readers or listeners.[33] But the main assumptions of Indian newspapers are urban; they focus on an urban classified advertising market. The people who distribute even the largest papers are invariably referred to as "hawkers." While large batches of copies do travel (by truck, train, or plane) to smaller cities, the assumption prevails that nearly all of the copies will be sold within a few miles of the city's central office.

Long before independence Indian newspapers relied heavily on advertising and subsidy. In the 1990s there was a sharply increased reliance on advertising. The *Times of India* (led by the business-oriented new young chief executive from the owning Jain family) cut its cover prices to semi-token levels (three U.S. cents, two U.K. pennies). The retail price thus has to be held sufficiently high to keep it just above wastepaper prices. Consequently, the elite English newspaper obtains some 90 percent of its revenue from advertising. In the early 1990s the newspapers were awash with a huge growth in advertising expenditure; however, from the mid-1990s onward much of this new consumer advertising went into television, and the newspapers had to revert to their traditional types of advertising. This has long meant, and still means today, heavy reliance on tender/contracts ads (often for government);

---

[33] Y. V. Lakshmana Rao, *Communication and Development: A Study of Two Indian Villages*, University of Minnesota Press, 1966; Paul Hartmann, B. R. Patil, and Anita Dighe, *The Mass Media and Village Life: An Indian Study*, New Delhi: Sage, 1989; Graham Jones, *The Toiling Word: Nurturing a Healthy Press for India's Rural Millions*, London: International Press Institute, 1979.

Figure 11.6
Selected matrimonial advertisements, *Times of India*. (Images provided by the author.)

classified advertising, especially for jobs and real estate; and "matrimonials," in which wealthier Indian parents have advertised for marriage partners for their children since the 1890s.

This salience of advertising revenue has several implications. The costs of Indian newspapers are dominated by newsprint (around 60 percent of total costs). The classified advertising ties the daily papers to the affluent and the urban. It forces big Indian newspapers to focus on specific city markets. It also puts a big emphasis on trying to be number one in that city because the market leading paper not only can charge more in absolute terms, but can also charge its advertisers more per thousand readers.

Consequently, the most successful papers have been the circulation leaders in the major language markets in the biggest cities. This phenomenon of the strong number one is very evident in most city-language newspaper markets. The *Times of India*, the *Hindustan Times*, and *The Hindu* were the dominant English papers in Bombay, Delhi, and Madras. Often there is one very dominant daily in the main language and main city of each state—for example, the Telugu-language *Eenadu* in Hyderabad. In other newspaper markets two leading newspapers are engaged in relentless competition with each other.

The leading English-language newspapers are mostly owned by traditional owning families. Some were launched by their owning families as instruments of nationalist opposition to the British; others were acquired from British owners 50 or more years ago. The *Times of India* and its group are owned by the Jain family. The *Hindustan Times* has long been owned by the Birla family, earlier generations of which were leading financiers of the Congress Party; Gandhi was actually assassinated in Birla House in Delhi, where the family company kept him in comfortable poverty. The *Indian Express* group has been controlled by the Goenka family, and *The Hindu* by the Kasturi family.

In the last quarter of the twentieth century total daily sales roughly trebled, which enabled the leading ownerships to become commercially strong. Concentration took place both between languages and between cities. Quite often a city's leading English-language daily and its leading Indian-language daily are owned by the same company; in some cases they occupy the same building and typically they offer advertisers combined rates. Big papers have become bigger by the second tactic of moving into additional cities. Several big newspapers also sold minority slices to foreign companies in the years around 2005.

The *Times of India*'s owning family company—Bennett Coleman—has been the most expansionist press force in India in recent decades. The company has a broad portfolio of magazines and other newspapers, including major Hindi and Marathi dailies; it is the dominant publisher in Mumbai and affluent Maharastra state. In 1961 the company launched a new daily, the *Economic Times*, which appears in pink; it looks like, and is quite similar to, the *Financial Times* of London. This financial daily has been extremely profitable and has helped to fund the company's second form of expansion into other cities across India. Between 1990 and 1997 the *Times of India* doubled its daily sale, with more than half of this sale now outside the base city of Mumbai. The *Times* was already strong in Delhi and other big northern cities, including Ahmedabad (Gujarat), Lucknow (UP), and Patna (Bihar). The *Times of India*'s successful invasions of other big city markets continued into the 2000s. India's computer software capital of Bangalore was the site of another *Times* triumph. The *Times of India* claimed in 2002 that it had just passed *USA Today* to become the world's largest selling broadsheet general English-language daily.

Three other large circulation English-language newspaper groups publish the *Indian Express*, the *Hindustan Times*, and *The Hindu*. Each of these papers has pursued a slightly different variation on the big city theme. The *Indian*

Express group prints in many locations (not always the largest city in the state) and was known for its belligerent opposition to a succession of governments. Both *The Hindu* and *Hindustan Times* have continued to focus on their big base city. All of these papers have a strong connection with Delhi (and with regional/local/city politics.) Also available in Delhi on the day of publication are several leading Hindi dailies and other English papers published in other northern cities.

Critics claim that today's big press is just the old "jute press" writ large. Most of these family companies are also major industrial and commercial players outside the media. There is a general understanding (one editor told me of an explicit agreement) that the paper does not criticize the owner's other businesses. This, however, is common international practice. The fact that they had other businesses did mean that newspaper owners felt vulnerable during Indira Gandhi's 1975–1977 emergency. But in more recent, and more freewheeling, times, this industrial backing probably makes these owners more (not less) formidable in the eyes of politicians. The leading family owners are significant players, not only in business and the media, but also in politics.

All Indira Radio, Soap, and Hindi Television-Cable-Satellite

Radio and television grew extremely slowly and were deliberately held back by successive Indian governments. Both radio and television took decades to progress from initial launch to effective mass medium.

Indian radio and television both awarded the English language an initial prominent role; as with film and press, there was a subsequent diminution of English language use and of Anglo-American media influence. In both radio and television an early phase of English and Hindi dominance changed into a subsequent phase of lone Hindi dominance. Finally, the 10 or so biggest regional languages became increasingly assertive in competition with Hindi; this sequence occurred first in radio and then in television.

Radio began in India in 1924 but it was only 50 years later—in the mid- and late 1970s—that Indian radio really became a mass medium. The Indian government deliberately held television back; it only became a big medium when, during 1987–1990, two (Hindi-language) religious soaps achieved super-popularity. From 1991 Indian television experienced a radical shift toward advertising finance and commercial entertainment. Initially the main competition was between new satellite/cable channels and the state broadcaster (Doordashan) for the Hindi-speaking audience. But increasingly in the later 1990s and onward the most dramatic change was a huge development of regional television output in the large regional languages.

Many Western, and Anglo-American, media accounts of Indian television have portrayed Rupert Murdoch as conducting a takeover of Indian television. This was an absurd exaggeration. The new channels of the 1990s only became seriously successful with biggish audiences when they Indianized their programming for the Hindi-speaking public.

Given successive Indian governments' policy of, in practice, preventing the growth of electronic media, change was likely to come from outside stimulus. This happened in radio, with the major early shaping done by the British BBC. Indian radio only moved toward popular programming when a station in Sri Lanka began transmitting Indian film music into India. India's eventual reluctant move into television was strongly influenced by Pakistan and the fact that Pakistani television, from across the border, could be received in nearby Indian cities such as Amritsar. Cable television in the 1990s was following in the traditional—foreign influence—pattern when it used new satellite channels uplinked from Hong Kong.

The pattern of extremely slow radio growth began under the British; but, in the first years of independence, radio's progress was agonizingly slow. Despite the Nehru government's earnest wish to build and consolidate the new nation, radio's potential for reaching out, relatively cheaply, to a mainly illiterate population was not seen as significant. The first five-year plans focused on agriculture, steel, and manufacturing. Radio was allocated between 0.1 percent and 0.2 percent of total government investment in the first three five-year plans. Radio was seen in the 1950s as an educational mechanism, but the emphasis was on the high and the classical, in both the Hindi (not Hindustani) language and in music (classical Indian).

The years 1960–1975 saw slightly quicker radio growth. India's super-popular film music at last got onto Indian radio, especially (following competition from Sri Lanka) with the Vividh Bharati music channel; however, even by 1975 it was only operating in larger cities and only for 13 hours a day. British/BBC terminology of the post-1945 period was still in evidence. In 1975 "news" and "spoken word (talks)" took up 32.7 percent of Indian national radio time, "classical" and "devotional" music had 20.5 percent, and "light" and film music only 9.3 percent.[34] Even as late as 1975 fairly little output was aimed at the then 80 percent of the population living in rural areas. Only 1.3 percent of radio programming was specifically aimed at women and 1.2 percent at children.

All India Radio was a monopoly service located within the Ministry of Information and Broadcasting. As a segment of this government department, AIR was part of Delhi's bureaucratic hierarchy. Indeed, AIR in 1972 (when visited by this writer) seemed still to be modeled on the BBC of the 1940s. AIR's headquarters behaved rather like the BBC during the 1939–1945 war; Delhi played the role of London, and multiple language transmissions were translated from a master English text—just as had happened in the BBC's transmissions in numerous languages to German-occupied Europe. Before AIR could broadcast any item (including the day's news) it seemed to require several signatures. In 1972 AIR was in quite a celebratory mood, with

---

[34] M. V. Desai, *Communication Policies in India*, Paris: Unesco, 1977: 56–64, 86–87.

much retrospective programming about "our war heroes" (from the previous year's victory over Pakistan). But seeking one's superior's signature was still a major activity; there were huge piles of faded buff files, some of which looked to be left behind by the British 25 years earlier.

Like many public broadcasting operations in the early 1970s, AIR was heavily politically influenced. Since the Congress Party had been in power for so long—and since the current Congress prime minister was Indira Gandhi—AIR was inevitably referred to as "All Indira Radio." Commenting on the 1975 emergency, the then director general of AIR later wrote that the new Gandhi censorship had little fresh impact, since AIR (unlike the press) was already censored.[35]

After the 1975–1977 emergency, AIR and radio grew more rapidly, especially until the late 1980s when, at last, the majority of Indian households had a radio set. By then radio/cassetteplayers were popular, but this also was an indication of AIR's failure. Many people wanted a radio set in order to listen to taped film music.

AIR's "development" and family planning programming was rather half-hearted; it was too urban, too Delhi, too bureaucratic. The music output also was half-hearted. And the news, its biggest single output, was widely regarded as politically biased toward Congress (and subsequently toward other incumbent governments).

The advertising industry was yet another relevant constituency that AIR antagonized. AIR carried its first radio commercials in 1967. In the 1970s decade AIR, as the only Indian outlet for broadcast advertising, did steadily increase its advertising. But already by 1985 television was beating radio as an advertising medium. In the 1990s radio had only about 2 percent of Indian advertising expenditure. By 1998 TV's audience was 1.5 times radio's audience, but television had 17 times as much advertising (34 percent versus 2 percent).

Above all, radio—as a medium—had failed to establish a positive image or reputation. The Mumbai media and advertising communities (by 1999) regarded it as old-fashioned, biased, partisan, bureaucratic, and rural; they complained that AIR did little audience research and then took one full year to make the results available. At the other the end of the hierarchy, radio was least listened to by the uneducated, by older people, by women, and by the rural people. Moreover (in contrast to TV) many people had a radio in the house but did not listen to it; they lacked the motivation and/or the cash to repair the set and to provide it with batteries. Radio entered a period of decline that continued through most of the 1990s.

It was not until around 1987 (four decades after independence) that television at last became a popular medium, primarily in northern India. In 1984 the state TV broadcaster (Doordashan) launched its first super-successful Hindi soap opera, called *Hum Log*. This triggered a soap explosion of many

---

[35] P. C. Chatterji, *The Adventure of Indian Broadcasting*, New Delhi: Konark Publishers, 1998: 254.

more Indian-made soap series and a boom in advertising; much of the advertising was for soap products. Then in the 1990s came another explosion of numerous new channels, which again bubbled over with Indian soap fiction programming. There were also massive quantities of advertising, up to 15 minutes per hour in prime time by the late 1990s; and, with many TV ads running for only 10 or 15 seconds, the Indian TV viewer was presented with thousands of soap, shampoo, and detergent commercials each year.

During these soap explosions after 1984 many Indian politicians and journalists complained about alien, global, and American influences. But to many outside observers, Indian television still seemed a remarkably inward-looking offspring of the inward-looking Indian film industry. India's decision not to have television for its first 25 years of statehood was both a cause and an effect of India's obsessively inward-looking gaze. In 1972 even people like editors of daily newspapers had only a sketchy idea of what TV was. In 1972 even advertising agency executives referred to TV advertising as a prospect for some uncertain future date. To the Indian elite—not traveling abroad and not yet having television or TV news—most of the world (beyond southern Asia) seemed a long way away. This elite had not seen the daily TV news from Vietnam in the 1960s. The one foreign medium that was often mentioned was BBC radio, welcomed especially for its accurate daily news (in English and Hindi).

The extremely slow Indian introduction of television went through four distinct stages. First was an experimental stage with one low-powered transmitter in Delhi; this phase finally ended when a second transmitter began operating in Bombay in 1972. Second, two stations were launched in 1973 in politically sensitive areas of the northwest, close to the Pakistan border; India was being dragged reluctantly into TV by the "threat" of Pakistan TV across the border, which could be received inside India. Third, in 1975–1977 television was extended to five other large cities. Fourth—after another very long pause of five years—television was extended to seven more major cities and state capitals. By 1982 (after a decade-long expansion), then, television was still only available in nine cities.

In 13 years (1972–1985) television was rolled out to just 16 cities. Most of these cities were state capitals, and television was located like radio, under the Ministry of Information and Broadcasting. Television was conceived as a service that (like Indian politics) would operate along an axis between Delhi and the state capitals. Overall the choice of location reflected a decision to give priority to the more politically delicate regions, (especially the north, southeast, and Assam). The urban emphasis was very marked. As late as 1982 India had only 19 TV transmitters—grossly inadequate for a large and mountainous country.

Doordashan (DD) in the 1980s had experienced what in retrospect some saw as a golden age of public service television. Between 1980 and 1990 India's total TV sets increased from 1.5 million to 28 million. Throughout the decade most TV viewers could receive just one DD channel, which carried a lot of news (in English and Hindi), plus factual and semi-educational programming. This pill was sugared with super-popular entertainment in the form mostly of cinema films.

The first super-popular Indian TV soap was the twice-a-week, 156-episode *Hum Log*, which ran on Doordashan in Hindi in 1984–1985. *Hum Log* had initially been designed as dispensing birth control advice in family fiction form. *Hum Log* was successful partly because it was the first really entertaining, long-running Indian TV drama. *Hum Log* also employed a superstar of the Hindi film industry, Ashok Kumar (who still found time to star in 12 movies in 1984); Kumar contributed an epilogue—a sage comment or two—at the end of each episode. *Hum Log* was also an early illustration of what would become a major problem for Doordashan, as the Delhi-based public broadcaster. *Hum Log* in Hindi was super-popular in the Hindi-speaking north; but despite the much discussed "event" status of this soap, one study showed that 52 percent of respondents in the big city of Madras (Chennai) had not viewed even one of the 156 episodes.[36]

After 1984, as the number of TV sets increased, numerous other new soap series (as well as movies and comedies) established new record TV-viewing numbers. But it was two religious soaps, *Ramayan* and *Mahabharat*, together running from early 1987 to mid-1990, that constituted the biggest landmark "event" in Indian television. Each Sunday morning, as the fresh episode was transmitted, the streets and fields of northern India were deserted. Many poor people, who did not own a TV set, listened outside the windows of people wealthy enough to possess a TV.[37]

To many Indian viewers these religious epic soap series constituted a religious experience. But the religious soaps had implications for several other aspects of Indian life beyond the purely religious. These soaps constituted a boost for television in general and for the public broadcaster, Doordashan, in particular. From 1987 to 1990 the number of television households doubled from 13 million to 28 million. The religious soaps also illustrated that Indian television had great potential, which had indeed been deliberately restrained by government policy. India's film industry created a substantial resource upon which TV could draw. The religious epics on TV followed one of Indian cinema's traditional genres—the religious-historical epic or "mythological" film. Indian TV could also draw upon the film industry's large supply of skilled actors, writers, singers, and technicians.

The religious soaps were also a boost for northern India, for Hindi, and for the nationalist political party, the Bharatiya Janata Party (BJP). These central

---

[36] Arvind Singhal and Everett Rogers, *India's Information Revolution*, Newbury Park, CA: Sage, 1990: 88–121.

[37] Christopher Thomas, "Normal Service After Indian TV Epic," *The Times* (London), July 13, 1990; Philip Lutgendorf, "All in the (Raghu) Family: A Video Epic in Cultural Context," in Lawrence A. Babb and Susan S. Wadley (eds.), *Media and the Transformation of Religion in South Asia*, Philadelphia: University of Pennsylvania Press, 1995: 217–51.

stories of the Hindu religion are indeed based in northern India, mostly in or around the state of Uttar Pradesh and near the Ganges (Ganga) River. In the *Mahabharat* series this northern Indian location was emphasized; the clothing worn by both men and women in the series was northern Indian; so also was the music and the dance. The language used was not just Hindi, but "a precise and refined Hindi that was representative of a small section of north central India."[38] These northern and Hindi emphases were consistent with a common preference at "The Centre" (Delhi), and in Doordashan, for Hindi as the major broadcasting language. But this was also less acceptable to the majority of Hindus outside northern India who did not speak or understand Hindi. Soon after the phase of the super-popular religious soaps in 1987–1990, Doordashan did make a sudden lurch toward providing new television channels in major regional languages. But Doordashan may have ignored this need (and popular demand) for too long, partly because it was startled by the degree of popularity achieved by its Hindi soaps.

Finally, the religious soaps were controversial simply because they were religious programming; Indian governments up to 1987 had striven with some success to maintain a secular, nonreligious state and government within a strongly religious society. Muslims were equal with Hindus. How then did "The Centre" allow this Hindu propaganda? As the public broadcaster, Doordashan needed the support of the incumbent government to engage in its religious soap project. The Congress Party, whose traditional coalition by the mid-1980s (with Rajiv Gandhi as prime minister, 1984–1989) was in very serious disarray, hoped that it might benefit from some positive, but tolerant, Hindu programming. However, it was two nationalist political parties that seemed to benefit more from the warm, pro-Hindu feelings. In fact, the Indian prime minister (Chandra Shekhar) of 1990–1991 was from the Janata Dal Party.

But it was the rise of the BJP that was most controversial. The BJP were the main new political force in India in the 1990s; from the 1998 election, the BJP entered a period of prime ministerial power (Vajpayee) and coalition leadership. It was widely believed by other Indian politicians that the BJP had exploited the warm pro-Hindu mood of the late 1980s. The BJP was accused of encouraging violent confrontations at Ayodhya (Uttar Pradesh) where, in December 1992, a Hindu mob destroyed a mosque and killed many Muslims. The subsequent rioting and death toll in 1992–1993 were especially bad in Bombay (Mumbai); a decade later in 2002 Hindus killed hundreds of Muslims (after Muslims had killed scores of Hindus) in another prosperous western state, Gujarat. The BJP was a national coalition leader from 1998; but the BJP was itself a coalition of more moderate Hindus and other fundamentalist zealots (especially in Maharastra and Gujarat). Critics could see the BJP as a party that flirted with violence because violence created helpful press

---

[38] Ananda Mitra, "An Indian Religious Soap Opera and the Hindu Image," *Media, Culture and Society*, Vol. 16, 1994: 149–55.

excitement and encouraged Hindi newspaper editors into active partisan support.[39]

One criticism of Doordashan was that its religious epics of 1987–1990 suffused an ethnic-cleansing political party with a warm glow of religious romance and respectability. Also, southern critics could assert, the religious soaps provided a glowing justification for Brahmin supremacy and for traditional—and unchanging—caste inequality.

Song, Soap, and Satellite: Hindi Television Goes Commercial

During the early 1990s both India and Indian television experienced a period of rapid change, an "opening" to economic liberalization, and a reduction in government ownership and controls. The Indian economy and Indian television became more commercially competitive, and both grew rapidly in the early 1990s. Doordashan was drastically changed from its previous dependence on public subsidy and its provision of a single channel across most of India. Coming from outside India in 1991 were that familiar odd couple of supposedly global importance, CNN and *The Bold and the Beautiful*. But although these foreign influences were important, their greater significance was as triggers of internal Indian change. Major newspaper groups, anticipating new media business possibilities, became increasingly critical of Doordashan, which they painted as monopolistic, arrogant, government-dominated, and unpopular.

This early 1990s opening to competition, and acceptance of foreign (English-language) channels, had led by the mid-1990s to a huge increase in the amount of Hindi-language programming. Only in 1987 did DD begin putting out morning and afternoon (1989) programming. But from 1980 audiocassettes, another way to hear film music, exploded in popularity, and there was also a boom in the recording of both old and new music within many different local traditions, dialects, languages, and political viewpoints. India became a significant audiotape manufacturer, making 217 million tapes in 1991.[40] Many thousands of "video parlours" were established as mini-cinemas, where a (pirated) Indian feature film could be viewed for a fraction of the theater entrance price. A similar service became common on longer distance bus journeys.

Cable TV began in India around 1981, and it also depended on the VCR and films on cassette. Especially in Bombay, small local entrepreneurs provided a cable movie service by stringing wires down streets to 100 or 200 homes. With pirated films, and a small weekly bribe to the local police, the

---

[39] Arvind Rajagopal, *Politics After Television: Religious Nationalism and the Reshaping of the Indian Public*, Cambridge, UK: Cambridge University Press, 2001: 151–211.

[40] Peter Manuel, *Cassette Culture: Popular Music and Technology in North India*, Chicago: University of Chicago Press, 1993: 60–63.

cable operator was in business. Four thousand such "cable operators" were believed to be active by 1989.[41] By late 1993 their trade association ambitiously claimed that India had about 100,000 local cable operators.[42]

Yet another indication of the inadequacy of the single Doordashan TV channel (and its news operation) was the brief appearance around 1990 of several services offering news coverage on videocassette. These news cassettes could be rented and in some cases were also played on cable. One such service was owned by the *Times of India* and another by *India Today* magazine.

In addition to cable and cassettes, the third key ingredient of televisual change was the satellite. During 1991 two English-language satellite services arrived in India, CNN and Star. CNN's coverage of the active phase of the Gulf War in the early weeks of 1991 was seen only in a few luxury hotels and in a few press newsrooms; but it received massive coverage in the newspapers. Also in 1991 the first Star channels (from Hong Kong) reached India via satellite; these had a wider impact via existing local cable operators who invested in the necessary dish antenna.

Calendar year 1993 saw a rapid expansion of commercial television and an aggressive, and sometimes chaotic, fight back by Doordashan, the previously somnolent giant of Indian television. Within a two-year period (1992–1993) cable expanded from 0.4 million to 7.3 million homes. Clearly by 1993 cable had gone beyond a small elite and into a wider market. Two new Hindi-language channels (Asia TV and Jain TV), added to Zee (which launched in 1992), meant that there were now three Hindi commercial channels showing mainly films and entertainment; this already pointed to the future of commercial TV with the use of Indian languages. Jain TV (controlled by a BJP politician) even carried some election programming for the 1993 state assembly elections—an early indication that commercial TV could also be political TV.

Doordashan was struggling in 1993 to generate fresh programming for fresh channels. Lacking the required investment cash, DD decided to hand over some TV slots to independent producers on a sponsorship basis. Using a "first-come, first-served" approach (common in tendering for Indian government contracts) DD found a line of prospective producers queuing in the street in late June 1993, some 10 days before the due date. This event was neatly timed for the late June start of the monsoon, which arrived on schedule to deluge the waiting day-and-night queue. Meanwhile the newspapers were actively involved in the first-come bidding process, which they headlined as "FCFS." The leading newspaper groups were involved as bidders, with their representatives out there in the monsoon-drenched queue. These top newspapers also bitterly attacked Doordashan and its incompetence; the four

[41] Indrajit Lahiri, "Era of Change: Broadcasting in India," *World Broadcast News*, November 1989: 30–36.
[42] S. C. Bhatt, *Satellite Invasion of India*, New Delhi: Gyan Publishing, 1994: 44–59.

leading English-language dailies also challenged some of DD's arrangements in court (and won).[43]

Doordashan had already (May 1993) begun its commercial sponsorship system; here the public broadcaster (driven by financial and competitive necessity) suddenly flipped into full commercial mode. The bidding producer was awarded the time slot and 10 minutes of advertising time per hour in return for a payment; the producer was then free to sell on the advertising minutes and fairly free also in making the programming. In 1993 Doordashan also launched five new DD channels; four specialist "themed" channels were soon canceled.

Only one new DD channel—the "Metro" entertainment channel—was a success. It was aimed at the large metro cities and was a youth-oriented, middle-class entertainment channel (soon officially renamed DD2). Doordashan largely dropped the approach of specialized "themed" channels. Doordashan's Metro/DD2 was a Hindi general urban entertainment channel (which left most of the rural and public service duties to DD1). Doordashan in 1994 introduced a major reorganization, involving 13 DD channels. Ten channels (DD4–13) would be entertainment channels in 10 different regional languages. Doordashan pointed out the future path both for itself and for the commercial channels—Indian entertainment programming in Hindi and in all of the major regional languages.

Indian television in the early 1990s thus switched from mainly public finance to mainly commercial finance. Doordashan was told in 1992 that in the future 80 percent of its funding was to come from advertising (instead of the previous 20 percent reliance on advertising). Consequently, in the early 1990s there was a need for huge new amounts of advertising revenue. Miraculously the government's 1991 "freeing" (or loosening) of the Indian economy did indeed lead to a massive increase in total Indian advertising expenditure. Television advertising expenditure quadrupled during 1993–1998 with a compound annual growth rate of 33 percent.[44] The biggest commercial advertiser in India had long been Unilever; other leading advertising spenders were Colgate Palmolive and Procter and Gamble—the full assault force of world soap, toothpaste, detergents, and shampoos.

The rapid growth of cable television in 1990s India has been described as a "Murdoch Revolution." But all of the main commercializing forces were in action before Rupert Murdoch arrived on the Indian scene. Murdoch was mainly important as a financier, as someone willing to put money into cable networks that were losing money. Indian finance for cable was in short supply.

In 1993–1995 Murdoch invested in several existing TV enterprises. The key pioneer of Indian commercial cable was Subash Chandra, who launched

---

[43] S. C. Bhatt, *Satellite Invasion of India*, New Delhi, Gyan Publishing, 1994.
[44] Source: Hindustan Thompson.

Zee TV in 1992;[45] by January 1994 Murdoch had acquired 49.9 percent of Zee. Murdoch also acquired 49.9 percent of the UTV production house,[46] which was already delivering to Zee 500 contracted episodes of a popular game show. Murdoch had also acquired, in late 1993, Hong Kong–based Star television. Initially Murdoch continued with Star's five (predominantly English) channels. Star only achieved significant success in India after Murdoch, in October 1996, appointed Rathikant Basu (a former head of Doordashan) as his Indian chief executive.[47]

Another key Murdoch investment was in a young Indian soap producer, Ektaa Kapoor, and her production company, Balaji Telefilms; Kapoor made successful TV soaps from 1993 onward and in 1999 launched, on Murdoch's Star Plus, *Because the Mother-in-Law Was Once a Daughter-in-Law*, which in the early 2000s was India's most popular cable soap. By 2004 Kapoor was producing 15 of Indian cable's 20 most highly rated weekly shows, and News Corporation now owned 26 percent of her company. Another big Murdoch/News success occurred in 2000 in the form of the *Millionaire* quiz show featuring movie superstar Amitabh Bachchan.

News Corporation, Star Plus, and other Indian Star channels were successful in the early 2000s because most cable operators (including ones with very low channel capacity) wanted to carry Star Plus. But Star India suffered a large loss during its first decade in India. Murdoch, from the start, hoped to distribute direct-to-home TV by satellite, which would avoid conventional cable's loss of revenue to greedy local cable operators and pirates. But Murdoch was kept waiting on this for over a decade. Eventually, when in 2004–2005 direct-to-home (DTH) satellite TV was approved by the Indian government, News/Murdoch was awarded 20 percent (while the Tata industrial group had 80 percent) of one of the four DTH licenses.[48]

Loosely defined "soap opera" drama was much the biggest category of new programming appearing on the new commercial channels and on the DD2 (Metro) channel. In India the distinction between daily and weekly series was less marked than in many other national systems. With so many time slots to be filled (and languages potentially to be dubbed into) the prospects for reshowing were especially salient; most obviously, a 104-episode weekly series could be stripped (reshown daily) in the afternoon. Many leading actors, directors, and writers wanted to follow movie precedent and to be in more than just one weekly (52 episodes a year) series. The Indian TV serial norm was to record a one-hour show in about 12 hours (or one and a

---

[45] Chris Dziadul, "The A-Zee of Indian TV," *Television Business International*, July/August 1994: 16–18.
[46] Meredith Amdur and Anita Katyal, "India Spawns Production Boom," *Broadcasting and Cable International*, October 1996: 45–50.
[47] Anil Wanvari, "Star in a Storm," *Television Business International*, October 1997: 82–83.
[48] "India Paves Way for Two New DTH Broadcasters," *Screen Digest*, June 2005; Jo Johnson, "TV Chief Hopes That Her Star Will Keep Rising," *Financial Times*, November 29, 2005.

half shifts) of studio time. Television actors obviously earned less per hour of finished product than did film actors; but a star TV actor, making 104 episodes a year of two successful series, could make more money than most film stars.

The prime-time soaps were aimed at the broad 15 percent of the urban middle class. The predominant form was the *family* series—often featuring one or more three-generational families with the emphasis on women characters and on such relationships as mother-in-law with daughter-in-law. As earlier inhibitions relaxed during the 1990s, plots tended to focus more on intrafamily conflict and extramarital relationships. For the casual foreign visitor, it was initially quite hard to differentiate between soap programming and soap commercials; both serials and commercials seemed to feature much the same families, the same cool and comfortable homes, the same consumer durables and furniture, and the same family conflicts—often resolved with the younger and older generations reaching smiling agreement in the closing seconds.

Soap and TV drama production gradually concentrated into a few big production houses. By 2001–2002 Balaji Telefilms was making over 20 soap drama series for Star, Sony, Zee, and other Indian networks. By 2002, 10 seconds of commercial time during a popular soap cost about $10,000.[49]

Although the Indian government was frequently surprised by the cassette/cable/satellite/new channels' offensive moves, the government still retained very significant powers. Like many other governments, it repeatedly changed its policy ideas and frequently postponed promised decisions. The Indian government for long continued to make the foreign channels up-link to their satellites from outside India. The government continued to decide Doordashan's broad strategy, to control key appointments, and to monitor the news. Senior DD executives themselves continued to have considerable power and to use it in an arbitrary manner.

During 1991–1995 "everything changed" in Indian television, but much also stayed the same. In terms of language, the main change was from one DD Hindi language channel to (for urban cable customers) several Hindi language channels. Most (rural) people, in fact, still in 1995 only had the option of the one, DD1, channel. But those city people who could afford cable had DD1, plus Metro (DD2) and a new Hindi channel from Zee, which specialized in Hindi films. Sony soon followed this Hindi path by acquiring the TV rights to a huge batch of Hindi films.

By the mid-1990s the overall Indian television picture was dominated by the Hindi language. A decade later, in 2005, many discussions of Indian

[49] Khozen Merchant, "Balaji Abandons Channel Nine Deal," *Financial Times*, May 10, 2001; Rashme Sehgal, "Queen of Soaps," *Multichannel News International*, February/March 2002; Shilpa Bharatan Iyer, "Kapoor's Sari Sudsers Hit Gold," *Variety*, September 20–26, 2004.

television asserted or implied that Hindi television—coming from Zee, Star, and Sony with some help from Doordashan—had a dominant Indian audience share. But English-language media—such as the *Times of India* and *India Today*—had financial interests in Hindi newspapers and magazines and Hindi television, and they tended to focus on the cable homes. However, in 2005 still only about 30 percent of India's households had cable TV. In round numbers India had 200 million households, 100 million households with television, and 60 million households with cable; Star TV was reaching about 40 million (or 20 percent of) Indian households. The cable share of population was actually less than the household share because affluent urban households had fewer people than did poor rural households. However, it was the affluent cable households—enthusiastic buyers of branded products—that most interested the big advertisers.

Much of the 2000–2001 ratings success of the Star Plus channel depended on a single super-popular quiz show; the Indian version of *Who Wants to Be a Millionaire?* offered 10 million rupees as the top prize and was hosted by the movie superstar Amitabh Bachchan. The show ran from 9 to 10 pm four nights a week. As with other super-popular TV shows, this one hugely boosted the network's entire evening prime-time schedule. Bachchan was reportedly paid $18 million for the first two years. This sum, together with the paid promotion, probably exceeded the entire advertising revenue attracted by the one-hour programming slot.

Why did Bachchan[50] (a bigger superstar in Bollywood than were either John Wayne or Clint Eastwood in Hollywood) agree to take on such a low status role as TV quiz host? Bachchan—after being the reigning superstar of the 1970s and 1980s—had suffered a career decline and had also lost heavily while operating his own movie production company. Bachchan badly needed the *Millionaire* money. He proved to be a professionally competent and sympathetic host; he read the questions both in exemplary Hindi and in perfect English.

Was this Americanization or Indianization? *Who Wants to Be a Millionaire?* was in fact created by the British Celador company. But its super-popularity in India depended on Bachchan as super-star (the TV show also reignited his movie and advertising careers); this was the first big prize Indian quiz show. One report claimed that after just two months on air, *Millionaire* was attracting 600,000 telephone calls a day. Moreover, the Indian public was familiar with quiz shows on both radio and TV. School quiz contests were popular in Calcutta by the early 1960s.[51] The entrepreneurial input for

[50] Lalit Vachani, "Bachchan—alias: The Many Faces of a Film Icon," in Christiane Brosius and Melissa Butcher (eds.), *Image Journeys: Audio Visual Media and Cultural Change in India*, New Delhi: Sage, 1999: 199–230.
[51] Labonita Ghosh, "Quizzical," *India Today*, metro section, March 29, 1999.

Millionaire was derived from Rupert Murdoch's experience with premium content on Sky in the United Kingdom and Fox in the United States.[52]

Regions Versus Delhi: Stars, Media, Political Bosses, Language

Dominance of both regional and central politics by Delhi and the Congress Party weakened in the 1960s and disappeared in the 1970s.

The 11 largest non-Hindi-speaking states have 55 percent of the Indian population; each of these states has its own film-TV, newspapers, magazines, and radio. Each of these states has its own leading language. Against these 11 states the four main Hindi-speaking states have 36 percent of population.

India's system of states is sometimes compared with the U.S. system of 50 states; but India's 28 states are in several ways more comparable to the 25 states of the European Union.

The state chief ministers and other leading Indian politicians operate alongside strong regional, as well as national, media. These media play a significant part in the Indian political tendency to throw the rascals out. Major state newspapers and other media that helped a politician to win one election often reverse their position and seek to throw the incumbent out at the next election.

Even in the largest states (both Hindi and non-Hindi) there is considerable media concentration. Often just two main newspaper groups oppose each other commercially and also attack each other's current political favorites.

Major regional language media are typically involved in numerous other conflicts—with the local Hindi media, with media in next door states, and with national media in English and Hindi. Many of the regional media are opposed to the public broadcaster, Doordashan. In several states there are media companies active in both print and electronic media and they tend shamelessly to promote their own company's interests while denigrating the competition.

---

[52] Amos Owen Thomas and Keval J. Kumar, "Copied from Without and Cloned from Within: India in the Global Television Format Business," in Albert Moran and Michael Keane (eds.), *Television Across Asia: Television Industries, Programme Formats and Globalization*, London: RoutledgeCurzon, 2004: 122–37; Melissa Butcher, *Transitional Television, Cultural Identity and Change: When Star Came to India*, New Delhi: Sage, 2003; Vanita Kohli, *The Indian Media Business*, New Delhi: Sage/Response Books, 2003: 59–107; R. Sukumar, "Murdoch vs Ambani vs Chandra," *Business Today* (Mumbai), March 14, 2004: 52–56; Norbert Wildermuth, "Negotiating a Globalised Modernity: Images of the 'New' Indian Woman on Satellite Television," in Gitte Stald and Thomas Tufte (eds.), *Global Encounters: Media and Cultural Transformation*, Luton, UK: Luton University Press, 2002: 195–215; Jane Fine and Arti Mathur, "Crowds Roar for Quiz Crore," *Variety*, July 17, 2000; Manjeet Kripalani, "Can Murdoch's Star Keep Rising in India?" *Business Week* (Europe), September 17, 2001: 26; Gupta Smita, "Star India's Focus on Innovation Pays Off," *Media* (Hong Kong), July 26, 2002; Wendy Goldman Rohm, *The Murdoch Mission*, New York: John Wiley, 2002: 195–214.

These conditions have helped to give very high media profiles to the leading politicians in the larger states. These high profile politicians—used literally to having their feet kissed by supporters and supplicants—tend to make preemptive political strikes in various directions. Accused of "corruption"— and of using the state police to pursue political vendettas—these high profile regional politicians are often in major legal difficulties and sometimes in prison; accusations of political assassinations (of journalists and others) are not uncommon. These high profile regional politicians become leading players in India's national political soap melodrama.

Many new media and political trends have begun in India's four southern states; each has its own language—Tamil Nadu has Tamil, Andhra Pradesh has Telugu, Karnataka has Kannada, and Kerala has Malayalam. These four states together had 222 million people at the 2001 census. These southern states have traditionally had levels of literacy and education above the Indian average.

The growth of new Indian media has typically occurred in English and then in Hindi; finally has come a boom in some 11 other languages, with the four southern languages in the lead. This happened in film; by the late 1980s over 60 percent of all Indian films were being made in the four southern languages. In daily newspapers a boom in Hindi daily sales was followed by a bigger boom of daily sales in 11 other Indian languages. By 2001, of the five highest selling non-English dailies, two were Hindi dailies published in the northern Hindi belt; the three others were all southern dailies—*Dina Thanti* published in Chennai in Tamil, *Eenadu* published in Telugu in Hyderabad, and *Malayalam Marorama* published in Malayalam in Kottayam. All of these big dailies in fact publish each day in numerous localized editions across their home state.

The four southern states were also in the forefront of the spread of satellite cable television across India. There were already three Tamil language channels by 1995. By 2000 there were seven channels in Tamil, five in Telugu, four in Malayalam, and eight in Kannada. Cable channels in languages other than Hindi and English numbered 46 (out of a total 100) in 2000[53] and about 100 (out of a total 200) in 2005.

The Tamil and Telugu media industries were the leaders in many non-Hindi and non-English media developments. Tamil Nadu was important not least because, even in the 1920s and 1930s, it was suspicious of the Congress Party as seeking to exercise Brahmin high caste dominance over all of India.[54] After 1947 Indian independence, Tamil Nadu—still the "Madras presidency"—showed some signs of separatism.

---

[53] Prasun Sonwalkar, "India: Makings of Little Cultural/Media Imperialism," *Gazette*, December 2001: 505–19.

[54] A. Ganesan, *The Press in Tamil Nadu and the Struggle for Freedom 1917–1937*, New Delhi: Mittal Publications, 1988; S. V. Rajadurai and V. Geetha, "Tamilnadu Claims Its Linguistic Heritage," *Media Development*, 1, 1992: 21–23.

In the years after 1947 many politicians in the Congress Party supported the notion of Hindi as the national language that would consolidate the new Indian nation. As prime minister, however, Nehru adopted the position that Hindi should not be forced on states that did not want it. In the meanwhile the Hindi film industry was popular across India and was helping the Hindi project. However, after Nehru died in 1964, some Congress politicians tried to push Hindi more strongly; this especially affected southern India, where Congress was in power, but where Hindi was not widely spoken. Tamil Nadu was in the lead in opposing the introduction of Hindi in the schools. "Language riots" began in early 1965 with the police killing 66 people, while several young men committed suicide. Much of the motivation behind the rioting was not so much in support of Tamil as it was against Hindi; professionals, civil servants, and students who spoke good English, as well as native Tamil, did not want to have to compete for Hindi-speaking jobs. A new political party, the DMK, came into being to challenge Congress Party dominance in Tamil Nadu. The DMK triumphed over Congress in Tamil Nadu in 1967. The DMK was highly successful at appealing to most caste, subregional, and ethnic segments. The DMK appealed to the rural areas, to the poor, and to women, without alienating the professionals and upper castes.[55] The DMK Party, and other breakaways from it, were clearly connected to the Tamil film industry. Five different film industry personalities served for a period as chief minister of Tamil Nadu during 1967–1990.

The most remarkable of these Tamil movie-politicians was M. G. Ramachandran, universally known as MGR. He was the Tamil film industry's all-time superstar and did much to deliver the combined film-political appeal. His fan clubs of young men[56] doubled as political helpers to the great star politician; MGR also appealed strongly to women (film fans and voters). In his films he played a fisherman, a road sweeper, a gardener, and other modest (low caste) roles. Despite much on-screen fighting and violence, his films (and his politics) supported education and motherhood while opposing alcohol and alcohol-induced violence against women.

MGR himself broke away from the DMK, founded his new ADMK party, and became chief minister of Tamil Nadu in 1977. The ADMK (like the DMK) was somewhat vague as to policy, but was adroit at positioning itself in the political marketplace. MGR was a flamboyant chief minister who specialized in heavily publicized acts of personal charity, such as the handing out of flood relief. His policy of providing free school meals was genuine and highly popular. His political life seemed miraculously to match cinematic

---

[55] Narendra Subramanian, *Ethnicity and Populist Mobilisation: Political Parties, Citizens and Democracy in South India*, New Delhi: Oxford University Press, 1999; Kanchan Chandra, *Why Ethnic Parties Succeed: Patronage and Ethnic Head Counts in India*, Cambridge, UK: Cambridge University Press, 2004: 275–81.

[56] Sara Dickey, *Cinema and the Urban Poor in South India*, Cambridge, UK: Cambridge University Press, 1993: 148–72; M. S. S. Pandian, *The Image Trap: M. G. Ramachandran in Film and Politics*, New Delhi: Sage, 1992.

requirements; he was severely wounded by a fellow actor (who had often played opposite him as a villain). MGR was seriously ill during three separate election campaigns. After his death there was a bitter political succession struggle between his widow and a former mistress. The winner was the former mistress, Jayaram Jayalalitha, who had herself been a glamorous movie star, making 49 films in one five-year period (1969–1973). She subsequently became a heavyweight 1990s politician in her own right, serving as chief minister of Tamil Nadu in two separate spells. Jayalalitha was a remarkably belligerent politician, even by Indian standards. She fought fiercely with the Karnataka government over the sharing of water from the Cauvery River; in this recurrent water war, movie stars from both states were prominent.[57] Jayalalitha had another war with *The Hindu* newspaper of Chennai and its distinguished editor, Narasimhan Ram.[58] She established her own cable TV channel, which, however, soon collapsed. When her AIADMK alliance with the BJP was heavily defeated in 2004, she still had several pending legal cases—including one that accused her of siphoning large amounts of cash out of the Tamil Nadu government finances.

Long before 2004, however, she was recognized across India by the single name Jayalalitha; on several occasions she demonstrated the power that an adroit regional power broker can exercise over "The Centre" in Delhi. For example, in 1999 while out of office at home in Chennai, Jayalalitha withdrew two AIADMK ministers from the BJP-Vajpayee central government in Delhi. She also threatened to remove all 18 AIADMK members of parliament from the BJP-led coalition. Under the prevailing Delhi conditions of coalition dependence on numerous small regional parties, Jayalalitha could—and did—strut the stage of the national media[59] and intimidate the incumbent prime minister of India. She also added another letter to the end of her name to become Jayalalithaa.

The neighboring state of Andhra Pradesh also saw a movie star turned politician, N. T. Rama Rao (NTR), become chief minister of the state (1983–1989) at the head of a new political party (Telegu Desam) and in opposition to the Congress Party. NTR only entered politics after a long career as the reigning superstar of the Telugu film industry; in the 1960s he starred in 107 films. He specialized in "mythological" films and played the role of Krishna 17 times. But in 1995 the movie star politician was deposed by his own son-in-law, N. Chandrababu Naidu, who became chief minister. Naidu was another high profile regional politician who claimed that he was the CEO, not just the chief minister, of Andhra Pradesh. Naidu was another remarkably belligerent politician[60] who campaigned tirelessly (in competition with

---

[57] B. G. Verghese, "The Ebb and Flow," *The Week*, October 20, 2002: 40–49; "Rivers of Discontent," *The Hindu*, October 13, 2002: 16–17.

[58] Narasimhan Ram, "Strong Constitutions," *Financial Times* magazine, November 22, 2003.

[59] "Everyone Loses," *India Today*, April 19, 1999: 18–25.

[60] "Creating Cyberabad," in Mark Tully and Gillian Wright, *India in Slow Motion*, London: Penguin 2002: 123–53.

Bangalore and Karnataka) to make Hyderabad and Andhra Pradesh the cybercapital of India. But although the urban voters liked him, the rural majority did not, and they threw the rascal out with a crashing defeat in 2004.[61]

Naidu was defeated despite having had much support from Ramoji Rao, the presiding media mogul of Andhra Pradesh. Rao's key media property was the Telugu daily *Eenadu*, which he launched only in 1974; in 1987 it was selling 264,000 daily copies and in 2002 passed the million daily sale mark. Rao became a major player in not only Telugu, but also in Indian, television. By 2004–2005 Rao controlled satellite television channels in 12 Indian languages.

In most of the larger Indian states the strong state media have helped to build up larger-than-life regional political bosses. West Bengal has some 8 percent of Indian population and its main city, Calcutta (now Kolkata), is the cultural capital not only of West Bengal but also of Bengali-speaking Bangladesh. West Bengal (like Kerala) has a strong communist tradition; Jyoti Basu was chief minister of West Bengal for 23 years (1977–2000), making him "the world's longest serving elected Communist politician."[62]

Regional power brokers and charismatic state chief ministers were also be found in the northern Hindi heartland. In 2001 the two most populated Hindi states—Uttar Pradesh and Bihar—together had 249 million people. Both states were poor, with low levels of literacy, short life expectancy, and high rates of population increase. Bihar suffered a major famine in 1968 and is still one of the two most "food insecure" states in India.[63] In both Uttar Pradesh and Bihar the Dalits ("untouchables") and the "other backward castes" increasingly flexed their political muscle; one consequence was the appearance of low caste political leaders such as Laloo Prasad Yadav in Bihar and Mayawati in Uttar Pradesh.

Laloo was a lower caste politician who served as chief minister in Bihar during 1990–1997. Laloo eventually went to prison in 1997 for his part in the "fodder scam"; $280 million was said to have been extracted from government schemes that provided animal feed to state-run farms. Before going to prison, Laloo firstly severely wounded the incumbent Delhi government by withdrawing 18 of "his" members of parliament; then Laloo designated his uneducated wife, Rabri Devin, to serve as chief minister while he was in prison. In 2004 Laloo joined the Indian government as railway minister.[64]

---

[61] Amarnath K. Menon, "Mega Byte Victory," *India Today International*, May 24, 2004: 24–26.

[62] "Basu the Marxist Bows Out," *The Economist*, November 11, 2000.

[63] "Portrait of a Famine—Bihar 1968," in *Khushwant Singh's India*, Bombay: IBH Publishing, 1969: 52–66; "Rural India in Ruins," *Frontline*, March 12, 2004: 16–29. An excellent account of Bihar politics and journalism in the 1980s is in P. Tharyan, *Good News, Bad News*, New Delhi: Pauls Press, 1999: 152–74.

[64] Mark Nicholson, "Hero of the Poor Ready to 'Fill India's Jails,'" *Financial Times*, July 31, 1997; Khozem Merchant, "Bihar's Boss Fights Bid to Oust Him," *Financial Times*, June 25, 1998; Ajit Kumar Jha, "Laloo's Dual Track," *India Today International*, September 27, 2004.

Uttar Pradesh, with 16 percent of the Indian population, is one of India's poorest states[65] but is a potential electoral prize. Uttar Pradesh state politics—once dominated by Congress—were in the 1990s contested mainly by the upper caste BJP party, the lower middle caste, socialist, Samajwadi Party (led by Mulavam Singh Yadav), and the Dalit-untouchable party, Bahujan Samaj Party (BSP). In 1995 the BSP took power under the leadership of the then 39-year-old Mayawati. Mayawati served as chief minister of India's most populous state for brief intervals in 1995, 1997, and 2002–2003. During these terms in office she made aggressive moves to transfer resources to her power base—the Dalit 20 percent of Uttar Pradesh's voters.[66]

Since the 1990s, politics in Uttar Pradesh and Bihar—and in other Indian states—has became increasingly caste-based. Caste-based regional parties focus on delivering benefits (jobs, money, access) to their caste-based electoral support. Charismatic political leaders of the regional subcastes, or caste fragments, develop a belligerent high profile political style, which achieves visibility with their electoral support. Larger-than-life politicians who are appealing to lower caste voters have to reach these voters without the sympathy of the major (Hindi, as well as English-language) press. The few big Hindi dailies (each of which prints in numerous locations across the northern Hindi heartland) and the English press, as well as the all-news cable-satellite networks, do not sympathize with low caste–populist politicians like Laloo and Mayawati. The elite media complain about political corruption and criminalization. Mayawati was condescendingly referred to as the "Dalit Queen," while Laloo was tagged as the "fodder scampster." But the politicians in question seem to adopt the all-publicity-is-good-publicity approach; a fair amount of positive publicity trickles through in the smaller local newspapers, in Hindi television, and perhaps especially in Hindi radio. The lower caste politicians may believe that denunciation by the elite press is positively helpful. Bravura gestures—such as Laloo's rule from prison via his wife or Mayawati's extravagant parties and diamond necklaces[67]—do not antagonize lower caste voters; these poor people expect politicians to be corrupt, but prefer the benefits of corruption to flow to their own leaders. Meanwhile, these regional power brokers maintain their significant power both in Delhi and in their home state. A power broker controls "my party," "my members" of the current Delhi coalition, "my subcaste," "my own name

[65] Edward Luce, "Growing Disparity Between India's Richest and Poorest States," *Financial Times*, "FT India" special report, December 9, 2003.
[66] Sudha Pai, "The State, Social Justice and the Dalit Movement: The BSP in Uttar Pradesh," in Niraja Gopal Jayal and Sudha Pai (eds.), *Democratic Governance in India: Challenges of Poverty, Development, and Identity*, New Delhi: Sage, 2001: 201–20; Edward Luce, "Caste Politics Dominates Uttar Pradesh Poll," *Financial Times*, February 7, 2002; "Caste Adrift in India," *The Economist*, February 9, 2002: 55–56; Subhash Mishra, "Maya Rules," *India Today International*, May 13, 2002: 16–19.
[67] Edward Luce, "Untouchables Left in the Cold by Leader Living Out of Reach," *Financial Times*, January 16, 2003; Subhash Mitra, "Happy Returns," *India Today International*, January 27, 2003: 18–19.

recognition," "my media image," and (to some degree) "my own loyal media."

India's Regional, National, and Southern Asian Media

In recent years India's regional media, and regional media owners, have become more powerful. In the Hindi-speaking states, and in the more populous non-Hindi-speaking states, the main regional media have had a big impact in shaping the dominant languages. After independence each of the major regional languages existed in numerous high and low, as well as very localized, versions. The regional transmissions of All India Radio tended to use the "high" form of each language. But when the big regional newspapers began—in the 1970s—to print numerous local editions, the more successful newspapers' success depended in part on their defining a simpler, more modern, and more user-friendly version of the language. This newspaper "house style" was often incorporated into a style guide for the journalists and then was published—and subsequently used by schoolteachers and others.[68] This enterprise of reshaping and steering the regional language—already pursued by regional film industries—was later pursued vigorously by regional television and cable.

It was the 11 or so largest non-Hindi languages that primarily benefited from this process of modernization and simplification. The most obvious losers in this were the many small languages. For the languages of intermediate size—perhaps from number 12 to number 20 in terms of number of speakers—the implications were more ambiguous. One consequence was an urge by smaller language groups to establish themselves as separate states. Three important new states that came into existence in 2000 were Chhatisgarh, Jharkhand, and Uttaranchal (whose combined 2001 census populations were 56 million). These three new states were sliced off from larger, and Hindi majority, states. Each of these changes can be seen as a rejection by a minority of membership of a Hindi-majority state. These cases also illustrate the political emergence of what official India still calls "the tribals," mainly hill- and mountain-dwellers who speak languages that, until recently, were not written languages. This obviously is politically delicate, not least because the Naxalites (Maoist-inclined insurgents whose depredations kill hundreds of people each year) are strong in mountainous and minority locations in 11 states from southern India to the Himalayan borders in the north. In India, as elsewhere in the world, their own independent mass media—in their own small local languages—are contributing causes, as well as political goals, of such groups. Inevitably innovations such as the new states of year 2000 lead to media and political campaigns that demand the creation of yet more additional new states.

---

[68] Robin Jeffrey, *India's Newspaper Revolution*, New York: Saint Martin's, 2000: 98–102, 182–83.

The main media and political tensions in India are those between "The Centre" (Delhi) and the regional state capitals. Here the radical commercialization of most Indian media during the 1990s is significant. This 1990s commercialization, which went still further in the years after 2000, left press, radio, and television between 80 percent and 90 percent dependent on India's still modest advertising expenditure. Since 2000 there has been some trend back to dependence on subscription (especially in cable-satellite TV); but the commercialization of the press has accompanied a trend toward the tabloid back sections of the newspaper invading the front section and the front page. The commercialization trend has occurred alongside a strengthening of caste in both politics and media. The BJP-led government that lost the 2004 election was a coalition of no less than 24 separate parties (claimed by some as a world record). Most of these 24 parties had their special relationships with local castes, caste fragments, and caste-friendly media. The Congress-led government of 2004 was a coalition of 15 parties. These parties are typically operating on a "spoils" system in which they seek tangible financial and other rewards for their caste constituencies. Some of these parties have racist, religious, and xenophobic agendas. However, paradoxically this system of narrow-minded parties leads to pluralistic—coalition—governments. Nevertheless, contained within the big plural coalition are some unpleasant, and indeed criminal, politicians[69] supported by some unpleasant and corrupt media.

If the main tensions faced by the Indian media operate along Delhi versus regional lines, the next most salient set of tensions (and ambitions) focus upon India's next-door nations in southern Asia. These countries include Pakistan (with a population in 2002 of 149 million); Bangladesh (143 million); Nepal (24 million); Sri Lanka (19 million); Myanmar, previously Burma (49 million); and Bhutan (2 million). India also has a border with China. Indian media and popular culture leak into the neighboring countries—mostly without any payment in return. Hindi and Mumbai movie Hindustani is quite easily understood by Urdu-speakers in Pakistan. Rajasthan (with Hindi and Rajasthani media) has the longest Indian state border with Pakistan. Punjabi is another Indian media language also widely spoken in Pakistan. India's Tamil media appeal to the Tamil minority in Sri Lanka, but the majority (of Sinhalese-speakers) also look toward India. Bengali is the main language on both sides of the India-Bangladesh border, and both governments are relatively relaxed about the cross-border media.

Satellite channels have, of course, added to transborder media leakages. David Page and William Crawley offer much detailed evidence on this.[70]

[69] Randeep Ramesh, "Criminal Candidates Hold Indian State Captive," *The Guardian*, April 26, 2004.
[70] David Page and William Crawley, *Satellites over South Asia*, New Delhi: Sage, 2001; David Page and William Crawley, "The Transnational and the National: Changing Patterns of Cultural Influence in the South Asian TV Market," in Jean Chalaby (ed.), *Transnational Television Worldwide*, London: I.B. Tauris, 2004: 128–55.

Indian movies have circulated across southern Asia since the 1920s. In subsequent decades the steadily rising crescendo of Indian popular culture made for a continuing one-way flow of popular culture out of India and into neighboring countries. This influence was widespread, incorporating *advertising* of Indian-branded products, *beauty* contests (as well as *Bollywood* and *Bengali* media), and *cricket*—India, Pakistan, and Sri Lanka are all cricket obsessed, and cricket and political stars like Pakistan's Imran Khan have had much Indian support and adulation. Moving on through the alphabet, Indian *democracy* (and its media consequences) are admired and envied across southern Asia. Indian-accented *English* is the lingua franca of all of the national elites across southern Asia. Indian *fashion*, which takes numerous regional forms, is also the southern Asian leader; the growth of both public relations and media commercialization have meant that the publicity photographs from the Mumbai and other Indian fashion industries increasingly adorn magazines and newspaper pages across the subcontinent. India is also the subcontinental leader in *glitz* of all kinds. And so on through the alphabet, not forgetting Hindi, Hindustani, and Hinglish.

So what of the Indian connection with the Anglo-American media? The people of India, like the people of many other nations, have ambivalent attitudes toward both the United States and the United Kingdom. There is certainly some admiration for, and envy of, the United States and for Indians employed by high technology companies in the United States. But the total extent of the Indian diaspora—in the United States, the United Kingdom, elsewhere in Europe, and the Arab countries—is quite small. The Indian media pay much attention to "global Indians" because they see this market as a potential revenue source.

Most Indians know little about America, much as most Americans know little about India. Indians (most of whom are vegetarians) don't much like burgers and fried chicken; Pizza Hut has been more successful in India, not least because its products remind Indians of their own breads.[71] But India has better, tastier, and cheaper fast food of its own. It's much the same with media. Hollywood still has only a very small audience in India. Foreign-owned cable-satellite operators such as Sony and Star are not perceived as Japanese or American but as 100 percent Indian, and mostly Hindi. Some U.S. English-language channels—such as Discovery and CNN—do attract a small elite audience; but this is little more than an updating of older BBC and other British influences and contents. BBC radio still has the largest daily Indian audience of any foreign media—but its audience is mainly in Indian languages.

While India does admire American wealth and technology, it does not envy the U.S. version of democracy. There has been strong resentment at U.S.

---

[71] Tulasi Srinivas, " 'A Tryst with Destiny': The Indian Case of Cultural Globalization," in Peter L. Berger and Samuel Huntingdon (eds.), *Many Globalizations*, New York: Oxford University Press, 2002: 89–116.

support for a longish sequence of Pakistani governments—several of which were military dictatorships. Most Indians welcomed the more friendly U.S.-Indian relationship that began in 2004.

Indian demonstrations and marches in December 2004 marked the twentieth anniversary of the Bhopal events of 1984. A Union Carbide chemical plant in Bhopal had a major explosion that killed some 7,000 people and led to the subsequent early deaths of another 10,000 or 20,000. Certainly Union Carbide (now part of Dow Chemical) was to blame, but the Indian government (and the state government of Madhya Pradesh) were far from totally innocent. The then chief executive of Union Carbide, Warren Anderson, visited Bhopal immediately after the disaster and accepted responsibility. Although the company eventually paid $470 million, Warren Anderson refused to return to India to face an Indian court, and the U.S. government failed to extradite him.[72] This complex story has not been forgotten in India; it is kept alive by, among others, the Hindi daily newspapers for which Bhopal is a major publishing site.

The Indian media are quick to see U.S. companies as seeking to exploit Indian poverty and backwardness. Enron's "cowboy operating style" was unpopular in India[73] before its American meltdown. Headlines such as "Illegal Tests Done on 790 Indian Women"[74] are part of a steady succession of Indian news stories that see the U.S. medical world as exploiting poor Indians.

India to Become a World News and Media Leader?

India is suitably positioned to become the news leader not only of southern Asia but of the whole of Asia. India is close, in time zone terms, to many of the world's people. India, with its big Muslim population, sits astride the major axis of Muslim peoples from northern Africa to Indonesia. India also has an open, dynamic, and democratic media scene.

India has a large and growing supply of high quality, English-speaking journalists. Mumbai and Delhi are especially strong in internationally relevant financial and economic news. Television news and actuality is another strength, emphasized by the proliferation of some 13 national and 15 regional all-news TV channels in India in 2005. India is immensely strong in all things

---

72 "Poisoned Legacy," *The Economist*, December 15, 1984: 67–68; Mark Nicholson and Rohit Jaggi, "New Flood of Bhopal Claims Expected," *Financial Times*, December 3, 1996; Dominique Lapierre and Javier Moro, *Five Past Midnight in Bhopal*, Delhi: Full Circle, 2001; Arun Subramaniam, "Bhopal: Eighteen Years On," *Far East Economic Review*, September 12, 2004; Saritha Rai, "Horror Persists Decades After Bhopal Leak," *International Herald Tribune*, December 1, 2004 (from *NY Times*).

73 Manjeet Kripalani, "Enron Switches Signals in India," *Business Week*, January 8, 2001; Anita Pratap, "Bad Connections," *Time*, June 26, 1995.

74 *Hindustan Times*, January 18, 2004.

visual and factual. There is likely to be a steadily increasing international focus on India as the exemplar of rich-poor extremes, environmental problems, and overpopulation (in which year will India's population overtake China's?)

There has been much anticipation that India will become a big industrial exporter in general and a cyberindustry exporter in particular; there are similar claims that India is becoming a big exporter of films, television, and music. But more probably Indian performance in these areas will be balanced roughly between export and import. Indian entrepreneurs such as L. N. Mittal, the world "king of steel,"[75] are internationally active; but foreign companies are increasingly active inside India.

In cyberindustry terms a rough balance is probable between high and low technology.[76] While India can expect further high technology successes, there will probably continue to be many thousands of lowly paid "cyber-coolies," forced to converse, in suitably rehearsed U.S. and U.K. English accents, with faraway customers during India's evening and early morning hours.[77]

Indian movies, music, and fashion are all quite widely exported. But Indian popular music incorporates American and world influences, with much Indian (and Indian regional) musical tradition.[78] Indian movies already have a big market in the relatively wealthy Indian diaspora; but the Indian movies that attract world audiences tend to be U.K.-Indian coproductions. Most Indian television entertainment will find its main foreign market in the Indian diaspora.

The Anglo-American advertising agencies were already strong in the 1960s and 1970s, and—with television—have become still stronger. Advertising seems likely to continue as the one important media field in which India is on the receiving end of globalization.

---

[75] Shankkar Aiyar, "L. N. Mittal: Steel King," *India Today International*, November 8, 2004: 18–21.

[76] "A World of Work: A Survey of Outsourcing," *The Economist*, November 13, 2004: 1–16; Stephen David, "The World is Calling," *India Today International*, August 22, 2005: 18–19.

[77] See two letters to the editor by Harish Trivedi, *Times Literary Supplement*, June 27, 2003, and August 22, 2003. This correspondence, titled "Cyber-Coolies, Hindi and English," was triggered by an article by Susan Sontag, "The World as India," *Times Literary Supplement*, June 13, 2003: 13–15.

[78] Vamsee Juluri, *Becoming a Global Audience: Longing and Belonging in Indian Music Television*, New York: Peter Lang, 2003.

12

China

Capitalist-Communist Media Stir-Fry

China and India have the world's largest populations and are also the most socially complex countries on earth. For centuries Europeans (and Americans) have marveled at the sophistication of many Chinese products (not least porcelain "china") and have wondered what would happen when China finally woke up. Now that it has woken up (or "stood up" in Mao Zedong's 1949 phrase) China puzzles the rest of the world, with its many paradoxes. Central Chinese paradoxes of relevance to the media include the following:

- While China has become in many commercial areas more capitalist than the capitalists, communism remains an important force. In China we see media that are aggressively capitalist in their pursuit of audiences and advertising while continuing to be Marxist and communist in terms of ideology and control.

- China remains a highly centralized country in which nationalism and national culture are strong and strongly encouraged. But regional power, regional sentiment, regional economies, and—not least—regional media are increasingly powerful.

- China is unique in having 900 million people who speak a single language, Mandarin; but about 400 million speak other languages. With the major exception of northeastern China, many of the people who live just inside China's lengthy borders (in southeastern, southern, western, and north central China) speak languages other than Mandarin. This causes much anxiety in Beijing and for Beijing's media regulators.

- The present regime in China politely and warmly welcomes foreign experts, foreign traders, and foreign media. However, the regime also pursues the old Chinese tradition of "making the foreigners serve China." The overall media importing strategy encourages controlled media

Figure 12.1 China's provinces.

importing as a means of learning to improve the audience appeal, and commercial strength, of Chinese media. This involves, for instance, an enthusiastic embracing of the Internet but also the employment of perhaps 30,000 people whose sole task is to build a Great Firewall of China against politically incorrect on-line materials.

Much China talk involves predictions about China's ability to maintain very high rates of economic growth. If quick economic growth does continue, China's media are likely to make further advances on the world stage:

- The size of China's middle class has often been exaggerated. But even if China's middle class was only about 130 million (or 10 percent of the population) in 2005, this might rise to 400 million (or 30 percent of the then Chinese population) by 2020. Should this happen, China would have more middle-class consumers and media consumers than the United States.

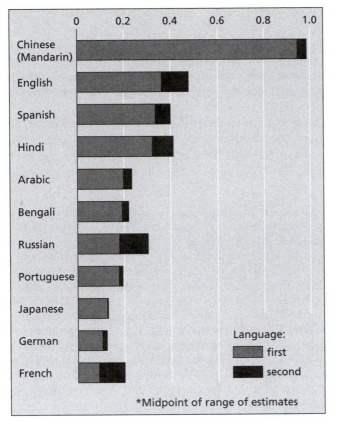

Figure 12.2 Most widely spoken languages, 2005, by number of speakers* (billion). *Source*: UNESCO, The Economist.

- Sixty years after the end of World War II, the Japanese were still not greatly loved in China. But if Japan and China increasingly accept each other's media, a new East Asian media order—or perhaps the China/Japan/Korea media—may move beyond East Asia to become a world media force.

- In the past, nations that became world leaders in manufacturing subsequently became world leaders in the mass media. This was true of Britain and France in the nineteenth century and the United States in the twentieth century. It could become true of East Asia (or East and South Asia) in the twenty-first century.

Madame Mao's Trial Boosts Chinese Television

The 1980–1981 televised trial of Mao Zedong's widow and the other members of the "Gang of Four" was a landmark in recent Chinese history. The trial was a political event because the Gang of Four had been Mao's kitchen cabinet through whom, in his last years, he orchestrated the disastrous chaos of the Cultural Revolution.

Madame Mao was the star performer at the trial, which became a landmark event also in China's media and television history. In other countries, it had often been a big sporting event that turned television into a mass medium. In China it was the deposing of Mao's widow that dramatized the combined political and entertainment potential of television.

Deng Xiaoping assumed full power in 1979 (Mao having died in 1976). Deng decided on a show trial with television cameras and lights. The Chinese were relatively unfamiliar with television because TV development was effectively frozen until Mao's death. Melinda Liu, who was a reporter in Beijing, recalled:

> It was the greatest show on earth at the time, a very cathartic thing. Of course, the party press was full of it. We heard the voices of Mrs. Mao and the others on radio. They also released a lot of still pictures of her shouting at the judges and witnesses. And it was on television; this was television in thrall to a political campaign. Long before the trial there had been street demonstrations, speeches, and denunciations of the Gang of Four.
>
> The television coverage was quite unlike anything seen in China before. Real events on the TV news each evening. It was a huge story, but not the whole story. The TV (and other) coverage was edited to focus on Mrs. Mao and the Gang of Four (and the other accused) as the bad guys. Mao's own leading role in the Cultural Revolution was not addressed. So they cut out Mrs. Mao's assertion that she was merely Mao's lapdog, doing his bidding.
>
> People were amazed at how much came out and especially were astonished by the television coverage. But in Beijing, at least, people realized that not everything was being revealed; there were tremendous rumours.[1]

As often with television, the impact on the audience was probably mixed and partly unintended. Madame Mao had herself been a film actress[2] in 1930s Shanghai, and she managed to upstage the judges by verbally abusing them loudly, interrupting, and asking embarrassing questions. Right at the start she made her key point: "Everything I did, Mao told me to do. I was his dog; what he said to bite, I bit."

Deng Xiaoping and other leaders of the new government watched the trial, in late 1980 and early 1981, via closed circuit television. They must have liked the edited trial extracts that appeared on TV on most (but not all) days of the trial. The trial seems to have strengthened their preexisting decision to expand television rapidly. In 1980 there were only five million TV sets in

---

[1] Melinda Liu (of *Newsweek*) in interview with this author, September 28, 2001, in Beijing.

[2] Ross Terrill, *Madame Mao: The White-Boned Demon*, Stanford, CA: Stanford University Press, 1999 rev. ed.; "The Smashing of the Gang of Four," in Immanuel C. Y. Hsü, *The Rise of Modern China*, New York: Oxford University Press, 2000 ed.: 763–74.

China, with Beijing ahead of Shanghai and a few other cities. But the huge interest probably ensured substantial numbers, perhaps up to 50 million, seeing at least some of the trial on television.

The number of TV sets in China increased tenfold between 1980 and 1985 (5 to 50 million) and trebled during 1985–1990 (50 to 160 million TV sets). Many other dramatic changes transformed urban China in the years after 1980. The one child policy was launched in 1980. Also around 1980 the physical transformation of the major cities began, with thousands of bulldozers and many millions of tons of steel. Beijing was rebuilt with eight-lane urban freeways à la Los Angeles (1980); Shanghai was rebuilt with skyscrapers.

In television the rapid takeoff involved an initial pattern of two television channels per large city. One was that city's own channel, the second was a national channel from Beijing. Less than 10 percent of programming was imported. BBC and other British material was prominent during 1978–1981. One of the first Chinese television stars was a young English woman, Kathy Flower, who presented a series of 60 30-minute English lessons, which began in January 1982.[3]

1900–1950: The Peak of Foreign Media in China

The peak of foreign, including American, media influence in China did not occur after 1980; it occurred before 1950. For example, Hollywood's impact in China since 1980 has been very modest, whereas in the mid-1930s Hollywood movies had a dominant (about 85 percent) share of the Chinese movie theater audience.

Even so, American movies were by no means the only foreign media in China before 1950. Both the British and the Japanese can also claim to have been foreign media leaders in China. The British were probably the leaders during 1900–1930; the Japanese military occupation of much of China made Japan the leading foreign media power during 1937–1945. The United States was unambiguously in the lead only for the brief civil war (communists versus nationalists) period of 1945–1948.

Throughout the half century from 1900 to 1950, Chinese film and radio were on a very small scale indeed. But especially after 1920 China had one of the world's largest selling newspaper industries; and over the whole 50-year period the United Kingdom was the biggest single foreign press force. During 1900–1950 China experienced massive political turbulence, rule by warlords, civil war between the communists and Chiang Kai-shek's nationalist Kuomeng-Tang (KMT), and the Japanese invasion and occupation (1937–1945) of large parts of China. During these years China had literally hundreds of daily (or several times a week) newspapers. Warlords, army commanders, and

[3] Kathy Flower, "China TV's First English Teacher Looks Back," *InterMedia*, December 1989: 12–15.

many businessmen published their own newspapers—almost all of which were very small, both in number of pages and in sales. There may have been as many as 358 dailies in China in 1925 and 910 dailies in 1935. The hundreds of small dailies relied heavily on news supplied first by the British Reuters news agency and second by the American UP, but also by the French, Japanese, German, and Soviet international agencies.[4] China was in fact the best single market for Reuters outside the British Empire from 1920 until 1935,[5] when the China-Japan War increasingly intervened.

During 1900–1950 many hundreds of Chinese newspapers were launched and then closed after a few months, or weeks, of publication. Many titles were closed by KMT or Japanese censorship only to be relaunched at a different location and under a fresh title. Nearly all of these small newspapers were owned and operated for reasons of political or commercial propaganda. Financial subsidies were the norm; most of the journalists accepted bribes as well as political constraints, and many journalists suffered violence. Often it was dangerous to sell these newspapers on the streets.[6] But Shanghai by the 1930s was publishing over 20 daily papers, while other larger cities were publishing 10 or more dailies. Against this background of corruption and propaganda a few foreign-supported newspapers set a (slightly) more elevated standard.

Many missionary newspapers had American support. The most important foreign journalist during 1897–1912 was George Morrison, the (Australian-born) Beijing correspondent of *The Times* (London).[7] Although American newspaper influence was important and Japanese press influence was dominant for nearly a decade, over the whole 1900–1950 period British press influence was probably strongest. British press influence was exerted not only in the Chinese press capital of Shanghai—through for example the "semi-official," British-owned daily, *North China Daily News*—but also through Hong Kong, which published both English/British and Chinese/Cantonese newspapers.

Hollywood was overwhelmingly dominant in the Chinese movie market.[8] But the Shanghai industry was making about 70 Mandarin movies a year, and Hong Kong was making about 45 Cantonese movies a year. However, the significance of this huge dominance of Hollywood movies in the mid-1930s was modified in two ways. First, China had very few movie theaters even in the movie capital of Shanghai, and there were literally only one or two movie theaters in most other Chinese cities. Second, in the years 1937–1945 the Japanese influence was strong; many Shanghai and Hong Kong films were

---

[4] Vernon Nash, "Chinese Journalism in 1931," *Journalism Quarterly* 8, 1931: 446–52.

[5] Donald Read, *The Power of News: The History of Reuters*, Oxford: Oxford University Press, 1992: 168–71.

[6] Lee-hsia Hsu Ting, *Government Control of the Press in Modern China, 1900–1949*, Cambridge, MA: Harvard University Press (East Asian Research Center, Harvard University), 1974.

[7] Cyril Pearl, *Morrison of Peking*, Sydney: Angus and Robertson, 1967.

[8] U.S. Department of Commerce, *Review of Foreign Film Markets*, 1937.

made under Japanese control and censorship.[9] Also both the KMT and the communists made their own wartime films deep in the Chinese hinterland.

In other media fields—notably radio and advertising—American influence was significant. But little money went into advertising—corrupt propaganda media were (and are) not attractive to advertisers. Commercial radio also existed on a small scale as early as 1931, but remained insignificant compared to the press.[10]

Public relations and propaganda methods reached high levels of sophistication and cynicism in China well before 1950. There may have been some American PR influence, but Lenin's writings, and communist media practice in general, were almost certainly bigger influences on Mao Zedong and the communists. Among the communist leadership, Chou-En-lai (Chinese prime minister, 1949–1976) was a virtuoso publicist (and diplomat) of great charm, courage, and insight. During 1938–1947 Chou edited the communist *New China Daily* from three different Chinese locations. At one desperate moment in January 1941, Chou-En-lai himself hawked copies of the *New China Daily* on a Chongqin street. Chou's formative press and publicity experience occurred when he was a student in Paris in 1920–1924.

The unambiguous period of the United States as leading foreign media influence began with the Japanese surrender in 1945. For a brief period there were significant numbers of American soldiers (and dozens of American journalists) inside China.

Some of these influences were carried over into the communist era after 1948. Jay Leyda recalled his "shock" at what he saw as obvious Hollywood influences in Chinese communist films. Early 1960s children's storybooks not only carried communist propaganda themes but also, he said, showed the stylistic influence of American products such as *Tarzan*, *Prince Valiant*, and *Terry and the Pirates*. He often observed adults reading these comics in Beijing, and "children read little else."[11] But Leyda, who lived in Beijing only after 1959, may have mistaken some Japanese for American influences.

Nevertheless, by 1949 many communist journalists and propagandists were familiar with, and had been influenced by, radio singing commercials, comic strips, Hollywood movies, the pyramid style of newspaper writing, and Western news agency war reporting. After 1949 the Chinese propagandists turned their backs on the origins of such techniques, but they also incorporated these imported techniques into their ensuing propaganda assaults on the domestic Chinese population. As elsewhere, European, American, and Japanese media practices were mixed with traditional local and national approaches.

---

[9] Poshek Fu, *Between Shanghai and Hong Kong: The Politics of Chinese Cinemas*, Stanford, CA: Stanford University Press, 2003.

[10] Lawrence D. Batson and E. D. Schutrumf (eds.), *Broadcast Advertising in Asia, Africa, Australia and Oceania*, Washington, DC: US Department of Commerce, 1932: 4–5.

[11] Jay Leyda, *Diarying: An Account of Films and Film Audiences in China*, Cambridge, MA: MIT Press, 1972: 334.

Thirty Million Unreported Famine Deaths . . . and Cultural Revolution

How could 30 million famine deaths in China, around 1960, have gone unreported? Why did this huge disaster get almost no media coverage at the time either inside, or outside, China? This was a manmade disaster, sustained primarily by the will of one man, Mao Zedong, who did not wish his catastrophic errors to be reported. But how could one individual, however powerful, have censored almost all news about such a massive disaster?

This famine disaster was only the third in a sequence of four events that— under Mao Zedong's leadership—involved massive loss of life through violence or death from nonnatural causes. First was the fighting against the Japanese and the KMT; this fighting certainly involved millions of deaths. Second, the successful seizure of power by the communists in 1948–1949 led to the violent deaths of large numbers of landlords (and large farmers) who were lynched by their former tenants. Also at this time—especially during 1950–1951—substantial numbers of Chinese soldiers were killed in the Korean War. Third, in the Great Leap Forward of the late 1950s, there was a huge pause in the rapid growth of the Chinese population. Famine was the main cause. Fourth, the Cultural Revolution around 1970 also claimed large numbers of deaths as Red Guards lynched or persecuted into suicide hundreds of thousands of people; others died in prison or undergoing various forms of punishment.

During the Mao years China was governed by a type of individual authority for which terms such as "charisma" or "dictatorship" seem to err by understatement. But Mao Zedong was, of course, the "Father of the New Nation"; his fathership was much closer to that of Stalin in the Soviet Union than to Nehru in India. Mao had earned his national father status by having led the famous 52-week "Long March" (of 1934–1935), which most of the marching fighters did not survive. Mao also led the communists and the People's Liberation Army (PLA) to a victory against the much larger forces of Chiang Kai-shek and the KMT. Mao was projected to the Chinese people as at once somewhat remote and unworldly as well as all-seeing, all-knowing, a communist demi-God who dressed in baggy peasant's clothing. It was an extreme case of the national cult of personality.

Behind Mao's somewhat shambling exterior and fierce words of vague meaning, was a significant steel strength. This strength was the People's Liberation Army, most of whose generals and soldiers always followed Mao, however bizarre his new enthusiasm. Most generals followed Mao because he had been their leader in the PLA's triumphant battles of the 1940s. Having seen such massive destruction, chaos, and suffering, the generals—like most Chinese—feared further civil war and saw Mao (even if he himself had created the chaos) as the best person to tidy up civil chaos and reunite the people.

Another obvious reason for following Mao was fear or terror. Like Stalin, Mao used terror as a political weapon. Communist Party members, from the highest to the lowest, had seen the terror process in action—an individual was denounced, forced to "struggle" and to confess; if you were lucky you were merely demoted and disgraced, but, if less lucky, you were imprisoned, tortured, and killed. Most people preferred to agree with Mao and to join in the denunciations of anyone designated as a capitalist roader or as an imperialist running dog.

Mao usually managed to get his way with China's huge Communist Party and its huge government bureaucracy. But some of Mao's biggest problems derived from the reluctance of senior people, especially in Beijing, to follow his latest campaigning enthusiasm. Old ways, Mao often said, tended to reassert themselves. But Mao was amazingly successful in small meetings and in confrontations with party and government leaders. He, of course, had made many of the initial appointments (around 1949). Mao was also good at getting his supporters not only into top army positions but also into the top jobs at the numerous police, secret police, security, and intelligence bureaucracies in Beijing. Mao was also careful to maintain contact with loyal Communist Party leaders in key provincial cities.

The mass media and propaganda apparatuses of the communist state were another area of Mao Zedong's dominance. A party leader or ministry bureaucrat denounced by Mao would subsequently be denounced by the dominant media—in the *People's Daily*, by the Xinhua national news agency, and on radio. These denunciations would quickly reach across the huge landmass of China and would then be repeated at the local level by provincial city press and radio. Such denunciations typically received no direct refutation and were usually followed by a confession of guilt from the target of the denunciation.

For most (but not quite all) of his 27 years as China's supreme leader, Mao was in the position of the only politician media mogul in a nation-state that had only one media conglomerate. All media were communist, and all communist media spoke the same words—words "suggested" by Mao (or one of his assistants) to the few top media editors. A few phone calls and conversations within the Beijing power structure became the single hymn sheet from which all Chinese media, and all Chinese people, must now sing. None of this is very mysterious. Even in the West, editors regard orders, or suggestions, from the chief executive (or owner) as being legitimate. Especially in 1950s China, editors expected to follow whatever the party line, and Mao, might require. One such editor was Deng Tuo, who edited *People's Daily* through most of the 1950s; Deng was an independently minded intellectual, historian, and creative writer, but he had also edited publications for the communists for the decade previous to 1949, and he regarded obedience to the party as normal and acceptable. In fact, he did become uneasy about the trend of policy during 1955–1956 and Mao duly sacked him. Deng was not initially denounced in public, but he did slip down the hierarchy;

eventually he became a victim of the Cultural Revolution and committed suicide.[12]

Under Mao one-way communication was taken to extremes. Mao behaved like a semi-divine figure who gave the key sermons and who literally made up the sacred hymns and the sacred summary. Not only did all Chinese media then repeat the latest sacred sayings, but eventually all Chinese citizens were expected to carry their copy of the sacred summary—the omnipresent Little Red Book.

Mao did not often personally address big rallies, and in his time there was almost no television. Mao preferred to orchestrate news and views across China via editors who hung on his every mumbled word. Meanwhile China was often in a state of chaos and turbulence, with many bureaucrats and party members wanting to follow policy but being somewhat unclear as to how Great Leap Forward or Cultural Revolution actually applied to their specific organization. Moreover, the courts and legal system, never strong in communist China, were sometimes genuinely mystified as to what the law was. In these turbulent circumstances one of the few certainties was that all of the central media carried the Great Leader's thoughts and orders.

In retrospect Mao's attitude, not only to his colleagues but also to the world at large, can perhaps be described as paranoid. But Mao had had some extremely painful bitter experiences with other nations. The KMT had fought and persecuted the communists over more than two decades. China had also suffered horribly at the hands of the Japanese. The 1931 Japanese attack on northeast China was still being recalled with considerable bitterness 70 years later, as newspapers published pictures of Japanese soldiers beheading Chinese victims.[13]

Many core beliefs of Mao Zedong and the Chinese communists derived from the civil war against the KMT during 1946–1949. These beliefs included the preference for short, but aggressive, propaganda campaigns; the central place of the military and of deified leadership; and hostility to intellectuals and the preference for Soviet models.[14] Mao's attitude to the United States was inevitably influenced by the Korean War and by American support for Chiang Kai-shek in the 1940s and for Taiwan from 1949 onward.

The Soviet Union was the new China's only major ally in its early years. The Chinese communists greatly admired Lenin's seizure of power and Stalin's defeat of the Germans. In the early 1950s China accepted hundreds of Soviet experts and significant Soviet investment. However, the Khrushchev anti-Stalin speech of 1956 was a big shock. After 1956, China turned against the Soviet Union. Consequently, by the 1960s China seemed (to Mao and

---

[12] Timothy Cheek, *Propaganda and Culture in Mao's China: Deng Tuo and the Intelligentsia*, Oxford: Clarendon Press, 1997.

[13] "Japan Urged to Repent for Slaughter," *China Daily*. September 18, 2001.

[14] Odd Arne Westad, *Decisive Encounters: The Chinese Civil War, 1946–1950*, Stanford, CA: Stanford University Press, 2003: 328.

others) to be surrounded by a hostile world including the Soviet Union and the United States, Japan, Taiwan, and even India. What Mao perceived as an extremely hostile international picture encouraged him (and the Chinese more generally) to think in terms of a widely spread defense. Just as in fighting the KMT small communist units had been effective, so also in resisting the United States, Soviet Union, and the others should China rely on decentralization. These defensive assumptions, and preference for broadly spread resistance, fitted neatly alongside Mao's general preference for villages, small groups, and peasant-soldiers. This decentralized thinking was significant in the Great Leap Forward and the Cultural Revolution.

Such thinking also affected planning for the media; strong local media in all significant cities would make resistance easier should China be attacked. Mao Zedong's preference for a broadly spread defensive posture is a key historical factor in the present-day strength of China's provincial and regional media.

It was against a turbulent international background that the new Chinese government, in the years around 1950, was seeking to consolidate its power across China. During the years of war and civil war the communists in general and Mao in particular had developed distinctive methods for persuading local peasants to support the revolution. From 1948 a huge land reform program was instituted; this involved first expelling landlords and then introducing communes. Not surprisingly, perhaps, in these revolutionary and warring times, many landlords and wealthier farmers lost not only their land but also their lives. Jack Belden's *China Shakes the World* (first published in 1949) contains a memorable account of these events.[15] After the People's Liberation Army (PLA) had captured a fresh area, the peasants were encouraged to deal with their landlords. Millions of peasants were eager literally to get their knives into their landlords.

The few foreign visitors in China in this period were astonished at the speed with which the new authorities were able to carry political education right down to the village level. One Chinese professor from Beijing, himself being "politically re-educated" in a rural area, was surprised in 1951 at the peasants' political vocabulary. Terms in common usage in 1951 included Chinese words for "to struggle," "oppression," "objective," "ideology," "feudalistic forces," "consciousness," "system of exploitation," and "task or assignment."[16] This indicated the ability of the authorities in Beijing to put words into hundreds of millions of rural mouths. Such "political education" was orchestrated from the center, especially through the *People's Daily* and other official publications. But in these early years the lowish circulation figures meant that the campaigns relied heavily on oral agitation, teaching sessions in village halls and schools, singing and chanting.

---

[15] Jack Belden, *China Shakes the World*, London: Pelican Books ed., 1973.
[16] Frederick T. C. Yu, *Mass Persuasion in Communist China*, London: Pall Mall Press, 1964: 91–92.

As the 1950s went on, the oral agitation continued, but the mass media component also increased, now reaching down to the leadership at the small town and village level. There was also a remarkably successful effort to get the basic media (especially press and radio) into semi-public places. In the 1950s newspaper circulations increased about sevenfold; there was an explosion in the use of large character posters. Serial picture books (or revolutionary comics) also expanded dramatically, reaching 100 million copies printed in the year 1956.[17]

Perhaps most remarkable was the use of radio in 1950s China. Throughout the 1950s there were very few radio sets in domestic households; but radio had been placed into village treetops, office buildings, and public transport, and—with loudspeakers switched to high volume—radio was an inescapable daily accompaniment for much of China's population. One Indian visitor, in 1959, reported that the loudspeakers tirelessly harangued the Chinese millions with official news, industrial output statistics, attacks on imperialist America, and details of current campaigns about cleanliness, correct diet, and comradely social activity. There was also much loud martial music and many martial songs, as well as deafening gongs and cymbals.[18]

These early years were also years of official "campaigns" proclaimed from the center; campaigns followed at very frequent intervals with a major, high profile campaign once every few years. The initial campaigning was designed to "eradicate the old order." A (briefly) more relaxed official attitude was evident in "The Hundred Flowers" campaigning of 1956–1957. Mao Zedong exhorted: "Let a hundred flowers bloom, let a hundred schools of thought contend." But Mao's timing coincided with the "thaw" in the Soviet Union. Mao quite quickly withdrew from his Hundred Flowers tolerance; some politicians and journalists who had accepted too literally the advice to speak out found themselves punished for rightist deviation.

The next big campaign was the Great Leap Forward of 1957–1959.[19] Both the comedy and the tragedy of the Great Leap seem to have been inspired by a wish to carry on without Moscow's technical support, to shake up the urban elite as well as the urban factory workers, and to revolutionize the countryside by showing that communes not only could farm the soil and replace the family but could also manufacture iron and make farming equipment, all at the village level. Orchestrated, as usual, by the top level newspapers—and backed up by the Xinhua news agency—all of the other national and local media joined the Great Leap Forward. Since one of the basics of the Great Leap was to go for hugely increased output, all media entities quickly announced their own plans for massive increases in production and productivity.

[17] Godwin C. Chu (ed.), *Popular Media in China*, Honolulu: University Press of Hawaii, 1978: 54.
[18] Frederick T. C. Yu, *Mass Persuasion in Communist China*, London: Pall Mall Press, 1964: 123.
[19] Frederick C. Teiwes with Wamen Sun, *China's Road to Disaster: Mao, Central Politicians and Provincial Leaders in the Unfolding of the Great Leap Forward, 1955–1959*, Armonk, NY: M.E. Sharpe, 1999.

But the countryside was most radically changed. Villagers were encouraged to construct dams and to smelt iron and steel. Not only was China to be self-sufficient, but each locality was to be self-sufficient. Communes were to be all-purpose local organizations, taking over most of the functions even of the family. Agricultural production was to be increased dramatically by the use of new (dubious) farming techniques. Food production did decline, but not enough to be the main cause of the subsequent famine. The main cause of starvation seems to have been a deliberate refusal to recognize how severe the famine was and deliberate refusal to move available food to worst-hit areas.

The population statistics indicate a remarkable population shortfall during 1959–1962. In the three previous years (1956–1959) the population increased by 44.5 million; in the subsequent three years (1962–1965) the population rose by 49.4 million. But in 1959–1962 a small population fall (200,000) is recorded. This suggests that between 40 and 50 million people went missing. Some of these were babies that did not get born (starving women are less likely either to become pregnant or to give birth to live babies). Many elderly and frail people died earlier than otherwise would have been the case. Jasper Becker in *Hungry Ghosts* points to similarities between the China famine of 1959–1962 and the Ukraine famine of 1932–1933, in that both were manmade. Reading Becker's book is as uncomfortable an experience as reading a book about the Jewish Holocaust. Two sets of Chinese peasant parents, as one example, agreed to eat each others' dead children as a desperate means of delaying their own starvation deaths. Becker argues that the great Chinese famine was not only made by, but effectively prolonged by, Mao Zedong and his inner circle. Mao did not want to admit this errors; he accepted phoney evidence concocted by fearful local officials. The only senior figure who gave early warning that the Great Leap Forward was becoming a disaster was then Minister of Defense Marshal Peng Dehuai; he reported back to Beijing in autumn 1958 that peasants were cutting down orchards to fuel furnaces and that the harvest was being left to rot. In early 1959 Peng Dehuai (rare among the communist leaders in himself having a poor peasant background) visited Mao's home village in Hunan "and found untilled fields, falsified production figures and peasants dying of starvation." Peng was quickly disgraced, forced into self-criticism, and put under house arrest; later, during the Cultural Revolution, he was imprisoned, tortured, and killed.[20]

How did this—one of the largest single famines in world history—fail to receive media coverage? One obvious reason was the lack of foreign journalists inside China in the period around 1960; some "China watchers" and journalists based in Hong Kong, who interviewed refugees leaving China, wrote about the famine, but their evidence was seen as unconvincing. The nearly complete failure to report the famine is a reminder of just how strong Mao's grip on the media had become. As starving peasants were

---

[20] Jasper Becker, *Hungry Ghosts: China's Secret Famine*, London: John Murray, 1996: 83–96.

Table 12.1 China: Politics and Media

YEAR	IN POWER	YEAR	POLITICS AND MEDIA	NUMBER OF TV SETS IN CHINA
1949	People's Republic of China	1949–1952	Campaign to eliminate old order	
	Mao Zedong (born 1893)		Media: revolutionary agitation	
		1956–1957	The Hundred Flowers	
1959–1963	Mao in semi-retirement	1957–1960	Split from Soviet Union	13,000 (1960)
		1957–1959	The Great Leap Forward	
		1964	China's atomic Bomb	
1976	Mao's death	1965–1977	The Cultural Revolution	
1979	*Deng Xiaoping* (born 1904)	1980–1981	"Gang of Four" trial including Madame Mao	3 million (1978)
		1981–1989	Rapid economic and media growth	50 million (1985)
		1989	Tiananmen Square (Beijing) uprising	160 million (1990)
1997	Deng's Death	1991–	Rapid economic and media growth continue	275 million (1995)
1997	*Jiang Zemin* (born 1926)			
2003	Jiang retires		Media reorganized to two main levels	
2003/2004	*Hu Jintao*			

eating human flesh, fear was eating the souls of Chinese politicians and journalists.

The Cultural Revolution (Table 12.1) was the next super-campaign, and it was another campaign in which both Mao Zedong and the Chinese mass media played prominent roles. Millions of Red Guards (mainly students and teenage schoolchildren) held mass meetings with Mao in the middle of Beijing. Red Guards occupied buildings and covered their walls in large character posters.[21] Red Guards also denounced their own parents and schoolteachers as reactionaries and worse. Many managers and bosses were thrown out of their offices and (if lucky) were dispatched either to cleaning

---

[21] Harriet Evans and Stephanie Donald (eds.), *Picturing Power in the People's Republic of China: Posters in the Cultural Revolution*, Lanham, MD: Rowman and Littlefield, 1999; Göran Leijonhufvud, *Going Against the Tide: On Dissent and Big-Character Posters in China*, London: Curzon Press, and Copenhagen: Nordic Institute of Asian Studies, 1990.

the streets or to be reeducated with farmwork. The youthful Red Guards were also allowed to travel free on the national rail system, allowing them to carry the Cultural Revolution across China.

Behind the flamboyant youthful demonstrators were struggles for survival between top party bosses and other equally bitter struggles at the regional and local levels. Mao Zedong was in his seventies during the Cultural Revolution. He was supposedly semi-retired from politics, but Mao kept returning with explosive force for positively his last devastating performance. Nevertheless, how did a temporarily retired Mao succeed in 1966 in overthrowing his successors, the new Beijing communist power elite? The main answer to this puzzle is simple: The army was loyal to Mao and through the army he regained control of the media and then of the Communist Party.

As the Cultural Revolution began to unfold, army units arrived at radio stations across the land. Radio, then the most mass of the Chinese media, was with Mao and with the army for the next 10 years. The other media were a little more difficult, but here also the Cultural Revolution moved rapidly. The army's own newspapers advocated the Cultural Revolution from the outset.

With Beijing as the base of the post-Mao new regime, the second city of Shanghai became crucial as a political, and media, location. A history of Shanghai in the Cultural Revolution records these events: In August 1966 local Red Guards set out to destroy the "Four Olds"—old customs, old habits, old culture, and old thought. They ransacked 150,000 of Shanghai's wealthier homes and removed cash, jewelry, and goods. Shanghai's then leading circulation daily paper, *Liberation Daily*, was asked to carry *Red Guard Battle News* as an insert in the paper; after a week of confrontation in late November and early December 1966, this was agreed and the *Liberation Daily* soon succumbed more fully. Also in December, Shanghai's high profile "Writers Group" (older cadres, young academics, journalists) joined the Cultural Revolution. In January 1967, the second of Shanghai's three largest newspapers, *Wenhui Bao*, was taken over by the rebels. Also in early January 1967, amidst large public demonstrations, the incumbent mayor of Shanghai was removed and assigned to "reform under rebel supervision."[22]

The remainder of the press and the media were quite soon under the control of Mao and in support of the Cultural Revolution.[23] Regional and local papers, for most of the decade 1967–1976, followed the central lead even more carefully than before. Many daily paper editors—anxious that significance should not falsely be read into the smallest printing idiosyncrasies—made up their pages to look almost identical to the *People's Daily*. According to (dubious) official figures, the total newspaper daily sale, which previously

---

[22] Elizabeth J. Perry and Li Xun, *Proletarian Power: Shanghai in the Cultural Revolution*, Boulder, CO: Westview Press, 1997: 12–18.

[23] Wang Shaoguang, *Failure of Charisma: The Cultural Revolution in Wuhan*, Hong Kong: Oxford University Press, 1995.

had grown rapidly, now stuck for a decade at the same figure, 30 million daily copies for the whole of China.

While the press and radio dominated, other media elements—notably both film and television—offered very little. Television, which was only present in China on a small scale, initially closed down altogether. One foreign observer noted in October 1970 that the 26-minute main evening television news included 18 minutes of rolling captions of Mao's thoughts on the screen,[24] with background music from *The East Is Red* ("The East is Red! The sun is rising! China has produced Mao Zedong!").

As the Cultural Revolution continued, now in full control into the 1970s, Mao (especially after 1973) handed over much detailed power to the "Gang of Four," which included his wife, former film actress Jiang Qing.

China's Regional-Capitalist and Nationalist-Communist Media

From around 1982 China took the capitalist road, under the leadership of Deng Xiaoping; increasingly there was a mixture of capitalism and communism. This, however, was not the only potentially awkward mix. As the

Figure 12.3 Cyclists and Volkswagen advertising, Beijing. (Mark Henley/Panos Pictures.)

---

[24] Timothy Green, *The Universal Eye: World Television in the Seventies*, London: The Bodley Head, 1972: 248–49.

regime became less communist, it also became more nationalist; and as it became more nationalist it also increasingly encouraged, or allowed, the regions of China to develop separately.

Much U.S. discussion of China highlights the challenge of trying to marry capitalism and communism. However, capitalism and socialism have cohabited peacefully in western Europe, India, and Latin America. The other combination—of nationalism and regionalism—may be more challenging. Certainly the regional mass media in China have developed considerable strength, and with some consequences not anticipated by the political elite in Beijing.

In both the 1980s and 1990s the Chinese economy produced a spectacular growth spurt. This was fueled with big foreign capital investment and was maintained by tens of millions of lowly paid workers. By the early 2000s China was the world leader in bicycle production, big dams, freshwater fish, furniture, microwave ovens, shirts, shoes, steel, personal computers, pigs, television receivers, toys, wheat, and much else. China was also generating a wave of new (dollar) multimillionaires (many of whom were in real estate).

By 2005 China had about 330 million households containing at least one television set. China was also at the top of several other communications and media big leagues. Advertising expenditure saw rapid growth. However, advertising expenditure back in the late 1970s was virtually nil; and

Figure 12.4 Chinese children (of the Miao ethnic minority) watching communal television at their school in a large cave, near Ziyun (Guizhou), July 2005. (AP.)

especially in the 1980s and 1990s there was not enough expenditure adequately to perform advertising's allotted task of funding most of the Chinese media.

From the early 1980s the Chinese media were increasingly allowed to be economically free; but the Communist Party and the state retained ideological control and ownership. Previous to 1980 all Chinese media were grey propaganda vehicles, offering only modest amounts of entertainment, rigidly controlled in terms of both finance and ideology. After 1983 the Chinese media increasingly lost their subsidy support, and now had to rely on advertising and sales revenue. Entertainment and noncommunist content now took up the bulk of press space and radio/TV time. Financial news, showbiz gossip, tabloid journalism, soap operas, and consumer advertising became ever more prominent. However, the Communist Party and the state retained firm control through several mechanisms. Although media could "go commercial," all media were ultimately controlled by the party or a state agency or company. All media had to give pride of place—including front pages and the top of the radio/TV news—to communist themes and politicians in power. In addition, the media were occasionally warned that they had gone too far. This was often done by the sacking or demotion of a few leading editors. More general clampdowns occurred in 1983, 1987, and especially in 1989[25] when hundreds of students and others were killed in Beijing's Tiananmen Square and when hundreds of media people were sacked or disciplined. There was another more subtle clampdown around 1999–2002.

Control was also exerted over the media by a complex set of regulations, operated by a bewildering number of different state agencies and government departments. The media regulators in the early 2000s included the Propaganda Department (Communist Party); the State News and Publishing Bureau; the Xinhua news agency; the State Administration of Radio, Film and TV (SARFT), whose remit included cable TV; the Ministry of Information Technology (in charge of telecommunications and Internet); the Ministry of Culture; the Ministry of Foreign Affairs; and the State Council Information Office. Also probably involved were two state security agencies—the Public Security Bureau and the Ministry of State Security.

As Communist Party ideology and rhetoric became less salient, the political leadership in Beijing was able to give more emphasis to the Chinese nation and nationalism. This was a relatively (compared with India) easy option because about 70 percent of all Chinese people speak some version of Mandarin; a still bigger proportion belong to the main—Han—ethnic group, which also includes most speakers of China's two other largest languages —namely Wu (the main language of Zhejiang, just south of Shanghai) and Yue or Cantonese (the main language in and around Guangdong, the boom area in southern China). Speakers of these three big languages totaled over 80 percent of the Chinese population. This relatively uniform linguistic

---

[25] Junhao Hong, "The Role of Media in China's Democratisation," *Media Development*, 1, 2002: 18–22.

background went along with common historical exploitation by European colonizers and by Japanese invaders.

With such a dominant main language and an even more dominant main ethnicity comes a strong majority sense of being Chinese and belonging to China, which has centuries of Confucian tradition and for centuries has also had a huge slice of the world's total population. The Communist Party leaders in China are able to call upon at least two major nationalist strands. There are official nationalist goals and sentiments such as consolidating the grip of the Han people (and of Beijing) on the (non-Chinese) mountainous western regions of Tibet and Xinjiang. But there is the rather different popular nationalism, especially of urban youth. Sometimes the regime deliberately manipulates these different strands of nationalism. For example, when university students communicate on the Internet about their objections to some current aspect of U.S. or Japanese policy, the regime can leave these nationalist outbursts to be observed by foreign journalists and diplomats; the students' nationalism reflects the teaching they received in the school system. Meanwhile, the Chinese government's own official reaction looks more restrained than that of the students.

Beijing deliberately cultivates an old Chinese nationalist tradition of "making the foreign serve China."[26] The approach here is to allow foreigners into China in various roles—as investors, as innovators, as teachers—but to limit such involvement. This approach can have a public relations aspect, as exhibited by Mao Zedong before he came to supreme power in 1949; the insurgent communists were extremely successful at inviting selected (mainly American) journalists—Edgar Snow and others—who then wrote books such as *Red Star over China*, which portrayed Chinese communism in a broadly positive light.[27] In recent decades the Beijing authorities, while inviting in foreign capital and foreign businesses, have been adroit in never losing control to the foreigners. Many foreign businesspeople (including media businesspeople) have arrived in China intending to make rapid commercial strides; most, but not all, of these foreigners have been disappointed. Many foreign businesses (including media businesses) continue to make financial losses in China and to shield from public (and shareholder) view the full extent of these losses.

The Chinese regime is anxious about any social movement that might attract support across China. The regime is anxious about Muslims, especially in the far west, and has encouraged Han Chinese to migrate there. The official fierce opposition to the Falun Gong[28] may indicate the communist leaders' anxiety that this religious sect could successfully attract widespread

[26] Anne-Marie Brady, *Making the Foreign Serve China: Managing Foreigners in the People's Republic*, Lanham, MD: Rowman and Littlefield, 2003.
[27] Chin-Chuan Lee (ed.), *Voices of China: The Interplay of Politics and Journalism*, New York: The Guilford Press, 1990: 163–295; "Covering China," *Media Studies Journal*, Vol. 13/1, Winter 1999.
[28] Danny Schechter, *Falun Gong's Challenge to China*, New York: Akashic Books, 2000.

national support through a nationalist appeal about the exploitation of poor Chinese people by wealthy foreigners and newly wealthy Chinese.

China's regions are strong—politically and economically, as well as in the media—and getting stronger. While China continues to operate a command economy and a centrally directed—and nationalistic—media, China's media also have a very strong regional element. This is without China having India's enormous strength and presence of regional languages. Here we will briefly consider four main areas of China—the northeast coast, the southeast coast, the inland east and south, and the west and the far west. Most of China's people live in the east and within 600 or 700 miles from the sea. But up to 10 separate locations (cities and/or provinces) have had some success in reaching television audiences outside their own localities.

The northeast coastal region stretches from Shanghai (China's precommunist media capital) past Beijing—the location of the top party newspapers and China Central Television (CCTV)—and also includes old coastal industrial areas to the northeast of Beijing. This is one of the richest Chinese regions; the population is Han, and the northeast has, in Beijing, the home of the Mandarin language.

The southeast is China's most dynamic region—in media as well as economically. This includes Zhejiang province and Fujian (opposite the island of Taiwan) as well as the Guangdong "new workshop of the world." This latter's Pearl River area contains several important cities—including Guangzhou, Shenzen, and Hong Kong. The Pearl River has been the leader in Chinese media innovation—especially in terms of independent newspapers, but also in radio and television. Hong Kong has been the location of a major film industry, using its own local Cantonese language. This southeast region is the main location of Han people who speak languages other than Mandarin. Not only is Guangdong more capitalist and less communist than Beijing, Shanghai, and the northeast; Guangdong's preferences in television programming, newspapers, and popular music also differ sharply from popular preference (and audience numbers) in Beijing and Shanghai.

Over one-third of China's population (some 450 million) live in the inland east and south at distances of 300 or 400 miles from the coast; major cities include Wuhan (inland from Shanghai on the Yangtze River). Several inland provinces—such as Hunan and Anhui—are significant media players. Even more than the coastal provinces, these inland provinces include very sharp contrasts between urban and rural and between affluent and poor Chinese.

The Chinese west and far west, with 60 percent of the land area and 20 percent of the population, have a few areas of substantial population. These include the Chongqing-Chengdu area, targeted for major growth; Chongqing (as the nationalist capital in the war against Japan) is a city with a unique media history. But much of the west and far west is very lowly populated.

Xinjiang, Tibet, and Quinghai—three vast western regions—have China's three highest proportions of ethnic minority people. Xinjiang in the far west is seen, by Beijing, as being especially sensitive because it is the main location for such Muslim peoples as the Uighurs and Kazaks. Unlike the Zhuang[29] (mainly near the Vietnam border in the southern province of Guangxi) these western Muslim peoples are seen by Beijing as potentially threatening, not least because their ethnic ties stretch across China's western borders into (former Soviet) Muslim central Asia. In addition to encouraging Han migration into these areas, Beijing also allows little local language media. Beijing politicians—fearing that the Uighurs will lapse into separatism and Muslim fundamentalist insurrection—approve of the packaging of Uighurs into the ethnic music and ethnic restaurant scenes within Beijing and other eastern cities.[30]

Beijing's restrictive media policies for sensitive ethnic minorities contrasts with the general policy of encouragement, or benign tolerance, toward most regional and local media in most of China. While Beijing retains its big force of media regulators, the broad policy is to allow the media to swim along with the tide of economic and business growth.

Major regional economic and social trends—upon which Chinese journalists report—also have consequences for the media industry and for journalism. Regional dispersal fits with Chinese tradition and with the Mao Zedong preference for a broadly spread defensive posture in face of enemy threats. But local autonomy has often led to excessive production because local politicians want to avoid unemployment. Regional government and industry often attract foreign investment into an already booming area, typically on the coast or somewhere in the inland southeast. Cities, especially coastal cities, which have been less successful at attracting investment, try hard to boost their image; such attempts have been made by Tianjin and Dalian, both of them large coastal cities not far from Beijing. This city-boosting can lead to major corruption.

Most of China's larger cities are significant media locations; the capital city of a province is typically the home base for both citywide and province-wide media. This media presence provides support, publicity, and power to local politicians and to major employers. But the media are now expected to rely primarily on advertising revenue; that advertising also comes primarily from local politicians and employers and is far from being transparent. With advertising being such a murky area, there has been a tendency toward corruption, kickbacks, under-the-table deals, and piracy of all kinds. Some

---

[29] Katherine Palmer Kaup, *Creating the Zhuang: Ethnic Politics in China*, Boulder, CO: Lynne Rienner, 2000.

[30] Robyn Iredale, Naran Bilik, and Fei Guo (eds.), *China's Minorities on the Move*, Armonk, NY: M.E. Sharpe, 2003: 89–138, 155–74; Rachel Harris, "Cassettes, Bazaars and Saving the Nation: The Uyghur Music Scene in Xinjiang, China," in Richard King and Timothy J. Craig (eds.), *Global Goes Local*, Vancouver University of British Columbia Press, 2002: 265–83; Christian Tyler, *Wild West China: The Taming of the Xinjiang*, London: John Murray, 2003; David S. Cloud and Ian Johnson, "Uighur Nationalism Tests the Boundaries of Security, Tolerance," *Wall Street Journal Europe*, August 3, 2004; Melinda Liu, "Trouble in 'Turkestan': Beijing's Crackdown on Uighurs in Xinjiang," *Newsweek*, July 10, 2000; "Go West, Young Han," *The Economist*, December 23, 2000: 95–96.

media consequently came to rely on subsidies, and some businesses, repelled by advertising corruption, preferred to set up their own media. This, in turn, contributed to oversupply—a surplus of weak media outlets, each one desperate for more advertising revenue.

Just as foreign businesses often wanted to build their factories in specific coastal locations, so also foreign businesses supported local media in these same locations. The southern boom area of the Pearl River also generated the highest levels of advertising finance, which in turn helped the local and regional southern media to produce high quality and popular output. This in turn provided an additional boost to the strong images of such boom cities.

There was also a temptation for local media to become involved in local corruption—alongside local politicians, local criminals, and local customs officials and taxation officers.

Newspaper Journalism, Envelopes, and the Internet

As the previously Marxist and Beijing dominated press marched toward regional commercialism, there were several unanticipated consequences in terms of circulation and advertising. The Internet unexpectedly had a major initial impact in strengthening the newspaper press, which was fragmented across numerous provinces and cities.

Around 1980 there was almost no television, no advertising, no film industry, and little media entertainment. By 1985 the Communist Party press was still dominant; the *People's Daily* still had an official circulation of five million (down from a previous seven million). China in 1985 had 26 dailies each with a circulation of over 500,000; at least 10 provinces had at least one daily with a sale of over 500,000 copies.[31] These were all the leading party papers in their province, with few pages, little news, and no advertising; the grey dailies depended on "circulation" revenue (including many "sales" into large offices). Other communist national dailies had faded into low circulations. In 1995 the predominant pattern was of province and city newspaper groups. Typically the morning paper was still the politically correct communist media leader in its province or city. But the political morning dailies were now subsidized by their much more popular stable companies, in the form of urban commercial (often afternoon) dailies. By 1985 advertising revenue was just exceeding sales revenue; by now also the Chinese audience saw press and TV as roughly equal in providing political news.

By 2005 the commercial papers had moved further ahead of the political party papers, and advertising was now the dominant source of revenue. The main trend of the press had continued to be toward regional entertainment, showbiz, crime, gossip, and sports; the television news was now regarded by most Chinese as the major form of political news.

---

[31] *Focus* (London), August 1985: 13–20.

From the 1980s the newspapers—while not criticizing the top communist leadership—did criticize at the provincial level, including (sometimes) the province's own political elite. Within a province of perhaps 60 million people, corruption and scandal cases could involve big numbers of people and big amounts of money. Some scandals crossed several provinces with combined populations of hundreds of millions of people. Financial scandals, lethal disasters, and major cases of social injustice were common targets for newspaper investigations.

Financial scandals could include the entire elite of a city or province. During 2000–2002 a major corruption case in Shenyang (a city of five million northeast of Beijing) included a former mayor's daughter fleeing abroad with big amounts of money. A corruption case in Guangdong in 2000 involved officials siphoning $1.9 billion from the province's finances. Another case involved officials and smugglers in Xiamen (Fujian province)—opposite Taiwan; 14 people involved in $6.4 billion worth of smuggling were sentenced to death and executed.[32] In such cases the family is billed for the cost of the bullets (two per person executed). In addition to the executed leaders, this case involved 600 government officials (police, customs officials, and Communist Party members).

The Chinese press also played a role in exposing a succession of banking and stock market scandals. Such stories are of importance to the Chinese government and to tens of millions of Chinese people who have had bad investment experiences; this includes initial public offer (IPO) privatization stocks. One financial scandal involved a group of China's leading mutual fund managers who were getting together in a Shanghai sauna to fix the market.[33]

Medical scandals also received some heavy press coverage, including government efforts to deny embarrassing epidemics, such as an AIDS epidemic around 2000–2002[34] and the SARS epidemic in 2003. Another area of medical scandal is the faking of drugs. A high proportion of antibiotics and other pharmaceuticals in China are fakes with "no active ingredient." Many purchased drugs have the wrong ingredients, and many thousands of Chinese people die each year from phoney "medication." Much of this activity is a cottage industry, involving peasants in their own homes assembling the supposedly high tech medications. These are "good" stories for journalists, not least because they raise obvious more general questions about health and medicine in China.

---

[32] Mark L. Clifford and Dexter Roberts, "Can China Tame the Corruption Beast?" *Business Week*, December 18, 2000; David Lague and Susan V. Lawrence, "Rank Corruption," *Far East Economic Review*, October 31, 2002: 32–34.

[33] Tiffany Wu, "China's Lapdog Financial Press Tests Watchdog Role," Reuters Business Briefing, China, December 24, 2000.

[34] Richard McGregor, "Beijing Acknowledges Aids Epidemic," *Financial Times*, March 3, 2001; Elisabeth Rosenthal, "China Acknowledges It Has an AIDS Epidemic and Asks for Help" (from *NY Times*), *International Herald Tribune*, September 7, 2002.

Other scandals concern schools and reflect the fact that even elementary education is not adequately financed and is not free to parents. Often schoolchildren are allowed by their parents to earn money by working at dangerous tasks such as assembling fireworks. A school fireworks disaster that kills children makes another explosive scandal story for the Chinese tabloids.

Industrial disasters in general, and coal-mining accidents in particular, provide another broad seam of scandal stories. In China some 60,000 coal miners died in mine accidents in the 1995–2004 decade; this was 115 dead coal miners per week. Thus mine disaster stories are a staple of Chinese newspapers, and relevant mine managers may try to evade blame or to dump the bodies in a nearby river.[35] These coal disaster stories also have wider significance beyond the high human death toll. China is short of fuel and is the world's biggest consumer of coal. As the industrial demand for coal continues to grow, miners are pushed to work beyond safe limits; local politicians thus get more tax revenue, businessmen get more profits, and journalists get more scandal stories.

Also providing yet another source of local scandal stories are the local police. One estimate is that during 1998–2001 15,000 people a year were executed, died in custody, or were shot by police.[36] According to the *China Police Daily* during a China-wide "Strike Hard" campaign against organized crime in 2001, a total of 443 police officers were killed.[37]

Scandal stories result also from the expansion of hundreds of China's cities onto farming land. Typically whole families live on, and cultivate, very small parcels of this land; under Chinese law their ownership is less than fully legally secure. City politicians may effectively confiscate such land and award it to real estate developers. Approximately one million Chinese men, women, and children are dispossessed in this way each year.[38] Such events, which typically happen within the circulation area of city newspapers, generate obvious scandal stories.

China's advertising expenditure showed big annual percentage increases in the 1980s and 1990s, but it was, of course, starting from almost nil expenditure in 1980. By 2003 Chinese newspapers still only attracted about $2 billion of advertising; of the then annual total of about $10 billion, a high proportion still went into nonmedia advertising. Partly because of the chaotic state of newspaper data and print advertising, some big advertisers (including Procter and Gamble) had become accustomed to taking time on CCTV and spending money on point-of-sale, outdoor, and other forms of nonmedia advertising. Most newspapers also, even after 2000, continued to sell their

---

[35] Richard McGregor, "Miners Pay High Price for China's Coal," *Financial Times*, July 17, 2002; Chris Buckley, "Scores Missing After China Blast," *International Herald Tribune* (from *NY Times*), November 29, 2004.

[36] Robert E. Gamer (ed.), *Understanding Contemporary China*, Boulder, CO: Lynne Rienner, 2003: 96–97.

[37] *Far East Economic Review*, January 17, 2002: 30.

[38] Jiang Xueqin, "Stealing the Land," *Far Eastern Economic Review*, February 7, 2002.

copies at semi-token cover prices. Under Mao Zedong the Chinese were used to subsidized four-page papers; by 2005 the most advertising-successful newspapers had expanded to 40 or 60 sectionalized pages.

The low level of newspaper finance in general and of advertising revenue in particular had had several consequences unanticipated by Deng Xiaoping. Systematic corruption was endemic in 1980s and 1990s Chinese newspapers. For many hundreds of publications, the price of advertising was extremely flexible. Moreover, weak publications could not afford a separate advertising sales force, so reporters were required both to report on, and to solicit advertising from, the same organization.[39] Some salesmen/reporters in effect sold "protection"—if you don't advertise we will write a critical story. It was not uncommon, also, for an advertising sales person to be paid in cash, in advance. Even in the case of successful publications with respectable printed rate cards, there could still be bribery—including bribery to obtain space in a successful publication with too much advertising and too few pages.

Journalists also received money payments direct from news sources, as one foreign journalist told this author:

> In addition to being a journalist, until 2000 I also worked for an investment consultancy. When you hold a press conference, you naturally invite journalists. You must pay each journalist between $12 and $35 (equivalent). If you don't do this, they won't write nice things about your factory opening. Often the journalist's driver gets some money and the journalist may get a second payment after a (friendly) story appears. Also the journalist is offered a free banquet.

It is not unknown for the man from the *Washington Post* or the observer from the British Embassy to be handed a red envelope; these people, of course, insist on handing back the envelope. In China the envelopes can be brown but are often red; this, some people say, is a reminder that in China (as elsewhere in Asia) it is customary to give small money gifts to guests. As in other countries where journalists accept envelopes, China has developed the practice of paying for editorial coverage that is not indicated as advertising or special supplement. Some unprofitable publications may only be able to attract journalists into employment by allowing them to supplement low salaries with regular envelopes and under-the-table payments.

Already by 1995 some commercial dailies were bringing in 10 times as much advertising as the leading ideological dailies in the same groups. With newspaper competition largely operating at the provincial and local levels, there was strong competition between rival dailies in the same city and also strong rivalry between the leading provincewide (mainly communist-ideological) dailies and the leading commercial dailies in that province's main city or cities.

---

[39] Chin-Chuan Lee (ed.), *Power, Money and Media: Communication Patterns and Bureaucratic Control in Cultural China*, Evanston, IL: Northwestern University Press, 2000.

From about 1990 there was official encouragement for financial and business publications; these were seen as necessary to make the commercial/capitalist economy operate more smoothly. Also tolerated or encouraged were magazines specializing in television, sport, and entertainment. In contrast to the newspaper situation, foreign companies were allowed entry into two specific magazine markets—consumer and technical magazines. Consumer magazines such as *Madame Figaro, Elle,* and *Cosmopolitan* appeared in Mandarin editions (with part foreign and part China-generated content). Also especially welcomed were selected technical magazines such as *China Computerworld* (which arrived in China in 1980) and an increasing number of business magazines.[40] But in each of these latter fields there was a strong element of "making the foreigners serve China." The fashion magazines might help the huge Chinese apparel industry to enter some more upmarket areas. Computer, other technical, and business magazines constituted a legal and cost-free way of using American and European expertise to educate China's computer specialists and businesspeople. In search of more efficient bookselling (not publishing) Beijing also welcomed the involvement of foreign companies such as Bertelsmann.

What, then, of the Internet? Here again the Chinese regulators had both defensive and offensive strategies, but there were also some unanticipated consequences. Defensive strategies reflected the Beijing government's anxiety that China might be flooded with inflammatory material that could cause general unrest and lawlessness; in particular Beijing worried that the Internet might be used to encourage aggressive demands for more democracy and to fan the flames of separatism in the far west and in other delicate border areas. The Beijing regulators developed a sophisticated and expensive "firewall" strategy; this was said to employ some 30,000 people and certainly also relied on Western defensive technologies (including technologies originally designed to protect child TV viewers and to protect American military secrets).

However, the Chinese authorities also wanted to encourage use of the Internet. As elsewhere, the Internet began slowly with business and government applications, then moved into affluent homes.[41] In the early 2000s the Internet café phenomenon quickly reached huge proportions. In early 1998 there were only 1.2 million Chinese Internet users,[42] but China's Internet users had passed the 100 million mark by 2005; however, the total number of computers lagged far behind. Internet use was still heavily concentrated in the larger cities. In Beijing in 2001 one study showed 31 percent of the population as Internet users, with the highest usage being among males between the ages of 16 and 24.[43] Most of these young males (and a rapidly increasing

[40] Dexter Roberts, "Newsstand Fever," *Business Week*, November 10, 2003: 26–27.
[41] Christopher R. Hughes and Gudrun Wacker (eds.), *China and the Internet: Politics of the Digital Leap Forward*, London: RoutledgeCurzon, 2003.
[42] Manfred F. Romich, "China," in Sankaran Ramanathan and Jörg Becker (eds.), *Internet in Asia*, Singapore: Asian Media Information and Communication Centre, 2001: 41–52.
[43] *2001/IMI Consumer Behaviours and Life Patterns Yearbook*, Phoenix, AZ: IMI, 2001: 662–63.

number of young females) in the Internet cafes were mainly playing computer games, e-mailing friends, and engaging in other such politically innocent pursuits.

However, the Beijing authorities on more than one occasion ordered the closure of many Internet cafés, often citing the fire hazards. In the worst episodes young Internet users died in late night fires because they were unable to escape through doors locked in order to protect the computers. There was probably a mix of official motives here. There was some genuine anxiety about safety, as well as continuing anxiety that young people were vulnerable to politically dangerous foreign and domestic messages. But the regime was probably only expecting to reduce (not entirely to eliminate) the threat of "dangerous" messages and of uninhibited political net chatter between students and urban youth.

Internet chat rooms and message boards were also useful to the regime because these provided a quick sampling—or sneak preview—of developing opinion among sophisticated Chinese youth (some of them literally the children, or grandchildren, of the Beijing elite). The Internet was also fine-tuned as part of the general Chinese mass media and performed (for the Beijing authorities) the useful functions of spreading information and sampling opinion, as well as reporting on injustice and potentially dangerous social and economic trends.

The Internet also influenced the print and electronic media in ways that Deng Xiaoping could scarcely have anticipated. Many commentators have seen the Internet as providing a route into China for foreign news that is not otherwise available. But most of China's daily newspaper readers are reading provincial and local city newspapers whose main focus is on local, provincial, and national news—not on foreign news.

The Internet has already had a major influence on the domestic Chinese press, simply by linking up geographically scattered daily newspapers with each other's news. No longer do journalists need to wait for newspapers to arrive from distant cities by mail. Many papers put material onto the Internet on a daily basis. For city dailies—short of cash and without reporters stationed across China—this is an important source of good additional news, which is both quick and cheap or cost-free. Journalists on weaker dailies get to look regularly at what bigger and stronger dailies in other provinces are saying. Through the net the daily press, which is fragmented across scores of separate city markets, achieves a loose unity.

Many dailies are reluctant to print negative stories about their own city administration and politicians. Both big and small negative stories about a particular city often appear, not in that city's press, but in newspapers in other nearby, or distant, cities. Internet and e-mail make this process much simpler for journalists and others who want to reveal things, which the local authorities may prefer to keep secret. Foreign correspondents also are helped by Internet and e-mail to get stories out of provincial Chinese newspapers ("Beijing authorities are denying it, but several dailies in central China are saying . . .").

The Internet as a news exchange system helps to establish reputations and prestige for specific publications and for specific editors and journalists. The Internet has also played a key role in disseminating news published in a succession of southern China dailies; in particular the Internet has enabled journalists across China to follow and to admire journalism from the Pearl River and from Guangzhou.

TV, Cable, Radio, Film: Most Eyeballs, Most Soap

Only in 1988 did China Central TV (CCTV) acquire its second channel. In 1985 CCTV1 still had almost all of the TV audience, whereas by 2005 this flagship first channel of CCTV had only 9 percent of the TV audience. By the early 2000s the audience was split into three roughly equal shares between national, provincial, and city/local television channels.

For the decade after Mao's death (1976–1986) the main mass media continued to be press and radio, while film struggled to get restarted. For four full decades (1949–1989) radio continued as the leading mass medium, which reached most Chinese people on a daily basis. Already in 1962 there were 6.7 million loudspeakers, meaning that a village of 300 people would have had about three loudspeakers. By 1984 radio was in most homes—220 million radio sets and 86 million loudspeakers; after a falloff during the Great Leap Forward, radio loudspeakers had advanced into tens of millions of homes, and many of these loudspeakers could not be turned off.[44] However, after about 1984 the radio audience declined quickly as television sets arrived. In a typical Chinese home of two smallish rooms the TV set drowned out the sound of radio, and by the 2000s more than half of all Chinese people said they never listened to radio.

Film, as a mass medium, had the strong support of Mao Zedong, but during the Cultural Revolution the film industry (under the personal direction of Madame Mao) was reduced to making, and reshowing, a handful of revolutionary dramas or communist musicals. Strangely, however, the fewer the number of films produced, the bigger the claimed total audience. Claimed Chinese movie attendance was 6 billion in 1971 and peaked at 29.3 billion in 1979.[45] These extraordinary numbers derived from the fact that, in the Mao era and after, most movie-viewing involved mobile movie facilities (with electric generators) that (it was claimed) visited most villages in China once a week or so. This was a free show in terms of money but a compulsory show in terms of attendance. After Mao's 1976 death these mobile movie shows continued, while Chinese producers were now again making 100 or more new movies annually. A big audience decline began in early 1980s, caused by

---

[44] Won Ho Chang, "Radio: China, the Last Hold-out of Wired Distribution," *InterMedia*, August–September, Vol. 18/4–5, 1990, 40–42.

[45] Zhang Li-Fen, "The Politics of Cinema in China," *Media Development* 1, 1993: 9–11.

television, by video (cassette) piracy, and perhaps by the continuing censorship. The entire mobile movie system was then disbanded. In the 1980s the Chinese film industry returned to make mainly entertainment movies, with more kung fu, more sex, and more slapstick; the 1980s films showed many fewer political meetings and fewer slogans and did less condemnation of class enemies. It was also during the mid- and late 1980s that the youthful "Fifth Generation" of Chinese filmmakers became internationally famous (and won numerous prizes) for *Yellow Earth* (1985), *Red Sorghum* (1987), and many other films. But in China itself these films stimulated neither official nor popular enthusiasm.[46]

During the 1980s Chinese television reached the majority of city homes and started to move out into more rural areas. The programs being shown on China's 160 million TV sets in 1990 were, by international standards, still very propagandistic, puritanical, and none too entertaining. Increasingly, however, more entertaining and viewer-friendly influences arrived at CCTV, via radio and via the south and Shanghai. Important influences of this kind came from Pearl River Economic Radio (PRER) in the mid-1980s; before PRER began transmission, some 85 percent of radio listening in Guangzhou City was switched to radio stations in nearby Hong Kong. Despite its "economic" label, PRER offered a local talk and music format; this format was then copied by a Shanghai radio station and later jumped across to a Shanghai TV station (Shanghai East TV).[47]

James Lull provides an excellent account of television in four of China's largest cities in the years 1986–1989. Initially most Chinese people who had television sets watched most of the available programming; during the hot urban summers many millions of Chinese viewed TV while sitting just outside their small homes. Chinese programming was much more popular than imports. Women preferred drama series specials, Chinese opera, and variety; men preferred sports, news, drama series specials, Chinese opera, and kung fu. For both men and women foreign drama specials were in seventh place; foreign movies were even less popular. Although there were some American imports (ranging from crime series and soaps to basketball)—mostly barter-financed—the majority of imports came from Japan, Europe, Taiwan, Brazil, and Mexico.

The most popular programming with the overall adult (men and women) audience was the soap opera (broadly defined) category. Several Chinese drama series were super-popular, but the most popular series shown in China around 1986 was the Japanese (NHK) telenovela *Oshin*, which was successfully exported to numerous countries. Lull notes that Chinese viewers felt culturally close to Oshin, a Japanese woman who strives bravely, over many

[46] Ni Zhen, *Memoirs from the Beijing Film Academy: The Genesis of China's Fifth Generation*, Durham, NC: Duke University Press, 2002; Kwok-kan Tam and Wimal Dissanayake, *New Chinese Cinema*, Hong Kong: Oxford University Press, 1998.
[47] Yuezhi Zhao, *Media, Market and Democracy in China*, Urbana: University of Illinois Press, 1998: 95–100.

years, against a daunting succession of challenges. Lull reports that around 1986 most Chinese people were longing for Japanese (not American or European) consumer goods; the most "abundant and desired" pop music came from Taiwan, Hong Kong, and Singapore.[48]

After the democracy demonstrations and killings in Tiananmen Square in 1989, all the Chinese media—and not least television—were disciplined in various ways; some people were dismissed. But by 1991 China's rulers were ready for another big expansion of television. Advertising expenditure on television overtook press expenditure for the first time in 1991. Many more new provincial channels were licensed to operate and were told that they must rely on advertising as their main source of finance. Also during 1991–1993 came a rapid growth in domestic satellite TV dishes.

However, direct-to-home (DTH) satellite TV soon experienced one of those regulatory flip-flops that have continued to affect Chinese television. As in many other countries, DTH TV initially existed in a grey area of uncertain legality. Direct reception of foreign satellite TV was made illegal in 1990, but the sale of the dishes only became illegal in 1993. This three-year pause resulted from lobbying by the People's Liberation Army, which was manufacturing most of the dishes at a nice profit. On October 11, 1993, however, the party spoke in *People's Daily*: China must be vigilant against foreign enemies,[49] so domestic satellite dishes are forbidden. Beijing wanted to maintain its satellite monopoly for the distribution of CCTV programming to the provincial stations. Beijing also wanted to maintain its veto against foreign media doing their own uplinking (as CNN[50] and many others had done in covering Tiananmen Square, 1989).

Because advertising revenue was now so important, audience maximization was vital, and as more ratings research became available (at least for the larger cities) Chinese television increasingly focused on ratings. Big foreign (coventure) companies followed their usual practice of only advertising when and where ratings data were available, as one advertising agency media buying executive told this author:

> Chinese companies, especially in inland China, are not interested in numbers. They work by hunch: "I've got some profit, so I'll buy some advertising." But the multinationals are like robots which need to be activated with numbers; no research numbers means no advertising spend. So the multinationals advertise mainly in big city media.

CCTV in the 1990s was losing audience in somewhat the same manner as public broadcasting systems in Europe and elsewhere, when competing against new commercial channels. From the viewpoint of the Communist Party bosses, the CCTV main evening news at 7 pm was crucial. Because the

---

[48] James Lull, *China Turned On: Television, Reform and Resistance*, London: Routledge, 1991; 92–126, 154–81.

[49] "China: Fear of Foreigners," *The Economist*, October 16, 1993.

[50] Mike Chinoy, *China Live: People Power and the Television Revolution*, Lanham, MD: Rowman and Littlefield, 2000: 183–289.

party could also control the entire TV scheduling apparatus, it could still ensure a big national audience; increasingly lighter, and more foreign, stories were placed toward the end of the news bulletin. But every evening several minutes directly after 7 pm were devoted to the top party bosses at that day's top party activities. There were many lengthy and reverential shots of these men sitting in large armchairs and listening as other elderly men in suits talked. This 7:00 pm–7:10 pm coverage did indicate the current party pecking order. But it was not "good television." The contrast with the commercials in the break before 7:00 pm was very marked. The commercials were dazzlingly inventive, dynamic, and funny, with a lightening fast pace (and short shot length) compared to the sluggish political coverage.

Between the early 1990s and the early 2000s Chinese television saw a big increase in production budgets available from booming advertising expenditure (especially for tonics, vitamins, and pharmaceuticals). There was also a major change in producer expertise and ability to generate popular entertainment. This led to an ever increasing tidal wave of new popular— broadly soap opera—drama.[51] Some of these were *telenovela*-style historical dramas, for example, following two families over several decades of recent history. The heroic "Long March" from the 1930s was still popular; but much soapy drama was linked to traditional problems in modern context (such as mother-in-law and daughter-in-law) as well as more recent obsessions such as soccer football and the striving young entrepreneur.

Chinese television also adopted its own versions of other cheap-to-produce formats. This included talk shows, cooking and domestic elegance programming,[52] quiz/game shows of many shapes and sizes, and the old variety show format with a mix of professional and amateur talent. There was a big expansion in animation production. China followed many recent U.S. and European trends—for instance, introducing in 2001 a reality show in which two teams competed against each other "to survive" in the high mountains of Yunan (and including cash prizes awarded via audience voting).

Such formats, when filled with Chinese people and recent Chinese history, were tapping into dramatic and often painful material. The death, destruction, dislocation, and rapid growth of recent decades mean that simple formats throw up an endless supply of truly tragic, high emotion human interest stories. Many "women's stories" report rape and other appalling abuse; a substantial proportion of all Chinese women in jail are there for murdering their husbands. A TV series called *We Are Friends*, which merely reports on a friendship of two people, could be gripping stuff; even a simple interview

---

[51] William C. Godby, "Televisual Discourse and the Mediation of Power: Living Room Dialogues with Modernity in Reform-Era China," in Randy Kluver and John H. Powers (eds.), *Civil Discourse, Civil Society and Chinese Communities*, Stamford, CT: Ablex, 1999: 125–52; Michael Keane, "Television Drama in China: Engineering Souls for the Market," in Richard King and Timothy J. Craig (eds.), *Global Goes Local*, Vancouver: University of British Columbia Press, 2002: 120–37.

[52] Howard W. French, "The Martha Stewart of China," *International Herald Tribune* (from *NY Times*), April 10–11, 2004.

about the family photographs can be a heart-rending saga of family loss, conflict, and survival.

All of these are prerecorded formats that can be both preplanned and postedited in line with current ideological guidelines. The many hundreds of hours of soaps are especially easy to control; for example, all soaps reflect family-size policy—the respectable urban soap family tends to have one child, two working parents, and a grandparent. Documentaries tend to be more politically sensitive, as are quiz/game shows involving nonmainland Chinese participants.[53] Another more ideological format was the compassionate consumer series, such as *Focal Point*, a super-popular CCTV show.[54] This type of show carries real stories often about people in conflict with uncaring government bureaucrats, officials, and police; such criticism, naturally, focuses on the failings of middle or low level bureaucrats and does not question the higher levels or the merits of one-party states and big government.

The search for (ideologically safe) popular material certainly led to much attractive programming across most of the provinces. Certainly CCTV was buying (or commissioning) programming from outside Beijing and Shanghai. CCTV was also syndicating out its own successful productions for reshowing by stations at province and city levels. There was also a significant number of independent TV producers making programming for city and other channels.

But around 2000 Chinese television was in a truly chaotic state. Much of Chinese television inhabited one or more "grey areas"—from piracy, via "legal" (paid) use of "illegally" produced material, and the station-zapping of commercials, through pornography and local politicians delivering unpaid self-promotion messages.

China joined the World Trade Organization (WTO) in late 2001 and the Beijing authorities radically reorganized the Chinese media during the years immediately before and after 2001.[55] The main approach was, first, to rearrange all significant media into a smallish number of large media groups. Second, all of the nonnational media—province, city, county, and small town —were reorganized into big regional groups.[56]

---

[53] Young Zhong, "Debating with Muzzled Mouths: A Case Analysis of How Control Works in a Chinese Television Debate Used for Educating Youths," *Media, Culture and Society*, Vol. 24/1, January 2002: 27–47.

[54] Wanning Sun, "The Politics of Compassion: Journalism, Class Formation, and Social Change in China," *Media Development*, 3, 2001: 13–18.

[55] Chin-Chuan Lee, "The Global and the National of the Chinese Media: Discourses, Market, Technology and Ideology," in Chin-Chuan Lee (ed.), *Chinese Media, Global Contexts*, London: RoutledgeCurzon, 2003: 1–31.

[56] Anke Redl and Rowan Simons, "Chinese Media—One Channel, Two Systems," in Stephanie Hemelryk Donald, Michael Keane, and Yin Hon (eds.), *Media in China: Consumption, Content and Crisis*, London: RoutledgeCurzon, 2002: 18–27; Zhengrong Hu, "The Post-WTO Restructuring of the Chinese Media Industries and the Consequences of Capitalisation," *Javnost: The Public*, Vol. 10/4, December 2003: 5–18; Chien-San Feng, "Is it Legitimate to Imagine China's Media as Socialist? The State, the Media and 'Market Socialism' in China," *Javnost: The Public*, Vol. 10/4, December 2003: 37–52; Brian Shoesmith and Kay Hearn, "Exploring the Roles of Elites in Managing the Chinese Internet," *Javnost: The Public*, Vol. 11/1, March 2004: 101–14.

A handful of the largest and most ideological media groupings now sat at the top of China's media system. One of the biggest was China Radio, Film and TV Group (CRFTG) incorporating all of CCTV (with its 12 TV channels), as well as China National Radio and the main international radio and TV propaganda organizations. The leading national press group included not only *People's Daily* but also some very un-Marxist publications such as *International Finance News*. Another major press grouping was led by the very popular *Beijing Youth Daily*. Xinhua remained as the national and international news agency, about whose intelligence and covert activities there continued to be little or no reliable information. Another new grouping of national significance was the capital city's "regional" electronic grouping—Beijing Radio, Film and TV Group (BRFTG)—which controls the main Beijing TV, radio, cable, and Internet activities.

But the more drastic reorganization was at the province level. The overall nonnational television pattern in the mid-1990s was so chaotic as to defy neat description, but there were four broad levels of regional/local TV output:

1. About 30 large regional groups each had several TV channels.

2. City channels; a large city such as Wuhan had three city channels.

3. New cable stations licensed during the 1990s. Shanghai Cable passed the three million subscriptions mark in 2001; Shanghai Cable in 2001 offered channels by satellite from seven other Chinese locations. Cable grew rapidly in all of the other larger (and in many smaller) cities. These new commercial systems offered up to about 40 channels.

4. Old cable stations, which had often grown up as part of the wired system of a factory or other enterprise; initially these had reached only the workers' homes, close to the factory. These systems also expanded in the 1990s but their technology was older and their capacity smaller.[57]

One of the new regional groupings of all electronic media was Shanghai Media and Entertainment Group (SMEG), which controlled three TV channels, several radio channels, important film and TV production studios, orchestras, two opera houses, a circus, several sports teams, and a convention center. By 2003 SMEG employed 5,200 people.[58]

During the 1990s the Beijing authorities promoted the use of China's satellite system for military, telecommunications, and television purposes. Satellites were seen as an especially efficient means of extending the reach of television across mountainous inland provinces. Three inland southern provinces—Guizhou, Yunnan, and Hunan—were among the first to utilize satellite distribution; the resulting footprints meant that their TV programming reached not only all of their own provinces but also stretched across

---

[57] Brian Shoesmith, "No Sex! No Violence! No News! Satellite and Cable Television in China," *Media Asia*, Vol. 25/1, 1998: 42–49.

[58] Mure Dickie, "China Tunes in to Foreign Channels," *Financial Times*, March 25, 2004.

China. Hunan TV took the lead in targeting the cable systems of more affluent coastal provinces and cities.

In 2001 CCTV's first channel (with its China-wide reach) was still the most popular single channel, with 9.1 percent of all TV viewing. But by 2001 it was apparent that the nonnational channels now had a bigger audience share than the national channels. While CCTV national television was still held back by ideological and educational tasks, the big regional stations were (via satellite) reaching audiences in other parts of China. With fewer ideological tasks, and a stronger focus on entertainment, the big regional channels were more popular.

In China in 2001 4 of the 10 most popular TV channels were CCTV channels (1, 5, 6, 8). But 6 of the 10 channels with the largest audience share across China were provincial stations from Shandong, Guizhou, Liaoning, Anhui, Fujian, and Hunan. The four top CCTV channels had 20.1 percent of all Chinese TV viewing; and the six top provincial channels together had 20.3 percent of total Chinese viewing.[59]

By late 2002 the reorganization had generated 20 TV-radio film groups, which collectively had the bulk of the TV audience. In the early 2000s CCTV's national audience share was slowly sliding down to one-third. Nearly two-thirds of all TV viewing in China involved province, city, and county TV and cable offerings.

The press also was reorganized along similar lines. In late 2002 there were 38 press groupings within China's 31 main regional government entities (22 provinces, four municipalities under direct Beijing control, and five so-called autonomous regions). A few other big cities were allowed a press grouping separate from that of the province, but in most cases a single provincial press group now includes everything from the main ideological publications of the province's Communist Party to the largest sale "commercial" dailies, as well as numerous regional magazines and smaller daily and weekly newspapers. Although there is a small trickle of province newspapers and news via Internet into other provinces, the readership of the provincial dailies (and especially of the popular afternoon dailies) remains overwhelmingly inside the province.

While reorganizing the press into just two levels, the authorities closed quite a large number of small publications, some of which were little more than publicity sheets for large commercial organizations. Also outlawed were all press subsidies.

The Beijing authorities thus forced a comprehensive conglomerization onto the media. This eliminated a lot of the preexisting competition. Now much competition is intragroup—for example, a struggle for resources between ideological and commercial, as well as between urban and rural, media offerings within the same group. Major disputes also lurk within the national media groupings, not least because the Communist Party awarded itself greater

---

[59] The Economist Intelligence Unit, *Business China*, May 21, 2001.

ownership and control over the media. The precise legal meaning of this media "ownership" still remains unclear.

Media competition now exists within groups, between print and broadcast groups, between city and province groups, and between different province groups (seeking to attract each other's audiences and to appeal via satellite to distant audiences). Who controls, and sets the rules for, this conglomeratized competition? Clearly it was Beijing that made the strategic plan; and since all media are now "owned" by the Communist Party, the Beijing authorities can still set censorship guidelines and can sack prominent editors.

But in practice it is now the provincial communist cadres who control the bulk of China's media. The provincial, or big city, authorities exercise financial control (via taxation and subsidy); they set the detailed guidelines and goals for specific publications and channels. Also it is those province and big city authorities (journalists say) who fine-tune the censorship rules and indicate each week which stories should be boosted and which ignored.

The media powers of provincial leaders were illustrated by events surrounding the *Southern Metropolitan Daily* in 2003. This successful daily, only launched in 1997, achieved rapid circulation gains across the province of Guangdong. The new province daily belonged to the provincewide Southern Media Group and was competing against a successful city daily in Guangzhou city; the *Guangdong Daily*, the lead publication in a major press grouping, in 2002 had a daily sale of 1.6 million. The *Southern Metropolitan Daily*'s circulation had also passed one million by 2002. In this city versus province daily competition the province paper, the *Southern Metropolitan Daily*, was by 2002–2003 more editorially aggressive and more politically daring; it was quickly acquiring a China-wide reputation. However, it ran into political difficulties with an April 25, 2003, story. This was a scandal story about a man, who the *Southern Metropolitan Daily* claimed, had been beaten to death in police custody. The scandal story went further; it reported that there was a network of custody-and-repatriation centers—in which undocumented rural workers (without permission to be in an urban area) were held under Soviet gulag-style conditions. The arrested workers, it was claimed, were even traded for money between custody centers. This scandalous story achieved national publicity and the Beijing authorities announced that the custody-and-repatriation centers would be closed. But the provincial government of Guangzhou subsequently arrested several senior personnel at the *Southern Metropolitan Daily*. The top manager and the top editor were both given long prison sentences for "embezzlement." In this case the provincial government and courts disciplined their own newspaper editors and managers; the provincial government also overruled the national government in Beijing.[60]

---

[60] Howard W. French, "China Tries to Muzzle Outspoken Newspaper," *International Herald Tribune* (from *NY Times*), April 16, 2004; Philip P. Pan, "Did China Tabloid Attain Pyrrhic Victory?" *Wall Street Journal Europe*, August 3, 2004; Frederik Balfour, "From Rag to Riches to . . . ," *Business Week*, December 30, 2002.

The province and city communist authorities make the senior media appointments; senior editors and provincial TV controllers are appointed by, and are part of, this regional communist power elite. Journalists' careers exist within a broader pattern of communist bureaucratic careers; a middle-ranking bureaucrat may be appointed into an important editorial post, and then may subsequently return to a more senior government bureaucratic post.[61]

Leading members of this provincial elite have very extensive powers; they exercise not only political power, but also commercial power, because many major businesses are owned by the provincial government. Moreover, all businesses depend on provincial regulators for permission to build new factories and much else. Furthermore, some successful businessmen are being accepted into senior levels of the Communist Party.

It may exaggerate to describe this as the dictatorship of the regional party, but some notorious cases do indicate that regional communist leaderships exercise not just political and commercial dominance; they also engage in large-scale organized corruption and crime. In the early 2000s some 150,000 communist officials were punished each year for corruption.

The notorious regional corruption cases in Shenyang and Xiamen indicate that the big regional media kept silent over big criminal activity. The mayor of Shenyang was shown in 2001 to have run a crime syndicate whose members included the local parliament leader, the head of the local tax bureau, the chief prosecutor, and the police chief; some journalists and editors must have been at least co-opted members of this organized crime syndicate. Even after the scandal went public, the Shenyang media did not report a major subsequent court case—reporting had to be left to journalists from other cities such as Wuhan, Guangzhou, and Beijing.[62] But for several years this massive scandal went unreported in Shenyang, a city of five million people.

From the viewpoint of central politicians in Beijing these provincial and city scandals must be preferable to possible provincial separatist breakaways. The army is organized quite differently from the provinces. The army has just seven large regional commands; and senior officers, who are moved frequently, are themselves kept apart from the province and city elites. While military intervention remains available as an option, even in 1989 the central authorities were reluctant to use military force in their own city of Beijing.

Although the top Beijing politicians and the numerous national regulators forcefully reshaped the Chinese media onto a strict two-level pattern, paradoxically these big changes of the late 1990s and early 2000s accompanied a decline in the overall importance of the national media. Beijing's main traditional control over the media was of news, factual output, and politics.

[61] Zhongdang Pan and Ye Lu, "Localizing Professionalism: Discursive Practices in China's Media Reforms," in Chin-Chuan Lee (ed.), *Chinese Media, Global Contexts*, London: RoutledgeCurzon, 2003: 215–36.

[62] James Kynge, "Cancer of Corruption Spreads Throughout Country," *Financial Times*, November 1, 2002; Mure Dickie, "A Free press for China: Will Beijing's Cautious Opening of the Media Herald a Triumph of Profit over Propaganda?" *Financial Times*, March 4, 2004.

Figure 12.5 The Super Girls achieved super-popularity during a singing contest on Chinese TV. Here the group performs at the People's Stadium, Beijing, October 2005. (AP.)

But, although an important political and news dimension continued at both the regional and national levels, the main thrust of Chinese media in the early 2000s was toward more entertainment, more advertising, and closer attention to the expectations and entertainment preferences of local audiences.

Whereas advertising expenditure in the 1980s and in much of the 1990s had been inadequate, by the late 1990s and early 2000s advertising expenditure was doubling every four years, which was at last providing enough finance to generate plenty of attractive TV entertainment programming at the regional level. There was now more regional soap-drama, while China's strength in regional music led to successful packaging of regional pop music for audiences across China.[63]

---

[63] Mercedes M. Dujunco, "Hybridity and Disjuncture in Mainland Chinese Popular music," Janet L. Upton, "The politics and poetics of *Sister Drum*: 'Tibetan' music in the global marketplace," Isabel K. F. Wong, "The Incantation of Shanghai: Singing a City into Existence," in Richard King and Timothy J. Craig (eds.), *Global Goes Local*, Vancouver: University of British Columbia Press, 2002: 25–39, 99–119, 246–64.

There was also a big regional development in reality entertainment formats such as the TV dating show. The mainland China dating show *Romantic Meeting* was launched by Hunan Satellite Television in 1998; this show was sponsored by a Japanese food company and used a group dating format based on a 23-year-old (1975) Japanese dating show. The Hunan show also followed a Taiwan offering, *Special Man and Woman* (distributed by Phoenix TV of Hong Kong to Chinese cable stations in 1997). The success of the Hunan dating show led at least 10 other regional TV stations to launch their own dating shows. These included *Saturday Meeting* (Shanghai TV), *The Square of Kindred Spirits* (Hebei TV), *Everlasting Romance* (Beijing Cable TV), *Good Man, Good Woman* (Shanxi TV), *Talking Marriage* (Hainan TV), and *Heavenly Fate* (Chongqing Satellite TV).[64]

Such popular, but cheap-to-produce, formats were obviously angled toward advertising concerns. Advertising, audience research, and regional entertainment marched on parallel tracks from the three preferred advertising locations of the early 1990s (Beijing, Shanghai, and Guangdong) to 10 cities, then 20, and then 30 preferred cities and provinces.

Increasingly by 2005 both the press and broadcast conglomerate groups were targeting the entire Chinese urban population of some 500 million. These people were the target for more and more entertainment output and for consumer advertising. City-based daily newspapers and weekly magazines, like city-based TV stations and cable TV operations, targeted these urban 500 million. These were also the Chinese people who welcomed TV programming from such exotic but not-too-distant locations as Hong Kong, Taiwan, Japan, and South Korea. Since between 15 and 20 million extra Chinese people are moving from rural to urban locations each year, this broad urban media focus will continue to strengthen.

Some 800 million people still live in rural China, and they are much less well served by the media.[65] These rural people are much more dependent on national CCTV television from Beijing, on provincewide television and radio channels, and on newspapers, which tend to reflect the political power of each province's Communist Party, government, and commercial elites. Rural incomes have risen slowly compared with urban incomes, and the rural-urban inequality gap has grown. China's rural millions lack adequate income after taxes; they also lack free education and adequate health services. Rural unemployment is a huge problem about which no reliable data exist.

The media intake of rural Chinese people is very different from the media intake of the national and regional elites. Elite individuals and their families number at most a few million—a fraction of 1 percent of China's population. These elite individuals have access to media not available to most people;

---

[64] Michael Keane, "Send in the Clones," in Stephanie Hemelryk Donald, Michael Keane, and Yin Hong (eds.), *Media in China: Consumption, Content and Crisis*, RoutledgeCurzon, 2002: 80–90.
[65] Yuezhi Zhao, "Transnational Capital, the Chinese State, and China's Communication Industries in a Fractured society," *Javnost: The Public*, Vol. 10/4, December 2003: 52–73.

many elite families live in special housing compounds or luxury apartment blocks where they are permitted to use satellite television, complete with numerous foreign channels. Elite individuals also have access to foreign publications, to foreign movies and music, and to special news services from Xinhua.

Making the Foreign Media Serve the Eastern Asian Media

Since the 1980s, American and European media exporters have discussed the massive potential of the Chinese media market.[66] But China has only accepted very modest quantities of media imports; even then, it has preferred to import from Asia rather than from Hollywood or Europe. Despite much Hollywood hoopla and publicity, and many personal visits by Western media moguls and barons, China has succeeded in making the foreigners help China to be media self-sufficient.

Hollywood has been especially successful in exporting expensive (to make) drama/fiction series around the world; but this success has not included China. A study of TV drama imports into China showed that, in 2000–2001, the U.S. share was only 18 percent; Taiwan, South Korea, Japan, and Singapore together outscored the United States by nearly 2 to 1 and, with Hong Kong

Figure 12.6 Jackie Chan, Hong Kong movie star, advertising Chinese-made computers on a street billboard in Fuzhou (Fujian). (Chris Stowers/Panos Pictures.)

---

[66] For example, "Media Projects to Link China and US," *The Wall Street Journal*, June 2, 1983.

added, eastern Asia was exporting three times as many TV episodes into China as was the United States. Moreover, American TV dramas were usually scheduled in lower audience times than were the eastern Asian drama episodes.[67]

The Hollywood companies were, from the 1980s, eager to reenter the China film market in some strength. But in 1992 of 222 movies shown in China only 12 came from Hollywood (versus 130 from China itself, 47 from Hong Kong, and 17 from Europe).[68] In the early 2000s, and despite the WTO, Hollywood still only had a very small fraction of the Chinese market.

A somewhat similar—semi-token—policy operated for the pronouncements of American politicians; President Bill Clinton, Vice President Dick Cheney, and President George W. Bush when on visits to China were all allowed to speak live on one of CCTV's channels. But on the main evening CCTV news their words were heavily edited, with references to sensitive topics removed. Similar treatment occurred in the newspapers, and even Chinese translations of American political memoirs were carefully edited to remove sensitive references.[69]

While American commentators noted the great difficulty of penetrating the Chinese media market, News Corporation (led by Rupert Murdoch and family) was often quoted as having successfully exported Star and Phoenix channels into China. But Star's main success (after a full decade in China) was on cable systems in parts of Guangdong province, where in winter 2002–2003 it had 1.3 percent of the province's prime-time TV audience.[70] Phoenix also was at best a rather ambiguous success. In fact, News/Murdoch controlled only 38.25 percent of Phoenix, while a similar share belonged to Liu Chang Le; the latter was widely known as being "close to" the People's Liberation Army and to senior Communist Party people in Beijing. Another view of this situation was that the Chinese authorities were once again sampling Western products while encouraging their owners to continue to subsidize these loss-making demonstrations.

China is unusual, as a big-population media power, in willingly importing from smaller nations. But in relying in the 1990s mainly on imports from Hong Kong and Taiwan, China was relying on overseas Chinese media enterprises. Taiwan and Hong Kong together accounted for more than half of

---

[67] Yik-Chan Chin, "The Nation-State in a Globalising Media Environment: China's Regulatory Policies on Transborder TV Drama Flow," *Javnost: The Public*, Vol. 10/4, December 2003: 75–92.

[68] "China Opens Doors to Foreign Films," *Variety*, March 7–14, 1994.

[69] Mei-Zhong, "Same Language, yet Different: News Coverage of Clinton's China Visit by Two Prominent Newspapers," in Randy Kluver and John H. Powers (eds.), *Civil Discourse, Civil Society and Chinese Communities*, Stamford, CT: Ablex 1999: 153–66; Joseph Kahn, "After the Fact, Chinese Prune Cheney's Speech," *International Herald Tribune* (from *NY Times*), April 18, 2004; Tsan-Kuo Chang, "Political Drama and News Narratives: Presidential Summits on Chinese and US National Television," in Chin-Chuan Lee (ed.), *Chinese Media, Global Contexts*, London: RoutledgeCurzon, 2003: 119–38.

[70] Mure Dickie, "Star TV Aims High in China," *Financial Times*, January 2, 2003.

all of the 60 million Han overseas Chinese.[71] The other main overseas Chinese locations were Indonesia, Thailand, and Malaysia—and these three locations were significant financiers of Chinese manufacturing.

Hong Kong was returned in 1997 by Britain to China, and Hong Kong, despite its special status, gradually became part of the broader Guangdong/Pearl River workshop of the world and dynamic leader of Chinese media innovation. From 1995 onward, China began gradually to increase its modest level of importing from South Korea and Japan. The year 2001 saw a big increase in South Korean TV fiction, movies, games, food, and fashion entering China.[72] Imports from Japan—especially of TV fiction and of TV reality formats—also increased significantly.

Some significant American and European media influence does remain in China. Probably the largest Euro-American media influence is exerted through advertising and Western advertising agencies.[73] There are also significant numbers of joint ventures and coproductions involving partnerships of Chinese with American and European media producers. Another notable Hollywood presence has been in pirated movies, at first on video cassettes, and then on DVD. "DVD-one dollar" was a common street-corner offer in large Chinese cities in the early 2000s.

But the broad international drift of Chinese media is toward neither California nor Europe. China is likely to remain broadly media self-sufficient. Increasingly China seems to be becoming one of the leaders of a China–Japan–South Korea–Taiwan–Indonesia–Thailand–Malaysia–Vietnam grouping, which has 30 percent of world's population and over 30 percent of the world's TV households.

[71] Robert E. Gamer, *Understanding Contemporary China*, Boulder, CO: Lynne Rienner, 2003: 155–94.
[72] Mi Hui Kim, "Cracking Wall: Korean TV Stars Propel New Openness in China," *Variety*, August 27–September 2, 2001.
[73] Jian Wang, *Foreign Advertising in China*, Ames: Iowa State University Press, 2000.

PART 3

WORLD MEDIA PECKING ORDER

13

World Media Pecking Order

There is a pronounced media pecking order within continents and across the world. Throughout the twentieth century the United States was generally seen as occupying the number one perch in this world media pecking order. Underlying the number one U.S. position was, of course, the commercial strength of its media industries and its large population (compared with other industrialized countries).

Media pecking orders also operate within world regions—with India as number one in South Asia and Mexico number one in Spanish America. Small-population nations typically import not only from the United States but also from the number one nation within their own world region. This chapter focuses on Japan's leading position in the East and Southeast Asian media pecking order. Also considered is South Korea, which since 1945 has ascended from a low to a much higher pecking order position.

Bigger-population countries tend to import media primarily from the United States; most bigger countries (except China) do not want to import media from smaller countries that are lower down the world, or regional, pecking orders. Larger countries in Europe—such as France, Germany, and the United Kingdom—do not want to import from each other (although they all import from the United States). The media trade pecking order involves cultural nationalism; in most countries, most politicians and most people want to export their national media. In particular most nations do not want to import much media from their main regional rivals, and they especially do not want to import from smaller neighbors. Belgium imports from France, and Guatemala imports from Mexico, but there is little or no media trade in the opposite direction.

The media pecking order is recognized by participating countries and remains relatively stable over time; this stability derives from established facts of population, language, and cultural tradition. The stability also reflects political and cultural alliances and antagonisms; consequently it requires a major war—or other major international turbulence—to generate speedy changes in the media pecking order. However, this does not stop specific nations from gradually rising in the pecking order, as South Korea has done in recent years.

World Media Pecking Order

Some evidence on the lack of rapid change in the world media pecking order was provided by studies of television trade in 1973 and in 1983, both conducted by Tapio Varis. In both 1973 and 1983 a few dominant patterns prevailed—including a "one-way flow" of TV programming from a few big exporters to the rest of the world. Entertainment material was predominant in this TV flow; around the world most countries imported one-third or more of their transmitted TV programming. But between 1973 and 1983 no huge changes in the flow of imported programs had taken place.[1]

Another facet of the relatively stable world TV trading picture was that, in both 1973 and 1983, the smallest population countries were the largest importers. The largest importers in 1973 included Guatemala, Singapore, New Zealand, Dubai, Malaysia, and Iceland, all of which imported at least two-thirds of their 1973 programming output.[2] Table 13.1 shows that in 1983 small-population countries typically imported a much higher percentage of their TV programming than did bigger-population countries.

Table 13.1   Percentages of Imported Television Programming in Big- and Small-Population Countries, 1983

	Percentage of TV Time That was Imported	
	BIG POPULATION	SMALL POPULATION
Eastern Europe	8	27
Asia and Pacific	10	43
Western Europe	21	40
Latin America	32	44
Near East	35	47
Africa	31	60
Totals	21	41
Number of countries	13	39

Note: The 13 big-population countries were the Soviet Union, China, India, Pakistan, France, Germany, Italy, Spain, the United Kingdom, Brazil, Mexico, Egypt, and Nigeria.
Source: Tapio Varis, *International Flow of Television Programmes*, Paris: UNESCO, 1985.

---

[1] Tapio Varis, *International Flow of Television Programmes*, Paris: UNESCO, 1985: 53.
[2] Tapio Varis, "Global Traffic in Television," *Journal of Communication*, 24/1, 1974: 102–9.

Table 13.2 Percentage of Imported TV Programming in Asia-Pacific, 1983

		PERCENTAGE OF TV IMPORTED, 1983	POPULATION, 1983 (IN MILLIONS)
Small imports	India	7	723
	China	8	1,023
Modest imports	Philippines	12	55
	Pakistan	16	94
	South Korea	16	40
Substantial imports	Sri Lanka	24	16
	Hong Kong	24	5
	Vietnam	34	57
	Australia	44	15
More than half imported	Malaysia	54	15
	Singapore	55	3
	Brunei	60	0.2
	New Zealand	73	3

Source: Tapio Varis, *International Flow of Television Programmes*, Paris: UNESCO, 1985.

In the single region of "Asia and Pacific" we can see (Table 13.2) four levels of media importing loosely linked to population size. India and China were small importers; but the four countries that imported more than half of their transmitted television had an average population of about five million people.

Another study shows that in 1989 two big-population Asian countries (Indonesia and Japan) imported 12 percent and 4 percent, respectively, of their TV transmissions from the United States; but the two small city-port states of Singapore and Hong Kong imported 40 percent and 34 percent of their TV from the United States.[3]

By 1989 Japan was starting to become a modest exporter of TV programming to East and Southeast Asia. Thailand, for example, was importing 19 percent of its TV programming; 8 percent of Thai TV come from the United States and 11 percent from elsewhere (mainly Japan and Hong Kong).

Japan and the Eastern Asian Media Pecking Order

By 1970 Japan was broadly self-sufficient in most aspects of media and popular culture; feature films were, and have remained, the one major exception, with Hollywood having a 50 percent or more share of the Japanese movie

---

[3] David Waterman and Everett M. Rogers, "The Economics of Television Program Production and Trade in Far East Asia," *Journal of Communication*, Vol. 44/3, Summer 1994: 89–111.

market in most years since 1970. However, from the mid-1990s onward, Japan increasingly became an East Asian media number one—either as the sole number one or sharing the number one slot with the United States. Japan was still reluctant to apologize for its acts of aggression during World War II;[4] but increasingly Japan was seen in East Asia and around the world as innovative, fashionable, and cool.[5] By 2004 Japan had some 60 beauty and fashion magazines aimed at affluent young women; it was increasingly said in the United States and Europe that Japanese females ages 15–25 (mostly living with their parents and with plentiful disposable incomes) were becoming the world's fashion setters.

Since 1989, when Sony acquired the major Hollywood studio Columbia Pictures (and Tristar), the United States–Japan showbiz connection has gone through many changes. Sony had major early problems with Columbia, and Matsushita's 1991 acquisition of MCA only lasted four years.[6] However, the United States–Japan relationship has continued to grow and change. There is much coproduction, especially in animation, but also in several other genres. American children have become used to cartoon characters designed to look American to Americans and Asian to Asians. Many American media people have worked in Japan, and Hollywood frequently buys up specialized Japanese talent. Sony is often classified as an American company; however, Sony may find itself—as in the struggle over high definition DVD—confronted by an alliance of both its Japanese and its Hollywood competitors.[7]

Opinions will probably continue to differ as to whether Sony was successful with its commercial policy of combining electronic hardware with entertainment software. What is perhaps less debatable is that the Japanese companies and the Japanese public together led the world in several marriages of new technology with old media. Japanese companies led the development of the VCR; Japan invented both the Walkman and karaoke, two new ways of replaying music. Japan was also ahead of the United States in various applications of digital technology, including broadband high speed Internet service.

Animation arrived on American network TV (ABC) in the 1960s and became an important element in the new satellite-cable channels after 1980; *The Simpsons* first appeared on the Fox network in January 1990 and animation

---

[4] "The Japan That Cannot Say Sorry," *The Economist*, August 12, 1995: 59–61; Jane W. Yamazaki, "Crafting the Apology: Japanese Apologies to South Korea in 1990," *Asian Journal of Communication*, Vol. 14/2, September 2004: 156–73.

[5] Gregory Beals, "Kings of Cool," *Newsweek International*, December 11, 2000: 38–42; Christopher Palmeri and Nanette Byrnes, "Is Japanese Style Taking Over the World?" *Business Week* (Europe), July 26, 2004: 96–98.

[6] "Matsushita Acquires MCA: A Marriage Made in Hollywood," *Broadcasting Abroad*, January 1991: 3; "Matsushita and Hollywood: Retreat from Tinseltown," *The Economist*, April 8, 1995: 90–93.

[7] Michiyo Nakamoto and Scott Morrison, "Hollywood Snubs Sony's New DVD Format," *Financial Times*, November 30, 2004.

achieved a growing prime-time presence.[8] Hollywood also continued to be the dominant force in animated feature movies. In addition to the strong movie and TV presence, Hollywood could build on a massive output of printed material including comic strips. But Japan had its own big printed *manga* output. Japan was also a volume producer of TV animation/anime, making between 1,500 and 2,000 TV episodes and films annually in the mid-1990s; this number had doubled to nearly 4,000 TV episodes and films in 2004.[9] The six leading Japanese networks showed 1,519 hours of animation in 1999, of which only 103 hours (7 percent) was imported.[10] In animation for TV, Japan imported little from, but exported much to, the United States.

Japan was adroit at the low profile approach, which often involved people elsewhere in Asia consuming Japanese animation without recognizing its Japanese origins. Japan was also good at finding new outlets for its massive animation, or anime, output.[11]

Sony and Nintendo became the leading world players in the provision of video game consoles—including portable consoles.[12] Japanese and American companies dominated the sales of the video games. While American video games tended to be unambiguously American,[13] Japanese video games tended to shield their national origins with their leading characters often given European-sounding names and American locations.

A study of *Television Across Asia*—which considers in particular the flow of television game programming formats around Asia—concludes that Japan is the key player in this Asian TV format exporting business. Japan (and not the United States or other Western countries) is the main supplier of TV game formats to the commercial television businesses of South Korea, China, Taiwan, Singapore, and Hong Kong.[14]

In the 1990s Japan became a substantial exporter to eastern Asia of television drama/fiction. *Tokyo Love Story* (1991) helped to launch a new type of Japanese television fiction that came to be known as "trendy drama." This fiction subgenre was targeted initially at affluent young Japanese women; the stories stress romantic relationships and encounters in affluent Tokyo settings. These trendy dramas appealed to young women and young people

[8] Carol A. Stabile and Mark Harrison (eds.), *Prime Time Animation: Television Animation and American Culture*, London: Routledge, 2003.

[9] "Hollywood Rules Toon Box Office," *Screen Digest*, October 2004: 294–95; Ian Rowley, "The Anime Biz," *Business Week*, June 27, 2005: 66–71.

[10] Denise Jeremy, "Drawing Lessons from Japan," *Broadcast International* (London), March 30, 2001: 4–5.

[11] Gwen Robinson, "Anime Territory: Japan Toons Boom Worldwide," *Variety*, June 19–25, 1995: 35, 62; Michiyo Nakamoto, "Lean Times in Japan's Golden Age," *Financial Times*, January 18, 2005.

[12] Michiyo Nakamoto, "Nintendo and Sony Showdown in War of Consoles," *Financial Times*, September 22, 2004.

[13] Michel Marriott, "The Color of Mayhem," *New York Times*, August 12, 2004: G1, 7.

[14] Albert Moran and Michael Keane (eds.), *Television Across Asia: Television Industries, Programme Formats and Globalization*, London: RoutledgeCurzon, 2004.

elsewhere in Asia because Tokyo was familiar from Japanese comics and magazines and was regarded as an affluent, sophisticated, romantic, and cool location; Japan was admired for its cuisine and fashionable clothes. The trendy dramas provided starring roles for young Japanese actresses and were attractive to advertisers (and for product placement). These Japanese dramas were often exported to China, Taiwan, South Korea, and Thailand through a specifically Asian form of media technology and piracy. This (made in Japan) technology was the VCD (video compact disc); pirated batches of episodes from Japanese TV drama series were sold across Asia and played on VCD players. In Hong Kong a very wide range of Japanese programming was pirated (via VCD)—including several varieties of TV drama, as well as animation, "adult" movies, and films. Perhaps the crucial appeal of this Japanese programming is that audiences elsewhere in eastern Asia see it as different but not very different, from their own country's television. The Japanese programming is seen as culturally closer, and more relevant, than imported American programming.[15]

Japan has also been a leader in mobile telephony and text messaging. While cell phones advanced in the United States relatively slowly (with an awkward mix of technologies) in Japan and Korea (and northern Europe) mobile telephony raced ahead. Japanese phones soon offered a variety of animated images; and Japan by 2003 was the world leader in another significant market—35 percent of Japanese people with handsets were using them to play video games.[16]

Sony's best years may already be behind it; but in 2004 Sony emerged as the most admired brand in a survey conducted in China, Hong Kong, Taiwan, the Philippines, Thailand, Malaysia, Singapore, and Indonesia. The second most admired brand was Nokia. Of the top 10 brands, three were American (Kodak, Coca-Cola, Nike) and six were Japanese (Sony, Panasonic, Canon, Toyota, Honda, Fuji).[17]

South Korea Ascends the Eastern Asian Media Pecking Order

South Korea has since 1945 ascended from near the bottom of the eastern Asian media pecking order to its current position near the top, behind only Japan and China. South Korea has been unique in several ways; with a population of nearly 50 million, it is larger than the three other "tiger economies"—Taiwan, Hong Kong, and Singapore. South Korea has a unique geographical proximity to three major powers—Seoul is close not only to

---

[15] Koichi Iwabuchi (ed.), *Feeling Asian Modernities: Transnational Consumption of Japanese TV Dramas*, Hong Kong: Hong Kong University Press, 2004.

[16] "Mobile Gaming: Gaming's New Frontier," *The Economist*, October 4, 2003.

[17] "Asia's Top Brands: Sony Rules in Asia," *Media Brand Portfolio* (Hong Kong), July 16, 2004.

Beijing and Shanghai but also to Tokyo and to Vladivostok on Russia's Pacific Coast. South Korean nationalism has been sharpened in twentieth-century conflicts with, and antagonism toward, not only China, Japan, and Russia but also the United States; and South Korea and North Korea have together developed a double-edged nationalism.

South Korea today is unusual as a smallish media power in doing some media exporting to the two nearby giants, China and Japan. South Korea has also been unusual in developing media technology; in particular, in the early 2000s, South Korea was the world leader in broadband fast Internet.[18]

In both political and media terms Korea spent most of the first half of the twentieth century under the ruthless colonial mastery of Japan. Following Japan's imperial expansion (and negotiations in the early 1900s with the European empires and the United States) Korea became in 1910 a recognized colony of Japan. For 35 years (1910–1945) Japan imposed both its military force and its own, Japanese, language and media on Korea. In the early colonial years the Korean people and media were forbidden to use the Korean language, which in 2005 (with some 23 million speakers in North Korea and 49 million speakers in South Korea) was one of the world's larger languages.

After liberation from Japan in 1945, all things Japanese were rejected by Koreans, North and South. But inevitably, many traces of the Japanese legacy lingered on. For example, of all the South Korean cabinet ministers from 1948 to 1981, 36 percent, had received education in Japan, versus 25 percent who had received education in the United States.[19]

After ceasing to be a Japanese colony in 1945, Korea endured another 15 years of turbulence that included war, civil war, and large scale destruction. Even before the Korean War began in 1950, Korea was split into a Soviet-protected North and an American-protected South. As the Russians tried to eliminate rightists in the North and the Americans attacked Leftists in the South, guerrilla fighting sprang up across Korea. Then in 1950 the major North-South confrontation began. Within less than 12 months Seoul was captured four times—twice by North Korea (and its Chinese ally) and twice by South Korea (and its U.S. ally).[20] By 1953 1.3 million Koreans had been killed and 1.5 million North Koreans had fled to the South; most Korean homes and 85 percent of industrial capacity had been destroyed. All Korean mass media in 1953 were either destroyed or seriously retarded.

Even before 1950, South Korea had been an extreme example of dependence on Hollywood movies. Of 75 countries in 1948, South Korea topped the list in terms of movie dependence—with 95 percent of its exhibited movies

---

[18] "DSL Becomes Mass Market in Korea. Japan Booms, but Growth in US Is Slow," *Screen Digest*, October 2002: 320.

[19] Kyong-Dong Kim (ed.), *Dependency Issues in Korean Development: Comparative Perspectives*, Seoul: Seoul National University Press, 1987: 434–58.

[20] D. S. Lewis (ed.), *Korea: Enduring Division? A Keesing's Special Report*, Harlow, Essex: Longman, 1988.

coming from the United States. The remaining 5 percent came from the United Kingdom.[21]

It was only during the 1960s and 1970s that South Korea first developed its own substantial press, broadcast, and film industries. During 1961–1979 South Korea was turned into an economic tiger under the military regime of General Park Chung Hee. Between 1960 and 1980 GDP per head (in standard dollars) increased by 373 percent. The Park military dictatorship was backed by a substantial continuing American military presence. In 1960 South Korea was still a largely agricultural country, intent on rebuilding homes and schools. By the time of Park's assassination in 1979, South Korea had been industrialized through an alliance of the Korean military, newly big state-supported (Chaebol) companies and foreign (mainly U.S. and Japanese) capital.

By 1975 a strictly controlled South Korean press was selling almost six million copies a day, while radio and TV also grew rapidly. In the 1970s South Korea had already become an off-shore producer of animation—some of it subcontracted direct from Hollywood animation companies, and some of it subcontracted from (or via) Japan.[22] South Korea was also making modest advances up the media pecking order in film.

The bizarre and antagonistic relationship between North and South Korea was reflected in their two separate movie industries, each dedicated to its own political ideology and belligerent nationalism. Kim Jong Il, who was designated the sole successor to his father, Kim Il Sung (1912–1994), as the dictator of North Korea, was obsessed by film. The then apprentice dictator was especially an admirer of the successful 1970s South Korean film director Shin Sangok. In 1978 Kim had Shin Sangok, and his actress wife, kidnapped and abducted to the North. The director and the actress remained in North Korea for eight years before their successful 1986 escape back to Seoul.[23]

During 1980–1993 South Korea made a slow transition to democracy[24] and by 1993 had political and media systems loosely comparable to those of Spain or Greece of the same period, or to Japan perhaps 15 year earlier. For example, Seoul had six big daily newspapers that in 1985 together sold 5.6 million copies and by 1993 sold almost 8 million copies—a smaller Seoul version of the Tokyo dailies' massive sales. But 1980 had been South Korea's most traumatic year since the 1950s. In 1980 widespread protests (or riots) in the provincial city of Kwangju led to Korean paratroopers killing several

[21] UNESCO, *World Communications*, Paris: Unesco, 1950.
[22] John A. Lent and Kie-Un Yu, "Korean Animation: A Short but Robust Life," in John A. Lent (ed.), *Animation in Asia and the Pacific*, Bloomington: Indiana University Press, 2001: 89–104.
[23] Hyangjin Lee, *Contemporary Korean Cinema: Identity, Culture and Politics*, Manchester, UK: Manchester University Press, 2000: 31–32.
[24] Kyu Ho Youm, "Democratization and the Press: The Case of South Korea," in Patrick H. O'Neil (ed.), *Communicating Democracy: The Media and Political Transitions*, Boulder, CO: Lynne Rienner, 1998: 171–93; Jon Vanden Heuvel and Everette E. Dennis, *The Unfolding Lotus: East Asia's Changing Media*, New York: Freedom Forum Media Studies Center, 1993: 6–21.

hundred demonstrators. The new military dictatorship (of President Chun Doo-Hwan) instituted a media purge; at least 700 print journalists were sacked and the previously part-commercial TV/radio system was effectively turned into a state monopoly—the Korean Broadcasting System (KBS). Massive student and trade union protests marked the entire 1980–1993 period, but (partly in anticipation of the 1988 Seoul Olympic Games) a new president (Roh Tae Woo) instituted big democratic and media reforms. South Korea's politics, economy, and media continued to receive comprehensive American support. South Korea (like Japan) was effectively allowed to develop its industries (such as ship-building), and its media, behind a protectionist wall. The South Korean economy was export driven. But imports—including rice and TV programming from the United States—were increasingly restricted.

However, during 1980–1993 South Korea continued to import substantial numbers of movies from Hollywood, and the U.S. military's American Forces Korean Network (AFKN) was allowed effectively to operate as a national TV network across South Korea.[25] But KBS, even after 1987, was restricted to 10.5 hours per day, meaning that it did not need to import cheap U.S. programming for the lowest audience hours. Hollywood movie imports were rationed with more severe quotas; movie theater owners were threatened that baskets of poisonous snakes would be released in movie theaters if they showed too many Hollywood movies.[26] As the South Korean economy grew, and as advertising expanded, journalists and broadcasters—supported by newly strong trade unions—found themselves in a strong position. Print journalists received good salaries and were also well supplied with envelope cash bribes (known in Seoul as *Chonji*).[27] Most of the press was controlled by old press families or by big Chaebol companies, including Samsung. South Korea made 116 feature movies in 1990, a substantial number for its population size.[28]

In 1993 South Korea elected its first civilian president and in the years after 1993 came to be widely regarded as a model of both economic and democratic virtue. The South Korean media industry has continued its progress up the media pecking order. It can now regard itself as ahead of most European nations as a media power; South Korea has become a media trendsetter—no longer 15 years behind Japan. Many Japanese people (especially young people) no longer regard Korea as a backward and inferior former colony, but now equate Korea with cool.[29]

[25] Jong Geun Kang and Michael Morgan, "Culture Clash: Impact of US Television in Korea," *Journalism Quarterly*, Vol. 65/3, Summer 1988: 431–38.
[26] Jeff Sipe, "Foreign Film Makers Run into East Asian Resistance," *Financial Times*, December 16, 1988; Bradley Martin, "Sex, Lies and Hegemony: A South Korean Campaign Against US Films," *Newsweek*, October 9, 1989.
[27] Kyu Ho Youm, "*Chonji* Journalism in Korea: An Issue for Press Ethics," *Media Asia*, Vol. 20/2, 1993: 100–1.
[28] "World Film Production Increases," *Screen Digest*, December 2001: 377–80.
[29] Brian Bremner and Moon Ihlwan, "Cool Korea," *Business Week*, June 10, 2002: 26–32.

Since 1993 (and especially since Korea's financial crisis of 1997) Samsung has come to be seen as a major electronics company, perhaps even a serious challenger to Sony.[30] Although its policy is to avoid big (Sony-like) involvement in media content, Samsung owns South Korea's largest advertising agency, as well as a big newspaper. In addition to Samsung's many digital products, South Korea's main claim to electronic world leadership has been in broadband fast Internet and on-line services. Korea, with its heavily urban population, quickly made broadband profitable; by 2003 over 70 percent of South Korean households were hooked up to broadband. This, in turn, enabled South Korea to become a world leader in MMORPGs massively multiplayer on-line role-playing games (MMORPGs); a Korean company, NCsoft, by September 2003 claimed to have the world's most popular on-line game—Lineage—a medieval fantasy in which (paying) customers could assume their own medieval roles and fight other players.[31] South Korea also seemed to be a world leader in juvenile addiction to on-line gaming and the Internet.[32]

South Korea increasingly made films other than its traditional output of horror movies. In 2003 Hollywood had less than half the South Korean movie theatrical market, and Korean movie exports to East Asia were on the increase.[33] The Pusan film festival became an Asian leader, and Japanese-Korean movie coproduction and cooperation became commonplace. Korea's very own Seoul Music began to reach a wider Asian audience,[34] and selected Korean TV series reached audiences in China and Japan. A few South Korean TV actors became celebrated as romantic stars in Japan.[35]

South Korean media output became more popular in East Asia, partly because it was now faster paced as well as more sexy and fashion-conscious.[36]

---

[30] "Samsung Electronics: As good as It Gets?" *The Economist*, January 15, 2005: 66–68.

[31] John Larkin, "Winners of the Monster Game," *Far East Economic Review*, September 5, 2002: 32–34; "Computer Games: Invaders From the Land of Broadband," *The Economist*, December 13, 2003: 65–66.

[32] "Gaming Addiction Rife in South Korea," *Screen Digest*, January 2004: 24.

[33] "South Korea," *Variety*, April 24–30, 2000: 53–59; Ahn Byung-Sup, "Korea: Troughs and Crests," in Aruna Vasudev, Latika Padgaonkar, and Rashmi Doraiswamy (eds.), *Being and Becoming: The Cinemas of Asia*, Delhi: Macmillan 2002: 273–300; Song Jung-a, "Movies Resist Dangers of Export Success," *Financial Times*, November 17, 2003, "Special Report: South Korea": 5; "Korean Film Exports Upward Trend," *Screen Digest*, August 2004: 305.

[34] Andrew Ward, "Seoul Music Strives for a Global Audience," *Financial Times*, February 8, 2002: 12.

[35] Norimitsu Onishi, "Korean Star Captures Fancy of Japan's Women," *International Herald Tribune*, December 16, 2004: 2; Ichiko Fuyuno, "Soap-Opera Diplomacy," *Far East Economic Review*, September 16, 2004: 66–67.

[36] Young-han Kim, "The Broadcasting Audience Movement in Korea," *Media, Culture and Society*, Vol. 23/1, January 2001: 91–107; Jae-Kyoung Lee, "A Crisis of the South Korean Media," *Media Asia*, Vol. 23/2, 1996: 86–89, 94; Sang-Chul Lee and Susan K. Joe, "Key Issues in the Korean Television Industry: Programmes and Market Structure," in David French and Michael Richards (eds.), *Television in Contemporary Asia*, New Delhi: Sage, 2000: 131–49; Myung-Jin Park, Chang-Nam Kim, and Byung-Woo Sohn, "Modernisation, Globalisation and the Powerful State: The Korean Media," in James Curran and M. Yun-Jin Park (eds.), *De-Westernising Media Studies*, London: Routledge, 2000: 111–23.

But there was also a related decline in the popularity of both United States foreign policy[37] and media. Older Koreans, who could remember the traumas of the 1940s and 1950s, still preferred American imports. But many younger Koreans, born in the 1960s or later, were more skeptical about the United States. After the collapse of the Soviet Union, many South Koreans wanted closer ties with North Korea. Television coverage of the 1992 Los Angeles riots—in which Korean shopkeepers were targeted—made a big negative impression. Some of the most popular Korean media output has involved reinspecting episodes in recent history, in some of which the American military had played leading roles.[38] After 1993, uncensored television analysis of the 1950–1953 Korean War was at last allowed for the first time. In early 1995 the Kwangju massacre (of 1980) was analyzed in a massive TV series of 24 episodes; the news coverage of foreign TV crews (censored by the Korean government in 1980) was now seen for the first time. This (and other) media coverage raised questions about the American military's role in encouraging (or at least not sufficiently discouraging) the lethal actions of the South Korean paratroops and of South Korea's military regime.

An August 2005 poll suggested that young South Koreans now rejected the U.S. view of North Korea as a rogue state. Two-thirds of South Koreans ages 16–25 said that, in a North Korea versus United States war, they would side with North Korea.[39]

Slow Change in the World Media Pecking Order

Nation-states and regional blocs at the top of the pecking order export to those below them; nation-states and regional blocs at the bottom of the pecking order import from those above them.

India does little importing, but its media exports (many unpaid for) go to big South Asia (Pakistan and Bangladesh); lower down the pecking order are small South Asian states such as Nepal.

China overall does little importing but is unusual in importing some media from smaller countries in its region (Taiwan, South Korea, Japan). Japan does only a little importing but is a strong exporter to other eastern Asian countries, big (such as Vietnam and Thailand) and small.

The larger Arab media players (Egypt and Saudi Arabia) do some importing—mainly from the United States and Europe—but do more exporting to small and poorer Arab nations.

[37] "Awkward Allies: South Korea Needs America, but Increasingly Wishes It Didn't," *The Economist*, April 19, 2003, "A Survey of South Korea": 11–13.
[38] Andrew Salmon, "At the Movies: South Korea's Battle with Hollywood," *International Herald Tribune*, November 15, 2004: 9–10.
[39] B. J. Lee, "The Unwanted General," *Newsweek International*, September 5, 2005.

Africa has its own pecking order, depending on imports from the United States and Europe. Two larger African countries (Nigeria and South Africa) do some exporting to other sub-Saharan African countries.

The United States remains at the top of the pecking order but less unambiguously so than previously. The United States now has to share the top end of the pecking order with the leaders of several other regional media blocs, especially in Europe. We now turn to Europe.

14

Europe and Euro-American Media

European and American media are increasingly becoming a single Euro-American media industry. Within this grouping, the United States leads in entertainment while Europe takes the lead in setting the world news agenda.

But while the United States has one main language, one educational system, and one national media industry, the European Union (EU) has 25 nation-states, all 25 of which are cultural nationalists. All 25 EU members defend and promote their own national media, national educational system, national culture, and national language. Most politicians and most voters broadly accept the combination of a Europe-wide economy with a national culture and national media system.

This chapter divides the European Union into three categories. First, the big five western European countries (France, Germany, Italy, Spain, the United Kingdom) had 66 percent of the EU's 457 million population in 2005. Led by France, all of these big five want to promote and to export their national culture and media; they are reluctant to import from each other. All of the remaining 20 countries (except Poland) have much smaller populations. Both the small western European and the ex-communist central European countries tend to import media both from the United States and from the European big five.

Despite their small size European countries tend to have highly distinctive internal regions, which often also have (or have had) their own distinctive languages. About 110 separate linguistic "peoples" can still be identified in Europe;[1] some apparently disappearing languages still have some media, especially radio. In other cases languages cross state boundaries; for example,

---

[1] Felipe Fernández-Armesto, *The Times Guide to the Peoples of Europe*, London: Times Books, 1997.

there are extensive French-language media in Belgium and Switzerland and Swedish-language media in Finland.

Citizens of EU countries are typically aware of the European economy but take little interest in Brussels politics. The European Union is a labyrinth of obscurity and complexity. Not many European citizens could accurately describe the functions of the European Commission, the Council of Ministers, the Council of Europe, the European Parliament or the Comité des Représentants Permanents (COREPER). The European Economic Community (EEC)/EU was not designed to be easily understood by voters or easily reported on by journalists.[2] Consequently, there is little in the way of Europewide, general audience, mass media—especially at the retail level.

Big differences also exist between the media of northern, southern, and central Europe. Western Europe's greatest media strength is in the north because the north includes not only Germany and the United Kingdom but also eight small-population Scandinavian and Benelux (plus Ireland) countries, where the mass media also are strong. These 10 northern countries are collectively strong in "old media" (especially the daily press and public broadcasting), in newer media such as commercial television and cable TV, as well as in new media. The early European leaders in digital television were the United Kingdom, Denmark, Sweden, and Norway.

Quite sharply distinguished from these 10 northern countries are four countries of the south—Italy, Spain, Portugal, and Greece. In these four countries less money (than in the north) is spent on media; both advertising expenditure and public funding are lower than in most of northern Europe. In these southern countries public service broadcasting is relatively weak and newspaper readership is low. Cable TV is weak in southern Europe; consequently, TV—and in particular commercial TV—is more dominant here than in the north.

Two authors argue that in Greece and Spain the connection between the media and the military dictatorship continued into the democratic era and can be seen in excessive present-day "intimacy" between the political elite and the media.[3] Two other authors point to five characteristics common to the media of southern Europe and Latin America: (1) low levels of newspaper circulation, (2) a tradition of advocacy reporting in which newspapers have

---

[2] Deirdre Kevin, *Europe in the Media*, Mahwah, NJ: Lawrence Erlbaum, 2003; Olivier Baisnée, "Can Political Journalism Exist at the EU Level?" in Raymond Kuhn and Erik Neveu (eds.), *Political Journalism*, London: Routledge, 2002: 108–28; David Morgan, "British Media and European News: The Brussels News Beat and Its Problems," *European Journal of Communication*, Vol. 10/3, September 1995: 321–43; Katharine Sarikakis, *Powers in Media Policy: The Challenge of the European Parliament*, Oxford: Peter Lang, 2004.

[3] Fotini Papatheodorou and David Machin, "The Umbilical Cord That Was Never Cut," *European Journal of Communication*, Vol. 18/1, March 2003: 31–54; David Machin and Fotini Papatheodorou, "Commercialisation and Tabloid Television in Southern Europe: Disintegration or Democratisation of the Public Sphere?" *Journal of European Area Studies*, Vol. 10/1, 2002: 31–48.

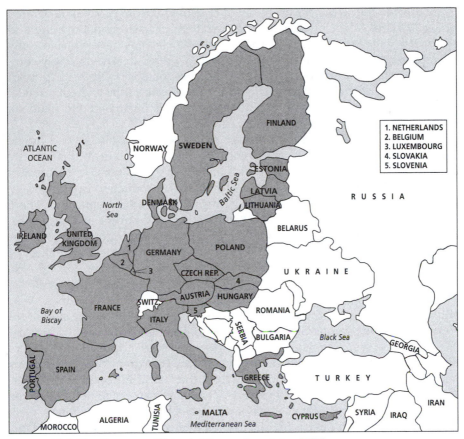

Figure 14.1 The European Union's 25 member states, 2006.

a strong partisan position and in which commentary and advocacy (rather than any attempt at neutral reporting) are emphasised, (3) privately owned media tend to reflect the interests of their big business and big industry ownerships, (4) the politicization of public broadcasting and also broadcast regulation, and (5) the limited development of journalism as an autonomous profession.[4]

The central European countries belong to another category, that of ex-communist countries. Following the collapse of communism in 1989, most of these countries experienced major changes, the mushroom growth of new media outlets, and then a period of consolidation (including substantial foreign ownership).

---

[4] Daniel C. Hallin and Stylianos Papathanassopoulos, "Political Clientism and the Media: Southern Europe and Latin America in Comparative Perspective," *Media, Culture and Society*, Vol. 24/2, March 2002: 175–95.

Obviously the media of Europe are very different from those of the United States. Whereas the United States has a pattern of local monopoly city and suburban daily papers, each European capital city has head-to-head daily newspaper competition. While U.S. radio and TV are overwhelmingly commercial, each European country has its own idiosyncratic tradition of "public" broadcasting, which has then changed into a mixed public and commercial system. Radio is also strong and idiosyncratic in Europe at the national, regional, and local levels.

Europe is the most lucrative market in the world for Hollywood movie exports. Meanwhile, each European country has its own industry that mainly makes low budget films, most of which are never shown outside the country of origin. This latter point also applies to most TV production in Europe.

The movie/film industry, however, is a unique and extreme case. There are more elements of Europe-wide media than may appear at first glance. Although European newspapers do not give massive attention to other European countries, one study of 11 European newspapers showed all 11 of them giving much more attention to Europe-wide news than did the *New York Times*.[5] There is a similar contrast in TV news coverage of Europe.

Any growth of European patriotism, loyalty, or sentiment occurs slowly. But the same is true of the European Union itself—growth is very slow from year to year, but substantial from decade to decade. Opinion polls increasingly suggest the emergence of a Europe-wide public opinion that differs sharply from U.S. public opinion. To many citizens of Europe the United States seems further away than previously, while the rest of Europe seems closer. Perhaps as important as the single euro currency is soccer football. Millions of football fans across Europe are knowledgeable about Barcelona's back four, Bayern Munich's midfield, Manchester United's strikers, and AC Milan's goalkeeper. The manager/coaches of the top European teams are better known across the continent than are most of the presidents and prime ministers.

One of the main motivations for subscribing to pay/extra TV sports channels is to watch more European football; another motive, however, is to watch more Hollywood movies. In terms of media trade, there have been three main phases since 1980:

- Until the mid-1980s European television continued with few channels, little advertising, and quite modest imports of American programming.

- By the mid-1990s, however, there was a big increase in both conventional channels and new satellite channels and a big increase in American programming hours.

- By the early 2000s European television had responded to the "American invasion" by making more of its own quite cheap, but very popular, programming. The American share of European audience time thus declined.

---

[5] Hans-Jörg Trenz, "Media Coverage on European Governance," *European Journal of Communication*, Vol. 19/3, September 2004: 291–319.

However—in the move from perhaps 2 to 200 national TV channels—it has become increasingly difficult to establish basic facts. The American share of European television audience time is no longer easy to establish. Some "American" programming is in fact Japanese or a copy of a European film or programming format. Programming that may look Italian or Spanish in fact comes from Hollywood.

The complexities of ownership, coproduction, and audience share also reflect transatlantic cooperation, coownership, translation, franchising, reversioning, and piracy. More broadly, this book argues that these complexities are evidence of the gradual emergence of a single Euro-American media bloc.

France and Cultural Nationalism

Since 1945 successive French governments have pursued a policy of cultural nationalism; this policy has aimed to support French culture and French media at home in France, but has also attempted to project French culture into a leadership position across Europe. French cultural nationalism, however, has had limited export success, primarily because other countries, initially in western, and subsequently in central, Europe, copied France and pursued their very own cultural nationalisms. Resistance against Hollywood media in particular, and against American culture in general, was a key plank of French cultural nationalism. While the quantity of U.S. imports varied —being especially high in the 1990s—French governments largely failed to wean either the French or European populations away from American entertainment.

In the mid-1980s France made a sudden leap into commercial television and media deregulation. But for 40 years, 1945–1985, the French media remained under strict regulation; in fact there were 10 successive new regulatory regimes for French broadcasting between 1945 and 1990. The regulatory regime changes reflected especially the political turbulence of the presidency of Charles de Gaulle (1958–1969).

1944–1945 became year zero when—with the German occupation now ended—everything supposedly began afresh, new and democratic. French film, French radio, and the Parisian press were quickly reinstated, free of the Nazi taint. France instituted a new highly (and technically) educated administrative elite. By 1950 French culture and French art were back in their number one place; Jean-Paul Sartre became the first philosopher-author superstar of the postwar world. Across Europe (and much of the world) France was again the leader in cuisine, wine, and fashion. France also led what became the EEC and later the EU. This was essentially a deal between French agriculture and German industry. But the new European governmental institutions were modeled on Paris; and—especially important—French was installed as the official lead language in Brussels (a mainly French-speaking city).

Film in particular was seen as an art form in which France and its filmic "authors" must take the lead. The 1950s and 1960s were glory years for the French film (not least because television spread slowly in France, only reaching 50 percent of French households in 1966). In the 1960s film attendance was still very high, while the government subsidized the entire industry.

Year zero, 1944–1945, saw the mushroom growth of many new Parisian newspapers. Especially significant was *Le Monde*, intended as a newspaper flagship for French political and cultural independence. *Le Monde*, which indeed did impress the rest of Europe, had several idiosyncrasies; it had no commercial ownership, and it appeared as an afternoon paper in Paris but as a next-morning daily in the French provinces. When much of the Parisian mushroom newspaper growth quickly shriveled and died, a newly powerful daily press emerged in the main provincial cities. But perhaps the proudest French press accomplishment was the launch of Agence France-Presse (AFP) as a new national and international agency to replace the old Havas (born 1835) agency, which had collaborated with the German occupation. AFP (with a substantial French government subsidy) quickly reestablished itself in Latin America and became the leading chronicler of the decline and fall of the French empire in Africa and Vietnam.

During the 40 years of 1945–1985, French broadcasting—first radio and then television—followed the public broadcasting route. When foreign commercial radio stations located outside France (in places like Luxembourg and Monaco/Monte Carlo), transmitted into France, the French government acquired these "peripheral" radio stations, but controlled them via a holding company (Sofirad) that allowed some semblance of independence. Meanwhile, the public system only provided quite limited amounts of television each day. In 1964 (20 years after the German occupation) France was transmitting only 11 hours a day of television and only 39 percent of households had television. French television was heavily factual; even by 1973 factual output (news, current affairs, documentary, educational, and sport) accounted for 59 percent of TV time. In 1973 France was only importing 9.2 percent of its television time; this was all in "series" and "long films,"[6] meaning that only about 5 or 6 percent of French television was American.

In the mid-1980s both French television and radio were transformed into a much less "public" and much more commercial system, with more advertising and commercialization, more channels, and more imported programming. The policy changes were far from simple as politicians of the left and right attempted to preempt each others' plans.[7] The biggest single change was the transformation of the number one "public" TV channel (which had mixed license fee and advertising funding) into a 100 percent advertising

---

[6] Kaarle Nordenstreng and Tapio Varis, *Television Traffic—a one-way street?* Paris: UNESCO, 1974: 22.

[7] Michael Palmer and Jeremy Tunstall, *Liberating Communications: Policy-making in France and Britain*, Oxford: Blackwell, 1990: 162–215.

financed and commercially controlled channel. The new commercial operator of the TF-1 channel was Bouygues, France's leading construction company. By 1988 the sole TF-1 channel had a 50 percent audience share and a rapidly growing advertising revenue. In a short space of time France went from two to six national TV channels. The new arrangements were intended to maintain a mix of public and private TV. Two public channels remained (France 2 and 3). But the commercial competition—with France's modest total advertising spend—was ferocious and one of the new channels (La Cinq) collapsed in 1992. Imports from the United States greatly increased in the late 1980s. In 1987 some 1,400 films were shown on France's six television channels; in contrast to previous years, only three of the year's largest viewing audiences were achieved by French films.

Radio also underwent a commercial revolution. In the 1981—1991 decade France went from no commercial radio stations (on French soil) to 1,200 local commercial radio stations.[8] Some 900 of these local stations were part of national commercial radio networks, such as NRJ. Then the Parisian policymakers noticed that these radio networks were playing much Anglo-American music. To combat this (somewhat predictable) state of affairs, a splendid new law was passed in 1994 that required that 40 percent of radio music must be French language "chansons." But this was not yet the full extent of the French state's pop music interventions. Micromanagement went further. Half of the 40 percent of French radio airtime must go to "young talent."[9] Another distinctly grey (if youthful) area had emerged.

The French film industry retained a majority share of the French movie theater audience until 1986. During the decade 1970–1979 Hollywood had only 26.3 percent of the French theatrical movie market; but during 1989–1993 Hollywood had a 56.7 percent share in France,[10] and continued at around that percentage in subsequent years. The French film industry was hit both by a decline in total audience numbers and by a decline in the French film share of the audience.

In order to grapple with this financial problem the new Canal Plus, launched in 1984, was a subscription-based terrestrial channel that was legally required to screen, and to part-finance, French movies. Canal Plus has successfully generated finance and (a TV showing) for hundreds of new French films.[11] Canal Plus has played a big patronage role in French film

---

[8] Raymond Kuhn, *The Media in France*, London: Routledge, 1995: 77–108.

[9] Marcel Machill, "The French Radio Landscape: The Impact of Radio Policy in an Area Defined by the Antagonistic Forces of Commercialisation and Cultural Protection," *European Journal of Communication*, Vol. 11/3, 1996: 393–415.

[10] Jean-Pierre Jeancolas, "From the Blum-Byrnes Agreement to the GATT Affair," in Geoffrey Nowell-Smith and Steven Ricci (eds.), *Hollywood and Europe*, London: British Film Institute, 1998: 47–60.

[11] "Canal Plus," *Variety*, October 10–16, 1994: 53–82; David Looseley, "Facing the Music: French Cultural Policy from a British Perspective," *International Journal of Cultural Policy*, Vol. 7/1, 2000: 115–29.

because once Canal Plus accepts a film, it becomes much easier to raise the remaining required finance—often from a mix of commercial, and public subsidy, sources. This French system of generating film finance has tended to support films that are more culturally (and nationally) virtuous than commercially compelling.[12] Another key component that attracted some five million subscribers to pay for Canal Plus was that the channel carried other attractive programming (from sport to pornography), and in particular Hollywood movies; in fact, for its first two decades Canal Plus had output deals with all of the Hollywood movie majors. Canal Plus was thus a display window not only for French film "authors" but also for Hollywood movie blockbusters, as well as for American "independent" movie output.

French journalism has a mixed record in support of France's national culture project. France is strong in a wide range of magazines from news magazines to women's magazines and cartoon publications. The French company Hachette Filipacchi, which publishes *Elle* and many other big magazines, makes more than half of its sales outside France—in the United States and Asia as well as in other European countries.

French newspaper journalism since 1945 has a rather weak record. The bulk of daily sales now belongs to big groups of monopoly provincial dailies. The biggest newspaper owner of the years since 1945 was Robert Hersant, who, between 1950 and his death in 1996, built a big group of dailies. His flagship paper, *Le Figaro*, was the main conservative competition to *Le Monde*. Robert Hersant had been an overt anti-Semite who collaborated with the Germans.[13] Hersant refused to apologize: "All those who know me a little are aware that I was the only Frenchman of my generation not to have been a resistance hero."

The eight Paris dailies (which included two business dailies, the Catholic *La Croix* and the sports daily *L'Equipe*) had a 2004 combined sale of 1.73 million (compared with a 11.8 million sale of London dailies). Despite some intellectual virtues, and some commercial success, the leading few Paris dailies (*Le Monde, Le Figaro, Libération*) tended to define themselves as part of a Parisian elite. These papers often failed to reveal huge political scandals, and also failed to report significant facts that "everyone" in the Paris elite already knew. The newspapers knew about but failed to report a massive scandal inside the Paris city hall, in which all the political parties (including the communists) were financial beneficiaries.[14] The Paris press was also slow to reveal another widely known scandal concerning the ELF oil company, from which successive French administrations siphoned hundreds of

---

[12] Dominique Bégin, François Colbert, and Ruth Dupré, "Comparative Analysis of French and French Canadian Willingness to Support the National Film Industry," *International Journal of Cultural Policy*, Vol. 7/2, 2000: 355–68.

[13] Dominique Pons, *Dossier H. . . . Comme Hersant*, Paris: Alain Mureau, 1977.

[14] Robert Graham, "The 'Juppé Effect': Chirac's Loyal Ally Is Convicted but Stays at the Head of French Politics," *Financial Times*, February 5, 2004.

millions of francs into their own pockets and into those of various West African dictators.[15]

The French press was extremely reluctant to reveal any personal information about incumbent French presidents. The great French public was unaware that both Georges Pompidou (president, 1969–1974) and François Mitterrand (president, 1981–1995) were suffering from deadly illnesses in their final years as president. For most of President Mitterrand's 14 years as president, the French public did not know several key facts about his past—including the fact that he had not only been a World War II resistance hero but had also collaborated with the Nazis. It was Mitterrand himself who revealed this (and the fact that he had an illegitimate child) in the closing weeks of his life.

So what of Le Monde and its mission to be Europe's leading elite newspaper? Sixty years after its 1945 launch, Le Monde was still one of the world's most highly regarded and most quoted newspapers. Content analysis would probably show that Le Monde had a good record on many colonial and foreign policy issues. Le Monde has remained the bulletin board of the French elite, whose members both love and hate their daily paper. While looking especially toward Europe and Africa, Le Monde has maintained a skeptical attitude toward the United States. However, Le Monde is increasingly accused of looking inward and backward. The newspaper's major continuing idiosyncrasy in 2005 was the old pattern of afternoon publication in Paris and next morning publication in the provinces. This constituted an extraordinary remembrance of things past in an era of 24-hour all-news television in which France has actively participated. Multilocation printing was demonstrated some decades ago in the Soviet Union, India, and elsewhere. Le Monde (like several Times elite newspapers) seems unsure of the role of an elite paper under today's conditions; and, like some of the others, it has suffered from a succession of revelatory scandal books and insider feuds. Le Monde's situation also involves trade union strength and its journalists' power to veto changes they dislike.[16]

French cultural nationalism reveres stars and creative celebrities of all kinds. Leading film auteurs are super-stars of French culture; a select group of TV news anchorpersons and presenters of political interview programming are seen as stars. Also accorded star status are leading philosophers, historians, sociologists, and novelists who condescend to become talking heads on French television. Yet another category of French media star is the charismatic media mogul or baron. Jean-Luc Lagardère (who died in 2003) exemplified the mogul media owner role after presiding over Matra (which

---

[15] Jon Henley, "Sleaze Scandal That Rocked France Ends in Jailing of Former Elf Oil Chief," The Guardian, November 13, 2003.

[16] Jean Planchais and André Fontaine, "Obituary: Hubert Beuve-Méry," The Independent (London), August 8, 1989; Paul Webster, " 'Hate-Filled' Book Rocks Le Monde," The Guardian, February 26, 2003; Nicholas Bray, "France's Le Monde Is Struggling to Avoid Filing for Bankruptcy," Wall Street Journal, November 27, 1984; Adam Gopnik, "The End of the World," New Yorker, November 15, 2004: 64–71.

made military aircraft and missiles). Lagardère subsequently controlled *Elle* magazine and the Hachette Filipacchi magazine colossus; he also built Formula One racing car engines, owned a big stable of race horses, and was a friend of French presidents from de Gaulle to Chirac.

Jean-Marie Messier was a French media manager who earned star ratings in the late 1990s and around 2000. He had a classic French elite background —he worked for a prime minister (Balladur) and became at age 29 a partner at Lazard's bank. He then rescued the scandal-ridden water utility Générale des Eaux and decided (as *Variety* observed) that there was no business like eaux business. The water company was transposed into a media giant that controlled, among much else, the filmic holy ground of Canal Plus. Messier became a French media star who miraculously seemed to be buying up big segments of Hollywood movies and music; Messier's newly named Vivendi became Vivendi-Universal Entertainment (VUE). In another deal, Messier paid over $10 billion for the USA Network cable company. Messier had paid too much in creating this Franco-American colossus; what went up came down, and that included Messier himself. Certainly his business decisions (over $100 billion spent on acquisitions during 1996–2001) were unwise. Even more unwise was Messier's decision to reside in New York City and to make contemptuous remarks about France and "cultural exception." Conquering America was admirable, but virtually becoming American—and doubting France's cultural mission—was not acceptable to the French elite, including the French banking elite. Messier lost his job and his star status.[17] Meanwhile, the long-time boss of Canal Plus, Pierre Lescure (whom Messier had sacked), was quickly moved up to cultural hero and (tragic) star status. Pierre Lescure was well qualified for French cultural heroism; he was a successful news anchorperson and a fanatical supporter not only of French films, but also of U.S. movies and jazz and rock music. His father had been editor of the communist daily *L'Humanité*; in 2001 Lescure published an acclaimed auto-biography, *Histoire de Desirs*.

After Messier's fall, the Universal Hollywood interests returned to American ownership and NBC became NBC-Universal. But the French media industry did retain several commercial strengths. France was an international power in magazines and in advertising agencies (Publicis and Havas); the Decaux outdoor advertising company competed with the U.S. outdoor giants. France has remained a leader in fashion, luxury goods, cuisine, and international supermarkets (Carrefour).

Agence France Presse has strengthened its position as the only non-Anglo world news agency. In many countries around the world AFP is now seen as the most objective (or least biased) source of fast world news—for newspapers, for Internet, and as a basic news service for radio and TV.

---

[17] Jo Johnson and Martine Orange, *The Man Who Tried to Buy the World: Jean-Marie Messier and Vivendi Universal*, London: Viking Penguin, 2003.

Another French international success is TV5,[18] a showcase for France and for French-language programming from Belgium, Quebec, and Switzerland. Supported especially by the French Foreign Affairs ministry, TV5 is available around the world.

However, French cultural and media nationalism has had several relative failures. Hollywood continues to make bigger incursions into the French market than the French media are able to make into the wider European market. Some French authorities worry that France, Quebec, Belgium, and Switzerland continue to have the only reliable cores of French speakers. Vietnam seems to be largely lost to French; and some people think that English-language South African and Nigerian media are a long-term threat to the survival of French in much of West Africa.

Western Europe's Big Five Cultural Nationalists

By 2005 the European Union had 25 member nation-states, but of the total 450 million population, about two-thirds (300 million) lived in the five bigger western European countries—France, Germany, Italy, Spain, and the United Kingdom. These five countries together are the leading world market for all of Hollywood's movie, TV, video, and music output.

In 1983 France, Germany, and the United Kingdom imported about 12 percent of their total TV output from the United States.[19] But by 1995 in these five big countries the American share of audience time had probably at least doubled to around 25 percent; by 2005 there had been a decline, perhaps to between 15 percent and 20 percent in different "big" countries. Much the heaviest European dependence was on American movies (in all windows—theatrical, TV, and video).[20]

In 1983 these five countries took more than two-thirds of their entire TV imports from Hollywood; and this broad pattern has continued. Each of the other four big countries are not much less idiosyncratic than France. Each of these big five had its own highly distinctive experiences in World War II. France and Britain both had very distinctive end-of-empire experiences. All five nations joined the European Union, but at different times. Each of the five nations sees itself as one of the great players in history. All five

[18] "Twenty Years of TV5," *Cable and Satellite Europe*, January/February 2004.
[19] Tapio Varis, *International Flow of Television Programmes*, Paris: UNESCO, 1985.
[20] Hans J. Kleinsteuber on Germany, Jean-Marie Charon on France, Gianpietro Mazzoleni on Italy, Rosario de Mateo on Spain, and Jeremy Tunstall on The United Kingdom in Mary Kelly, Gianpietro Mazzoleni, and Denis McQuail (ed.), *The Media in Europe: The Euromedia Handbook*, London: Sage 2004; Jeanette Steemers, *Selling Television: British Television in the Global Marketplace*, London: British Film Institute, 2004; Stylianos Papathanassopoulos, *European Television in the Digital Age*, Oxford: Polity Press, 2002; Richard Collins, *Media and Identity in Contemporary Europe*, Bristol: Intellect, 2002; Leen d'Haenens and Frieda Saeys (eds.), *Western Broadcasting at the Dawn of the 21st Century*, Berlin: Mouton de Gruyter, 2001.

have truly unique artistic and cultural heritages, which they wish to project internationally.

In terms of the media, Germany was unusual in having, for decades, a radio/TV system that was regionally, not nationally, based. Britain's media have seemed (at least to outsiders) to be polarized between five national tabloid dailies and several prestige dailies, and between the BBC and the Murdoch/Thatcher-created BSkyB. Meanwhile, control of huge swathes of the Italian media by one man—Silvio Berlusconi—has been an embarrassment to many Italians and to many Europeans.[21] Spain is also distinctive, not least in its rapid switch from dictatorship (General Francisco Franco, who died in 1975) to democracy; Spain is unusual, also, in having a significant terrestrial TV and radio output not only in Spanish but also in important regional languages.[22]

Nevertheless, we can list a number of media characteristics that Germany, Italy, Spain, and the United Kingdom share with France. In all five of the big western European countries there was a huge change between 1980 and 1990 in the amount of television available to the national audience. The overall picture was of each country going from three channels in 1980 to eight channels in 1990. This was accompanied by a substantial increase in hours-per-channel because in 1980 there was not yet much daytime TV in Europe. Also during 1980–1990 there was a big increase in cable and satellite TV.

National decisions to deregulate public broadcasting and to introduce additional commercial channels were encouraged from several directions. The American example was important, although in 1980 the American "cable revolution" was still in its infancy; in Brussels (and Belgium) cable had penetrated a bigger percentage of households. A very important precedent was established in Italy; following a 1975 Constitutional Court decision, local entrepreneurs were free to establish unregulated local radio and TV stations. Initially local stations sprang up, featuring local news, sports, talk, music, and, of course, local pornography. It was from this "only in Italy" chaotic tragicomedy that a former cruise crooner and real estate developer, Silvio Berlusconi, emerged to control Italy's three leading commercial TV channels. The national governments—both at home and in Brussels—were persuaded by the "Italian example," by the spread of cable in Belgium and the Netherlands, and by the American example.

Each of the five big European countries lurched into injudicious deregulation without much concern for the overall European picture. In each country enthusiasts for deregulation (which included politicians of the right, newspaper owners, and the advertising lobby) argued that new cable/satellite technologies made deregulation inevitable. Italy was the first, falling into deregulation by accident. Next came France and Germany—with media

---

[21] Tobias Jones, *The Dark Heart of Italy*, London: Faber and Faber, 2003.
[22] "Territory Guide to Spain," *Television Business International*, November/December 2001: 3–22.

policy the football of long-running left versus right squabbles; both France and Germany were committed to massive deregulation by 1986. Next came Britain, where television was deregulated during 1988–1992. Last of the big five was Spain, which deregulated in the early 1990s, on a mainly French model.[23]

However, in none of the big five countries did commercial (100 percent advertising-financed) broadcasting drive "public" broadcasting to its death. In all five countries a mixed commercial and public system emerged. Public television (and radio) had suffered its biggest loss of audience by 1995 and during 1995–2005 its continuing audience loss was quite small. In 2005 the big five countries each had two or three major public channels; these were still quite well funded—with a combination of license fee and advertising. These two or three public channels in 2005 still had a combined national audience share of over 35 percent. The public channels typically had continually revised, rethought, and retuned their programming. Each public TV broadcaster had a different programming mix on its different channels (such as one majority and one minority channel). But public broadcasters typically concentrated on factual television (news, documentary, information, and sports) plus some expensive, high profile, national scripted drama and/or comedy. The terrestrial commercial channels typically fought fiercely for the mass audience (and advertising revenue); these commercial channels also had higher levels of importing.

Daily newspaper sales were quite substantial in all five countries at both the provincial and national levels; this was despite lower sales in the south —not only in Italy and Spain but also in the south of France. Slow daily circulation declines were common to all countries. Total daily sales in the early 2000s in these five countries were about 60 million—slightly ahead of the United States. Each of the five countries has strong head-to-head national newspaper competition, plus at least one free daily in each of the very largest cities.

All five of these countries have important magazine industries; France, Germany, Spain, and the United Kingdom all export substantial quantities of magazines. These countries also boast the world's biggest collection of major news agencies, including four world class agencies—Reuters, AFP, EFE (Spain), and DPA (Germany). ANSA (Italy) is one of the world's larger agencies.

All five countries have national movie industries that are long on ambition, nostalgia, numbers of movies produced, and numbers of movie theater screens; all five are, however, short of paying audiences—either at home, elsewhere in Europe, or around the world. Across these five bigger countries about two-thirds of all movie theater visits are to see Hollywood movies.

---

[23] Jeremy Tunstall and David Machin, *The Anglo-American Media Connection*, Oxford, UK: Oxford University Press, 1999: 189–99.

Another common characteristic is that, with the boom in commercial television since 1950, press ownerships have crossed over into television;[24] consequently, there has been a new wave of cross-media companies, media moguls, media mogul families, and media barons. There have also been several mogul-to-mogul sales of big media companies. In the United Kingdom, the presiding chief media mogul from the 1980s onward was Rupert Murdoch, who—with the crucial partisan (and dubiously legal) support of Margaret Thatcher—crossed over from being the United Kingdom's leading press owner to becoming also the controlling mogul-owner of BSkyB; the latter company became in practice the monopoly satellite-to-home TV supplier and the monopolistic gatekeeper for premium (sports and movie) content going to cable. Murdoch's bizarre preeminence in Britain was exceeded only by Berlusconi's even more bizarre mogul dominance in Italy. Berlusconi by the early 2000s was a monopolist of Italian commercial TV; he was the dominant force in Italian advertising and Italian movies. He was also the owner of a big newspaper, a big magazine group, and a big football team (A.C. Milan). Finally, Berlusconi as prime minister quickly exerted significant partisan influence over the three public, RAI, channels.

A common strand in several different Euro-mogul careers was some kind of special relationship with Hollywood. In France Hollywood connections were vital to Canal Plus and to the rise and fall of Messier's Vivendi-Universal. Rupert Murdoch was himself a Hollywood owner and BSkyB depended on Hollywood movies for one of its main revenue streams. Berlusconi had also been especially dependent on Hollywood in the years around 1980.

In Germany dependence on TV fiction imports from Hollywood was fundamental to the collapse of KirchMedia and related companies. Kirch controlled major elements of the German media, including the second largest commercial TV company, ProSiebenSat1, and the major press group, Springer. ProSiebenSat1 alone had 2001 revenues of over two billion U.S. dollars.[25] But the company collapsed because of rights purchasing. Leo Kirch had spent 46 years (1956–2002) trading in rights, especially German rights for Hollywood films and TV series. In Kirch's corporate structure it was rights trading (not his two TV networks) that occupied the key position. Kirch's big problem in the late 1990s was *Premiere*, his digital TV "pay" subscription channel. In the competitive German TV market a new high tech "pay" offering needed premium exclusive programming; Kirch invested heavily in sports rights but even more heavily in Hollywood films. Supported to unwise lengths by state-owned Bavarian banks (and despite his weak digital technology), Leo Kirch in 1995–1997 signed 10-year contracts for virtually the entire future movie output of the Hollywood majors. His 10-year contract with Paramount

---

[24] For example, Sat-1 was launched in January 1985 by a consortium of German publishers. Vanessa O'Connor, "The Publishers' Channel," *Cable and Satellite Europe*, January 1985: 54–55.

[25] ProSiebenSat1 Media AG, *Annual Report 2001*: 102.

was worth $2 billion, and two other contracts (with Disney and Columbia-Tristar) were each worth $1 billion.[26] In early 2002, Kirch's impending disaster was already causing consternation in both southern Germany and southern California.[27] The next year ProSiebenSat1 became even more Hollywood dependent when it acquired a new chief owner in the person of Haim Saban, the Egyptian-Israeli-Hollywood cartoon mogul.[28]

Nevertheless, the appeal of Hollywood movies to European audiences can easily be exaggerated, as can the appeal of all, or any, American programming. In the United Kingdom, for example, the television ratings were increasingly dominated by domestic productions in general and by early evening British soap series in particular. In the second week of January 2006, 15 of the top 20 ratings slots were occupied by British soaps (*Coronation Street, EastEnders, Emmerdale*), while not one American production appeared in the week's top 75 ratings.[29]

In the other larger western European countries the big effort to produce cheap-but-popular shows only really began during the 1990s. Germany's first five-days-a-week soap, *Good Times, Bad Times*, only appeared in 1992. The first genuine Italian and Spanish soap series only began in 1996. In 1989 western Europe only had eight domestic soaps (six U.K., one German, one Irish). By 1994 there were 20 and by 1997 over 40. By 2005 even France had its own popular prime-time soap, *Plus Belle La Vie* on France 3 at 8:20 pm five nights a week. A major force in introducing domestic soap production to Europe was the Australian Grundy company.[30]

In the early 2000s the European-produced soaps were joined by a huge wave of domestic reality programming.

Cultural and Media Nationalism in Smaller Western European Countries

Western Europe's lesser-population countries do, indeed, have very small numbers of citizens. Four Scandinavian countries (Denmark, Finland, Norway, and Sweden) together have only 24 million; the Netherlands, with 16 million, has the largest of western Europe's small populations. But each of these small countries has its own, highly distinctive, national identity. Portugal has a unique history, including empire-building in Latin America, Africa, and Asia; has a distinctive geographical location in Europe's extreme

---

26 "European Television Movie Rights," *Screen Digest*, May 2002: 149–54; Ed. Meza, "Kirch Kingdom Takes a Tumble," *Variety*, June 17–23, 2002: A1, A8.

27 "H'W'D Feels Heat as Kirch Burns," *Variety*, March 4–10, 2002.

28 ProSiebenSat1 Media AG, *Annual Report*, 2003: 62–63.

29 "Week Ending: 15 January," *Broadcast*, January 20, 2006.

30 Hugh O'Donnell, *Good Times, Bad Times: Soap Operas and Society in Western Europe*, London: Leicester University Press, 1999.

southwest corner; is traditionally Roman Catholic; and has in Portuguese one of the world's largest languages. Portugal has a geographical big brother in the form of Spain and is the best foreign market for Brazilian *telenovelas*.

The Netherlands, three centuries ago, was a European leader in both commerce and art; it is geographically unusual with much of the Netherlands being below sea level; traditionally it has a mix of Roman Catholicism and Protestant-Calvinism. Dutch, also, is a big world language not least because of the former Dutch empire in Indonesia. The Netherlands has a nearby big brother in Germany; the Netherlands gave the world *Big Brother* and much reality TV.

Finland also has a very special history, having been invaded and colonized at various times by Sweden, Russia, and Germany. The main religions are Protestantism and (Greek) Orthodox. Linguistically Finnish is unrelated to other Scandinavian languages, although Swedish is a second official language. Finland's nearby big brothers are Russia and Sweden. Finland has significant Swedish-language, as well as Finnish-language, media. Finland is also unique for a small country in being a world leader in developing its knowledge and information society and being the home of Nokia, the early world leader in mobile telephony.[31]

Each of these small-population countries is eager to defend its own national culture, and does so through its educational system and mass media. As elsewhere, national identity has a strong us-against-them element. "Them" in national media terms are both U.S. media and also the media of the big-population European nations such as France, Germany, and the United Kingdom. In most cases there is one major local rival—such as Sweden for Finland and Spain for Portugal; for the Netherlands there is Belgium, whose mass media use the Dutch language, as well as French and German.

For a full 40 years after 1945 the national media of the small countries were quietly protected and reflected their national identity. Press, film, and broadcasting were all on a small scale compared with the big-population countries.

In Scandinavia, Netherlands, Belgium, and Switzerland the press was strong and strongly partisan. In several countries the daily press was also assisted by subsidies. A similar paternalistic attitude prevailed in relation to "public service broadcasting." The BBC and the British model were admired, especially in the northern countries in the post-1945 years. But, in each of these small countries, public broadcasting was nationally idiosyncratic. In most smaller countries, television was not a significant force during 1945–1960, and broadcasting consisted primarily of a limited radio output. In Norway television did not start until 1960 and by 1967 there were still only four hours of TV per 24 hours; in 1967 nearly half of Norwegian TV was imported, with the United Kingdom and other Nordic nations the main

---

[31] Timo Saari, "Researching the Future of Media in 'Wireless Valley,'" *InterMedia*, Vol. 27/5, October 1999: 4–6.

sources. When the Hollywood prime-time soap opera *Dynasty* arrived in Norway in 1983, it was experienced as if coming from outer space.[32]

In Portugal television did not begin until 1957 and was controlled by the dictatorship of Salazar until his death in 1970. Very different things happened in the Netherlands, where both radio and television were operated under a unique Dutch system of "pillarization." Initially there were four "pillars"—Catholic, Calvinist, socialist, and liberal conservative—each of which controlled a generous slice of broadcasting time.

Whatever the details of the particular public service system, these national broadcasters typically had a monopoly of national radio and TV output. They all had to decide how to treat the specific national experience of World War II. What should be said about collaborating with (or fighting) the Germans? Dutch broadcasters had to say something about the fate of Dutch Jews, three-quarters of whom died in the Holocaust. What should Swedish and Swiss broadcasters say about their national record of neutrality? Also in the later 1940s, the start of the Cold War raised many fresh questions, such as how the national broadcasters should report on their own national Communist Party.

In such political areas, national broadcasters inevitably looked toward the main contending forces in the legislature and tried to steer some "neutral" course between them. The public broadcasters were also confronted by big cultural issues, such as selection of the precise version of the national language or languages to be used in radio and later in television. In Belgium, for example, the Flemish public broadcasters deliberately used the pure or standard version of Dutch spoken in the Netherlands. The German-Swiss public broadcasters, by contrast, decided not to follow German German but deliberately to adopt Swiss versions of German. Both of these policies were subsequently modified.[33]

During the 1985–1995 decade "everything changed" in these small-population countries—public radio and television lost their monopoly and the press lost its monopoly of advertising. But much stayed the same—television, especially, remained in a few hands; the big new winner, in most cases, was a big new commercial television channel. By 1995 Norway's three-year-old TV2 already had a 30 percent audience share; in Sweden TV4 had a 29 percent share. In the Netherlands the new RTL4 channel went from nothing in 1989 to a 32 percent audience share in 1993. In Portugal the new SIC channel signed an exclusive contract with Globo of Brazil and in the later 1990s had an audience share of almost 50 percent.

In these small countries television deregulation was even more sudden and radical than in the large population countries. In these small countries

---

[32] Jostein Gripsrud, *The Dynasty Years*, London: Routledge, 1995.

[33] H. Van den Bulck and L. Van Poecke, "National Language, Identity Formation and Broadcasting in the Modern-Postmodern Debate. The Case of the Flemish and German-Swiss Communities," paper presented at the International Association of Mass Communication Research (IAMCR) meeting in Dublin, 1993.

public broadcasting had (previous to 1985) involved few hours of transmission and little, or no, TV advertising. When these small countries launched new channels they had fewer resources with which to generate additional programming. The small countries were heavily influenced by their big brother nations; Germany's increasingly commercial TV programming leaked across the borders into Denmark, Netherlands, Belgium, and Switzerland. These latter four small countries were also already more committed in 1985 to cable systems (bringing channels from nearby countries). This is discussed later in this chapter.

During 1985–1995 leading national print media groups took the opportunity to expand into national television; another move then took several press-TV groups across into neighboring countries. Egmont (Denmark), Bonnier (Sweden), Schibsted (Norway), and Kinnevik-MTG (Sweden) all acquired media properties in other Scandinavian countries.

The years 1985–1995 saw American involvement increase in two separate ways. First, the new commercial TV channels were more dependent on imports in general and on American imports in particular. While the public broadcasters in the northern countries had previously imported programming mainly from the United Kingdom and other northern countries, some of the new commercial channels now imported 30, 40, or even 50 percent of their entire output from the United States. Second, of the new trans-European companies the largest (CLT-RTL) was German, but some others—such as Scandinavian Broadcasting System (SBS)—were American controlled.

In the two decades from 1985 to 2005, national public broadcasting in these smaller countries declined from a 100 percent to a 35–40 percent audience share; most of that drop had already occurred by 1995. There has also been a decline in daily paid-for newspapers, especially provincial dailies; today there are strong monopoly ownerships of local weekly newspapers and magazines and also a few big owners of national dailies. These countries' media systems have been nationalized, Europeanized, and Americanized all at the same time. Many media owners in the smaller countries seem to pursue a mogul business style by both selling and buying media properties. When the Dutch VNU company decided in 2001 to sell its magazines, other companies from several other countries were involved. VNU sold its big collection of magazines (not only in the Netherlands but also in Belgium, Hungary, and the Czech Republic) to the Finnish newspaper and TV group Sanoma.

Endemol was another small company based in a small country (the Netherlands) that grew into worldwide significance during the 1990s, before being acquired by Telefonica of Spain. John de Mol and Joop den Ende combined their names and companies into Endemol and became a media mogul partnership.[34] Their initial triumph was to supply cheaply produced

---

[34] Nick Bell, "Major Men," *Television Business International*, April 1994: 18–24; Debra Johnson, "Holland's Endemol Broadens Horizons," *Broadcasting and Cable International*, April 1996: 36–37.

programming to two separate RTL commercial TV channels, one in Germany and one in the Netherlands. They supplied soaps, quiz/game shows, and variety entertainment. They achieved economies by using the same studio set for both the Dutch version and the German version of the same show. Endemol's studios (in the Amsterdam area) were close to major German media locations. By 1995–1996 Endemol had revenue of $400 million and was making development deals with numerous European broadcasters; an early strength was relationship and dating shows such as *All You Need Is Love* and *The Honeymoon Quiz*. In 1996 Endemol floated on the Amsterdam stock market; it used the extra cash to acquire successful independent production companies across Europe. Subsequently Endemol increasingly moved into the licensing of its "reality" shows, such as *Big Brother*. The success of numerous such formats in numerous countries indicated that Endemol shows included very little Dutch cultural idiosyncrasy and even less strict Calvinism. However, the Endemol mogul partners did themselves perhaps exemplify some traditional Dutch characteristics. The Endemol partners quickly grasped how television functioned in nearby bigger countries such as Germany, France, and the United Kingdom; they were within the long Dutch tradition of international commerce. Their shows were in the 1990s more innovative, more worldly-wise, and more commercially viable than competing cheap entertainment shows in both Europe and the United States.

For most of television's history up to the 1990s there had been only two main forms of television—fiction (drama, comedy, movies) and factual (news, actuality, education, and sports). Endemol showed that "unscripted" (but carefully planned) programming could become a third way. Reality shows have, of course, been dismissed as nasty, brutish, and much too long. But these shows were able to obtain high audience shares in both big and small countries. These unscripted shows put "ordinary" (although selected) people onto television; the language was the stumbling language of everyday talk; and the reality shows both created new national stars and recycled old national stars. The trade in TV formats involved selling the same format to numerous countries; but when each national version appeared on television, the unscripted participants spoke, cursed, and misbehaved in their common national language. Endemol and reality programming showed how small (and larger) countries could produce more cheap programming and import less.

Another interesting small country media innovator was Swedish Kinnevik and its Metro International subsidiary. In the decade 1995–2005 Metro launched free daily newspapers in 15 languages in over 100 cities across the world. In London and New York City the Metro invaders experienced belligerent well-funded competition, but the resurgence of the free daily was inspired by Stockholm.

Meanwhile, public broadcasting seems likely to continue in most, but perhaps not all, small European countries. Public broadcasters specialize in factual programming; the national news is popular with audiences across Europe, and most politicians share good political and career reasons for wishing to retain a big national news effort. Public broadcasters are also widely seen as supporting, and perhaps as subsidizing, the nation's traditional high, or higher, culture. Even in the small European countries public broadcasters make special provision for expensive orchestral music and for coverage of the arts. Several small countries have substantial international radio efforts, supported by special government funding. Public broadcasters are also actively involved as national book publishers.

Public broadcasters in small countries play a key role in financing the small national movie industry; typical movie budgets in small countries are about half the size of movie budgets in much larger countries (Germany, France, Spain, Italy).[35] To obtain a typical movie budget of $2 million, a small country movie producer may need to presell the project both to the public broadcaster and to a national arts-subsidy or film-subsidy body. These small countries in the past generated outstanding moviemakers; but Ingmar Bergmann, for instance, made his most famous and revered films in the 1950s and 1960s, when Swedish television provided little real competition. Each of today's film subsidy systems reflects national priorities, national arts policy, and cultural nationalism in general. Some projects are excessively national-nostalgic, while other projects strive awkwardly toward artistic innovation. But most small-budget films from small-population countries appeal only to the national audience that understands their national concerns and references.

While high culture attracts national finance and while reality television attracts both new audiences and new digital revenue pathways, what happens to immigrants and minorities? In Belgium, Netherlands, Sweden, Denmark, Norway, and Switzerland recent immigrants constitute about 10 percent of the population; many are from Muslim countries such as Morocco and Turkey. In several larger cities—including Amsterdam, Brussels, Malmo, Stockholm and Zurich—recent immigrants make up more than 10 percent of the population. Nevertheless, there has been rather little local media in Arabic, Turkish, or other relevant languages. One consequence, or cause, of this is a high level of tuning in to satellite services from the immigrants' homeland. Meanwhile, these small-population countries have seen the emergence of single-issue political campaigning (and parties) opposed to immigration and/or immigrants. How can immigrants be encouraged to participate in the local national culture and the local national media? How can the inevitable us-against-them element of national culture keep us from being against immigrant cultures? Here again, although recent immigration has occurred in all European countries, the precise components are specific to each small nation and its national culture.

---

[35] "Average Film Budgets in the US Soar Ahead," *Screen Digest*, August 2003: 228.

Media Nationalists of ex-Communist Central Europe

The collapse of the Soviet Union, of Yugoslavia, and of communism created to the west of Russia some 21 newly assertive nation-states, each with its own freshly assertive national media and national culture. The ex-Soviet and ex-Yugoslavian nation-states are discussed in Chapter 19; here we focus on Poland, Hungary, and the Czech Republic,[36] three of the most western of the central European countries; all three adjoin Germany or Austria. Each of these countries has had a turbulent twentieth- and nineteenth-century history. In each country politicians, people, and media have much to remember and to forget. Poland, Hungary, and the Czech Republic can all claim to have been places where World War II began, where Hitler was defeated, and where the Soviet Empire began to crumble.

Poland, with a population (39 million) four times that of either Hungary or the Czech Republic, is accordingly higher up the media pecking order. Poland has also been the quickest of these nation-states to "join" the Western media. Poland has one of Europe's most tragic national histories—removed from the map for over a century, brutally invaded by Germany and then fought over again by the Soviet Union, and the main site of the Nazi Holocaust. It was not an accident that the collapse of communism in Europe began in Poland in 1980. Poland was a European, even a world, leader in two media fields—print journalism and film. Polish journalists did not take strike action against the communist regime, even when such strike action (against food prices) occurred in summer 1980 in the Gdansk shipyards and elsewhere across Poland. However, Polish journalists pursued their version of professional journalism with dogged determination. Their quiet resistance to censorship made Polish journalists a number one target when martial law was introduced in 1981. All but three major newspapers were closed down, while radio and TV were subjected to military control. Many journalists lost their jobs. Under martial law proportionately more journalists were arrested than members of any other profession.[37] Because journalism was a respected occupation in Poland—and many journalists bravely continued to resist censorship and to speak out in public—this surely contributed to the military-communist regime's loss of legitimacy.

Poland also had one of the world's most admired film industries. The Polish people could be proud to have such a large (home and abroad) stable of auteur film directors, including Andrzej Wajda, Krzysztof Kieslowski, and Roman Polanski. Wajda in particular was both admired and feared by the

---

[36] This section relies heavily on two books: Brankica Petković (ed.), *Media Ownership and Its Impact on Media Independence and Pluralism*, Ljubljana, Slovenia: Peace Institute, 2004; and Mary Kelly, Gianpietro Mazzoleni, and Denis McQuail (eds.), *The Media in Europe: The Euromedia Handbook*, London: Sage, 2004.

[37] Jane Leftwich Curry, *Poland's Journalists: Professionalism and Politics*, Cambridge, UK: Cambridge University Press, 1990: 205–42.

communist government. His films *A Generation* (1954), *Kanal* (1957), *and Ashes and Diamonds* (1958) carried implicit, but forceful, critiques of both Russia and Germany and their armies. Wajda made a remarkably direct attack on Polish Stalinism in *Man of Marble*, which in 1976 attracted large Polish audiences;[38] this was part of a Polish film trend, called cinema of moral concern, that repeatedly questioned the Polish communist state. Four years after *Man of Marble*, the beginning of the end of communism occurred in Gdansk.

Czechoslovakia, created at Versailles in 1919, split into two states—the Czech Republic and Slovakia—in 1993; each new country had its own national media system. Also crucial to the Czech Republic's self-image was the Prague Spring of 1968, which included a freer media and led to brutal suppression by the Soviet army in August 1968. While the Czech Republic's media in the 1990s celebrated Czech freedom and democracy, these national media were less keen to celebrate two big Czech injustices. The substantial Roma (Gypsy) population of the Czech Republic did not receive fair and equal treatment from the Czech state or media. Another piece of Czechoslovak history, which the 1990s media preferred not to remember, was the 1945 expulsion from the Sudetenland (northwest Czechoslovakia) of 2.5 million ethnic Germans, as well as many Hungarians.

In Hungary itself, governments and media were confronted with the fact that the old Austro-Hungarian Empire had left over 20 percent of ethnic Hungarians in 1990 living outside Hungary (especially in Romania). But in 1990 the Hungarian people and media could at last celebrate the end of 55 years of foreign domination—first by Germany, then by the Soviet Union.

In each of these countries the old communist-slanted school history texts were rejected; massive projects began to rewrite national history and to celebrate previously banned writers and artists. In the universities also there were huge changes in the teaching of social science, history, and the arts. While waiting for the new textbooks to arrive, individual teachers had to present their own versions of national culture, national history, and national goals.

Meanwhile, despite their very different recent histories, each of these peoples—the Poles, Czechs, and Hungarians—saw their domestic mass media move through a similar sequence during the 1990s and into the next century.

Before the collapse of European communism and the fall of the Berlin Wall on November 9, 1989, the media across communist Europe had been following the Polish lead in small hesitant steps toward freedom. Most of the communist regimes made some concessions well before November 1989. Advertising and western pop music were growing. Hungarian television by early 1989 was reducing eastern imports and letting in more western programming. All of these countries in 1989 had a substantial array of thin daily

---

[38] David Caute, *The Dancer Defects: The Struggle for Cultural Supremacy in the Cold War*, Oxford, UK: Oxford University Press, 2003: 365–75.

papers controlled by the government, the Communist Party, and associated elements of the regime. A big majority of households had television sets; the normal pattern was of one Russian TV channel (Gostelradio1) and two public-state national TV channels.[39]

During 1989–1992 everything changed. The economy went from communist planning to extreme capitalist economic shock therapy. Many state-owned corporations were sold at low prices. The media went from communist control to capitalist freedom, but advertising revenue only expanded from a very low base; this was capitalism without much capital. The newspaper press went through the standard new freedom phase of mushroom growth. While some journalists and press workers seized control of their publications ("spontaneous privatization"), other journalists and nouveaux entrepreneurs launched new publications. Poland, for example, went from 53 dailies in 1989 to 80 dailies in 1992 and back down to 49 dailies in 1999. Political excitement fueled anarchy and chaos; in some cases two separate dailies were using the same one old communist newspaper name. The new democratic papers were initially nearly as thin (and light on advertising) as the old communist ones. The dailies that survived tended to be those run by more experienced journalists with good connections to the printers and to the old state monopoly distribution system.

While the press grappled with financial as well as editorial freedom, state-sponsored public television continued. These early chaotic years of 1989–1992 saw a redefinition of "public" broadcasting from communist to democratic western European public broadcasting. But around 1990 western Europe itself was challenging and confronting its own separate national traditions of public broadcasting. Initially the new democratic regime gave TV and radio journalists very much more freedom. Who would occupy the top positions and define what public service broadcasting meant in practice? One influential suggestion came from Czechoslovakia, where Václav Havel —a playwright twice jailed for his anti-communist writings—was elected president in December 1989. Across central Europe local equivalents of Havel—writers, intellectuals, academics—were given top positions in public broadcasting. This quickly led to confrontations and conflicts between newly elected politicians and newly appointed public intellectuals in charge of newly free (but undefined) public service broadcasting. Repeated clashes and repeated rounds of broadcasting legislation followed, up to and beyond year 2000.

A new phase of broadcast commercialization and competition began in the Czech Republic in 1993, in Poland in 1994, and in Hungary in 1997.

---

[39] Karol Jakubowicz, "Advertising in Poland—A Time of Transition," *Media Development*, 3, 1987: 16–18; Karol Jakubowicz, "Poland: Media Systems in Transition," *InterMedia*, Vol. 17/2, June–July 1989: 25–28; Graham Norwood, "Hungarian Television Is First Away from Eastern Bloc," *Broadcasting* (London), February 10, 1989: 27; "East Europe," *Broadcasting Abroad*, May 1989: 48–56.

The consequent changes were even more dramatic than similar changes in western Europe a few years earlier. In the Czech Republic the new commercial TV Nova was launched in 1993 and by 1995 had an audience share of 71 percent. Czech television advertising expenditure went from 5 million euros in 1991 to 95 million in 1995; TV advertising spending passed press spending for the first time in 1998. However around year 2000 the broad television audience picture in small central European countries was quite similar to the picture in small western European countries. The big new winners typically were one or two new commercial channels; however, the public broadcaster typically retained two national channels and a third or more of the national audience. All of the new commercial broadcasters tried to increase their advertising revenue and to impress the new local offices of the big western advertising agencies. Initially some of the new channels relied heavily on Latin American *telenovelas*; in the longer term there has been heavy importing of programming from Hollywood and from western Europe.

During the 1990s there was little international consensus as to what did, and did not, constitute correctly democratic journalism. In these highly politicized but newly democratic countries, national political warfare tended to outgun independent professional journalism.[40] Most journalists were reluctant to criticize key advertisers such as major telephone companies. Journalists in central Europe (as in western Europe) were puzzled by "investigative journalism" and how this might differ from "dossier journalism" (merely printing leaked documents). Was the Hungarian daily *Magyar Nemzet* justified in June 2002 in revealing that the new prime minister Peter Medgyessy had been an agent for the counterintelligence service of the former Hungarian communist state?[41]

Adam Michnik, chief editor of the Czech Republic's leading newspaper, *Gazeta Wyborza*, was involved in his newspaper's bid for the license to run a new television channel. He was approached in July 2002 by Lew Rywin— a celebrated movie producer—who offered to assist the television application in return for $17.5 million; Rywin was a close associate of the then Polish prime minister, Leszek Miller, and the scandal became known as "Rywingate." Editor Michnik audiorecorded Rywin's bribery attempt, and some saw his refusal to accept the bribe as exemplary. But should the country's most powerful newspaper have been seeking to enter television? Moreover, why did Michnik only reveal the bribery attempt some five months later? How credible was Michnik's claim that he did this so as not to

---

[40] Tomasz Goban-Klas, "Politics Versus the Media in Poland: A Game Without Rules," in Patrick O'Neal (ed.), *Post-Communism and the Media in Eastern Europe*, London: Frank Cass, 1997: 24–41.

[41] "Hungary's Embattled Prime Minister: He Admits He Spied but It Was Long Ago," *The Economist*, June 22, 2002: 45.

prejudice Poland's application to join the European Union?[42] Had Michnik been justified in informing both the prime minister and the president about this scandal long before, through the newspaper, he informed the great Polish public? There is, of course, no definitive answer to such questions. These Polish events and personalities related back to 1980s confrontations between the then communist government and the Solidarity opposition. In Poland, as elsewhere, the norms and values of national journalism are rooted in the specific national culture and history.

There were more open and more obvious anxieties about foreign ownership. The huge early success of (the U.S.-controlled) TV Nova in the Czech Republic in 1994–1995 occurred alongside a big foreign invasion of western print companies, including Bertelsmann (Germany), Mirror Group (UK, Maxwell), News International (UK, Murdoch), and Socpresse (France, Hersant). However, after several loss-making years most of these foreign print owners sold out and went home.

The foreign ownership element in television was relatively modest; taking Poland, Hungary, the Czech Republic, and Romania together and weighting for population, the U.S. companies had the largest foreign audience share —about 12 percent—in 2003. The only other significant foreign share in television was German. Compared with the press, the foreign element was quite small; public television remained state controlled and most of the successful new commercial networks were under domestic national control.

The newspaper and magazine picture was quite different. By 2003, German companies had 34 percent of daily newspaper sales across the four countries, and Swiss companies had 20 percent. This 54 percent German and Swiss circulation share did involve the giant Springer company of Germany; but the most successful single company in circulation terms was the Swiss Ringier company. Also successful were a number of regional press groups from Germany; regional German companies were especially successful in the ownership of small regional daily papers in central Europe. These German companies had had relevant experience inside East Germany when it became reunited with West Germany. There are many German-speakers in central Europe, and 10 years after the end of communism across Poland, Czech Republic, and Hungary, a national average of 50 percent of secondary school children were learning German, versus 67 percent learning English.[43]

Nevertheless, the more news-inclined public broadcasters were still national; most of the leading newspapers were nationally controlled and either independent or aligned with political parties and major politicians.

---

[42] Stefan Wagstyl, "Bribery Case Deepens Crisis," *Financial Times*, "World Report: Poland," April 15, 2003: 1; Peter Popham, "Poland Puts Producer on Trial in Political Sleaze Drama," *The Guardian*, December 3, 2003: 15.

[43] "The European Union: After Babel, a New Common Tongue," *The Economist*, August 7, 2004: 33–34.

European Cable and Satellite: America's Ambiguous Involvement

From the 1970s onward, the move from a few TV channels to many TV channels in Europe was heavily influenced by American companies, American policy, American programming, and American investment. The main thrust of the developments was a one-way flow from the United States into Europe. Nevertheless, there were many paradoxes; the "American threat" led, in some cases, to strengthened European defenses. Much of what happened, especially since 1990, has also been shrouded in ambiguity—not least because it is increasingly difficult to distinguish between what is American media and what is European media.

Cable television in 1975 was concentrated, in both Europe and the United States, away from the largest centers of population. U.S. cable subscribers in the 1970s were mainly located in remote rural areas and small towns or in mountain valleys. Cable television (CATV) typically used one high antenna to receive the local stations. In addition, CATV often brought into a lowly populated state (such as Iowa) a few extra stations from a bigger city in the same region (such as Chicago). These early American cable systems had low channel capacity, as did European systems. In Europe early cable also offered a few additional channels from nearby cities—often cities just across the national border. Local cable systems in Netherlands and Belgium (mostly controlled by the municipality) brought in additional channels from France and Germany. Cable was a local or regional phenomenon; however, in Belgium and the Netherlands the foreign channels, from across the border, offered a wider selection of films and series, including Hollywood exports.

In the 1970s important policy changes were occurring. In the United States space satellites were ceasing to be a military monopoly; and in Europe, Italian parliamentary and court decisions in 1975–1976 effectively deregulated television and allowed the Berlusconi revolution to begin. However, in 1975 there was still a scarcity of fresh programming with which to fill fresh channels. Berlusconi and his competitors relied on heavy importing from North and South America. With hindsight, perhaps the key development of the year 1975 was Home Box Office's live transmission of the Ali-Fraser heavyweight boxing contest from the Philippines. Only two cable systems (in Mississippi and Florida) scheduled this fight, but by 1977 HBO was available on 350 local systems in 45 states. Also important was the 1976 launch of the "superstation"; Ted Turner made his Atlanta station, WTCG (later WTBS), available by satellite to local cable systems. But what would later be called "platform" investment was still very limited because profitability was still uncertain. These new U.S. offerings in the 1970s still had no customers in Europe.

In the 1980s cable television was still developing differently in Europe and America. In 1981 only 10 percent of homes in western Europe had cable; but

75 percent of Belgian and 60 percent of Dutch homes had cable.[44] U.S. cable was an increasingly widespread phenomenon, advancing from the small towns into the cities. By 1985 the average American cable subscribing household could only receive about 25 channels, but the local system operator could choose from about 55 nationally available services. This included some 30 "basic" services (such as CNN, ESPN, MTV, USA, and Nickelodeon), 4 superstations, about 11 "pay" (mainly movie) services, and about 9 text services (such as AP and Reuters). However, the basic services, especially, had great difficulty generating either advertising or fee income,[45] and they soon began looking hopefully toward Europe.

Europe in late 1986 had 11 satellite TV services operating across national borders, and all 11 were losing money; the London-based Sky Channel and Superchannel were in the most European homes (seven and five million, respectively). But these British-English channels were commercial failures. However, in 1986 there were three small German-language satellite channels; these three—RTL-Plus, Sat-1 and 3-Sat—were the leaders of what was to become a big German-language satellite industry.[46]

Throughout the 1980s the main satellite-cable Brussels policy focus was what eventually became the *Television Without Frontiers* directive. This began in the European Parliament in 1980, while the directive finally came into force in 1991. The title reflected the early 1980s mood of anxiety about an American invasion and an optimistic hope that European countries would import TV programming from each other. The directive lacked teeth and specified that all European channels should carry at least 50 percent "European content," and even then only when this was "practicable."

As late as 1989 only 5 percent of western European viewing was of whole channels from other countries; and the bulk, even of this 5 percent of viewing, involved channels coming from next-door countries (and not by satellite). The biggest importer of whole channels in 1989 was Switzerland (from Germany) followed by Belgium (mainly from France). Only 1.59 percent of western European viewing in 1989 involved international satellites, and most of this viewing was in Sweden, Finland, Norway, and Denmark—all were importing London-based channels in their own national languages. These Scandinavian channels were taking advantage of Britain's earlier moves into satellite deregulation.[47]

Despite European anxieties dating back to the 1970s, by 1990 the big American channel invasion had still not arrived.

[44] Kees Brants, "Policing the Cable," in Denis McQuail and Karen Siune (eds.), *New Media Politics*, London: Sage 1986: 55–71. The U.S. figure (for 1980) was 19.9 percent. Eli Noam, *Television in Europe*, New York: Oxford University Press, 1991: 322.

[45] *Cablevision*, September 10, 1984: 100; Jeremy Tunstall, *Communications Deregulation*, Oxford: Blackwell, 1986: 121–41.

[46] Jeremy Tunstall and David Machin, *The Anglo-American Media Connection*, Oxford, UK: Oxford University Press, 1999: 200–14.

[47] Jan Perry (Young and Rubicam), "The Big Spill?" *Media Week* (London), May 25, 1990: 22.

U.S. Satellite and Cable in Europe: 1996–1997 Peak, Then Decline

Cultural nationalism and media nationalism prevailed across Europe in 1995 and 2005, as in 1975 and 1985. The old pecking order also continued. Each European country gave preference first to its own domestic output; second, a substantial minority of all video and television came from the United States; in third, and last, place came imports from other European countries, and, once again, this was mainly small countries importing from larger European countries.

Between 1985 and 1995 Hollywood's revenues from Europe greatly increased; the demands of new movie channels (such as Canal Plus in France and Sky in the United Kingdom) boosted the cash totals. There was also a big increase in the number of satellite channels across Europe—from 10 in 1984 to 130 in 1992. European policymakers and researchers emphasized the big amounts of network time occupied by American fiction (mainly movies and drama series).

Table 14.1 shows that Hollywood movies and series were taking up big quantities of prime time on terrestrial network TV in Europe in 1997. Even in the bigger population countries, some 20 percent of all television time was taken up by imported Hollywood fiction; this excluded other, nonfiction, imports. Moreover, the proportions of American content on many of the new satellite channels was even higher. Many small satellite channels were in the mid-1990s failing to schedule European productions in at least 50 percent of their time.

The broad 1997 picture, then, was of even the major channels in the major countries scheduling at least 30 percent of their time with American programming; some other countries, including Italy, were scheduling well over 30 percent.

Table 14.1 The U.S. Proportion of Television Fiction Screened in Selected European Countries, 1997

	U.S. PERCENTAGE OF PRIME-TIME TV FICTION	U.S. PERCENTAGE OF ALL TV FICTION
United Kingdom, Germany, and France	36.5	52.8
Belgium and Netherlands	49.6	58.1
Italy	62.6	52.1

Note: Based on 36 stations in six countries during January 1997.
Source: Els De Bens and Hedwig de Smaele, "The Inflow of American Television Fiction on European Broadcasting Channels Revisited," *European Journal of Communication*, Vol. 16/1, March 2001: 51–76.

However, there was already around 1995–1997 strong evidence of some countertrends. Some of the biggest importers around 1990 were new major channels such as the main RTL channel in Germany, which devoted only 30 percent of its programming budget to its own productions in 1990 but had increased this to 80 percent by 1994.[48] Despite the big quantities of Hollywood fiction, 1994 data show that in each of six European countries the top 20 programming ratings and shares were dominated by domestic productions and by football games involving the national team. The only exceptions were (a few) Hollywood films. There was not one Hollywood TV series in these 120 top-rated shows.[49] In France in 1996 all of the American shows achieving high audience shares (e.g., *The Young and the Restless*) were scheduled in early afternoon. Nor did the recently arrived American satellite offerings lack local competition; an analysis of 52 European satellite channels in early 1997 shows that U.S. channels achieved 28.8 percent of household penetration, national movie channels (with much U.S. content) achieved 2.5 percent, while EU satellite channels achieved 68.78 percent of total household penetration.[50]

The prime American strength in European TV around 1995–1997 was Hollywood movies; this included movies reaching audiences via a succession of market windows. Other American strengths were music television and children's channels.

The big American strength in fiction and scripted series did not carry over into factual and nonfiction programming. CNN in 1997 was in more European households (44 million) than was any other single satellite offering; but CNN (and several American financial news offerings) subsequently fell behind local all-news competition—both nationally and across Europe (Euronews). There was also a parallel growth in nonscripted talk, as well as game and reality programming. Oprah Winfrey attracted big afternoon audience shares in several European countries in and around 1992, but this also stimulated local competition. In the mid-1990s the big German commercial channel, RTL, had its own popular three hours of afternoon German talk each weekday.

In the early 2000s domestically produced reality programming was prominent in prime time across Europe. For instance, on Thursday evenings in 2003 there were 21 reality shows on the top 18 networks of France, Germany, the United Kingdom, and Italy.[51]

The steady growth in the number of channels meant that, both in Europe and America, even the largest channels increasingly had smaller market

---

[48] Meredith Amdur, "Programmers Bank on Markets Old and New," *Broadcasting and Cable International*, October 1994: 3–5; François Godard, "Homegrown: European Channels Banking on Their Own Series," *Broadcasting and Cable International*, February 1995: 3.

[49] Tim Westcott, "Aim High," *Television Business International*, April 1995: 188–90.

[50] "The Cable Penetration Chart: 1997 First Quarter," *Cable and Satellite Europe*, June 1997: 56–60.

[51] Georgina Higham, "Reality Bites Back," *Television Business International*, March/April 2004: 67–69.

shares. But in Europe in 1997 the largest four channels in most countries still had the great bulk of the audience. In four countries (France, the United Kingdom, Sweden, and Denmark) the largest four channels on average had 87 percent of the 1996 national audience. But in countries where cable and satellite had reached the majority of homes the four-channel total was much smaller; in both Germany and the Netherlands it was only 59 percent.[52]

The United States was, of course, the most striking example of audience loss by the few leading networks. The three traditional U.S. networks each went from a prime-time share in 1975 of nearly 30 percent to a 2005 share of about 10 percent; but in Europe popular series still often achieved much higher prime-time shares—such as 25 or 30 percent. For example, in the United Kingdom in January 2005, the top 75 programs of the week had an average share of 29.4 percent.[53]

With U.S. audience shares on average much smaller than in Europe and with production budgets linked to audience size and share, most Hollywood TV series by 2005 no longer had much bigger production budgets than those of TV series in the larger European countries. With as much or more money, per production hour, television production values (in the larger European countries) were now as high as those of Hollywood television. The one main Hollywood exception was, of course, the major movies with their much higher budgets and production values. A partial exception were lower budget American made-for-TV movies. Another exception was Home Box Office, which, because it was a premium "pay" channel, had high revenues and high budgets; even HBO series, however, were often carried by European networks that were only the fourth or fifth in national audience numbers.

In the early 1990s the most successful American satellite channels in Europe were "broad niche" offerings. Both in 1995 and 2005 MTV was probably the most successful and profitable. MTV had the advantage of much free content and the appeal of American (plus British) music in Europe. Not until January 1997 did MTV decide to break away from its London-based English-only service;[54] this initially led to MTV North (still in English), MTV Central (in German), and MTV South (in Italian). In 1998 MTV's German service was offering 70 percent German-language music; MTV's stable-mate, VH-1, was also available in a German version. By 2002 the parent company, Viacom, had 35 European channels (including 14 versions of MTV, 6 of VH-1, and 10 of Nickelodeon). This rapid escalation occurred because Viacom was now slicing its music and youth programming by language as well as by genre and subgenre (MTV Pop, Base, Extra Hits, Live, and Dance, as well as "older" VH-1 offerings). These MTV variations, however, faced strong competition; for example, Viacom by 1998 had only two of five German-language pop music video channels. Other American channel providers were also offering

---

[52] *European Television Analyst*, June 4, 1997.
[53] "Week Ending 30 January," *Broadcasting*, February 18, 2005: 38.
[54] Janine Gibson, "MTV Europe Axes 80 Jobs in London," *Broadcast*, November 21, 1997.

subgenre alternatives; by 2002 Discovery was available in 11 Discovery and Animal Planet versions.

The situation confronting American cable and satellite offerings varied greatly both between, and within, groups of European countries. The three leading European media countries—Germany, France, and the United Kingdom—had a combined population of 200 million and big differences from each other. Ninety percent of German households had satellite or cable by 2001; one consequence was six biggish German TV channels, none with a share larger than about 16 percent. France was unique in having one major subscription TV service (Canal Plus) and a low penetration of cable and satellite (despite a big national satellite effort).

Britain was by 2005 a European and world leader in digital television (available via Sky satellite, cable, or terrestrial digital); by early 2005 over 60 percent of all British homes had digital TV. In 2002, when BSkyB had already digitalised almost all of its then six million British (and Irish) customer households, it was offering about 175 channels. If "one hour plus" and other repeats and subvariants were included the total was over 200. BSkyB itself claimed 377 channels, but this included digital radio. The 175 total included 8 BBC TV channels, 4 part-BBC owned, 10 Viacom, 7 Discovery, and 8 channels in Asian languages and Arabic.

The group of small northern countries included such cable pioneers as the Netherlands and Belgium. The Netherlands public even in 1992 was devoting about one-sixth of its TV viewing time to German, Belgian, and British channels.[55] The Scandinavian countries came relatively late to cable and imported both from each other, and from the United States and United Kingdom. Most predigital households in this northern Europe group were limited to quite a low maximum possible number, such as 20 channels, which reduced the opportunities for U.S. cable offerings.

The southern European countries—Spain, Italy, Portugal, and Greece—both in 1995 and 2005 were among Europe's biggest importers of American programming; in Portugal's case Brazilian material continued in 2005 to loom large. But in these countries, also, both cable and satellite had only modest household penetration—again limiting the entry of multiple U.S. channels.

In ex-communist central Europe the penetration of cable and satellite was already quite high in 1995; by 2005 about half of all homes in Poland, Hungary, the Czech Republic, and Slovakia had cable or satellite TV.

Apart from the issue of American programming in European cable and satellite homes, Europe has performed weakly in two other important dimensions, namely, platforms and policies. The term "platform"—like other important communications concepts—lacks a standard definition. Here the term is used to describe major satellite offerings such as BSkyB in Britain and major cable companies that control local systems across whole European countries. Cable systems, in Europe as elsewhere, are normally local monopolies;

---

[55] Netherlands Broadcasting Corporation (NOS), *Hilversum Summary*, December 1992: 5.

also in Europe satellite provision involves either national monopoly or very limited competition. In the early 2000s in both Spain[56] and Italy two competing satellite operations merged into a sole national monopoly operation.

There has been a big American involvement since the 1980s in the establishment of satellite platforms for Europe. A key pioneer was Clay Whitehead, an MIT engineering graduate who worked in the Nixon White House (1969–1974); Whitehead ran the Office of Telecommunications Policy (OTP).[57] He subsequently became the leader of the Astra satellite project at the American-Luxembourg financed Societé Européenne des Satellites (SES). The first Astra-SES satellite was launched in 1988 and was used to carry BSkyB. By 1995 SES-delivered channels were in 64 million European homes.[58]

"Platform" was a term often used by Rupert Murdoch. The Murdoch-controlled BSkyB was Europe's most successful and profitable satellite operation; BSkyB was the dominant force in both satellite and cable in Britain in both 1995 and 2005. The Murdoch-controlled News Corporation also received European Commission approval in 2003 to merge its Stream operation into Telepiu to establish a monopoly satellite provider in Italy.[59] Murdoch quickly introduced some of his familiar tactics (such as heavy investment in expensive Italian football rights), and Telepiu soon made significant subscriber increases.

Three other American companies established a commanding position in European cable ownership in the late 1990s and early 2000s. The New York–based NTL company was a major player, especially in British and French cable. The Denver-based Richard Callahan by 2001 controlled 8.7 million cable subscriptions in Germany, Belgium, and Spain.[60] Third, UPC/UnitedGlobalCom—controlled by John Malone, the Denver-based king of cable—was involved in numerous European cable systems. By 2001 Callahan and Malone together controlled nearly one-quarter of all cable homes in Europe. But in a 24-month period (2000–2002) UPC shares—on the Amsterdam stock market—fell from 80 euros to 0.17 euros, losing 99.8 percent of their value. As it entered the bankruptcy pipeline, UPC had 8.4 million customer households in 13 European countries.[61] John Malone subsequently made a bid to become the dominant cable owner in Germany but was repulsed by the cartel authorities. Yet other American investment interests became involved in European cable, partly because of the low prices following the disastrous slump in the value of cable companies.

[56] David del Valle, "Spain: Merger Moves," *Cable and Satellite Europe*, April 2003: 18–22.

[57] Jeremy Tunstall, *Communications Deregulation*, Oxford: Blackwell, 1986: 206–12.

[58] Denis McQuail and Karen Siune (eds.), *Media Policy: Convergence, Concentration and Commerce*, London: Sage, 1998: 64–65.

[59] Fred Kapner, "Italian TV Gamble Spells All Change for Murdoch," *Financial Times*, June 12, 2002; "EC Gives OK to Italian Pay TV Merger," *Screen Digest*, April 2003: 102.

[60] Stanley Reed and Jack Ewing, "Cable's New Contender," *Business Week*, September 3, 2001: 16–17.

[61] United Pan-Europe Communications, *Annual Report 2001*, Amsterdam: 2001.

Cable across much of Europe continued in a state of bankruptcy and failure, mainly because Europeans seemed reluctant to pay high prices for the American "triple play" concept of telephone and on-line services, combined with digital television and the opportunity to view more (American and other) channels.

This cable situation was one of several cable-satellite broadcasting areas in which the European Union's policy had been weak to the point of being almost nonexistent or merely symbolic. The "Television Without Frontiers" policy was largely ineffective, since even the 50 percent European programming requirement was not effectively enforced. The EU's tendency to make policy about new technologies and to fix its policies too early and too rigidly was evident also in Europe's chaotic development of digital television.[62]

Josef Trappel observed in 1996 that in view of the dynamic developments within the sector, Brussels involvement and decision-making was at best "hesitant."[63] It continued to be hesitant, as during the next decade media policy was increasingly subordinated to telecommunications and competition policy; the EU also leaned toward commercial, and away from public, broadcasting.[64] Competition and monopoly policy tended to become the only effective policy.

The European Union was, since 1980, very well aware of the "American threat"; but the EU lacked the unity, the motivation, and the determination to oppose the invasion. This invasion included not only big inflows of programming, but also ownership of satellite platforms, cable platforms, and a major European broadcaster in the form of ProSiebenSat1. The European Union did not even attempt to persuade the Congress and the FCC in Washington to make matching concessions. Washington continued to forbid foreign ownership of broadcast stations and, effectively, of cable system operators.

However, satellite-cable channels that seek a Europe-wide audience continue to face formidable difficulties. Back in 1988 Rupert Murdoch guessed correctly that he could make more money by concentrating on the United Kingdom (and Ireland) with BSkyB than he could by spreading satellite channels across Europe. Nearly all of the American satellite enterprises have followed the pan-European route; but the audience in most countries, and for most satellite channels, is receiving American programming with local language subtitling. By 2002 the leading pan-European channels were being broadcast, on average, in eight languages.[65] For many of these channels there

---

[62] Stylianos Papathanassopoulos, *European Television in the Digital Age*, Oxford: Polity, 2002.

[63] Josef Trappel, "EU Media Policy: Recent Features," *Irish Communications Review*, Vol. 6, 1996: 70–82.

[64] Karol Jakubowicz, "A Square Peg in a Round Hole: The EU's Policy on Public Service Broadcasting," in Ib Bondebjerg and Peter Golding (eds.), *European Culture and the Media*, Bristol, UK: Intellect, 2004: 277–301.

[65] Jean K. Chalaby, "The Quiet Invention of a New Medium: Twenty Years of Transnational Television in Europe," in Jean K. Chalaby (ed.), *Transnational Television Worldwide*, London: I.B. Tauris, 2004: 43–65.

are no reliable published audience data; it is of course difficult to measure audience shares as low as 0.1 percent (or one-thousandth of the current viewing audience). This in turn means little or no advertising revenue.

By 2005 Europe had 1,703 channels—with 155 sports channels, 93 all-news channels, and 84 "adult" offerings. Europe's channels were in 50 separate languages (500 in English, 244 in French, 59 in Arabic, and a total of 71 channels in 16 Asian languages).[66]

Meanwhile, the German RTL company remains very much the largest TV and radio broadcaster in Europe. RTL was originally a Luxembourg company but came under Bertelsmann control in 2001. By 2005 RTL had 23 television stations—not only in Germany, Luxembourg, and the Netherlands but also in France, Belgium, Spain, Hungary, and the United Kingdom. As terrestrial operations, these various national companies had significant market shares; for instance, Channel 5, the RTL-controlled British offering, had a U.K. TV market share of 6.5 percent in 2005. RTL also had a chain of important radio stations across Europe.[67]

Europe and America: Who's Winning?

The list that follows includes 16 separate elements of the media. This is a guess, not even a guesstimate; some of the points are discussed at greater length elsewhere in the book. According to this author's guess, the overall picture has 7 examples of the United States beating Europe and 3 cases of Europe beating the United States. Six items are scored as equal; this generates a grand U.S. total of 10, while Europe scores 6. Most readers will disagree with some, or perhaps most, of this author's guesses. Certainly, it would take a massive study to research the topic in full detail. This list is not just about ownership, or revenue, or ratings, or political impact. It is intended to focus mainly on media exports/imports, but it does not do so in any systematic way.

In *fast general news* Europe wins because its big collection of big news agencies easily outpoints America's lone Associated Press. In addition, Eurovision is the core member of the daily news exchange between continental groupings.

In *factual output other than fast general news*, the United States is a winner through its newsmagazines, business news services (including Bloomberg), and documentary output from Discovery and other channels.

In televised and other *media sport*, Europe is the winner because it is the leader in soccer football, which is by a long way the world's most popular sport in general and in the media.[68]

---

[66] Boomtime for European Channels, *Screen Digest*, August 2005: 237–44.

[67] Peter Iosifidis, Jeanette Steemers, and Mark Wheeler, *European Television Industries*, London: British Film Institute, 2005: 85–86.

[68] Shawn W. Crispin, "Moving the Goalposts. Satellite TV Has Turned European Soccer into Asia's Sport of Choice," *Far East Economic Review*, June 10, 2004: 50–53.

In *movies*, Hollywood makes the United States an easy winner.

In *scripted TV* series the United States is also well ahead of Europe; these are drama-fiction, sitcom, and other continuing series that traditionally make about 20–25 episodes per year.

In *unscripted TV* the contest is equal. The transatlantic trade here has been two-way in recent years and the trade largely consists of format acquisition. Talk, games, and reality shows are nationally made.

Public broadcasting differs between different European countries, but most European countries have public broadcasters that receive some public (license fee or state grant) finance and in return produce some noncommercial programming. American PBS and NPR cannot match the combined efforts of the Europeans—which include extensive classical music played by house orchestras, arts programming, and arts channels such as Arte.

Radio is equally massive across Europe and across the United States; a draw.

Cable is a fairly obvious U.S. win both on its home territory and through its export effort into Europe.

Popular music is American led in most respects.

The Internet has also been American led and is a U.S. win; but Europe is catching up, not least in generating major offerings in languages other than English.

Advertising is another U.S. win, although Europe is catching up.

The *magazine* efforts of the United States and Europe are about equal. Many significant American magazines are owned by German, French, and British companies. But the reverse is also true.

Books also constitute a drawn contest between the United States and Europe. Substantial segments of the American book publishing industry are owned by German, British, and other European companies. Europe publishes more new titles; in the early 2000s the larger European countries together published about 400,000 new titles per year; however, the United States is a leader in best-selling books, hundreds of which are translated each year into European languages.

Newspapers are yet another difficult contest to score, but another draw is the fair result. The United States has more newspapers that are big in pagination, advertising revenue, political clout, and monopolistic domination. Europe has more newspapers that compete with each other and more newspapers that employ their own foreign correspondents (and do not depend heavily on syndicated material).

In *market research* the United States and Europe are scored as equal. In several respects market and audience research drives the entire American media, including movies, TV, and newspapers. But several leading research companies are now European owned. In addition to commercial broadcasters, European public broadcasters are also active at research, which includes research designed to help initiate future productions.

To repeat: The United States beats Europe 10 to 6, or 5 to 3.

Euro-American Media

European media are part of a largely integrated media industry that encompasses both the United States and Europe; increasingly this is a combination that also includes Latin America. There is a triangular media trade—between the United States and Europe, between Europe and Latin America, and also between the United States and Latin America; there are now big Mexican television exports into the United States. This Euro-American grouping has about one-quarter of world population, has a common Christian cultural history, and, in financial terms, accounts for more than half of all the world's media (more on this in Chapter 18).

It is the increased merging of the media industries of Europe and the United States that makes it so difficult to decide whether Europe or America is winning.

In media technology the United States has been the traditional leader, and this has continued with the computerization of much media production and reception. But while the United States developed the Internet, the growth of mobile telephony was led by European companies in general (such as Vodafone) and by Scandinavia (and Nokia) in particular. Mobile telephony is important for the media, not least in its opening up of a big new stream of media finance. However, Japan has also been a world leader in many aspects of new media technology.

Although Hollywood has long been, and still is, the one incontrovertible media example of American dominance, Hollywood's big export earnings also imply an element of dependence. Since the 1920s European financial (and talent) participation in Hollywood has taken many forms from "blind-buying" to Hollywood production in Europe.

Hollywood-European "coproductions" of various kinds have been common in all decades since the 1920s, with the exception of the 1940s. The peak of such movie coproduction was in the 1958–1968 decade, when Hollywood had been hit by television but when movie audiences were still big in Italy and France. Films like Fellini's *La Dolce Vita* (1960) were seen by big American audiences; Hollywood producers employed European stars and tapped into Italian and French subsidies. But as television grew in Europe this "golden age" of European cinema came to an end.

Germans and other Europeans continued to part-finance Hollywood in various ways such as preproduction sales; some European investors invested millions of dollars in Hollywood projects on a high-risk/high-return basis. The new American satellite TV channels began to seek out European coproducers from the late 1980s onward, and movie coproduction also increased in the 1990s. Output deals (to take all or most of a studio's movies) generated strong flows of European cash into Los Angeles.

"Ownership" itself is a flexible concept and is not always the same as "control." Many, or most, American media companies that are seeking to establish production subsidiaries in Europe will be looking for "local partners" to invest in the project. Disney successfully persuaded French banks and other European investors to put up more than half the capital for the Euro-Disney projects near Paris. Other media companies and media moguls also like to hold a big minority (but not a majority) of the shares. Mr. Mogul himself may actually only own 38 percent of the big company; "his" big company, The Mogul Corporation, may itself only own 38 percent of a subsidiary company, which is nevertheless branded as "A Mogul Corporation Company." Thirty-eight percent of 38 percent is a mere 14.44 percent, but as long as confidence remains in Mr. Mogul's entrepreneurship, this 14.44 percent represents "control." However, differing European and American interpretations of such situations can lead to acrimonious disputes and changes in both ownership and control.

Increasingly since the 1980s European and American media policies have been coordinated. Brussels policy sentiment has supported the notion of European-wide, European-owned, media; but in practice Brussels media policy has tended to focus mainly on competition, and anti-monopoly, issues. This anti-monopoly policy has increasingly been coordinated between the European Union's current competition commissioner and the anti-trust people at the Justice Department in Washington. As one example, Mario Monti, the European competition commissioner, in the early 2000s made three decisions that significantly influenced the shape of the recorded music business. First, he vetoed the sale of Time-Warner music to EMI; second, he also vetoed a merger of EMI and Bertelsmann Music (BMG); and third, he allowed the merger of BMG with Sony Music. More broadly, the Washington-Brussels combined stance supported copyright and opposed piracy—not only in music, but also in movies and TV recordings. Obviously the major American and European companies had a big interest in protecting their valuable copyright. The support of Brussels and Washington helped to confirm the contrast between Euro-America, where copyright was widely (if not universally) observed, and the rest of the world, where piracy broadly prevailed.

There was media lobbying in Europe long before there was a Brussels competition commissioner. The Hollywood majors first established their lobbying body in 1922; subsequently, the Motion Picture Association operated under several titles, including MPA, MPAA, and (in Europe) MPEA. The MPA lobbied aggressively in Europe from the 1920s onward. A second internationally significant media lobby consisted of newspaper trade associations from the United States and Europe; this grouping was influential in the introduction in the 1970s and 1980s of computerization against the will of newspaper trade unions. Third, another group of trade associations—in this case, advertising ones—were the most effective lobbyists during the Brussels 1980s debates on Television Without Frontiers (TWF). When a second phase of TWF policymaking occurred in the 1990s (resulting in a new directive in 1997) it was a commercial television grouping (ACT) that was most influential.[69]

---

[69] Daniel Krebber, *Europeanisation of Regulatory Television Policy*, Baden-Baden: Nomos Verlagsgesellschaft, 2001.

Across eight decades of European media lobbying, American lobbyists—battle trained in Washington—have usually been in the forefront. These American lobbies have often felt themselves to be on the winning side, but not always; it seems that Jack Valenti and the MPA, with their Hollywood-Washington belligerence, antagonized many Brussels people in the 1980s. In the 1990s it was the European commercial broadcasters, not the American satellite interests, that were most effective.

Certainly American media lobbyists have been more successful in Europe and Brussels than European lobbyists have been in Washington. Nevertheless, representatives of European companies have increasingly found themselves giving evidence at the FCC and in congressional committee and subcommittee hearings.

15

Africa

Bottom of the Media Pecking Order

Africa's many small population countries are at the bottom of the world's media pecking order. This chapter focuses on three former British colonies—Nigeria, Kenya, and South Africa—which are subregional media leaders in western, eastern, and southern Africa. Also considered are the turbulent media and political histories of such former French and Belgian colonies as Congo (Zaire), Cote d'Ivoire, and Rwanda. The chapter concludes that Nigeria and South Africa are becoming Africa's media leaders.

Distinctive characteristics of Africa's media include the following:

- Africa has the world's lowest levels of income per head; this affects everything else, including media consumption.
- Africa is fragmented into numerous lowish population countries, with arbitrary boundaries—many of which were drawn on the map at a European conference in 1884.
- Africa has in recent years been the continent most ravaged by civil war and internal conflict, by corrupt unelected regimes, by military coups, by poverty, by high infant mortality, and by major diseases including HIV/AIDS and malaria.
- Africa in 2005 was receiving financial aid to the tune of about $35 per African per year. However, Africa has also suffered from "unfair trade" in the form of huge Euro-American agricultural subsidies, whose impact effectively has wiped out any beneficial aid impact.
- Africa has a very different history from Asia, in that Africa had no pre-1900 tradition of literacy (outside Arabic).
- The modern media in non-Arab Africa were largely established by European colonizers; Africa was, and is, the continent most subject to media colonization.

Table 15.1 1950–2005 Growth in a Typical African Country

	1950	2005	1950–2005 INCREASE
Population	4.5 million	15 million	3.3 times
Capital city population	75,000	1.5 million	20 times
Literate adults and children	100,000	8 million	80 times
University graduates	50	500,000	10,000 times
Daily press readers	40,000	2 million	50 times
Radio listeners	50,000	10 million	200 times
Television viewers	—	8 million	—

Note: These numbers are illustrative or guesstimated.

- In 1950 Africa had very low levels of media compared with other continents; however, between 1950 and 2005 there was huge media growth.

Table 15.1 provides some illustrative (guesstimated) figures, showing changes in the 55 years after 1950. Incidentally, most African statistics, including media statistics, are unreliable. In Africa most of the economy involves subsistence farming and street trading or other economic activities for which no reliable record is kept. Even national population figures tend to be highly suspect. Media statistics are unreliable because in most cases the data relate only to larger urban areas; and even in urban shantytown areas there are formidable research problems in terms of sampling, interviewing, and language.

In Table 15.1 the biggest increase is in the number of university graduates, but the increases in media audiences are also huge. Television had not yet arrived in 1950 and only started to achieve big audiences in the 1990s; but the number of radio listeners increased by about 200 times. Incidentally, the number of all literate adults and children is intended to include children who may read to their parents. In African countries about half the population is younger than 18.

Despite such spectacular change, much has stayed the same. The Europeans who came to Africa in the eighteenth century were looking for gold, diamonds, and slaves. In the twenty-first century the Europeans and Americans are looking for gold, diamonds, and oil. From a media standpoint, recent African history can be divided into three distinct phases.

During 1900–1960 Africa was colonized mainly by the British, French, Belgians, and Portuguese. During a few years around 1960 nearly all of these colonies achieved independence, typically with little previous preparation. As they became formally independent, these countries were still dependent in many ways on their recent imperial masters in London, Paris, and Brussels. Some press and radio already existed, but it had largely been developed as an extension of the European press and radio.

During 1960–1990, the first 30 years of independence, nearly all of the newly independent African countries came under one-party rule, military rule, or both. In most countries there were military coups, and some countries had a succession of coups; at least 79 governments were overthrown by force during 1960–1990.[1] These years coincided with the Cold War, and there was rivalry in Africa between the Soviet Union and the Euro-Americans. Successive French and British governments worked to keep Africa looking Northwest, rather than Northeast. The United States became a significant player on the African media scene, for the first time, during 1960–1990. In particular infant African television services imported Hollywood entertainment series. While selling *I Love Lucy* and other old TV series to Africa, the United States also actively supported some of the most corrupt and autocratic regimes in Africa—for example, the Mobutu Sese Seko regime in Congo-Zaire and the apartheid regime in South Africa.

During 1990–2005 big changes occurred. As the Cold War ended, Africa moved toward more democratic regimes, including genuinely contested elections and much more media freedom. In the years after 1990 there were also strong trends toward economic liberalization and the privatizing of previously state-controlled companies and assets. In the 1990s fewer African media were owned and operated by the government; many new newspapers and other publications appeared. A small handful of commercial and private radio stations had by 2000 expanded to over 1,000 (mainly FM) commercial radio stations.

African media, although established by Europeans, differed considerably from European models. In Europe in the 1950s the press was heavily linked to political party discourse and radio followed some kind of "public broadcasting" model. In Europe both radio and press operated broadly within the traditions of the legislature and laws of libel and defamation. But these latter traditions and understandings did not take immediate root in Africa. Around 1960 the experience of most African journalists consisted primarily of attacking the colonial government; many of these journalists had been not unhappy to go to prison for their intemperate language. These journalists may also have worked on missionary publications, in which aggressive language could be given a biblical (or Old Testament) justification. Then when the independence-seeking nationalists came to power, their journalist colleagues initially wanted to support, and not to attack, them. African journalism around 1960—like African political debate—tended toward extremes of criticism or praise. Judicious "balanced" reporting seemed inappropriate to the political excitement of the early months and years of independence.

Since 1960, African media talk has often tended toward either strong (or extreme) praise or strong (or extreme) criticism. One extreme can be described

---

[1] "The Rule of Big Men or the Rule of Law," *The Economist* survey of sub-Saharan Africa, January 17, 2004: 4–6.

as *praise singing*—the journalist follows a traditional African path and has only praise and flattery for chiefs, or politicians, in power. Second was *heavily pro-government talk*, such as, during 1960–1990, could be heard on state-controlled radio across Africa. Third was *critical talk*, which tended toward no-holds-barred and no-language-barred attacks; this characterized government media attacks on their domestic political opponents. Fourth, and even more extreme, was *hate talk*, which went beyond cursing its opponents to racist/ethnic abuse, threats of violence, and incitement to kill opponents.

All independent African governments from 1960 have seen the media, along with education, as a key instrument in developing the nation-state and national consciousness. In most individual African countries there have been a few major languages as well as many smaller and lesser languages. A key policy issue in the 1960s concerned the way in which radio time should be divided up between languages. The most common solution was to give the largest single radio time share to French or English or Portuguese; most of the remaining radio time went to perhaps the three or four largest (or politically most crucial) local languages. Often an additional 10 or 20 smaller languages received no radio time at all. Similar choices had to be made in education.

By 2005 most Africans seem to have developed some kind of double identity—my ethnic group (or tribe) and its language, but also my nation-state and its language (either colonial or national). A 2004 BBC survey in 10 African countries found about 30 percent of respondents saying their "strongest feelings" were for country; about 20 percent were for "ethnic/tribal group," and about 50 percent were "equally for both."[2]

What about a third identity level—as an African? Music, religion, and football are three spheres of activity that may enable Africans to think of themselves as Africans. Several large countries (such as Nigeria, Congo, and South Africa) have super-popular music that is listened to in other countries. More than half of all Africans are either Muslim or Christian; there are more Christians in Africa than in the United States. A quite different sphere of pan-African interest is soccer football; just as many Europeans are aware of Europe through football, so also similar sentiments are appearing in Africa.

Nevertheless, common language is often the biggest single component of national sentiment; and in Africa the most widely spoken languages are English,[3] French, and Arabic. It is, of course, these very languages that assist the media export efforts of Anglo-American, Franco-Belgian, and Arab-Muslim media producers. Many African languages do cross borders; but only Hausa (western Africa), Kiswahili (eastern Africa) and perhaps one or two others have large cross-border audiences.

---

[2] Based on interviews with 7,671 people. *The Independent*, review section, October 18, 2004: 1–4.
[3] Alamin M. Mazrui, *English in Africa: After the Cold War*, Cleveden, UK: Multilingual Matters, 2004.

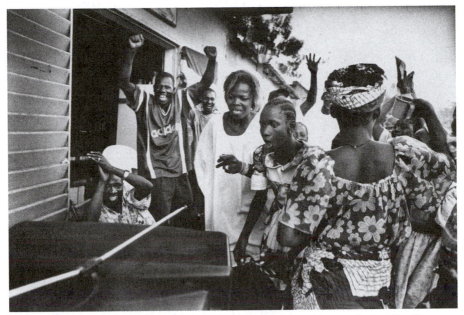

Figure 15.1 Football fans in Mali watching their national team playing South Africa, February 2002. (Dieter Telemans/Panos Pictures.)

In this chapter "Africa" excludes the northern tier of countries from Morocco to Egypt whose populations mainly live near the Mediterranean Sea and most of whom speak Arabic.

Media in Nigeria and Western Africa

The British and French empires had an especially dominant position in western Africa. The mass media of western Africa also were closely modeled on those of London and Paris; in Nigeria at least 10 separate daily newspapers adapted their titles from London publications. The French and English languages still today have a dominant position in western African media.

One former British colony, Nigeria, has about the same population as western Africa's 16 former French colonies; while Nigeria in 2005 had 129 million people, the most populous former French colony, Cote d'Ivoire, had only 17 million. (See Table 15.2.)

The first colonies in western Africa to achieve independent nationhood were Ghana (1957) and Senegal (1958). Both France and Britain surrendered their western African colonies without much struggle. Even in pioneering Ghana (then Gold Coast) the independence campaign caused very few deaths; and Nigeria, following in Ghana's footsteps, had an even quieter passage to independence. In both Ghana and Nigeria the largest cities, the media, and

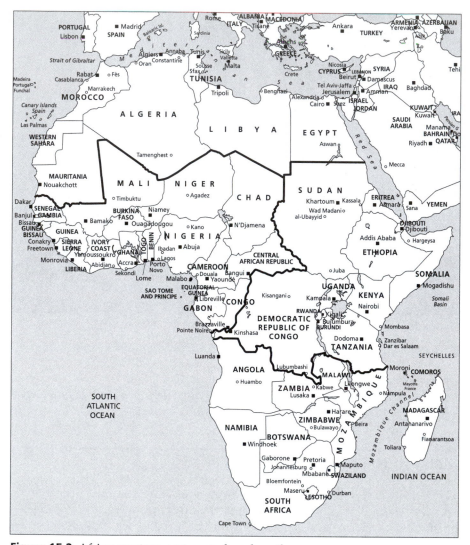

Figure 15.2 Africa: western, east-central, and southern.

the most fertile land were near the coast. Mali, Niger, Chad, Burkino Faso, and Central African Republic were all land-locked, and mainly desert, countries. In the desert nations the very small media (at independence) were based mainly in the capital city.

As the colonial powers departed, they expressed pious hopes for democracy, contested elections, a free press, and responsible broadcasting. But the new African elites preferred to follow what the French and British had done, while ignoring what they had said. Pre-independence government and media had been nondemocratic and authoritarian; this would continue unchanged

Table 15.2 Western African Populations, 2005

NUMBER OF COUNTRIES		2005 POPULATION, MILLIONS	PERCENTAGE
1	Nigeria	128.8 ⎫	54.4
3	Other former British colonies	29.4 ⎭	
16	Former French colonies	129.5	44.6
1	Liberia	2.9	1.0
Total 21		290.6	100

Source: CIA, *The World Factbook*. July 2005 population estimates.

after independence. London and Paris supplied training, free material, recorded radio programming, and music. First Ghana, and then a number of francophone new nation-states, established new national news agencies—with London (Reuters) or Paris (Agence France-Presse) providing advice, equipment, training, and, of course, news. London and Paris news agency executives saw the Ghana News Agency (GNA), and the others, as convenient subcollectors of news about the brave little new nation; newly formed Ministries of Information in western Africa (and their new national news agency) obtained a supply of world fast news. Thus GNA was able to supply (Reuters) world news to its first three 1957 customers—the prime minister's office, Radio Ghana, and the *Daily Graphic* (the leading newspaper).[4]

In both Ghana and Nigeria, British hopes were quickly shown to be wildly optimistic. Kwame Nkrumah and his Convention People's Party (CPP) quickly took control of Ghana's media; Nkrumah himself was deposed by a military coup in 1966. By 1966 Nigeria's "democratic experiment" was also in major trouble. During 1967–1970 Nigeria experienced a major secessionist civil war; "Biafra"—much of southeast Nigeria—attempted to break away from Nigeria. Up to one million people were killed; the domestic Nigerian media were ferociously partisan. Britain, the imperial mother, supplied arms (and news) to the Nigerian government throughout the three-year civil war.

Nigeria in 1960 was unusual in already having media competition in the form of competing daily newspapers in Lagos. Nigeria had separate daily newspapers in each of its three regions, in addition to federal newspapers. There were also separate regional radio services. Moreover, television in Nigeria began as a West regional service (in 1959), before independence and before federal government TV.[5] The East region also launched its own

---

[4] Rosalynde Ainslie, *The Press in Africa*, London: Victor Gollancz, 1966: 199–211.

[5] Mike Egbon, "Western Nigeria Television Service—Oldest in Tropical Africa," *Journalism Quarterly*, Vol. 60/2, Summer 1993: 329–34; Ebele N. Ume-Nwagbo, "Politics and Ethnicity in the Rise of Broadcasting in Nigeria, 1932–62," *Journalism Quarterly*, Vol. 56/4, Winter 1979: 816–21, 826.

TV (as well as radio) on independence day in 1960. The central (federal) government would face obvious regional difficulties, if it wanted to dominate the media.

Nigeria had already developed a tradition of press criticism. Much of this criticism, of course, had been aimed at the British, but Ghana's independence (1957) ensured that Nigeria's independence would not be long delayed. Some of the pre-independence press criticism was between insurgent politician-journalists in the three regions of colonial Nigeria.

In media terms the (largely Christian) south was ahead of the (largely Muslim) north. The media reflected the main ethnic and political divisions in Nigeria. About two-thirds of all Nigerians speak one of the three major languages—Igbo mainly in the southeast, Yoruba in the southwest, and Hausa-Fulani in the north. Because the Hausa-Fulanis have the biggest population, they have dominated Nigerian politics; but they have struggled to control Nigerian media. With political power based in the north and the press based in the south (especially in Lagos), the bulk of the press has tended to be anti-government, anti-north, and anti-Muslim.

During Nigeria's early independent years in the 1960s, the national political leadership came from three main sources. First were "traditional rulers" (or tribal chiefs), some of whom, before 1960, effectively administered Nigeria for the British. Second were army officers who led the first coup in 1966; army officers subsequently ruled Nigeria for 28 of the next 32 years (1966–1998). Most of the initial coup leaders had received officer training in Britain and were lieutenant colonels at the young age of about 32. Yakubu Gowon, who became head of the federal military government at the 1966 coup, was age 32 and the youngest head of state in Africa; he had attended officer training courses at several U.K. military locations.

In addition to traditional rulers and army officers, a third main category of Nigerian leaders were the journalists and press entrepreneurs. Two of the leading four Nigerian politicians of the early 1960s fit this latter category—Nnamdi Azikiwe and Obafemi Awolowo.[6] Azikiwe was both the father of the new nation of Nigeria and the father of Nigerian newspaper journalism. Azikiwe ("Zik") was a man of much charisma and of many talents; he spoke all three of Nigeria's main languages (Igbo, Hausa, and Yoruba) as well as English. He attended college in the United States; returning to western Africa, he edited the *African Morning Post* (in Accra, Ghana) and then in 1937 established the *West African Pilot*. He worked for Reuters and was prime minister of the eastern region (from 1954), as the British prepared Nigeria for independence. During 1960–1963 he was governor general and then until 1966 the first president of Nigeria.[7]

---

[6] Reuters News Agency and Sidney Taylor (eds.), *The New Africans*, London: Paul Hamlyn, 1966: 315–51.

[7] "Nnamdi Azikiwe: Obituary," *The Economist*, March 25, 1996; B. Akintunde Oyetade, "Nnamdi Azikiwe," *The Independent*, May 15, 1996.

Obafemi Awolowo was a Yoruba and the first premier of western Nigeria; he trained as a lawyer in London. He worked as a journalist and editor from 1944 onward. In 1959, as independence was arriving, Awolowo and his party (the Action Group) controlled 14 small newspapers, while Azikiwe (and his NCNC party) controlled 10 papers.

Unfortunately, in the early 1960s, political discourse both in the elected legislature and in the Nigerian newspapers quickly descended into abuse and extreme denunciations; it then descended still further into racist hate talk between ethnic and religious groups. Malcolm Brynin, who content analyzed what was said in the legislature and written in the newspapers, commented: "As the political conflict of the time was ethnic in nature, so was the political propaganda of the press, and it engaged itself in the ethnic battle with extraordinary intensity."[8]

The January 1966 coup, led by a group of young Igbo army officers, killed the two top politicians of the northern region. A countercoup in July 1966 involved the killing of numerous Igbo officers; this in turn was followed by mass killings of Igbo civilians living as small minorities in Lagos and in northern cities. Surviving Igbos fled to their native southeast, and this pogrom led to the Igbo-Biafra secession and the 1967–1970 Biafran secessionist war. Newspaper owners and editors shared, with politicians and army officers, some responsibility for the slaughter and death of about one million of the then Igbo population of about nine million. The media war of vitriolic words continued through the civil war of 1967–1970; it involved not just the press but also the broadcasters (primarily radio) of the federal government, plus the north and the west, against the east. The east ("Biafra") generated a large international media offensive, not least because it paid for a significant European public relations campaign.

The first long period of military rule lasted 13 years (1966–1979). But at the end of the Biafra War in 1970, the then military rulers made serious attempts at national reconciliation. In 1975 a (third) coup removed General Gowon, who had presided over the Nigerian government in the war against Biafra. Despite this long period of military rule, Nigeria in 1975 had some 15 daily newspapers with a total sale of about 750,000 copies. In the 1970s the Nigerian media behaved with more constraint—partly because of the military censorship and partly from some genuine hope for reconciliation. A relatively moderate military government matched a more restrained media; and in 1979 the military government (under General Olusegun Obasanjo) handed over rule and elections to civilians; but civilian rule lasted only four years (1979–1983) before the next coup.

By the end of the civilian rule period in 1983 there were three distinct types of Nigerian newspaper. First were papers owned or controlled by the federal government, a category that included the *Daily Times* (Lagos)—the long-time

---

[8] Christopher Malcolm Brynin, "Conflict and Communication in the Third World," unpublished Ph.D. dissertation, City University, London, 1983: 198–99.

circulation leader. Second, some of the larger dailies were controlled by larger state governments based in cities such as Ibadan and Enugu. Third, several important newspapers were controlled by individual politician/media owners. The most significant newcomer in this continuing Nigerian tradition was Moshood Abiola, a successful businessman who launched *National Concord* in 1980. Abiola was clearly a newspaper owner with distinct political ambitions; he hoped to be elected president of Nigeria in 1983. Abiola was soon engaged in a newspaper rivalry with his fellow Yoruba and fellow newspaper owner, Obafemi Awolowo. Adjectives used by *National Concord* to describe Awolowo included "dictatorial, holier-than-thou, inconsistent, power monger and illusionist."[9] Subsequently, however, the two newspaper owner antagonists formed a new political partnership. *National Concord*'s descriptions of Awolowo then included "far-sighted, dogged and principled fighter, democratic and consistent."

Moshood Abiola might, perhaps, have been Nigeria's greatest leader. He was another larger-than-life charismatic entrepreneur–politician–newspaper owner. Abiola was both a Yoruba (born near Lagos) and a Muslim—perhaps the perfect combination for a Nigerian politician. He somewhat overstepped Muslim rules by having about 18 wives and more than 60 children. He qualified as an accountant (University of Glasgow) and quickly became Nigerian chief executive of the American ITT telecommunications company. Subsequently he became a shipping magnate and sponsor of many charities. At age 43 he launched his *Concord* newspaper and he later owned other publications. In 1993 he won the presidential election, and while the generals refused to publish results, his *National Concord* (with Nigeria's second highest daily sale) proclaimed him as the presidential winner. The generals returned (with leader Sani Abacha) and sent Abiola to prison, where, five years later, he died in July 1998.[10]

Successive Nigerian governments increased the number of states within the federal system; initially there were just 3 states, but in 2005 there were 36 states (plus the federal capital in Abuja). As the political system was broken into smaller pieces, so also was the broadcasting system. As early as 1977 Nigeria had domestic radio broadcasting in 34 languages—9 at the federal level and another 25 languages at the state level.[11] By 1985, for example, Nigeria had 19 states and in each state capital there was one federal government TV station, one federal government radio station, and one state government radio station; there were also 10 television stations controlled by

---

[9] This quote comes from a larger "case study" of *National Concord*: Luke Uka Uche, *Mass Media, People and Politics in Nigeria*, New Delhi: Concept Publishing, 1989: 101–8.

[10] Richard Synge, "Bearer of Nigeria's Hopes for Democracy," *The Guardian*, July 8, 1998; "Abiola's Dangerous Death," *The Economist*, July 11, 1998: 67; Michael Holman and Michela Wrong, "Deprived of Victory and Robbed of Freedom," *Financial Times*, July 8, 1998.

[11] Olu Ladele, V. Olufemi Adefela, and Olu Lasekan, *History of the Nigerian Broadcasting Corporation*, Ibadan: Ibadan University Press, 1979: 158–60.

state governments.[12] These arrangements were subsequently expanded into another 17 states, and there was also, by the 1990s, a significant element of private commercial TV and radio.

As experienced by the Nigerian people and media, the regime of Ibrahim Babangida (1985–1993) was repressive, but the regime of Sani Abacha (1993–1998) was even more repressive. Babangida had intended to hand over from a military to a civilian government. The majority of the electorate in June 1993 voted for Moshood Abiola to be their new civilian president. When the military regime refused to announce the election results, they appointed another civilian as president; then, later in 1993, a new (and fiercer) military regime, under General Abacha, took power. Abacha was thus confronting several of Nigeria's key political elements, not only Moshood Abiola the politician/newspaper owner, but also Muslims, the Yoruba, and the military. Abacha abolished political parties, the national legislature, and the cabinet. Abacha shut down the leading newspapers—Abiola's *National Concord*, as well as *The Punch* and *The Guardian*. Several radio and TV stations were also closed; in some cases the personnel from a closed publication courageously relaunched under a different title.

Abacha's repressive political and media decisions attracted condemnation from inside Nigeria, from African and other members of the Commonwealth, and in the United States.[13] But Abacha continued the repression; in November 1995 internationally known writer Ken Saro-Wiwa (who was also an active and outspoken newspaper columnist) was executed with eight colleagues in a Port Harcourt jail.[14] Abacha earned a reputation as not only the most repressive, but also as the most corrupt, of Nigeria's succession of military dictators. After Abacha died suddenly in 1998, his widow was stopped at Lagos airport with 38 suitcases that contained huge quantities of cash. Subsequent legal investigations suggested that Abacha had deposited some $3 billion in private bank accounts in Europe.[15]

During 1985–1998, the military dictatorships of Generals Babangida and Abacha exacerbated a number of major structural problems within Nigeria. The two military dictators frequently shuffled their supporters (and rivals) into and out of key positions in the army. Prominent retired (potential plotter) army officers were rewarded with prominent civilian roles in newly privatized companies, which the Nigerian military government was selling off in line with the "structural adjustment" policies of international aid providers. The

---

[12] Laolu Ogunniyi, "Legislating for African Television," *InterMedia*, Vol. 13/2, March 1985: 33–34.

[13] Howard M. French, "Nigerians Fear New Strife Could Blow the Country Apart," *New York Times*, August 14, 1994; Barry Hillenbrand: "Nigeria: 'Brink of an Abyss,'" *Time* (International), August 9, 1993: 26–27.

[14] Steve Crawshaw, "Nigeria Defies the World. Commonwealth Is Thrown into Turmoil," *The Independent*, November 11, 1995.

[15] David Pallister, Jamie Wilson, and Ed Harriman, "Money Laundering: The Nigerian Connection," *The Guardian* (London), October 4, 2001.

military regime's overall economic policies were ineffective, leaving Nigeria with only one significant export—oil. Many individual journalists (on numerous small publications) did publish and broadcast many highly critical news stories and comments. Some newspaper offices were burned down, and numerous journalists were arrested; some media people died in jail, including (in 1998) Moshood Abiola.

While military rule held back Nigerian news and other factual forms of radio and television, several categories—including music, comedy, and film —all grew and prospered. As early as 1976 the majority of the music played on Lagos radio stations was Nigerian or African. Nigerian radio and television generated some extremely popular comedy material. By 1976 a comedy series, *Masquerade*, had become a TV "event" in Nigeria; it featured the household of Chief Zebrudaya, one of whose "temporary wives" was called Appolonia Godgive Nwogbo.[16]

Nevertheless, Nigerian media grew fastest during two periods of civilian rule—1979–1983 and 1998 onward. Four years of civilian rule, 1979–1983, were a high point for Nigerian democracy, media freedom, and licensed irresponsibility. With numerous radio and television stations now controlled by regional (state) governments, many contending regional voices could also be heard and viewed by people living across the border in another state. But it was the newspapers that explored the limits of the new freedom with the most enthusiasm: "To an outsider the liberties taken by Nigeria's press come close to anarchy as rival parties, politicians and states push their cause with no holds barred."[17]

Many new weeklies and several new dailies appeared during this civilian rule period,[18] but, after military rule returned in 1983, most of these ceased publication. However, two important survivors were *National Concord* and *The Guardian*, which became major Nigerian newspapers. Graham Mytton wrote at the time: "Nigeria has a pluralist mass media system. It is nevertheless a fractured kind of pluralism which reflects the political situation and in turn helps, to a large extent, to define and create the situation it reports."[19]

Civilian rule returned once again in 1998–1999. The new president (reelected in 2003) was Olusegun Obasanjo—the previous military dictator (1976–1979) who had stepped aside in 1979 to allow a return to civilian rule. Obasanjo and his administrations faced Nigeria's formidable problems, now greatly

---

[16] Michael R. Real, "Broadcast Music in Nigeria and Liberia: A comparative Note," Theo Vincent, "Television Drama: A Critical Assessment," and O. O. Oreh "Masquerade: And Other Plays on Nigerian Television," in Frank Okwu Ugboajah (ed.), *Mass Communication, Culture and Society in West Africa*, London: Hans Zell, 1988: 95–112.

[17] Peter Blackburn, "Read All About It but Check Who Is Telling the Story," *The Guardian* (London), October 25, 1982.

[18] Ad'Obe Obe, "Freedom of the Press; a Licence to Abuse?" *The Guardian*, October 6, 1981; Sylvanus A Ekwelie, "The Nigerian Press Under Civilian Rule," *Journalism Quarterly*, Vol. 63/1, Spring 1986: 98–105, 149.

[19] Graham Mytton, *Mass Communication in Africa*, London: Edward Arnold, 1983: 117–26.

exacerbated by nearly three decades of military rule, military corruption, oil dependence, and Anglo-American support.

The newspaper press (which had doubled its sales during 1975–1995), saw further rapid growth. Television and radio continued to grow. But Nigeria's biggest media growth was in its brash new film industry (see later in this chapter). Two Nigerian news magazines ran a series of exposé stories that led, within two years of civilian rule, to the resignation of one speaker of Nigeria's House of Representatives and two Senate presidents.[20] But much Nigerian journalism (print and broadcast) has become relatively restrained and broadly supportive of both federal and state governments.

Less restrained, however, are the leaders of another new Nigerian media genre, televangelism. Since the 1980s, millions of (mainly southern) Nigerians have been attracted by American-style evangelism and born-again protestant Christianity. This evangelism has generated large cash flows for the more popular Nigerian sects and for the leading charismatic preachers, who typically control the sect and flaunt their resulting wealth. Evangelistic religion had, by 2005, became a major funder of TV and radio. At the national, state, and local levels the evangelistic sects buy radio and TV time. Many individuals obey the requirement to contribute a 10 percent tithe from their earnings.[21]

Similarly in northern Nigeria, much Saudi and Gulf Arab money flows into support for Muslim TV and radio. Consequently, Nigerian broadcasting depends on a financial triad—governmental subsidy, commercial advertising, and religious sponsorship. Some observers claim that recent northern Nigerian moves toward strict Shariah law are partly a defensive response to Christian fundamentalist televangelism growth in television (from a low base in the 1980s).[22] The rapid growth of 1990s radio in western Africa was celebrated in a collection of impressive anthropological studies that included several field studies from francophone countries such as Benin, Burkina, and Niger.[23] There was also much optimistic comment on new technologies; call centers in places like Senegal enabled educated Senegalese to become part of French service industry. Mobile telephony helped to make national elections more transparent and less corrupt.

---

[20] Emmanuel O. Ojo, "The Mass Media and the Challenges of Sustainable Democratic Values in Nigeria: Possibilities and Limitations," *Media, Culture and Society*, Vol. 25/6, November 2003: 821–40.

[21] Walter Ihejirika, "Media and Fundamentalism in Nigeria," *Media Development*, 2, 2005: 38–44; Leslie Goffe, "God, Gospel and the Dollar," and Sola Odunfa, "Miracles and Money," in *BBC Focus on Africa*, July–September 2005: 10–18; Dino Mahtani, "Vast Market for Salvation Superstars," *Financial Times*, special report: "FT Nigeria," April 26, 2005: 5.

[22] Jo Ellen Fair, "Francophonie and the National Airwaves: A History of Television in Senegal," in Lisa Parks and Shanti Kumar (eds.), *Planet TV: A Global Television Reader*, New York: New York University Press, 2003: 189–208.

[23] Richard Fardon and Graham Furniss (eds.), *African Broadcast Cultures: Radio in Transition*, Oxford: James Currey, 2000.

French and British postcolonial policies differed markedly in western Africa. One simplistic distinction claimed that France treated its ex-colonies as children, while Britain treated its ex-colonies as adult (if sometimes wayward) offspring. The French connection between Paris and western Africa was close and narrowly targeted. French western Africa had its own two currency regions (both tied to the French franc). Several western African countries (such as Senegal and Cote d'Ivoire) had sizeable numbers of expatriate French men and women who continued to eat food, drink wine, and consume media shipped and flown in from France.

After 1960 two of the most "successful" ex-French regimes in western Africa were those of President Léopold Senghor in Senegal and President Félix Houphouet-Boigny in Cote d'Ivoire. Dakar (Senegal) had been the old French administrative headquarters for western Africa, and Cote d'Ivoire (next to Ghana) had the most successful economy in western Africa from 1960 to 2000. These two presidents closely matched the French ideal of the highly educated and accomplished "African Frenchman." Both men had outstanding records inside the French educational system. Senghor was a published poet (in French); Houphouet-Boigny was an elected politician in Paris and was briefly the French minister of health (1957–1958). Both men achieved the presidency of their respective nations at independence in 1960. Both became African "enlightened despots," who used their superior abilities and superior French experience to maintain relatively benign autocracies. Both men, however, did use force to put down a succession of violent and rebellious internal challenges during the 1960s. Senghor was distinctly unusual in voluntarily giving up the presidency of Senegal after a mere 20 years in office (1960–1980), when he was only 73 years old.[24]

In Cote d'Ivoire, President Houphouet-Boigny decided in 1990 (after 30 years in office) to hold a democratic election, which he won. For his last three years in office "Houph" was a democratically elected president. Shortly after his December 1993 death, Cote d'Ivoire seemed a relatively happy and prosperous country. The media were growing; there had been only two daily papers (both state controlled) in 1989, but in 1995 there were five dailies, one of which was completely independent of government. Television and radio, already well developed in Cote d'Ivoire, were growing; there were new FM radio stations.[25] However, this mid-1990s democratic tranquillity obscured underlying problems that later emerged into large scale violence and incipient civil war in 1999. Cote d'Ivoire's domestic ethnic mix involved major tensions not least between the Muslim north and the Christian south; these problems had been made more complex by the Cote d'Ivoire policy of welcoming immigrants from nearby countries. Tensions had been largely

---

[24] Kaye Whiteman, "The Paradoxes of Senghor," *Africa Today*, February 2002: 32–33.
[25] André Jean Tudesq, "Problems of Press Freedom in Cote d'Ivoire," in Festus Eribo and William Jong-Ebot (eds.), *Press Freedom and Communication in Africa*, Trenton, NJ: Africa World Press, 1997: 291–302.

contained by Cote d'Ivoire's economic success, by financial infusions from France and the international donors, and by the political prestige and political finesse of President Houph.[26] But President Houphouet-Boigny had been unwise to remain in power for so long; he died in office officially at 88 years old. When he died, the entire Parisian political elite attended the funeral; he had probably believed too much of the Parisian flattery and he had accepted too easily the fawning publicity in his domestic media. Houph also exhibited another unfortunate trait—an obsessive concern with his own poor rural origins; he was born in a small inland village called Yamoussoukro. He subsequently made this village the new capital city of his country.

Not all of the francophone western African countries were ruled by (relatively) enlightened despots. Some of these countries were among the poorest and worst governed nations on earth. One extreme example was the self-styled "emperor" of the Central African Republic, Jean-Bédel Bokassa, from 1965 to 1979. Bokassa was a pioneer of the unhappy tradition by which African presidents channelled large amounts of public (and foreign aid) money into their foreign bank accounts.

Togo provided another extreme example. In Togo the brutal dictatorship of Gnassingbe Eyadema lasted 38 years (1967–2005). His dictatorship, which began when he was 31 and ended when he died at age 69, illustrates some of the factors behind such extended periods of dictatorship. Eyadema as president had so many people eliminated, and had so many enemies, that there was no safe way in which he could retire from office. His enemies tended either to escape into exile or to die in mysterious ways. He was also, like other dictators, dependent on his own ethnic (Kabye) group, which comprised only one-quarter of Togo's population but was dominant in Togo's army and security service.

The media were another key ingredient of these extended dictator careers. In a very small country like Togo, with its small population (which reached three million in 1985), it was especially easy to exercise rigid control over the media. The Togo media were based in the coastal capital, Lomé. Provincial media were very modest indeed. Eyadema kept a suspicious eye on the media, and the rulers, of nearby states. But he could rely, for most of his dictatorship, on French support. There was occasional criticism in the French media. When he came to power in 1967, *Le Monde* reported that Eyadema had personally assassinated Sylvanu Olympio, Togo's first president (1960–1963).[27] In a small country, however, with only one main airport, it was not difficult to seize incoming copies of French newspapers.

---

[26] "Ivory Coast," *BBC Focus on Africa*, January–March 2003: 10–17; Cameron Duodu, "Ivory Coast: Descent to Chaos," *Africa Today*, October 2002: 14–17.
[27] Kaye Whiteman, "Gnassingbe Eyadema: Dinosaur Dictator Who Ruled Togo for 38 Brutal and Fearful Years," *The Guardian*, February 7, 2005; Martin Ekeke, "Togo: Till Death Do Them Part," *Africa Today*, June 2003: 24; Martin Luther King, "Togo: Transition Blues," *Africa Today*, March 2005: 12–14.

From about 1990 there was a major change of atmosphere across western Africa. The collapse of communism in eastern Europe in the late 1980s made a particularly big impression in francophone western Africa, where French Marxist discourse had been prevalent. From 1990 onward coups became less frequent and more enlightened; some military regimes handed over to civilians, multiparty elections became common, and the media became bigger and freer. In Mali, for example a brutal military regime (Moussa Traoré, 1976–1991) was terminated by another coup, which then led to Mali becoming "a model of democracy." Liberia, which received much American Cold War support, was the main CIA base for Africa; but in 1990 most of this support was withdrawn.

However, all was not economic sweetness and democratic light. After 1990 both Liberia and Sierra Leone suffered a decade of civil war and civil turbulence. These two civil wars also helped to destabilize both Cote d'Ivoire and Guinea. Although Liberia's and Sierra Leone's civil wars each had its distinctive (and highly complex) features, there were several common characteristics. In both Liberia and Sierra Leone there were high levels of antagonism between ethnic and religious groupings; in both countries in the 1990s there was additional polarization between poor farmers (struggling with locusts, desert, drought, illiteracy, and hunger) and what they saw as the urban fat cats, driving Mercedes and dealing in diamonds, gold, and foreign aid. Both civil wars resulted in big displacements of population; many war refugees crossed borders into neighboring countries, carrying with them the seeds of civil war. The fighting in both civil wars involved what foreign journalists reported as surreal and grotesque features; many soldiers were recruited as children and some were required—as an initiation—to kill their own parents or their local village chief. Already in 1992 there were reports of Liberian boys and young men going into battle, stoned on drugs and wearing fancy costumes—including women's dresses.[28] By 2003, a decade later, there had been numerous accounts of Liberian soldiers carrying guns but also with wigs, lipstick, toys, human bones, masks and wedding dresses, or bath robes.[29]

These civil wars involved battles between rival ethnic warlords. Stephen Ellis argues, in considerable detail, that there was a strong element of religion in the Liberian civil war.[30] Christianity came with the freed American slaves, who established Liberia as a Republic in 1847; over the ensuing decades Christianity mixed with local African religions, resulting in belief and ritual that included human sacrifice and the eating of human flesh, especially the human heart or "engine." Liberia's chief 1990s warlord, Charles Taylor, had important media and diamond trading connections; but he emphasized the

---

[28] "Horror Story," *The Economist*, November 21, 1992.
[29] "Goodbye to All That?" *The Economist*, August 16, 2003.
[30] Stephen Ellis, *The Mask of Anarchy: The Destruction of Liberia and the Religious Dimension of an African Civil war*, London: Hurst, 1999: 220–80.

religious dimension of his rule, and when he finally left Liberia (in 2003) his farewell address included specific comparisons between himself and Jesus Christ.

In the 1990s Cote d'Ivoire drifted into its own civil war. When Houphouet-Boigny died in 1993, he was succeeded by Henri Konan Bédié, who was subsequently reelected in 1995. However, in order to ensure his election, Bédié challenged the nationality of the large number of immigrants who had been attracted by Cote d'Ivoire's relative economic success; Bédié thus managed to exclude all of his main political rivals from the 1995 election. There was a successful military coup in 1999. No longer the relatively tranquil, ethnically inclusive, and economically successful creation of Houph, Cote d'Ivoire in the early 2000s was involved in civil war against a background of economic decline and ethnic antagonism.[31] Like most African conflicts, this was a conflict over wealth and land—in particular the land on which Cote d'Ivoire's cocoa crop generated most of the country's exports (and filled nearly half of the world's chocolate bars). By 2003 Cote d'Ivoire was split into two main segments—the southern half, mainly Christian and ethnically Bété, the main cocoa growing area and the location of President Laurent Gbagbo's government; and the northern segment, mainly Muslim, ethnically Dioula, and with less fertile land. A sizeable slice of western Cote d'Ivoire was controlled by two other ethnic-military-political party groups.[32]

Media, or lack of media, seems to have played a significant part in the civil war turmoil of Liberia, Sierra Leone, and Cote d'Ivoire. Sierra Leone's small TV service was launched in 1963 but ceased to operate at all during 1987–1993.[33] Often radio was the only form of mass media still operating, and very often this radio was actively participating hate radio, involved in ethnic turmoil, ethnic targeting, and aggressive wartime propaganda. Previous to the 1990s era of civil wars, the media in Sierra Leone and Liberia had been quite weak. The civil war period saw frequent trashing and torching of buildings, including major media locations such as newspapers and TV stations.[34] Also trashed and looted were provincial government buildings and retail stores of all kinds. Some people managed to loot new television sets, which, however, were useless because the national television broadcaster's buildings or local transmitters had been destroyed.

Radio in 1990 had the largest national reach and became more salient; in comparison with TV and newspapers, radio—both its transmission and

[31] "Ivory Coast," *BBC Focus on Africa*, January–March 2003: 10–17; Cameron Duodu, "Ivory Coast: Descent to Chaos," *Africa Today*, October 2002: 14–17.
[32] Thalia Griffiths, "Striking at the Empire," and Jarves Copnall, "United in Anger," in *BBC Focus on Africa*, January–March 2005: 18–21.
[33] Patricia A. Holmes, *Broadcasting in Sierra Leone*, Lanham, MD: University Press of America, 1999.
[34] William Reno, "Sierra Leone: Warfare in a Post-State Society," in Robert I. Rotberg (ed.), *State Failure and State Weakness in a Time of Terror*, Washington, DC: Brookings Institution Press, 2003: 71–100.

reception—is cheap and flexible. Radio also survives conflict, or can be relaunched, more easily. Both Liberia and Sierra Leone were products of Anglo-American empire in which English was the senior language; it was widely believed that BBC radio gave the most reliable news. However, there was also a chaotic radio propaganda war at the local level. Charles Taylor in Liberia built up his personality cult through radio; he liked to phone into live radio with dramatic assertions and attacks on his enemies, whom he often compared with Hitler.

Even so, many people in Sierra Leone and Liberia still did not hear any radio. For example, many people in the Liberian capital still had not heard of Charles Taylor's August 2003 departure (to Nigeria)[35] when it had already been shown on TV screens around the world.

However, this imperfect access, even to radio, probably gave added emphasis to such radio news as was heard. Much of this "news" was actually hate radio, a phenomenon that in the 1990s was not limited to Rwanda.

Radio: Genocide in Rwanda and Democracy in Kenya

Radio continued to be the leading mass medium in the heart of Africa throughout the late twentieth century. This was most starkly illustrated in Rwanda, where in 1994 a single radio station took the lead in orchestrating the killing of some 800,000 people, about 10 percent of the population. Central and eastern Africa (as defined here) had in 2005 about the same total population—and the same area—as the United States. In the largest three countries—Congo, Sudan, and Ethiopia—both newspapers and television have been less developed than in Nigeria; all three of these countries experienced secessionist civil wars, in which radio was prominent. Radio was also the leading medium in Somalia and in mountainous Rwanda and Burundi. Only in Kenya were press and television as developed as in Nigeria. We will focus here mainly on the disaster and genocide in Rwanda and the contrast with "democratic success" in Kenya.

One radio station played a key role in the Rwandan genocide of 1994; RTLM Radio actually instructed its listeners to kill Tutsi "cockroaches," and it announced the names and addresses of target individuals, in order to assist the local death squads. In addition to the 800,000 who were killed, many thousands were raped or lost arms or legs. Machetes and clubs were the most widely used weapons, but guns were also employed.

It has been argued widely that democratization (political and media) "came too quickly" in Rwanda. Even the principle of multiparty democracy was only accepted in 1990; four years later, in April 1994, the genocide began.

[35] Rory Carroll, "Conflict Reignites in Monrovia Despite Taylor's Departure," *The Guardian*, August 13, 2003; Martin Ekeke, "End Game in Liberia," *Africa Today*, August/September 2003: 40–41.

The genocide took place against a background not only of democratization but of continuing civil war. During 1990–1994 new political parties came into existence. The number of print publications (mostly weekly) increased from about 12 to about 60. Radio Rwanda, the state broadcaster, actually allowed some opposition politicians onto the air during 1992–1994. But a new commercial radio station (RTLM) began transmission in July 1993. RTLM ("One Thousand Hills Free Radio") was new, "commercial," youth-oriented; RTLM played popular music (Congolese, Cameroon, Caribbean), used irreverent jokey talk, and eventually issued frequently repeated advice on the killing and maiming of "cockroaches."[36]

Dictatorship was the main Rwanda political fact of the 21 years previous to the 1994 genocide. General Juvénal Habyarimana was in power during 1973–1994. He came to power in a military coup of mainly north Rwanda army officers, who overthrew the previous regime, led by mainly central and southern army officers. Habyarimana won "elections" in 1978, 1983, and 1988. In 1990 he accepted multipartyism, and the last D of his governing party, MRND, was made in 1991 to mean Democracy. Like other dictators embracing democracy, he planned to retain power, not least by manipulating the newly democratized media. The newly democratic dictator (previous to his assassination in April 1994) was planning the genocide in which hate radio was to play a leading role. Like many military dictators, Habyarimana was eliminated by a military-versus-military coup, the very same path by which he had come to power in 1973. While Habyarimana had merely planned the genocide, those who briefly succeeded him were ready (the day after his death in a plane crash) to carry out the genocide plan.

Many (but not all) "foreign observers" saw the genocide as in fact a civil war. There was, indeed, a civil war in Rwanda. Lowish intensity civil war was present in Rwanda from even before the 1962 independence and for most of the years to 1994. The Belgians had officially labeled the slightly wealthier (mainly cattle-herding) Rwandans as "Tutsis," and these latter (about 15 percent of the population) were allied with the Belgian administration in ruling the "Hutu" (mainly cultivating) 80 percent majority. Shortly before independence, however, the Belgians switched their preference and encouraged the (previously subordinate) Hutus to take power with their Parmehutu political party. In 1959 the first big exodus of Tutsis—to Uganda,

[36] Gérard Prunier, *The Rwanda Crisis: History of a Genocide*, London: Hurst and Company, 1997; Julienne Nyirankusi Munyaneza, *The Rwandan Conflict: Radio and Language as Tools of Propaganda and Weapons of War*, London: City University Department of Sociology, unpublished M.A. dissertation, 1999: 75–84; Christine L. Kellow and H. Leslie Steeves, "The Role of Radio in the Rwandan Genocide," *Journal of Communication*, Summer 1998, Vol. 48/3: 107–28; Philip Gourevitch, *We Wish to Inform You That Tomorrow We Will Be Killed with Our Families*, London: Picador ed., 1999; Johan Pottier, *Re-Imagining Rwanda: Conflict, Survival and Disinformation in the Late Twentieth Century*, Cambridge, UK: Cambridge University Press, 2002; Roméo Dallaire, *Shake Hands with the Devil: The Failure of Humanity in Rwanda*, London: Arrow Books, 2004 (first publ. by Random House, Canada, 2003): 105–6, 183–84, 379–41, 420–22.

Tanzania, Burundi, and Congo (Zaire)—took place. Between 1959 and 1994 there were numerous other exoduses from, and returns to, Rwanda by (mainly) Tutsi refugees. Hundreds of thousands of Rwandan Tutsis lived abroad, especially in Uganda, for long periods. In 1993 a Tutsi-led political party in exile—the Rwandese Patriotic Front (RPF)—which had acquired military expertise with (President) Yoweri Museveni's forces inside Uganda, began fresh attacks inside Rwanda. This led to peace talks in Arusha (Tanzania) and a "power-sharing" government in which RPF (led by "minority" Tutsis) obtained, through its fighting performance, about half of the top government positions. The "majority" Hutus—and especially the extremist nationalist Hutus—regarded the RPF as "foreign" (many now English-speaking) invaders. These extremist elements apparently planned to assassinate their President (Habyarimana) and to eliminate the "Tutsi invaders." Lack of success in the civil war would be circumvented by the use of civilian militias, who were trained in killing fellow civilians. From early April 1994 for some 100 days, the civil war continued at the same time as the genocide. Most "foreign observers" (observing from outside Rwanda) could only see the civil war. They failed to recognize the villagers-kill-villagers genocide although the genocide was evident also in the capital, Kigali, in the form of many dead bodies rotting on the streets.

Before RTLM Radio came onto the air in July 1993, the path to genocide was prepared by other media. In 1990 (December 10) a new extremist weekly publication, *Kangura*, printed "The Ten Hutu Commandments," two of which stated:

4. Every Muhutu should know that every Mututsi is dishonest in business.

8. The Bahutu should stop having mercy on the Batutsi.

During 1991–1993 Radio Rwanda echoed these sentiments in a slightly more restrained language.

For some nine months previous to the genocide of April 1994 there was a continuous barrage of hate radio. Beginning in July 1993 RTLM Radio went much further into ethnic condemnation of, and hatred for, the Tutsis. Then there was another escalation, which began immediately after the presidential assassination of April 6, 1994. It was now that RTLM called openly for the elimination of the "cockroaches" (the hate term it had repeatedly used to describe the Tutsis). The ensuing blitzkrieg of Hutu radio and mass killings indicated detailed previous planning in which RTLM Radio had participated; the "commercial" RTLM Radio was in fact owned by a group of extremist Hutu businessmen who were in alliance with the extremist army officers (who both carried out the coup-assassination and orchestrated the genocide). RTLM Radio personnel had names and addresses of targeted individuals, which they systematically read out on the radio. The genocide leaders were especially keen to eliminate the Tutsi elite; Tutsi car owners' license numbers were collected and these were also announced on RTLM Radio. Specific buildings were named as well as places where some Tutsis had found temporary refuge. Phrases used over RTLM Radio included the following:

> Fight the cockroaches, pound them. Stand up . . . take your spears, clubs, guns, swords, stones, everything, sharpen them, hack them, these enemies. . . .
>
> To get rid of weeds, you uproot them: kill the father, mother, children. . . .
>
> When you kill a rat, don't spare the pregnant one either.

From 1994 General Paul Kigame presided over a tense, but largely nonviolent, decade. With the support of praise-singing media, Kigame won Rwanda's first "democratic" presidential election in 2003, with 95 percent of the vote. Rwanda was deeply involved in even more deadly events in Congo/Zaire. Meanwhile, everything seemed to be radically different in Kenya—just across Lake Victoria from Rwanda. In Kenya there were increasingly democratic and multiparty elections in 1992, 1997, and 2002.

Kenya's largest ethnic group, the Kikuyu, are only about 20 percent of the population. The two main Kenya-wide languages are English and Swahili. An impressively large fraction of the population speak English to a high standard. British colonial influences are still strong and highly visible in Kenyan politics, life, and media. The United States presence adds to the British and is most noticeable in imported television programming. The combined Anglo-American presence spans Christian religion, military training, commerce, and education.

Nevertheless, Kiswahili is Kenya's most widely spoken language. Swahili radio has Kenya's biggest media audience, and Swahili with a strong admixture of English—referred to as "Sheng"—is prominent in everyday conversation, on the urban street, and on the Internet. Swahili combines inland Bantu elements with coastal Arabic; it is not an elite language but a language carried by trade, military, and other outside-the-home use.[37]

In 1954–1959, Kenya's end-of-empire was violent; 1,090 Mau Mau rebels were executed by hanging, and up to 20,000 Africans died in combat. At least 150,000 Kikuyu men spent a year or more in a detention camp without trial; very few European settlers died.[38] But after Kenya's 1963 independence, Jomo Kenyatta, recently seen by the European settlers and politicians as a "leader to darkness and death," was quickly transformed into an international statesman, the benign leader of the new nation. Kenyatta had in fact always been a moderate, an amateur journalist, a professional intellectual.[39] He was a speaker and leader of real charisma. He had been convicted in an unfair trial, but Kenyatta did not worry about this. He told large audiences

[37] An outstanding analysis is Ali A. Mazrui and Alamin M. Mazrui, *Swahili State and Society: The Political Economy of an African Language*, Nairobi: East African Educational Publishers, and London: James Currey, 1995.
[38] David Anderson, *Histories of the Hanged: Britain's Dirty War in Kenya and the End of the Empire*, London: Weidenfeld and Nicolson, 2005.
[39] Jomo Kenyatta, *Facing Mount Kenya*, London: Secker and Warburg, 1938.

of both black African and white (British) settler-farmers that moderation, reconciliation, and Kenyan nation-building were the goals. Everyone now loved him, the wise old man.[40]

Kenyatta was the big man for the first 15 years of Kenyan independence (1963–1978). The white settlers caused no trouble—the small and mid-sized farm owners took the compensation, providing (initially) plenty of land for African farmers. The main Kenyan mass media up to 1963 had included *The Standard* newspaper, which from the beginning of the twentieth century had been the voice of the white settlers; this leading newspaper (now under Lonrho big business ownership) switched its pro-government allegiance to the new Kenyatta regime. In 1960 a new daily appeared, *The Nation*, owned by the Aga Khan; the Nation group included also the *Sunday Nation* and a Swahili daily, *Taifa*. These two foreign press ownerships and President Kenyatta supported and sustained each other. The other main mass media outlet was radio from the government-controlled Voice of Kenya.

During the Kenyatta years, Kenya was a "success story" especially because the economy grew at up to 10 percent a year. Coffee, tea, and tourism all did well. Meanwhile, Kenya's previously strong two political parties were effectively reduced to one; the KANU party and Kenya were now dominated by Kenyatta and his fellow Kikuyu (based just north of Nairobi) and the Luo (based in the west, near Lake Victoria). The leading Luo politician, Tom Mboya, was sadly assassinated on a Nairobi street six years after independence. Soon after this, by the early 1970s, Kenyatta had established a one-party state with little freedom of expression. On a 1972 visit this author was told by journalists of a list of unmentionable topics. Most severely forbidden was any discussion of the succession—a classic focus for authoritarian unease.

Kenyatta followed the already common African pattern of ruling through a small group or court of men from precisely his own (Kikuyu) ethnic background. Jomo Kenyatta, so admirable in so many ways, unfortunately also fell into the common African pattern of the political big man who decides to become big in personal wealth. Kenyatta's eventual successor was Daniel arap Moi, a school teacher by background, who was from a small Rift Valley ethnic group, the Kalenjin. Moi's political strategy during 24 years in power (1978–2002) was to unite the numerous smaller ethnic groups against the much larger Kikuyu and Luo. Moi's strategy was thus the mirror image of Kenyatta's. During his first four years in power (1978–1982) President Moi focused on additional educational spending. His somewhat more relaxed regime allowed more protest voices to be heard; the University of Nairobi and other campuses were closed several times. In August 1982, however, there was an attempted coup by junior elements in the small Kenya air force. Although several hundred people died, this was modest by coup standards;

[40] Keith Kyle, *The Politics of the Independence of Kenya*, London: Macmillan Press, and New York: Saint Martin's Press, 1999.

many of those who died were slumdwellers engaged in looting Indian-owned (and other) shops in downtown Nairobi.

During the 1980s President Moi clamped down on various dissident forces; his methods included prison without trial, harassment of various kinds, and a few assassinations. By 1990 many lawyers, academics, writers, politicians, and journalists were either in prison or in exile. Nevertheless, a pro-democracy movement was gradually coming together in Kenya. The general election of 1988 was (like those of 1979 and 1983) not a genuinely democratic election. There were loud complaints from various bodies, including the Law Society of Kenya and the National Council of Churches of Kenya (NCCK). In 1992 Kenya had its first genuinely multiparty, more or less democratic, elections.

Vital to the democracy movement in Kenya was the existence of the two major newspaper groups that provided low key, but factual, reports of the democratizing events. The established print media followed behind the radical lead of several high quality nondaily publications, especially *Nairobi Law Monthly* and *Finance*.[41] Also important were the forces of international finance and western diplomatic pressure (led by the then U.S. ambassador, Smith Hempstone, who, however, did not arrive in Kenya until 1989). Although Anglo-American, western European, International Monetary Fund, and World Bank pressures were significant, the ending of the Cold War was more important. Events in South Africa were also influential; the wives of several prominent political detainees sent a message to Nelson Mandela when he visited Nairobi in July 1990. This protest against prison without trial received big publicity in Kenya and abroad.

When President Moi reluctantly agreed to the genuinely multiparty elections of 1992, he was seen by some as certain to lose power. Moi, however, recognized that new democracy would require fresh electoral tactics. The self-styled "professor of politics" decided that new democracy would, paradoxically perhaps, require new forms of repression. Under conditions of democratic contested voting, the "small tribe" strategy now (Moi effectively decided) would require more (not less) corruption and more (not less) violence. Consequently, from around 1990—and for most of the next 12 years—there was a rising crescendo of increased government corruption, increased political violence, and increased political and media protest.

The increased political corruption of the 1990s involved President Moi allowing "his" politicians to enrich themselves. They were allowed to benefit from privatizations of previously state-owned companies, to accept bribes from foreign companies, and to help themselves to pieces of disputed land. The more corrupt a KANU politician was, the more he stood to lose by falling out with Moi; such a politician might be sent to prison or meet a sudden and

---

[41] B. A. Ogot, "Transition from Single Party to Multiparty Political System, 1989–93," in B. A. Ogot and W. R. Ochieng' (eds.), *Decolonisation and Independence in Kenya, 1940–93*, London: James Currey, 1995: 239–61.

unexplained death. Corruption also allowed Moi himself to establish his own personal wealth. Corruption was useful too in that it was easy to channel funds into KANU for use in wholesale bribery of voters in key election districts and constituencies.

President Moi resorted to political violence in several forms, from police beatings to systematic ethnic cleansing in selected areas; special election violence was also used at appropriate times. In Kenya the police were well known themselves to be corrupt; they routinely stopped motorists and extracted cash. The police were also known to be violent both toward criminals and political protesters; during 1997–2000 of all Kenyan firearms deaths, 60 percent were due to shots fired by police[42]; in 2001 (before the 2002 election) this rose to 90 percent.

Systematic ethnic cleansing was also used by Moi and KANU, both in order physically to remove potential opposition voters from their homes and land and to reward loyal KANU voters. This electoral ethnic cleansing was used especially in the area of the Rift Valley (about 150–200 miles northwest of Nairobi), where Moi's own Kalenjin people were traditionally located. Some of the worst violence of this kind happened previous to the December 1992 "democratic" election. A church (NCCK) report documented this violence, as did a report from a committee of 13 of KANU's own members of parliament. There was an established price list for "fighters" who killed people or burned grass-thatched or permanent homes.[43]

President Moi's 1992 tactics were broadly successful. A multiparty national election took place in December 1992 and was duly won by KANU. A strong group of national and international election monitors concluded that the 1992 elections were an improvement, although still not "free and fair." The monitoring unit did list many undemocratic details and also referred to "situations of immense provocation such as the persistent ethnic clashes."[44] The national election monitoring unit also agreed with the opposition accusation that the main Kenyan mass media were heavily biased. The Kenya Broadcasting Corporation (KBC), the new name for the old Voice of Kenya had been heavily biased in support of Moi's KANU governing party; KBC reporting of the opposition had focused heavily on the "split opposition" theme. Somewhat less biased was the now KANU-controlled *Standard* newspaper group; least biased of the major media were *Nation* group publications.

President Moi hung onto power for another decade (1992–2002). But the demands on his political survival skills became steadily more severe. Soon

---

[42] A study by Kenya's Chief Government Pathologist, Dr. Kirasi Olumbe, *Africa Today*, February 2002: 7.

[43] Republic of Kenya, *Report of the Parliamentary Select Committee to Investigate Ethnic Clashes in Western and Other Parts of Kenya*, Nairobi: Republic of Kenya, September 1992: 75; see also Mark Huband, *The Skull Beneath the Skin: Africa After the Cold War*, Boulder, CO: Westview Press, 2001: 238–48.

[44] National Election Monitoring Unit, *The Multi-Party General Elections in Kenya, 29 December 1992*, Nairobi: National Election Monitoring Unit, 1993: 90–92.

after the December 1992 election, traditional repressive measures were again being used. Ethnic arithmetic would continue to be central to Kenyan politics. Moi was evidently embarrassed by some of the excesses of the recent past, not least the February 16, 1990, murder of the then foreign minister (Robert Ouku); while President Moi's closest ethnic and political friend, Nicholas Biwott, was never tried for the murder of his cabinet colleague, Biwott was widely regarded as the chief suspect. By now, however, all such events were very fully reported. *The Nation*, Kenya's leading daily paper, had gradually developed into a consistently skeptical voice, although the editors were careful to make their criticism seem moderate, responsible, and positive.[45] For example, an anonymous editorial article would first criticize the opposition parties before pointing out that "KANU has probably the greatest credibility problem of all, if only because it is the party of Government."[46]

In 1997 KANU and Moi again won the election. But political and other problems continued to escalate. World commodity prices moved against the Kenyan economy; international financial lenders and donors were increasingly skeptical—especially of corruption in Kenya. After 1997, Moi came to be seen as a "lame duck" who must leave office in 2002. The media gradually became more skeptical.

Radio was still the most important mass medium in Kenya. A large 1998 survey[47] showed radio accounting for about 60 percent of "media activity engaged in yesterday"; the KBC Swahili radio service was by far the largest and was the only Kenyan medium reaching two-thirds of the population. Next was English-language radio, including new FM local radio. In 1998 television had only about 20 percent of the media audience. More than half of this television was made in Kenya; but American, Australian, and Latin American soaps and British imports (including football) were also quite prominent. Finally, newspapers also accounted for about 20 percent of media activity, with 25 percent of the sample claiming (somewhat unconvincingly) to have read the *Daily Nation* yesterday; the high figure probably reflected an urban-biased sample but also indicated the prestige and reputation of this (quite serious) newspaper.

The *Daily Nation* in fact continued into the election year of 2002 to offer fairly neutral factual coverage of a non-Nigerian style; however, the *Daily Nation* by 2002 had developed a stable of African columnists who wrote well and often wrote columns critical of the Moi government. By 2002 the *Daily Nation* also routinely carried political cartoons that were fairly uninhibited in attacking the Moi government. In competing with the independent and higher sale *Daily Nation*, the KANU-controlled *East African Standard* had also

---

[45] Mark Huband, "Kenya Tense as Hopes of Democracy Are Dashed," *The Guardian* (London), July 18, 1994.

[46] "Credibility and Political Parties," *Daily Nation*, September 27, 1993.

[47] Research International East Africa, *Media Survey 1998*, "Based on 1,660 random interviews with African adults (15+)."

become more critical; *Standard* pieces about police corruption, land owner-ship, or the destruction of Kenya's forests became routine.

It was not until summer 2002 that President Moi finally lost his dominance of Kenyan politics.[48] Moi indicated that he would support Uhuru Kenyatta in the end-of-year presidential elections. This device of choosing the politically inexperienced son of Jomo Kenyatta angered many KANU politicians, who saw Moi as trying to hold onto power by manipulating his successor. For many Kenyans the Moi-Kenyatta partnership carried the smell of yet more corruption. Moi's choice of the younger Kenyatta led to a major breakaway from the KANU party. This big breakaway, which included several of Moi's main political friends and enemies of the last two decades, established the National Rainbow Alliance (Narc); the new alliance, and its presidential candidate Mwai Kibaki, easily won the December 2002 elections. Power changed hands through a genuinely contested democratic election, helped along by the Kenyan media.

So what conclusions can be drawn from a comparison between Rwanda and Kenya? One basic conclusion is that Kenya has been very far from a total success; Kenya's road to democracy—while not interrupted by genocide—was strewn with hundreds, or low thousands, of violent deaths. Moreover, after 1994, Rwanda was in some respects a success.

Clearly important were basic facts of geography and history. Rwanda was perched up in the hills alongside the African crossroads of Lake Victoria; many of Rwanda's problems were imported from, and reexported to, Uganda and Congo/Zaire. Rwanda was unfortunate in its German-Belgian colonial history and also illustrates the point that even an African country with few genuine ethnic differences can still suffer from class war and civil war. Rwanda also suffered from the interference of so many foreign powers as well as the lack of interference of the same powers, and the United Nations, in 1994.[49] Kenya was supremely fortunate in the father of the new nation Jomo Kenyatta, who exhibited in Kenya some of the same personal qualities and political skills that Nelson Mandela subsequently used to such effect in South Africa.

Kenya was especially fortunate, also, in aspects of its mass media. Kenya was fortunate in the relatively smooth way in which its main media "changed sides" at independence. Kenya was probably fortunate, and certainly unusual, in its two major newspapers—both the *Standard* and the *Nation* were strong national daily newspapers; the element of foreign (but low profile) foreign ownership was also unusual. The *Daily Nation* in particular behaved with caution and moderation, which in retrospect seem well judged and adroitly exercised. Kenya was also perhaps fortunate in having two major, nontribal, languages—Kiswahili and English; this enabled the media in general (and

---

[48] For excellent coverage of Kenyan politics in 2002, see *Africa Confidential* throughout the year.
[49] Linda Melvern, *A People Betrayed: The Role of the West in Rwanda's Genocide*, London: Zed Books, 2000.

Daily Nation, August 8, 1998   The EastAfrica, August 10, 1998

Figure 15.3 Two Nairobi newspapers report the August 1998 bombing of the United States embassy. (Images provided by the author.)

radio in particular) to focus on these two languages. One consequence, of course, was the weak media position even of the largest Kenyan languages, including Kikuyu.

The Kenyan media were influenced by the use of Nairobi as a hub location for international news agencies. Reuters, Associated Press, and Agence France-Presse all have their main eastern African bureaus in Nairobi. Both AP and Reuters cover 13 or 14 African countries (and off-shore island nations) from Nairobi; these include conflict cases such as Somalia, Rwanda, and Ethiopia. Some coverage of the civil wars in Congo and Sudan was done from Nairobi. Major foreign newspapers (especially American and British) have correspondents based in Nairobi. The Reuters and Associated Press Nairobi bureaus in 2002 together employed about 20 full-time (or nearly full-time) journalists for their text, TV, and picture services. They also together employed an additional 50 part-time "stringers"—most of whom were citizens of the eastern African countries from which they were reporting. This significant journalist presence has some unintended consequences. Although on most days correspondents are in, or focusing on, other countries in eastern Africa, Kenya still gets more news coverage than it "deserves." This probably has meant that political violence in Kenya (dozens killed) gets as much coverage as, or more coverage than, violence elsewhere in turbulent eastern Africa (often involving hundreds or thousands killed). Unfair or unbalanced though this may seem, the international media presence probably encouraged

President Moi to move cautiously when pursuing his political opponents. The Kenyan government wanted to promote Nairobi and Kenya as the eastern African regional hub, one offering political stability.

During the late 1990s and early 2000s, Kenya's media continued to gain strength. There was rapid growth in TV advertising and in the production of original Kiswahili TV soap and comedy. But President Mwai Kibaki's new government experienced only a brief 2003 honeymoon. Both Kenya's low intensity violence and high intensity political corruption were soon again attracting heavy criticism from the domestic and foreign media. The *Nation* and *Sunday Nation* newspapers, in early 2006, published an explosive corruption report by John Githongo (a former Kenyan journalist and Transparency International analyst). The Githongo report accused the finance minister and the energy minister of large scale corruption. The central role of the media in Kenyan politics was emphasized when President Kibaki responded by attacking, not the foreign-owned Nation group, but the Standard group; masked police arrested *Standard* journalists, burned newspapers, and temporarily closed Standard-owned KTN television.[50]

Mobutu, State Failure, and Radio Survival

Four countries—Congo, Sudan, Ethiopia, and Uganda—have been plagued, over the decades since 1960, with civil war and secessionist attempts. Radio survives better than TV or newspapers under conditions of civil conflict and when there is no electricity supply. Radio also can be heard from other countries in Africa and beyond.

The three largest of these countries—Congo, Sudan, and Ethiopia—all have other characteristics that work against television. Their combined population density is only one-fifth of Nigeria's. The terrain is also awkward for television—most of the Congo is rain forest, much of Sudan is desert and semi-desert, while Ethiopia has major mountain ranges that block TV signals. Each of these countries can also claim to be among the world's most ethnically diverse; each has 100 or 200 distinct languages.

Radio already occupied an unusually prominent place in Congo in the 1930s; this continued for the next seven decades. In the 1930s the Belgians were busily developing the Congo's fabled wealth—which included copper, diamonds, timber from the rain forest, cobalt, and uranium; Congo also has extremely fertile soil and plenty of rain. The Belgian colonists were widely dispersed across this large territory and by 1939 the colonial government had

---

[50] Andrew England, "Kenya Tests Out Its Democracy with Satire and Adultery on Screen," *Financial Times*, September 2, 2005; Michela Wrong and Duncan Campbell, "Top Ministers Face Inquiry into Corruption Allegations in Kenya," *The Guardian*, January 20, 2006; Marc Lacey, "Masked Kenyan Police Stage 2 Raids on Media," *International Herald Tribune* (from NY Times) March 3, 2006.

established radio stations in eight provincial cities for the benefit of their mining engineers and other expatriate Belgians.

Radio gave substantial coverage to Congo's independence celebrations in 1960. The new president, Joseph Kasavubu, generously praised and thanked the departing Belgians. But the new prime minister, Patrice Lumumba, denounced the departing Belgians in a highly undiplomatic, angry speech; Lumumba listed some of the Belgians' (many) imperial sins.

A feud between Kasavubu and Lumumba was a major feature of the Congo's early weeks of independence. They denounced each other over Radio Leopoldville and each man announced—over the radio—the dismissal of the other man from office. UN personnel temporarily stopped both men from using the national radio; but President Kasavubu was allowed to use the radio of Congo Brazzaville (just across the Congo River).[51] Prime Minister Lumumba not only lost radio access but, later in 1960, lost his life; he was tortured and killed, with Belgian army and American CIA involvement.

Radio was also involved in the Congo's first serious attempt at regional secession. Moïse Tshombe in July 1960 declared himself president of the new secessionist state of Katanga; this southeast region of Congo had important copper and other mineral wealth;[52] it also had a radio station that became the voice of the separatist state. Tshombe and Katanga were persuaded back into the Congo, but the fragility of the Congo was plain for all to see.

It was also in the eventful year of 1960 that Joseph-Désiré Mobutu launched his first coup; Mobutu was one month short of his thirtieth birthday. After handing the country back to its civilians, he launched another coup and ruled the Congo for the next 32 years (1965–1997). Mobutu had many talents and many weaknesses. He had worked as a journalist after he left the army at age 25; he edited two magazines, *L'Avenir* and *Actualités Africaines*. Perhaps his greatest talent was as a media manipulator and self-publicist. Much of Mobutu's celebrated personal imagery was visual—the leopard-themed clothes and hat, the heavy glasses. But much of this visual imagery went into live performances; Mobutu was an outstanding public speaker. He also had great courage; he frequently appeared in front of rioting soldiers, who could easily have gunned him down.

But it was radio that carried Mobutu's doctrine of "authenticity." He renamed the country Zaire, he renamed himself Mobutu Sese Seko, and the capital, Leopoldville, became Kinshasa. For two long decades the radio carried large amounts of Zaire authenticity talk; it also carried Congolese music—super-popular, not only in the Congo, but in the surrounding countries. A major theme of the music was praise-singing for President Mobutu.[53]

---

[51] Minabere Ibelema and Ebere Onwudiwe, "Congo (Zaire): Colonial Legacy, Autocracy and the Press," in Festus Eribo and William Jong-Ebot (eds.), *Press Freedom and Communication in Africa*, Trenton, NJ: Africa World Press, 1997: 303–21.

[52] Conor Cruise O'Brien, *To Katanga and Back: a UN case history*, London: Hutchinson, 1962.

[53] Gary Stewart, *Rumba on the River: A History of Popular Music of the Two Congos*, London: Verso, 2000; "Congolese Music: Rumba in the Jungle," *The Economist*, December 20, 2003: 83–85.

Figure 15.4 President Mobutu speaking to the media at one of his palaces, Kinshasa, April 1997. (AP.)

Mobutu quickly became skilled at playing off his benefactors against each other. While the Belgians were still in charge, Mobutu became very friendly with the CIA—as the then CIA boss in Leopoldville, Larry Devlin, has often recounted.[54] Mobutu was happy to play off the Americans against the French and Belgians; he also flirted with the Soviet Union.

Despite his many talents, Mobutu was inept at running the Congo or even the Congolese army.[55] There were important uprisings, not only in 1964–1965 but also in 1977–1978 and 1991–1992. Mobutu seemed unable to get his generals to pass on the pay to the soldiers; without regular pay, the soldiers "lived off the country," raped women, and terrified the population.

---

[54] Michela Wrong, *In the Footsteps of Mr Kurtz: Living on the Brink of Disaster in the Congo*, London: Fourth Estate, 2000: 61–68, 77–82.

[55] René Lemarchand, "The Democratic Republic of the Congo: From Failure to Potential Reconstruction," in Robert I. Rotberg (ed.), *State Failure and State Weakness in a Time of Terror*, Washington, DC: Brookings Institution, 2003: 29–69.

Journalists began to call Mobutu a kleptocrat who presided over a kleptocracy; Mobutu lived in absurd luxury in a country of unrelenting poverty. In his later years he spent much of his time at Gbadolite in the remote north, where he constructed his Versailles-in-the-bush; one of numerous presidential palaces, this one was very convenient should a quick hop across the frontier (into the Central African Republic) become necessary.[56]

Collapse of the Congo accelerated after 1991, as the old Cold War financial infusions from abroad suddenly ceased.[57] The 1994 violence in Rwanda and Uganda spilled over into the Congo and eventually led to Mobutu being removed in 1997 by Laurent Kabila and his Rwandan-based army.

After Mobutu's departure (and death), a bigger Congo conflict began. During 1998–2004 this conflict was widely claimed to have killed between three and four million people. It was described as the world's most deadly conflict since 1945. Some journalists also referred to it as "Africa's first world war"[58] because military forces from several neighboring countries were sucked into the conflict. Much of the reported violence occurred in the extreme east of the Congo—close to the border with Uganda, Rwanda, and Burundi. Most of the news stories also originated either from towns in this area (such as Bunia, Goma, and Bukavu) or from Kinshasa in the far west. Few foreign news reports came from the 900-mile-wide area in between.

Once again, in this Congo civil war, many of the combatants were children. Many of the fatalities resulted from untreated wounds and from epidemics derived from the war. Many terrified people retreated into the rain forest and never emerged. These were not obvious TV-viewing or newspaper-reading conditions; radio was again the leading medium—with radio hate talk also prevalent.

In the years around 2000 the Congo experienced state failure. "How people respond to state failure in Kinshasa"[59] is the research topic of a large team of Belgian and other social scientists. In Kinshasa most public services had collapsed; this included health care facilities, hospitals, and schools. Even water (in a city that has 55 inches of rain per year and is on the bank of a huge river) was in weak supply. Food (which used to come down the Congo River in big quantities) was scarce; many people lived on one meal per day, or every two days. Families kept animals inside their homes and planted vegetables on the street verges and in the parks. In Kinshasa there was an increased following for evangelical Christianity and a strengthened belief in witchcraft. Accusations of witchcraft between parents and children were common.

---

[56] Kaye Whitman, "Obituary: Mobutu Sese Seko: Thief Who Stole a Nation," *The Guardian*, September 9, 1997; "Mobutu Sese Seko: Africa's Last Cold War Despot," *Financial Times*, September 9, 1997.

[57] "Zaire: The Last Days of Mobutu," *The Economist*, March 22, 1997.

[58] Mark Turner, "Africa's First World War," *Financial Times*, November 14/15, 1998; Colette Braeckman, "The Looting of the Congo," *New Internationalist*, May 2004: 13–16.

[59] Theodore Trefon (ed.), *Reinventing Order in the Congo: How People Respond to State Failure in Kinshasa*, London: Zed Books, 2004.

Kinshasa was, and is, a big city—with a population somewhere between four and seven million. Even under conditions of state failure and government collapse, some media continued. Newspapers, magazines, and irregular printed matter (including locally produced strip cartoons) were published and widely read. In 1997–1999 Kinshasa had at least five daily papers, three news agencies, and numerous weeklies. Television did still operate although frequently interrupted by power failures; TV had to compete with air conditioning, fans, and refrigerators for scarce electricity. Radio again was the biggest medium in Kinshasa—and, even more so, outside Kinshasa. The Kinshasa music scene continued to function. Radio talk and street gossip intermingled; indeed the Kinshasa slang for gossip was *Radio Trottoir* (literally sidewalk or pavement radio).

One other failed state—Somalia—deserves a brief mention. Somalia was another African nation where democratization, radio, civil war, and genocide combined into a "failed state." In Somalia "radio has been an intensely popular medium since its introduction in the early 1950s." A military dictator, Mohamed Siad Barre, was in power for 22 years (1969–1991);[60] when he eventually was removed from power in 1991, Somalia entered a phase of state collapse. A 1993–1995 UN effort, under American military leadership, attempted to introduce democracy. A sizeable force of U.S. Marines marched up the beach in 1993 and marched down the beach in abject failure in 1995. Somalia continued to lack central government but was instead controlled by several competing warlords, each of whom had his own belligerent radio station.[61]

South African Media: Apartheid and After

In 1975 apartheid was still well established in South Africa, and the two main European groups (Anglo and Dutch) controlled the press and the monopoly state radio broadcaster. There had been no television because the Afrikaaner-Nationalist-Apartheid governments feared that television might encourage the big African, "coloured," and Indian majority to demand equality and democracy.

But in 1975–1976 several changes occurred. South Africa did (at last) launch television. There was a major black uprising in Soweto (Johannesburg) in 1976. Also, the Portuguese dictatorship was overthrown, and the two big southern African Portuguese colonies—Angola and Mozambique—were given their independence. As the South African politicians looked to the north, they saw

---

[60] I. M. Lewis, "Why the Warlords Won: How the United States and the United Nations Misunderstood the Clan Politics of Somalia," *Times Literary Supplement*, June 8, 2001: 3–5; Richard Greenfield, "Obituary: Mohamed Siad Barre," *The Independent* (London), January 3, 1995.

[61] "Somalia: A State of Utter Failure," *The Economist*, December 17, 2005.

these two newly independent states as enemies, which they would need to destabilize with internal armed resistance (or terror).

Consequently, South Africa took on a more forward, more aggressive, strategy, which involved a newly active working alliance with the United States. South Africa and the United States together gave support to armed resistance in the two former Portuguese colonies. During Ronald Reagan's presidency (1981–1989) this alliance strengthened. A de facto alliance could also be seen in the mass media; South Africa, which had previously feared television in general and Hollywood television in particular, now became an enthusiastic importer of American TV series. Moreover, in South Africa Hollywood did not have to face much British competition. In London the musicians' and actors' trade unions had agreed with the boycott proposals of the anti-apartheid movement; British musicians and actors boycotted the South African market, just as British sports people refused to play cricket or rugby football with South Africa.

The Anglo-Boer War (1899–1902) was won by the British, but the subsequent peace was won by the other European settler group of Dutch-Afrikaner farmers. From the 1920s these farmers built up their own Afrikaans language newspaper press, and by 1950 South Africa had two strong groups of daily newspapers. It was at this time that the (Afrikaner) Nationalist Party introduced apartheid.

During the three decades of 1945–1976, such foreign media influences as entered South Africa were predominantly British. The strong newspaper press looked toward London. The SABC (loosely modeled on the BBC) was the monopoly radio broadcaster, and many English-speaking South Africans listened to the BBC's world service. Some black journalism did exist, often linked to the Anglican or Roman Catholic churches. The most politically significant black-oriented 1950s weekly publication, *Drum*, was a focus for African readers and journalists and for African National Congress politicians, including Nelson Mandela, Oliver Tambo, and Walter Sisulu. Launched in 1951, *Drum* carried plenty of sports, sex, and crime as well as anti-apartheid politics. All of its reporters and photographers were "nonwhites." *Drum* was launched by two Oxford graduates; the owner was Jim Bailey, a poet and former RAF Battle of Britain pilot. *Drum*'s editor in the early 1950s was a young Englishman, Anthony Sampson.[62]

In 1955 South Africa had more radio receiving sets than the whole of the remainder of Africa. By 1976 South Africa had 5 million of Africa's then only 19 million radio sets. In response to the 1960s African independence wave, South Africa developed a substantial external radio effort—in 1970 it was transmitting 150 hours a week targeted to other nation-states in southern Africa.[63]

---

[62] Anthony Sampson, "Sophiatown," in "Johannesburg" survey, *Financial Times*, August 7, 2002.

[63] *BBC Handbook*, London: BBC, 1978: 75.

Television began—with great caution—in January 1976, ushering in an era which, in retrospect, was late apartheid (1976–1994). It was a financially weak television service initially funded by a highish license fee ($40) deliberately intended to discourage most "nonwhites." The early SABC service was a single channel, which initially transmitted for five hours per weekday, with alternate hours in English and Afrikaans. By 1978 there was some programming in Zulu, Xhosa, and other African languages; more languages (and channels) followed. Television advertising was introduced for the first time in 1978, when it accounted for 16 percent of total advertising spending.[64] As a smallish TV system required to transmit programming in several different languages, SABC's television operation was inevitably dependent on programming imports.

The 1976–1994 late apartheid period saw a big swing toward importing, mainly from the United States. The newspaper press continued to have the main media political impact; indeed the English-language newspapers (with their strong U.K. links) were perhaps the most effective opposition force—not least because the two major newspaper groups, Times and Argus, were both ultimately controlled (like much else in South Africa) by the giant Anglo-American Corporation.[65] Consequently, the closure of the leading oppositionist daily, the *Rand Daily Mail* (in 1986), was a key event in the history of late apartheid; this was an indication that the Nationalist Party government was withdrawing from white democracy as well as denying "nonwhite" democracy.

By 1980 the United States dominated both music imports and TV imports into South Africa, with, for example, *Murder She Wrote* as the most popular TV series in 1980. Not only were large quantities of U.S. soaps, drama series, and comedies imported into South Africa, but much U.S. television religion was also approved—by the Afrikaner Apartheid Christians—for filling up many empty hours outside prime time. In South Africa, Hollywood TV also had an especially strong double offer—white U.S. series for white South African audiences and some black (but politically bland) U.S. TV series that were especially popular with "nonwhites." A similar double offer existed in music.[66]

The South African media have had a dominant position across southern Africa for several reasons. South Africa's population is twice that of

[64] C. Anthony Giffard, "The Impact of Television on South African Newspapers," *Journalism Quarterly*, Summer 1980, Vol. 57/2: 216–23.
[65] William A. Hachten and C. Anthony Giffard, *The Press and Apartheid: Repression and Propaganda in South Africa*, London: Macmillan, 1985; Keyan Tomaselli, Ruth Tomaselli, and Johan Muller, *The Press in South Africa*, London: James Currey, 1989 ed.; Keyan Tomaselli and P. Eric Louw (eds.), *The Alternative Press in South Africa*, London: James Currey, 1991; Les Switzer and Mohamed Adhikari (eds.), *South Africa's Resistance Press*, Athens: Ohio University Center for International Studies, 2000.
[66] Rob Nixon, *Homelands, Harlem and Hollywood: South African Culture and the World Beyond*, New York: Routledge, 1994: 11–41.

Mozambique, the second most populated country. South Africa throughout the twentieth century had diamond, gold, and agricultural wealth. South Africa also had the region's only major commercial and industrial center.

The Kalahari desert covers two of South Africa's immediate neighbors —lowly populated Namibia and Botswana. The more significant southern African countries are the island state of Madagascar, the two former Portuguese colonies of Angola and Mozambique, and Zimbabwe and Zambia. Zimbabwe suffered considerable violence and political turbulence both before and after its 1980 independence, and its media were government dominated.

Both Mozambique and Angola suffered civil wars of extraordinary ferocity and both conformed to the familiar African civil war pattern in which press and TV were curtailed by the conflict, while radio was the leading mass medium and the leading outlet for civil war propaganda and hate. In Mozambique the Marxist Frelimo government was opposed by Renamo (backed by South Africa and the United States). This conflict was especially fierce during the Reagan, late apartheid, and late Cold War years of 1981–1986.

Angola was an extreme case in several respects—including the length and brutality of its civil war and the prominence of propaganda radio. An attempt to substitute democracy for civil war occurred in 1992, but the loser in the first round of the election, Joseph Savimbi, immediately restarted the civil war. The Marxist MPLA Party was founded in 1956 and took power in Angola in 1975, when Portugal granted independence; during the struggle for independence, the MPLA was helped by Congo (Brazzaville) where it had a rebel radio station. Roberto Holden, leader of the rival FNLA rebel party, was a brother-in-law of President Mobutu, who provided radio facilities in Kinshasa. Angolan independence in 1975 marked the beginning of another civil war in which UNITA, led by Joseph Savimbi, opposed the Marxist MPLA government. It is now clear that the United States (in the person of Secretary of State Henry Kissinger) decided to throw CIA support behind UNITA, mainly because of its opposition to the Marxist government. This U.S./CIA support was provided in alliance with military support from apartheid South Africa, with South African soldiers posing as mercenaries. American-sponsored forces also entered Angola from Congo/Zaire; this support was provided in anticipation of, and also before, Soviet and Cuban military support for the MPLA.[67]

---

[67] Odd Arne Westad, *The Global Cold War: Third World Interventions and the Making of Our Times*, Cambridge, UK: Cambridge University Press, 2005: 207–49. A number of sources were summarized by Howard W. French, "CIA Reports Show US Helped South Africa in Angolan Civil War," from *New York Times* service, in *The East African*, April 8–14, 2002. One key source of this information was Robert Hultslander, who served as CIA station chief in Angola from August to November 1975. See Andrew Buncombe, "CIA 'Ran Covert Missions' to stop Communist Coup," *The Independent* (London), April 5, 2002.

Joseph Savimbi led UNITA in a civil war against the MPLA in most of the 27 years (there were a few cease-fires) between 1975 and 2002 (he was killed in 2002).[68] During this war about one million people died (out of a 1990 population of 8.4 million) and some 40 percent of Angola's total land area was covered with landmines and other unexploded munitions. Joseph Savimbi's UNITA was remarkable also for its extremely aggressive propaganda radio, The Voice of the Black Cockerel; it produced a very strong sound, it seemed to move its location or locations, and it probably had CIA assistance. American CIA assistance to UNITA in fact ended in 1993, but the Black Cockerel's loud voice continued.

Malawi and Zambia are the only two other mainland countries in southern Africa (as defined here). Malawi is a small, poor, mountainous country with weak mass media. Somewhat more formidable were the media of Zambia with its copper wealth. Both Zambia and its media were for some decades widely admired in Europe. Kenneth Kaunda presided over Zambia's first 27 years of independence (1964–1991). Kaunda was another "enlightened despot" who ran a one-party regime, which avoided civil war as well as large scale violence. Kaunda lost Zambia's 1991 election and left office peacefully. There are several excellent studies about the Zambian media,[69] a significant market for, not rival to, the much stronger South African media. In 1993 South African radio was listened to "regularly" by 33 percent of the Zambian population; the next most popular of the foreign radio stations in Zambia were the BBC (23 percent) Malawi radio, Zimbabwe radio, Voice of America (7 percent), and Tanzania radio.

From 1993–1994 onward, major changes took place both in South Africa's domestic and export media. In the newspaper press, domination by two large newspaper groups continued; but in one group, the Irish Independent/ Tony O'Reilly company became the chief owner, and all of the newspaper groups (including the two long-time leading Afrikaans-language press groups) acquired significant black African shareholdings. The English-language press—and the Afrikaans press more reluctantly—"changed sides" to support President Mandela and his ANC government. There followed the obvious dilemma: Under newly democratic conditions, how far should a free (and still largely white) press go in criticizing a democratically elected

---

[68] Sousa Jamba, "Portrait of a Rebel," *BBC Focus on Africa*, April–June 2002: 11–13; "War, Peace, War," *The Economist*, November 7, 1992: 73–77; Muyiwa Moyela, "Angola: Wealth and Poverty in the Mix," *Africa Today*, February 2002: 42–47.

[69] Graham Mytton, *Mass Communication in Africa*, London: Edward Arnold, 1983: 73–92; Francis Peter Kasoma, *The Press in Zambia*, Lusaka: Multimedia Publications, 1986; Robert C. Moore, *The Political Reality of Freedom of the Press in Zambia*, New York: University Press of America, 1992; Francis P. Kasoma, "Press Freedom in Zambia," in Festus Eribo and William Jung-Ebut (eds.), *Press Freedom and Communication in Africa*, Trenton, NJ: Africa World Press, 1997; Debra Spitulnik, "Mobile Machines and Fluid Audiences," in Faye D. Ginsburg, Lila Abu-Lughod, and Brian Larkin (eds.), *Media Worlds*, Berkeley: University of California Press, 2002: 337–54.

government?[70] On several issues—not least HIV/AIDS—the press found itself in conflict with Mandela's successor, President Mbeki.

In both TV and radio there were other post-apartheid dilemmas. Although white power was diluted by new legislation and regulation, the spirit of "reconciliation" was still extended not only to English, but also to Afrikaans, radio and TV. So South African broadcasting finance was split between large amounts of English, Afrikaans, and multi-African-language broadcasting. Because so many South Africans (especially blacks but also Afrikaners) spoke English—as a non–mother tongue language—the senior broadcasting language was English. The combination of extensive broadcasting hours, and English as the lead language, created ideal conditions for Hollywood exporters.

A second dilemma concerned "public service" programming and funding. Post-apartheid South Africa developed its own mix of public and commercial broadcasting. Public service rules required broadcasters to follow the goal of national reconciliation; in some cases this generated somewhat formulaic programming, as fictional characters from contrasted ethnic backgrounds learned to live, argue, and laugh together. But, as elsewhere, commercialization accompanied democracy, and a trend toward privatization (especially in radio) made advertising ever more important. The license fee had become somewhat ineffective in the last days of apartheid—as both rebellious blacks and rebellious whites had refused to pay up. When advertising became the dominant source of revenue, the programmers were forced to target much programming at whites and the affluent black minority (for whom advertisers were willing to pay higher rates). The leading public channel in the early 2000s was SABC1, which carried mainly English-language programming. It also carried a lot of imports, especially from Hollywood.[71]

Toward a Nollywood–South Africa Media Connection

Africa will probably continue to provide Hollywood with some of its highest audience shares. As more African households get more television channels, Hollywood will be invited to play its traditional export role of filling some of the otherwise yawning gaps in the TV schedule. Many educated Africans

[70] Douglas Foster, "Letter from Johannesburg: The Trouble with Transformation," *Columbia Journalism Review*, September/October 2004: 39–45.
[71] Eric Louw and Naren Chitty, "South Africa's Miracle Cure: A Stage-Managed TV Spectacular?" in Abbas Malek and Anandam P. Kavoori (eds.), *The Global Dynamics of News*, Stamford, CT: Ablex, 2000: 277–96; Abebe Zegeye and Richard Harris, "Media, Identity and the Public Sphere in Post-Apartheid South Africa: An Introduction," in Abede Zegeye and Richard Harris (eds.), *Media, Identity and Public Sphere in Post-Apartheid South Africa*, Leiden: Brill 2003: 1–25; Robert B. Horwitz, *Communication and Democratic Reform in South Africa*, Cambridge, UK: Cambridge University Press, 2001.

will probably prefer to pick and choose among imports from Euro-America rather than follow the simple offerings on the local national channels. CNN and the BBC appear to receive especially strong attention from African political elites. These (and other Anglo TV news offerings) may provide an attractive mix of political entertainment, information, and education. African countries can neither afford big diplomatic services nor employ many foreign correspondents. CNN, BBC, and other news services can perhaps fill some of the gap.

But Hollywood and the other Anglo-Americans will not be the only exporters. Another exporter may be the Nigerian film industry, while a third exporter may be South African–based satellite services. Lagos/Nigeria and Johannesburg/South Africa have the critical mass, and the commercial experience, to expand their considerable media export activities.

Nigeria's most remarkable media innovation of the 1990s was a new film industry that rapidly produced many hundreds of "feature films" made cheaply on videotape. These were something very different from what had previously passed for "African film." Before they departed, the British had set up several colonial "film units" that were modeled on the British public information films of 1939–1945 and reflected the colonial government's information priorities;[72] these British efforts obviously ceased at independence. Most "African films" after 1960 were made in former French colonies and were produced (and given limited distribution) with French government cultural finance. "African film" effectively became a minor genre within French film.[73]

Differing radically from francophone African Film, the Nigerian video film industry was not subsidised. These Nigerian films were commercial and entertainment oriented; they filled an entertainment gap between imported feature film and a Nigerian television industry, which suffered financially in the mid-1990s. By the late 1990s, Nigeria was making over 200 video films per year, typically between two and six hours in length; the annual total may have reached 2,000 by 2004.[74]

These films incorporated typical soap-melodrama themes, including plenty of sex and marital discord, expensive clothes and Mercedes, as well as magic, witchcraft, and other supernatural elements. Many films were made in Lagos, sub-Saharan Africa's largest city. By 1999 most cinemas in Lagos were showing these video films. The video films were also distributed via

[72] J. M. Burns, *Flickering Shadows: Cinema and Identity in Colonial Zimbabwe*, Athens: Ohio University Press, 2002.

[73] Roy Armes, "Film as an Authentic Expression of Francophone Africa," *Media Development*, 1, 1993: 3–5; Angela Martin, *African Films: The Context of Production*, British Film Institute (BFI Dossier, number 6), 1982; Manthia Diawara, "Senegal," in Gorham Kindem (ed.), *The International Movie Industry*, Carbondale: Southern Illinois University Press, 2000: 117–39.

[74] Bryan Pearson, "Nigeria: Rebounding Biz Goes Straight to Video," *Variety*, July 9, 2001; Nosa Owens-Ibie, "How Video Films Developed in Nigeria," *Media Development*, 1, 1998: 39–42; Christelle de Jager, " 'Brother' Star in Feature," *Variety*, March 1–7, 2004.

retail video shops (both for sale and rental). There was by year 2000 plenty of film publicity on radio and TV, in the general press, and in a spate of magazines devoted to video and video stars. Most videos were produced within seven days. Often actors received no payment; actors performed in each others' films without pay, with the individual lead filmmaker perhaps selling all rights in the film to a distributor. This movie industry had elements similar to the Indian film industry of the 1940s. Most facts and numbers in this Nigerian film business were, in the early years, either inflated or deflated, often in order to attract publicity or to defraud partners.

Most of the mid-1990s video films were in Yoruba, but both Igbo and Hausa film production businesses followed. A video film may be predominantly in Yoruba but can also include English phrases and sentences as well as some characters who speak urban Nigerian "pidgin English." The major foreign influences on Nigerian video film are American and British soap operas, Brazilian and Mexican *telenovelas*, and Indian feature films. The main domestic influences are Yoruba traveling theater and Nigerian television; film plots are often taken from newspaper stories or from Nigerian novels or plays.

The Indian film industry connection is especially strong in the northern, Hausa-language, branch of Nigerian video film. Hausa films (like Indian films) focus heavily on such themes as arranged marriage versus romantic love. Indian films have been popular in the Hausa-speaking north, partly because they appeal equally to the young male cinema audience and the young female home video audience. Young Hausa men may watch an Indian film in a cinema where prostitutes openly solicit customers. But video has also enabled young Muslim women to view Indian films at home and to adopt some of the dress styles of Indian movie stars.[75]

In the early 2000s, the new Nigerian film industry became more organized both internally and externally. Within Nigeria the film industry gradually introduced better (and slightly less cutthroat) business practices. Also the Nigerian films increasingly developed strong export markets in other Anglo countries, such as Ghana and Zambia. The Nigerian, or Nollywood, films carry themes that resonate across the continent; the witchcraft theme, common in Nigerian films, resonates as a possible explanation for the tragedy, ambition, kin conflict, and deprivation of urban Africa.

As Nigerian films have reached out to other countries across Africa, so also have satellite TV services based in South Africa. By 2002 there were already some 250 TV channels being transmitted by 22 satellites across Africa; 86 of these channels were in French, about 100 in English, and 30 in Arabic. Despite this big available array of satellite channels, less than 2 percent

---

[75] Brian Larkin, "Hausa Dramas and Video Culture in Nigeria," in Jonathan Haynes (ed.), *Nigerian Video Films*, Athens: Ohio University Center for International Studies, 2000 ed.: 209–38; Françoise Balogun, "Booming Videoeconomy," in Françoise Pfaff (ed.), *Focus on African Films*, Bloomington: Indiana University Press, 2004: 173–84.

of African households were receiving whole satellite channels (by any technology).[76]

However, multichannel television was already well established as part of the affluent African lifestyle. Moreover, most television viewers across Africa were receiving smaller doses of TV via satellite. The South African satellite services had retransmission agreements with many television services across Africa to carry a few hours per day or per week.[77]

In 2002 the leading South African satellite service was Multichoice, which had contracts with TV services in over 30 African countries. Four of the most popular genres of transnational African television were sports, game shows, soaps, and films. Many people watched both African and European football.

Reality television was beginning by 2003 to exploit some of the continental possibilities. In May 2003 Africa was offered *Big Brother Africa*, with 12 young men and women, each from a different African country; all but one (Angola) of these countries were former British, and thus Anglophone, countries— including Nigeria, Ghana, Kenya, Uganda, and Tanzania. This first (Endemol produced) *Big Brother Africa* ran for 106 days; M-net (Johannesburg) claimed a daily 30 million audience across 46 countries. The winner, a 24-year-old Zambian woman, received $100,000.[78]

Also popular across Africa were soap operas. South Africa had quite a strong supply of soaps, but satellite offered soap drama series from western Africa, from France, from Britain, and from Globo in Brazil; in addition most African TV viewers could view American five-day-a-week soaps.

These multichannel services provided great opportunities, also, for other American programming, including Hollywood movies. It is against these Hollywood movies that Nigerian movies will have to compete. The Nollywood movies cannot compete with Hollywood in terms of traditional expensive production values. However, the Nigerian films have been created and market-tested in Africa's most populous country. Many Africans— including even South African university students—prefer African drama, music, and sports to American drama, music, and sports.[79]

---

[76] Helen Muchimba and Modupe Ogunbayo, "Nollywood Special," *BBC Focus on Africa*, October–December 2004: 46–50; Ike Oguine, "Nollywood Looks to the Future," *New Internationalist*, October 2004: 372; Sarah Duguid, "Tales from the Backyard," *Sight and Sound*, October 2004: 8–10.

[77] Graham Mytton, Ruth Teer-Tomaselli, and André-Jean Tudesq, "Transnational Television in Sub-Saharan Africa," in Jean Chalaby (ed.), *Transnational Television Worldwide*, London: I.B. Tauris, 2004: 96–127.

[78] Sara Bakata, "What Chance for EA in the Big Brother House?" *East African*, June 2–8, 2003; David Short, "Formats Prove S. Africa's Strongest Link," *Television Business International*, October/November 2003: 24; Marc Lacey, "Reality TV Houses Africa Under One Roof," *International Herald Tribune* (from *NY Times*), September 10, 2003; Christelle de Jager, " 'Big Bro' Gives Reality New Meaning," *Variety*, September, 15–21, 2003.

[79] Larry Strelitz, "Media Consumption and Identity Formation: The Case of the 'Homeland' Viewers," in Gitte Stald and Thomas Tufte (eds.), *Global Encounters: Media and Cultural Transformation*, Luton, UK: University of Luton Press, 2002: 153–71.

In some francophone Western African countries multichannel television is better established than in any of the anglophone countries except South Africa. Multichannel TV is cheaper in the francophone countries, partly because most of it is financed (and subsidized) by France in particular, but also by Canada (Quebec) and Belgium.

The significance of price can also be seen in mobile telephony. The mobile cell phone revolution in Africa (and especially in South Africa) has been dramatic, not least because subscribers can pay in advance, even if they lack credit cards and bank accounts.[80]

In sub-Saharan Africa, the United States, France, and Britain all seem likely to have their most impressive media export performances—at least in terms of market share, although not in revenue.

---

[80] Mark Ashurst, Arnaud Zaijtman, Will Ross, and Joseph Warungu, "Mobile Revolution," *BBC Focus on Africa*, January–March 2004: 19–25.

PART 4

NATIONAL MEDIA AND WORLD REGION MEDIA

16

National Media System as Lead Player

Three chapters in this last part of the book consider additional world regions (or subregions)—the Arab countries, Spanish America, and the former Soviet Union (and Yugoslavia). Each of these regions is an additional example of the pecking order analysis of previous chapters.

In each of these cases, there is some kind of common language and a significant element of regionwide media in that language. However, the break-up of the Soviet Union (and Yugoslavia) has replaced 2 nation states with 21 nation states. Meanwhile the Arab bloc, Spanish America, the former Soviet Union, and the former Yugoslavia now constitute 56 nation-states, each with its own national media projecting its own national culture (old and new).

This chapter argues that, over the last 200 years, the nation-state has been the leading media player. The media have typically had a salient role in conflicts (and alliances) between nation-states and empires. Small weekly newspapers played a leading role in the 1770s, as the North American colonies asserted their independence from London and the British Empire.

Around 1880–1914 many of the now large national newspapers in France, Britain, and other European countries expressed their belligerent patriotism with loud enthusiasm for further imperial expansion.

In the two decades after 1945, European empires handed over to insurgent nationalist movements, in which newspapers played a salient part. After independence the new national media were required to participate actively in strengthening government power and in establishing a new national culture. In most cases a specific colony was transformed into a new nation-state, with the same boundaries, the same ethnic composition, and the same colonial name.

But this chapter also considers two other examples—the "Asian Tigers," Malaysia and Taiwan—where an exact colony-into-nation-state transfor-mation did not occur. In both of these more "accidental" new nation-states, strong government-guided media were given an especially prominent role in combining two or three major ethnic identities into a single nation-state.

Here we see the mass media as occupying no less than five levels, from a *world* level down to a *local* level that may involve fewer than one million people.

The *world*, or global, level is clearly significant for the media; it is especially important for finance and trade. The world level is also vital for media finance and media technology. Clearly American media in the mid-twentieth century had a significant amount of global reach. But, even by 1950, Hollywood and U.S. media were almost completely shut out of China, southern Asia, and the Soviet bloc. Since then, this book argues, the American share of the world media audience has (despite an upward blip or two) been in decline. Technology and "new media" continue to be important and to spread globally; so also do media genres such as soap drama or all-news television. But what is actually consumed continues to be very different in different parts of the world; and what is perceived, for example, by most Arabs or most Indians or most Chinese, is very different from what is perceived by most Americans or Germans.

Four other "lower" levels are collectively much more important than the global or world level.

- *The world region, or group of nation-states.* Examples of regions include eastern Asia, southern Asia, the Arab world, and Euro-America. Overlapping with these are some former empire-based groups.

- *The nation-state level* continues to be the most important level; the nation-state is especially salient in the 11 biggest population countries (from China to Mexico and including the United States), which have about 60 percent of the world's people. The nation-state level is also the key level for most middling states of 40–100 million population, in which 20 percent of the world's people live.

- *The national regional* level is significant for most of the world's people; these regions include regional "states" or provinces within federal systems such as India, Nigeria, and Germany. Distinctive languages, histories, and religions may be relevant. In both large and medium population countries substantial mass media elements exist at this level.

- Finally, *the local level* can be extremely important and often involves a distinct language spoken by one million people or less. At the end of the twentieth century there were said to be some 6,000 languages—many of them in remote areas of New Guinea, in India and Pakistan, in the two big archipelago nations (Philippines and Indonesia), in the Congo and Amazon river basins and tropical forests, and around the Himalayan and Andes mountains. The local level can also involve local population fragments left behind—as in Eastern Europe—by previous empires. At this level there is typically at most only a modest media element (such as weekly newspapers and perhaps some radio);[1] often there is no formal education in the local language. These local enclaves and their media are under threat; however, they are under threat not by global or American media but from the national government, the national media, and the national education system. They may also, as in the Philippines,[2] be under threat from the national army and police, perhaps on a "terrorist" threat, or separatist threat, basis.

Individual human identity is, of course, a separate issue. Many people have two or more identities. Especially common is a twin identity such as Tamil Indian or Catalan Spanish.

The nation-state is usually the most important media level because the media are linked to political power, education (including language teaching), and general culture. The nation-state level is also especially important because the national media typically incorporate some news, entertainment, and education from the other levels. A national newspaper or national TV channel typically includes some world and world region material; many national media also provide some regional and/or local material in the form of locally printed editions, local TV news, weather, sports, and local politics.

The nation-state itself is very far from being a fixed entity. But Benedict Anderson's concept of "imagined communities" lacks clarity. Both "community" and "imagined" are notoriously vague terms. National histories and identities are not just imagined; some media term such as "versioned" might be more appropriate. Many nation-states in Africa and Asia are exact successors to previous colonies; this is historical fact, not imagination. In some respects the older social anthropology concept of the "mythical charter" may be more valid; a tribe or people explained their relationship to other tribes, to the animals, to the mountains and rivers in a spoken "history" that in some cases sounded like the biblical Genesis. The "mythical charter" is an explanation for facts—including ethnicity and kinship—that exist on the ground.

Nation-states educate their children, and fill their media, with a biased selection, or self-regarding version, of established history. New regimes often decide to introduce a different version of that national history; this can lead to rewritten school history books, fresh "advice" to the media, and the temporary closure of national museums (while the exhibits, and explanations, are rearranged). But the key facts of the colonial history, and the territory of the ex-colonial nation, typically remain; its inhabitants and ethnic groups also remain the same (at least in the short run).

The media have played a major role in the conduct of wars and civil wars; the media are significant in anointing the winners and the losers in war.

---

[1] Donald R. Browne, *Ethnic Minorities, Electronic Media and the Public Sphere: A Comparative Study*, Cresskill, NJ: Hampton Press, 2005.
[2] Carlos H. Conde, "Reporting Without Understanding," *Media Asia*, Vol. 29/2, 2002: 67–70.

The media are also deeply involved in diaspora, the spreading out—and sometimes pulling back—of migrants. All three of these often happen on a nation-state-to-nation-state basis, and within a specific world region.

Most recent wars have been between close neighbors (such as Germany against France, Japan against China, or Israel against Arab states). The most obvious losers in war tend to be kept in subordination or are ethnically cleansed and then expelled across a nearby border; the media typically applaud, or simply ignore, what's happening.

Diasporas are often claimed to exemplify the role of satellite television, and other modern media, in accelerating globalization. True, some diasporas are long distance. But the biggest diasporas of recent decades have been within single world regions—for example, the Chinese diaspora in Southeast Asia and the southern Asian diaspora in the Indian Ocean and the Persian Gulf regions. Turkey-to-Europe or Mexico-to-United States diasporas are relatively short distance. The big European migrations into North and South America have helped to sustain what this book sees as a single Euro-American world region.

1776: Newspapers and a New Nation

It is sometimes assumed that the newspaper started locally and only later became international. The reverse is more accurate—the newspaper was initially international, as foreign news moved around Europe, especially through Venice in the sixteenth century and through Amsterdam in the seventeenth century. Later (after 1800) the newspaper became more national; and finally it became local as well.[3]

Before 1776 much American news was about Britain and Europe.[4] On the continent of Europe, the largest newspaper press was in French, but, previous to the French Revolution of 1789, most French-language newspapers were published outside of France—especially in Germany, Holland, and Britain.[5] Governments censored domestic news, which they saw as politically dangerous, but foreign news was regarded as relatively harmless. Even in Britain, where government control was fairly relaxed, it was still safer to publish foreign, rather than domestic, news; provincial weekly newspapers published a lot of foreign news (usually taken out of the London dailies).[6]

---

[3] Hannah Barker and Simon Burrows (eds.), *Press, Politics and the Public Sphere in Europe and North America, 1760–1820*, Cambridge, UK: Cambridge University Press, 2002; Anthony Smith, *The Newspaper: An International History*, London: Thames and Hudson, 1979.

[4] Al Hester, Susan Parker Humes, and Christopher Bickers, "Foreign News in Colonial North American Newspapers, 1764–1775," *Journalism Quarterly*, Vol. 57/1, Spring 1980: 18–22, 44.

[5] Jack R. Censer and Jeremy D. Popkin (eds.), *Press and Politics in Pre-Revolutionary France*, Berkeley: University of California Press, 1987; Bob Harris, *Politics and the Rise of the Press: Britain and France, 1620–1800*, London: Routledge, 1996.

[6] Jeremy Black, *The English Press in the Eighteenth Century*, London: Croom, Helm, 1987: 238.

Both Britain and its North American colonies experienced rapid growth in newspaper sales in the eighteenth century. In Britain severe censorship was replaced with taxes and subsidies (to government-friendly publications). By the 1770s London published some nine daily papers, as well as three-times-a-week newspapers intended for delivery to the provinces. Probably about 250,000 London-printed newspapers were sold each week. London coffeehouses were regarded with astonishment by European visitors because the London coffee drinkers seemed to talk so little and to read the newspapers so obsessively; when they did talk—it was also observed—these London coffee drinkers' conversation tended to focus on topics provided by the newspapers.[7]

An obsessive fixation on newspaper news was also starting to appear in the American colonies. By 1776 there were still no American dailies, but in the port cities (especially Boston and Philadelphia) there was a weekly newspaper publishing explosion. There were 17 American weekly papers in 1760, 39 by 1780, and 210 in 1800.[8] In the early 1770s there were about 360,000 households that purchased about 60,000 newspapers per week. With newspapers being passed between households (and also read aloud), probably the majority of American adults read (or heard read) at least one newspaper per month.

These American newspapers helped to build up and then to break up the British Empire. Previous to the early 1760s the British (and their newspapers) and the Anglo-American colonists (and their newspapers) were allied in the French and Indian wars of 1756–1763. The American papers deferred to the London papers by reprinting much London news and comment; the colonial printers pirated the work of London celebrity-essayists, political commentators, and radical critics. The flow of newspaper material was almost entirely a one-way flow, meaning that London politicians knew relatively little about the colonies (especially quick-changing public opinion), whereas the colonists were better informed about London politics and London disputes over colonial policy. The Stamp Act[9] (passed by the London Parliament in March 1765) was unintentionally, but perfectly, designed to antagonize (and to unite) several key colonial occupations—especially the lawyers, the printers, and the merchants. In the decade 1765–1775 something happened that has been crucial in many subsequent colonial independence movements; the American newspapers "changed sides," from approving of empire to opposing empire.

The newspapers helped to create the new nation and went on to sustain the new United States; the newspapers helped to convert broadly contented

[7] Michael Harris, "The Structure, Ownership and Control of the Press, 1620–1780," in George Boyce, James Curran, and Pauline Wingate (eds.), *Newspaper History*, London: Constable, and Beverly Hills: Sage, 1978: 82–97; Michael Harris, *London Newspapers in the Age of Walpole*, London: Associated University Presses, 1987.

[8] Bruce M. Owen, *Economics and Freedom of Expression*. Cambridge, MA: Ballinger, 1975: 64.

[9] Theodore Draper, *A Struggle for Power: The American Revolution*, London: Abacus, 1997.

colonists into often passionate patriots of the emerging new nation. A big majority of the colonists originated from Britain and were demanding that, although resident in America, they were entitled to British rights. The majority spoke English as their mother language and were Protestant Christians. Few of the colonists were very rich or very poor; most were farmers working on land not far from a big river or the sea. The leaders of the colonists were colonial gentry landowners (like George Washington), lawyers, merchants, and printers. In addition to more formal meetings, these leaders often met in newspaper offices where they could smell both printers' ink and salt water. John Adams moved around the colonies, mounting a sequence of newspaper attacks on the governors of specific colonies. Benjamin Franklin had been another highly mobile member of the colonial elite;[10] in addition to his Renaissance man accomplishments (as diplomat, sage, and inventor) Franklin was instrumental in launching new newspaper titles and became America's first important press entrepreneur. In 1775–1776, at the start of the insurrection, Franklin was a leader in transforming some small scattered newspapers into a formidable revolutionary machine.

Previous to 1750 the small American newspapers had been more concerned with religion than with political news; but after 1760 the papers increasingly concerned themselves with political news about the latest British outrage.[11] The colonial newspapers orchestrated the many voices of protest, as Arthur Schlesinger wrote:

> The press, that is to say, instigated, catalyzed and synthesized the many other forms of propaganda and action. It trumpeted the doings of Whig committees, publicized rallies and mobbings, promoted partisan fast days and anniversaries, blazoned patriotic speeches and toasts, popularized anti-British slogans, gave wide currency to ballads and broadsides, furthered the persecution of Tories, reprinted London news of the government's intentions concerning America and, in general, created an atmosphere of distrust and enmity that made reconciliation increasingly difficult. Besides, the newspapers dispensed a greater volume of political and constitutional argument than all the other media combined.
>
> As Benjamin Franklin pointed out, the press could present the "same truths" repeatedly in "different lights" and hence not only "strike while the iron is hot" but "heat it continually by striking." . . .
>
> Perhaps most important of all, the press bore the principal brunt of the struggle for liberty of expression and so emboldened patriots everywhere to speak their minds.[12]

10 *The Autobiography of Benjamin Franklin, and Selections from His Other Writings*, New York: Random House, 1950.

11 Thomas L. Leonard, *The Power of the Press: The Birth of American Political Reporting*, New York: Oxford University Press, 1986: 13–59; Jack P. Greene and J. R. Pole (eds.), *A Companion to the American Revolution*, Oxford: Blackwell, 2000.

12 Arthur M. Schlesinger, *Prelude to Independence: The Newspaper War on Britain, 1764–1776*, New York: Knopf, 1958: 46–47.

The Declaration of Independence was signed and agreed on July 4, 1776. The Declaration was printed on a Philadelphia newspaper press; Thomas Jefferson and Benjamin Franklin helped the printer in the correction of typographical errors. Printed copies were dispatched to all of the colonial newspapers and, by July 20, most of the newspapers had printed the Declaration of Independence in full.

The Revolutionary War found the American and the British newspapers giving very different accounts of the fighting. The war effectively commenced at Lexington and Concord (near Boston) on April 19, 1775 and lasted until 1783. Many years later Ralph Waldo Emerson wrote:

Here once the embattled farmers stood,
And fired the shot heard round the world.

The shot was "heard" through newspapers that crossed the Atlantic to London, Amsterdam, and other European locations. News of the American war received big coverage, not least in French-language newspapers. The gallant colonists resisting the evil British redcoats (and their German mercenary allies) made a wonderfully "good story" for editors around Europe. Casualties were heavy; the fearless George Washington and the Marquis de Lafayette made excellent war heroes; most of the fighting took place close to the main coastal newspaper publishing locations. Just as the American military eventually won the war, the American newspapers won the publicity battle.

As occurred after many other subsequent colonial independence struggles, the American newspapers also played a part in dealing with losers. After independence, the Indians lost their protected areas across the Appalachians, and the newspapers were enthusiastic boosters for this western expansion. African slaves were not beneficiaries of the bold words and high ideals of the Declaration of Independence.[13] The newspapers were part of the slavery system, and slave advertisements (dealing both with fresh young slaves for sale and requests for the return of escaped slaves) were common in newspapers as far north as Philadelphia.[14] Also among the losers were the Tories, who had remained loyal to London and opposed independence. In the build-up to the war, the newspapers increasingly printed excerpts from the private correspondence of prominent Tories; since most newspaper printers were also official postmasters, this mail intercept operation was easily achieved. While Tories were abused and humiliated, few were killed; however, unrepentant Tories were forced to flee (to Canada or the West Indies or back to Britain) and they thus lost their homes and other property. As in many independence movements, the largest local group (the expatriate

---

[13] Simon Schama, *Rough Crossings: Britain, the Slaves and the American Revolution*, London: BBC Books, 2005.

[14] Darold D. Wax, "The Image of the Negro in the *Maryland Gazette*, 1745–75," *Journalism Quarterly*, Vol. 46/1, Spring 1969: 73–80, 86.

British) won; they controlled all the key resources, including the media. Several significant minority groups lost.[15] In 1788–1789 a Constitution was agreed, the first U.S. Congress met, and George Washington was inaugurated as president. At this time the famous *Federalist Papers* were appearing; most of the papers were originally published as newspaper articles and were then widely reprinted. In 1791 the first 10 amendments to the Constitution were adopted, and one of these amendments provided for the freedom of speech, religion, and the press. This was also before the French Revolution had yet had any significant impact on America.[16] The newspapers celebrated a freedom that did not apply to blacks, Tories, or the indigenous population.

The central role of the newspaper press in North America—especially in generating and guiding new nationalist enthusiasm—is relatively unambiguous. The press was also important in independence in Mexico and in other Latin American countries; but this overall picture was much more chaotic, and the precise role of the press less clear. Mexico was effectively more remote because news from Europe took much longer to reach (inland) Mexico City than to reach Boston. In 1800 New Spain (soon to become independent Mexico) included much of the present-day United States west of the Mississippi; of its total seven million population only one million were Spanish whites. There were really two conflicts—one between the Indians and the Spanish and another between Spanish settlers and the Spanish officials and soldiers. Mexico City, with 170,000 inhabitants in 1810, was the largest city in the Americas and a high proportion of its male residents were entitled to vote. There were also substantial numbers of very small circulation newspapers, which were party and election oriented. Mexico City newspapers could report on the activities of the American continent's oldest opera house and most ancient university.[17] These newspapers were active in the 1810–1830 Mexican independence era.

Several media aspects of the American independence era have also been present in other eras, and in the present time. The media both help to build up, and to knock down, empires. The national media tend to operate alongside both new and old nation-states. The media are involved in what happens before, during, and after war. Export or diaspora media can lead to immigrant media, which then become the established national media of a new nation-state.

---

[15] Ray Raphael, *The American Revolution: A People's History*, London: Profile Books, 2001.

[16] Lloyd S. Kramer, "The French Revolution and the Creation of American Political Culture," in Joseph Klaits and Michael H. Haltzel (eds.), *The Global Ramifications of the French Revolution*, Washington, DC: Woodrow Wilson Center Press and Cambridge University Press, 1994: 26–54.

[17] Eric Van Young, *The Other Rebellion: Popular Violence, Ideology and the Mexican Struggle for Independence, 1810–1821*, Stanford, CA: Stanford University Press, 2001; Richard A. Warren, *Vagrants and Citizens: Politics and the Masses in Mexico City from Colony to Republic*, Wilmington, DE: Scholarly Resources, 2001; Robert Harvey, *Liberators: South America's Savage Wars of Freedom, 1810–30*, London: Constable and Robinson, 2002.

Big in 1900: Press, Nation-States, Empires, Diaspora

Before the 1914–1918 war, larger newspaper industries had grown up alongside a number of new, or newly assertive, nation-states—including the United States, Britain, France, Germany, Japan, and Russia. In all of these nation-states, large popular newspapers loudly supported not only the nation but also the nation's new and growing empire. Press censorship had been greatly reduced;[18] European monarchies indulged in refurbished ritual and in increasingly media-oriented ostentatious display. This was an era of wars, most of which the new big national presses stridently supported. The period around 1900 saw the biggest migrations in modern history (on a percentage of population basis) and some of the largest diaspora and emigrant media movements.

The first daily newspaper to sell one million copies was the Parisian *Le Petit Journal* in 1890, following the removal of the last French newspaper tax in 1886. By 1915 Japan—with a 4.5 million daily sale—was, along with the United States, France, Britain, and Germany, one of the five leading press powers. In tsarist Russia in 1915, Saint Petersburg and Moscow dailies together sold 1.6 million daily copies; the Moscow daily, *Russkoe Slovo*, briefly sold one million daily copies in 1917.[19] These newspapers grew alongside some big increases in the electoral franchise.

New populist newspapers in Europe and Japan tended to copy especially New York, but also London and Paris, models. Serial fiction was extremely important; so were crime, court cases, women's pages (including fashion), advice columns, gossip, Did You Know? trivia, wars, elections, and sports.[20]

Similar in their broad content categories, these populist newspapers were nationalistic and jingoist in their coverage, not only of war, but of their monarchies. The British monarchy was active in relaunching, or inventing, traditional ceremonies;[21] this was believed to be essential in order to attract the public, the newspapers, and the photographers. But the German, Austrian, Hungarian, and Italian governments in 1910 all spent more money on their monarchies than Edward VII received from his government in London. The next highest spenders on their monarchies were Spain (sixth), Japan (seventh), and Bavaria (eighth). Royal reporting before 1914 was stridently nationalist, international, and highly sensitive. Edward VII (who in 1901

---

[18] Robert Justin Goldstein, *Political Censorship of the Arts and the Press in Nineteenth Century Europe*, London: Macmillan, 1989.

[19] Louise McReynolds, *The News Under Russia's Old Regime*, Princeton, NJ: Princeton University Press, 1991.

[20] Michael Oriard, *Reading Football: How the Popular Press Created an American Spectacle*, Chapel Hill: University of North Carolina Press, 1993.

[21] David Cannadine, "The Context, Performance and Meaning of Ritual: The British Monarchy and the 'Invention of Tradition,' c. 1820–1977," in Eric Hobsbawm and Terence Ranger (eds.), *The Invention of Tradition*, Cambridge UK: Cambridge University Press, 1983: 100–64.

succeeded Queen Victoria) was not seen by London editors as a big problem
—since "everyone" knew about his affairs with married women, and the
press did not report such things. Wilhelm II, the German kaiser (1888–1918),
posed more difficult reporting problems. First, he also had affairs with
married women. Second, "everyone" in the European elite knew that his
"best friend," Philipp Eulenburg, and other close friends, were homosexual.
Third, the kaiser worried his relatives (including his grandmother Queen
Victoria) because he was unstable and given to extreme anger.[22]

The late nineteenth century saw the emergence of important new
nation-states (such as Germany and Italy) and newly industrializing
important states (notably Japan). These "new" (but old) nations quickly
became important military and industrial powers. They had monarchies
and modern newspaper industries. But, to be like France and Britain, they
also needed empires.

Jingoistic nationalism, empire building, and a populist newspaper press
reinforced each other—and not least in Britain and France. Even France,
before 1870, was scarcely yet a nation; many French people in the 1860s did
not in fact speak French or think of themselves as French, and very few of
the big rural population yet read a newspaper. But by 1914 most French
adults did speak French, were literate, had been to school, and did think of
themselves as French; many read one of the four large sale Parisian daily
papers—*Le Petit Journal*, *Le Petit Parisien*, *Le Figaro*, and *Le Matin*. Readers of
these newspapers received regular news from France's extensive colonial
empire. News from much of Africa, and from Indo-China, reached the world
largely through the Paris-based Havas news agency.[23]

The years before and after 1900 saw the "Scramble for Africa" with Britain
and France leading the charge.[24] Although much less than universally popular
in Britain, the empire played a major role in the general elections of 1895 and
1900. Schools and homes were adorned with imperial imagery and on the
walls hung maps that (with Canada and Australia overblown) seemed to
award Britain a large fraction of world real estate. Children's comics, the
music halls, and most of the newspapers (popular and serious) kept up a
steady drumbeat of imperialism. For the 1897 Diamond Jubilee (60 years)
of Queen Victoria's reign, the *Daily Mail* (launched the previous year) offered
its readers a "golden extra," whose main headline was "Queen and Empire—
Pageant of Unparalleled Meaning and Significance." Inside were short
messages (dated the previous day) from 30 separate locations in the empire.
"Our own correspondent" claimed from Bombay that people met in

[22] John C. G. Röhl, *The Kaiser and His Court*, Cambridge, UK: Cambridge University Press, 1994 (first publ. in German in Munich by C.H.Beck, 1987).
[23] Michael B. Palmer, *Des Petits Journaux aux Grandes Agences*, Paris: Aubier Montaigne, 1983; "Le Papier Qui Parle," in Eugen Weber, *Peasants into Frenchmen: The Modernisation of Rural France, 1870–1914*, London: Chatto and Windus, 1977: 452–70.
[24] Thomas Pakenham, *The Scramble for Africa, 1876–1912*, New York: Random House, 1991.

"mosques, temples and churches and prayed long life and blessings on the benign reign of the Queen Empress."[25]

Most of these messages came from the Reuters news agency, whose historian describes it as an "imperial institution" in its "heyday" years of 1878–1914. The British state was the main owner of the world cable system, and Reuters news agency was a leading user of those cables. Reuters' imperial coverage specialized in short sharp facts, quotes from speeches made by colonial governors, stock market prices, and disasters (usually only reported if European lives had been lost). Reuters also specialized in "Queen Victoria's Little Wars"; during 1850–1900 British forces were engaged each year in an average of three or four separate actions, wars, or punitive expeditions in various remote corners of Africa and Asia.[26] The most spectacular colonial war coverage was of the South African Anglo-Boer War (1899–1902); the casualties (military and civilian) were huge and constituted more than a little war. Reuters deployed a large force of full-time correspondents and stringers;[27] the *Daily Mail* and other popular dailies also had their own correspondents. New heights, or depths, of patriotic jingoism were achieved by the London press. Reuters and other news was replayed around Europe, and around the world, under anti–British Empire headlines.

By 1914 the British, who had been among the first to pioneer (and then to stop) their Atlantic slave trade and "punitive expeditions," could lick their South African wounds and self-righteously decry the barbarity of several late-arriving imperialists. For patriotic British journalists the worst offenders here were the German colonizers (in what are now Tanzania, Cameroon, and Namibia) and the Italians (in Eritrea and Somalia).

Japan, also impatient to have its new empire, fought successful wars against China (1894–1895) and Russia (1904–1905). The rapidly growing Japanese press followed the New York and London models. As happened elsewhere, Japanese newspapers that worried about the wisdom or legitimacy of colonial wars tended to lose circulation and to collapse. The Japanese popular press liked to criticize the Japanese government for not being aggressive enough. Occasional massacres by Japanese soldiers were excused by the newspapers on the grounds of youthful patriotic exuberance. Fast news of Japanese victories went by cable (and generated extra editions), while background pieces (about our brave boys at the front) went by mail. Newspaper editorials and poems cheered on the gallant war effort.[28]

Yet another new imperial power was the United States. While the newspaper mogul William Randolph Hearst did not really cause the war to

[25] *Daily Mail*, June 23, 1897.
[26] Byron Farwell, *Queen Victoria's Little Wars*, London: Allen Lane, Penguin, 1973.
[27] Donald Read, *The Power of News: The history of Reuters*, Oxford, UK: Oxford University Press, 1992.
[28] J. L. Huffman, *Creating a Public: People and Press in Meiji Japan*, Honolulu: University of Hawaii Press, 1997.

happen, the Spanish-American War did overlap with the Hearst versus Pulitzer newspaper circulation wars in New York and other big U.S. cities. By 1903 the United States had picked up a modest colonial handful—the Philippines, Guam, Hawaii, Samoa, Cuba, and Puerto Rico. The American newspapers sent unprecedented numbers of foreign correspondents to these smallish wars. Literally hundreds of American correspondents, photographers, and artists covered the small Cuban War.[29]

The New York popular papers had already invented a completely new type of "foreign story"; newspapers financed and promoted most of the larger African and polar expeditions of this period. It was James Gordon Bennett (owner of the *New York Herald*) who in the early 1870s "discovered" both Africa and the Arctic. Bennett financed Henry Stanley's pursuit and finding of Dr. David Livingstone on the shore of Lake Tanganyika in November 1871. Bennett also became a financier of polar expeditions. These expeditions typically stretched over at least two years and were a kind of factual *telenovela* genre of the era. Competition to be first (with the news) led to exaggeration, dubious claims, and outright falsehood.[30] These stories were syndicated especially between the United States and Britain, but they also appeared in newspapers in other countries. There were large elements of American and British patriotism and self-congratulation, although Norwegians were the most consistently successful (polar) explorers.

While nationalism and press jingoism often accompanied the growth of empires around 1900, in the same period other empires were collapsing and new nations were being launched. The Russian, Austro-Hungarian, and Ottoman empires were all in trouble in the early twentieth century. At the end of the 1914–1918 war there was a massive rearrangement of national boundaries, nationalisms, and national media. The Austro-Hungarian Empire, in particular, was split up. The Versailles Treaty (1919) and the new League of Nations established new nations, including Finland, Estonia, Latvia, Lithuania, Czechoslovakia, Yugoslavia, and Ireland (Irish Free State). There were also new frontiers (Poland, Romania, and others); and several pieces of the tsarist Russian Empire were temporarily independent around 1917–1921 (Armenia, Georgia, Azerbaijan, Ukraine, and "White Russia").

The map of eastern European nationalisms and nation-states shifted drastically, not only before and after 1914–1918, but also during the war. The Germans and Austro-Hungarians made their biggest military gains to the east and captured all or most of today's Poland, Ukraine, Belarus, and Lithuania. Here, for a brief period, the German army engaged in some

---

[29] Robert W. Desmond, *The Information Process: World News Reporting to the Twentieth Century*, Iowa City: University of Iowa Press, 1978: 386–402; Nathaniel Lande, *Dispatches from the Front: A History of the American War Correspondent*, New York: Oxford University Press, 1998 ed.: 125–65.

[30] Beau Riffenburgh, *The Myth of the Explorer: The Press, Sensationalism and Geographical Discovery*, Oxford, England: Oxford University Press, 1994.

interesting nation-state and national media engineering. The Germans introduced into Poland and Lithuania a policy for dealing with subordinate nationalisms; this was a two-level and two-language policy—involving the positive encouragement of the local national language and culture, alongside German as the overarching language and culture. This two-level policy probably reflected recent German experience in Africa. The policy may also have influenced Lenin and Stalin, who introduced a similar two-level (local nation plus Russian) policy in the infant Soviet Union. The German nation builders (of 1915–1918) in Poland and Lithuania proclaimed one agreed standardized version of each local language; this extended to the German acceptance of Yiddish as the approved national language for Polish Jews. The official version of the local national language was to be taught in schools at the lower levels. For the Ober Ost (northeast) region of German occupation, seven local languages were accepted and standardized for school teaching. The German language was also compulsory in each ethnic group's schools. The German Ober Ost occupiers published their own newspapers in the seven languages; in September 1917 one independent Lithuanian language newspaper was allowed, but it was subject to censorship. Nevertheless, the Germans organized a conference intended to establish Lithuania as a political nation within the German Empire. The conference elected a council of 20 members, who audaciously (but unsuccessfully) declared Lithuania fully independent.[31] This heavy educational and political focus on the Lithuanian nation—and the appearance of Lithuanian language newspapers (at a time of high political excitement) strengthened Lithuanian identity and nationalist sentiment.

Not only was the 1870–1920 period an era of nationalist and imperialistic newspapers, it was also an era of "great" press moguls and "great" journalists. These seemingly towering figures personified the rise of the mass press. Often the "great" press individuals were journalists first and chain newspaper owners subsequently. Some of the "great editors" were journalists in partnership with a mogul owner; this was true of Hearst's relationship with his key editor, Arthur Brisbane. A somewhat similar partnership ran tsarist Russia's circulation leader *Russkoe Slovo*; the owner was I. D. Sytin (Russia's major book publisher), and the "great editor" was V. M. Doroshevich, whose only instruction was not to antagonize the censors.[32] This great editor's commentaries on his frequent travels also helped to divert attention from his dependence for foreign news on the agency cartel.[33]

[31] Aviel Roshwald, *Ethnic Nationalisms and the Fall of Empires: Central Europe, Russia and the Middle East, 1914–1923*, London: Routledge, 2001.

[32] Louise McReynolds, *The News Under Russia's Old Regime*, Princeton, NJ: Princeton University Press, 1991.

[33] Terhi Rantanen, *Foreign News in Imperial Russia*, University of Helsinki doctoral dissertation, 1990; see also Robert A. Bartol, "Alekse Suvorin: Russia's Millionaire Publisher," *Journalism Quarterly*, Vol. 51/3, Autumn 1974: 411–17, 462.

Another aspect of some "great journalists" was that they were not really journalists at all. Famous writers (such as Leo Tolstoy and Émile Zola) wrote for the papers; so also did the young soldier-politician Winston Churchill, who while an army officer reported on northwest frontier (India) campaigning for the *Daily Telegraph*; later he covered the South Africa War (1899–1902) for the London *Morning Post*.[34] These great writer-journalists tended to be great patriots, great nationalists, and great imperialists.

This pre-1914 era of combined nationalism and imperialism can also be seen as an era of globalization; there were huge international flows of capital, goods, and people. The biggest single population flow was from Europe into North America. As a percentage of the U.S. population in 1870 and 1950, the net migration into the United States was more than twice as big (39.3 percent) in 1870–1913 as the migration into the United States in 1950–1998 (16.4 percent).[35]

The American emigrant or diaspora media phenomenon in the years around 1900 was also on an impressively large scale. In 1914 the United States had 160 foreign-language daily newspapers; a big majority were in European languages—55 German-language dailies; 12 each in French, Italian, and Polish; 10 in Yiddish; 8 in Spanish; and 8 "Bohemian" (Czech) dailies. There were also over 2,000 English-language dailies at this time.[36] At least one American German and one Yiddish daily each had a circulation of over 200,000, but a more typical sale was 10,000 daily copies. The classic work on this topic (and on migrating media in general) is Robert Park's *The Immigrant Press and Its Control*,[37] published in 1922. Park, a founding father of academic sociology, was at the University of Chicago and physically close to one of the major immigrant press locations. The immigrants came especially from central, eastern, and southern Europe, where newspapers had been much censored. The press in eastern Europe had also been retarded by radically different high and low forms of the language. High language forms repelled ordinary readers; low forms were often spoken forms only.

In America the immigrants used the immigrant papers for many purposes. They were an Americanizing agency; readers of the immigrant paper learned American ways of thought, of commerce, of behavior. The immigrant papers were also commercial enterprises—sometimes set up by the very steamship companies that brought the immigrants over and now wanted to sell them return passages; many papers were political enterprises. Some battled for independence movements and wars of liberation back in Europe; many had connections with the American big city political machines and the

---

[34] Martin Gilbert, *Churchill—A Life*, London: Minerva, 1992: 76–113.

[35] Angus Maddison, *The World Economy: A Millennial Perspective*, Paris: OECD, 2001: 128.

[36] Michael Emery and Edwin Emery, *The Press and America*, 8th ed., Boston: Allyn and Bacon, 1996: 230–31, 293.

[37] Robert E. Park, *The Immigrant Press and Its Control*, New York: Harper, 1922.

Democratic Party. The immigrant papers were also carriers of "old country" sentiment—increasingly purveying a nostalgic and dated view of back-in-Europe reality. There were Yiddish papers evolving a popular written form of the language of the Jewish ghettoes of Europe; German papers fat with department store advertising; Marxist papers in many languages, most of which purveyed Marxism in excessively abstruse terms; Magyar papers devoted to Slovak-baiting; Norwegian papers devoted to Luther and God; and many papers devoted to making money.

Despite the enormous profusion of papers—and their profusion of worldviews—the most successful papers (Park says) were the "Americanizing" papers, pursuing news, entertainment, and advertising with all-American zeal. The German papers especially were prosperous, and the most prosperous of these, like the *New York Staatz-Zeitung*, were really American papers written in German. Robert Park called his book *The Immigrant Press and Its Control*. The "control" referred first to the importance of revenue, of delivering readers to advertisers. Second, Park was referring to political controls exercised by the U.S. federal government during World War I. This control was fairly subtle by contemporary European standards. The federal government, well before 1917, was worried about the loyalty of immigrant papers and of German-language papers in particular. The government supplied large quantities of free patriotic news and feature stories in the appropriate languages; the government also placed advertising in approved immigrant papers. These dangled carrots were on the whole effective. The German-language press reluctantly switched from German nationalism to American nationalism, and after 1918 it descended into steep decline.

While this Europe-to-America media migration was much the largest of the pre-1914 era, there were other migrations, not least out of Asia. There were 10 Japanese and 5 Chinese dailies in the United States in 1914. By 1920 there were 5 Arabic-American dailies; these Arabic papers were part of a print diaspora that was escaping the Ottoman Empire.

Also before 1914 there was an Indian diaspora in eastern Africa, southern Africa, and elsewhere in Southeast Asia. Most of these Indians initially went to construct railways or to work in mines. By 1914 there was also a Chinese diaspora, thinly spread across Southeast Asia. In Indonesia (Dutch East Indies) the Chinese increased from 0.5 percent of the population in 1820 to 1.5 percent in 1913 (and 2.3 percent in 1929).[38] Between 1881 and 1906 daily Chinese newspapers were launched in Singapore, Thailand, and Indochina.[39]

---

[38] Angus Maddison, *The World Economy: A Millennial Perspective*, Paris: OECD, 2001: 87.
[39] John Lent (ed.), *The Asian Newspapers' Reluctant Revolution*, Ames: Iowa State University Press, 1971.

Radio and Print, 1945–1965: New Nationalism Replaces Old Imperialism

A print and radio combination was central to the emergence of new nation-states after 1945. China, India, Pakistan, Indonesia, and the Philippines all became independent during 1946–1948. Between 1954 and 1963 most of the remaining Asian colonies and nearly all of the African continent's present-day 57 nation-states also achieved their independence.

At first glance the radio numbers look very small, especially in Africa. Across the entire African continent in 1955 there was only 1 radio per 100 people;[40] there were 4 per 100 in 1965 and only 7 per 100 in 1975 (after transistor radios had finally become widely used in Africa). Still fewer people read daily newspapers. Even as late as 1971–1972, countries selling fewer than two daily papers per 100 people included India, Algeria, Saudi Arabia, Angola, Ethiopia, Ivory Coast, Mozambique, Senegal, and Zambia.[41]

But at the height of the African independence surge, around 1960, both radio and daily press already reached large fractions of the then smallish population of most capital cities. Radio broadcasts and the (perhaps one) daily newspaper might only be reaching 10,000 households in a capital city of 200,000 people. But with large families in each household—and with others sometimes hearing the radio and hearing the newspaper read aloud—the majority of the capital city's population even in 1955 (and more certainly in 1965) was receiving some radio and/or press messages.

A huge literature on nationalism exists. Anthony Smith, Benedict Anderson, Gopal Balakrishnan, Miroslav Hroch, Ernest Gellner, Eric Hobsbawm, and others have put forward many fascinating arguments about the nation.[42] This nationalism literature places heavy emphasis upon the role of an intellectual elite, of higher education, and of printed books in the emergence (and early history) of ex-imperial new nation-states. A more balanced view might give greater weight to newspapers and radio; in many, or most, cases basic education, newspapers, and literacy were heavily intertwined in the story of most independence struggles. Although some independence leaders—especially in French colonies such as Senegal and

---

[40] Graham Mytton, "From Saucepan to Dish: Radio and TV in Africa," in Richard Fardon and Graham Furniss (eds.), *African Broadcast Cultures: Radio in Transition*, Oxford, UK: James Currey, 2000: 21–41.

[41] UNESCO, *World Communications*, Paris: UNESCO, 1975.

[42] Anthony D. Smith, *Nations and Nationalism in a Global Era*, Oxford, England: Polity Press, 1995; Gopal Balakrishnan (ed.), *Mapping the Nation*, London: Verso with New Left Review, 1996; John Hutchinson and Anthony D. Smith (eds.), *Nationalism*, Oxford, UK: Oxford University Press, 1994; Benedict Anderson, *Imagined Communities*, London: Verso, 1991 ed.; Benedict Anderson, *The Spectre of Comparisons: Nationalism, Southeast Asia and the World*, London: Verso, 1998.

Cote d'Ivoire—were heavyweight intellectuals, most independence leaders had more modest intellectual and academic accomplishments. Many were schoolteachers (like Kwame Nkrumah in Ghana), junior civil servants, or colonial army soldiers.

"New nations" and new nationalism were prominent on the world news agendas of the 1940s and 1950s. Indian "national" independence had been demanded for decades and especially after the Amritsar massacre of 1919; in 1947 national independence was achieved, not for one nation, but for two— India and Pakistan. The obvious message for many African independence seekers was that the nationalism-and-independence formula convinced the European imperial powers. The "mother" nations (especially Britain and France) wanted strong new national governments to lead new national independence. What mother wanted, independence-seeking politicians duly demanded. The waning imperial power and the eager independence leaders agreed on new nation-states. There was much disputation as to the constitution, the pre-independence election, the preliminary trial government period, and then full independence. Both sides talked optimistically; the imperial mothers hoped that the new nations would stick close to mother. The insurgent leaders tried to calm mother's fears and promised to preserve the Westminster model or French political culture.

The new nation-states came into being against a background of high profile media coverage, which took a triangular form. Not only the local colonial media and the imperial capital media were involved; there was a third media force—world and U.S. media. Much of the media action occurred in the colonial capital city; newspapers and "external" radio from London and Paris reached Africa, but many independence leaders themselves spent time in London or Paris, where they could have their independence discussions relatively secure from arrest. Kwame Nkrumah became prime minister of (not yet fully independent) Ghana (Gold Coast) in 1952. He was in prison during 1950–1951 and previous to that (1945–1947) was in London, where he was active in the West Africa Students' Union. Many future leaders of French ex-colonies spent time in Paris in the late 1940s and 1950s. Available to them each day were French and British media full of the end of empire story. In both British and French domestic politics and media around 1950 there was also much discussion of socialism, nationalization of major industries, and so on.

In addition to the imperial capital and colonial capital media axis were also the world media. Outside the orbit of France and Britain, the "world media" in the 1950s was mainly U.S. media, especially in the form of the AP and UP news agencies.

In India, Reuters' dominance declined as both AP and UP carried their domestic rivalry onto the world scene. American newspaper correspondents also began to appear in India in the 1930s, and during 1940–1945 there was a major U.S. media interest in India. In the last few years before 1947 independence, Indian politicians deliberately focused on U.S. media and adopted current American journalism practices, such as the pre-announced press conference.[43]

After India's and Pakistan's independence, American media interest turned to Africa. In most cases the additional publicity in American media probably had little impact on the independence timetable; in the 1950s both London and Paris became increasingly committed to quick strides in an independence direction. However, in selected cases, such as Algeria and Kenya (where white settlers opposed independence), American media and political concerns were more significant. Paradoxically perhaps, one of several reasons why French governments could not lock up Jean-Paul Sartre (and other French leftist advocates of Algerian independence) was that it would have caused so much fuss in the American media.

As discussed in previous chapters, there were broadly similar media phases during and after most independence struggles. At the height of the independence struggle, the major media typically changed sides—nearly all of the media came to support the imminent independence, and most of the media typically supported the national party, or nationalist coalition, that was about to achieve both independence and power. A second common phase was a media honeymoon period, which then dissolved into an angry media war of words. Third was often some kind of violent crisis—either lethal rioting or civil war, followed by a government crackdown on violence —supported by most of the media. Fourth typically followed an attempt (or attempts) at establishing a coalition against violence; this latter was often accompanied by some kind of explicit charter of national unity, in which the media and the schools were expected to play leading roles.

In some smaller countries this charter of national unity involved a coalition of the two largest ethnic groups; in Malaysia (later in this chapter) this involved a coalition of Malays and Chinese. In Nigeria it required some kind of understanding between the Muslim north and the (mainly Christian) south. Whether this coalition of major groupings was or was not successful, there were still substantial minority groups that were effectively losers. These losing groups were largely excluded from the media; their smaller languages usually received no more than a few token hours of radio time. Any newspaper in a small language (spoken by perhaps less than one million people) would probably only be a nondaily newspaper published by the central government. There would be very few school textbooks in its own language for such a small ethnic nation. Meanwhile, the major national media tended to portray these smaller ethnic pockets as problematic and inclined to separatism.

Were there significant examples of ethnic national diasporas and ethnic diaspora media in the 1945–1965 period? Some big population movements, such as the spread of ethnic Russians into non-Russian parts of the Soviet

---

[43] Milton Israel, *Communications and Power: Propaganda and the Press in the Indian Nationalist Struggle, 1920–1947*, Cambridge, UK: Cambridge University Press, 1994: 246–316.

Union, are perhaps best classified as continuing Russian imperial expansion. "Long distance" diaspora expansion continued, for example, from Europe into Australia and Canada. But the biggest population movements were relatively "short distance" movements. There were big post-1945 population movements in eastern and central Europe. Turks, Algerians, and Mexicans (and Central Americans) moved short distances into Germany, France, and the United States; in each of these three cases there were also the beginnings of big diaspora media.

Some of the biggest cross-border movements in 1945–1965 occurred in Africa and Asia. Many rural people in Africa, southern Asia, and the Middle East probably did not even realize that they were crossing international borders; often the same language was spoken on both sides of the border. Many Africans moved across borders to capital cities, and other urban locations, in search of work. Here the media must often have been active in attracting the cross-border migration; the familiar radio plus print combination (plus messages between kin) emphasized the ethnic nation while encouraging international migration.

Asian Media Tigers: One Nationalist State, Two Ethnic Identities

Both Malaysia and Taiwan were Asian "tiger" fast-growing economies of the 1970s and 1980s; and both by 2005 had populations of about 23 million. Both countries have struggled with more than one major ethnic identity. In Malaysia a little over half the population are Malay Muslims, while about 30 percent are Chinese.

In Taiwan the main distinction has been between the over 80 percent who are Taiwan "natives" and about 15 percent who are the families of Chinese mainlanders who came to Taiwan with Chiang Kai-shek (and his KMT party and army) in the late 1940s. In both 1992 and 2004 nearly half of Taiwan's people saw themselves as "both Taiwanese and Chinese." But during 1992–2004 the proportion seeing themselves as purely "Chinese" fell from 26 percent to 6 percent, while those seeing themselves as "Taiwanese" increased from 17 percent to 41 percent.[44]

Similarities also exist between the mass media in Malaysia and Taiwan. In both cases there is a recent history of a strong, or autocratic, regime that dominated both press and radio/TV. In both countries the media have been required to support, indeed to propagate, the official national ideology and approved social charter.

In both countries, American and European media have had only a limited significance. Perhaps more important has been the media relationship with

---

[44] "Turning Taiwanese, a Survey of Taiwan," *The Economist*, January 15, 2005: 4–6.

other Asian nations, including mainland China. Both Malaysia and Taiwan have had their own film industries and have been major export markets for the Hong Kong film industry.[45] Other similarities include the following:

- Both have an ex-imperial history. Malaysia was part of the British Empire. Taiwan's traditional connection with mainland China was broken by Japan, and during 1895–1945 Taiwan was a Japanese colony.

- In both Malaysia and Taiwan the media were owned and controlled for decades directly by the government and by politically friendly businessmen.[46]

- Both countries found themselves confronting two nearby big brother countries. Taiwan was geographically close to mainland China and Japan; Malaysia was very close to Indonesia and within the "greater China" orbit.

- Both of these small countries—so successful in high tech electronics manufacturing—were keen to impress the world; both wanted to have the world's tallest building.

- Some of the ethnic tensions in both Taiwan and Malaysia were channeled into the educational system—resulting in obsessive concern with passing examinations and with the fine detail of the current equal opportunities (or quota) regulations.

- Neither Malaysia nor Taiwan is a direct successor to a previous colony. Both countries were unanticipated consequences of post-1945 violence and were not the result of carefully laid plans. Both were also early products of the Cold War and of communist versus noncommunist conflict.

Taiwan during 1945–1949 became not fully, but nearly, independent, and then remained in this state for over half a century. The communist victory over the nationalists left Taiwan as an island bolt-hole for Chiang Kai-shek's army and his KMT Party. February 28, 1947, began a sequence of events that made "2-28" a key date in recent Taiwan history. Several local Taiwanese were killed in street confrontations with mainland KMT police. Members of the local Taiwan crowd managed to seize the main radio station (in Taipei) and to broadcast their Taiwan nationalist, and anti KMT/mainland, demands.

The majority of the Taiwan population in 1947 were the descendants of people who had come mainly from (non–Mandarin-speaking) Guangdong in

---

[45] Hassan Muthalib and Wong Tuck Cheong, "Malaysia: Gentle Winds of Change," and Liao Gene-Fon "Taiwan: In and Out of the Shadows," in Aruna Vasudev, Latika Padgaonkar, and Rashmi Doraiswamy (eds.), *The Cinemas of Asia*, Delhi: Macmillan, 2002: 301–28, 418–40.

[46] Zaharom Nain and Mustafa K. Anuar, "Ownership and Control of the Malaysian Media," *Media Development*, 4, 1998: 9–16.

southern China, 200 and 300 years earlier. During 1945–1948, much of the KMT nationalist Chinese elite left Shanghai and other mainland locations and took refuge in Taiwan. One commentator describes this exodus of China's industrialists, bankers, doctors, administrators, professors, artists, and chefs as "the largest single movement of an elite in world history.[47] After February 28, 1947, it took a week for additional KMT military forces to arrive from the mainland; these forces then killed between 10,000 and 20,000 Taiwanese. By 1949, when the KMT were defeated by the communists, there were some two million mainlanders—and four million locals—on Taiwan. But the local Taiwanese population grew much faster, and by 2000 constituted not 65 percent, but over 80 percent, of the total.

Chiang Kai-shek, with his mainland elite and the remnants of a once huge army, took power and established a new official ideology; Taiwan was claimed to be the real and only China. Chiang Kai-shek effectively ruled in Taiwan for 30 years (1945–1975) and was succeeded by his son (Chian Ching-kuo), who was president for a further decade until 1988.[48] The official ideology made Mandarin the one and only official language; Taiwanese children were educated entirely in Mandarin and were not allowed to speak their own Taiwanese language, even on the school playground. There was a personality cult of Chiang Kai-shek as the "Great Helmsman" and head of the only political party (the KMT). A big boost was given to the Taiwanese mass media. There were strong efforts in radio and press, entirely in Mandarin. Taiwan also quickly built up its own large film industry. The Taiwanese film industry was making over 100 films a year by 1957; in the late 1960s it averaged 200 films a year. The films were allowed to use the Taiwanese language[49] and—in the longer term—seem to have played a key role in sustaining a Taiwanese national cultural sentiment, separate from the mainland and from Mandarin.

The KMT regime in Taiwan continued with its oddly conceived national ideology in all education and most mass media for 40 years. All school textbooks were in mainland Mandarin; Taiwanese children learned about the history, literature, art, and geography of (mainly northern) China—a place they had little prospect of ever visiting. The media policy involved the familiar autocratic formula of a small number of large audience media. Newspapers were restricted to 12 pages. Taiwan maintained a big external media propaganda effort; after Taiwan in 1971 lost its UN seat to the People's Republic of China, the media were seen as now needing to fill some of this diplomatic gap. Taiwan became known as the most generous financier of free

---

[47] Christopher Anderson, "In Praise of Paranoia: A Survey of Taiwan," *The Economist* (18-page section), November 7, 1998: 5.

[48] Stéphane Corcuff (ed.), *Memories of the Future: National Identity Issues and the Search for a New Taiwan*, Armonk, NY: M.E. Sharpe, 2001.

[49] John Lent, *The Asian Film Industry*, London: Christopher Helm, 1990: 61–91.

foreign trips for American politicians; an "ad hoc Taiwan caucus," which appeared in Washington, DC, in 2002, claimed 87 congressional members.[50]

During 1985–1988 the (still KMT) government at last began to loosen Taiwan's ideological and media straitjacket. After 40 years it was increasingly difficult to explain to Taiwan's youth that, despite their island's nearly-nation having less than 2 percent of the mainland's population, Taiwan would ultimately prevail. By 1985 (and 10 years after his death) Chiang Kai-shek's reputation as father of the nation was in decline. Some democratization was introduced; an important opposition political party, the DPP, emerged from the staff and readership of radical magazines. In 1988 newspaper restrictions were reduced and the two largest dailies (*China Times* and *United Daily News*), each with a million plus daily circulation, doubled their pages from 12 to 24. During 1988 Taiwan experienced a publishing explosion, with 57 new newspapers (or editions) launched in the year.[51] There was also some modest restriction on the firm grip of the KMT on the existing television channels; local cable TV now began on a biggish scale, in the usual legal limbo-land and reluctant to obey the wishes of government regulators, copyright holders, or the advertising industry. Cable, initially insurgent and chaotic, later concentrated and commercial, was seen by the DPP (and other opposition political parties) as an important alternative to government-dominated regular television.[52] In December 1992 Taiwan had its first fully democratic general election; the DPP got 31 percent of the vote.[53]

Although both the Taiwanese "nation" and media are highly complex, by comparison, Malaysia and its media are a fabrication of greater complexity. Under various permutations of Malaysia, the Malays were always the largest single ethnic group; second were the Chinese, and third the Indians. But whether the Malays were a dominant majority depended upon which geographical version of Malaysia was in operation. At independence in 1957 (after a major Chinese insurgency against the British), the country was just the Malay Peninsula with Malays in the majority. However, in 1963 there were three geographical additions—Singapore (about 80 percent ethnic Chinese) and two former British colonies in North Borneo, namely, Sabah and Sarawak (both lowly populated and predominantly non-Chinese); in this version of Malaysia the Chinese population loomed large and the Malays did

[50] Murray Herbert, "Taiwan: No Big Deal," *Far East Economic Review*, May 2, 2002: 19; Jason Dean, "Taiwan: Keep a Secret?" *Far East Economic Review*, April 11, 2002: 21.
[51] Yun-Ju Lay and John C. Schweitzer, "Advertising in Taiwan Newspapers Since the Lifting of the Bans," *Journalism Quarterly*, Vol. 67/1, Spring 1990: 201–6; Kuldip R. Rampal, "Press and Political Liberalisation in Taiwan," *Journalism Quarterly*, Vol. 71/3, Autumn 1994: 637–51.
[52] Peilin Chiu and Sylvia M. Chan-Olmsted, "The Impact of Cable Television on Political Campaigns in Taiwan," *Gazette*, Vol. 61/6, December 1999: 491–509; Ping-Hung Chen, "Market Concentration in Taiwan's Cable Industry," *Media Asia*, Vol. 26/4, 1999: 206–15; Ping-Hung Chen, "The Role of the State in Shaping Taiwan's Cable Television Industry," *Media Asia*, Vol. 29/1, 2002: 37–41.
[53] "Taiwan Breaks the Mould," *The Economist*, December 26, 1992–January 8, 1993: 77–78.

not have a secure majority. The latter disadvantage (from a Malay viewpoint) was removed in 1965, when Singapore (then population: two million) left Malaysia to become a separate nation-state.

From its 1957 independence onward Malaysia continued to have elections and a frequently reshuffled governing coalition. Under various names this governing coalition normally included Malays, as well as some Chinese and Indians. But tensions existed especially between the Malays (then mainly rural peasants or "Bumiputras") and the Chinese (mainly urban and dominant in trade and business). In the late 1960s, The "Alliance" included major leaders and politicians of all three main ethnic groups. But there were always political and other differences within each ethnic group; most of the Chinese spoke some version of Mandarin. Most of the "Indians" were Tamils from India or Sri Lanka. There were also significant cleavages among the Muslim Malays, not least between fundamentalist Muslims and others. At the 1969 elections the Alliance, the three-ethnic coalition, faced opposition from several smaller single-ethnicity parties.[54]

The 1969 elections led to the worst rioting and violence in Malaysia's independent history. On May 13, 1969, the election results caused Malays to celebrate, in Kuala Lumpur, the (Malay-led) Alliance victory in terms of legislative seats won. But other opposition (Chinese and Indian) parties also celebrated their increased shares of the total vote. Two rival victory celebrations clashed, leaving between 200 and 800 people dead. The Chinese bore the main force of the violence in deaths, injuries, and commercial premises destroyed.[55] This led to a new deal agreed mainly between Chinese and Malay leaders; the Chinese would continue to run the modern economy and would receive protection and security for their language and culture. The (Muslim) Malays would be the leaders of the political and cultural coalition and would receive positive discrimination in government employment and in education; Malay would be strengthened as the main language. The press, which was seen as having used its freedom irresponsibly, would be curbed.

A new official ideology was introduced, under which ethnic criticism and prejudiced statements (and employment practices) were outlawed. The New Economic Policy (NEP) was designed to produce economic growth and to eliminate (especially Malay) poverty. Finally, there was a crackdown on press and broadcasting irresponsibility (or freedom) through a new Sedition Act. Another (implicit) element was hostility to foreign media, not only Western media but also Chinese-language media in nearby Singapore. The major ethnic rioting was not repeated, and the next national election (1974)

---

[54] Karl von Vorys, *Democracy Without Consensus: Communism and Political Stability in Malaysia*, Princeton, NJ: Princeton University Press, 1975.

[55] "Riots and Rukunegara Politics," in Gordon P. Means, *Malaysian Politics*, London: Hodder, and Stoughton, 1976 ed.: 391–416.

passed peacefully with the English-, Malay-, Chinese-, and Tamil-language newspapers all conforming to the new national ideology guidelines.[56]

The United Malays National Organisation (UMNO), the main Malay political party, continued to dominate Malaysian politics in the years 1970–2000. But UMNO still faced a series of crises. Mahathir Muhammad as prime minister (1981–2003) faced what he saw as crises in 1983–1984 (over the powers of the traditional feudal rulers), in 1987 (over a party breakaway), and in 1998 (when Mahathir dismissed and imprisoned his finance minister, and chosen successor, Anwar Ibrahim).[57]

Mahathir himself was not only an accomplished tactician but also a ruthless autocrat. In addition, Mahathir was a capable journalist, pamphleteer, and propagandist. At the time of the 1969 riots, Mahathir had denounced the policies of the then prime minister (Tunku Abdul Rahman). The following year Mahathir expanded his critique into a book, *The Malay Dilemma*, which had to be published abroad (in Singapore).

Mahathir's polemical talents were influenced by his experiences in the early 1950s as a medical student in Singapore. In 1950s Singapore a disparate group of Malay intellectuals, journalists, poets, singers, writers, politicians, and filmmakers were reinventing and modernizing the Malay language; by importing many new words, by altering the script, and by adapting the Malay language to city (Singapore) life, these young Malays were turning a traditional peasant language into a modern language suitable for an independent nation-state.[58]

By the mid-1970s the new national ideology was firmly in place. The new policy confirmed Malay as the main language for school education. The production of school textbooks in Malay by the mid-1970s accounted for about 70 percent of all Malaysian book publishing.[59]

While big economic growth steadily transformed Malaysia into an economic tiger, so also Malaysia became a media tiger with an overall media system increasingly similar to the media system of a two-language European country, such as Belgium. However, as the Malaysian media grew commercially stronger, governmental controls remained as strong or stronger. Television, radio, and the press were all dominated by government or UMNO ownership or by friends (or relatives) of the regime leaders. In the 1970s it was still the Chinese who were most constrained by this because a higher percentage of Chinese than Malays were reading daily newspapers

[56] Elliott Parker, "The Malaysian Elections of 1974: An Analysis of Newspaper Coverage," in John Lent (ed.), *Case Studies of Mass Media in the Third World*, Williamsburg, VA: Department of Anthropology, College of William and Mary, 1980: 79–97.
[57] R. S. Milne and Diane K. Mauzy, *Malaysian Politics Under Mahathir*, London: Routledge, 1999.
[58] T. N. Harper, "The Politics of Culture," in *The End of Empire and the Making of Malaysia*, Cambridge, UK: Cambridge University Press, 1999: 274–307.
[59] Ronny Adhikarya, *Broadcasting in Peninsular Malaysia*, London: Routledge, 1977: 11.

and had television sets; another irritation for the Chinese was that most television programming was in Malay or English.[60]

Malaysian newspapers remained the most ethnic-specific medium. There was a strong supply of daily newspapers in English, Chinese, and Malay plus a small Tamil-language press. Both the Chinese- and English-language presses had obvious similarities to each other and to European models; both English and Chinese newspapers aimed for some kind of consensual neutrality and by the early 2000s had about three readers per copy. But Malaysian newspapers were still being read in a more extended family manner with about six readers per copy.[61] Malay-language newspapers also tended to be more partisan (in support of ethnic Malays).[62]

From the 1970s the Malaysian government was seeking to cut down on media imports but was also struggling with the familiar programming requirements of new TV channels and more hours per day. The Mahathir government of the 1980s and 1990s had strong views as to specific countries from which it did not wish to import. The most important negative preference of the Malay-led government was to avoid Chinese imports—and thus to minimize imports from China, Hong Kong, Taiwan, or Singapore. India was also suspect as the main mother country of Malaysia's Tamils. With highly populated Indonesia also suspect (since its main language was so close to the Malay language) Malaysia's one and only preferred Asian media source was Japan (despite its 1940s occupation). Mahathir was also suspicious of Britain as the bad old imperial power and of the United States—as a source of too much violence and sex.

Since the early 1990s, both Malaysia and Taiwan faced new problems, as highly directed national cultures and national media were challenged, explicitly and implicitly, by increasingly educated and affluent populations. In Taiwan there were moves toward a less autocratic system from the mid-1980s, and by the early 2000s Taiwan was being acclaimed as a multiparty democracy.

Both Malaysia and Taiwan had by the early 2000s fabricated and developed new nation-states; there was also significant national sentiment attached to these new nation-state entities. In both new countries nationalism and national sentiment operated on two or more levels. Many Malaysians—especially Chinese and Indians—saw themselves as being both Malaysian and also either Chinese or Indian.

---

[60] Newell Grenfell, *Switch On: Switch Off. Mass Media Audiences in Malaysia*, Kuala Lumpur: Oxford University Press, 1979.

[61] Shaila Koshy, "Living in Interesting and Trying Times," *Media Asia*, Vol. 28/2, 2001: 111–12.

[62] Khor Yoke Lim and Adnan Hussein, "Perceptions of Ethnic Identities in Malaysia: A Media Study," in Anura Goonasekera and Youichi Ito (eds.), *Mass Media and Cultural Identity: Ethnic Reporting in Asia*, London: Pluto Press, 1999: 101–28; Balan Moses, "Ethnic Reporting in the Malaysian Media," *Media Asia*, Vol. 28/2, 2002: 102–6.

The mass media had played a leading role (along with the educational system) in developing these highly complex, but basically two-level, patterns of cultural identity. In both Taiwan and Malaysia, authoritarian governments had imposed new national ideologies, new language policies, and their ethnic nationality policies. But in the 1980s and 1990s an important element in the drift toward more democracy was the familiar pattern of new media, with a more commercial and populist approach. Malaysia's existing multiethnic TV, satellite, and radio systems expanded, meaning that Chinese and Indian Malaysians (already heavy viewers of Chinese and Indian films on video) could now follow mainly Mandarin or mainly Tamil radio and TV, as well as newspapers in their own language.

In Taiwan there was a big development of cable TV (fed by Mandarin, American, and Japanese and Chinese channels). There was a significant relaxation of media relations with mainland China, meaning that Taiwan increasingly participated in film co-productions with Hong Kong and China.[63] There was a significant pop music industry in Taiwan, which—although heavily interested in the mainland—did also record and distribute many local Taiwanese musicians.[64] Indeed, these "international" developments stimulated much new Taiwanese media output. There were many talk shows and much phone-in programming on both radio and TV.[65] There was a huge development of Taiwanese TV *telenovelas*; the normal pattern was five half-hour episodes per week.[66] Much more American and Japanese material was now available, but little American programming was shown in prime time on the bigger networks. A late 1990s study of Taiwanese teenagers found that American films were the fourth most popular genre. Both Taiwanese and Hong Kong films were more popular, as were Japanese cartoons. The most popular genre with teenagers was the Taiwanese "live variety show."[67] Six of the top nine genres were Taiwanese. Some Taiwanese talk show hosts, singers, and actors have become local superstars, and increasingly they are also being seen in China.

[63] Junhao Hong and Jung Kuang Sun, "Taiwan's Film Importation from China: A Political Economy Analysis of Changes and Implications," *Media, Culture and Society*, Vol. 21/4, July 1999: 531–47.

[64] Alan Wells, "The International Music Business in Taiwan," *Media Asia*, Vol. 24/4, 1997: 206–13.

[65] Rueyling Chuang and Ringo Ma, "(Re)Locating Our Voices in the Public Sphere: Call-in Talk Shows as a Channel for Civic Discourse in Taiwan," in Randy Kluver and John H. Powers (eds.), *Civic Discourse, Civil Society and Chinese Communities*, Stamford, CT: Ablex, 1999: 167–68.

[66] Yean Tsai, "Cultural Identity in an Era of Globalisation: The Structure and Content of Taiwanese Soap Operas," in Georgette Wang, Jan Servaes, and Anura Goonasekera (eds.), *The New Communications Landscape*, London: Routledge, 2000: 174–87.

[67] Herng Su and Sheue-Yun Chen, "The Choice Between Local and Foreign: Taiwan Youths' Television Viewing Behaviour," in Georgette Wang et al. (eds.), *The New Communications Landscape*, London: Routledge, 2000: 225–44.

Both Taiwan and Malaysia are small (invented or fabricated) nations that also have a role in the Chinese diaspora. As small nations, they could be expected to be big media importers; but these are both small nations that are anxious about their massive Asian big brothers. The newly created Malaysian and Taiwanese nationalisms are being challenged both from "above" (by China, Japan, the United States, the United Kingdom, Indonesia, and India) and from "below" by ethnic nationalism and ethnic media. There have also been some unintended consequences of national media and languages. In Malaysia the forced teaching of Malay in the schools has persuaded many ethnic Chinese and Indians to send their children to fee-paying schools where they can learn their mother language; one result has been a weakening of English speaking in Malaysia, which is at odds with Malaysia's international economic policies.[68] Taiwanese politicians are anxious about the flight of much of their electronics industry to China; and since the late 1980s Taiwanese has become steadily more popular—and more used in schools in some areas—at the expense of Mandarin.

National Diaspora Media in the Satellite Television Era

The flows of Mexicans and eastern Asians into California and the flows of Turks and northern Africans into Germany and France are sometimes quoted as examples of unprecedented globalization. Surely their use of satellite TV, as well as e-mail and other electronic services, has no real precedent? Well, yes and no. Obviously back in 1900 there was neither satellite TV nor e-mail, and immigrants then had to rely on newspapers, magazines, and letters if they wanted to maintain contact with their families still in the "old country."

Much of today's migration is not global but rather more nation-to-nation. These migrations—and the accompanying media—tend to flow along much the same pathways as a century ago; in some cases the direction of flow has been reversed—as Europe's big outflows are replaced by a preponderant in-flow. Nation-to-nation flows also lie behind the double identity that many recent migrants experience.

However, only about 3 percent of today's world population live outside their country of birth or citizenship. The biggest population movements are within the large population countries. The migration of China's rural population into urban areas exceeds—in sheer millions of people—all previous migrations. There are other huge migrations inside India, Pakistan, Indonesia, Brazil, and Nigeria. These internal migrations may often involve

---

[68] S. Jayasankaran, "Malaysia: A Plan to End Extremism," *Far East Economic Review*, December 26, 2002–January 2, 2003: 12–16; Zaharom Nain and Mustafa K. Anuar, "Marketing to the Masses in Malaysia: Commercial Television, Religion and Nation Building," in David French and Michael Richards (eds.), *Television in Contemporary Asia*, Delhi: Sage, 2000: 151–77.

two languages, and two sets of media—with many people experiencing the double identity situation. Non-Cantonese speakers migrate into Cantonese-speaking southern China cities; many Indians move within India, but across the border line between Hindi and another language. In both China and India, migrants are able to access print and electronic media from their original home region and locality.

The biggest players in international migration—both as receivers and senders of migrants—are the largest population countries. The United States is still the biggest single national "receiver" of migration, although Europe overall has a larger number of foreign-born inhabitants.[69]

The biggest "senders" of migrants are China, India, Mexico, and other large population countries. These big senders also generate the biggest and most high profile migrant media. Big audience numbers are nearly always commercially beneficial in the media. "Overseas" Chinese people or "nonresident" Indians can use three types of their own national media and communication. First, they can receive publications and recorded movies as well as Indian or Chinese domestic TV channels, via satellite or local cable. Second, these emigrants create their own new media in their new host country; this is especially true of the Chinese communities across Southeast Asia. Third, there are various "two-way" media, such as e-mail, Internet, and cheap phone calls; and in some cases there is a mix—for example, newspapers-by-satellite from India or Turkey appear in Europe with added "local" European news.

Much migration has been more nation-to-nation than global. For instance, there are probably about 30 million Chinese people living outside China; 80 percent of these are in Southeast Asia and about 65 percent of the total are in Indonesia, Malaysia, or Thailand (and mostly in urban areas of these countries).[70] More than 20 million Indians[71] lived abroad in 2005, mainly in English-speaking countries and/or former British colonies—Myanmar

---

[69] Stephen Castles and Mark J. Miller, *The Age of Migration*, London: Macmillan, 2000; Frances Cairncross, "The Longest Journey: A Survey of Migration," *The Economist*, November 2, 2002; Martin Wolf, "Humanity on the Move: The Myths and Realities of International Migration," *Financial Times*, July 30, 2003.

[70] Paul J. Bolt, *China and Southeast Asia's Ethnic Chinese*, Westport, CT: Praeger, 2000.

[71] Raminder Kaur and Ajay J. Sinha (eds.), *Bollyworld: Popular Indian Cinema Through a Transnational Lens*, New Delhi: Sage, 2005; Marie Gillespie, *Television, Ethnicity and Cultural Change*, London: Routledge, 1995; Sadanand Dhume, "From Bangalore to Silicon Valley and Back: How the Indian Diaspora in the United States is Changing India," in Alyssa Ayres and Philip Oldenburg (eds.), *India Briefing*, Armonk, NY: M.E. Sharpe, 2002: 91–120; Stuart Cunningham and John Sinclair (eds.), *Floating Lives: The Media and the Asian Diaspora*, Lanham, MD: Rowman and Littlefield, 2001; *The Global Indian: Doing Us Proud*, special issue of *India Today International*, January 13, 2003; Amol Sharma, "Come Home, We Need You," *Far East Economic Review*, January 23, 2003: 28–32; Aminah Mohammad-Arif, *Salaam America: South Asian Muslims in New York*, London: Anthem Press, 2002; Vijay Prashad, *The Karma of Brown Folk*, Minneapolis: University of Minnesota Press, 2000; Shilpa Davé, Leilani Nishme, and Tasha G. Oren (eds.), *East Main Street: Asian American Popular Culture*, New York: New York University Press, 2005.

(Burma), the United Kingdom, the United States, Canada, Malaysia, South Africa, and Saudi Arabia.

Emigration is often point-to-point, as migrants establish small ethnic communities (and media) in the receiving country. Pakistanis have moved to the north of England and Bangladeshis have settled in east London; Turks have settled in Amsterdam,[72] Frankfurt, and other German cities. Migrants from the Dominican Republic, Ecuador, and El Salvador—as well as from Mexico—all have their preferred locations in particular suburbs of New York City. Iranians prefer Los Angeles.[73] Detroit's large Arab population originates especially from Lebanon and is equal to about 5 percent of Lebanon's total population.[74]

Point-to-point movement involves not only people, but also money; indeed, financial remittances (often via Western Union) are a major factor in the economies of some sending nations.[75] This point-to-point pattern also maximizes the opportunities for media to flow. A tightly packed ethnic enclave can offer video stores that supply old country entertainment, movie theaters that show the movies, and other retailers that sell satellite editions of home country newspapers; retailers supply appropriate satellite dishes, and local cable companies can make a realistic profit by supplying (premium priced) whole TV channels from the mother country. All of this media material then plays a substantial role in structuring the immigrant community's conversation, leisure time, and worldview. In addition, many larger immigrant communities generate, and organize, their own new media in the receiving country. Small local papers in some cases grow into small daily papers; a few hours per week of radio time may expand into entire radio channels. As the migrant community expands, it becomes increasingly easy for small newspapers, magazines, and radio stations to acquire suitable syndicated material. Much material—today as a century ago—is material

[72] Nezar AlSayyad and Manuel Castells (eds.), *Muslim Europe or Euro-Islam*, Lanham, MD: Lexington Books, 2002; Asu Aksoy and Kevin Robins, "Banal Transnationalism: The Difference That Television Makes," in Karim H. Karim (ed.), *The Media in Diaspora*, London: Routledge, 2003: 89–104; Christine Ogan, "Communication, Politics and Religion in an Islamic Community," in Russell King and Nancy Wood (eds.), *Media and Migration*, London: Routledge, 2001: 127–43; Christine Ogan and Marisca Milikowski, "Television Helps to Define Home for Turkish Women in Amsterdam," *Media Development*, 3, 1998: 13–21; Marisca Milikowski, "Exploring a Model of De-ethnicization: The Case of Turkish Television in the Netherlands," *European Journal of Communication*, Vol. 15/4, December 2000: 443–68; Andy Bennett, "Hip Hop am Main: The Localization of Rap Music and Hip Hop Culture," *Media, Culture and Society*, Vol. 21, 1999: 77–91; Bertrand Benoit, "Germans Wake Up to the Call of the Muezzin," *Financial Times*, November 4, 2003.
[73] Hamid Naficy, "Narrowcasting in Diaspora: Middle Eastern Television in Los Angeles," in Karim H. Karim (ed.), *The Media of Diaspora*, London: Routledge, 2003: 51–62.
[74] Nikki Tait, "Arab-American Community: Immigrants Earn Their Rewards," *Financial Times*, February 28, 2000.
[75] Devesh Kapur and John McHale, "Migration's New Payoff," *Foreign Policy*, November/December 2003: 49–57.

taken from major media (both in the receiving and sending countries) and then reedited, reframed, and translated for the specific local audience.

Some of these nation-to-nation and point-to-point flows also involve return flows of the migrants themselves. Some very long distance migration does exist—for example, from Europe to Australia or from Indonesia to Europe. But most migration is within the same world region or is comparatively short distance. Among major receiving countries, the United States gets it biggest flows from the most nearby parts of Latin America; both Germany and France receive most of their immigrants from within the Mediterranean area and Europe. If the sending and receiving points are only two or three hours' flying time away, this can lead to a pattern of regular (perhaps annual) return visits. Many Mexican migrants in Texas visit their old home each year. Moroccans and Turks have a choice of several kinds of travel to and from France or Belgium and to or from Germany or the Netherlands.

Not all migrant groups are supplied with abundant media in their mother language. There is huge variety even within migration from one country to one country. There is a big social class dimension between Indian medical doctors in the United States and United Kingdom (who probably learned English at home) and poorer migrants from the same country; many migrants come from poor rural backgrounds. There are also ethnic differences, for example, between Muslims and Hindus; even black and white migrants from the same Latin American country tend to live in separate U.S. localities.

In many (but not all) cases the receiving country's educational and media systems ensure that the second and third generations become increasingly assimilated into the receiving country's language and culture. Audience studies tend to show that the third generation, especially, lacks facility in the old country language and, of course, follows less print and electronic media from the old country.

However, there is some official anxiety that in certain specific cases of large scale migration—such as Mexicans in California, Algerians in France, and Turks in Germany—assimilation is not so easily achieved.[76] If assimilation does not occur—and the second and third generations continue to cling to their parents' and grandparents' ethnic identity—this is yet again a specific nation-to-nation and point-to-point phenomenon.

Digital television with its big increase in channel capacity is having a strong impact within the bigger migrant populations—such as Mexicans, Indians, and Chinese. Both digital satellite and digital cable operators can offer a big bundle of Indian or Chinese channels; this is a broad niche market, and many emigrant Indians, for example, are willing to pay a premium price for a generous bundle of Indian movie and entertainment channels. By year 2001 Indians and Pakistanis resident in the United Kingdom could already

---

[76] Jörg Becker, "Multiculturalism in German Broadcasting," *Media Development*, 3, 1998: 8–12.

subscribe to 18 South Asian satellite or cable channels (mostly from Zee, Sony, and Star).[77] By 2004 Chinese residents in the United States could receive 17 Chinese channels (including 5 from the state broadcaster, CCTV; another 7 regional Chinese channels; and several Cantonese channels from Hong Kong).[78]

In addition to their large offerings for eastern Asian and southern Asian customers, satellite TV operators in the United States, the United Kingdom, and Europe also offer channels in up to an additional 20 languages. In the United States this, of course, includes the big Spanish/Mexican offering but also involves channels from a number of other Asian and European countries. French, German, Italian, Japanese, Turkish, Filipino, Vietnamese, and Russian channels are widely available. Local digital cable operators in southern California, greater New York, and greater London offer a bewildering array of language channels.

Two broad conclusions seem valid. There is an important distinction between small and large ethnic national migrations. The impact of imported media seems to be strongest in the case of large local ethnic groups that originate from large sending nations—such as China, India, Mexico, or Turkey. The overall impact depends heavily upon education, including religious education and mother tongue education. Where the ethnic migrant community is strong—such as Turks in Germany, Pakistanis in northern England, or Mexicans, Koreans, and Vietnamese in California—then a big bundle of media and TV channels from the mother country can be expected to have a significant impact.

Second, these satellite TV and other current media phenomena do, certainly, exist within a "global" framework. But the main players here are nation-states and their national media—often just two nation-states, one sender and one receiver. This can be seen as a struggle between the sending culture and the receiving culture, with the individual person having to choose which identity is to be his or her prime identity. But the majority of today's migrants are not involved in a Herculean contest of national versus global. The connection—although within a global setting—primarily involves only two nation-states (and often just one or two localities within each nation-state).

---

[77] Andy Fry, "Multichannel Melting Pot," *Cable and Satellite Europe*, January 2001: 16–21.
[78] Linda Haugsted, "Satellite Ops Make Asian Push," *Multichannel News*, November 8, 2004.

17

A Separate Arab Media Bloc

Most of the 300 million Arabs of 2005 lived in some 20 different countries, spoke quite different versions of Arabic, and followed differing branches of the Muslim religion. Nevertheless, the majority of these 300 million people lived in a different mental world from most Europeans and Americans.

Take, for example, the September 11, 2001, suicide plane attacks in New York and Washington, DC. Gallup research indicated that most Arabs and Muslims did not believe that these attacks were carried out by Arabs; 89 percent of respondents in Kuwait rejected the standard American and European account.[1]

The Western world has its own history of accepting, or propagating, myths about the Middle East. Edward Said elegantly dissected misleading "western conceptions of the orient."[2] A "Lawrence of Arabia" legend was constructed partly by T. E. Lawrence himself, but also by a succession of book authors, journalists, and Hollywood movie makers.[3] According to Melani McAlister, the United States, after 1945, viewed Egypt and the Middle East through a haze of biblical romance and pro-Israeli sentimentality, combined with unrealistic strategy, commercial self-interest, and racism.[4]

Although American movies arrived in the Arab world in the early 1900s, American media in general have been weaker in the Arab countries than in most other world regions. Taking the twentieth century as a whole, Western media influence in the Arab countries was shared between France, Britain,

[1] Brian Witaker, "Muslim Countries Doubt Arab Role in September 11," *The Guardian*, February 28, 2002.
[2] Edward W. Said, *Orientalism: Western Conceptions of the Orient*, London Penguin Books, 1995, first publ. 1978.
[3] Lawrence James, *The Golden Warrior: The Life and Legend of Lawrence of Arabia*, London: Weidenfeld and Nicolson, 1990.
[4] Melani McAlister, *Epic Encounters: Culture, Media and US Interests in the Middle East, 1945–2000*, Berkeley: University of California Press, 2001.

Figure 17.1 The Arab countries.

and the United States. Moreover, there were strong domestic Arabic language media, especially in the larger population countries such as Egypt.

This chapter will mainly consider Egypt (the biggest media producer), Saudi Arabia (the biggest media financer) and the small Gulf states, and the ex-French colony Maghreb countries (primarily Algeria).

Each Arab country can be seen in terms of several levels. "Arabs" effectively are people who speak (some version of) the Arabic language and Arab countries have a majority of such people. Most Arabs are Muslims by religion. There are some broad Arabic media (especially since the era of satellite TV); but there are few Muslim media and the countries with the biggest Muslim populations (Indonesia, India, Pakistan, and Bangladesh) have their own media in their own languages. Most media in the Arab world are at the nation-state and national level and are controlled by the national government or ruling national party. Freedom House (of New York) classifies as "not free" most of the Arab countries, including Egypt, Algeria, Iraq, Saudi Arabia, and Syria.[5]

In addition to the Arabic language, the Muslim (Sunni or Shia) religion and nation-state loyalty and identity focus also on two other levels. There are significant ethnic minorities within most Arab countries; these minorities include separate ethnic/language groups such as the Kurds in Iraq and Syria, Christians in Lebanon and Egypt, and "Berbers" in northern Africa. There were, in the past, sizeable Jewish minorities in several countries.

---

[5] Freedom House, *Freedom in the Middle East and North Africa*, New York: Freedom House and Lanham, MD: Rowman and Littlefield, 2005.

Another level is the "tribe" or "clan." Some of these tribes claim to be able to trace their ancestry and their leaders' ancestry back to the prophet Mohammed. It is not correct to assert that most of these Arabs were, only a few decades ago, really just groups of Bedouin families wandering around the desert on their camels. It is, however, true that these "tribes" have a distinctive location and a tradition of local peasant agriculture. Many tribes, and most Arabs, have resided on quite narrow fertile strips along coastlines, near to oases and along major rivers (such as the Nile and the Tigris and Euphrates). Many Arabs derive from tribes that lived close to, but not in, both the desert and a nearby town. There are few significant tribal media as such. But politicians and soldiers from one specific locality may control and operate both the national government and the national media. Saudi Arabia is dominated by the Wahabi tribe (or sect), which derives from the central desert area of what is now Saudi Arabia. The leader of the Wahabis, Ibn Saud, named the country after himself, and, with numerous wives, fathered the 36 Saudi princes whose offspring today control and finance the Saudi media and much of the pan-Arab media.

A study conducted by Zogby International in May 2004 found that, across six Arab countries, the largest proportion of respondents, 42 percent, saw their most important identity as "citizen"; 37 percent said "Muslim" and 15 percent said "Arab." But "Arab" was the most quoted choice (38 percent) as second important identity; here "Muslim" came next with 29 percent, while "citizen" had 22 percent. So, while the most popular choice was citizen as first identity and Arab as second identity, the Muslim religious identity was also very important.[6]

Despite a lengthy history, Arab mass media were held back throughout most of the twentieth century by several factors. A major restraint was the lack of media freedom and the heavy hands of political domination and censorship control.[7] Another restraint has been the huge difference between the separate street Arabics spoken by the mass of the people and the "high," classical and scholarly, version of Arabic; classical Arabic is the language of the Koran and since this is seen as the word of God, it cannot be altered.[8] These very different versions of Arabic are one element in the lowish levels

[6] The six countries were Jordan, Morocco, Lebanon, Saudi Arabia, United Arab Emirates, and Egypt. Interviews were conducted only in each country's three or four largest cities. Forty-eight percent of respondents were women. The percentages quoted here are based on a simple average of the six countries and are not weighted for population. Zogby International, "Arab Attitudes Towards Political and Social Issues, Foreign Policy and the Media," Utica, NY: Zogby, 2004.

[7] Ami Ayalon, *The Press in the Arab Middle East: A History*, New York: Oxford University Press, 1955; William A. Rugh, *The Arab Press: News Media and Political Process in the Arab World*, Syracuse, NY: Syracuse University Press, 1987 ed.; Trevor Mostyn, *Censorship in Islamic Societies*, London: Saqi Books, 2002; Nabil H. Dajani, "An Analysis of the Press in Four Arab Countries," in *The Vigilant Press: A Collection of Case Studies*, Paris: UNESCO, 1989: 75–88.

[8] Georges Khodr, "Script, Word and Image in Arabic Culture," *Media Development*, 2, 1985: 33–35.

of literacy; most education is carried on in standard classical Arabic, which is a separate language from what schoolchildren and students speak on the street and in the home.

Another inhibition to media development is that, although the Arab world has its oil billionaires and many thousands of dollar millionaires, most Arabs are nearly as poor as most Indians and most Africans. Continuing mass poverty, in most areas away from the Persian Gulf oil fields, is also linked to rapid population growth. Across the Arab countries population grew by about 400 percent between 1950 and 2000. It tends to be the poorest countries that have the faster growth. For instance, Yemen's population doubled between 1981 and 2000, when it reached 17.5 million. It is predicted to increase by another five times, reaching over 100 million by 2050.

The exceptionally restricted position of women in the Arab world has been yet another factor restricting media growth. For many decades more women than men were illiterate, and even a literate urban woman could not go out to buy a magazine.

The long period of 1800–1950 was an era of empire and imperial decline. The late nineteenth and early twentieth centuries saw the Ottoman Empire collapse and fade back into what became modern Turkey. As the Ottoman Empire declined, the French and the British stepped in;[9] also involved were the Italians and the Germans. The first modern Arab newspaper was established by Napoleon in Egypt. Throughout the nineteenth and early twentieth centuries, a growing Arabic newspaper press, which used classical Arabic, attacked the French and British empires. Many pioneering Arabic publications were published in Egypt by journalists who were fleeing the stricter censorship in Lebanon, Syria, and elsewhere.

The French and British were still expanding their Middle East empires around 1920; France acquired Syria as a League of Nations mandate and Britain acquired Iraq. The claim that it took Winston Churchill only one afternoon to invent Iraq is an exaggeration. But Churchill, as British colonial secretary, did chair the March 1921 meeting (in a Cairo Hotel) that fixed Iraq's borders and deliberately included Shias, Sunnis, and Kurds; Churchill also selected the Hashemite dynasty (and Faisal I) to rule Iraq.[10]

From 1930 onward a new Arabic movie industry established its main base in Cairo. These talkie movies followed popular singers and became pioneers of the use of local (Egyptian) Arabic in the mass media.

The two decades of 1950–1970 were an era of Arab independence and nationalism. Lebanon achieved independence in 1943 and Egypt in 1952. A key event was the combined 1956 attack on Egypt by France, Britain, and

---

[9] Bernard Lewis, *What Went Wrong? Western Impact and Middle Eastern Response*, London: Phoenix, 2002.

[10] Christopher Catherwood, *Winston's Folly: Imperialism and the Creation of Modern Iraq*, London: Constable and Robinson, 2004; Tariq Ali, *Bush in Babylon: The Recolonisation of Iraq*, London: Verso, 2003: 42–65.

Israel. The 1956 events dramatized the decline of the French and British empires and the increased importance of the United States and Israel in the Middle East. By 1962 Algeria achieved its independence and became an important new Arab power. The 1950s and 1960s saw a big growth in Arab radio in general and in Egyptian radio in particular. Newspapers continued on an elite path; in the 1960s new Arab TV stations followed the common pattern in importing American TV series. The main media focus, however, was upon the achievement of independence and upon supporting the new nation state.

The next two decades, 1970–1990, were an era of continuing nationalism and new oil wealth. Following the Israeli-Arab wars of 1967 and 1973, the Arab-led OPEC (Organization of Petroleum Exporting Countries) in 1973 quadrupled the price of oil. The years 1979–1980 saw another huge oil price increase, the collapse of the shah's regime in Iran, the arrival of Ayatollah Khomeini, and the 444-day siege of the American embassy in Teheran. The year 1982 found the Israeli army and air force in action in Lebanon, followed in 1983 by the killing of 300 U.S. marines, French paratroopers, and others in Beirut. These events gave the Middle East greatly enhanced economic, political, and media significance.

During 1978–1983, new satellite facilities made it possible to film and transmit TV news pictures around the world within a few hours. One consequence was a continuing flow of dramatic "earlier today" news coverage. The Teheran crowds that ousted the shah in 1979 were the largest yet seen on TV; there was no precedent to the night-after-night coverage of the U.S. Teheran embassy humiliation. TV news coverage of the Israeli bombing and shelling of Beirut in 1982 was more vivid, dramatic, and shocking than almost anything previously seen in the "sitting room war" genre.[11] A further flood of dramatic TV news pictures began to flow in 1987 with the start of the Palestinian "intifada" against Israel. In 1973 there were still only one million TV sets in Egypt and Iraq combined, but the number grew rapidly[12] and by 1990 probably the majority of Arab citydwellers had some kind of access to a TV set. This TV coverage certainly helped to focus both world and Arab attention on the Israel-Palestine issue and the role of the United States in support of the Israeli military.

Paradoxically, however, while the United States was increasingly unpopular for its support of Israel, the 1980s also were a high point for American television market share inside the Arab world. Hollywood was assisted in the 1980s by an Arab boycott against the importation of TV programming from Egypt, the Arab world's leading producer of TV programming. The 1980s boycott was intended to punish Egypt for having made

---

[11] For an account of Beirut in 1982, see Robert Fisk, *Pity the Nation: Lebanon at War*, Oxford, UK: Oxford University Press, 2001 (first publ. 1990): 199–400.

[12] Yahya Abu Bakr, Saad Labib, and Hamdy Kandil, *Development Communication in the Arab States: Needs and Priorities*, Paris: UNESCO, 1985.

Table 17.1 Sources of Transmitted Television Programming, 1983

SOURCE OF PROGRAMMING	TV Transmitted by (Percentage)	
	EGYPT	FOUR OTHER ARAB NATIONS (ALGERIA, SYRIA, TUNISIA, YEMEN)
Domestic production	65	52.5
United States	19	9.5
Other Arab countries	5*	14.7
United Kingdom, France, Germany	7	9.2
Other†	4	14.1
Total	100	100

* All from United Arab Emirates.
† Includes Japan, Soviet Union, and "other socialist" nation-states.
Source: Tapio Varis, *The International Flow of Television Programmes*, Paris: UNESCO, 1985: 45–47.

peace with Israel. However, even during this period, Arab TV imports from Hollywood were less than massive—as Table 17.1 shows. Following a common pecking order pattern, the biggest regional media power, Egypt, was also the biggest importer from America. A simple unweighted average across five Arab countries showed each one importing 11.5 percent of its TV programming from the United States in 1983.

Post–Cold War nationalism increasingly prevailed from 1990 onward across the Arab world. This period saw a growth in Islamic fundamentalism. In media terms the 1990s saw the consolidation of Arab and Arabic television; this was increasingly an era of satellite television, much of it financed from Saudi Arabia (discussed later in this chapter). The era also saw two U.S. (and their allies) wars against Iraq, in which the media again played prominent roles.

The previously quoted 2004 Zogby study showed that across six Arab countries, 53 percent of respondents saw "Arab" as either their primary or secondary identity. Sixty-five percent of respondents quoted the current Israeli prime minister, Ariel Sharon, as the world leader they "disliked most." These, and other, data indicate the emergence of broad Arab public opinion and a widespread (but far from universal) sense of Arab identity, or pan-Arab nationalism. As with many other categories and examples of nationalism, this pan-Arab nationalism emphasized antagonism toward opponents and enemies. The sense of Arab identity seemed to rely heavily on opposition to Israel and the United States, but was also fueled by resentment against autocratic governments and elite oil wealth.[13] Much of this antagonism was

---

[13] Fouad Ajami, "How Oil Fuelled the Middle East's Rage," *International Herald Tribune*, October 18–19, 2003.

then directed into traditional (Muslim) religion[14] and support for selected Arabic media. Fifty-three percent of respondents in the 2004 Zogby poll said that Al-Jazeera was their top choice among international TV news channels.

Egypt: Leading Arab Media Power

Egypt has been the leading Arab media power for the last 200 years. Although Hollywood movies were significant especially in 1920s and 1930s Egypt, over the last 120 years British and French media influences have probably outweighed American influences. However, Egyptian national media and Egyptian national culture have been more significant than any foreign influences. For over 120 years Egypt has attracted journalists and media from other Arab countries; and Egypt has exported to other Arab countries its own books, movies, newspapers, magazines, popular music, and TV series.

Egypt can claim to be the world's oldest nation. However, the air passenger approaching Cairo at first sees nothing but empty light brown desert; then there is the smog of Cairo and a dark green strip of fertile land along the Nile. Most of the population still lives along the Nile and in the Nile delta; some 20 million people live in greater Cairo. Egypt celebrates its unique location at the "corner of Africa, Asia and Europe."

In Egypt the mass media in general exercise an unusually commanding position. Egyptian entertainment stars are known across the Arab world; the Egyptian daily *Al Ahram* was the leading Arabic newspaper throughout the twentieth century, and Egypt's total daily sale always surpassed the total combined daily sale of the next three largest national Arab newspaper industries. Moreover, Egypt's three leaders during its first 50 years of true independence (Gamal Nasser, Anwar Sadat, and Hosni Mubarak) were men of the media. It was radio that made President Nasser the leading Arab political personality of the late 1950s and the 1960s. President Sadat relied heavily on the media,[15] and the gunfire that killed him (in 1981) was broadcast live. President Mubarak was also an active media performer, both through major speeches transmitted live and through "big interviews" on TV and in the press.

Egypt has changed hugely since the 1950s. During 1950–2005 the population grew from 21 million to 74 million. But while "everything changed" in Egypt, much also stayed the same. Despite considerable internal turbulence, there was no civil war, and only sporadic fundamentalist violence and assassinations; no further military coups occurred after the two birth-of-the-new-nation army coups of 1952 and 1954. In the early 2000s

---

[14] Clifford Geertz, "Which Way to Mecca?" *New York Review of Books*, June 12, 2003: 27–30, and June 26, 2003: 36–39.

[15] Desmond Meiring, *Fire of Islam*, London: Wildwood House, 1982.

much was the same as in the early 1950s. The Egyptian population was growing at 2 percent annually in the early 1950s and still at 1.7 percent in the early 2000s; the Egyptian president in 1955 (Nasser) was a soldier, while the 2005 president (Mubarak) was a former head of the Egyptian air force; in both 1955 and 2005 Egypt was a poor country with only modest amounts of oil and natural gas. Income per head did increase after 1985. The radical landholding reforms of the 1950s had been reversed by the 1990s. In 2005 Mubarak did face a more "democratic" presidential election, which he won with 88.5 percent of the vote.

Egypt in both 1955 and 2005 was an authoritarian state with only a few democratic trimmings;[16] press and religious freedom existed only on a minor scale. In both 1955 and 2005 the conservative religious group the Muslim Brotherhood was forced to maintain a very low profile. In the 2005 parliamentary elections the Brotherhood won 17 percent of the seats. In both 1955 and 2005 some media opposition was tolerated, but small opposition publications struggled against severe financial disadvantages. During the 2005 elections both police and army units harassed journalists (and other professionals) who demonstrated against the regime in central Cairo.

In both 1955 and 2005 Egypt continued to operate two quite different versions of Arabic. Classical Arabic was used for serious newspapers, in books, and in most formal education; "Egyptian Arabic" was used in movies, music, and much of radio and TV (outside news and religious programming). This was like modern Italy using both Latin and Italian; in both 1955 and 2005 the perverse language combination exacerbated inequalities in education and literacy, while cementing differences between social classes and between the rich and poor. Inflexibility in language also helped to maintain the yawning gap between Muslim fundamentalism and the facts of modern life in Cairo and in Egypt.

For their first 150 years (1800–1952) the Egyptian media operated against a background of fluctuating empire and fluctuating nationalism. Egypt was a semi-official part of the British Empire during 1882–1952, but this happened mainly because of a British wish to defend the Suez Canal. Following policies somewhat similar to those they operated in India, the British discouraged political opposition but tolerated moderate press criticism. An Egyptian (classical) Arabic press grew very slowly; from the 1860s this press relied upon Reuters for its foreign news.[17] In the 1920s Hollywood's silent movies achieved popularity but mainly with the expatriates (Greeks, Italians and Germans, as well as French and British). As in India, the arrival of the talkie movies stimulated the emergence of Egyptian cinema, using street (not

---

[16] Maye Kassem, *Egyptian Politics: The Dynamics of Authoritarian Rule*, Boulder, CO: Lynne Rienner, 2004; Anthony McDermott, *Egypt from Nasser to Mubarak: A Flawed Revolution*, London: Croom, Helm, 1988; Ahdaf Soueif, "Egypt Awakes," *The Guardian* weekend magazine, December 3, 2005: 96–105.

[17] Donald Read, *The Power of News. The History of Reuters*, Oxford, UK: Oxford University Press, 1992: 81–84, 165–66, 270–71.

Figure 17.2 Hand-painted advertising for an Egyptian film, Cairo, 2004. (Mark Henley/Panos Pictures.)

classical) Arabic. Hollywood movies in Egypt achieved their peak market share in the 1920s and 1930s. In the years after 1945 the Egyptian industry was making about 60 films a year.[18] In a detailed analysis, Robert Vitalis concluded that by 1950 Hollywood had only about a 20 percent share of the Egyptian movie audience.[19] Egyptian films attracted much bigger audiences than did the large number of exhibited Hollywood films.

The years 1952–1970 were the years of Egypt's new independence and newly assertive nationalism. Egypt's nationalism previous to 1952 was primarily nationalism against Britain; there was a love-and-hate element in that many Egyptians admired British "fair play" and democracy but despaired of Britain ever granting these luxuries to Egyptians. After the British departed—once in 1952–1953 and again in 1956–1957—Egyptian popular nationalism was focused increasingly against the United States and against Israel.

Nasser became Egyptian prime minister in 1954 (and was president during 1956–1970). Nasser was not greatly interested in the Egyptian movie industry, which was especially strong in the 1960s. Nasser's prime media

---

[18] Georges Sadoul, *The Cinema in the Arab Countries*, Beirut: Interarab Centre of Cinema and Television, 1966: 69–97.

[19] Robert Vitalis, "American Ambassador in Technicolor and Cinemascope: Hollywood and Revolution on the Nile," in Walter Armbrust (ed.), *Mass Mediations: New Approaches to Popular Culture in the Middle East and Beyond*, Berkeley: University of California Press, 2000: 269–91.

concern was with radio.[20] In 1951 Egyptian radio was on a modest scale with a total of about 300,000 radio sets, mostly in Cairo and Alexandria. Foreign radio in 1951 was relatively strong, with British radio (BBC and also a "gray" British station in Cyprus) in the lead. Next came other Arab countries' radio, followed by U.S. and then French and Monte Carlo radio.[21] Nasser was himself a virtuoso radio performer, effectively combining street Arabic with Koranic and poetic overtones. Nasser rapidly expanded radio services aimed both at domestic and foreign audiences; transmitter power was greatly increased. The Cairo-based "Voice of the Arabs" became in the later 1950s the first successful attempt to address all of the Arab national publics as a single audience. In 1956 Egypt did 101 hours a week of radio broadcasting to foreign audiences. This had trebled by 1960 and doubled again to 589 hours a week in 1966.[22] To Arab peoples still under colonial governments, the Voice of the Arabs preached armed struggle, assassination, and crowd violence. French and British military forces, attempting to contain violent independence movements in places such as Algeria and Aden (later Yemen), discovered the Egyptian radio to be a potent antagonist. During the years 1957–1959, Egypt was the fifth biggest external radio broadcaster in the world. But as many other nations—both Arab and non-Arab—developed Arabic language external radio, the impact (and credibility) of Voice of the Arabs declined.

Nasser died in 1970, and the next two decades saw several changes of direction. During his presidency (1970–1981) Sadat attempted to make permanent peace with Israel. Sadat refashioned official Egyptian nationalism away from Nasser's socialism and toward cautious containment of Islamic fundamentalism. During 1970–1990 Egypt developed a strong domestic television industry; Egypt could build upon its recent radio strength and upon its film industry, which by 1980 had made about 2,000 films. Egyptian films (like those in India) stressed music and song, and Egypt by 1980 had a substantial national team of music and acting stars. One such acting star was Amina Rizq (1910–2003), who appeared in 250 films and, from 1958, in television; she was also a celebrated stage actress and appeared in many Arabic translations of classic European drama.[23]

Egypt is a complex, ancient and modern nation that struggles to bridge a number of linked contradictions, both in its mass media and in its broader national culture. The Egyptian media offer both commercial entertainment and devout Muslim programming. This apparent contradiction is especially evident at Ramadan each year. During the daytime fast, both radio and TV offer religious programming; however, after dusk, when the fast is broken,

[20] Sydney W. Head (ed.), *Broadcasting in Africa*, Philadelphia: Temple University Press, 1974: 15–28; Douglas A. Boyd, *Broadcasting in the Arab World*, Philadelphia: Temple University Press, 1982: 13–50.

[21] Daniel Lerner, *The Passing of Traditional Society: Modernizing the Middle East*, New York: Free Press, 1958: 214–63.

[22] *BBC Handbook*, London: BBC, 1966, 1971.

[23] Adel Darwish, "Obituary: Amina Rizq," *The Independent*, September 13, 2003.

Egyptian television fills the evening schedule with much of its strongest commercial entertainment of the year. Advertisers also like these Ramadan evenings because the audiences are large and in a relaxing consumer-happy mood. Egypt and Cairo claim to be the home of the belly dance, a tradition that seems somewhat contrary to Islamic norms of decorous female deportment and dress. Cairo also has a Holy Koran radio station, which might seem to pose few challenges to the censors; however, the regime has sometimes disciplined Koran radio for allowing its Koranic commentaries to become too rabidly fundamentalist.

Another potential contradiction exists between Egypt as a secular state (which includes a substantial Christian minority) and Egypt as a traditional home of Muslim orthodoxy and scholarship. An analysis by Walid Abdelnasser of an Islamist Egyptian newspaper, *Al-Mukhtar Al-Islami*, in the 1990s, indicated a number of repeated themes and assumptions. *Al-Mukhtar* saw the West as a source of enmity and threat; the West, and especially the United States, was seen as intervening to assist Christian minorities in Muslim countries, as well as to support Israel. The West was seen as unfairly praising Muslim critics of their own religion and as unfairly equating Islam and Muslims with terrorism.[24]

In another Egypt-based analysis, Karin Werner studied a group of devout Islamist women who advocated nonviolence and religious studies. They also saw the West as engaged in imperialist exploitation. These women saw the commercial Egyptian media in general as seductive and dangerous, while satellite TV dishes were the source of much evil. These Muslim women followed self-denying rules by which they deliberately avoided contact with popular Egyptian mass media. Nevertheless, these same women had seen horribly explicit pictures of the dead bodies of Bosnian Muslims, whom they regarded as the victims of 1990s Western imperialist aggression. The pictures reached this Egyptian religious group with the help of Saudi Arabian finance. Thus military action in Bosnia, which the West had seen as rescuing Bosnian Muslims from Serb ethnic cleansing, was seen by these devout women as Western genocide against Bosnian Muslims.[25]

There has long been what looks like a contradiction between Egypt's foreign policy and Egypt's mass media assumptions, on the issue of relations with the United States and Israel. In 1979 Egypt was expelled from the Arab League for participating in the 1978–1979 United States–Israel–Egypt Camp David meeting hosted by President Jimmy Carter and in the subsequent 1979 Camp David Accords. Egyptian foreign policy continued to pursue peace with Israel, and Egypt (along with Israel) accepted significant U.S. financial

---

[24] Walid M. Abdelnasser, "Islam and the West: Perspectives from the Egyptian Press with Particular Emphasis on Islamist Papers," in Kai Hafez (ed.), *Islam and the West in the Mass Media*, Cresskill, NJ: Hampton Press, 2000: 141–56.

[25] Karin Werner, "'Coming Close to God' Through the Media: A Phenomenology of the Media Practices of Islamist Women in Egypt," in Kai Hafez (ed.), *Mass Media, Politics and Society in the Middle East*, Cresskill, NJ: Hampton Press, 2001: 199–216.

support. But in Egyptian films and TV series the Israelis and Americans were routinely presented in a much more negative light; for example, Egyptian fiction has been well supplied with female Israeli spies who aimed to seduce vulnerable Egyptian males.

Another contradiction was the continued survival of both classical Arabic and popular Egyptian Arabic. Because classical Arabic was the main medium of education, the entire activity of reading was, in practice, discouraged; this in turn skewed the Egyptian media against print media and books and toward radio and television. Very few Egyptians use classical Arabic for everyday conversation. But classical Arabic prevails in the newspapers and in broadcast news; this in practice means that all news in censored twice— once for politics and then again for correct use of Koranic language and grammar.

The Arabic language divide even affects the pronouncements of leading politicians. For example, when President Mubarak was interviewed on Egyptian television, the questions were posed in classical Arabic; Mubarak then replied in Egyptian Arabic, but for press publication his answers were translated into classical Arabic.[26] This two-language convention seems unlikely to facilitate efficient, or accurate, political communication; but it could be said that Egypt is still in a better position than other Arab countries, which effectively have to use three versions of the language—classical Arabic, their own national popular Arabic, and Egyptian Arabic (the language of imported Egyptian films, TV, radio, and music).

Another Egyptian source of contradiction or polarization is between the wealthy and the poor. Politics, commercial life, education, and the mass media are all highly polarized. Power in Egypt is concentrated into the president's executive office, the army, the internal security apparatus, and the ruling National Democratic Party's patronage machine.[27] The 1992 law that reversed Nasser's farm reforms[28] of the 1950s is a relevant example; this 1992 law strengthened the large landlords and radically weakened the position of six million small tenant farmers and their families. This law was passed by a national Egyptian legislature that included many farm landlords and no tenants; the legislation reflected World Bank and International Monetary Fund polices of the early 1990s. The land reform law received strong support from *Al-Ahram* and other major newspapers.[29]

---

[26] Niloofar Haeri, *Sacred Language, Ordinary People: Dilemmas of Culture and Politics in Egypt*, New York: Palgrave Macmillan, 2003: 68–69, 99–100; Yasir Suleiman, *The Arabic Language and National Identity: A Study in Ideology*, Edinburgh: Edinburgh University Press, 2003; Yasir Suleiman, *A War of Words: Language and Conflict in the Middle East*, Cambridge, UK: Cambridge University Press, 2004; Navid Kermani, "Silent Sirens: The Language of Islam and How Osama bin Laden Betrays It," *Times Literary Supplement*, October 1, 2004: 12–15.

[27] Max Rodenbeck, "Egypt: God's Choice," *Foreign Policy*, November/December 2003: 41–42.

[28] Keith Wheelock, *Nasser's New Egypt*, New York: Praeger, 1960: 74–108.

[29] Ray Bush (ed.), *Counter-Revolution in Egypt's Countryside: Land and Farmers in the Era of Economic Reform*, London: Zed Books, 2002: 107–11; David Hirst, "Egypt's Peasants Yearn for Nasser," *The Guardian*, October 7, 1997.

372 NATIONAL MEDIA AND WORLD REGION MEDIA

Television has undoubtedly helped to extend the range of the Egyptian media beyond the elite. Egyptian television's most popular programming since the 1970s has been an endless flood of fictional melodrama. These melodramas depend on advertising revenue and typically portray middle-class Cairo, or other big city, families. In 2004–2005 a single Cairo location (Media Production City) was producing about 800 TV drama episodes per year.[30]

But print media continue to be primarily elite media. The chief editor of the leading daily paper, *Al-Ahram*, has—since the Nasser era—always been close to the incumbent president; editors are changed but *Al-Ahram* sails serenely onward.[31] Some eight large publishing organizations dominate both book and newspaper publishing; they operate in classical Arabic and attract most of the publishing finance.[32] There are other elite media, including a small but impressive European-style art movie sector.[33]

However, the elite publishing effort and the affluent (and politically bland) television still leave other sources of demand unsatisfied. One consequence is a collection of shrill tabloid weeklies and gossip magazines. In Cairo (as in China) some journalists both sell advertising and write stories; blackmail by the press is commonplace, and cash in envelopes changes hands.

Another consequence of the overall media apparatus is that poor and/or religious Egyptians feel underrepresented by Egypt's largish media industry. Not only the Muslim Brotherhood but also the more intellectual and sophisticated "New Islamists"—despite some media access—feel excluded from the mainstream media.[34] This leaves a continuing role for the traditional mode of communication in the mosque, or the role of the Islamic pulpit.[35] There are 3,000 mosques in Cairo alone.

The Egyptian government also knew that about half of all adult women and a third of all adult men were still illiterate in the early 2000s.

---

[30] Amanda Cuthbert, "Egyptian TV: A Cultural Oasis?" *Broadcast*, December 10, 1979: 14–15; Lila Abu-Lughod, "Egyptian Melodrama—Technology of the Modern Subject?" in Faye D. Ginsburg, Lila Abu-Lughod, and Brian Larkin (eds.), *Media Worlds: Anthropology on New Terrain*, Berkeley: University of California Press, 2002: 115–33; Fiona Symor, "'White Elephant' Starts to Pay Off," *Financial Times* special report: "FT Egypt," December 7, 2005: 4.
[31] Munir K. Nasser, *Press, Politics and Power: Egypt's Heikal and Al-Ahram*, Ames: Iowa State University Press, 1979.
[32] Stefan Winkler, "Distribution of Ideas: Book Production and Publishing in Egypt, Lebanon, and the Middle East," in Kai Hafez (ed.), *Mass Media, Politics and Society in the Middle East*, Cresskill, NJ: Hampton Press, 2001: 159–73.
[33] Ibrahim Fawal, *Youssef Chahine*, London: British Film Institute, 2001.
[34] Raymond William Baker, *Islam Without Fear: Egypt and the New Islamists*, Cambridge, MA: Harvard University Press, 2003.
[35] Asghar Fathi, "The Role of the Islamic Pulpit," *Journal of Communication*, Vol. 29/3, Summer 1979: 102–6; Asghar Fathi, "The Islamic Pulpit as a Medium of Political Communication," *Journal for the Scientific Study of Religion*, Vol. 20/2, 1981: 163–71.

French Versus Arabic Media and Culture in Algeria

The three former French colonies of Algeria, Morocco, and Tunisia have a combined total population that is similar to Egypt's. These countries are geographically close to Europe. All three of these countries continue to have close connections with France, involving migration, trade, culture, and language. In all three countries French-language media compete for supremacy against Arabic-language media.[36] American and Anglo media are very much less significant.

In recent decades in Algeria, American movies and television have had about 15 percent of audience time.[37] But over half of Algerian TV has been made in Algeria; the remainder was split into three segments—from France, from other Arab countries, and from the United States. However, the U.S. programming has been dubbed into French in France, while the Algerian-produced programming is in both French and Arabic. In terms of language the proportion is about 50 percent Arabic, 35 percent French, and 15 percent American-French.

The close connection between France and Algeria continues despite the ferocity of the independence struggle in 1954–1962. Both the French military and the Algerian insurgents resorted to deliberate killings of civilians and used torture on a large scale and over an extended period. There are both higher and lower estimates, but if we accept an estimate of one million Algerians killed, this was about 10 percent of the 1954 population—with many other people permanently affected by major injuries and torture. Why was France so fiercely determined to stay in Algeria? Both Morocco and Tunisia had relatively peaceful paths to independence (achieved in 1956). But Algeria was different because of its nearly one million French (and other European) settlers in 1954. France claimed that Algeria was part of France, while the French-Algerians (most had been born in Algeria) regarded themselves as French people permanently residing in Algeria.

A French army of 37,000 men arrived in Algeria in June 1830. After heavy fighting (especially in the early 1840s) Algeria was officially proclaimed as an integral part of France in 1848. Resistance continued, especially from the non-Arab "native" Berbers. Resistance was strongest in Kabylia, a primarily Berber area of coastal hills and mountains to the east of Algiers. In 1871 the French announced their final conquest in Kabylia, where 1.5 million acres

---

[36] Lise Garon, *Dangerous Alliances: Civil Society, the Media and Democratic Transition in North Africa*, London: Zed Books, 2003.

[37] Michael Pilsworth, "Algeria," in Douglas A. Boyd (ed.), *Broadcasting in the Arab World*, Philadelphia: Temple University Press, 1982: 170–83; François Chevaldonné, "Globalisation and Orientalism: The Case of TV Serials," *Media, Culture and Society*, Vol. 9, 1987: 137–48; François Chevaldonné, "Nationalization, Market Economy and Sociocultural Development: The Structures of Audiovisual Communication in Independent Algeria," *Media, Culture and Society*, Vol. 10, 1988: 269–84.

374 NATIONAL MEDIA AND WORLD REGION MEDIA

of the best land were confiscated. French farmers increasingly took over all of the most fertile land along Algeria's Mediterranean Coast. The French authorities made French the official language of Algeria; the use of Arabic was forbidden in much of education and administration.

A fairly small fraction of the population of Algerian boys were put through the standard French school education of the period. The boys were being trained (along common imperial lines) to acquire manual skills, to perform clerical work in the French administration, and to fill the lower ranks in the colonial army.

A summary of the language situation—at the start of the Algerian independence struggle in 1954—might be as follows: Most Algerians spoke local versions of Arabic, while a very small minority were literate in classical Arabic. A small, mainly urban and military, minority could both read and write better in French than in Arabic. Another minority, of Berbers, spoke one of several Berber dialects (or languages) but could speak no Arabic or French.

However, despite about 80 percent of the Algerian population having some facility in spoken Arabic, the French language continued to advance both during and after the 1954–1962 independence struggle.[38] Arabic was designated after independence as the sole official language of Algeria. But the French language advanced for two main reasons. First, it would have been difficult to make Arabic the sole language of education; there were the problems of "high" and "low" Arabic and the sheer scale of the problem of creating sufficient Arabic printed materials. The regime became reluctant to import educational materials from Egypt, not least because an early consignment of Egyptian Muslim Brotherhood schoolteachers were regarded as having been too Muslim fundamentalist. A second reason was that most of the political and military elite had been educated in French; indeed, many of the military and political elite were themselves of Berber origin and had jumped from Berber families into French education without acquiring much Arabic. In fact, the Algerian elite is Berber-Algerian more than it is Arab-Algerian. The army, whose members have dominated Algerian politics, has been led by the Chaouis; another northern Algerian Berber people, the Kabyles, have dominated industry, state administration, and the prestige francophone media.[39] These latter facts help to explain both why French has prospered in "Arab" Algeria and why French-language newspapers have retained such a strong position against the Arabic language press. Moreover, the skewing of power toward an ethnic minority was not unusual, but was common across the post-colonial world, including the Middle East.

[38] Jacqueline Kaye and Abdelhamid Zoubir, *The Ambiguous Compromise: Language, Literature and National Identity in Algeria and Morocco*, London: Routledge, 1990; Yahia Mahambi, "Tradition, 'National' Culture and Television in Algeria," *Media Development*, 2, 1989: 28–31.
[39] Hafid Gafaïti, "The Monotheism of the Other," in Anne-Emmanuelle Berger (ed.), *Algeria in Others' Languages*, Ithaca, NY: Cornell University Press, 2002: 19–43.

Throughout the twentieth century both the mass media and political violence played salient roles in Algeria. The French never completely succeeded in pacifying either Algeria or Morocco; outbreaks of Muslim violence (against the French, the Jews, or other Muslim groups) were frequent occurrences. The 1914–1918 war was significant; 173,000 Muslims joined the French military and 25,000 Muslim Algerians died in France.

In the interwar period Muslim Algerians were allowed to join political parties; party newspapers were set up, some local elections were won, and then the French reversed direction. For example, in early 1919 Emir Khaled launched a newspaper (*Ikdam*) and later in the year his list of candidates won the local municipal elections; the French government then rejected the election results.

World War II had a significant impact because Algerians were well placed to observe the Germans, the Vichy French, the de Gaulle French, the Americans, and the British—all of whom were active in northern Africa. During 1939–1945, and after, Algerians seem to have received more news from both home and abroad than did the citizens of many African and Middle Eastern countries. French radio (both domestic and external) could be heard along the Algerian coastline. Newspapers and magazines arrived regularly from France.

During the 1954–1962 independence war there was a huge international media interest in the violent happenings. Most of the violence involved Muslim Algerians versus the French and their Muslim assistants. When the French army finally departed, they left behind some 263,000 Algerian Muslim "auxiliaries"; several tens of thousands of these auxiliaries were massacred, mostly in December 1962.

Another form of Algerian violence on Algerians involved the two separate armies of soldiers that had fought against the French. There was a regular Algerian army formation, which operated from across the borders in Morocco and Tunisia and came to power with Colonel Houari Boumedienne's government of 1965–1978. But initially it was the soldiers of the internal insurrection, under Ahmed Ben Bella, who took power (1962–1965). These two sets of forces were involved in Algerian versus Algerian civil war, both before and after the French departure. Algeria's eight-year war of independence became the subject of a justly famous movie, *The Battle of Algiers* (1966), directed by the Italian Gillo Pontecorvo.

Following his 1965 coup against Ben Bella, Boumedienne asserted that fewer pro-Western policies were required. During his relatively peaceful period in power (1965–1978),[40] Boumedienne became one of the acknowledged leaders of the "nonaligned" group of countries that proclaimed a "third world" separate from the Cold War East-versus-West confrontation. In line with this international perspective, the Boumedienne regime allowed

---

[40] Adam Shatz, "Algeria's Failed Revolution," *New York Review of Books*, July 3, 2003: 52–56.

some diversity among Algerian newspapers (but not in radio-TV). In 1966 this author observed Algerians reading *Le Monde, Le Figaro,* and other Paris publications in downtown Algiers cafés, which had been preferred targets for anti-French bombings only a few years earlier.

The media were again prominent during a fresh Algerian crisis that began in 1988 and lasted for more than a decade. This crisis turned into a low intensity civil war that claimed some 150,000 lives—many of them women and children whose throats were slashed.[41] The full ferocity of these events was, once again, hard to comprehend, although the single central event was unambiguous. The governing Front de Libération Nationale (FLN) had been in power for nearly three decades when it called national legislative elections. A new legal Islamic party, the Islamic Salvation Front (FIS), which had previously triumphed at the 1990 municipal elections, scored a big success in the first round of the national legislative elections of December 26, 1991. This was to be a (French-style) two-round election, but on January 11 and 12, 1992, the National Assembly was dissolved and the second round of legislative elections were canceled. On January 14 the regime reshaped itself into a new government with a new president, Mohamed Boudiaf; less than six months later on June 29, 1992, Boudiaf was assassinated.

A major insurrection now began; new anti-terrorism measures were introduced; several prominent Algerians were murdered; in March 1993 Amnesty International denounced the widespread use of torture in Algeria.[42] The insurrection proclaimed its Muslim and Arab authenticity against what was seen as the non-Muslim and Westernized government and its military backers. The insurrection targeted the police, other government personnel, and government buildings. The police and government special forces targeted members of the insurrection and their families; both sides put up fake roadblocks and killed the passengers of cars and buses.[43]

Worth noting are two media aspects of these events that throughout the 1990s averaged at least 10,000 violent deaths per year. First, journalists played a very prominent role during the insurrection. Fifty-one journalists were killed in Algeria during 1994–2004, more than in any other single country. Many editors of small publications bravely took advantage of such press freedom as existed. Both the regime and the insurgents used the mainstream press and the "mushroom press" to carry their fight to the enemy. Some new publications that were closed for daring to criticize Algeria's military godfathers then reappeared on the Internet.

---

[41] For example, see Robert Fisk: " 'I felt the knife at my neck. My wife was so brave. She tried to help. So they cut her throat in front of me,' " *The Independent,* October 22, 1997.

[42] Benjamin Stora, *Algeria, 1830–2000: A Short History,* Ithaca, NY: Cornell University Press, 2001; Mark Huband, *Warriors of the Prophet: The Struggle for Islam,* Boulder, CO: Westview Press, 1998: 46–72, 94–139.

[43] Robert Fisk, *The Great War of Civilisation: The Conquest of the Middle East,* London: Fourth Estate, 2005: 631–719.

Second, the media made a major contribution to the mind-set and worldview of the young Islamist insurgents. Evidence for this is to be found in a book by Luis Martinez about the war. Martinez lived among the insurrectionists in a southern suburb of Algiers, Les Eucalyptus; his anthropological fieldwork and interviewing must have required courage comparable to that of outspoken journalists. Martinez argues that the otherwise inexplicable ferocity of the confrontation became easier to comprehend when seen as a struggle for both political power and entrepreneurial success. The conflict of the police and the special forces (and their informers) against the Islamist insurrection had some of the qualities of conflict between mafia factions or rival drug cartels.[44]

According to Martinez, ordinary people in the Algiers suburbs relied heavily on media images to construct their "imaginaire," or worldview.[45] He refers frequently to Algerian television, which most young Arab men could see in their family homes or in cafés.[46] It seems to have been the TV news and other frequent shows that made the biggest impression; also significant were newspapers and music, while state radio probably reinforced the images of state television.

Two different categories of young Arab males had their own media relationships; religious young men were advised to avoid all French and foreign media. Foreign satellite TV was known as "paradiaboliques" and the French Canal Plus as "Canal Blis" (Satan Channel). Devout Muslims also saw the Algerian media as promoting corrupt Western consumer culture and sexual permissiveness.

Most young Algiers males, however, were less devout and many were unemployed "hittistes" (those who "prop up the wall"). These youths were typically involved in casual work and/or casual crime; they were much more enthusiastic about football, entertainment, and especially Raï music (from the large coastal city of Oran).

Both categories of young men agreed in seeing the military-backed Algerian regime as too close to France and too reliant on the French language. The regime was also seen as still socialist or even communist, at a time (around 1990) when eastern Europe was rejecting communism. The military-backed regime was seen as insufficiently Arab and as rejecting the Sunni Muslim religion.

Most of these young men and their parents were engaged in reinterpreting images offered to them by Algerian state media. News from eastern Europe was seen as showing the Algerian military regime as socialist and out of touch with the world. But news of the conflict between Israelis and Palestinians

---

[44] Committee to Protect Journalists, quoted in *The Economist*, August 14, 2004.

[45] Luis Martinez, *The Algerian Civil War, 1990–1998* (first publ. as *La Guerre Civile en Algérie* in 1998) London: Hurst, in association with the Centre d'Etudes et de Recherches Internationales, Paris), 2000: 38–39, 43–46, 64–69, 113, 157–61.

[46] In 1989 Algeria had about 12 million adults, about 3 million (mainly black and white) TV sets, and about 35,000 satellite antennas. "The Maghreb," *Variety*, May 9, 1990: 41–58.

reflected Algerian state television's own anti-Israel framework—which most of its viewers were happy to accept.

The state media's repeated portrayals of the heroic independence struggle of 1954–1962 were seen by these young Algiers men as indicating the dangers of the present closeness of the regime to France. Current news coverage was seen as indicating that France was giving military and other assistance to the hated Algerian military regime.

Daily TV news coverage of the Algerian insurgency was seen as heavily biased against the insurgents. People who had themselves observed violent clashes claimed that subsequent official television portrayals were untrue. Many viewers were also unconvinced when the regime put captured (and probably tortured) insurgents onto television to confess their mistakes and crimes. Even bland fictional portrayals—for instance, a comedy series about a loveably incompetent policeman—were given a negative reinterpretation.

Martinez's account takes the story up to 1998. At that time the Algiers insurgents' worldview seems to have focused almost entirely on Algeria itself, the wider Arab world, Israel, and France. Interest in the rest of Europe was quite modest, and the United States was only glimpsed as a far distant land of California shopping malls and Chicago mafia gangs. Up to 1998 satellite television had still had only a modest impact. But this was soon to change.

Arab Satellite Television

Al-Jazeera, the Qatar-based satellite TV news channel, soon after its 1996 launch was reaching audiences right across the Arab world. While Al-Jazeera set new standards of independence for Arab television news, it nevertheless also reflected some ancient media traditions. Al-Jazeera relied heavily on Arab journalists previously employed by a BBC-Saudi Arabian (Orbit) satellite service that collapsed in April 1996. BBC Arabic radio had maintained a strong following in the Middle East from the 1930s[47] into the 1990s. Also in the 1980s and 1990s some of the most respected Arabic (and Arab-owned) newspapers and magazines were based in London; indeed, the "satellite revolution" began in newspapers before it reached television. Big Saudi Arabian financial subsidies were behind both the London-based newspapers and also some early London-based satellite TV offerings. Al-Jazeera, too, was launched with a big subsidy—from the ruler of Qatar.

Various satellite efforts in general, and Al-Jazeera in particular, were widely seen as likely to have an especially big impact in the Arabic language and across the Arab countries. In four main locations—Egypt, Saudi Arabia, the small Gulf states, and Lebanon—politicians, princes, and entrepreneurs saw huge possibilities in satellite television (and in other new technologies

---

[47] Peter Partner, *Arab Voices: The BBC Arabic Service, 1938–1988*, London: BBC, 1988.

such as the Internet). Satellite TV seemed to offer dramatic possibilities for the projection of governments and of personalities, including insurgent/terrorist leaders such as Osama bin Laden.[48]

In the late 1990s, Al Jazeera quickly became popular across the Arab world with audiences and unpopular with governments. Like other news and talk satellite-delivered TV channels, Al-Jazeera offered a combination of international news agency video plus video from its own camerapersons, correspondents, and stringers. But it also offered discussions, debates, and confrontations involving studio guests and interviewees. Both news and discussion featured conflict on several levels. Al-Jazeera offered conflicting news coverage and discussion on domestic issues within Arab nation-states; this involved conflicts between rich and poor, men and women, the religious and the secular, inside Saudi Arabia and inside other Arab nation-states. Equally likely to worry Arab governments was a focus on conflicts between Arab states. Yet another focus was on conflict between Arab states and non–Arab states—especially Israel, the United States, and Europe. This pursuit of conventional Western news values (with emphasis on negative events and conflict) led most Arab governments by year 2001 to have complained bitterly to Al-Jazeera and to the Qatar government. Advertisers tended to avoid a TV channel that was so unpopular with so many governments and politicians in power. Al-Jazeera correspondents were harassed, news bureaus were closed down, and news access was denied.

In 2000–2001 an already high profile and popular Al-Jazeera was presented with fresh news and conflict raw material. The second intifada began in 2000, enabling Al-Jazeera to spend many hours showing daily clashes between Palestinians and Israelis. Then came September 11, 2001; next was Afghanistan; and in 2003 the U.S. invasion of Iraq. For Al-Jazeera this provided plenty of news about conflicts within, and conflicts between, Arab states. But the early 2000s were especially strong on Arabs and Muslims versus the Americans and Europeans. The U.S. government (and military) joined the long list of governments that made bitter complaints; several of Al-Jazeera's offices and personnel were on the receiving end of American fire power. However, one content analysis of Iraq War TV news coverage found that Al-Jazeera was as "objective" as ABC, CBS, NBC, and CNN and was more objective than Fox News.[49]

---

[48] Jason Burke, "Theatre of Terror," *The Observer*, November 21, 2004: Review 1–2; Jason Burke, *Al-Qaeda: The True Story of Radical Islam*, London: Penguin Books, 2004.

[49] Sean Aday, Steven Livingston, and Maeve Hebert, "Embedding the Truth: A Cross Cultural Analysis of Objectivity and Television Coverage of the Iraq War," *Press/Politics*, Vol. 10/1, Winter 2005: 3–21; Mohammed El-Nawawy and Adel Iskandar, *Al Jazeera*, Cambridge, MA: Westview/Perseus, 2002; Naomi Sakr, "Maverick or Model? Al Jazeera's Impact on Arab Satellite Television," in Jean Chalaby (ed.), *Transnational Television Worldwide*, London: I.B. Tauris, 2004: 66–95; Hugh Miles, *Al Jazeera: How Arab TV News Challenged the World*, London: Abacus/Time Warner, 2005; Mohamed Zayani (ed.), *The Al Jazeera Phenomenon: Critical Perspectives on New Arab Media*, London: Pluto Press, 2005; William Wallis, "Al Jazeera; 'It Is Not Up to Us to Decide Who Is the Good Guy and Who Is the Bad,'" *Financial Times* special report, Qatar, May 18, 2005: 5.

Figure 17.3 Satellite dishes in Morocco (Marrakech). (Michael Morgensen/Panos Pictures.)

The Arab-Israeli six-day war of 1967 had revealed the weakness of communications between Arab countries. But the resulting Arabsat project lacked finance and the first Arab satellite was not launched until 18 years later, in 1985.[50] Previous to 1985, Algeria and Saudi Arabia were leaders in the use of Intelsat for domestic telecommunications. But the Europe-based video news suppliers (Visnews, UPITN, EBU, and French TV) established dedicated daily satellite news feeds, initially to the Gulf countries, from 1978.

First to make entire television channels available in other Arab countries were the Egyptians and Saudi Arabians; these two countries had the resources with which to make expensive channel launches, without any realistic expectation of significant revenue. In 1990 Egypt began to put onto Egyptian Space Channel (ESC) some of its popular domestic TV output. In 1991 the first Saudi Arabian satellite TV offering appeared in the form of Middle East Broadcasting Centre (MBC); MBC was based in London and generously financed by two Saudi billionaires (Saleh Kamel and Walid al Ibrahim).

Arabic satellite television has continued to be a high cost and low revenue activity. Despite big financial losses, satellite TV in the Arab world (as

---

[50] Elham Khali, *The Arab Satellite and the Flow of Information in the Arab World*, University of Amsterdam, unpublished doctoral dissertation, 1983; Nihal Rizh, "First Arab Satellite Launched," *World Broadcast News*, April 1985.

elsewhere) just grew and grew.[51] There was only one Arabic satellite channel in 1990, but by 2005 there were about 150 Arabic satellite TV channels.[52] The two financing (or subsidizing) modes remained broadly the same. By 2005 the Egyptian state broadcaster, Egyptian Radio and TV Union (ERTU), had 25 channels; most of the other Arab state broadcasters were also offering one or more of their channels via satellite to other countries.

The original Saudi subsidy-by-billionaire pattern had also grown and grown. Two other major Saudi-backed offerings were Orbit and Arab Radio and Television (ART), both launched in 1994 by wealthy Saudi entrepreneurs. MBC, Orbit, and ART (later combined with ANN) continued to be leading providers of satellite TV.

These mainly Saudi-backed channels were commercial in style (if not in profitability) and they aimed mainly at a premium "pay" market; but the premium subscriptions (especially in the 1990s) were similar to U.S. or European rates—too expensive for all but the top few percent of Arab households. These Saudi-backed channels by 2005 had lost big (but unknown) sums of money; estimates for their total losses varied between one billion and several billion dollars.

Egypt launched its first satellite (Nilesat 101) in 1998.[53] The leaders of Arab television, and pan-Arab satellite TV, continued to be Egypt and Saudi Arabia. Egypt (after the 1980s boycott) was not only the biggest satellite provider, but Egyptian programming was also exported to other countries on both domestic channels and via pan-Arab satellite broadcasting.

Also from around 1996 other smaller players began to export their programming via satellite. During the 1980s anti-Egypt boycott, many Egyptian TV actors and producers moved to the small oil-rich Gulf states; some of these made-by-Egyptians television series were then exported as Dubai or Abu Dhabi television. Some of these countries' wealthy princes wanted to become television players (even if in nonprofit mode). When Qatar-based Al-Jazeera was launched in 1996, it broadly fitted this financial pattern.

At least three other models of pan-Arab television originated from Lebanon, from Hollywood, and from Europe. Lebanon had in the 1960s and 1970s performed a sort of Hong Kong role for international news media. In the 1990s Lebanon became an active television production location, and two Lebanese channels were available on satellite from 1996; one was a Christian channel (LBC), while the Future channel was Sunni Muslim and controlled

---

[51] Naomi Sakr, *Satellite Realms: Transnational Television, Globalization and the Middle East*, London: I.B. Tauris, 2001; Jon B. Alterman, *New Media, New Politics? From Satellite Television to the Internet in the Arab World*, Washington, DC: The Washington Institute for Near East Policy, 1998; Sétareh Ghaffari-Farhangi, "The Era of Global Communications as Perceived by Muslims," *Gazette*, 1998, Vol. 60/4: 267–80.

[52] "Arab Satellite Television: The World Through Their Eyes," *The Economist*, February 26, 2005: 23–25.

[53] Sarah Callard, "Nilesat 101 Launched," *Cable and Satellite Europe*, June 1998: 12; Julian Clover, "Jewel of the Nile," *Cable and Satellite Europe*, February 1998: 22–23.

by Rafiq Hariri (Lebanon's top businessman and politician, who was assassinated in 2005). By 2005 tiny Lebanon had these two, plus four other, domestic TV channels;[54] two were Shia Muslim—NBN and Al Manor (the Hezbollah channel, seen by many opponents as terrorist TV).[55] Lebanon also has a reputation for producing much of the Arab world's least Muslim, least clothed, and most sexy television. Lebanon-based Future TV launched the first pan-Arab musical talent show in 2003. *Superstar* (based on the U.K. *Pop Idol* format, licensed by Fremantle) was carried by TV networks across the Arab world. The 12 finalists included amateur singers from seven Arab countries.[56]

Available to the Arab satellite audience are various American, British, French, and other Western television offerings, including versions of MTV. Already by 2000 there were 16 Showtime and 10 Star channels. The main audience for MTV, as for CNNI and BBC World, was and is the few percent of wealthiest households—and especially those who speak English or French.[57] More popular, by 2005, were at least a dozen Arabic music channels, featuring new young singing stars from Lebanon and Egypt. The most popular 2005 program in Iraq was a talent competition show, *Iraq Star*, transmitted by Lebanon-based Al-Sumariyah TV.[58]

Enigmas: Saudi Arabia, Conflict, and the Arab Public

Saudi Arabia in 1950 was almost entirely starved (for religious reasons) of movies and moving images; but by 2000 it was a television-saturated country. The Saudi GDP increased by 1,900 percent and the population by 570 percent in the same 1950–2000 period.

[54] Ali Jaffar, "Crossing the Great Divide," *Variety*, May 2–8, 2005: 32–33.
[55] Graham Usher, "Islamic Faithful Calls Hizbollah's Faithful Across Lebanese Airwaves," *The Guardian*, February 24, 1997; Andrew Muller, "We're Coming to Get You," *Independent on Sunday*, April 7, 2002: 20–23; Adam Shatz, "In Search of Hezbollah-II," *New York Review of Books*, May 13, 2004: 26–29; Roula Khalaf, "French Court Blocks Way for Hizbollah TV," *Financial Times*, December 15, 2004; Victoria Firmo-Fontain, "Power, NGOs and Lebanese Television: A Case Study of Al-Manar's TV and the Hezbollah Women's Association," in Naomi Sakr (ed.), *Women and Media in the Middle East*, London: I.B. Tauris, 2004: 162–79.
[56] Marwan M. Kraidy, "Globalization Avant La Lettre? Cultural Hybridity and Media Power in Lebanon," in Patrick D. Murphy and Marwan M. Kraidy (eds.), *Global Media Studies*, New York: Routledge, 2003: 276–95; Cecilia Zecchinelli, "Rivalry and Riots Make Arab 'Superstar' a Hit," *Variety*, August 25–31, 2003.
[57] In October 2003 satellite "pay" television was present in only 1.5 percent of Arab homes. Most subscribing homes were in Saudi Arabia, Kuwait, and United Arab Emirates. The most successful of these offerings were Orbit and Showtime, followed by ADD (Arab Digital Distribution) and ART. The slow "pay" take-up was attributed to the large number of "free" satellite services. *Screen Digest*, November 2003: 345.
[58] Ali Jaafar, "Rockin' in Iraq," *Variety*, October 24–30, 2005.

For many non-Arabs Saudi Arabia summons up conflicting images—a country split between the twenty-first and twelfth centuries; the American ally[59] that was also home to most of the September 11 suicide attackers.

Saudi Arabia can be said to have pioneered a new form of media finance—massive continuing subsidies from princely billionaires. While portraying the wealthy Saudi elite, the Saudi media have—it seems—largely ignored the huge gulf between the poor and the rich. Saudi royal vacations, costing more than one million dollars a day, do not receive the tabloid revelatory coverage devoted to the excesses of, for example, the British royal family. Meanwhile, in 2005 the Saudi princes and their friends controlled all the dozen Saudi daily papers, all domestic Saudi TV, two of the leading London-based Arabic dailies, and most of the most popular pan-Arab satellite TV channels.[60]

Another area of Arab television innovation seems to lie in the relentless portrayal of violent reality. Al-Jazeera and other TV channels (available in Saudi Arabia and elsewhere) do not edit out the most violent news images in the Euro-American manner. Consequently, Arab viewers can see more death and destruction—often about culturally close events and people—than can Westerners. Moreover, viewers are directed toward the websites (of Al-Jazeera and other Arab channels) if they wish to view further detail, such as a hostage being killed.

There is a marked shortage of reliable data on the Arab audience; both newspaper sales, and TV audience numbers, are unreliable. We seem to know more about the (limited) advances of Arab women as journalists, TV producers, and filmmakers[61] than we know about women as TV viewers. But across the Arab world, and especially in Saudi Arabia and the Gulf, many women (including women with university degrees) spend most of their time in the home; most women neither drive cars nor go out to paid employment.

Men also spend much time at home. Many Arab males are unemployed,[62] and in Saudi Arabia much of the paid work is done by foreign guest workers. Across the Arab world millions of young men sit at home—and not only in the midday heat—watching violent factual and fictional material; some of these young men will also be watching imported pornographic videos and Internet sites. Different individuals will draw different lessons from such viewing. Some viewers will obey religious instructions and focus on Islamic channels and videos; however, even this material can (according to Egyptian government authorities) encourage religious violence against the ungodly.

Another continuing dilemma for Arab governments is that positive nationalist sentiment tends to imply, or to accompany, other negative and hostile national sentiments. The Saudi Arabian population is concentrated in

[59] Craig Unger, *House of Bush, House of Saud*, New York: Scribner, 2004.
[60] "A Long Walk: A Survey of Saudi Arabia," *The Economist*, January 7, 2006.
[61] Naomi Sakr (ed.), *Women and Media in the Middle East: Power Through Self-Expression*, London: I.B. Tauris, 2004.
[62] Roula Khalaf, "Saudi Jobs' Desert That Feeds Terror," *Financial Times*, October 19, 2001.

an east-west band running from the Gulf oil areas through Riyadh to Jeddah on the Red Sea. But Saudi Arabia has at least 20 significant tribal ethnicities, especially in the lowly populated north. Official Saudi media inevitably play down such ethnic differences and promote national Saudi sentiments. This, however, leads to some neighboring countries—such as Iraq and Yemen— being presented by Saudi media in a negative light. Najran, on the Saudi side of the border with Yemen, is one notoriously sensitive area. Saudi Arabia seems committed to building an Israeli-style barrier along its border with Yemen. Politicians have noticed that by about 2010 the Saudi population will have fallen behind that of Yemen (as well as Iraq). The Gulf area where most of the Saudi oil is located is also highly sensitive because the local people are mainly Shia Muslim and thus far removed from the dominant Saudi brand of Sunni Muslim; also the oil area is delicate because of the large numbers of foreign workers (and their accompanying foreign media).

Whatever does and does not happen in the Arab world, it seems safe to predict yet further turbulence and a continuing central role for pan-Arab (not Western) media. The worldview of most Arabs will continue to be radically different from the worldview presented in the Euro-American media.

18

Spanish-Language Media in Latin America

The decline of U.S. political and media influence, in the years after 1950, was especially clear in Spanish Latin America. Throughout the four decades of the Cold War, the United States supported numerous Latin American military dictators, opposed any signs of socialism or communism, and deliberately undermined democratic politics and media. The U.S.-supported invasion of Cuba (April 1961) was one of the most inept of the CIA's many bungled exploits; but Washington policy in the region after 1961 remained obsessed with the eccentric Castro regime on the smallish island of Cuba. From the late 1980s, Washington's Latin American policies gradually switched to the promotion of free trade and privatization, with specific campaigns on drugs and terror. By 2005 the military regimes were gone and most Latin American countries had centrist or moderate left governments.

Spanish America exemplifies the media pecking order within a major world region or subregion. Mexico is today's Spanish American media leader. Lower down the pecking order are Colombia, Peru, and Venezuela. At the bottom are small Central American countries such as Guatemala, El Salvador, Nicaragua, and Honduras. These countries are the main focus of this chapter.

In the 1950s and 1960s U.S. media were very strong in Spanish America; television was Hollywood dominated and most world news came from U.S. news agencies. But by the 1990s and 2000s, Latin America was providing most of its own TV programming; and by the 1990s most world news came to Latin America via European (no longer U.S.) news agencies.

Spanish American countries typically have strong national media based in a dominant capital city (which may have up to one-third of the entire national population). Political parties have tended to be weak and military coups have been common. Even under today's apparently more democratic conditions, elected governments can still struggle to survive their full time span.

Figure 18.1 Selected Latin American countries.

Endemic political turbulence has enabled the big media to become leading political players. In Spanish America the leading media owners have often been members of one of the nation's "oligarchy families." Some individual editors, journalists, and broadcast personalities also achieve extraordinary prominence.

The media in each country tend to promote a highly romanticized and patriotic version of the national history. Historical names, such as Simón Bolívar (1783–1830), may be frequently cited; complex historical border disputes with neighboring nation-states are quoted and requoted. The media typically also provide tabloid coverage of less romantic aspects of modern life; blood-on-the-streets coverage can be very bloody indeed.

Latin America is unique in consisting of 18 nation-states, each of which has Spanish as its main language. Obviously there is an exchange of media, old and new, between these 18 countries. But in each of the 18 nations, the national media promote their own national culture and their own patriotism.

Since the nineteenth century, U.S. (and, to a lesser degree, European) interests have been prominent in Latin America's politics, economies, and media. In the nineteenth century the national populations were still small; communications between some countries were inhibited by sheer distance, by the Amazon rain forest, and by the Andes, the world's second highest mountain range. Communication by sea to North America or Europe was often easier than communication between, say, Chile and Venezuela. Even today the quickest air route between two Spanish American cities may go through Miami.

During the nineteenth century the United States developed a "forward strategy" toward Latin America. Washington politicians were anxious about possible European incursions. The British built rail systems in several Latin American countries, and *The Times* (London) was seen as the model for would-be prestige daily papers. The turn of the century saw the U.S. Marines in repeated expeditions to Cuba, Panama, the Dominican Republic, Haiti, and Nicaragua.

In the late nineteenth century, Havas (the French agency) was the main supplier of world news to Latin American papers. But the Pulitzer-Hearst popular news developments of the 1890s started to influence newspaper owners and editors, first in Mexico and then further south.

From 1900 onward, U.S. politicians were increasingly anxious about European influences in Latin America. They were not too worried by the British, the French, or the Italians (even though Argentina's press rose to prominence on a crest of Italian journalism influence). It was the Germans who were widely seen in Washington as the big threat to the Monroe Doctrine. This "threat" was more imagined than real.

During 1900–1940 the United States expanded its forward strategy. The U.S. government and media supported numerous military dictators across Latin America. President Franklin Roosevelt was following this tradition in his support for the notorious Trujillo dictatorship (from 1930) in the Dominican Republic. In the early decades of the twentieth century there was big investment by Wall Street banks, by oil companies such as Standard Oil, as well as by large scale agricultural companies such as United Fruit. The U.S. media were even more assertive. U.S. popular magazines and movies developed strong export markets. The U.S. news agencies—especially UP, but also AP—overtook the Europeans to become the lead suppliers of international news in Latin America. Moreover, in the 1930s, commercial radio achieved financial success, supported by U.S. advertisers and advertising agencies.

The 1938–1945 period saw a big escalation in U.S. media propaganda of all kinds. The British conducted an extensive secret propaganda campaign whose initial goal was to bring the United States into the war against Germany; there was another large (and largely secret) British propaganda campaign especially in Brazil, Argentina, Colombia, and Ecuador.[1] There was also a much larger, and much less secret, U.S. campaign, which aimed to beg, to bully, and to bribe the entire Latin American media into opposing Germany

[1] *British Security Coordination: The Secret History of British Intelligence in the Americas, 1940–45,* London: Saint Ermin's Press, 1998: 273–344.

and into supporting the allies. The American campaign was located in the office of the Co-ordination of Inter-American Affairs (CIAA) at the State Department; CIAA was run by Nelson Rockefeller, whose family had a leading role in Latin American oil and banking.

Nelson Rockefeller's Latin American campaign in the early 1940s had some similarities to the domestic U.S. immigrant press campaign of 1916–1918. Rockefeller received very generous U.S. government funding and quickly discovered that financially weak Latin American newspapers and radio stations were easily persuaded by dollars and advertising. Rockefeller's CIAA effort incorporated elements of a major news agency, and of a national election campaign, supported by public relations and market research. A large news operation supplied 30,000 words a day of Spanish and Portuguese editorial-news-features to 1,200 newspapers and 200 radio stations; friendly newspaper editors were given vacation trips to the United States. Rockefeller persuaded American businesses active in Latin America (including Coca-Cola, Colgate-Palmolive, and pharmaceutical and oil companies) to advertise only in pro–United States publications. U.S. advertisers received a subsidy (tax exemption) for this and for including CIAA slogans in their advertising. Pro-German publishers were blacklisted and could obtain neither advertising nor newsprint from North America. The Rockefeller operation also persuaded NBC and CBS to join the campaign. NBC (RCA owned) was especially interested both in selling radio receivers and in keeping the U.S. government out of U.S. radio (and TV). After a bumpy start, RCA and CBS combined to offer comprehensive Spanish and Portuguese services; NBC-CBS shortwave transmissions as well as radio advertising, news, and recorded music were designed for use by local national radio chains. Rockefeller's CIAA provided a weekly service to 13,000 Latin American "opinion leaders"; CIAA was, of course, also assisted by Hollywood's current crop of patriotic wartime movies and newsreels. Because the French Havas was now under Nazi control, the U.S. news agencies acquired enhanced strength. By 1943–1944 the CIAA calculated that 75 percent of all international news reaching Latin American audiences came from the United States. Already by 1943–1944 CIAA was toning down its aggressive anti-Axis propaganda; the dominant Rockefeller message now was merely pro–United States.[2]

In 1945 Nelson Rockefeller's CIAA came to an end, but the U.S. media and the U.S. government quickly discovered a fresh Latin American media target, namely communism and/or socialism. Juan Peron (president of Argentina, 1946–1955) was seen first as a dangerous fascist and then subsequently as a dangerous socialist. Peron did introduce some major attempts at welfare reform, but his closing down of opposition newspapers (especially *La Prensa*) attracted the antagonism of the American news agencies.

---

[2] Joy Elizabeth Hayes, *Radio Nation: Communication, Popular Culture and Nationalism in Mexico, 1920–1950*, Tucson, AZ: University of Arizona Press, 2000: 97–114; Edward Jay Epstein, "Power Is Essential . . . ," *Sunday Times* (London), December 14, 1975.

During 1950–2000 the CIA, and other U.S. agencies, targeted the politics, economy, and media of at least 13 (and probably all 18) Spanish-speaking countries.[3] Brazil and Haiti were also targets, and so was British Guiana (later Guyana); the British prime minister (Harold Macmillan) tried unsuccessfully at a meeting on June 30, 1963, to argue President John Kennedy out of his (Cuban-related) decision to overthrow the elected government of Cheddi Jagan.[4]

The 1970–1973 presidency of Salvador Allende is the best documented case of U.S. targeting of the domestic media system (and economy) of a Latin American country.[5] The Chilean case is remarkable politically, not only because the U.S.-supported military coup of General Augusto Pinochet had so many negative consequences, including a major political assassination in Washington, DC.[6] The Chilean case is also remarkable for the deliberate targeting (and death) of a democratically elected president, who (by world standards) was a moderate socialist; Allende was a medical doctor by background who was deeply committed to democratic change and to improving the lot of Chile's poor and disadvantaged. The anti-Allende policy of the United States was, of course, the policy of another elected president (Richard Nixon). But perhaps especially remarkable and reckless was the targeting of Chile's mass media by the U.S. government. This targeting spread across at least 1964–1973, starting six years before Allende was elected president. The U.S. media campaign against Allende was controlled by the CIA and incorporated many of the conventional techniques and dirty tricks of Nixon-era electioneering. Money played a big role, not only in bribing journalists but also in establishing fake publications, running radio disinformation campaigns from neighboring countries, and creating false rumors through street handouts. Deeply involved in this corrupt and anti-democratic campaign was *El Mercurio*, generally regarded as Chile's leading prestige daily newspaper; *El Mercurio* played a leading role in persuading the Chilean military to support a coup. In retrospect, it is still remarkable that the Washington decision-makers were so naive and short-sighted as not to recognize that such blatant, and such cynical, intervention would eventually prove counterproductive.

After 1975 the United States continued its forward strategy in Latin America—not least in Central America and Colombia. But many other

[3] William Blum, *Killing Hope*, London: Zed Books, 2003.
[4] Stephen G. Rabe, *US Intervention in British Guiana: A Cold War Story*, Chapel Hill: University of North Carolina Press, 2005.
[5] United States Senate, *Covert Action in Chile, 1963–73*, Staff report of the Select Committee to Study Governmental Operations with Respect to Intelligence Activities, Washington, DC: US Government Printing Office, December 18, 1975; Jussi Hanhimäki, *The Flawed Architect: Henry Kissinger and American Foreign Policy*, New York: Oxford University Press, 2004: 100–5, 429–31, 474–81; William Blum, *Killing Hope: US Military and CIA Interventions Since World War II*, London: Zed Books, 2003: 206–15.
[6] John Dinges and Saul Landau, *Assassination on Embassy Row*, New York: McGraw-Hill, 1981.

changes have occurred since 1975; Mexican media have become big in the domestic U.S. market, and the Latin American media have increasingly become part of the broader Euro-American media.

Mexico: Leader of the Media Pecking Order

Like the other Spanish American nation-states, Mexico has a highly distinctive national history and national geography, as well as a unique national media system. Mexico's population reached 106 million in 2005 (having increased 3.5 times since 1950). Ways in which Mexico has differed from the remainder of Spanish America include the following:

- Mexico (like other countries with over 100 million population) is not a net media importer. Both in terms of audience time and cash expenditure, Mexico exports more media than it imports.
- Mexico has Spanish America's biggest single media organization, in the form of Televisa (and linked companies).
- Mexico is top of the Spanish American media pecking order.
- Across Mexico's long northern border with the United States there have been big flows of print, radio,[7] and TV as well as big flows of investment, work, manufactured goods, migration, drugs, crime, and much else. But Mexico has another important, southern, border—mostly with Guatemala. Straddling this border live several million native Americans who for centuries have been exploited by, but not educated by, Spanish-speaking people. Millions of Maya people, who have had little exposure to the mass media, live alongside a media-saturated Spanish-speaking majority. Mexico has some of Latin America's poorest people, while Mexico City has a number of dollar billionaires.[8]
- Mexican politics, and national history, focus heavily on violence. The "Mexican Revolution" (which began in 1911) was the most deadly event in twentieth-century Latin America. Since then, Mexico has only had "small massacres" of various kinds—in which typically hundreds (but not thousands) died. The Mexican media have long had an obsessive concern with the Mexican Revolution; the early 2000s saw strong media interest in digging up the truth about selected "small massacres" of previous decades.

The five decades between 1880 and 1930 were politically turbulent. The lengthy Porfirio Diaz dictatorship (1876–1911) was followed by the Mexican

---

[7] Gene Fowler and Bill Crawford, *Border Radio*, Austin: Texas Monthly Press, 1987.
[8] John Authers and Sara Silver, "Slim's pickings: Latin America's Richest Man Eyes Up His Next Undervalued Target," *Financial Times*, April 25, 2005.

Revolution led by, among others, Emiliano Zapata (1879–1919), whose slogan was "Land, liberty and death to the landowners." The 1920s were yet another turbulent decade. Fifty years of political oppression and turbulence opened the way for major United States media influence—especially in newspapers and movies, but also in the 1920s in radio. During the Mexican Revolution of the 1910s many young Mexican newspapermen went into exile in Texas and California; after 1918 they returned to Mexico to develop such major Mexican newspapers as *El Imparcial, El Universal*, and *Excelsior*. Mexico's own movie industry struggled to establish its national independence. In 1930–1934 Mexico imported 96 percent of its exhibited films from Hollywood.[9]

U.S. media influences in Mexico peaked in the years 1930–1970 and then subsequently declined. Mexico continued to have numerous daily newspapers with low circulations and little advertising; these newspapers imported large quantities of news, features, comic strips, and pictures from the U.S. news agencies and syndication services. Talkie films in midcentury were a minor exception to the general pattern. The Mexican industry did quite well in numbers of domestically produced movies. Production peaked during 1949–1958, averaging 99 films a year. Mexico made about 4,000 feature films during 1930–1990.[10]

Radio in Mexico followed United States commercial radio very closely; radio receiving sets, programming styles, and advertising were all heavily imported from the United States.[11] Mexican television followed the commercial practices of the new U.S. television industry. In 1954 Mexico was seventh, equal with France and the Dominican Republic, in terms of numbers of television sets per population. But this television service, entirely dependent on advertising, was badly underfunded. As the U.S. TV industry developed the recorded TV series, so Mexico became an eager importer, not least of "action adventure" television series. In the early 1970s Mexico was importing about 40 percent of its television output, predominantly from the United States. However, this proportion decreased during and after the 1970s; Mexico produced its first *telenovela* in 1956 and has subsequently rivaled Brazil as a producer of TV soaps. Mexico also was a major producer of comedy, variety entertainment, game shows, and several types of super-popular music, as well as government-friendly news and political talk.

Both Mexican radio and Mexican television have been dominated by a single family to an extent unusual even by Latin American standards. Much of the history of Mexico's large radio and television industries is also to be found within one leading radio station and one leading TV company, Televisa.

[9] Kristin Thompson, *Exporting Entertainment*, London: British Film Institute, 1985: 220.
[10] Octavio Getino, "The Audio-Visual Scenario in Latin America," *Media Development*, 2, 1997: 28–31; Jorge A. Schnitman, *Film Industries in Latin America: Dependency and Development*, Norwood, NJ: Ablex, 1984.
[11] Joy Elizabeth Hayes, *Radio Nation: Communication, Popular Culture, and Nationalism in Mexico, 1920–1950*, Tucson: University of Arizona Press 2000: 103–15.

Three men—father, son, and grandson, each named Emilio Azcarraga—have been the currently dominant broadcasting owners and entrepreneurs in Mexico.

Emilio Azcarraga Viduarreta became the dominant figure in Mexican radio; he also pioneered and dominated Mexican television until his death in 1972. This Azcarraga was adroit at working initially with his brothers, and then with other business partners; he was also close to each successive Mexican president. Early in their radio careers in the 1920s, the brothers were engaged in retail sales of U.S.-made radio receivers; in the 1930s and 1940s they had close connections with the dominant U.S. radio networks (NBC, CBS). When television began in Mexico in 1950, Emilio Azcarraga again took the lead. Following the huge commercial success of his key radio station (XEW), Azcarraga established the key TV station in Mexico City (XEW-TV). He also formed a partnership with Romulo O'Farril, who launched a TV station across the border from Brownsville, Texas; a jointly owned Azcarraga-O'Farril TV station was established in Tijuana (XETV), across the border from San Diego, California.[12]

In 1972 the son (who had been chairman since 1964) took over the family business; Emilio Azcarraga Milmo in 1972 found himself involved in a new business partnership, called Televisa, which controlled most of Mexican television, including the three most popular national networks and a number of provincial stations. Televisa became one of the world's largest television production organizations. In 1990, Televisa was producing 95 hours per day of national and local TV; by 1997 it was producing 137 hours of TV programming per day. In January 1995 Televisa's four popular networks (2, 4, 5, 9) still attracted 79 percent of all Mexican weekday TV viewing. Throughout his time in control of Televisa (1964–1997), this (second) Azcarraga demanded absolute obedience from all employees and from most people in Mexican public life. He cultivated a lavish lifestyle (huge yachts, private jets, five wives). Like some other media monsters, he was also obsessively secretive; he kept quiet the fact that he was not born in Mexico, but in San Antonio, Texas.

In 1997 control of the family media empire passed to the grandson, Emilio Azcarraga Jean, who was then age 29.[13] By 1997 the Grupo Televisa empire included four TV networks, 300 local TV stations, a still strong collection of radio stations, several record companies and labels, a substantial slice of the Mexican film and cinema business, two football teams, the Aztec stadium, and the Museum of Contemporary Art in Mexico City. Televisa had major newspaper and magazine interests; it also owned slices of important TV companies in Chile, Peru, and the United States.

---

[12] UNESCO, *Television: A World Survey*, Paris: UNESCO, 1953: 51–56.
[13] Joel Millman, "Mexican TV Leader Reprograms Itself," *Wall Street Journal*, May 14, 1997; Elisabeth Malkin, "Son of El Tigre," *Business Week*, October 18, 1999: 34–37.

Each Emilio Azcarraga relied upon the same three crucial connections—in advertising, with the United States, and in Mexican politics. Behind the radio/TV semi-monopoly lay a near monopoly of advertising; in Mexico the bulk of advertising (82 percent in year 2000) has gone into radio and the various forms of TV. The U.S. connection has long been evident in advertising. Most importantly, the first two Azcarragas were close to, and obedient to, the PRI party, which governed Mexico for 71 years (1929–2000). By allowing Televisa to be commercially free but politically controlled, the successive presidents and the PRI party could make themselves look less dictatorial than they really were. Whereas most Mexican newspapers loosely followed the incumbent government, Televisa followed the government more slavishly and with only minimal signs of objectivity. This was especially noticeable in the news[14] and the prestige *24 Hours* evening political talk show. For example, in *24 Hours* coverage of the 1988 presidential election, the PRI government candidate (Salinas de Gortari) received 140 minutes of coverage, while the five other candidates averaged 5 minutes and 27 seconds each.[15]

Until 1996–1997 all of the Mexican mass media were subservient to politicians in power. Mexico has a long newspaper tradition, and the leading newspapers have always looked much like the leading newspapers of a western European country. But Evelyn Stevens, observing the Mexico City daily newspapers in 1965–1966, noted much glorification of the incumbent president and many references to the heroes of Mexican history; at the same time many Mexico City journalists and columnists also wrote publicity releases for public relations companies.[16]

There was generous "envelope" cash for journalists and paid announcements presented as editorial material. These paid stories are known as *gacetillas*, and rates were quoted alongside straight advertising rates in advertising business publications. This author was told in Mexico City in 1973 that paid "news stories" cost two or three times as much as normal paid advertising. Advertising agency personnel were dismissive of all Mexican newspapers (including the then most respected paper, *Excelsior*) as politically subservient and commercially corrupt; published circulation data were inflated. Advertising agency personnel (often U.S. or U.S.-trained) said that they advised clients to avoid the press, but to spend their advertising pesos first in TV and second in radio. Thus commercial weakness, U.S. influence, and dependence on government were closely linked; newspapers behaved

---

[14] Gabriel Molina, "Mexican Television News: The Imperatives of Corporate Rationale," *Media, Culture and Society*, Vol. 9, 1987: 159–87.

[15] Ilya Adler, "The Mexican Case: The Media in the 1988 Presidential Election," in Thomas E. Skidmore (ed.), *Television, Politics and the Transition to Democracy in Latin America*, Washington, DC: The Woodrow Wilson Center Press, and Baltimore: The Johns Hopkins University Press, 1993: 145–73.

[16] Evelyn P. Stevens, *Protest and Response in Mexico*, Cambridge, MA: The MIT Press, 1974: 30–36, 40.

subserviently toward government[17] in return for government advertising and other subsidies.

Radio came to prominence in Mexico at the same time as the PRI party began its long political reign. The first Emilio Azcarraga and his colleagues developed a style of commercial radio that was extremely close to advertisers (not least U.S. advertisers), to the PRI government, and to radio listeners, who in the 1930s and 1940s were still mainly in Mexico City and a few other larger cities. Mexican radio presented a version of Mexican history in which the Mexican Revolution of the 1910s was seen as a heroic uprising somewhat akin to the U.S. American Revolution of the 1770s.[18] The radio account deliberately glossed over the fact that the Mexican Revolution had been a peasants' revolt and an uprising of the native people against the big landowners and the Mexico City elite. Joy Hayes has shown how Mexican radio also packaged a semi-official Mexican national popular culture within the guidelines of political requirements and commercial radio realities. In particular, Mexico's strong and varied popular music was given support from Cuban, Brazilian, and other popular music and then presented to the Mexican public as their own entirely domestic Mexican musical tradition.[19]

When television appeared in Mexico in the 1950s, it built upon theatrical, film, press, and radio precedents. The huge *telenovela* output was influenced by the Mexican radio soap, already strong by 1950. Mexican *telenovelas* typically ran to between 40 and 90 episodes (less than Brazilian *novelas*). The Mexican *novelas* drew on Mexican theater and film and on the photo-comics that continued to be super-popular in the TV era. Mexican television also built on, and further developed, a national tradition of comedy. Several of the superstars of Mexican TV were comedians. One was Cantiflas, the movie and TV star;[20] another was Bozo, the circus clown.

The scene that confronted the 29-year-old Emilio Azcarraga Jean, when he took control of Televisa in 1997, contained several rapidly changing elements. Televisa itself was losing market share to the freshly aggressive Azteca, the privatized commercial successor to a previous small public service TV effort. Linked to this emerging Televisa-versus-Azteca television rivalry was a more open approach to Mexican politics. In 1997 the PRI party's long monopoly of power was drawing to a close. The PRI did badly in the 1997 elections and lost the presidential election of 2000 to Vicente Fox. There is strong evidence that Televisa's much more politically neutral approach in 1997, and

---

[17] William A. Orme, Jr., *A Culture of Collusion: An Inside Look at the Mexican Press*, Miami: University of Miami, North-South Center Press, 1997.

[18] Robert N. Pierce, "Mexico's Undying Myth," in *Keeping the Flame: Media and Government in Latin America*, New York: Hastings House, 1979: 96–118.

[19] Joy Elizabeth Hayes, *Radio Nation: Communication, Popular Culture and Nationalism in Mexico, 1920–1950*, Tucson: University of Arizona Press, 2000.

[20] Jeffrey M. Pilcher, *Cantiflas and Chaos of Mexican Modernity*, Wilmington, DE: Scholarly Resources, 2001.

subsequently, had a direct impact on the voting.[21] There was a related tendency to dig up the (plentiful) suppressed political scandals of recent decades. In 2004, for example, Luis Echeverria (president of Mexico, 1970–1976) was accused of being responsible for the deaths of student demonstrators killed by soldiers in Mexico City on June 10, 1971.[22]

Other important Mexican media changes after 1990 included the greatly increased volume of media exporting into the United States and the growth of satellite, cable, and Internet.

Meanwhile, as "everything changed," much stayed the same. For example, the North American Free Trade Association (NAFTA) agreement came into effect in January 1994—but without many of the benefits anticipated by Mexico. January 1994 also saw the emergence in the Mexican far south (Chiapas) of the Zapatista movement—a native American (Mayan) protest against oppressive central and regional government. The Zapatista rebellion certainly had some new elements, not least its leader "Subcomandante Marcos," a highly sophisticated modern revolutionary costumed to attract television audiences. Marcos' stagy props included balaclava, tobacco pipe, AK-47 rifle, handgun, spare ammunition, and, of course, a cell phone. Marcos correctly calculated that both international and Mexican TV would find him irresistible. However, the Chiapas uprising also involved that old Mexican custom, the small massacre.

Neither President Fox nor the newly open Mexican media were entirely free of past media-related problems. President Fox (a former chief executive of Coca-Cola, Mexico) did better at advertising himself and winning the 2000 election than he did in governing the country. Fox continued the overintimate and commercially corrupt presidential relationship not only with Televisa, but also with TV Azteca.[23] Meanwhile, the Mexican media have reported on Mexico's high rates of drug crime, police corruption, torture, political assassination, and kidnapping.

Unanticipated Consequences of Political and Media Democratization in Peru and Venezuela

Peru and Venezuela are middle-ranking countries in Spanish America; each has only about one-quarter of Mexico's population level. Both have

---

[21] Chappell H. Lawson, *Building the Fourth Estate: Democratization and the Rise of a Free Press in Mexico*, Berkeley: University of California Press, 2002: 157–209.

[22] Ginger Thompson and Tim Weiner, "Mexican Leader Indicted," *International Herald Tribune* (from *NY Times*), July 24–25, 2004.

[23] Henry Tricks and Andrea Mandel Campbell, "Parties Launch Bold Democratic Experiments," *Financial Times*, October 5, 1999; John Authers, "How Fox Threw Away a Golden Opportunity," *Financial Times* special report, "Mexico and Globalisation," December 13, 2005: 5.

been heavy importers of U.S. and, increasingly in recent years, Mexican media. Venezuela is also a successful exporter of TV series to its neighbors; the Venevision company claims to have exported its *telenovelas* to over 100 foreign countries.

Both Peru and Venezuela have been ruled in the past by military regimes (including military regimes that claimed to be left of center). Since 1980 both countries have been broadly democratic; however, during the 1980s and 1990s the increasing populations of both Peru and Venezuela actually got poorer. Economic growth was outpaced by population growth.[24] Wealth and income are also extremely unequally distributed. The majority of people in Peru and Venezuela are urban dwellers. A minority are rural people, and, especially in Peru, most of these rural people speak indigenous languages, not Spanish. There is a smallish "middle class" that includes, for example, trade unionized employees in Venezuela's large oil industry. This "middle class" may constitute only 15 percent of the national population, but perhaps 30 percent of the large capital city population. The middle class provides the main readership for the more established daily newspapers.

At the end of the twentieth century there were many political and media changes. Power had traditionally been shared between one or two major political parties and the military; there had been a group of oligarchy families that typically owned the leading newspapers. In recent decades there have also been small groups of television-owning families (some being both major press and TV/radio owners). In addition to the Brazilian and Mexican media dynasties, there have been Grupo Clarin (Argentina), Grupo Cisneros (Venezuela), and Corporación Caracol (Colombia).[25] While such media families continue to exist, the media have become more commercialized; there has been a decline in noncommercial "public" broadcasting and in media controlled by elements of the Roman Catholic church.

There has also been a trend away from the "military strongman" (or dictator) and toward the rise of maverick political personalities (some began as soldiers) who are said to "govern by television." A number of national politicians began their national TV careers as the winners of beauty queen competitions. (Venezuela claims to have won more Miss Universe and Miss World competitions than has any other country).

After 1990 both Peru and Venezuela experienced a mix of democratic and authoritarian rule, marked by a succession of "crises" and a frenetic pattern of continuous electioneering and volatile opinion polls. Television and tabloid newspaper coverage became ever more central to national politics. Prominence was often given, in live news coverage, to street demonstrations, protest marches, and strikes. Both Peru and Venezuela had high murder rates, which the media accentuated in (lightly edited) blood-soaked detail.

---

[24] Angus Maddison, *The World Economy: A Millennial Perspective*, Paris: OECD, 2001: 288.

[25] Alfonso Gumicio Dagron, "Media, Freedom and Poverty: A Latin American Perspective," *Media Development*, 2, 2004: 8–12.

Another common media focus was on corruption; in Peru and Venezuela, endemic bribery and corruption involved politicians, journalists, TV stars and producers, and media owners. Some major owners (such as the wealthy Cisneros family, owners of Venevision of Venezuela) were buoyed up by their diversified business interests. But there was not enough advertising revenue to fund the many media outlets, and some media owners became dependent on government, political, and commercial bribes. Television also relied heavily on cheap, or free, factual material in the form of amateur street video as well as secret video recordings of bribery and corruption in action.

Alberto Fujimori and Hugo Chávez were the leading personalities in Peruvian and Venezuela politics since 1990. Fujimori was elected president of Peru in 1990 and finally fled in disgrace a decade later, in 2000; he sent his resignation letter by fax from Japan. Part of Fujimori's electoral appeal was that in 1990 he was largely unknown; even his place of birth was a mystery (was he born in Japan, in which case he was not legally qualified to be president of Peru?). Fujimori was presented on television and across the Peruvian media as the strongman who assumed semi-dictatorial powers in 1992 and then successfully confronted the Shining Path Marxist insurgents. (This insurgency killed about 69,000 people, mostly Quechua-speaking Indians, during 1980–2000.[26]) Behind Fujimori was a mysterious senior aide —Vladimiro Montesinos—who (it later transpired) had been in the pay of the CIA and of certain drug cartels.

In the mid-1990s Montesinos presided over a massive phone-tapping campaign[27] and coordinated the Peruvian government's relations with four major (contending) U.S. agencies—State, Defense, CIA, and the Drug Enforcement Administration (DEA). In the late 1990s Montesinos was paying about $2.4 million a month to TV channels 2, 4, 5, and 9 for their support of Fujimori. In a sting operation Montesinos was videoed (and shown on TV) handing over $619,000 in cash (for one month's support) to a vice president of Channel 4 TV. Montesinos (and his boss President Fujimori) also dictated daily newspaper front page stories for $3,000 a time (more if a cartoon was included).[28]

Hugo Chávez, elected president of Venezuela in 1998, was another maverick politician who "governed by television." Chávez had led an unsuccessful military coup and spent 1992–1994 in prison. All of Venezuela's four major commercial television networks and most of the leading

[26] Juan Forero, "Report Says 69,000 Died or Disappeared in Peru," *International Herald Tribune*, August 29, 2003 (from *NY Times*).
[27] Sally Bowen, "Peru TV Report on Phone Tapping Prompts Protests," *Financial Times*, July 15, 1997.
[28] Sally Bowen and Jane Halligan, *The Imperfect Spy: The Many Lives of Vladimiro Montesinos*, Lima: Ediciones Peisa, 2003: 309–37, 383–88; Catherine M. Conaghan, *Fujimori's Peru: Deception in the Public Sphere*, Pittsburgh: University of Pittsburgh Press, 2005.

newspapers were bitter opponents of President Chávez.[29] He soon became famous for answering back with lengthy (several hours) appearances especially on public (noncommercial) radio and television. He projected himself as a blunt, vulgar, but loveable and funny man-of-the-people who could mix childhood anecdotes and cooking advice with lengthy denunciations of his political opponents; the U.S. oil industry; Washington, DC; and the Venezuelan press. Opinion poll research indicated that most Venezuelans either loved Chávez or hated Chávez; electoral results suggested that—at least for several years—more Venezuelans loved than hated this larger-than-life media personality.[30]

While he was undoubtedly influenced by Fidel Castro in Cuba, Chávez was a baseball fan who had visited the United States and was also copying North American models. For at least a century, Spanish Americans had looked toward the United States; Washington—which had previously provided much military and intelligence advice and finance—in the 1990s, especially, increased its flow of democracy and electoral advice and finance. Various Washington government agencies, the two main political parties, the U.S. trade unions—and, of course, the U.S. media—were generous dispensers of such democratic advice and finance.[31]

However, Spanish American copying of U.S. models often had unanticipated (or un-U.S.) consequences. Spanish Americans tended to follow the U.S. practice of spending large sums of money on buying media exposure and support. The North American idea of the recall election, and the U.S. practice of packing the Supreme Court with political appointees, were also copied. But Spanish American politicians were less likely to adopt the detailed regulation (and checks and balances) that in the United States places limits on such political practices.

Similarly, the Spanish American media (while following U.S. models) somehow managed to out-trash U.S. TV entertainment and also to out-sleaze U.S. political consultants in the deployment of electoral dirty tricks. "Attack" publicity tended to prevail, and suitable scandal scenarios were prepared for most electoral situations. Another alarming tendency was a drift into hate speech, including—on some occasions—media incitement to kill political opponents.

Peru, Venezuela, and other Latin American countries have turbulent histories and are experiencing a turbulent present. Politicians themselves

---

[29] Phil Gunson, "A Bitter War of Words: Chávez and the Private Press Can't Seem to Get Along," *Newsweek*, August 9, 2004.
[30] "Hugo Chávez's Venezuela: Oil, Missions and a Chat Show," *The Economist*, May 14, 2005: 23–25; Jennifer McCoy (Carter Center), "What Really Happened in Venezuela?" *The Economist*, September 4, 2004: 52–54; Richard Gott, *In the Shadow of the Liberator: Hugo Chávez and the Transformation of Venezuela*, London: Verso, 2000; Damarys Canache, *Venezuela: Public Opinion and Protest in a Fragile Democracy*, Miami: University of Miami, North-South Center Press, 2002.
[31] Andrew Buncombe and Phil Gunson, "US Revealed to Be Secretly Funding Opponents of Chavez," *The Independent* (London), March 13, 2004.

face the possibility of kidnap or assassination and the probability of tabloid scandal revelations. The prevailing crisis atmosphere has an element of self-fulfilling prophecy; winning the next election tends to become an all-consuming goal, and politicians are willing to subvert both the economy and the media in order to win. Politicians who win elections may be quickly confronted with the (economic or media) consequences of their previous corrupt and rash behavior. Elected presidents are often removed before their full term in office is complete; in Ecuador, three elected presidents were removed from office over an eight-year period (in 1997, 2000, and 2005)—two were ousted by the Congress and one in a military coup. Lucio Gutiérrez was removed by Ecuador's Congress in 2005, first for tampering with the Supreme Court and second for failing to handle huge street protests led by Quito's middle class; both the army and the police refused to intervene.[32]

TV and radio stations in heavily populated capitals such as Lima or Caracas can quickly entice onto the streets crowds of a size that are only seen in Washington, DC, once in a decade or two. This urban crowd is often a middle-class crowd of the kind that frequently demonstrated against President Chávez. For a financially weak TV station, a big city crowd makes cheap and popular programming material; added amateur video enhances the impression of immediate actuality. The prominent role given to big crowds on national TV can also help to stimulate massive rural crowds. This happened in Bolivia, where the large indigenous rural population elected one of their own (Evo Morales) to the presidency in late 2005.

These media and political developments have tended to strengthen, rather than to soften, strident nationalism. As ever, nationalism needs an opponent or enemy. This enemy may be a neighboring nation (and/or its football team), but a favorite enemy are those *gringo* Americans. As U.S. Spanish American policy is increasingly shaped with a view to electoral consequences in Florida, California, and Texas, some U.S. foreign policy has been extraordinarily inept. An example is the famous April 11–13, 2002, military coup in Caracas, which the Bush White House bizarrely welcomed as a "return to democracy"; within hours the coup leaders dissolved the Venezuelan Congress and began to arrest elected politicians. Within a few more hours the elected President Chávez returned in triumph. The entire coup lasted about 47 hours, during which time both the White House and much of the U.S. media (including the *New York Times* on April 13) unintentionally enhanced Chávez's political charisma and illustrated his claims of U.S. political intervention and media meddling.

Also deeply involved in the U.S.-backed failed coup in 2002 were leading members of the Cisneros family, which controlled (among many other companies) Venevision, the leading television company. It was claimed

---

[32] "A Coup by Congress and the Street," *The Economist*, April 23, 2005; Andrew Gumbel, "Ecuador's Parliament Removes President After Popular Uprising," *The Independent* (London), April 21, 2005.

subsequently that some of the coup plotters' meetings took place in Cisneros family offices.[33]

While some U.S. entertainment remains popular in Spanish America, there has been a decline in the popularity of Washington and of American news. Also, despite the "trend toward democracy" the Latin American public's opinion of democracy declined during 1996–2005; across 13 countries a declining percentage believed that "Democracy is preferable to any other kind of government." In only four countries did the pro-democracy vote increase; the biggest increase (62 percent in 1996 and 76 percent in 2005) occurred in Venezuela. In Peru faith in democracy declined steeply (from 63 percent to 40 percent). Other countries in which there was a big 1996–2005 decline in people preferring democracy to any other form of government included Colombia (from 60 percent to 46 percent) and Guatemala (from 50 percent to 32 percent).[34]

From Guatemala to Colombia: The United States Loses Control of the News Agenda

Between the 1950s and the 1990s the United States lost control of the international news agenda in Central America (as across the world). By 1990 Latin American newspapers were relying primarily on European, and not U.S., news agencies for their foreign news. By 1997 this trend had gone still further. A study of eight Latin American newspapers showed them overwhelmingly relying in 1997 on the European news agencies. By 1997 UPI was virtually dead as an international news provider. *El Mercurio* (Chile) was Associated Press' best customer (in the 1997 study), but even here the European agencies accounted for 64 percent of that paper's foreign news. At *Excelsior* (Mexico) the European agencies (especially EFE of Spain) outgunned AP by 72 percent to 1 percent. The European agencies (especially Agence France Presse) had a huge lead at the only two Central American papers in the study.[35]

---

[33] Steve Ellner and Daniel Hellinger (eds.), *Venezuelan Politics in the Chavez Era: Class, Polarization and Conflict*, Boulder, CO: Lynne Rienner, 2003: 7–26; Michael McCaughan, *The Battle of Venezuela*, London: Latin American Bureau, 2004: 84–115. Interview with Chávez in Isabel Hilton, "The Venezuelan Great Survivor Rides His Luck," *The Guardian*, October 18, 2002. Phil Gunson, "Director's Cut," *Columbia Journalism Review*, May/June 2004: 59–61; Tim Westcott, "Cisneros Jumps Ahead," *Television Business International*, January/February 1998: 85–6; Leslie Hillman, "Cisneros Toughs It Out," *Television Business International*, March/April 2003: 22.

[34] Latinobarómetro poll data: "Democracy's Ten-Year Rut," *The Economist*, October 29, 2005: 63.

[35] Fernando Reyes-Matta, "Journalism in Latin America in the '90s: The Challenge of Modernization," *Journal of Communication*, Summer 1992, Vol. 42/3: 74–83; Jose-Carlos Lozano et al., "International News in the Latin American Press," in Abbas Malek and Anandam P. Kavoori (eds.), *The Global Dynamics of News: Studies in International News Coverage and News Agendas*, Stamford, CT: Ablex, 2000: 75–93.

This was a big decline since the 1950s when the U.S. agencies were dominant; by the 1990s it was Europe that had three big news agencies in Latin America (EFE, AFP, Reuters) while the United States had only one (AP). Latin American editors appear to have lost confidence in news supplied from the United States. Between 1950 and 1990 the U.S. media, while showing some skepticism, had "neutrally" reported huge quantities of Washington misinformation. The CIA and State Department tactic of "plausible deniability" continued to have some success with some people, but it was inadequate to convince averagely skeptical journalists in Latin America; these journalists were familiar with their own governments' not-so-plausible untruths.

Central America was, of course, the United States' traditional backyard—loosely similar to Ireland and Algeria for the United Kingdom and France. During 1853–1933 the U.S. Marines invaded Nicaragua on 20 separate occasions. Some subsequent interventions (notably the CIA Bay of Pigs attempted invasion of Cuba, 1961) were unsuccessful. But Guatemala (1954) and the Dominican Republic (1965) could be seen as successful. It was not until the 1970s that such interventions became more difficult and more controversial at home. Roman Catholics and Protestants (bishops, Jesuits, nuns, and missionaries) began to speak up for the *campesinos* (country people) and against the corrupt dictatorships. A number of church people (including some U.S. citizens) were assassinated. Both Roman Catholic and Protestant publications in the United States and Europe became, from the 1960s, increasingly critical of Washington's support for Spanish American dictatorships. The religious press was often better informed than were the mainstream U.S. media.[36]

Although the death toll in Guatemala and Central America was much higher, the well-documented horrors of Chile and Argentina alerted the world to the realities of routine U.S. support for military dictatorships; it was all too evident that many leaders of coups, and of death and kidnapping-squads, had received military training in Panama, Georgia, North Carolina, and other U.S. locations.[37] Revulsion against such connections was expressed by some leading politicians, such as President Jimmy Carter, and by some leading U.S. journalists.

In the 1950s U.S. dominance of Central America extended to the economies, the politics, and the media. Guatemala (the most populated Central American country) did not pass the 3 million population mark until 1951, but had quadrupled to 12 million by 1998. Guatemala in 1950 was indeed a banana (or coffee) republic; the (U.S.) United Fruit company had a huge slice of the Guatemalan economy and a monopoly of the national rail system. The

---

[36] Edward T. Brett, *The US Catholic Press on Central America*, South Bend, IN: University of Notre Dame Press, 2003; See also *Media Development* and other publications of the World Association of Christian Communication (WACC).

[37] "The School of the Americas and Terror in El Salvador," in Frederick H. Gareau, *State Terrorism and the United States*, Atlanta: Clarity Press, 2004: 22–42.

United States also dominated the Central American media in the 1950s. Each (very small) capital city had a very small press. Television was arriving (too early). Inevitably these very small, very weak TV systems quickly became heavily dependent on U.S. programming.

Radio was the only strong medium in these poor countries, where mountains inhibited the reach of both newspapers and television. Many Central American politicians and church leaders first became nationally known through radio. Washington followed up its 1940–1945 commercial radio onslaught with an additional onslaught of white, grey, black, and religious radio stations. The peak of this radio propaganda effort probably occurred in Nicaragua on behalf of the Contras.[38] In the 1980s there was a bewildering maze of (legal and illegal) U.S.-financed radio stations transmitting across the international frontiers of Central America.

Nicaragua in the early 1980s also exemplified two aspects of U.S. policy. First, Washington's Central America policies tended to reflect current domestic American policy obsessions—1950s Cold War concerns, 1960s Fidel phobia, and in the 1980s President Reagan's insistence on preventing the Soviet Union's Evil Empire from infecting Central America. Second, interagency policy rivalry was extreme, even by Washington standards. Reagan's White House—in order to bypass resistance in the U.S. Congress—entered into the bizarre Iran-Contra labyrinth, which, to be effective, required the silent goodwill of key players in Israel, Iran, Lebanon, and Nicaragua.[39] A substantial slice of the Contra money was intended for media manipulation.

Ronald Reagan is said to have expressed mild surprise that all of those little Spanish-speaking places were in fact separate countries. How many North Americans or Europeans even today could correctly list each of the Central American nation-states? Meanwhile, each of these small Spanish-speaking countries has its own cultural nationalism. Because of the very different impact of Reagan (and other U.S.) policies, each country has added to its portfolio of cultural and historical idiosyncrasies.

In Guatemala more than half of the population are indigenous Mayans, most living in extreme poverty. Guatemala has Central America's most tragic recent history. Some 200,000 Guatemalans (nearly all Mayans) died violent deaths during decades of civil violence, after the CIA-assisted 1954 coup[40] against the moderate left elected government of President Jacobo Arbenz. Guatemala in 1954 still had a plantation economy in which the Mayans

---

[38] Howard H. Frederick, "The Radio War Against Nicaragua," *Studies in Latin American Culture*, Vol. 6, 1987: 217–35; Howard H. Frederick, "Media Strategies Stifle Democracy in Central America," *Media Development*, 2, 1985: 32–38; Lucinda Broadbent, "Communication Freedom in War-Torn Nicaragua," *Media Development*, 1, 1988: 5–7; Robert A. White, "Participatory Radio in Sandinista Nicaragua," *Media Development*, 4, 1990: 10–16.

[39] Lawrence E. Walsh, *Firewall: The Iran-Contra Conspiracy and Cover-up*, New York: W.W. Norton, 1997.

[40] Nick Cullather, *Secret History: The CIA's Classified Account of Its Operations in Guatemala, 1952–1954*, Stanford, CA: Stanford University Press, 1999.

provided the cheap labor. Greg Grandin's *The Last Colonial Massacre* documents the recent history of the Coban area in central Guatemala. In 1953–1954 the big farmers bitterly opposed the Arbenz land reforms, through pamphlets, flyers, radio, and newspapers. After the 1954 coup, the *New York Times* agreed to a CIA request not to send any reporters into the countryside. Today the Guatemalan media are on a significant scale, with large imports of television series from both Mexico and the United States. The newspaper press is also hugely bigger than in 1954. But, writes Greg Grandin, throughout the twentieth century the Guatemalan press played on newspaper readers' fears of machete-wielding rural Indians.[41] During a violent seven-year period (1978–1985) 47 Guatemalan journalists were murdered and another 100 fled abroad. Media offices were bombed, and, even in the relatively peaceful 1990s, some journalists continued to receive death threats.[42] In 1998 Roman Catholic Bishop Juan Gerardi published a report (on human rights abuses in the recent civil war) that blamed the army for most of the deaths; two days later the bishop himself was assassinated. The following year, 1999, President Bill Clinton apologized for past U.S. involvement in Guatemala, saying that American "support for military forces and intelligence units which engaged in violence and widespread repression was wrong."

In El Salvador a U.S.-backed military coup took place in 1979. The following year the Roman Catholic archbishop was assassinated (by a military hit team) while celebrating Mass;[43] that led to a coalition of opposition parties called the National Liberation Front (FMLN), which fought a civil war against the government for the next 11 years (1981–1992). This war also saw newspapers bombed and journalists (including five Dutch journalists) killed. A feature of these El Salvador events was the prominence of the radio word war; the FMLN had two strong radio stations, one of which, Radio Venceremos, became famous for its anti-government news and its very local music.[44] In Nicaragua (1980 population: 2.8 million) there was yet another

---

[41] Greg Grandin, *The Last Colonial Massacre: Latin America in the Cold War*, Chicago: University of Chicago Press, 2004: 59, 67, 139; Greg Grandin, *The Blood of Guatemala: A History of Race and Nation*, Durham, NC: Duke University Press, 2000; Jeremiah O'Sullivan, "Guatemala: Marginality and Information in Rural Development in the Western Highlands," in Emile G. McAnany (ed.), *Communications in the Rural Third World*, New York: Praeger, 1980: 71–106; Edward S. Herman and Noam Chomsky, *Manufacturing Consent: The Political Economy of the Mass Media*, New York: Pantheon, 2002 (first pub. 1988): 71–116; David McCreery, *Rural Guatemala, 1760–1940*, Stanford, CA: Stanford University Press, 1994; Deborah J. Yashar, *Demanding Democracy: Reform and Reaction in Costa Rica and Guatemala, 1870s–1950s*.

[42] Trish O'Kane, *Guatemala in Focus*, New York: Interlink Books, 1999: 50–52.

[43] Richard Higgins, "Archbishop Oscar Romero: The Martyr of El Salvador," *International Herald Tribune*, March 26–27, 2005 (first pub. in the *Boston Globe*); Andrew Buncombe, "The Archbishop, the Death Squad and the 24-Year Wait for Justice," *The Independent* (London), August 24, 2004: 24–25.

[44] José Ignacio López Vigil, *Rebel Radio: The Story of El Salvador's Radio Venceremos*, Williamatic, CT: Curbstone Press, 1995; Elizabeth Jean Wood, *Insurgent Collective Action and Civil War in El Salvador*, Cambridge, UK: Cambridge University Press, 2003.

lengthy 1980s civil war. But after the notorious Somoza García dynasty, which ruled Nicaragua for 42 years (1937–1979), finally collapsed, the subsequent government—the Sandinistas (or FSLN)—moved to the left; here in Nicaragua the rebels (the Contras) were to the political right and were seen by President Reagan as requiring his freakish funding support.

One revealing aspect of Nicaragua was the extraordinary prominence of the Chamorro family. Pedro Joaquín Chamorro Cardenal inherited, from his father, *La Prensa*, Nicaragua's leading newspaper (founded in 1926). Pedro Chamorro edited *La Prensa* throughout 1952–1978, when it was the main press opponent of the (U.S.-backed) Somoza dictatorship; he was arrested (and tortured) several times. In 1978 Pedro Chamorro was assassinated, a key event leading to the Sandinista uprising; *La Prensa*'s offices were destroyed in the early fighting in June 1979. Pedro Chamorro had been an internationally celebrated newspaper hero; he was the descendant of no less than four conservative presidents of Nicaragua.

But what happened after Pedro's death perhaps revealed even more about Nicaragua and its media. In the early 1980s, during the early years of the Nicaragua civil war, all three of Nicaragua's leading daily newspapers were being edited by Chamorro family members. *La Prensa* itself (with the largest circulation) was inherited by Pedro's widow, Violeta, who initially supported the Sandinista government; but Violeta appointed her elder son (another Pedro Chamorro) as editor, and the widow-and-son team subsequently took *La Prensa* into opposition against the leftist Sandinista government. In the early 1990s, while Violeta Chamorro was president of Nicaragua, both of the leading pro-Sandinista Nicaraguan dailies were also edited by Chamorro family members. *Barricada* (the official socialist voice of the Sandinistas) was edited by Carlos, another son of Pedro Chamorro and Violeta. Most of the original *La Prensa* staff migrated to a new daily, *El Nuevo Diario*, which also supported the Sandinista government and was edited by Xavier Chamorro, a brother of Pedro and brother-in-law of Violeta.[45]

During the 1980s *La Prensa* inevitably remained highly controversial. Many Nicaraguans, including the Contras (whose military activities, and main U.S. support, were based in Honduras), saw *La Prensa* as the free media voice that the Marxist Sandinistas didn't dare to close down permanently. The Sandinistas saw *La Prensa* as a U.S.-subsidized newspaper and referred to it as *La PrenCia*.

The Nicaraguan news in the domestic U.S. press and TV has been quite heavily studied.[46] Robert Leiken's full length book, *Why Nicaragua Vanished*,

---

[45] David Kunzle, "Nicaragua's *La Prensa*—Capitalist Thorn in Socialist Flesh," *Media, Culture and Society*, Vol. 6/2, April 1984: 151–76; "Pedro Joaquin Chamorro Winner of the Golden Pen of Freedom 1982," *FIEJ Bulletin* (Paris), March 1982: 14; Peter Ford, "Tenacity Pays Off at La Prensa," *Financial Times*, September 23, 1987.

[46] Robert S. Leiken, *Why Nicaragua Vanished: A Story of Reporters and Revolutionaries*, Lanham, MD: Rowman and Littlefield, 2003; "Discussion of Media Coverage in Central America," in Landrum R. Bolling, *Reporters Under Fire*, Boulder, CO: Westview, 1985: 95–142.

asks why the U.S. media wrongly predicted the result of Nicaragua's February 1990 elections. The (U.S.-backed) Contras won the election, although most U.S. media predicted that the leftist Sandinistas would triumph. Leiken convincingly argues that most U.S. journalists were looking at Nicaragua through an outdated post-Vietnam framework. But one might argue that merely predicting one election incorrectly was quite a modest failure compared with other inadequacies of U.S. reporting of Nicaragua.

Most American correspondents in Nicaragua—as in El Salvador—appear to have been impressed by the high journalist death rate; they were mostly discouraged from more than rather tentative day trips into the countryside, where most of the fighting and the best informed observers (such as Roman Catholic priests) were located. Mark Pedelty, who studied journalists at work in El Salvador, says that the correspondents of the big U.S. media relied too heavily on the U.S. embassy and its diplomats (and presumably CIA people). Pedelty suggests that other journalists in El Salvador—correspondents for European and Latin American media and Salvadorean (part-time) "stringers" —had a better grasp of local reality. Pedelty notes a "classic" article by a British journalist (John Carlin of *The Independent*) who quoted a U.S. Marine colonel's dismissal of human rights abuses as: "After all: it's only little brown men shooting at little brown men." American correspondents, says Pedelty, did not report such revealing racist remarks because they too easily accepted U.S. military and intelligence off-the-record rules.[47]

During the 1990s there was a return of peace, if not of tranquillity, to most of Central America. While each small nation incorporated its own recent horrors into its own national collective memory, the U.S. (and the world's) media spotlight turned to another nearby nation—Colombia. This country of large size (twice France's) and largish population (46 million in 2005) has long been known for violence in the cities and especially in the countryside. A political murder and a Bogotá riot in 1948 led to "La Violencia," in which at least 100,000 people were killed. Ten years of this violence was only ended by an agreement in 1958 of the two big parties (conservative and liberal) to alternate in power.

When this author arrived at the Hilton in Bogotá in 1973, it was a surprise to find heavily armed soldiers on every floor of the tall hotel. In interviews with international news agency and other media personnel, there were frequent references to the local "oligarchy families,", also known as "the Garchs." Colombia had two famous, oligarchy family–owned dailies —El Espectador and El Tiempo. But these newspapers were traditionally highly partisan and belligerent;[48] in terms of potential for further violence

[47] Mark Pedelty, *War Stories: The Culture of Foreign Correspondents*, New York: Routledge, 1995; Peter Chapman, "El Salvador: Journalists on the 'Bang-Bang' Trail," *Broadcast* (London): April 19, 1982: 10–11; Jon Snow, *Shooting History*, London: HarperCollins, 2004: 177–94.
[48] Vernon L. Fluharty, *Dance of the Millions: Military Rule and Social Revolution in Colombia*, Pittsburgh: University of Pittsburgh Press, 1957: 263–64.

these prestige newspapers were more a part of the problem than of the solution.

In the 1970s there were many Hollywood series on Colombia's TV channels. Today there is a lower proportion of U.S. material and more from Mexico. Colombia itself is a significant TV producer and exporter. But U.S. concern in Colombia has increasingly involved drug production and trade and has increasingly also involved U.S. military training, U.S. helicopters, U.S. chemical defoliants, U.S. courts, and Washington finance. The Colombia policy conundrum and the ferocious three-sided confrontation have been famously controversial. But less disputable is the failure of the U.S. government and media to control the news agenda. Much U.S. domestic comment—from many different political angles—is critical.[49] The professional dedication and writings of some American civil rights workers are exemplary.[50] But inevitably even friendly foreign media commentators suggest that the forward U.S. strategy in Colombia has failed to restore stability to Colombia, while distracting attention from the main drug problem, which lies within U.S. domestic policy. Many critics in many countries condemn what they see as the inadequacies and self-delusion of U.S. politicians and media in relation to Colombia.

This is very far indeed from the successful North American control of the 1950s Latin American news agenda.

Spanish-Language Media in the United States

Spanish-language media inside the United States experienced explosive growth in the years after 1995. In 1995 a representative Hispanic family could only receive two or three Spanish-language television channels;[51] by 2005 there were some 75 Spanish-language (cable and satellite) networks operating inside the United States. This spectacular growth reflected increased demand and increased supply. There simply were more Spanish-speaking people and households, a fact underlined by the 2000 U.S. census. On the supply side, the expanded channel capacity of digital television transformed the possibilities of getting a new offering onto both digital satellite TV and local cable TV. From 2003 digital cable operators were offering up to 30 Hispanic channels, selected to appeal to the specific local Hispanic community.

There were some Spanish-language offerings by the late 1920s—both in press and radio—but the scale was very small. Today's Spanish-language

---

[49] Joseph Contreras, "Colombia: Failed 'Plan,'" *Newsweek International*, August 29, 2005: 36–39; Peter Dale Scott, *Drugs, Oil and War and the United States in Afghanistan, Colombia and Indochina*, Lanham, MD: Rowman and Littlefield, 2003.

[50] Such as Robin Kirk, *More Terrible Than Death: Violence, Drugs and America's War in Colombia*, New York: Public Affairs/Perseus, 2003.

[51] América Rodriguez, *Making Latino News: Race, Language, Class*, Thousand Oaks, CA: Sage, 1999.

daily newspaper circulation leader, *La Opinion*, was launched in Los Angeles in 1926, but most Spanish papers were small weeklies struggling against the fact that Mexican immigrants typically were illiterate and were striving to assimilate quickly. In the southwest, by the 1930s local radio stations' Spanish programming was confined to an hour or two per day.

Even around 1980 U.S. Hispanics were only just beginning to be seen as a market worth pursuing. Radio was in the lead with more than 500 radio stations carrying at least some Spanish-language programming.[52] The Hispanic press was, at last, starting to show strong signs of life. *La Opinion* doubled its small daily sale during 1975–1980.

Hispanic television was showing the most impressive growth because by 1980 satellite technology enabled the Spanish International Network (SIN) to become a real U.S.-wide operation. SIN was controlled by the Mexico City Azcarraga/Televisa company, and SIN's owned and affiliated stations were heavily programmed with Mexican *telenovelas* and other Televisa product. SIN depended on being effectively owned, operated, and subsidized from Mexico City. KMEX (Los Angeles) and KWEX (San Antonio) had been the original basis of the SIN operation. But this author (and coauthor David Walker) were told in Los Angeles in 1979 by KMEX's then general manager, Danny Villanueva, of the reluctance of advertisers to buy into Spanish-language TV; although 44 percent of small children in Los Angeles had Spanish names, KMEX got no baby food advertising.[53]

Of the 75 Hispanic networks that existed in the United States in 2005, most had been launched in the previous four years. The overall scene was dominated by two large United States–Mexico combinations. Much the larger of these two was the Univision (U.S.) and Televisa combination. Univision had been owned and operated (against U.S. law) by Televisa/Azgarraga; but after some legal action, and a brief ownership by Hallmark (1986–1992), Univision was acquired by a group led by a former Hollywood agent (and owner of Embassy TV), Jerry Perenchio. Univision had a dominant position in U.S. Spanish television through a portfolio of Univision networks and a new batch of five mainly movie and music networks (TuTv) co-owned with Televisa.[54] In 2002 Univision was also allowed to acquire the largest U.S. chain of (55) Hispanic radio stations.[55]

---

[52] Jorge Reina Schement and Loy A. Singleton, "The Onus of Minority Ownership: Fee Policy and Spanish-Language Radio," *Journal of Communication*, Vol. 31/2, Spring 1981: 78–83.

[53] Jeremy Tunstall and David Walker, *Media Made in California*, New York: Oxford University Press, 1981: 86–93.

[54] Martha M. Hamilton, "New Dispute Erupts over Sale of Spanish-language TV stations," *Washington Post*, September 21, 1986; Jennifer Pendleton, "Perenchio Buys Univision with Mex, Venezuela Partners," *Variety*, April 13, 1992; Cynthia Littleton and Andrew Paxman, "Univision's Perenchio Hablas Success," *Variety*, May 24–30, 1999: 5, 87; Ronald Grover, "The Heavyweight of Latin Airwaves," *Business Week*, August 9, 2004: 70–71.

[55] Demetri Sevastopulo and Alison Beard, "Univision Hispanic Deal Approved," *Financial Times*, September 23, 2003.

The second biggest player in this market was Telemundo, owned by NBC/GE; it claimed to be in 92 percent of US Hispanic homes.[56] Next in importance was the Azteca America network, showing programming from the second Mexico City TV company. Following these networks came Spanish offerings from American majors—such as Discovery en Espanol, Fox Sports en Espanol, and various Turner Animation networks. Several other networks were themed to Spanish-language movies, music, sport, kidvid, and entertainment—mostly drawn from Latin America, but packaged in New York or Miami. Nearly all of these networks made some programming —especially news, talk, and celebrity interviews—in the United States.

Finally there were some 20 additional networks from specific countries; here Spain (and especially the Madrid public broadcaster, RTVE) was in the lead both in terms of households reached and a more upmarket audience. Next came networks from Argentina, Chile, Colombia, Venezuela, Puerto Rico, Costa Rica, Ecuador, Uruguay, and the Dominican Republic; most of these national networks reached not more than 500,000 U.S. homes.[57]

In addition to digital technology and the sheer size of the U.S. Hispanic population (41 million in 2005), another important factor was the general media turbulence in the 1995–2005 period. The Internet and related innovations had motivated all media managers to anticipate the future and—in an uncertain world—one of the safest predictions was the continuing growth of the U.S. Hispanic population. Increasingly, the major network providers wanted to have their own Hispanic offerings. The big newspapers also, facing circulation and Internet conundrums, were reviewing their Spanish-language strategies. *La Opinion* was by 1989 half owned by the Los Angeles Times group (and subsequently by the Chicago Tribune group).[58] There was a tendency to drop the approach of a Spanish news insert and to focus on a separate Spanish newspaper—such as *El Nuevo Herald* (Knight Ridder) in Miami. Another approach was Tribune's chain of *Hoy* newspapers, appearing in separate big city local editions.[59]

But all of these Spanish-language operations were financially quite cautious. One key inhibition was that the most affluent Hispanics were typically the longer-stay and more professional people, who spoke better English than Spanish. There was a large middle group, many of whom spoke both English (perhaps at work) and Spanish (perhaps at home), or "Spanglish" (a mix); many of these people followed both Anglo and Spanish TV. But the core audience—the heavy viewers of, and listeners to, Spanish TV and radio— was the most recent immigrants, who also had the lowest incomes. This latter point goes some way to explaining why, while "Hispanics" made up

[56] Davied Tobenkin, "Univision vs Telemundo," *Broadcasting and Cable*, October 6, 1997: 34–42; Mary Sutter, "Telemundo's Major Makeover," *Variety*, July 11–17, 2005.
[57] *Multichannel News* and *Broadcasting and Cable* supplement, "Hispanic Television Summit," December 6, 2004: 18A–24A.
[58] Mark Fitzgerald, "One Man's La Opinion," *Editor and Publisher*, October 1, 2001: 10–14.
[59] Mark Fitzgerald, "Newspaper Roc en Espanol," *Editor and Publisher*, March 2004: 26–31.

14 percent of the 2005 U.S. population (and had 8 percent of total U.S. buying power), Spanish advertising only accounted for about 3 percent of the U.S. advertising spending.[60]

The "Hispanic audience" was, of course, highly fragmented—not only in terms of language, social class, and income but also in country of origin. So great were, and are, the differences between Cuban Americans, Mexican Americans, and Chilean Americans that the term "Hispanic audience"[61] reflected marketing hype rather than cultural reality. This was recognized as a problem by Univision, whose leading performers (such as news anchor Jorge Ramos) tried to drop their Mexican (or other national) Spanish and to use a standard (nonnational) Spanish.[62] The linguistic diversity within the "Hispanic" community[63] was also one factor inhibiting the development of U.S.-Spanish serious movies and of more artistically ambitious, and less commercial, television genres.[64]

Has the big growth of U.S.-Hispanic media had much impact on the United States? There is still little Anglo exposure to Spanish TV, radio, or music. Indeed, paradoxically, the increase in Spanish networks may have accompanied decreased Anglo exposure to Hispanic TV. To get access to the big bundles of Spanish TV programming, it is necessary to subscribe to the relevant tiers offered by cable and satellite operators; very few Anglos make that investment.

The Hispanics are ever more visible in certain states such as California, Texas, Florida, and New York/New Jersey.[65] But the now less numerous African Americans still seem more visible than Hispanics. How many Americans remember that in the Los Angeles riots of April–May 1992, Hispanics outnumbered African Americans by 44 to 42?[66] One criticism has been that the salience of Mexican youth gangs in the United States has been exaggerated on local U.S. TV news.[67] But how much interest is there in the expulsion of Los Angeles gang members back to Central America where they further destabilize countries trying to recover from civil war, and then, perhaps, return to the United States?[68]

---

[60] George Winslow, "The New Multiethnic Math," *Multichannel News,* July 11, 2005: 34–36.
[61] Louis E. V. Nevaer, *The Rise of the Hispanic Market in the United States,* Armonk, NY: M.E. Sharpe, 2004.
[62] Jorge Ramos, *No Borders: A Journalist's Search for Home,* New York: Rayo/HarperCollins, 2002.
[63] Michael A. Morris, "Effects of North American Integration on Linguistic Diversity," in Jacques Maurais and Michael A. Morris (eds.) *Languages in a Globalizing World,* Cambridge, UK: Cambridge University Press, 2003: 143–56.
[64] Chon A. Noriega, *Shot in America: Television, the State and the Rise of Chicano Cinema,* Minneapolis: University of Minnesota Press, 2000.
[65] Mike Davis, *Magical Urbanism: Latinos Reinvent the US City,* London: Verso, 2000.
[66] Charles E. Simmons, "After the Los Angeles Riots: New Challenges Face US Media," *Media Development,* 3, 1992: 19–21.
[67] Raúl Damacio Tovares, *Manufacturing the Gang: Mexican American Youth Gangs on Local Television News,* Westport, CT: Greenwood, 2002.
[68] Ana Arana, "Central American Gangs Head North," *International Herald Tribune,* May 16, 2005; "Criminal Gangs in the Americas," *The Economist* January 7, 2006: 23–26.

In terms of world media, and media trade, the key significance of Hispanic media is that the United States now imports (and produces) "foreign-language" media on a substantial scale. In media terms the United States is no longer a completely impregnable Anglo Fortress America.

Latin America, North America, and Euro-America

Latin America has become less U.S.-dependent (or U.S.-dominated) in terms of media than was the case in the 1940s and 1950s. Latin American media are now engaged in complex two-way relationships with the media of Europe, as well as with the media of the United States.

Perhaps the biggest single element in this change has been the Latin American *telenovela*—both the short Mexican-style *novela* and the somewhat longer Brazilian *novelas*. These *telenovelas* have dominated television prime time across Latin America since 1980. *Novelas* have enabled Latin America to achieve something that western Europe has not achieved—domestic dominance in prime evening time drama. The *telenovelas* have played a prominent role in bringing Latin American and European media closer together. Meanwhile, Europe has come to play a bigger role in Latin American media and the leading role in Latin American international news.

At least five nations strive (unsuccessfully) for the media leadership of their continent. But Latin America has both a clear Spanish-language pecking order and also two large (100 million plus population) nations—Mexico and Brazil—which are nevertheless not very direct competitors.

Within both Mexico and Brazil there has been a very high degree of media ownership concentration. Both Televisa and Globo have combined enough political, marketing, and production strength to be able to control or limit fresh U.S. incursions into their national markets.

There is a clear second tier in the Spanish American pecking order. Colombia, Argentina, Peru, and Venezuela have 25 percent (and together with Mexico and Brazil 69%) of the population of Latin America and the Caribbean. These four countries rely heavily on their own TV production, and they all do some exporting. These four approximately balance imports from the United States with imports from Latin America (mainly Mexico).

In the 1990s U.S. media companies generated a huge publicity barrage about the imminent takeoff of multichannel TV across Latin America.[69] But the results achieved fell very far short of the early and mid-1990s hype. Eight percent of Latin American households had cable or satellite in 1994 and the penetration rate only grew by about 1 percent a year over the next decade. Half of all Argentine households (especially in Buenos Aires) were cabled by

---

[69] "Special Report: Latin America," *Variety*, March 28–April 3, 1994: 37–67; "Cable and Satellite Focus on Latin America," *Broadcasting and Cable International*, October 1995: 56–65.

1998, but all the other countries had very low levels of cable.[70] Argentina's subsequent financial catastrophe held back its further cable growth.

But two satellite direct-to-home offerings also experienced big losses. One satellite consortium involved News Corporation (Murdoch) in alliance with both Televisa and Globo; the second consortium was led by Hughes/General Motors (with Galaxy Latin America and DirecTV), Cisneros (Venezuela), Multivision (Mexico), and Abril (Brazil). U.S. publicity presented this as another triumphant step for U.S. media; more cynical commentators saw these two consortia as smart moves by the Latin American media moguls, who correctly anticipated the big financial losses that duly ensued. The two satellite combinations largely failed to overcome several familiar difficulties. While research showed that wealthy Buenos Aires families especially viewed Cartoon, Fox, and Nickelodeon,[71] there was little effective demand from the great bulk of the (low income) populations. As found elsewhere, there were two huge marketing hurdles to be jumped. First, average-income Latin Americans could not afford even basic subscriptions to either cable or satellite. Second, as the digital offers became available, especially after 2000, the cost of the digital box (and of the multiple programming tiers) was still more prohibitive. Even in the United States and United Kingdom an effective subsidy was required in the 2000s to spread the digital boxes. In Latin America the satellite providers found themselves providing massive digital subsidies and also facing big piracy rates.

The most obvious result of these business plans gone wrong was the 2003 collapse of the DirecTV Latin American operation; in Latin America, as in North America, DirecTV collapsed into the arms of Murdoch/News Corp. So the winner was Murdoch? Again, the new combined (monopoly) service was somewhat ambiguous financially; some analysts believed the real winner to be the increasingly belligerent Televisa,[72] which was also pressuring its partners in Univision.

Since the 1970s a two-way media connection between Latin America and Europe has gradually developed. *Telenovelas* (and other entertainment) from Latin America have been imported by many TV schedulers, especially in southern, central, and eastern Europe (including Russia). Spain has become a significant player in Latin America—not least in banking and telecommunications. The privatized Telefonica has had a significant presence not only in telecoms but also as owner of Argentina's leading TV network of the 1990s (Telefe) and as a seller (through Endemol) of television formats. Prisa (the owner of the leading Madrid daily, *El Pais*) acquired a network of 450 radio stations across Latin America, from Buenos Aires to Miami.[73]

---

[70] Andrew Paxman, "Disputes Stall Cable in Brazil, Colombia," *Variety*, March 23–29, 1998.
[71] "US Based Ad-Supported Channels in Buenos Aires" (August 1997), *Advertising Age International*, September 1997: 126.
[72] Ken Bensinger, "Televisa Wins Big in Rupe Deal," *Variety*, October 18–24, 2004.
[73] Carlta Vitzthum, "Prisa Wants to play Conquistador," *Business Week*: June 27, 2005.

The biggest media role of Europe and Spain in Latin America has been in news—through the EFE,[74] AFP, and Reuters news agencies. As more Latin American countries have become more democratic, they have tended to prefer European (rather than U.S.) models of democracy, news, and media. But Elizabeth Fox pointed out in 1997 that national, rather than international, factors were more significant in Latin American media.[75]

The United States continues to have much the strongest single national media system in the world and in Euro-America; however, the U.S. media position, especially in Latin America, has significantly weakened since the mid-twentieth century.

There is much ambiguity in these relationships. Are Europe and the Americans influencing each other, or are their media systems simply developing along parallel lines? In a major business relationship, such as that between Televisa and Univision, is the Mexican exporter or the U.S. importer in the stronger position? Have the U.S. news agencies really lost news leadership—in both Latin America and Europe—to the European news agencies, or are all big international agencies constituent parts of a Euro-American news cartel? The difficulty of answering such questions itself reflects the fact that media America and media Europe have, at least partially, merged.

[74] Soon Jin Kim, *EFE: Spain's World News Agency*, New York: Greenwood, 1989.
[75] Elizabeth Fox, *Latin American Broadcasting: From Tango to Telenovela*, Luton, UK: University of Luton Press, 1997: 129.

19

Twenty-one New Media Nations Replace Communist Media Empire

Many people in 1991 asked why the Soviet Union had collapsed. A more relevant question was: When the British, French, and Dutch empires had all collapsed during 1945–1965, why did the Russian Empire not collapse until 1985–1991?

This chapter argues that, like other empires, the Russian Empire was eventually unable to resist the challenge of insurgent nationalism and of ethnic-nationalist media. After the Soviet break-up, 15 new post-Soviet nation-states now exist, in all of which national culture and national media are salient. But in Russia, and in 11 other former republics (out of 15), the existing elements of democracy and independent media are outweighed by authoritarian government and government-dominated media.

The Russian Empire up to the death of Stalin had been held together by terror. After the 36 Lenin-Stalin years (1917–1953), terror continued, but on a lesser and lesser scale. By the 1980s the Russian Empire lacked the big stick, which continuing empires seem to require.

Moscow politicians and bureaucrats believed their own propaganda (in their own media) to the effect that the Soviet Union was a single nation-state and not a EurAsian empire-on-the-land. An oddity of sustained propaganda is that even many normally skeptical members of the audience (and the propagandists themselves) believe much of the invention and untruth. Very few Western politicians, diplomats, or political scientists predicted the break-up of either the Soviet Union or Yugoslavia; they also believed some of the disinformation.

In both the Soviet Union and Yugoslavia, regional languages were sustained by regional media and regional education, which, in turn, sustained regional mythology and loyalty. Both Stalin and Tito (and their

413

Figure 19.1 The 15 successor states of the former Soviet Union.

successors) encouraged regional languages and culture. But they failed to recognize that they were imperialists in an end-of-empire era.

Regional politicians and journalists were well aware of the seductive appeal of regional loyalty and regional nationalism. Many of them bided their time, suspecting (like Indian politicians and journalists of the 1920s and 1930s) that time was on their side. A key 1950s decision in both the Soviet Union and Yugoslavia was to allow television in regional languages.

From 1985 onward, Mikhail Gorbachev's freeing of the media allowed Soviet citizens to view Soviet politics more realistically, to learn about corruption and inadequacies in their own republic and in Moscow, and to observe the dissatisfaction of many Russians with a fractious, and expensive, non-Russian Empire.

Subsequently, six Baltic and South Caucasus republics moved toward independence, and the television coverage revealed that Moscow was reluctant to gun down demonstrators and marchers. When the regional media "changed sides" to support regional independence (and lived to tell the tale), then independence was already achieved.

The main American media influence in the Soviet Union occurred in the silent cinema of the 1920s. American, British, and German radio played only a very small part in the collapse of the Soviet Union and Yugoslavia. It was domestic print, radio, and television that encouraged people to believe that they were Serbs or Croats (not Yugoslavs) and Uzbeks, Georgians, Lithuanians, or Russians (not Soviets).

The Russian Empire has been described as seeking to be (especially in the 1920s and 1930s) an equal opportunities empire. Moscow made a big effort to improve the economies of the non-Russian republics. Stalin operated a two-level, two-language policy. Each of the 14 non-Russian republics had two official languages—Russian and its "own language." The Russian Empire made a much bigger attempt (than did the British and French empires) to educate and to modernize all of the citizens of all of its 15 republics. However, this policy eventually came unstuck when well educated, and fairly well-fed, regional elites were able to use the regional language to promote regional nationalism. Regional nationalism gradually developed and—tolerated by Moscow for three decades (1953–1985)—grasped the new opportunities offered in 1985.

Misinformation, propaganda, and mass media manipulation played a big role in sustaining the Russian Empire until the 1980s. One key purpose of misinformation was to hide from Soviet citizens the very fact that they resided in a police state, and a police empire, which systematically misinformed them about the outside world. This systematic misinformation was less viable in the 1980s, with the Soviet Union's now highly educated population.

Because the public media carried misinformation on an industrial scale, the Communist Party elite had to be supplied with doses of more genuine news and more reliable information. This was done by allowing the communist elite access to foreign news and more objective Moscow news. Consequently, Communist Party elite members increasingly recognized that their entire regime and their Russian Empire were built on misinformation.

Misinformation involved denying the people of one republic accurate information about what was happening in other republics. This practice collapsed in the more open media conditions after 1985. The previous presentation of tranquillity across the entire Soviet empire could no longer be sustained; during 1985–1991 people across the Soviet Union learned, through the media, of civil war in the South Caucasus and of nonviolent, but determined, civil disobedience in the Baltic republics.

Was economic failure the root cause of the Soviet Union's collapse? In fact, Soviet GDP per capita grew by 27 percent during the 1965–1975 decade; taking a 20-year period—1965–1985—Soviet GDP per capita growth was well behind that of the United States and far behind that of western Europe. However, perhaps more importantly, GDP per capita fell by over 7 percent during 1986–1991. So, while Mikhail Gorbachev was telling the people that things were getting better, Soviet GDP per head in 1991 was back to the level of 1976–1977—no growth in 15 years.

During his period in power (1985–1991) Mikhail Gorbachev was at first seen as a television superstar, who promised better, freer, times. He was a television revelation after the three Soviet bosses of the previous decade; during 1975–1985 Leonid Brezhnev, Yuri Andropov, and Konstantin Chernenko came across on Soviet television as mumbling and stumbling, buttoned-down bureaucrats from some former age. After them Gorbachev was a television natural; but from 1985 onward, Gorbachev appeared for more and more hours on television; and the more Gorbachev talked, the worse the overall political and economic picture seemed to become. By 1991, Gorbachev had lost much of his previous popularity, and so had the Soviet Union.

National Media and End of Empire

In the Soviet Union, the major media distinction was between big Russian language media, which were edited in Moscow (and went to the entire Soviet Union), and the regional media of particular republics, which were edited and produced in each republic in that republic's main language (and also in Russian).

Table 19.1 shows the 1990 populations of the Soviet republics, with Russia containing 51 percent of the population and the 14 non-Russian republics having 49 percent. However, this table simplifies a much more complex reality. During both the tsarist and communist eras, there had been huge movements of population. Consequently, in most republics, not only the main titular language (Ukrainian in the Ukraine or Kazakh in Kazakhstan) and Russian, but several other languages, were spoken as mother tongues. The religious map was also extremely complex, despite (or because of) Soviet attempts to abolish or play down religious ties.

The media hierarchy was one of several overlapping hierarchical grids. The senior (political) hierarchy was the Communist Party, the all-knowing and all-powerful force in a one-party state. Alongside the party hierarchy was the government hierarchy with a bureaucracy stretching from the Kremlin in Moscow across 11 time zones to small settlements on the Pacific. Alongside party and government was a language hierarchy; all languages were supposedly equal, but Russian was the senior "All Union" language across the whole Soviet Union. Leading titular republic languages were highly placed in the regional hierarchy.

The Soviet media hierarchy is set out (in greatly simplified form) in Table 19.2. At the very top was the Communist Party of the Soviet Union (CPSU). The media hierarchy was anchored into the communist hierarchy by placing key editors and media executives on the relevant party committee; the small town editor would be on the small town communist committee and the current chief editor of *Pravda* was on the Central Committee in Moscow. Each level of the media took the ideological and policy lead from the entities above it in the hierarchy. The Communist Party normally published major policy statements, speeches, and ideological interpretations in *Pravda*, which was in charge of ideology, policy, and comment; TASS was the engine for news, including fast news. There were also other elements, including more weighty magazines and "heavy journals" such as *Kommunist*. Radio and TV

Table 19.1   Populations of Russia and the 14 Non-Russian Republics of the
Soviet Union in 1990

	POPULATION (IN THOUSANDS)	MAIN LANGUAGE(S)	MAIN RELIGION(S)
Russian Federation	148,290	Russian	Russian Orthodox
Baltics			
Estonia	1,582	Estonian	Protestant
Latvia	2,684	Latvian	Protestant
Lithuania	3,726	Lithuanian	Roman Catholic
Total	7,992		
West/Asia, South Caucasus			
Armenia	3,335	Armenian	Armenian Orthodox
Azerbaijan	7,134	Azeri	Shia Muslim
Georgia	5,460	Georgian	Georgian Orthodox
Total	15,929		
Eastern Europe			
Belarus	10,260	Russian and Belorussian	Belorussian Orthodox
Moldova	4,365	Romanian	Moldovan Orthodox
Ukraine	51,891	Ukrainian and Russian	Ukrainian Orthodox and Roman Catholic
Total	66,516		
Central Asia			
Kazakhstan	16,742	Kazakh and Russian	Sunni Muslim
Kyrgyzstan	4,395	Kirghiz	Sunni Muslim
Tajikistan	5,303	Tajik	Sunni Muslim
Turkmenistan	3,668	Turkmen	Sunni Muslim
Uzbekistan	20,515	Uzbek	Sunni Muslim
Total	50,623		
Soviet Union TOTAL	289,350,000		

became very important, but they continued to follow the print media in terms
of comment and news agenda. Both *Pravda* and *Izvestia* were very thin, six- or
eight-page publications priced at a few kopeks (equivalent to two or three
U.S. cents). Millions of Communist Party members and government office
workers received free copies.

A second (regional or republic) hierarchy was, of course, subordinate to
the first (Soviet) hierarchy. Here the regional languages were much more
important. But people living in a particular republic had a choice not only of

Table 19.2   Hierarchy of Soviet Union–wide Media, 1984

TYPE	NAME	SALES
Ideological press	*Pravda, Izvestia*	10.2 million daily sales
		6.4 million daily sales
National and international news agency	TASS	
Soviet Union–wide radio and television	Gostelradio	
Film industry		About 14 annual visits per person

Other newspapers distributed across the entire Soviet Union

Trade union daily	*Trud*	18.0 million daily sales
Young adult	*Komsomol Pravda*	13.6 million daily sales
Children's	*Young Pioneer Pravda*	9.7 million daily sales
Army	*Red Star*	3.1 million daily sales
Sports	*Soviet Sport*	4.6 million daily sales

newspapers (and radio and TV) in local languages. In addition to Russian print and broadcast media coming from Moscow, each republic had its own radio and TV output in Russian, as well as in the main local language or languages.

Stalin himself came from Georgia (an ethnically diverse region) and spoke Russian with a Georgian accent. His nationalities and language policy adopted a positive attitude to regional languages; in Georgia, for example, the Georgian language was encouraged alongside Russian.

Lenin wrote enough about the press to fill a 474-page book.[1] From his lengthy experience of political exile, Lenin stressed the primacy of the communist newspaper (its editors, sellers, and readers) as the basic activity and organizer of the party. Lenin also directed Soviet news values toward positive and "exemplary" stories of virtuous workers' achievements.

However, across the entire Soviet Union the nationalities policy was more complex. A huge effort was made to codify dozens of languages that were still mainly only spoken languages. Many languages—especially in the Soviet east—were converted to the Latin alphabet and not into the Russian (imperial) Cyrillic alphabet. Soviet policy was to select one or two languages in each area for development, publication, education, and use in press and radio. These policies inevitably exacerbated conflicts between "developed" and "undeveloped" local languages. This collection of nationality policies generated a steep new hierarchy of Soviet languages and Soviet media. First

---

[1] *Lenin About the Press*, Prague: International Organisation of Journalists, 1972.

was Russian spoken as a mother tongue by about half of all citizens and as a second language by many others. Next were major "western" languages such as Ukrainian. Third were large languages such as those spoken in Muslim central Asia. Fourth were "indigenous" and small tribal languages. Finally, Stalin invented a fifth, negative category of "diaspora" nationalities, languages, and media; the main examples—reflecting Stalin's 1930s anxieties— were Poles, Finns, Germans (mainly in the western Soviet Union) and Koreans (in the east).[2]

Lenin's conception of a positive news agenda continued throughout the whole history of the Soviet Union. Several preferred Western news categories—such as civil riots, earthquakes and environmental disasters— received little or no media coverage. Civil disorder and local rioting were common in the Soviet Union. Police stations were attacked, ethnic clashes were not unusual, while local bureaucracy and shortages often induced alcohol-fueled public rage; but the death toll only occasionally rose above 20.[3] Such unseemly events were seldom reported. Earthquakes, common across much of the Soviet Union's southern regions, were not reported. Also unreported were environmental disasters such as the now notorious shrinkage of the huge Aral Sea; Kazakhstan was the location of numerous unreported environmental "problems" such as nuclear bomb testing.

Right up to 1985, Soviet television had a certain resemblance to the more old-fashioned monopoly public broadcasting systems of western or northwestern Europe. Entertainment on TV relied heavily on old Russian films and music programming (some classical). There was a distinct shortage of soap operas and entertainment series. News was normally scheduled across all channels so that there was no available alternative viewing.

The average age of the leadership was quite high, and neither Khrushchev (in power 1953–1964) nor Brezhnev (1964–1981) was a natural TV performer. Khrushchev offended many Russians with his vulgar peasant language and undignified histrionics. Great care went into the smooth presentation of Brezhnev, who, toward the end of his 17 years in power, tended to mumble and stumble. Where Brezhnev mumbled inaudibly, Soviet TV editors were expert in techniques for clarifying his diction; this included substituting recordings of Brezhnev, when younger, saying the same (or similar) words more clearly. As with any ageing star, there was a preferred type of TV shot. Brezhnev was always to be filmed in medium shot, showing the top half of his body; presumably in close shot he looked too ancient and in long shot he looked small and insignificant.[4]

---

[2] Terry Martin, *The Affirmative Action Empire: Nations and Nationalism in the Soviet Union, 1923–1939*, Ithaca, NY: Cornell University Press, 2001.

[3] Vladimir A. Kozlov, *Mass Uprisings in the USSR*, Armonk, NY: M.E. Sharpe, 2002.

[4] Reino Paasilinna, *Glasnost and Soviet Television*, YLE (Finnish Broadcasting Company) Audience Research 1995: 126–30.

Meanwhile, in each of the 14 non-Russian republics there were two separate language media systems running alongside each other. About half the locally available television time was in Russian (coming both from Moscow and from the republic itself) and about half was in the main local language of the republic; the same was broadly true of daily newspapers and magazines. Cheaper media (such as weekly newspapers and radio) were available in Russian, in the main republic language, and in other languages. Although this system looked superficially equal as between the two languages, a specific example, such as Azerbaijan, revealed that the Russian half of television received more generous finance, despite Russians being only 8 percent of the local population. The Azeri language had equal time, but it did not have equal finances.

This somewhat awkward compromise seemed to work quite well from a Moscow elite viewpoint. The majority Azeri population could watch local Baku produced programming—much of it ethnic (Middle Eastern) music or educational-style documentaries. The alternative was slicker and more expensively made Russian output.[5] Many Azeri-speaking viewers must have found this mixture both frustrating and boring. Meanwhile, Moscow had developed, within each of the 14 non-Russian republics, a regional media system (press, radio, and TV) that in 1991 quickly "changed sides" in classic independence-seeking revolutionary style. During the 1970s a few top Moscow politicians recognized this danger. But it was too late.

The National Media Sequence

The 15 republics of the former Soviet Union are now all separate nation-states. All of these 15 nation-states can be seen as following a somewhat similar sequence from the late nineteenth century to the early twenty-first century. This is a sequence from imperial media into new nation-state media; the sequence, consequently, has similarities to the sequence experienced by independent nation-states that broke away from the British, French, Dutch, and Portuguese empires. In addition, there are some similarities to the sequence of stages that characterized the break-up of Yugoslavia into (at least) six nation-states:

- Most of these nation-states of today were part of tsarist Russia and looked toward Moscow both in political and press terms.
- The Lenin-Stalin years (1917–1953) were years of extraordinary turbulence, including two world wars (and the aftermaths), agricultural collectivization, mass terror, forced migration, and death by labor camp.

---

[5] Ellen Mickiewicz, *Split Signals: Television and Politics in the Soviet Union*, New York: Oxford University Press, 1988: 7, 208.

The media were slavishly propagandistic in support of the Russian Empire and Stalin.

- The years between Stalin and Gorbachev (1953–1985) were somewhat less turbulent; it was in these years that each of the republics acquired a substantial media system in its own language.

- The six Gorbachev years (1985–1991) saw the break-up of the Soviet Union. These were years of high political and media excitement, at the regional and Moscow levels.

- Around 1989–1992 the media "changed sides" to support, and to lead, the brave 15 new nation-states. Many new media appeared and some established media went into steep decline. But many (previously communist) politicians crossed over into the new regime, as did many media voices.

- Independence was typically accompanied by, or followed by, violent confrontation within the new nation-states. In some cases there was civil war, while in other cases whole population fragments were "encouraged" to move out. Under newly democratic conditions, political language—and media language—could take extreme forms and could deteriorate into hate speech.

- During the 1990s most of the new nations—with diverse mixes of democracy and dictatorship—won support for some kind of constitutional accord or charter of agreed principles. The media—as revealed in election coverage and in everyday output—tended to be highly partisan in support of those in power.

Singing Revolution: The Baltic Sequence

The three small Baltic republics played a key early role in the break-up of the Soviet Union. Estonia, Latvia, and Lithuania had a combined 1990 population of eight million—less than 3 percent of the Soviet Union's total. The late 1990s challenges from these three small republics to the Soviet Union were based on democratic support and peaceful passive resistance. These were also nationalist challenges. Each of the three countries had its own proud national tradition of resistance to the Russian Empire in the east and to German imperialism in the southwest.

Each of the three Baltic republics/nations was asserting its national distinctiveness, based not least on its own language and its own religious tradition. Lithuania had its own language and was predominantly Roman Catholic. Latvian (like Lithuanian) was a Baltic language, but Latvians were predominantly Protestant. Estonian is related to Finnish, and Estonia was, like Latvia, mainly Protestant. All three of these countries had traditions of wanting to be Baltic nation-states; one might say that the three Baltic countries are today becoming part of greater Scandinavia. All three countries have long looked, enviously, toward Scandinavia for media models.

These Baltic countries have a history of being colonized by Poland, Sweden, and Denmark as well as by Germany and Russia. But, in the nineteenth century, tsarist Russia was the relevant imperial power. The Russian Empire also imposed the Russian language and Russian script. Following the tsarist collapse and the Russian revolution of 1917, the three Baltic countries escaped into a national independence that lasted two decades, until 1939. These years, 1918–1939, were not years of golden democracy; but subsequently these years were looked back to as a period during which each of the three nations had been a sovereign nation-state. The media (mainly the press) were active in each of the three traditional national languages; in the 1920s and 1930s each of the three published thousands of books—for the first time achieving a significant quantity of its own national printed literature.

The worst years in the recent history of the Baltic countries were 1940–1953; there were three brutal occupations—Russian, German, and Russian again. First, for about 12 months (1940–1941) the Baltics were occupied by the Soviet army under the conditions of the Hitler-Stalin agreement (of 1939). The Soviet occupation was so brutal that many Baltic people initially welcomed the arrival of the German army, whose merciless occupation lasted three years (1941–1944). Third, the Baltics also experienced occupation, once again, by the Soviet army during the last nine years of Stalin (1944–1953). This third occupation was perhaps even more deadly than the previous two, not least because active guerrilla resistance, against the Red army, continued for many months after the peace of 1945. Soviet repressive measures against this insurgency (of "forest brothers") were savage, even by Stalin's horrific standards.

In 1940 the three Baltic countries were annexed into the Soviet Union and—apart from the German phase of 1941–1944—the Baltics constituted three republics within the Soviet Union for the five decades, 1940–1990. After 1944 the Russian language was again imposed across the Baltics, and the Stalin regime attempted to obliterate the entire independent national cultural expression of the 1920s and 1930s. In Estonia alone nearly 20 million Estonian-language books were destroyed—a dozen printed books for each man, woman, and child.

After the Khruschev anti-Stalin speech of 1956, the Soviet imperial regime relaxed considerably across the Baltics. During 1956–1985 there was a big development of the two-language policy in both education and the media. The Moscow policymakers transformed these three republics from mainly agricultural (and collective farm) economies into industrial economies. Along with the industry came many Russians; by 1980 about one-third of the three Baltic populations were Russians. This big in-migration—plus the strong Russian media (both Moscow and local republic)—made many Baltic people fear that Russianization might become so dominant as to destroy the Baltic languages. However, the three Baltic republic languages did continue, with a strong secondary role in both education and media.

In all three Baltic republics Gorbachev's new regime was seen as a unique opportunity. The Baltics seized the opportunity in subtle and peaceful ways for which Gorbachev had only the traditional brutal option of suppression, an option he was reluctant to use. The Estonian, Latvian, and Lithuanian media (mainly press and radio) "changed sides" quietly but decisively; more precisely the media abandoned the Russians (both in Moscow and locally) and increasingly sided with their local national politicians. In August 1987 big demonstrations took place in all three countries to commemorate the forty-eighth anniversary of the 1939 Nazi-Soviet pact. This was a well chosen focus because it followed the now acceptable Soviet practice of criticizing Stalin; but it was also a reminder that during 1918–1940 Estonia, Latvia, and Lithuania had been independent.[6]

One year later, in 1988, an even more ambitious demonstration was organized—a human chain of demonstrators stretching 600 kilometers through the three capitals—Vilnius (Lithuania), Riga (Latvia), and Tallinn (Estonia). Two million people took part, one-quarter of the entire Baltic population. This massive peaceful demonstration depended upon publicity in the local national (non-Russian) media. Radio played the lead role, and the radio broadcast the huge crowds singing and chanting. National popular music had itself been central to the gradual reawakening of nationalism and patriotism in Estonia and the two other Baltic nations since the mid-nineteenth century. A strong tradition of choral singing had also developed; in the long Russian Empire era, Baltic choirs had often been required to sing the praises of Lenin and the brotherhood of all the Soviet peoples. In their singing revolution the Baltic peoples sang patriotic songs, which were picked up by Western media and broadcast around the world. The singing revolution was also heard across the Russian Empire, both directly and indirectly.

The three Baltics were ahead of the other 11 non-Russian republics. In November 1988 Estonia's Supreme Soviet voted for a Declaration of Sovereignty. In 1989 Lithuania (May), Estonia (May), and Latvia (July) all declared their independence. This was followed by the two million singers' demonstration (August 1989). After anxious months of nearly independence, Soviet Interior Ministry troops attacked a television antenna tower in Vilnius (Lithuania's capital) in January 1991. About one dozen people were killed, but the troops were then withdrawn. The Baltics were now effectively independent; five months later, Boris Yeltsin won the presidential election in Russia.

Independence, so long desired, when it arrived brought many problems. In all three new nation-states, GDP per capita declined; all three nations were faced with the presence of substantial Russian minorities. All three nations eventually joined NATO and the European Union—having satisfied Brussels of their democratic credentials.

---

[6] Graham Smith (ed.), *The Nationalities Question in the Soviet Union*, London: Longman, 1990.

The media of all three independent Baltic nations went through some broadly similar phases after 1991. Initially the newly independent media stuck close to the newly independent government; there was a mushroom growth of many small publications, while radio and television remained "public." Next followed a phase of privatization in the general economy and across the media. Radio and television changed toward a predominantly commercial system. In the mid-1990s there was a huge increase in regular TV channels and an even bigger increase in the total hours of transmitted television.

The national media in the three Baltic countries have tended broadly to follow Scandinavia. Media subsidy, including press subsidy, was significant after 1990 and was only phased out quite slowly. Scandinavian companies are important owners within the Baltic national television industries.

The three Baltic nation-states share many characteristics, as well as economic and social problems. But all three are also competing with each other—not least in new service industries, including tourism. All three still face their "Russian problems," even though Russians are a much smaller slice of the population in Lithuania than in Latvia and Estonia. Like all newly independent nations, these nations are nationalist in their domestic media and nationalist against their former imperial parent (Stalin's Soviet Union).[7]

Violent Revolution: The South Caucasus Sequence

Violence marked the breakaway from the Russian Empire by the three South Caucasus countries of Georgia, Azerbaijan, and Armenia. While television viewers across the Soviet Union saw a peaceful progression in the Baltics, the TV images from the South Caucasus showed major interethnic violence between, and also within, the three republics.

These three small countries, located between the Black Sea and the Caspian, were at the borders of the Ottoman and Russian empires. Azerbaijan is predominantly Shia Muslim, while both Armenia and Georgia have their own branches of Russian Orthodox Christianity. Each has its own language, or rather, languages. Georgian can claim to be an older language than either French or English; and at least 10 other languages are spoken within particular corners of present-day Georgia.[8]

---

[7] This Baltic section relies primarily on the following: Svennik Høyer, Epp Lauk, and Peeter Vihalemm (eds.), *Towards a Civic Society: The Baltic Media's Long Road to Freedom*, Tartu University, Estonia: Baltic Association for Media Research, 1993; Peeter Vihalemm (ed.), *Baltic Media in Transition*, Estonia: Tartu University Press, 2002; Taivo Paju, "Estonia," Ilze Nagla and Anita Kehre, "Latvia," and Audrone Nugaraite, "Lithuania," in Brankica Petković (ed.), *Media Ownership and Its Impact on Media Independence and Pluralism*, Ljubljana: Peace Institute, Institute for Contemporary Social and Political Studies, 2004: 165–89, 249–65, 267–84.

[8] Graham Smith, Vivien Law, Andrew Wilson, Annette Bohr, and Edward Allworth, "Language Myths and the Discourse of Nation-Building in Georgia," in *Nation-Building in the Post-Soviet Borderlands*, Cambridge, England: Cambridge University Press, 1998: 167–96.

Figure 19.2 Georgia, Armenia, Azerbaijan, and Russia.

The tsarist Russian Empire started to take control of these three territories during 1801–1804. Armenia experienced major massacres (1895–1897, 1909, and 1915) in which Turks and Kurds killed more than half of the entire Armenian people. The Russian Empire was especially active in Georgia, where it attempted to impose the Russian language; a series of Georgian uprisings were brutally suppressed, giving Georgians a heroic history of opposition to the Russian giant. Azerbaijan also had a violent nineteenth century, including several uprisings against Russian rule.[9]

During 1914–1917 the South Caucasus saw further independence uprisings put down by a brutal Russian army. The Russian Revolution of 1917 tempted all three countries to declare themselves independent, but the Soviet army reconquered the region in 1922. All three territories became separate Soviet republics in 1936.

The South Caucasus countries were ruled continuously from Moscow for over 150 years with a small heroic phase of national independence around 1920. Under continuous Soviet rule from 1922 until 1985, the three republics had a happier history than did some of other Soviet regions. Stalin (and his secret police chief, Beria) came from Georgia, and his Georgian background must have influenced the Stalin "nationalities" policy. All three South Caucasus republics (with their Mediterranean-like climates) supplied the Soviet Union with fruit, wine, and vegetables. This pattern was broken after 1990, resulting in major economic dislocation.

---

[9] Charles van der Leeuw, *Azerbaijan: A Quest for Identity*, London: Curzon, 2000.

From the start of the Gorbachev period (1985–1991) and the relaxation of Moscow dominance, the bitter resentments of all three South Caucasus territories quickly emerged into two main violent conflicts. The great Soviet public—which had been kept ignorant of these, and other, regional conflicts —were astonished to see on their TV screens what amounted to civil war within the Soviet Union. More specifically, this was war between Armenia and Azerbaijan about a small enclave of Christian Armenians within the territory of Muslim Azerbaijan. The obscure enclave, Nagorny Kharabach,[10] played a leading role in the collapse of the Soviet Union. For two years (1988–1990) the television news showed warfare and massive protest crowds in the two capitals—Yerevan (Armenia) and Baku (Azerbaijan). The TV audience could also see few signs of Moscow performing its traditional role of (brutally) restoring order. When Red Army units did finally intervene in Baku in January 1990, it was difficult to understand why the army was slaughtering Baku citizenry.

All three of these Soviet republics drifted toward independence from 1989. In April 1989 Soviet Interior Ministry troops dispersed a popular demonstration in Georgia's capital of Tbilisi; at least 20 people were killed by blows from the soldiers' spades. But as Georgia moved toward independence, other violence broke out; this came from several areas within Georgia that had long desired their own independence and whose leaders did not want to be part of an independent Georgia. TV viewers across the Russian Empire could see in Georgia two separate levels of independence-seeking and again—after the repressive Tbilisi events of April 1989—little response from Moscow.

All three South Caucasus territories saw their local republic media "switch sides" to support the newly high profile nationalism. Indeed, these local media contributed to the civil war atmosphere with strident denunciations of their local enemies.

In contrast to the Baltics, these newly independent nations after 1991 did not arrive at a nationally agreed compact or accord. But in both Azerbaijan and Georgia, a strong element of continuity (if not of stability) was provided by two politicians whose careers spanned the Soviet and independence eras.

Geidar Aliyev was Azerbaijan's leading political personality for 34 years (1969–2003). He was the communist boss (first secretary) of Azerbaijan for 13 years; then he was promoted to the Moscow Politburo for 5 years; finally, he was the elected president of independent Azerbaijan for 10 years (1993–2003). Shortly before he died in 2003,[11] Geidar Aliyev was succeeded by his son Ilham Aliyev. Independent Azerbaijan retained many features of the Soviet period, including very strict control of the media. The October 2003 election, which brought the younger Aliyev to the presidency, was extremely one-sided, with overwhelming media support for the dynastic succession. Meanwhile, Azerbaijan's changing national orientation was symbolized by

---

[10] Neal Ascherson, "In the Black Garden," *New York Review of Books*, November 20, 2003: 37–40.
[11] Felix Corley, "Geidar Aliyev" (obituary), *The Independent*, December 15, 2003.

another succession—of scripts. Under the tsars the Azeri language used the Arabic script, but under Moscow rule the Cyrillic (Russian) script prevailed. In 2001 President Aliyev (Senior) ordained another switch—to Roman script.

In Georgia some continuity was maintained through the long political career of Edward Shevardnadze, who was Georgia's top politician for 31 years (1972–2003). He was the Georgian communist boss (first secretary) during 1972–1976. He was a senior Moscow politician (1976–1985) and, as Mikhail Gorbachev's foreign minister (1985–1990), was much admired especially by journalists inside and outside the Soviet Union. Shevardnadze resigned in 1990, predicting an attempted Moscow military coup (which duly happened in 1991). For another decade (1992–2003) he was president of newly independent Georgia. During this decade he struggled unsuccessfully against mounting corruption and against three important separatist movements. Two of these separatist areas occupied more than half of Georgia's Black Sea Coast—Abkazia[12] to the north and Ajaria to the south. The third separatist area was South Ossetia opposite North Ossetia and Chechnya in Russia; each of the three Georgian separatist movements involved complex Muslim-Christian and language polarities.

All three of these separatist movements were still active when Shevardnadze's 11 years as Georgian president ended in late 2003. Shevardnadze resigned (at age 75) after a particularly corrupt parliamentary election and huge protest crowds in Tbilisi. The media played a prominent role. By the standards of the other recently independent former Soviet republics, Georgia's media remained relatively free.[13] Both press and broadcast media leaned heavily toward Shevardnadze, whose family, it was said, controlled more than half of the entire Georgian economy. But there were usually at least a few dissenting media voices. In July 2002 a prominent oppositional journalist, at the Rustavi-2 TV channel, was murdered. In October 2002 a punitive raid by tax police against Rustavi-2 triggered large demonstrations on the Tbilisi streets. Over the next 12 months a Latin American pattern developed by which large street demonstrations (against Shevardnadze) received huge television coverage. During these months the Georgian media "changed sides"; this process peaked with the publication of the fake results of the parliamentary election (November 20, 2003).[14] Three days later Shevardnadze resigned.

Most of the Georgian media changed sides to support 35-year-old Mikheil Saakashvili, who was duly elected president of Georgia in December 2003; he won 96 percent of the vote and was supported by a similar proportion of the Georgian media. This level of support raised expectations to unrealistic

12 Neal Ascherson, *Black Sea*, London: Vintage 1996: 244–56.
13 Robert Parsons, "Revolution Haunts the Land of Monsters and Poets," *The Guardian*, November 24, 2003.
14 Tom Warner and Stefan Wagstyl, "Georgians Brace Themselves as Leaders Talk of Civil War," *Financial Times*, November 20, 2003.

heights; by 2003 some people were describing Georgia as "failed state" that might require decades to get back to where it had been in 1985.

The successful Saakashvili electoral campaign of late 2003 exhibited considerable sophistication (and generous funding) in its use of advertising, its commissioning of exit polls (which make fake vote counting unconvincing), and its courting of the foreign press.[15] It was also said that the U.S. Tbilisi embassy had been active in persuading all of the main opposition parties to unite behind (the American-educated) Saakashvili.[16]

In these three ex-Soviet Caucasus countries, nationalism is encouraged by three underlying forces. First are the contrasting religious layers—Muslim (Russian-Georgian border), Christian (Georgia), Muslim (Azerbaijan), and Christian (Armenia). Second, nationalist anxieties focus on opposed sponsors. The United States and the West are strong in Georgia and Azerbaijan—both seen as key to Caspian-to-Mediterranean oil pipeline politics; but Armenia looks toward Russia. Third, shifting clan/ethnic alliances are crucial within these nation-states and nationalisms. Across this Caucasus chessboard the media may continue to play the queen.[17]

Hesitant National Revolution: Ukraine's Media Sequence

Ukraine and Russia together had 69 percent of the Soviet Union's population and most of its industry and agriculture. When Ukraine's 52 million people departed in late 1991, the Soviet Union was finished. Ukraine, however, departed somewhat hesitantly; while many Ukrainians in the west were Catholics and spoke Ukrainian, most people in the industrial east spoke Russian as their first language.

Ukraine had been part of the Polish and other empires before being a main component of the tsarist Russian Empire. But the tsars looked down on Ukrainians, the great majority of whom in 1914 were still illiterate—meaning that there was only a small Ukrainian press.

For four years (1918–1922) Ukraine was independent, before being reoccupied by the Red Army and incorporated into the Soviet Union. During the Stalin years, Ukraine's suffering was worse even than that of Russia itself. Stalin's collectivization of agriculture, and the related famine, killed several million Ukrainians. Several more million Ukrainians died in the German-Soviet War of 1941–1945. Ukraine also suffered from massive forced evacuations of several ethnic groups that Stalin suspected of disloyalty.

---

[15] "The Last Word: Mikhail Saakashvili," *Newsweek International*, December 8, 2003; Mikheil Saakashvili, "Why Georgia Is Serious About Democracy," *Financial Times*, December 2, 2003.

[16] Ian Traynor, "The People Smoke Out the Grey Fox," *The Guardian*, November 24, 2003.

[17] "Special Report, The Caucasus: A Moment of Truth," *The Economist*, November 29, 2003: 23–25.

However, despite this tragic history, the Stalin regime—during 1923–1939 —operated, especially in the Ukraine, what Terry Martin calls an "affirmative action empire"—"a strategy designed to avoid the perception of empire." A massive official effort was made to Ukrainize the Ukraine. The many Ukrainians who spoke Russian as their mother tongue were ordered to learn Ukrainian. Both primary and secondary education were successfully Ukrainized. Also Ukrainian newspaper production switched from 88 percent in Russian in 1923 to 92 percent in Ukrainian in 1932.

Nevertheless, the initial attempt to make Ukrainian the sole dominant language in the Ukraine eventually failed. During the 1930s the Ukrainization effort remained strong; but sales of Ukrainian newspapers were still outnumbered by Russian-language newspapers coming from nearby Russia and Moscow. By 1939 Ukrainian had become the main language of school, home, and general culture. But Russian remained the main language of office, factory, and university.

In 1945 Stalin pushed Poland's boundaries to the west and added a big chunk of eastern Poland (around the city of L'viv) into an expanded Ukraine. During 1945–1985 Ukraine was, after Russia itself, the Soviet Union's most important agricultural and industrial republic. There was a substantial element of Ukrainian-language media, although Russian-language media (both from Russia and from Ukraine) were more prominent.

During the Gorbachev years (1985–1991) the Ukraine's ultimate destiny was unclear. There was the continuing Ukraine versus Russia split; many Ukrainians had complex attitudes not only toward Russia but also towards Poland as a former imperial power and as a leading source of national independence sentiment. As elsewhere in the Soviet Union, religion recovered in the Gorbachev period, but in religion the Ukraine traditionally looked three ways—Ukrainian Orthodox, Ukrainian Catholic (Uniate), and Russian Orthodox. A key experience for Ukraine was the April 1986 "world's worst nuclear disaster" at a power station in Chernobyl, 60 miles north of the Ukrainian capital, Kiev. The communist authorities in Kiev and Moscow attempted to keep this disaster secret, until several neighboring governments (including Sweden and Poland) and their media revealed the evidence. The Chernobyl events said much about Moscow's attitude to news—the insistence on denying that a massive, and deadly, disaster had happened. Moscow's reluctant acknowledgment of the Chernobyl disaster also seemed to reveal an attitude of contempt for ordinary people in general and for Ukrainians in particular.

Both before and after its 1991 independence, Ukraine avoided violence— although Ukraine-Russian relations were frequently tense. The main post-independence understanding allowed much of the old communist hierarchy to stay in power.[18] This was especially true of the 1994 elections, in which

---

[18] "Unruly Child: A Survey of Ukraine," *The Economist*, May 7, 1994.

many former communists were elected and Leonid Kuchma became president of Ukraine. But the Ukrainian economy sank and sank during the entire 1990s. The media were strictly obedient to government;[19] an initial period of mushroom press growth, which began around 1990, had largely faded by 1993.

Ukraine in the early 2000s had one of Europe's larger media industries.[20] But while there were plenty of opposition politicians—and several opposition parties—they found it hard to get time or fair treatment (especially before elections) on television.[21] Ukraine was well provided with corruption, scandals, and the murder of the occasional politician and journalist. Ukrainian President Leonid Kuchma was himself accused in December 2000 of having a journalist murdered. *The Economist* published a list of six prominent people who died in car crashes in Ukraine during 1997–2002. Were these political assassinations, or did these deaths merely reflect Ukrainians' tendency to drive too fast?[22]

Another political dirty trick scarred the face of Viktor Yushchenko, eventual winner of Ukraine's late 2004 presidential election; Yushchenko had apparently been poisoned by his political opponents. This election result was widely seen as a win for (Ukrainian-speaking) western Ukraine and the western democracies—and a loss for eastern Ukraine and Russia.

However, central to the rapid political changes of 2004 was a "change of sides" by the Ukrainian media. Most critical of the old regime were some newspapers and websites that supported Yushchenko and his glamorous political ally (and 2005 prime minister), Julia Tymoshenko (the "Orange Princess"). Also eager to change sides were many television journalists from the government Inter station and from commercial stations such as ICTV, Novy Kanal, NTN, Tonis, and 1+1.

By 2004 most of Ukraine's television output was controlled by new oligarchs, who had benefited from the rapid privatization of Ukraine's steel and other traditional heavy industries. Each oligarch operated simultaneously in three spheres—big business, legislative politics, and media ownership. During 2004 these oligarch media moguls began to "change

---

[19] Olga Zernetskaya, "Broadcasting Reform in Ukraine," *Media Development*, 1, 1994: 32–34.

[20] Andrei Richter, "The Partial Transition: Ukraine's Post-Communist Media," in Monroe E. Price, Beata Rozumilowicz, and Stefaan G. Verhulst (eds.), *Media Reform*, London: Routledge, 2002: 133–54.

[21] Louk Hagendoorn, Hub Linssen, and Sergei Tumanov, *Intergroup Relations in States of the Former Soviet Union*, Hove, Sussex: Psychology Press/Taylor and Francis, 2001; Paul Kubicek, "Regionalism in Post-Soviet Ukraine," in Daniel R. Kempton and Terry D. Clark (eds.), *Unity or Separation: Center-Periphery Relations in the Former Soviet Union*, Westport, CT: Praeger, 2002: 227–48; Ann Lewis (ed.), *The EU and Ukraine: Neighbours, Friends, Partners?* London: Federal Trust, 2002; Taras Kuzio and Andrew Wilson, *Ukraine: Perestroika to Independence*, London: Macmillan, 1994.

[22] "Ukraine's Election: Stumbling Along," *The Economist*, April 6, 2002; "Ukraine's Politicians: If You Think, Don't Drive," *The Economist*, March 30, 2002.

sides." One such oligarchic media mogul, and owner of big confectionary interests, was Petr Poroshenko ("the Chocolate King"); his Channel 5 was already supporting Viktor Yushchenko's Orange cause. Another new media mogul oligarch was Viktor Pinchuk, the son-in-law of President Kuchma. After the disputed second round of the presidential election, Pinchuk's TV outlets switched away from loyalty to his father-in-law, Kuchma. Five weeks after Pinchuk's change of sides, Yushchenko (on December 27, 2004) won the court ordered rerun of the second round of the presidential election. Members of other key professions—judges, senior diplomats, and civil servants—also changed sides. Senior people in the security services were crucial in discouraging violent confrontations between the demonstrators and the police.

This "Orange Revolution" had several similarities to other revolutions in Latin America, Russia, and elsewhere. Yushchenko subsequently spoke to appreciative audiences in Washington and London, but he sank to a 20 percent domestic approved rating after less than 12 months in office. Like other charismatic election winners, he was unlucky with his relatives; both his wife and his son ("Son of God") were accused of blatant corruption. In September 2005 he fired his prime minister and the entire cabinet.[23]

Despite this turbulence, Ukraine seems likely to continue as one of the least fervently nationalist of the ex-Soviet countries. There has been a modest recovery in Ukrainian-language media. Many people will continue to speak both Russian and Ukrainian; and the Ukraine will continue to be one of the world's most genuinely bilingual nations.

Reluctant Revolutions: Uzbekistan, Kazakhstan and Central Asia

The five central Asian republics all departed from the Soviet Union in 1991; most of their people and their elites showed every sign of wanting to remain—but by late 1991 there was no Soviet Union to belong to. However, each of these five countries during the 1990s developed its own highly idiosyncratic nationalism, mythology, and media.

---

[23] Judy Dempsey, "Economic Clans Broke Deadlock in Kiev," *International Herald Tribune*, December 9, 2004; Tom Birchenough, "Sign of the Times for Ukrainian TV," *Variety*, December 6–12, 2004; Stefan Wagstyl and Tom Warner, "Oligarchs Hedge Bets as Political Fortunes Swing," *Financial Times*, December 1, 2004; Judy Dempsey, "In Ukraine, TV Shakes Off Some Shackles," *International Herald Tribune*, December 13, 2004; Nick Paton Walsh, "Television Becomes Attuned to a New Spirit," *The Guardian*, November 29, 2004; Timothy Garton Ash and Timothy Snyder, "The Orange Revolution," *New York Review of Books*, April 29, 2005; "Special Report: Ukraine," *Financial Times*, June 1, 2005; Tom Warner, "Ukraine President Sacks PM and Cabinet," *Financial Times*, September 9, 2005; Judy Dempsey, "Ukraine's Dance of the Oligarchs," *International Herald Tribune*, December 24–25, 2005: 11–12.

The tsarist empire acquired most of today's Kazakhstan in the early nineteenth century; Russia by 1876 controlled most of what are now Uzbekistan, Turkmenistan, Kyrgyzstan, and Tajikistan. The tsars only ruled these areas for between 50 and 100 years (previous to 1917). Little tsarist education or print media penetrated central Asia, and the overall literacy level was below 5 percent in 1917.

In the Lenin-Stalin era (1917–1953) central Asia was transformed. The present lines on the map that indicate the five nations' boundaries were originally drawn by Stalin in 1924 and revised by him in 1929 and 1936. Stalin (according to Olivier Roy) was determined to give each of his five creations "the trappings of statehood." Several previous empires had left behind many ethnic fragments and many languages. Stalin constructed his five new Asian republics and designated one main language (apart from Russian) for each. But Stalin cautiously included several divide-and-rule features; for example, in each designated capital the majority of the population would not be speakers of that republic's main titular language. Stalin deliberately created eccentric boundaries—with the capital cities of three of the republics all in a small area of mountains and valleys near the border with China.

Stalin also set out to transform the five republics.[24] The Muslim religion (and mosques) were discouraged; agricultural collectivization was introduced; such Islamic customs as veiling and polygamy were made illegal. In his analysis of the anti-veil campaign in Uzbekistan, Douglas Northrop shows that this head-on attack was largely unsuccessful. Despite massive publicity campaigns—led by the major Russian newspaper, *Pravda Vostoka* —the veiling campaign inadvertently reinforced the seclusion of Uzbek women; if they had to be unveiled in public, they would not appear in public. It took the 1941–1945 war and its aftermath to abolish the veil.[25]

But Stalin's educational reforms achieved considerable success against formidable difficulties. As late as 1926, literacy levels among Tajiks, Turkmen, Uzbeks, Kirgiz, and Kazakhs were 2 percent, 2 percent, 4 percent, 5 percent and 7 percent, respectively. In the 1920s the Tajik language, for example, was still largely unwritten. There were very few schools or teachers and nothing much for the teachers (let alone any pupils) to learn. In the promotion of the Tajik language and the attack on illiteracy, newspapers were given a leading role in teaching the teachers not just to teach, but to read. These official Tajik newspapers, launched between 1926 and 1928, also pioneered the roman script.[26]

After Stalin's death (1953) there was continued rapid growth in education and mass media (in both the republic languages and in Russian). Kazakhstan,

---

[24] Olivier Roy, *The New Central Asia: The Creation of Nations*, London: I.B. Tauris, 2000: 78–84; Ronald Grigor Suny and Terry Martin (eds.), *A State of Nations: Empire and Nation-Making in the Age of Lenin and Stalin*, New York: Oxford University Press, 2001.

[25] Douglas Northrop, *Veiled Empire: Gender and Power in Central Asia*, Ithaca, NY: Cornell University Press, 2004.

[26] Mohammed-Reza Djalili, Frédéric Grare, and Shirin Akiner (eds.), *Tajikistan: The Trials of Independence*, London: Curzon 1998, 14–41.

for example, was expected to tolerate the massive testing of nuclear weaponry and the growth of new crops such as wheat and cotton (on probably unsuitable soil). Partly because of these huge dislocations, and partly based on his own experience as the boss (first secretary) of Kazakhstan during 1954–1956, Brezhnev, during his years of supreme power in Moscow (1966–1982), established a fresh policy understanding with the central Asian leaders. First secretaries (and holders of other top jobs) in the central Asian republics should be natives of the particular republic. Dimukhamed Kunaev was a Kazak who served two terms as first secretary in Kazakhstan and also served on the Politburo in Moscow.[27] Very few central Asian politicians did have successful Moscow careers. But in the five republics the local Russians did not play a big role in the republic's government and politics. Each Asian republic's native political elite was subject to Moscow's five-year planning and military policy but was given much latitude in running the republic's affairs, including its mass media.

As seen by Brezhnev (and the Moscow elite) the potentially awkward Muslim central Asian republics were growing economically and were being efficiently (and peacefully) governed by Moscow's chosen, but local, men. However, behind this quiet exterior there was a big output of press, radio, and television in each republic's lead language. An equal opportunities policy prevailed in education with the great majority of fresh university graduates being ethnic locals (not ethnic Russians). The Muslim religion (like religion across the Soviet Union) had largely gone underground (or into private homes), but was still there.[28] Presiding over all of this were powerful local (republic) political bosses who were happy with the growth of the republic's economy and media; they were probably willing to look the other way, as long as local nationalism was not overt or strident. By 1985 regional cultural nationalism had been encouraged by Moscow for over six decades and was now increasingly internalized by individuals. When in December 1986 Gorbachev appointed a Russian (rather than a Kazak) to the new boss of Kazakhstan, there was rioting in the Kazak capital of Alma Ata.

The central Asian media passed through several phases during the Gorbachev years and the 1990s.[29] In Uzbekistan the Communist Party largely lost control during 1989. The years 1989–1992 saw the Uzbekistan media "change sides" or switch from supporting the communist power elite to

---

[27] Ingvar Svanberg, *Contemporary Kazaks: Cultural and Social Perspectives*, London: Curzon, 1999: 1–16.

[28] Ahmed Rashid, *Jihad: The Rise of Militant Islam in Central Asia*, New Haven, CT: Yale University Press, 2002.

[29] Willem Van Schendel and Erik J Zürcher (eds.), *Identity Politics in Central Asia and the Muslim World*, London: I.B. Tauris, 2001; Sally N. Cummings (ed.), *Power and Change in Central Asia*, London: Routledge, 2002; Boris Rumer (ed.), *Central Asia: A Gathering Storm?* Armonk, NY: M.E. Shape, 2002; Shireen T. Hunter (ed.), *Central Asia Since Independence*, Westport, CT: Praeger, 1996; Martin Hadlow, "Central Asia Media Audit: Where New Nations Need New Media," *InterMedia*. Vol. 21/1, January–February 1993: 41–45; Beatrice F. Manz (ed.), *Central Asia in Historical Respective*, Cambridge, MA: Harvard University Russian Research Center, 1994, and Boulder, CO: Westview, 1998.

supporting the same people under the different banner of the democratic and independent nation-state of Uzbekistan. The number of published newspapers and magazines tripled during 1988–1990. *Pravda Vostoka*, the Soviet ideological newspaper, was taken over by its editorial staff. There was some expansion of Uzbek-language radio and TV and some reduction of Russian radio and TV. Until the end of 1991 big media subsidies continued to operate; the old system, in effect, subsidized an explosion of interest in Uzbek national culture, literature, and arts and in the Sunni Muslim religion.

The years 1991–1993 saw the emergence of a new phase. Islam Karimov, previously communist first secretary, took advantage of the euphoria to get himself elected president of Uzbekistan in 1991. He (and other quick-footed politicians in central Asia) then used the excuse of a major civil war in Tajikistan (1992–1993) to crack down on political freedom. At the same time, much of the media subsidy apparatus was abolished, leading to newspaper circulation losses and the quick demise of many new press titles. Karimov and other autocrats in the region chose television as their preferred mass medium.

In a seven-year period (1992–1999) seven previously "national" Uzbek newspapers lost 85 percent of their combined sales. Paper supplies from Russia were now much more expensive and there was little advertising. Newspapers had gone from semi-token to genuine market prices.

Television had been in almost all Uzbek households by 1985, and in the 1990s it became ever more the leading mass medium. By 2000 about 80 percent of TV was in Uzbek (much of it subtitled or dubbed) with only 20 percent in Russian. Uzbek TV in year 2000 was still government dominated. There were big programming imports—mainly Latin American *telenovelas*, entire Russian channels, and Hollywood movies; some programming also came from Turkey, Egypt, and India. About 10 percent of programming was religion (Muslim).[30]

In the early 2000s the central Asian republics entered yet another new phase. The United States, Russia, and China—and the world's major oil and gas companies—were now increasingly interested in a new twenty-first century version of the nineteenth-century Great Game (mainly between Russia and Britain).[31] This has provided opportunities for central Asian dictators to use their political skills on a larger stage. A group of political scientists, looking back at the 1990s, described Kazakhstan as exhibiting "hybrid authoritarianism," Kyrgyzstan as displaying "an economy of authoritarianism," Uzbekistan offering "benign authoritarianism," Tajikistan

[30] Lutfulla Kabirov and Scott Smith, "Uzbekistan," in Monroe E. Price, Beata Rozumilowicz, and Stefaan G. Verhulst (eds.), *Media Reform: Democratizing the Media, Democratizing the State*, London: Routledge, 2002: 47–68.

[31] Ahmed Rashid, "Central Asia: Trouble Ahead," *Far East Economic Review*, May 9, 2002: 14–18; Caroline Lambert, "At the Crossroads: A Survey of Central Asia," *The Economist*, July 26, 2003.

as operating "ineffectual authoritarianism," and Turkmenistan as exhibiting "semi-sultanism."[32]

In central Asia, incumbent presidents used television to win elections. Television was also used to build personality cults. Perhaps the most un-inhibited personality cult was that of President Saparmurad Niyazov of Turkmenistan. A huge statue of this great man was constructed to tower over the capital city and to rotate slowly in time with the sun. President Niyazov also looked out, unblinking, from the top right-hand corner of every switched-on TV screen in Turkmenistan.

Another authoritarian ruler, President Narsultan Nazarbayev of Kazakhstan, had followed a practice common in Africa; one television channel, and other media properties, were owned by his daughter. A similar example also existed in Kyrgyzstan.

Meanwhile, Gulnora Karimova, daughter of the president of Uzbekistan, in 2002 owned 51 percent of the leading Uzbek mobile phone company.[33] When, in August 1991, Islam Karimov ceased to be first minister of the Uzbek Soviet Republic and became president of independent Uzbekistan, he continued to use the same office space. Karimov established himself as the benevolent leader of a democratic and apparently multilayered government system that in practice was highly autocratic and highly centralized. Karimov also introduced a fresh version of Uzbek history, celebrating the achieve-ments of a new national icon, Tamerlane, during the 1330s decade. Karimov in his own writing set out to "replenish our national spiritual treasury with new names and works by our great ancestors—philosophers, scholars and creators of beauty."[34] In May and September 2005, President Karimov suppressed two armed uprisings; he used a mix of new methods (his security forces had received American training) and old methods such as boiling people alive.[35]

The new rulers of central Asia did make some major cultural changes. In Kazakhstan there were only 66 mosques in 1990, but by 1996 (with some financial help from Saudi Arabia) there were 4,000 mosques. Other changes included a new national flag, a new constitution, new passports, a national bank, a new currency, and a new national anthem (with words by President Nazarbayev). Streets, towns, and regions were renamed, with Marxist names

---

[32] Sally N. Cummings (ed.), *Power and Change in Central Asia*, London: Routledge, 2002: 1–23.

[33] David Stern, "Uzbekistan Offers Rich Pickings for Leader's Daughter," *Financial Times* August 19, 2003.

[34] Lawrence R. Robertson and Roger D. Kangas, "Central Power and Regional and Local Government in Uzbekistan," in Daniel R. Kempton and Terry D. Clark (eds.), *Unity or Separation: Center-Periphery Relations in the Former Soviet Union*, Westport, CT: Praeger, 2002: 265–90.

[35] "Uzbekistan: The Blood-Red Revolution," *The Economist*, May 21, 2005; C. J. Chivers and Thom Shanker, "Uzbek Units Linked to Deadly Crackdown Got US Training," *International Herald Tribune*, June 30, 2005 (from *NY Times*); Craig Murray (U.K. ambassador to Uzbekistan, 2002–4), "Why the US Won't Admit It Was Jilted," *The Guardian*, August 3, 2005; "Uzbekistan: A Show Trial," *The Economist*, October 1, 2005.

succeeded by traditional-sounding Kazak names.[36] However, President Nazarbayev was reluctant to make major changes in the Kazak mass media. By 2002 most people across Kazakhstan had several TV channels, but the bulk of the programming still came from Russia. By 2004 80 percent of programming had to qualify as Kazak, but anything with Kazak subtitles or dubbing met the definition. Also available in Kazakhstan were entire Russian domestic channels (as in the days of the Soviet Union). Mexican *telenovelas* were present in force on Kazak prime-time TV. Among Kazak-produced programming were reality offerings, such as a Kazak version of *Who Wants to be a Millionaire?*[37]

Central Asia is Russian television's strongest export market. Russian television importing is cheap and familiar; Kazakhstan still has a sizeable (but dwindling) ethnic Russian population, and most adult Kazaks have some understanding of Russian. But this heavy reliance on Russian TV probably also indicates a reluctance to stir up possibly fundamentalist Muslim sentiment.

Russian Media: Nationalist, At Last

Russia in the 2000s shared some common features with the eight Caucasus and central Asian new nations. In each country a small elite largely controlled, or owned, politics, government, the economy, and the media. Within a broadly authoritarian system there was an element (or Potemkin village façade) of genuine democracy. Some free media were allowed, but opposition politicians often faced physical harassment and an array of inhibiting dirty tricks. Before and during elections, opposition politicians were awarded semi-token amounts of television time. But the dominant media tended to caricature both political opponents and ethnic minorities as unpatriotic and as potential separatists or terrorists. In Russia the Muslim population (of about 20 million) received much negative media coverage.

In two decades, 1985–2005, the Russian media were commercialized and Russianized. Various commentators claimed that the Russian media after 1985 became Americanized, or Europeanized, or advertising-dominated. More accurately, the Russian media went from a subsidized communist system to a supposedly market-driven and advertising-driven system. But Russia acquired commercial media that generated very little revenue. Total Russian advertising expenditure in 1999 was still only a negligible $760 million[38]

---

[36] Sally N. Cummings, *Kazakhstan: Power and Elite*, London: I.B. Tauris, 2005: 88–90.

[37] Amos Owen Thomas, "Television Dependency in Independent Kazakhstan," *Gazette*, Vol. 67/4, August 2005: 325–37.

[38] Olga Tretyak, "Advertising in Russia," in Ingomar Kloss (ed.), *Advertising Worldwide*, Berlin: Springer, 2001: 185–222; Terhi Rantanen, *The Global and the National: Media and Communications in Post-Communist Russia*, Lanham, MD: Rowman and Littlefield, 2002: 107–26.

—less than the total advertising spending of each of eight Latin American countries in the same year. Russians—long accustomed to heavily subsidized print media—were not eager to pay commercial subscription rates. Moreover, this was happening while Russians' incomes were falling steeply. By 1998 Russian GDP per capita stood at only 58 percent of 1990 levels.

With little state subsidy, little advertising revenue, and little subscription revenue, the Russian media had to be financed in other ways. These ways included ownership by super-rich oligarchs, special government support for politically friendly media, and cash in envelopes for journalists. In election periods cash in suitcases put in a predictable appearance. "Commercialization" of the Russian media took some rather noncommercial, and unprofitable, forms.

But Russianization was much more genuine. Throughout the communist years (1917–1991) the media had normally been required to play down Russian patriotism and nationalism; this restraint was needed in order to support the myth that the 14 non-Russian republics (and their languages) carried equal status with Russia and Russian. Exceptions to this prevailing rule had been rare, but included the years 1941–1945, when Stalin called upon Russian patriotism to oppose the Nazi German invaders. Mostly, however, Russian nationalism had to remain covert. Then around 1990–1991 Russian nationalism ceased to be covert and became overt. Several new political parties—whether leaning toward capitalism or communism—wanted "Russia" or "Russian" in their official title. Throughout the 1990s there was suspicion of foreigners both from the West and in the former Soviet republics, now independent states. Also widespread was suspicion of the approximately 10 percent of ethnic "non-Russians" in Russia, including both Jews and Muslims.

The 1990s saw the collapse of much of the old Soviet media system. In the 1990s the Russian film industry and the old Soviet habit of going to the cinema virtually ceased to exist.[39] The average Russian had visited the cinema 14 times a year in the mid-1980s, but by the mid-1990s this had fallen to less than one visit per year. Hollywood annual movie revenue was only a few cents per Russian.

While many new weekly publications were published[40] and exhibited the sudden mushroom growth of titles always seen when censorship is relaxed, numerous new publications quickly folded. Sales of the big communist newspapers collapsed; for example, *Pravda, Komsomol Pravda*, and *Izvestia*—whose combined 1984 daily circulation was 30.2 million—in 1994 were together selling 1.68 million daily copies. These prestige publications of the Soviet era thus lost 96 percent of their circulation in a single decade.

---

[39] George Faraday, *Revolt of the Film Makers*, University Park: Pennsylvania State University Press, 2000.

[40] Jukka Pietiläinen, *The Regional Newspaper in Post-Soviet Russia*, University of Tampere, Finland, 2002, academic dissertation.

State support for television was also sharply cut back. The early and mid-1990s were the period when Russian television showed huge numbers of *telenovelas* from Brazil, Mexico, Colombia, and other Latin American countries; fortunately for the TV managers, the Latin American *novelas* were both super-cheap and super-popular. U.S. imports—especially *Santa Barbara* —were also popular (though not quite as cheap to import). The Latin American *novelas* seem to have provided just the riveting combination of romance, sunshine, and escapism that Russians wanted—when little new Russian TV programming was on offer.

Russia, in the 1990s, had just lost an empire and went through some of the same disorientation experienced in Britain and France in the 1960s after their empires had gone. Post-imperial Russia also suffered some of the traumas experienced by many newly independent nations. Much journalism was very aggressive; young journalists who had become famous by attacking Gorbachev now turned against the new Russian president, Boris Yeltsin. The Russian Parliament (Duma) and Yeltsin were in conflict. Hyperinflation in 1993 was combined with a big shrinkage of the Russian economy. The year 1993 saw Yeltsin winning a national referendum and also saw Yeltsin using military force to bombard the Russian parliament building.

Older Russians could still remember the carnage of 1941–1945. Now they saw their Parliament bombarded in 1993, while in 1994 the Russian army unsuccessfully attempted to pacify Muslim Chechnya. Television covered these events and also the big rise in violent crime in Moscow and many other cities. Journalists themselves were especially attuned to violence; some 200 media employees were killed in Russia during 1991–2004, and many more local journalists were attacked and beaten (often for writing stories critical of new commercial businesses).

Not least because of limited finances, one individual journalist might dominate an entire factual television series. Thin newspapers often gave generous space to a few high profile journalists, who specialized in dramatic revelations without too much concern for balance, fairness, and accuracy. While most journalists (like most Russians) were struggling to maintain a meager existence, a few individuals were doing well professionally and financially. Some television producers and personalities were setting up their own independent TV production companies with a linked advertising agency. But both national television and newspapers were grubbing for finance by selling "editorial" space and by accepting commercial advertorial programming.[41]

Already by 1994, Yeltsin was beginning to break the public monopoly in radio and television. Especially remarkable was the 51 percent privatization of ORT1, Russia's leading TV channel and the only channel reaching virtually 100 percent of Russian TV households. As this partial privatization occurred,

[41] Olessia Koltsova, "News Production in Contemporary Russia," *European Journal of Communication*, Vol. 16/3, September 2001: 315–35.

an energetic businessman (from the car industry), Boris Berezovsky, became the leading figure in ORT1. Also in 1994 a new commercial channel, NTV, emerged under the control of Vladimir Gusinsky. Both of these new television entrepreneurs soon also controlled newspapers.

These two groups—the journalists and the new media "oligarchs"—were helpful to Boris Yeltsin in the parliamentary election of late 1995, and especially in the two-round presidential election of June–July 1996. Yeltsin was not in the best of health either physically or politically. According to opinion polls, less than 1 Russian in 10 approved of Yeltsin's performance; millions of Russians blamed him for their falling living standards. His tendency to behave drunkenly, on both domestic and foreign TV, was not a vote catcher. Yeltsin's two main opponents emerged in the first presidential round as Gennady Zyuganov (an aggressive traditional communist) and Alexander Lebed (an Afghanistan war hero who also played a key role in defeating the 1991 attempted coup against Gorbachev).

How then did a drunken, unwell, and unpopular Yeltsin defeat these two charismatic opponents in 1996? Heavy overt media bias and a sustained dirty tricks campaign both helped. But there were also some astute political moves. Yeltsin campaigned actively (and often soberly) in early 1996. Moreover, after the first round (June 1996) he did a deal with the third-placed candidate, offering Alexander Lebed a senior government post (secretary of the state security council).

Yeltsin's 1996 election campaign stressed the potential horrors of a return to communism, and some commentators have claimed that this brilliant idea came from American political consultants.[42] But both the anti-communist theme, and the dirty tricks, were commonplace in Russia and other ex-communist countries at this time. Most media oligarchs, media managers, and journalists were sincerely unhappy at the prospect of the media (and the state) returning to communism. Consequently, the Yeltsin campaign received more free air-time than its opponents. The Yeltsin campaign also did a big paid commercial advertising blitz with money supplied by friendly oligarchs, businesspeople, and managers; probably some money, at least, did come from (and through) foreign companies. Many free newspapers and posters warned against a return to the bad old communist days. The dirty tricks campaign spread negative stories about competing candidates. There were extensive payments to journalists to write slanted stories; in addition, many stories were placed in the press on a paid-for editorial content basis. There was probably also some miscounting of the final votes. This elaborate operation was especially active in the period between the two voting rounds. Between the June and July rounds Yeltsin added 18.5 percentage points (for a final 53.8 percent total) while Zyuganov, his communist opponent, added only 8.3 percentage points. Yeltsin's achievement was also remarkable in

---

[42] Ivan Zassoursky, *Media and Power in Post-Soviet Russia*, Armonk, NY: M.E. Sharpe, 2004: 57–114.

that he suffered from at least one heart attack between the two elections. Naturally this fact was concealed from the media and the electorate.[43]

Only a few months later, the great Russian public once again had a low opinion of Boris Yeltsin. By January 1997 Yeltsin had spent 10 of the past 19 months in the hospital. In an opinion poll, 69 percent of Russians replied that they had not been getting reliable information on Yeltsin's health; 82 percent replied that, had they received reliable information on Yeltsin's health in 1996, they would not have voted for him.[44]

Nevertheless, Yeltsin served all but three months of this four-year term as Russian president. These years 1996–1999, were the years in which the "oligarchs" reached the height of their power in several major industries, including oil. These were also the years in which the oligarchs reached their peak of power in the media. Indeed, the Russian media industry had switched from massive subsidy by the communist state of the Soviet Union to massive subsidy by the newly super-rich oligarchs of Russia. This was the period during which the Russian media were most critical of, and independent from, the Russian state. The commercial channel NTV achieved a reputation for editorial independence, not least for its hard-hitting criticisms of Russian army atrocities in would-be breakaway Chechnya.

The next presidential election was to be in March 2000. Again Yeltsin's electoral strategy was effective; Boris Yeltsin resigned on December 30, 1999, leaving his temporary successor, Vladimir Putin, a three-month honeymoon period before the presidential election.[45] Yeltsin's and Putin's people had also cleared the way with another preemptive dirty tricks campaign against Putin's two most threatening opponents. ORT, the TV ratings leading channel, raised questions about the health of Yevgeny Primakov (former prime minister and leader of Fatherland-All Russia); Yuri Luzhkov, the popular Moscow mayor, was accused of corruption.

Before the 2000 election, pressure was increasing on newspaper editors to toe the line. The Yeltsin-Putin government also lost patience with the TV channels associated with the two media oligarchs, Berezovsky and Gusinsky. Their channels—ORT, NTV, and TVG—had 64.4 percent of the total Russian audience and 85.7 percent of Moscow audience time in July 1997.[46] By 2001

[43] Sarah Oates, "Russian Television, Political Advertising and the Development of a New Democracy," in Lynda Lee Kaid (ed.), *Television and Politics in Evolving European Democracies*, Commack, NY: Nova Science, 1999: 147–69; Ellen Mickiewicz, *Changing Channels: Television and the Struggle for Power in Russia*, New York: Oxford University Press, 1997: 164–89; David E. Hoffman, *The Oligarchs: Wealth and Power in the New Russia*, Oxford: Public Affairs, 2002: 325–64; Chrystia Freeland, *Sale of the Century: The Inside Story of the Second Russian Revolution*, London: Little, Brown, 2000.

[44] ISM-Research Centre, Moscow, reported in "Leaderless Russia," *The Economist*, January 18, 1997: 41–42.

[45] Richard Sakwa, *Putin: Russia's Choice*, London: Routledge, 2004: 15–33.

[46] Hedwig De Smaele and Sergej A. Romashko, "Russia," in Leen d'Haenens and Freda Saeys (eds.), *Western Broadcasting at the Dawn of the 21st Century*, Berlin: Mouton de Gruyten, 2001: 381.

both of these media oligarchs were living outside Russia and both had lost control of their TV channels; Berezovsky saw his properties returning to his (previously passive) partner Gazprom, the gas giant.

Putin was able to wrap these moves in nationalistic and patriotic rhetoric. The continuing Russian campaign against Muslim separatism in Chechnya could also, after September 2001, be portrayed as Russia taking a leading role in the worldwide war against terrorism. Putin went on to win a second presidential election in 2004 and to establish a pattern of government that was remarkably stable by comparison, at least, with Yeltsin's government in the turbulent 1990s.[47] The Putin post-2000 regime established Russia with what can be called a normal autocratic democracy (even though it was run by a slightly odd mixture of market reformers and secret policemen).[48] Television had returned to state control, partly exercised by Gazprom, the energy giant that has one-quarter of the world's natural gas. But the media are not a state monopoly because the (now smallish) press and the Internet are broadly free.

Russia's media benefited through the substantial economic growth from the year 2000 onward. The Russian movie industry revived.[49] Russian television also had much more money to produce programming other than news, talk, games, reality, and music shows. The Internet, mobile phones, and cable TV spread rapidly. Most significantly—in terms of media finance—Russian advertising expenditure rose steeply in the early 2000s.

But not everything in the Russian media was tranquil. Journalists continued to be murdered. One such murder was of Pavel Klebnikov, the U.S.- and U.K.-educated editor of a new Russian edition of *Forbes* magazine; he was murdered in July 2004. His magazine had published the first Russian "rich list," which showed that 36 Russian (dollar) billionaires had assets equal to one-quarter of Russian GDP.[50]

Since 1990 the Russian language media have been less concerned with reporting on, and supplying media to, the world beyond Russia. The Russian language has ceased to be the lingua franca of a communist world, which stretched from Berlin to Beijing. In the 14 ex-Soviet countries where Russian was the senior language in the communist years, Russian is now much less widely taught in the schools. Russian, however, remains the first language

---

[47] Jonathan Becker, "Lessons from Russia: A Neo-Authoritarian Media System," *European Journal of Communications*, Vol. 19/2, June 2004: 139–63.

[48] Neil Buckley, "Market Reformers and Former Spies," *Financial Times* special report: "Russia," April 5, 2005.

[49] "Russian Cinema: Not Since Battleship Potemkin," *The Economist*, August 28, 2004: 74–75; "World Report: Russia," *Variety*, January 30–February 5, 2006; 81–86.

[50] Andrew Osborn, "Editor Who Unmasked Super-rich of Russia is Shot Dead in Moscow," *The Independent*, July 10, 2004; C. J. Chivers, Ervin E. Arvedlund, and Sophia Kishkovsky, "Russia in Transition: Troubling Questions. Killing of Editor Casts Doubt on Future." *International Herald Tribune*, July 19, 2004 (from *NY Times*).

of millions of ethnic Russians still resident in the ex-Soviet new nations.[51] These new nations continue to import some (but much less) Russian TV programming.

The Russian media, and people, now look more toward life within Russia. Opinion polls frequently show that Russians are cynical about politics and politicians; democratic elections—as experienced in Russia—have understandably made Russians skeptical about democracy. According to one 2000 opinion poll, the Brezhnev years (1966–1982) were now widely seen as Russia's best.[52] But despite their media and despite their "democratic" politicians, the Russians still seemed to love Russia. The Russian people, and to some extent the Russian media, are aware that Russia is one of the great nations of history. Russia has, at last, rediscovered cultural nationalism.

Yugoslavia's Regional Media and Six New Nations

Quickly following the break-up of the Soviet Union (1985–1991) into 15 nation-states, Yugoslavia broke up (1991–1995) into 6 nation states. Yugoslavia had less than 10 percent of the Soviet Union's population, and Yugoslavia's land area was only 1 percent of the Soviet Union's.

In both the communist Soviet Union and communist Yugoslavia there was a nationalities (or regional) policy that encouraged regional language, regional government, and regional media. In both cases the strong regional media "changed sides" around 1990–1991 and became the stridently nationalist media of the new infant nation-states.

The media in general, and television in particular, played central roles in the break-up of both the Soviet Union and Yugoslavia. The detailed (often live) televizing of the 1985–1991 Soviet break-up surpassed anything seen in any previous major revolution. But the extent of the TV coverage of the Soviet break-up was then quickly surpassed by the Yugoslav break-up. In no civil war previous to this Yugoslav war had television—especially regional television—carried so much hate talk and so much news coverage of the enemy's atrocities and ethnic cleansing.

Central to the television image war were the Croatian (Zagreb) broadcaster HTV and the Serbian (Belgrade) broadcaster RTV.[53] These new nationalist TV services used the output of the international video agencies (Reuters and AP) and their own camerapeople's output; they also used (with fresh commentary) each other's news output. The Yugoslav broadcasters, in

---

[51] Vida I. Mikhalchenko and Yulia V. Trushkova, "Russian in the Modern World," in Jacques Maurais and Michael A. Morris (eds.), *Languages in a Globalising World*, Cambridge, UK: Cambridge University Press, 2003: 260–90.

[52] Robert Service, *Russia: Experiment with a People. From 1991 to the Present*, London: Macmillan, 2002: 109–10.

[53] Misha Glenny, *The Fall of Yugoslavia*, 3d ed., London: Penguin, 1996: 66; Marcus Tanner, "I Watched as 'Sloba TV' Turned into Voice of Hate," *The Independent*, April 24, 1999.

addition, used amateur video. Families who had bought video cameras to record weddings and other family events now used their cameras to film burned homes, dead bodies, and shallow graves; some of this family video material reached television.

In both Yugoslavia and the Soviet Union a multinational and multilingual communist state got into serious difficulties. Long-repressed regional nationalism broke into public view in increasingly virulent forms, cheered on by nationalistic regional media.

In both Yugoslavia and the Soviet Union the reigning Communist Party emerged from the 1939–1945 war having triumphed against Germany and its allies. In 1945 the regime had enormous prestige and power; in the early post-1945 years the economy was rebuilt and living standards improved. In the 1980s both countries lost their long-time political leaders; Brezhnev died in 1985, and President Josip Broz (aka, Tito) of Yugoslavia died in 1980 after 35 years of postwar power. In both countries by the 1980s the economy was stagnating. In both cases the old Communist Party and police state apparatus was still in place. In both Yugoslavia and Soviet Union, the army, once heroic, was now in decline. There had been a big loss of popular legitimacy.

In both countries the communist regimes had tolerated regionalism, regional languages, regional sentiment, and regional media. The regional media were poorly financed, but this encouraged them to engage in regional populism. Regional journalists, editors, and producers were adept at slanting, biasing, and fabricating stories. As daily students of their own national and capital city media, regional media people had learned the tricks of systematic disinformation. When the time seemed ripe for counterbias, counterfabrication, and counterdisinformation, many (but not all) media people—especially in Yugoslavia—were ready to use the media to encourage ethnic cleansing, expelling and/or killing members of a minority ethnic group.

Tito could congratulate himself on having outfought and outthought the Germans in their particularly savage occupation (1941–1945) of Yugoslavia. He had called Stalin's bluff by distancing Yugoslavia from the Soviet sphere. Tito had also dealt with the British, Americans, and Italians in war and peace. In addition to being one of the twentieth century's most successful guerrilla leaders, Tito was a skilled diplomat, communist politician, and self-publicist. He persuaded the Western media—as well as visiting liberals and tourists—that Yugoslavia believed in workers' control and local democracy. He rewarded himself with several palatial villas, where he hosted visiting communists and capitalists.

But Tito, the retired guerrilla commander, continued to be a ruthless domestic politician. When Milovan Djilas began to develop his "New Class" critique—initially in the Communist Party newspaper *Borba* (The Struggle)—he was denounced, humiliated in the Central Committee Plenum in 1954, and dispatched to prison.[54]

---

[54] Milovan Djilas, *Tito: The Story from Inside*, London: Weidenfeld and Nicholson, 1981.

Tito's ruthlessness, prestige, and unrivaled power enabled him to maintain a delicate balance between Yugoslavia's fractious ethnicities. Yugoslavia was a product of the 1914–1918 war, Versailles, and the collapse of the Habsburg and Ottoman empires. Initially the new nation was known as the "Kingdom of the Serbs, Croats and Slovenes."[55] These were Yugoslavia's three most prominent ethnic groups, but there were several other substantial ethnicities (including Muslims, Albanians, Macedonians, and Montenegrins) as well as spillovers (especially Hungarians) from nearby nation-states.

The two key groupings, which Tito knew he must keep in balance, were the Serbs (about 40 percent of Yugoslav population) and the Croats (about 22 percent in the 1971 census). Superficially there was little difference between Serbs and Croats—they spoke the same language (Serbo-Croat), they belonged to the Christian tradition, and they had intermarried in the past. However, there was still fierce rivalry between Croats and Serbs, not least because of World War II. The Serbs had suffered the worst of the German onslaught, whereas many Croats had fought with the Italians and Germans. The Serbs saw the Croats as fascist "Ustashas" while the Croats saw the Serbs as terrorist "Chetniks." Also, the Serbs were by religion Serbian Orthodox, while the Croats were predominantly Roman Catholic.

These Serb versus Croat rivalries were evident in their common language, Serbo-Croat. In Serbian the Cyrillic (Slav, Russian) alphabet was used, whereas Croatia used the roman alphabet. But essentially this was one language—easily comprehensible to the radio and TV audiences in both Croatia and Serbia.[56] Tito himself was a Croatian with some Serb connections, but he knew that while the Croatians must be placated, Serbia had to be number one.

In addition to 40 percent of the population being Serbs, the capital city (Belgrade) was in Serbia and the army was heavily Serbian. Yugoslavia was the Serbs' empire on the land. But although the Serbs predominated (Table 19.3), they were also thinly spread (and thus potentially vulnerable) across much of Yugoslavia. Serb minorities were present especially in Croatia, in the mixed Muslim-Croat-Serb republic of Bosnia-Herzegovina, and in Kosovo (where the Serbs were a small minority, in effect a colonial elite presiding over a big majority of Albanian-speakers).

During the 1970s Tito deliberately relaxed the central control of Belgrade and allowed more power and regional autonomy to the republics. This trend was confirmed in a new 1974 Constitution for Yugoslavia, which gave added autonomy to Serbia's two "provinces" of Kosovo and Vojvodina; effectively these two now became republics, taking these extensively self-governed regional entities from six to eight. The regional loosening was very apparent

[55] Misha Glenny, *The Balkans, 1804–1999. Nationalism, War and the Great Powers*, London: Granta, 1999: 402–12.
[56] Robert D. Greenberg, "Language, Nationalism and the Yugoslav Successor States," in Camille C. O'Reilly (ed.), *Language, Ethnicity and the State*, Basingstoke: Palgrave, 2001: 17–43.

Table 19.3 Ethnic Composition of Yugoslavia's Population and Working
Journalists, 1971–1972

	PERCENT OF POPULATION (1971 CENSUS)	PERCENT OF JOURNALISTS (1972)
Serbs	39.7	37.0
Croats	22.1	19.6
Muslims	8.4	9.6
Slovenes	8.2	11.5
Albanians	6.4	3.1
Macedonians	5.8	10.6
Others	9.4	8.6
Total	100	100
Total number	20.52 million	5,895

Source: Zdravko Lekovi and Mihalo Bjelica, *Communication Policies in Yugoslavia*, Paris: UNESCO, 1976: 54, 61.

in the mass media; in the 1970s the still relatively new television service saw a downgrading of Yugoslav-wide television news and an expansion of regionally based news.

This added media regionalization reflected Tito's confidence, in his old age, that he had previously made the right decisions in his nationalities policy. In 1945 he had broadly followed Lenin-Stalin Soviet tradition. But Yugoslavia also had a long tradition of daily newspaper publication especially in Slovenia, Croatia, and Serbia—three provinces that accounted for 86 percent of newspaper sales in 1975. There had in fact been a steady increase in daily titles from 33 in the late 1920s to 50 dailies (in six languages) in 1937.[57]

Gertrude Robinson in her book *Tito's Maverick Media* perceptively expressed doubts as to the long term viability of such a decentralized media system within Yugoslavia's delicately balanced (or unbalanced) ethnic composition.[58] The media contribution to the ultimate break-up of Yugoslavia must derive from 70 years (1920–1990) of daily journalism in several republics and languages. Some of the multiethnic, multicultural, and multi-identity character of Yugoslavia must also derive from radio broadcasting during 1930–1990. By 1939 there was radio broadcasting from five different locations and by 1946 from eight.

Even Yugoslavia's small movie production industry was decentralized into several centers and languages. In 31 years, 1960–1990, Yugoslavia made 776 feature movies (25 per year). The first film was made in Serbia in 1910 and

[57] Kenneth E. Olson, *The History Makers: The Press of Europe from Its Beginnings Through 1965*; Baton Rouge: Louisiana State University Press, 1966: 414–28.
[58] Gertrude Joch Robinson, *Tito's Maverick Media: The Politics of Mass Communication in Yugoslavia*, Urbana: University of Illinois Press, 1977.

portrayed heroic Serbian resistance to Turkish oppression; many later Serb "partisan" movies glorified Serbian resistance to the Germans. Zagreb (Croatia) specialized in animation, and Ljubljana (Slovenia) was an active production location; some movies were made at other centers.[59]

When television arrived—passing one million sets for the first time in 1967 and three million in 1975—it was building upon the decentralized models of press, film, and radio. Despite the small population of about 20 million people, Yugoslav television was established on a strongly regional basis. Typically in both the 1970s and 1980s each of Yugoslavia's six republics produced one-third or more of its own TV output and "imported" a similar proportion from elsewhere in Yugoslavia (with subtitles added). Yugoslavia imported about one-quarter of its TV programming[60] from eastern and western Europe and from the United States. It was possible for TV viewers largely to avoid programming from the Yugoslav (and Serb) capital of Belgrade. Moreover, with both local media personnel and local politicians coming from the same specific ethnic background, there was a strong coincidence of interest and sentiment between journalists and politicians; they met each other at local communist and other meetings.[61]

The regions were gradually getting stronger—in both political and media terms—while Belgrade got weaker. Meanwhile, most people in Croatia and Serbia described themselves as Croats (75.1 percent) and Serbs (64.4 percent) while in the same 1981 census only 8.2 percent and 4.7 percent saw themselves as "Yugoslavs."

After Tito died in 1980, the regional media became stronger in asserting their region's claims to national identity.[62] One Yugoslav academic wrote in 1985 of a "tendency towards decentralisation and partitioning into eight systems" in the mass media.[63] Another Yugoslav academic, also in 1985, claimed that in "a country which has two alphabets, three main languages, and in addition about ten major ethnic minorities," the decentralization of television was inevitable.[64]

In April 1987 a previously obscure Serbian politician named Slobodan Milosevic gave a speech in Kosovo that was shown prominently and repeatedly on Serbian television news in Belgrade. Milosevic was deputy to

---

[59] Daniel J. Goulding, *Liberated Cinema: The Yugoslav Experience 1945–2001*, Bloomington: Indiana University Press, 2002 ed.

[60] Tapio Varis, *International Flow of Television Programmes*, Paris: UNESCO, 1985: 20.

[61] Gertrude Joch Robinson, *Tito's Maverick Media: The Politics of Mass Communication in Yugoslavia*, Urbana: University of Illinois Press, 1977: 195.

[62] Spyros A. Sofos, "Culture, Media and the Politics of Disintegration and Ethnic Division in Former Yugoslavia," in Tim Allen and Jean Seaton (eds.), *The Media of Conflict: War Reporting and Representations of Ethnic Violence*, London: Zed Books, 1999: 162–74.

[63] Miroljub Radojkovic, "The Information and Communications System in Yugoslavia," in L. Danjanovic and Dan Voich (eds.) *The Impact of Culture-Based Value Systems on Management Policies and Practices*, New York: Praeger, 1985: 300–25.

[64] Tomo Martelanc, "Television in Yugoslavia: Content and Usage," *Intermedia*, Vol. 13/4–5, July/September 1985: 79–80.

the president of the Serb republic and was launching a (soon to be successful) bid for the Serbian leadership. He made a deliberately inflammatory speech in Kosovo, calculated to exacerbate tensions between local Serbs and Albanians; according to Serbian tribal (school and media) history, Kosovo rightly belonged to the 13 percent of colonizing Serbs and not to the 85 percent of colonized Albanian-speakers. This Milosevic speech was a key event in raising the ethnic temperature and in stimulating Serbian ethnic belligerence. But the repeated showing on Belgrade television did not happen accidentally. It was, in fact, a piece of political theater carefully prepared and rehearsed by Milosevic with his friends in Belgrade TV and on the ground in Kosovo. Milosevic's inflammatory speech—accompanied by stone throwing from a huge crowd—took place on Friday April 24, 1987. But Milosevic had in fact made a quiet visit to Kosovo four days earlier (Monday). Local Serb supporters agreed to place two trucks full of throwable stones in the intended crowd area. Milosevic himself alerted television contacts in Belgrade, who agreed to send their camera crew to a story that would normally have been filmed by a local Kosovo crew.[65] Milosevic in April 1987 had thus already shown himself to be an astute manipulator, not only of ethnic hatred, but also of the television presentation of ethnic hatred.

As Serb leader, Milosevic worked closely with Belgrade television—which was shamelessly one-sided across the early 1990s years of ethnic cleansing. This was mostly a war of soldiers against civilians. It was also a media contest of television portraying the horrific results of the other side's ethnic cleansing, while not showing the horrific results of our side's ethnic cleansing. Serb television dwelt endlessly on the (genuine) sufferings of ethnic Serbs just across the border into eastern Croatia. But the slaughter of thousands of Muslim civilians in Bosnia by both Croats and Serbs was ignored by both Zagreb and Belgrade television.[66]

National idiosyncrasy, national culture, and national mythology have been plentifully apparent in the evolution of Yugoslavia's successor states. Slovenia (with its central European connections) moved quickly to join the European Union. Serbia—still obsessed with its Kosovan mythology— invaded Kosovo and was bombed (in 1999) by NATO; the bombing was of more symbolic than destructive significance, but Milosevic lost the 2000 Serbian election and was extradited in 2001 for trial at the International Criminal Tribunal for the Former Yugoslavia (ICTY) in the Hague. This gave Milosevic another stage on which to deploy his television performance talents.

---

[65] Adam LeBor, *Milosevic: A Biography*, London: Bloomsbury, 2002: 75–84; Laura Silber and Allan Little, *The Death of Yugoslavia*, London: Penguin/BBC, 1996: 38–39. The TV series (on which this book is based) includes videotape of the Milosevic speech and interviews with other participants in the Kosovo speech event. Noel Malcolm, *Kosovo: A Short History*, London: Papermac, 1988: 341–44.

[66] James Gow, Richard Paterson, and Alison Preston (eds.), *Bosnia by Television*, London: British Film Institute, 1996.

Franjo Tudjman—Croatia's boss for a decade (1989–1999)—was another Yugoslav politician who benefited politically from projecting nationalist mythology and ethnic hatred. Like Milosevic, Tudjman became adroit at playing to his regional/nationalist media. Tudjman's taste in clothes (white uniform, gold braid, many self-awarded medals, imposing military headgear) could make him look like a Hollywood Ruritarian dictator. Tudjman was a skilled debunker of Serbian historical exaggeration, but he was also a propagator of Croatian mythology. Tudjman revered Tito, who had twice put him in prison. In pursuing the Croatian national cause, Tudjman ethnically cleansed tens of thousands of Serbs, while he was both anti-Semitic and anti-Muslim.[67]

Like other post-communist nationalist politicians, Tudjman became adept at winning (or fixing) elections. His right-wing (some said fascist) political party (HDZ) became skilled in the new electoral arts, including attracting electoral finance from the sizeable anti-communist Croatian diaspora in the United States, Germany, and Australia. He also tolerated small amounts of freeish media (including some privatized radio and TV) while controlling the big media.[68]

Since Tudjman's death (in 1999) political power in Croatia has changed more than once. Like some other ex-Yugoslavian new nations, Croatia looked toward future membership of the European Union. The citizens of Serbia also increasingly wanted to be accepted by Brussels. But Serbia still exhibited several unacceptable characteristics, such as the mafia assassination in March 2003 of Serbian Prime Minister Zoran Djindic.[69]

Although some foreign media (including newspapers) were available in Belgrade throughout the Milosevic years and later, many, or most, Serbs maintained their ignorance of the grisly deeds done in their name. The most popular TV channel in Serbia in 2004 was very commercial and apolitical.[70] A decade after 7,000 Muslims were massacred by Bosnian Serbs in Srebrenica (in July 1995) most people in the Serbian capital, Belgrade (less than 100 miles from Srebrenica), were unaware of the massacre. Indeed, a video showing six Muslims being killed by Bosnian Serbs in Srebrenica in 1995 caused a sensation when shown 10 years later on Belgrade TV in June 2005.[71]

---

[67] Stjepan Malovic and Gary W Selnow, *The People, Press and Politics of Croatia*, Westport, CT: Praeger, 2001; Branka Magas, "Franjo Tudjman: Obituary," *The Independent*, December 13, 1999; "Franjo Tudjman: Obituary," *The Economist*, December 18, 1999; Ian Traynor, "Franjo Tudjman: Obituary," *The Guardian*, December 13, 1999; Tom Walker, "Croats Wake to the End of a Cruel Reign," *Sunday Times* (London), December 12, 1999.

[68] Gavin Gray and Laura Silber, "Media: The Door is Shutting on Criticism," *Financial Times*, May 30, 1996: survey, Croatia: 3; Ian Traynor, "Croatian Press Counts Cost of Spurning Party, *The Guardian*, November 14, 1997.

[69] Eric Jansson, "Serbia Detains Hundreds and Gags Media," *Financial Times*, May 20, 2003.

[70] Jared Manasek, "Letter from Belgrade: The Paradox of Pink," *Columbia Journalism Review*, January/February 2005: 36–42.

[71] Roger Cohen, "Years After Milosevic: Serbia's Illusions Persist," *International Herald Tribune*, August 31, 2005.

20

American Media Decline to Continue?

This book has discussed the importance of large nation-states; the top 11 nations in population (including the United States) contain over 60 percent of world population, and all 11 are broadly media self-sufficient. Media imports in these big countries typically account for between 5 and 10 percent of audience time; the United States itself fits this pattern because probably between 6 and 7 percent of U.S. domestic audience time goes to Spanish-language media, with a total "foreign" share of perhaps about 8 percent.

Nearly one-fifth of the world's people live in countries with a population between about 40 million and 100 million, and several of these countries (such as Germany, France, the United Kingdom, and Spain) have their imports and exports (in terms of audience time, if not money) roughly in balance. It is only in the remaining 150 countries—which have about 20 percent of the world's population—that media imports are large in terms of national audience time.

In very rough numbers, the world audience (outside the United States) devotes:

10 percent of its time to U.S. media

10 percent of its time to other media imports

80 percent of its time to domestic, national media

Most of the 10 percent of "other media imports" come from within the importing country's world region, continent, subcontinent, or language area. Examples include the Arab world, Spanish America, and Europe. There is also much media trading within southern Asia and within eastern Asia.

Euro-America (minus Russia) is in practice a single world region. The American media industries rely for the bulk of their export earnings on Europe, Latin America, and Canada. Half of all Euro-Americans are native

English- or Spanish-speakers. Much media trading that is described as "global" can more meaningfully be classified as taking place within Euro-America.

This does not mean that Europeans and Americans (north and south) agree about all media and political issues. They do not. There are big disputes and conflicts within the United States, within Europe, within Latin America, and between Europe and the Americas. But nearly all Euro-Americans do live in the same mental world, which is one mental world different from the mental worlds inhabited by most Arabs, by most Indians, and by most Chinese.

China and India

Three major groupings—China, southern Asia, and Euro-America—together have about 66 percent of the world's population (and a bigger proportion of media production and consumption). Another smaller population grouping —the Arabic-speaking countries—have about 5 percent of the world's people. These four media groupings—containing over 70 percent of the world's people—all seem likely to strengthen.

Both Chinese and Indian media will become more prominent, both within their own regions and in the world. If the Chinese economy continues to grow rapidly, the world will increasingly want to know more about it. The Chinese media—including the Xinhua news agency—will then increasingly be a leading source of world economic news.

If India also continues to grow rapidly, the Indian media will become more important. India's current pattern of exporting entertainment—mainly within Asia and to Africa—can be expected to expand. India also has another international strength in its English-language capabilities and media. The *Times of India* claimed by 2003 to be the world's largest sale English-language broadsheet daily. The world increasingly will want to know more about India's economy and politics. Moreover, journalists and politicians around the world, where trust in American media has been damaged, may look toward democratic India as a more congenial source of news and comment.

National Media: The Dominant Level

The national level of media is dominant in the countries where 90 percent of the world's people reside. Audiences today prefer their own news, weather, sports, comedy, soaps, games, reality, and other cheap factual programming. The public, the producers, and the politicians agree that national is to be preferred. The politicians like national programming because this helps the politicians themselves to remain prominent.

Both school textbook writers and media journalists have to decide what to say about recent politics, recent violence or wars, a nation-state's ethnic mix, and so on. Both textbooks and the media give current explanations and assessments of the "father of the nation," the nationalist movement that achieved independence, the post-independence violence, and the new charter of national values.

The national media level dominates audience time not only in television and radio but also in newspapers and magazines. The national media level also incorporates elements from the levels both "above" and "below" the national level. Global or American media materials reach the national audience through national newspapers and national TV channels; imported radio music is packaged alongside national music and national radio talk, news, weather, and sports.

The world regional level of media also often reaches the audience with some national trimmings attached. When media are traded within a world region, there may be some co-production participation. Sometimes "our" national stars (of entertainment or sports), who appear on the foreign programming team, are a key appeal. Some television imports are "versioned" or edited to give the impression that this is a national product and not an import from a big brother nation.

The national media level also often incorporates material from the "lower" levels of national region or locality. In countries like India, national newspapers print regional editions in which some regional news is provided. Many national television networks include some time in the schedule for regional or local news and sports. Bundles of cable programming offer channels devoted to regional sports. Many national media also carry nonnational advertising, including local retail advertising.

This national mixing of levels means that the same piece of media output might be classified as either global, or world regional, or national, or national regional or local. The simple quiz show is enormously popular around the world. But how to classify *Who Wants to Be a Millionaire?*, a British quiz format sold to many other countries (including the United States and India) in the early 2000s? There is no correct answer to this particular quiz question. This can be seen as yet another example of global plus local, or glocal, media; but the logic is strongly national. The TV quiz show is related to the trivia quizzes that appeared in many newspapers and magazines around 1900 (name the tallest woman, shortest man, longest river—and so on). Game and reality shows echo Euro-American Victorian charades, amateur dramatics, and home music-making.

The more global the economy becomes, the more national politicians will continue to use their cultural and educational powers (legislation, regulation, license allocation, artistic subsidy, and technology promotion). These national politicians will still want the national media to defend, to reflect, and to promote the nation-state, the national culture, the national history, the national ethnic mix, and the national religion or religions.

Alongside national media dominance, the pecking order tradition seems likely to continue. National media systems will still be reluctant to import media from countries that are below them in the pecking order. Thus many countries in the world may well still expect to take perhaps one-third (but no longer a half) of their media imports from the United States. Many countries will continue to prefer U.S., European, or Japanese imports, rather than taking programming from (and awarding finance to) a nearby rival located at a similar elevation in the pecking order.

The United States Loses Control of World News Agenda and History

Between 1950 and 2005 the United States lost control of the world news agenda. Around 1950 the then three U.S. international news agencies carried the then current major American themes—democratic America against Soviet and Chinese communism, democratic America against French and British imperialism, democratic America as the rebuilder of western Europe and Japan. In 1950 neither Reuters nor Agence France-Presse provided many significantly different themes.

After 1960 the British Reuters and French AFP news agencies acquired a somewhat bigger share of this world news flow leadership. The British and French also played a significant role in writing and publishing history for the world, including the world's new nations. In the 1960s many newly independent countries were still importing school textbooks from their former imperial mothers or were publishing textbooks in association with mother country book publishers.

Around 1990 CNN was seen by some people as having extended American news leadership. But 1990 in fact marked a declining trend in American news leadership. By now Associated Press had lost the world news lead to Europe's Reuters, AFP, EFE, and DPA. CNN increasingly lost its 24-hour all-news leadership to national news channels in Europe and elsewhere. The U.S. forces in Iraq from 2003 onward found that Arab-region Arabic-language news media dominated the Middle East news agenda.

History, especially national history, has slipped out of the hands of the Anglo-Americans, who still, however, publish thousands of volumes of history each year. Especially since the 1970s, even small nations such as Malaysia have been publishing all of their own school textbooks; this textbook publishing operation is often controlled by one or more government departments. History and politics textbooks now present the new nation's own approved version of its own national birth. India inevitably has a negative view of many British colonial actions. In many countries, also, American historical intervention is inevitably seen in a very negative light. Textbooks in Congo (Zaire), in Angola, in Indonesia, in Chile, in Guatemala, in Iran—and elsewhere—are unlikely to praise the United States and the CIA interventions of recent decades. In many school textbooks around the world both the former colonial power and the United States will be portrayed as high profile bad guys.

When the Democratic Republic of Congo celebrates 50 years of independence (from Belgium) in 2010, it may perhaps be recalled that Louis (Satchmo) Armstrong toured the Congo in November-December 1960; his tour was sponsored by Pepsi Cola and the U.S. State Department. At the 2010 anniversary it seems unlikely that Congo's politicians and media will fail to recall the CIA's role in the assassination in January 1961 of Patrice Lumumba, the recently elected youthful prime minister of the new nation of Congo.[1]

International news agencies—AP, AFP, and Reuters—will continue to provide fast news to newspapers, to television, and to Internet news offerings; even Internet bloggers will be commenting on, and reframing, mainstream news, much of which comes from the big news agencies. The current A team of AP, Reuters, and AFP may be increasingly challenged by a larger B team of news agencies from western Europe, Japan, Russia, India, China, Brazil, and perhaps Africa.

These international news agencies will want to become more genuinely international and less dependent on their headquarters nation. Many agency correspondents and camerapersons who work in the Middle East have Arab names. Increasingly, journalists in a specific world region are reporting on their region to the rest of the world via an international news agency.

Some big news agencies are more national than others. Agence France-Presse is very French, but in today's world many people expect French news to be more reliable than American news.

Haunting Inconsistencies of American Policy

Most governments pursue inconsistent policies. The United States has a very big government machine that exhibits some big inconsistencies, in the media as elsewhere.

Media protectionism is especially noticeable in the ownership of local television stations. While U.S. citizens are allowed to own and operate major television companies in Europe, only U.S. citizens may control U.S. TV stations. Money, all agree, is crucial to getting elected in the United States —at both federal and state levels; much of this money goes to buying commercial time on the electronic media. Major city stations are also crucial in giving massive local news coverage to political incumbents. Major local TV stations have long been, and still are, highly profitable; this has allowed owners of TV stations to invest their profits elsewhere in the media. Why is

[1] Penny M. Von Eschen, *Satchmo Blows Up the World: Jazz Ambassadors Play the Cold War*, Cambridge, MA: Harvard University Press, 2004: 66–70.

this important area protected from foreign involvement? Because the National Association of Broadcasters (NAB) is a belligerent group that frightens American politicians with lobbying tactics similar to those of the National Rifle Association (NRA).

Another big contrast in America's media policy has been between its overt pursuit of democratic sweetness and light and its covert policies of undermining other nations' democratic media. Major tools in undermining existing media have been false news reports, cash bribes to editors and politicians, and incitement to the military to initiate a coup. Also used were many paid marches and riots and some destruction of media buildings. A final component was "plausible deniability"—the relevant U.S. embassy should try to project a mask of innocence; inevitably, many such denials were implausible and damaged U.S. credibility.

One of the first of what may prove to be a big new wave of CIA revelations was a book by Steve Coll, the Pulitzer Prize–winning journalist. His book, *Ghost Wars: The Secret History of the CIA, Afghanistan and Bin Laden,*[2] dealt with CIA intervention over a 22-year period (1979–2001). More revelatory accounts of U.S. covert action in Afghanistan, Pakistan, Iraq, and other Arab and Muslim countries can be expected. Such critiques of American intervention will usually seem significantly more critical when extracted into, and translated into, Arabic and other languages.

Hard to Predict

The further rise and rise of media in southern and eastern Asia seems probable. Both are already the world leaders in their numbers of television households. But neither seems likely to surpass Euro-America in the scale of international media trade. While Asia will have the largest audiences—and the most millions of eyeball hours—Euro-America will continue to generate bigger dollar amounts from media trade. Within Euro-America there are several national players that see themselves as significant media exporters as well as media importers. France, Germany, Britain, Spain, Italy, Brazil, and Mexico—like the United States—have good commercial reasons for observing and policing copyright and intellectual property rules and laws.

Future technology developments are especially difficult to predict. The ultimate technology outcome has often been different from most predictions; quite often it is the second or third placed horse that eventually wins the technology race. The leading participants—manufacturers, government departments, programming producers, regulators, monopoly authorities —themselves cannot predict what will happen, and which company or

---

[2] Steve Coll, *Ghost Wars: The Secret History of the CIA, Afghanistan, and Bin Laden*, New York: Pengiun, 2004.

technology will achieve market leadership, without running foul of competition law. Within this huge range are several key areas of uncertainty:

- What will be the main means of delivering home entertainment—satellite, cable and/or phone line, mobile devices, or digital radio?
- Will today's 100 or 500 cable/satellite channels be replaced by tomorrow's 100,000 or 500,000 channels?
- Will new payment technologies or new pirate technologies prove the stronger?
- The Internet will surely continue to expand, will become less American, and will take bites out of other media technologies. But which technologies in particular? Will newspaper news largely migrate to the Internet, and, if so, how will these Internet news services generate enough revenue?
- The future of smaller languages may depend quite heavily on the success, or failure, of translation technologies.

Such uncertainties as these add up to high total levels of uncertainty. The United States still seems well placed to handle these uncertainties better than almost any other country. Quite possibly U.S. media innovation will be able to balance out other declining trends. The United States may be able to retain much (but not all) of its current level of worldwide media prominence. However, it will be ever more difficult to determine what is American media and what is Euro-American media.

INDEX

Abacha, Sani, 295
Abdelnasser, Walid M., 370n
Abiola, Moshood, 294
Abu-Lughod, Lila, 372n
Aday, Sean, 379n
Adhikarya, Ronny, 352n
Adler, Ilya, 393n
Advertising, 34–38
    agencies, 37–38, 132
    brand, 35
    media buying agencies, 37–38
    United States, 36–37
The Affirmative Action Empire, 419, 429
AFN (American Forces Network), 74
Africa, 285–325
    Africa Confidential, 310n
    Big Brother Africa, 324
    corruption, 307–08
    Daily Nation, 308–11
    film, 322–25
    hate talk/radio, 288, 293, 301–05, 315
    Hausa, 288, 323
    Indian films, 323
    journalists, 287, 296, 311
    Kiswahili (and Sheng), 288, 305–12
    languages, 288, 292, 294, 309–12, 317–18, 321
    military coups, 287, 292–93, 303
    National Concord, 294–96
    Nairobi, as news hub, 311–12
    newspapers, 289, 293–94, 298, 307
    praise singing, 288, 313
    radio, 287–88, 291, 294, 298, 301–06, 309, 312–16, 319
    religious TV and radio, 297
    RTLM radio, 302–05
    television, 294–96, 305, 308, 317
    United States media, 287, 317–18, 321
Agee, Philip, 119
Aggarwal, S. K., 163n
Ahn, Byung-Sup, 244n
Ainslie, Rosalynde, 291n
Aksoy, Asu, 357n
Albarran, Alan B., 27n
Algeria, 373–78
Ali, Tariq, 156n
Aliyev, Geider, 426–27
Allen, Robert C., 15n, 16n
Allende, Salvador (President, Chile), 389
Alterman, Jon B., 381n
Amnesty International, 118
Ananda, Prakash, 158n
Anderson, Benedict, 331n, 344
Anderson, Christopher, 75n
Anderson, David, 107n, 305n
Ang, Ien, 86–87
Angola, 319–20
Animation, 48, 238–39

Arab countries and media, 9, 360–84
    Al-Ahram, 366, 371–72
    Al-Jazeera, 366, 378–382
    Arab public opinion, 365
    Arab worldview, 360, 370, 377–78, 384
    British media, 366, 369, 378, 382
    films, 363, 367–69, 372
    French media, 366, 373–77, 382
    journalists, 118, 367
    London as Arab media center, 378, 380
    Muslim Brotherhood, 367, 372, 374
    Muslim religion, 362, 365–66, 370–72, 377
    national identity, 365, 368
    newspapers, 363, 366, 370–72, 374–76
    radio, 364, 369
    satellite television, 378–82
    television, 364, 369, 372, 377–82
    United States media, 364–68, 370, 381–83
    Voice of the Arabs, 369
Anuar, Mustafa K., 355n
Arbenz, Jacobo (Guatemala, Prime Minister), 90, 403
Argentina, 387–88, 410–11
Armenia, 426–28
Armes, Roy, 322n
Arnheim, Rudolph, 15n
Ascherson, Neal, 65n, 426n, 427n
Australia, 4, 45–46, 49
Awolowo, Obafemi, 292–94
Ayalon, Ami, 362n
Ayres, Alyssa, 162n
Azcarraga, Emilio, dynasty, 392–95
Azerbaijan, 420, 426–28
Azikiwe, Nnamdi, 292–93

Bachchan, Amitabh, 148, 179–81
Baker, Raymond, 372n
Bakr, Yahya Abu, 364n
Balakrishnan, Gopal, 332n
Balogun, Françoise, 323n
Baltic countries, 421–24
Bandit Queen, 142
Banks, Jack, 103
Barker, Hannah, 332n
Barnard, Christopher, 80–81
Barnouw, Eric, 48n
Bartol, Robert A., 341n
Batson, Lawrence D., 197n
Batten, Frank, 39
BBC (British Broadcasting Corporation), 195, 378
    World (TV), 101
    World Service (radio), 41, 62, 101, 171, 188, 302, 322
Becker, Jasper, 203
Becker, Jonathan, 441n
Bégin, Dominique, 254n
Belden, Jack, 73n, 201